Canadians in the making

Arthur R. M. Lower *has also written:*

COLONY TO NATION

CANADA, NATION AND NEIGHBOUR

THIS MOST FAMOUS STREAM

UNCONVENTIONAL VOYAGES

Canadians

1958

in the making

a social history of Canada

by Arthur R. M. Lower

Longmans, Green and Company, Toronto

971
407712

Printed and bound by
T. H. Best Printing Company, Limited
Don Mills, Ont.

101062506

ad manes
patris matris fratris

Contents

Illustrations, xiii

Diagrams, xiv

Preface, xv

Part I: New France, 1

1: FRANCE COMES TO AMERICA, 1
A new world, 2
Indians and Frenchmen; the past and the future, 5
Champlain, 7

2: THE FIRST IMPACT OF THE WILDERNESS, 10
Indian filth and Indian carnality, 11
The 'noble red man', 12
Why the French came: the appeal of freedom, 15

3: THE FOUNDATION STONES OF NEW FRANCE, 18
The colony begun: the sixteen-thirties, 20
'Upon this rock—', 22

4: A COMMUNITY FORMED, 27
New France not a replica of old, 28
Reproductive valour in New France, 33
The Canadian 'gentleman', 36

5: THE COMMUNITY ESTABLISHED: A DESCRIPTION OF
NEW FRANCE ABOUT 1700, 40
Frontier aberrations, 43
Seventeenth-century town planning, 46
The spirit of New France, 48
The harsh French law, 51

6: NEW FRANCE AND ROMAN CATHOLICISM, 56

  The various aspects of French Catholicism, 60
  The struggle for dominance in and over the
  Catholic Church of French Canada, 62
  The Catholicism of the humble, 66

7: NEW FRANCE REACHES THE PROVINCIAL STAGE, 71

  Cultural growth, 72
  Eighteenth-century government, 75
  French soldiers and Canadian morals, 77

8: THE LILIES COME DOWN, 81

  The various meanings of the Conquest, 84
  What the Conquest meant for the Canadians, 86

Part II: British North America, 93

9: AFTERMATH OF CONQUEST: TWO WORLDS IN
  ONE, 95

  The English ruling class, 95
  Middle- and lower-class British, 99
  French and Catholic conceptions of society, 100
  Church and clergy, 102
  The Canadian upper classes, 105
  The new French middle class, 108
  The anonymous mass, 110

10: THE FIRST ATTEMPT AT LIVING TOGETHER, 116

  The period of racial myth-making, 1760-1775,
  117
  From the American Revolution to the French
  Revolution, 121
  The period of the French Revolution, 123
  The early nineteenth century, 127

11: THE PRIVATE QUARREL OF THE ENGLISH, 135

  What the American Revolution meant for Can-
  ada, 135
  The heritage of ritualism, 137

12: THE FIRST WAVE OF ENGLISH SETTLEMENTS, 143

  The Maritime Provinces: Newfoundland, Prince
  Edward Island, Cape Breton, 144
  Nova Scotia, 145

New Brunswick, 151
Quebec—Lower Canada, 154
Upper Canada, 155
The 'climate' of the times, 163
Red River, 168

13: THE WAR OF 1812, CONSTRUCTIVE CONFLICT, 173
The American attempt to conquer Canada, 174
French Canada and the war, 176
The war turns Loyalists into Canadians, 179
Effects of the war, 181

14: THE GREAT DAYS OF SETTLEMENT, 1820-1850, 187
Growth in numbers, 189
The immigrant British, 194
The officer and gentleman, 197
The shortcomings of the pioneer, 202
The solid citizens, 205
From atoms to community, 206

15: VICTORIA REGINA, 212
From the eighteenth to the nineteenth century, 213
Romanticism, 214
Romanticism in religion, 215
Romanticism, imperialism, nationalism, 220
Romanticism in architecture, 225
Romanticism and colonial literature, 231
The coming of the nineteenth century in politics, 234

16: MID-CENTURY, 240
The Maritimes, 240
Lower Canada—the English, 244
Lower Canada—the French, 251
Upper Canada, 254

17: THE HEIGHT OF PROSPERITY: BRITISH NORTH AMERICA DURING THE EIGHTEEN-FIFTIES, 259
A healthy local rural culture, 260
The end of good land: the perpetual frontier of the North, 263

The rising cities and their life, 264
Old men and new, 266
The first provincial university, 269

18: THE PERIOD OF CONFEDERATION, 273
    Hatred as a virtue: Canada as a melting-pot of belief and prejudice, 274
    The Southern threat, 278
    Dissensions in retreat before political union, 282

Part III: Canada, 287

19: A NATION BEGUN, 289
    Carpentering or smelting? 289
    The roots of Confederation, 292
    Ottawa, symbol of nationalism, 296

20: THE NEW NATION: THE CRITICAL YEARS, 299
    Why did the Dominion survive? 301
    Canada in 1871—the cities, 303
    The excellence of Toronto, 306
    Dawn of a local urban culture? 312
    The talk of the times, 314
    Crusaders and sceptics, 319
    Sport, organized and unorganized, 321

21: A STURDY YEOMANRY: CANADA IN THE 'HORSE AND BUGGY AGE', 327
    The Canadian country-side, 329
    The typical Canadian farmer, 332
    The clash between rural and urban values, 337
    The dispersion of the farm boys, 341

22: THE BIRTH OF MODERN CANADA, 345
    The revival of nationalism, 346
    A schooling in imperialism, 349
    A nascent culture, 353

23: THE TRANSCONTINENTAL COUNTRY, 358
    The country beyond the Lakes, 358
    The men who made the West, 361
    The new western society, 365

24: NEW CANADIANS, 371
    The 'New Canadians', 372
    Consequences—political, social, religious, 278

25: THE IMMIGRANT STOCKS IN CANADA, 384
    Comments on the diagrams, 386

26: WAR'S RUDE ALARMS, 395
    The call to arms—and the response, 396
    War's consequences, 400
    Rank, class, and Sam Hughes, 402

27: YESTERDAY AND TO-DAY, 408
    Science and religion, 409
    The post-war revolution, 410
    The change in sexual morals, 411
    Is the world getting better or worse? 417
    Is social justice a criterion? 420

28: NEW GODS FOR OLD, 423
    The great god CAR and his associates, 424
    Men like gods: British style and American, 426
    The god Equality, 429
    The old culture and the new civilization, 434
    The goddess Canada, 438

Index, 447

Illustrations and diagrams

ILLUSTRATIONS

The seventeenth and eighteenth centuries, 162
    The church of St. Laurent, 1696
    St. Andrew's Presbyterian church, 1831

Domestic architecture in the eighteenth and nineteenth centuries, 163
    The White House, 1793
    The Campbell house, 1822

The new style and the old: Gothic revival and classical, 194
    The dining-room of "Elmwood", 1839
    The City Hall, Kingston, 1843

Victorian occasions, 195
    Bishop Strachan's funeral, 1867

Upper class Victorian domesticity, 290
    The Allen family at home, 1871

The familiar surroundings of our fathers, 291
    Eaton's catalogue, 1905-1906

The imitations of the imitations, 322
    St. Paul's College, Winnipeg
    Casa Loma, Toronto

Aspects of the frontier, 323
    "Goddesses of Liberty", 1898

DIAGRAMS

1. Three centuries of births and deaths: the Roman Catholic population of New France and the French population of Quebec, 34

2. Census of New France, 1665-1765, showing population, land under cultivation, agricultural production, head of livestock, 41

3. Population growth in British North America, 1820-1850, for all the provinces and for each province, together with immigration, 191

4. Population history of the Township of Wilmot, Ontario, 1821-1951, illustrating the rise and decline of a rural area, 260

5. "Cowgram", 1871-1946; "acregram", 1871-1946 — showing per capita amounts of cattle and land under cultivation in Canada, 332.

6. British Isles and French racial stocks, showing areas of assimilation the one to the other, 1871-1951, 386

7. Growth of the foreign stocks showing areas of assimilation, 1871-1951, 386

8. Growth of the Italian stock, 1881-1951, 387

9. Growth of the Jewish stock, 1881-1951, 387

10. Growth of the Scandinavian stock, 1871-1851, 388

11. The foreign stocks: a special case, the Icelanders, 1901-1951, 388

12. Growth of the main foreign stocks, 1901-1951, 388

13. Percentage increase of the major origins by decades, 1871-1951, 389

14. The Ukrainians in Canada, 1941, and their characteristics, 390

15. Birth and death rates, rate of natural increase, 1921-1951, for British, French, German-Dutch, Scandinavian, Russian, Polish, Ukrainian, Italian, and Jewish stocks, 391

16. The intermingling of the Canadian people: marriages of Roman Catholics with Roman Catholics as a percentage of all Catholics marrying, 1921-1951—all Canada (except Quebec) and British Columbia, 392

17. Principal religions of the principal racial origins, 1951, 393

Preface

THIS BOOK IS EXPERIMENTAL and, as far as I know, a pioneering effort. A good many types of history have been written about Canada—constitutional, economic, and political—and there have been plenty of articles and small books lighting up the life of a countryside or city. But as yet no one has tried to put things together in an effort to depict the growth of the country as a whole, and throughout its history.

I have kept a few fixed points in view. First of all, I have tried to distinguish sharply between economic and social history by telling myself that economic history consists of the story of what man does to his environment, whereas social history has to do with what his environment does to man. The economic historian looks at the axe in the settler's hands and he traces its effects through clearings to ploughed fields, crops, statistical returns of crops, and the towns that such efforts eventually bring into existence. The social historian looks at the settler and tries to estimate what effects new conditions have on him and the subtle changes in his relations to his fellows which eventuate in a new social group. Or, again, the economic historian will be interested in the raft of logs got out of the bush in the spring and the processes of its conversion into lumber—such as the techniques of river-driving, of the operation of lumber-mills—but the social historian will be interested in the new type of man all this activity produces, the river driver.

Secondly, I have had to wrestle continuously with that protean notion 'progress'. It would have been easy to accept the continental norm of 'progress' as that which is bigger and newer than that which went before, but that would seem to be to throw away all critical, philosophical detachment. And it would probably reduce social history to some kind of boring statistical success story. Yet the alternative to finding a theme that can be systematically developed and which will support appropriate general positions is to go on giving endless, more or less picturesque, descriptions and more or less relevant anecdotes. This would require a writer to sustain interest from page to page and he would probably end up in a tide of small talk.

Perhaps a way out of the quandary can be found in a non-committal definition of 'progress' as 'increase in complexity'. There can be no question of the increase in the complexity of Canadian society in the last three centuries. Yet a mere description of three centuries' increase in complexity would be neither interesting nor important: something more must be furnished. One line of analysis that will supply a good framework, if nothing more, is that which attempts to distinguish the various stages marking the evolution of society and to group its material around them. If there is one thread binding the contents of this book together, it is this conception of the stages in a community's development. I have found it hard to apply to every situation and I have not attempted to be rigorously logical in shaping my material over this precise mould but, since it comes close to furnishing the thesis on which I have written, I must attempt to explain it.

We begin with the trading post: a few men in a make-shift house, clinging to the shore and with nothing further from their thoughts than passing the rest of their lives in such a situation, far from home and families. Then comes interest in the new land for itself and the thought that it might be possible really to live in it and to make something of it. At that point the trading post gives way to what might be called pioneer settlement. Anyone who has been in a fur-trading post knows the sharp psychological line which separates it from the settlement. When women come, we clearly get into this next stage, for women are hostages to the new world. And when they are followed by children we have crossed the line from mere settlement to colony. A colony has some aspects of permanence: some of its people have committed themselves and cease to think of themselves primarily as exiles. But a colony draws most of its life from its mother country. It is dependent upon it for most of the necessities of life beyond the simplest, even for food, and particularly for defence and for recruits. Colonials still think of themselves as severed parts of 'the nation', to which they refer lovingly as 'home'. About a colony, as the word is used here, there is always the final problem: will it or will it not endure?

When the new settlement gets beyond the point of mere survival and its society takes on some form and shape, it may be thought of as having become a province. A provincial society remains economically and emotionally attached to its mother country and leans on it as the centre of its way of life. Its 'culture', in both the restricted and unrestricted sense, springs from it.

In the United States, the phrase 'provincial society' has been used with a time tag attached. 'Colonial society' more or less coincides with the first two generations on American soil: the period in which the big adaptations were being made and settled social life getting under way. 'Provincial society' is a term for communities which already have discernable characteristics of their own, as had, say, Massachusetts Bay in the eighteenth century. The English phrase 'the provinces' introduces the antithesis *province-metropolis*. Between this sense of the word and those arising out of the settlement of a new country (which carry both evolutionary and political connotations), there are both similarities and differences: ambiguity is almost unavoidable. Thus in America, in both the United States and Canada, while the provincial stage (referring to growth from first settlement on) is clearly discernible, the moment new urban nuclei come into existence the antithesis between centre and circumference arises also. Provinces as organized communities are both self-conscious and dependent and also 'provincial' in the sense that they have no satisfactory metropolitan centre of their own, that is, no dynamic, creative centre, where every activity flourishes, especially the higher ranges of culture, and where life's patterns are consciously fashioned, and set! One of our problems is to decide whether New France, like New England, passed into the provincial stage and when.

'The provinces', 'provincial', 'provincialism', all these terms come with derogatory undertones. 'Provincial' communities wear second-hand cultural clothes. A 'provincial' person is one who is 'behind the times'—behind the current fashion of the metropolis! A 'provincialism' is an outmoded expression or habit. How white a light is thrown on European civilization in its earliest stages by such words as 'pagan' and 'heathen' to describe people whose major sin was that they were not city folks but lived 'in the country'. Later, 'pagan' passes into 'peasant' with scarcely lessened intensity.

In the societies with which our own has been most intimately associated, the domination of the great centre has long been complete. France and England (which country itself remained for long culturally provincial to Paris) emerged from the Middle Ages as the two nations *par excellence* and their undisputed foci were their capital cities, Paris and London. After the English Conquest, New France slowly found a new metropolitan centre in Rome, and gradually New York—or even Hollywood— usurped London's hegemony over English Canada. It is the failure of modern Canada to find a satisfactory centre within itself which leads to ambiguities in its structure and doubts about its future.

Between metropolitan centre and provincial hinterland a tension exists which it is impossible to get rid of. This is one of the enduring themes of literature. Is there, it may be asked, a non-metropolitan individual in existence, however erudite, cultured or wealthy, who has not felt small tremors of diffidence or assertion pass through him when he has come into the company of his metropolitan opposite numbers? If such an individual moves to the metropolis, he himself becomes a metropolitan and those left behind manifest the same unconscious attitude towards him. Endless correlations of greater or less worth have been made between great capital and sharp smartness, the province and innocent worth, between metropolis and sin, provincial town and virtue. As a popular song of about 1890 had it:

> I came to this great city
> To find a brother dear
> And you wouldn't dare insult me, sir
> If brother Jack were here.

The prestige of metropolitanism has nothing to do with the individual person: it is simply something that attaches to him by reason of his association with the centre. There has been many a 'provincial' who has had nothing of the 'provincial' about him except his place of residence, many a one who has made his independent contribution to culture. The poet Wordsworth was such a one. Nevertheless this attitude of those who do not live in a metropolis reaches into the depths of being, for basically it is the fear and distrust of the smaller for the larger which we find on every level of animal life. Canada, it must be remembered, in adjudging the pertinence of these remarks, has through most of its history been clearly 'provincial'.

Nothing can be done about the antithesis. If a person is a 'provincial', he had better make up his mind to accept the fact, knowing that to-day modern communications make it irrational to attach much importance to it. There was a time when, unless their social class swept them into realms above such considerations, not being 'Londoners' or 'New Yorkers' or residents of some other recognized centre, could make people unhappy—especially people of creative abilities—by making them feel 'out of it', 'old-fashioned', not 'up-to-date'. Often such people sought to dissociate themselves from their provincial surroundings and to pose as sophisticated metropolitans—one thinks of poor Madame Bovary. If a man had a youthful experience of the great city, he might cherish it all his life, for that put a special character on him—he 'had been around'. The immortal expression of the would-be metropolitan's desire to associate himself with the actual 'man-about-town' is that of Mr. Justice Shallow in Shakespeare's *Henry IV*. Shallow, it will be remembered, has as his guest a distinguish recruiting agent fresh from the Court, no less a person than Sir John Falstaff. Shallow is an old fellow-student of Falstaff, and he makes much of the times they used to have together. As he says to his fellow-justice, Silence:

"Ha, cousin Silence, that thou hadst seen that that this
    knight and I have seen! Ha, Sir John, said I not well?"
Falstaff takes it all in at a glance and puts it in a nutshell:

"We have heard the chimes at midnight, Master Shallow."

Shallow's genuinely provincial attitude is as common in the new world as in the old. Possibly even the inhabitant of Chicago feels just ever so slightly second-rate in the presence of an inhabitant of New York and covers up his feeling by a small extra pinch of assertiveness. The provincial has always been fair game for the dramatist and the novelist (for example, Bob Acres in Sheridan's *The Rivals*)—the innocent up from some distant town with a funny but familiar name, the 'country cousin', the 'rube.' But there is another side to provincialism in North America, albeit a transient one. In the new world, every cross-roads expects to become in due course the largest city on the continent. This confidence puts its inhabitants on a level with those of the cities which have already attained this status, and the cross-roads remains for them the satisfactory centre of the world. It takes ages to make a village realize that its fate is—to remain a village!

As yet, few of our villages have reconciled themselves to their fate. Their inhabitants are thus metropolitans *in posse*.

Provinces, former colonies, invariably hope to advance and become something else, something which they do not clearly define to themselves but which, with the help of history, we can see to be nations. The American Revolution occurred because the American colonies were growing beyond the provincial stage and no longer rested easily in dependence on the mother country. It may be that the federation of the British North American colonies into Canada arose from the same cause: at the time there was a good deal of talk about national life. The political line from province to nation is easy to follow because it is usually accompanied by outward changes that force themselves on anyone's attention. Growth into nationhood in the sphere of culture is a much longer and more intricate process, one much harder to see, usually a much more tantalizing one, than the mere acquirement of political independence. The United States itself until recently retained some aspects of provincial cultural dependence upon England, as perhaps, indeed, it still does. Few would be so naïve, of course, as to assume that any culture can be complete within itself, unaffected by creative developments elsewhere. But cultures tend to hover round the great centres, which influence more than they are influenced. English Canada throughout its history has been clearly in tow of both the two senior English-speaking countries (which have often pulled in different directions!). For a time after the Second World War, it looked as if the country might go on to genuine cultural nationhood (the present writer would identify the phrase with 'genuine nationhood'), but as this is written it seems to be drifting back again into its old provincial position, this time with the United States replacing England as the major metropolitan centre of gravity, though with Rome (and to a lesser extent Paris) providing a certain counter-weight through French Canada.

Is there a stage beyond nationhood? It may be that there is and that it lies in this attractive and creative power inhering in the vast modern world-cities. So Oswald Spengler contends. Canada probably is not much more provincial to New York city than is, say, Ohio. Over the vast hinterland that modern communication reaches, the world-city seems to gather everything into itself: economic control, cultural control, political control, and that without much respect to political boundaries. Even linguistic boundaries are far from sure barriers, as the penetration of American radio into Quebec indicates.

The different British American colonies reach the various stages of development at different periods and within all of them there exist numerous sub-communities, each of which also differs in its rate of development and in the aspects it presents at any given time and which distinguish it from its neighbours. Yet this is what makes the interest of our story—its variety, added to its continuous expansion of scale. The interest of our story and also its difficulties! How is unity to be imposed on a scene that unrolls through three centuries and which must shift about from Newfoundland to the Pacific coast? Each of the new communities, as it comes into the picture, resembles the others but each is also different from the others. In New Brunswick, for example, how can one picture emerge from the differing portraits of the St. John Valley and the North Shore? In Upper Canada, has not the Ottawa Valley at mid-nineteenth century a life of its own? And hardly any two of these regions march abreast: Nova Scotia is half a century in advance of Upper Canada, and Upper Canada itself, beginning to be settled in 1783, is to this day engaged in settling its northern edges. In this building of societies it is not 'Anno Domini' which counts, so much as the succession of the generations. Northern Ontario to-day is the contemporary of Niagara of yesterday, though separated from it by a century and three-quarters of time.

Nothing confirms the huge place of colonization and settlement in Canadian affairs more emphatically than the equally huge place these stages hold in the Canadian mind. We have hardly yet begun to examine the life of our cities and its place in our history. It would still be difficult for the average Canadian to think of a Canadian civilization, for he has just moved into his house, which has hardly yet become the old family home. Civilization is something the Canadian expects to come from outside. Yet however little we may have of our own, it would seem worth while examining it, and to this several chapters are devoted. Here lies much unmined wealth.

For New France, the problem of tracing society's evolution throughout its various stages is relatively easy, since the people are homogeneous and live in a limited region. They advance logically through all the stages—from trading post to pioneer settlement, from settlement to colony and from colony to province. The Conquest interrupts but does not destroy the evolution, and after a generation of adjustment, French-Canadians emerge as a self-conscious people. They reach this stage years before any English section of British North America, and part of the difficulty between them and the English arises from this time difference in social evolution. Throughout the nineteenth century the question remains open as to whether this new people goes on to become a separate entity, a nation, or enters into partnership with dissimilar communities to build a still more complex society. Confederation seems to supply the answer, though everyone knows that to this day, no complete answer has been given. Is modern Canada a nation or is it a state containing an approximation to two nations?

It is only when a high degree of self-awareness arrives, when the old past ceases to absorb the new society's own past, when readiness comes to make the biggest decisions—those involving peace and war, that is, existence itself—that provincial society is displaced by national society. As suggested above, whether Canada has entered this stage, or having entered it, can remain in it, is uncertain. There have hitherto been two common wills in Canada, not one, a poor situation for decision making. Neither English nor French have forgotten their separate pasts, though they are moving towards the point where they will be able to make a common decision on the great fundamentals. The Korean War represented something close to a national decision; the decision of September 1939 (World War II) was mainly an English-Canadian one. Yet modern technology gives the metropolitan community enormous power: it may be the fate of Canada, like other societies in the same situation, to be sucked dry and then to decline again into that barren parochialism from which it has had so much trouble emerging. Or it may be that the very brittleness of a mechanical world will bring about that nemesis which after many years and much suffering, may restore significance to the smaller communities.

In addition to the framework of social stages, I have kept in mind other large forces which the panorama of Canadian history displays. One of these is race: what study of Canada would be worth anything that did not attempt to depict the complex mentalities behind the labels 'English' and 'French' (to say nothing of the more recent immigrant groups)? I have tried to analyze these in *Colony to Nation* and have consequently more or less taken them for granted here, illustrating them as best I could where the need arose, but never allowing them to be far from my thoughts. Yet I have not felt it appropriate to turn this book merely into a history of race relationships.

Add to race, religion: here, again, is a topic that shouts for inclusion in any social study of Canada, where the clash of creeds has been so prolonged and so noisy. Our own secular age has been inclined to look for historical causation in the materialistic areas of economics and geography, to push political explanations into second place and to neglect the role of religion. Yet it should take little reflection to convince us that it is the intangibles even more than the tangibles over which men quarrel, and that religion, fitting men and society like an old suit of clothes, whether as a deeply-held faith or a mere set of prejudices, has usually been the most divisive and most formative of social forces. A religion in itself is a way of life. It stamps its nature on those within it—a plain statement as between Mohammedan and Christian, or even Catholic and Protestant—but one not so evident when it comes to mere Protestant denominations. Yet these, too, create ways of life of their own. Anglicans, Methodists, Presbyterians, Baptists, Lutherans, Quakers and others, even minor sects, all engender different attitudes towards the world, towards economics, culture and fellow-humans. Adjustment between them all has not been easy. I hope I have illustrated some of the ways in which denominationalism, together with the theologies and philosophies that underpin it, has shaped our history.

A third great determinant is class. It is probably blasphemous to suggest that we in Canada have given any recognition to the class line, since we all believe so ardently that we have a classless society, but it does not take more than a glance at our history to reveal the monster's existence. At certain times and places it had a vast importance. The struggle of privilege and equality, in fact, has given us most of our social dynamic for many years and it will continue to do so, though the forms of privilege will change greatly from time to time.

Apart from following large, heavy lines on the chart such as the above, I suppose I have worked from rule of thumb. I have tried to paint a portrait, and as I studied my materials I became more and more absorbed in them. For I saw in my mind's eye an interesting picture, an absorbing picture—the grain of mustard seed (to which that preacher at the founding of Montreal three centuries and more ago referred) which was cast into the ground and which has brought forth abundantly, with wide variety of limb and foliage. To try to follow the process, still more to try to understand some of the mystery of growth—of how a new people is born—is what I have attempted. It may well be that I have not been able to put on paper what was in my mind's eye, or having put it there, have managed merely a smudge. As to that the reader may decide. I may be allowed to warn him that he must not expect to find any completeness to what I have attempted to do. If I had tried to discuss everything I would never have ended and a dozen volumes would not have sufficed to incorporate the relatively limited amount of material I have gathered. For example, I have not said much directly on the huge question of the growth of a free society, its maintenance and extension. The life of a people is indescribably intricate and in reasonable compass no one can do more than put down a few bold brush strokes. It is to be hoped that what I have done will encourage others to go on beyond the point I have reached—the attractions of our development have not been exhausted, but are just coming into view.

I would like to thank all those authors and publishers who allowed me to quote from their works. My own publishers, too, have been considerate in giving me a contract for this book without limit of time and in their efforts in bringing it into the light of day. To Mr. Bernard McEvoy of the firm I owe a special debt, as it was his original suggestion which prompted me to undertake the work.

The grateful obligation remains of adding some words of

thanks to those who have helped me in this long task. Queen's University and my Principal, Dr. W. A. Mackintosh, greatly facilitated my work by giving me a talented assistant for a year in the person of Mrs. Joyce Dingle (who has continued her interest since, has given me valuable criticism and has worked like a Trojan doing the bulk of the index), by awarding me the Mc-Laughlin Research Chair, by providing the efficient secretarial services of Miss Eleanor Smith and the assistance of the library staff, especially Miss Melva Eagleson. Henry Adams used to say that it costs as much to write a history as to keep a racing stable: this book provides a certain corroboration of his observation. I hope the University authorities will feel their choice of activities justifies itself. Elizabeth Harrison has given some of her artistry towards the decoration of the book, and my friends the Harrisons and Phelps's have provided, free of charge, patient audiences from time to time on which I have foisted the reading aloud of portions of this manuscript. My wife has had to endure still more intensive experiences of the sort. This should be counted unto all of them for righteousness.

A.R.M.L.

Canadians in the making

Part I: New France

Part I: New Types

1: France comes to America

THE COMPLETELY URBANIZED MAN, if such a man exists, will avoid his native earth: he will confine himself to those parts of it which are safely battened down under concrete. Urbanism, a term not to be confused with another, civilization, is a matter of pavements, buildings, books and gas fumes. But a history of Canada, any history, must have much to do with untamed nature and with the countryside. Cities will come into it, too, but late, though with emphasis. The first acts of the Canadian drama are played outdoors. Will the completely urbanized man avoid Canada and Canada's history? He may find the country big but boring: man makes civilization, he may say, mountains do not. He may, however, be a bit tired of his pavement, his gas fumes—and even of his books. If so, something simpler may attract him. If he is not intrigued with mere simplicity, he may still find in a young country and its story something of satisfaction, not only for his nerves, but also for his intellect.

What is that something? It is the element of vision. He who has imagination enough can catch the vision of new communities forming, of new men shaping new doctrines, the vision of what may be.

Those who live in twentieth-century Canada are fortunate enough to be able to see this making of a country still going on beneath their eyes. They can feel the thrill of accomplishment and know what hope the words 'new world' inspire. No Canadian needs go far to find again the peace of the wilderness. Happy people, perhaps, if they could stay in that position, heirs of perpetual youth!

Canadians, if they are men of the canoe and the portage, can well enough understand the distant days when all the continent was wilderness. If they are men of trade, they can remember that traders explored a continent. If they are men of books, there have been countrymen of theirs who could wield both axe and pen. Even if they know no history, they can understand their forest background better than those for whom the ancient life in the woods, the forest that no man owned, is now only a thin folk memory. But can they, or anyone today, understand the full impact that must have been made on sensitive souls, less sophisticated than modern man, when first they looked upon the new world?

A new world

A new world! A world wherein the tired old heart of Europe, cooped up in its fixed, restraining limits, could renew itself. A world capable of containing anything—spitfire Amazons fierce only to the moment of conquest, and in abundance;[1] "anthropophagi and men whose heads do grow beneath their shoulders"; a world where Prospero, the great magician, could create his cloud-capped towers and gorgeous palaces, a world wherein might exist people larger than ships and where gold and freedom lay just over the western horizon.

When at the beginning of the seventeenth century the French first turned in earnest towards that portion of the new world which Canadians have made their own, the corner of the veil had already been lifted. Cartier in 1534 could credulously hear Indians' tales of the Kingdom of the Saguenay, where oranges and gold abounded. In the belief that he had got an easy cargo of gold, he could load his ship up with iron pyrites.

Three-quarters of a century later, Champlain, a man whose name and reputation not even Canadian schools can entirely strip of their attraction, did not repeat that particular mistake. He sought something more rooted than wealth. He sought (to adapt Mrs. Hemans' lines on the Puritans of New England) not "rich jewels of the mine," but rather "a faith's pure shrine." That faith, clothed in Catholic dress, was deeper than Catholicism. It was faith in the French race; above all, faith in his vision. Here in America, with which he fell in love, would arise a new community of mankind, with hope ahead of it! "The pleasure that the French will enjoy when settled in these parts, leading a comfortable, quiet life with complete freedom to hunt, fish, house themselves and settle at their sweet will. . . ."[2]

There speaks the heart of that old world which had long put behind it the freedom and flexibility of youth. The Forest of Arden was but a poet's dream. It was in the new world that Champlain received his vision. And now that vision has been fulfilled, the new community has arisen, and history, kinder than circumstances, has bestowed its approval upon him, with its proud title of "The Father of New France."

Champlain, the man, is not difficult to understand—the perpetual adventurer and builder, the essentially constructive mind, a mind turned outward, not inward; observant and executant, not contemplative, the curious mind, eager to find out new mysteries. He was what the necessity of the hour imposed upon him—hydrographer, sea-captain, warrior, official, explorer, anthropologist, governor. In each of these capacities, he distinguished himself. His survey of the New England coast was an excellent piece of work. He made the ocean crossing many times. He fought the Iroquois—bravely, if not too wisely. As governor, he brought the colony through trying times and secured its re-establishment after it had been lost to the English. As explorer, he gave us the first account of the Great Lakes. And as anthropologist, he has left a mass of detailed material on the customs of late Stone-Age man. Champlain's energy and versatility, the many parts he played, are a preview of the kind of man the continent was to demand.

Versatility it was for which a *new* world called above all else: a man had to be prepared for anything, and nothing was too strange for some kind of credence. Champlain met at Isle Percée on his first voyage to the St. Lawrence a certain Monsieur Prévert of St. Malo, who had been down in what is now New Brunswick, looking for a mine of which rumour was going about. This gentleman described the Indians of that land, the Armouchiquois. They were, he said, "most unnatural in shape . . . their head small and their body short, their arms as thin as those of a skeleton, and their thighs the same, their legs thick and long and all of a size, and when they squat down on their heels, their knees are more than six inches higher than their heads. . . ."[3]

These fellows were nothing to what was to come: Prévert reported to Champlain a wonder that made Shakespeare's men with heads growing beneath their shoulders seem mild indeed, and Champlain, apparently, took him seriously. At least he says that,

"There is another strange thing worthy of record. . . . To the southward, near Chaleur Bay, lies an isle where lives a dreadful monster called by the savages Gougou, which they told me, had women's shape, but very terrible, and so tall, said they, that the top of the masts of our vessel would not have reached her waist . . . and that she has often devoured, and still devours, many savages, whom she puts in a great pouch when she can catch them, and then eats them; and those who had escaped the peril of this direful beast said that this pouch was so large that she could have put our vessel in it. . . . The said Monsieur Prévert of St. Malo himself told me that on his way to explore the mines that he and all his crew heard strange hissing noises made by it, and that the savages told him it was the same beast, and were so afraid that they ran everywhere to hide themselves . . . and I am led to believe their tale by the general fear which all the savages have of it. . . . I hold it to be the haunt of some devil who torments them in this fashion. . . ."

Evidently Champlain was a man of his age.

There was one among the companions of those early years who was not so easily fooled. This was the young Parisian barrister, Marc Lescarbot, who came out to Port Royal with de Poutrincourt in 1606, armoured with metropolitan and legal scepticism. He himself met the Armouchiquois and he says that "they are as good-looking men as ourselves, well built and agile. And as to the Gougou, I leave its credibility to the reader."[4] Lescarbot goes on in charmingly discursive fashion to comment on signs and wonders nearer home—the 'Mad Monk of Paris', visions secured by fasting, the way some "sick people talk of seeing the Virgin Mary or the devil," and so on. "Many people when alone, are afraid of spirits if a mouse moves." Lescarbot gave to a wide range of material on early Canada a much-needed 'debunking'. People who wrote of 'royal palaces,' or 'the fifty palaces of Hochelaga' had evidently not seen the miserable huts which were the reality. On the other hand, Cartier, when he picturesquely said that all the ships of France could be loaded with the birds flying about Bird Island, was just being "a little hyperbolical." As to the two-footed beast, one-legged men, the pygmies, people who never need to eat food and men who have no recta, all of whom Cartier had duly reported, Lescarbot simply notes that he "had as his authority, an old man whom he had forced to come before the King [chief] to recount these things." He says there are stranger things in nature than two-footed beasts, but he makes no comment on the likelihood of meeting men without recta. Nor is there anything inherently improbable in the rumour about a freshwater sea (Lescarbot wrote before anyone had been beyond Lachine). As to the little tricks the Indian women had, such as divesting themselves *en masse* of all their clothes on occasion, and the advantages many of the French took of their engaging accessibility, he passes by these new world scenes without remark: though marvels, they were not the kind of marvel that depended on credulity.

Lescarbot is one of the most interesting writers we have on the days of the beginnings, for he puts down his inner thoughts.

From his pages it is possible to see something of what brought these men out, away from the familiar life they knew, across the stormy Western Ocean, and thus to discern the shape of the foundations on which New France was to be reared. "Fair eye of the universe, nurse from of old of letters and of arms, help of the afflicted, strong stay of the Christian religion, dearest Mother—France!"[5]

Was it to be patriotism, then, which attended Canada's founding, the love of *la belle France*, the strong consciousness of *gesta Dei per Francos*? Or was it another vision? With France fading over the ocean's rim, he put his feelings into verse:

"Just as one sees the vigour of a plant enfeebled
At change of soil in lively way wake up
And scatter richer flowers upon the lawn,
Thus German Franks in Gaul replanted,
Thus ancient Saxon, on England's isle engrafted,
These new peoples, thus their new homes making,
Their rule and efforts did redouble. . . .

And so go we where heaven and fortune call us
To found afar another France more fair,
Turning our backs upon the faint of heart
Upon the soulless mass, upon disease and hunger,
The conqueror's ravages, old vices, old despair
The worn-out countryside itself—these we shall
all forget!
Oh, what ramparts in my mind's eye I see!
What towers rise up! What golden floods of rivers
bathe new walls!
What kingdoms rise from honourable achievement!
What laurels generous heads caress . . . !"[6]

"This province we are about to found will be worthy to be called your daughter, the colony of men of courage and the retreat of those of your children who are not contented with their lot,"[7] continues the enthusiastic maker of new peoples in his apostrophe to France. Some can see nothing in the new world but its difficulties—the perils of the ocean crossing, the dreariness of the wilderness, the absence of civilization. They are those without vision. "Fear not, ye men of Israel," he quotes, "I will help you, saith the Lord." The ramparts and towers would in due time rise. The history of Canada, then, as now, lay in the future. "America is promises."

Indians and Frenchmen; the past and the future

But were there not already people in America, men who had

immemorial title to it? In the regions into which he had come, the Spaniard had made short work of such, and their title. The cruelties of the Spaniard would not be repeated by the French. If it had been intended that the conquered should be destroyed, "God would not have commanded his apostles to go into all the world and preach the gospel." The only honourable course for the French to pursue, Lescarbot contended, in coming into the new world, was to attempt to preserve the inhabitants and bring them into the Christian religion. Thus at the very lifting of the curtain, the problem presented itself which has never been resolved: how can European civilization expand without injustice to those who encounter the expansion? When the inferior culture is overwhelmed, are the inferiors to find sufficient compensation for its destruction in 'the blessings of civilization'? For this problem, each of the colonizing nations was to present its own semi-solution. None was more humane, more genuinely Christian, than that of seventeenth-century France. And yet it was a failure, like the others. The Indian may occupy a large space in the annals of those dark and bloody times, but we know now that from the day the first white man stepped ashore, he was doomed. The history of the future did not lie with him.

For New France, the future would be decided by the men whose restlessness drew them across the Western Ocean and whose tenacity enabled them to stick out cold, starvation, and disease until the feeble transplanted root of which the verses speak began to show new signs of life. Why should they come? Prospect of gain, yes; excitement, yes; Indian souls, yes; Indian women, yes; France, yes; failures left behind, yes; hope, and a new and wider life, yes. There are few motives which may not be propounded, and few of which we can be sure.

At any rate, they came, the transplanted root struck, and a new experiment in human society began.

The first French ashore, whether sea-captains, traders, or priests, were men of action, though the strangeness of the passing scene gave them much to talk about and made some of them also men of the pen and as such put posterity under their debt. As men of action, the French built and traded, sowed natural and spiritual seeds, and acquainted themselves with the conditions of the new world. They learned the art of the canoe, they learned to face the winter, they even learned to meet that still greater peril, the scurvy; they learned Indian languages. They learned the Indians' ways, in all their filth and carnality, and in their occasional nobility. Some of them, like Etienne Brulé, learned to become Indians. From the first, they showed a surprising adaptability.

Like those of the other colonial peoples, their objectives in the new world were immediate, unplanned, changing from day to day. In the sense in which we understand the word, there was no *national* effort. To-day under the pressure of war and industry, nations vibrate like taut drums, but how could there have been national effort in the weak France of the early seventeenth century, a France only slowly recovering from a generation of miserable civil war, a France in which the cause of the strife, religion, still sharply divided men?

Division was reflected in all the first efforts of the French. A succession of individuals kept wheedling favours out of government, finding great names to grace their actions and pitting themselves and whatever resources they could collect against the Atlantic and what they hoped they could get out of what lay beyond it. Some of them were Protestants, some Catholics. If laymen, they got on well enough with each other, but if professional exponents of either of the two creeds, they felt called upon to carry their contentions to the recesses of the forest. To all of them, Catholic or Huguenot, the new world was a mine from which the European had already dug such materials as gold and codfish. Perhaps there would be other metals, or at any rate something valuable 'out there'. There might even be that which was piously rated as the most precious of all commodities—human souls.

And so were launched the innumerable little expeditions of our school-book days, and their promoters—the La Roches, the Pont-Gravés, the de Chastes, the De Monts, the Poutrincourts, the Caens, and the rest. A few of them grabbed quick profits in beaver skins, most of them were failures. The French efforts of these early days would not have got far had it not been for the appearance of a *man*, the man Champlain.

Champlain

No history of Canada can pass over Champlain as colonizer. Without his persistence and wisdom, the sound of the French tongue would not have continued to be heard on the banks of the St. Lawrence. It is fitting that each new modern generation should pay fresh tribute to him. Let us therefore hope that from some high cross-trees his mariner's eye can still discern these signals made from distant horizons: they will constitute his chief reward, for he had little enough during his mortal life.

Champlain had, roughly speaking, three main tasks: he had to get his men ashore and housed, he had to establish relationships with the aborigines, and he had to keep his employers satisfied. Of these, no doubt the last was the most difficult. For the crucial early years, he was not 'The Representative of France': on his first expedition to the St. Lawrence, he was little more than a passenger, and it was not until the second, in 1608, that he obtained command of a ship. But as he came up the St. Lawrence in that fateful year, he was to prove to be, in Parkman's fine phrase, "the Aeneas of a destined people and in his ship lay the embryo life of Canada."[8] The profit-and-loss accounts of those early beaver voyages have long since been cast, the Indians have ceased to be more than picturesque embroidery on the margin of Canadian life, but the men who went ashore at Quebec in 1608 have still their life in the French-speaking people of Canada.

It would be impossible for the most enthusiastic Francophile to close his eyes to the minor scale of the enterprise thus begun. An uncertain ship's company and some building supplies—these were the beginnings of Canada. The supplies were used to erect a structure that has since become as famous as it must have been uncomfortable, the 'Habitation', built where now stands the 'Lower Town' of Quebec. The ship's company celebrated the beginnings of France overseas by a conspiracy against Champlain, which he ended by hanging the leader and putting his head upon a pike. For the information of those who at present bear the name, this first man hanged in Canada was called Duval.

After the buildings had been completed and winter came, the scourge of the pioneer descended—scurvy. The simple remedy learned from the Indians by Jacques Cartier—spruce-needle tea—was unknown to Champlain. Consequently by spring most of his men had died: Canada thus began, like other colonies, in disturbance, disease and starvation. The fortunes of the colonization venture were still further lowered through the loss by its backer, De Monts, of his fur-trading monopoly. This reduced Champlain again for several years to the status of a mere sea-captain, and it was not until 1613 that the revival of the old Roberval charter under one of the grandees of France secured his advancement for the first time to official position—he became *Lieutenant-in-America* of the newly formed chartered company. From that time until his death, although the authority under which he operated constantly varied, Champlain was the heart and soul of 'New France', and before his death the trading post which he had established had become a little knot of settlement.

Notes to Chapter 1.

1. Samuel Eliot Morison, *Admiral of the Ocean Sea* (Boston, 1942), p. 417.
2. *The Works of Samuel de Champlain* (Champlain Society Edition), Vol. III, p. 257.
3. Ibid, pp. 180 ff.
4. Marc Lescarbot, *The History of New France* (1615) (Champlain Society Edition), Vol. II, p. 172.
5. Ibid., Vol I, p. 12.
6. Ibid., Vol II, p. 387, present author's translation.
7. Ibid., Vol I, p. 144.
8. Francis Parkman, *Pioneers of France* (Boston, 1898), p. 325.

2: The first impact
of the wilderness

FOR NEARLY TWO HUNDRED YEARS after Columbus, most Europeans who came to found colonies in America ended up rotten with scurvy or dead of starvation: only by slow degrees did men learn to wrest a living from the land itself. Down to Penn's Philadelphia (1682), nearly every colony in North America presents the same doleful tale.

New France was no exception to the rule. In 1535, Cartier starved at Stadacona. In the fifteen-sixties, French Huguenots starved in Florida. In 1605, Champlain's Frenchmen starved and died of scurvy on the Ste. Croix river, and in 1608-1609 at Quebec, his men once again were starving or dying. About the same time in the much more genial climate of Virginia, few Englishmen came through the winter. It was not until they had been on the St. Lawrence for thirty or forty years that the French passed beyond immediate danger of starvation.

The men who starved and died while getting Europe transplanted to America were just as intelligent as we are, just as brave, and probably a good deal hardier. Why then all the misfortune? Every schoolboy will stand ready with an answer, and the sum of the answers will be—lack of the technical progress we have made since those days. Among the Pilgrims who settled at Plymouth in 1620, some there were who had brought with them a scarce and novel commodity—soap. When the accounts were reckoned up at the end of the first winter, it was asserted that mortality had been much greater among those who had washed with soap than those who had gone dirty in the good old-fashioned way. Soap, nevertheless, was to become one of the main pillars of our North American civilization.

The French at Quebec had no excessive prejudice in favour of soap. By our fastidious standards, their cleanliness left much to be desired, but they were more particular than the Indians. The accounts they left behind them are full of the disgust they experienced for the more revolting aspects of native beastliness. Sucking raw corncobs which had been rotted in mud and water until they stank was bad enough, though if you were going to go among the Indians, it had be taken as all in the day's work; but eating a dead dog that had been thrown out to rot weeks before, as Champlain saw some Indians do, was carrying things a bit far.

Indian filth and Indian carnality

Equally common are the observations on the Indians' carnality. Even by the standards of our own pornographic age, some of the practices recorded bear printing only in the staid columns of the learned books.[1] These were not all merely the animal simplicity of primitive men; there was a touch of sophistication in them. When the braves were about to go off on a war party, their women, in serving them their departing meal, all stripped naked. This may have been religious ritual but the children of the forest were careful to warn the good missionaries of what was about to happen, in order to give them time to beat an orderly retreat. Other Frenchmen were not as shocked as the missionaries: like the questing male everywhere, they lost no time in turning such occasions to good account.[2] White blood must have begun to pass into the wigwams from the first but this does not argue a return current: interbreeding was confined to the Indian mother's side.[3]

Apparently the cruelties of the Indians shocked the French, especially the missionaries, rather less than their sexual performances. Europe itself was still in the age of cruelty and what would revolt us to-day, people of the time were able to take in their stride. Moreover, for missionaries who had schooled themselves in the belief that the heavenly kingdom was the goal and this life but a transient experience, perhaps best lost quickly, tortures represented a brief moment before eternity: the important point was to be sure that you came out on the right side of eternity—hence the insistence on baptism and conversion, and hence the extraordinary fortitude shown by the Jesuit martyrs. No one, nevertheless, must jump to the conclusion that the French were not affected by Indian cruelties: there is plenty of evidence to show that they did their best to prevent them when they could. The classical case is that of the Iroquois being tortured by the Indian allies of Champlain after the Lake Champlain foray of 1609.

"... Each took a brand and burned this poor wretch (the Iroquois prisoner) a little at a time. . . . Sometimes they would leave off, throwing water on his back. Then they tore his nails out and applied fire to the ends of his fingers and to his *membrum virile*. Afterwards they scalped him and let hot [spruce?] gum drip on the crown of his head. They then pierced his arms near the wrists and pulled out his sinews with sticks by main force, and if they could not get them out, they cut them off. This poor wretch uttered strange cries, and I felt pity at seeing him treated in this way. Still he bore it so firmly that sometimes one would have said that he felt scarcely any pain. They begged me repeatedly [to join in]."

Champlain then said that the French did not commit such cruelties but killed people outright, if they had to kill. This seemed a strange point of view to the Indians, who argued that in that case people would not feel any pain, but after some discussion, Champlain got permission to shoot the victim, which he did.[4]

Champlain was a great and good man, but he had been a soldier and he was a man of his time, and the times rolled on against a backdrop of hardship, hardness, dirt, cruelty, and violence quite out of the experience of those of us moderns fortunate enough to live west of the Atlantic. This background, which conditioned all Europeans of the period, made it easier for them to meet the hard conditions of life in the new world than it would have been for us, and put them closer to the primitives.[5] Man-hunting was not far from just another form of sport. On de Poutrincourt's voyage down the coast of New England in 1605, there seems to have been a constant fusilade kept up against natives, the reason always being 'self-defence', but with no sentimentality over 'another redskin biting the dust'. And of all the colonizing peoples, the French had the best record. Now at mid-twentieth century, Europeans find it less easy to crowd into native territories, pre-empting lands and making new white societies: they have grown squeamish about the bloodshed (but only within a generation or so) and as a result, are losing their colonies. Among whites, only hard-bitten Russians indifferent to world opinion, and possibly Afrikaners, still seem able to act in the old ruthless way.

The 'noble red man'

Once the white man had pushed back the forest and the dangers it contained, among which the Indian was the greatest, he could afford to begin to romanticize the situation: the fiends in human shape could be thought of as children of nature. In Europe the myth of the 'noble savage' in his free-dom, simplicity, and essential dignity, was to go far and become a major factor in the political thinking of advanced minds. What would Rousseau have done without the American Indian? "Man is born free, but everywhere he is in chains." It was civilization which had done the dirty job: the Indian was free and innocent before the white man began to corrupt him. The state of nature, powerful recourse of the great thinkers of both seventeenth and eighteenth centuries, was conveniently far away across the seas and only one of them, Thomas Hobbes, had the piercing vision which enabled him to descry it as one wherein man's life was "solitary, poor, nasty, brutish and short."

For the whites in America, to whom the Indian was always more or less visible, sentiment never grew to romantic heights: the best that could be done out here was to make the Indian an expert hunter and trail-blazer, the hero of a 'wild west show', a *Last of the Mohicans*, a picturesque, rather than a romantic, figure. The French term for 'Indians' was realistic, *les sauvages*.

The first comers were under no illusions about the noble red man, his traits and his capacities: they described him as they found him, and the description are seldom flattering. His dirt, his carnality, and his cruelty have been touched on. He did not show up too well, even in those arts in which he was supposed to excel. On every count, the French were better warriors. When they had learned the ways of the bush, they became just as good canoemen and bushmen—and it did not take them long to learn. Indians at first were more or less reliable providers of meat and fish, usually less rather than more: the French after some serious initial fumbling, learned to do their own hunting and fishing, and when there was anything to be found they apparently did it just as well as the Indians.

And they were infinitely more flexible and adaptable. An interesting example of this quality was furnished by de Poutrincourt at Port Royal in the spring of 1606. After building a pair of boats, the expedition found they had no pitch for paying the seams. De Poutrincourt began to collect spruce gum and solved the problem of melting down and purifying the gum by an ingenious arrangement of cooking pots, one inside another, to make an alembic, or primitive still. "This was wonderful in a person who had never seen such an operation," says Lescarbot,[6] and the astonished savages said . . . "The Normans know many things."

This kind of inventiveness turns up on every page of the old voyages. During the famous winter at Port Royal when the Order of Good Cheer was helping to pass the time, and everybody apparently was able to stuff to bursting, conservative French artisans actually began to discover that they could do things beyond the range of their own trades: "certain masons and stone-cutters turned their hands to baking, and made as good bread as that of Paris. So, too, one of our wood-sawyers several times made us a great quantity of charcoal."[7] Right at the beginning, the new world began playing one of its biggest tricks, peeling off the careful specialization of the generations left behind and making the master of one trade a jack of all. Jacks of all trades Canadians have continued to be ever since, and every nook and cranny of their social, economic, and political organization still bears witness to the fact.

The French, then, had not met natives for whom they could have much respect. Treacherous, thievish, and cruel they were —the epithets pile up. Had they no redeeming qualities at all? Of course they had souls, and these theoretically brought the same price in heaven as did those of the whites. This was the missionary angle, but until the missionary day of dominance came, it was an angle that did not get overmuch attention. Did not the laymen then find anything commendable in the Indians? Yes, they did, and they seem to have been ready to give credit where credit was due. Champlain actually came upon a clean tribe, the Andatahouate, living near Georgian Bay: at least, he referred to them as "the cleanest savages in their household affairs that I have ever seen"[8] which is perhaps like the testimonial to the excellence of the cook—"the tallest cook I have ever employed." Lescarbot affirms of the Micmacs around Port Royal "as for our savages, I never saw amongst them any immodest gesture or look. . . ."[9] Sagard, who devoted a good deal of space to retailing their moral shortcomings, declared that Huron women "usually love their husbands better than the women here. If they were Christians, there would be families among whom God would take pleasure to dwell."[10] Nor did he fail to experience genuine kindness from some of his Indian fellow travellers: "Although his only covering was a bear-skin, he made me share it when it was raining at night, without my asking; and in the evening he even arranged a place for me to sleep at night. . . . In compassion for my difficulties and weakness, he would not let me row or wield a paddle. . . ."[11] Such extracts make plain that it was not only lack of gravity and of restraint in speech which caused the Indians at first to call the Frenchmen 'women': Champlain was bad enough with his squeamishness over the good old Huron custom of chopping out enemy hearts, but here was a whole class of Frenchmen who when it came to looking after themselves were as helpless as women, Frenchmen who dressed rather like women, too, who logically must be women!

Why the French came: the appeal of freedom

When the Frenchman first came upon the Indian, he found not indeed 'the noble savage,' but a stalwart man, above all a free man. Yet the subtle poison lying in metal cooking pots began at once to sap both the stalwartness and the freedom. The Indian remained, not conquered and enslaved, merely pushed aside. How could the first French know that within a century and a half their descendants would suffer a fate with unwelcome aspects of similarity?

For twenty years after they began to renew their interest in America, the French did little more than disport themselves in regions of unaccustomed freedom. They built a couple of small trading posts (which have been romanticized out of recognition by our English popularisers), sent various ships along the coast and penetrated a respectable distance inland along the obvious line of the St. Lawrence-Ottawa-Lake Huron route. Their fur trade did not amount to much and their missionary effort had hardly started. Many of the 'gentlemen' among them, of whom Lescarbot is the sole vocal, but delightful, example, probably came over out of curiosity, attracted by that nostalgia for the wilderness which crops up in most of us, that desire to escape from restraints of civilization which has propelled the white man all over the globe and which has a good deal to do with his zest in war. One can see the appeal of 'the lodge in some vast wilderness' in the way in which de Poutrincourt fell in love with Port Royal: he secured a grant of it *en seigneurie* from de Monts (later confirmed by the Crown) and had every intention of making it his home. And why not? "When at last within the harbour"—i.e., inside the Annapolis Basin—"it was a wondrous sight for us to see its fair extent and the mountains and hills which shut it in, and I wondered that so fair a spot remained desert, and all wooded, seeing that so many folk are ill-off in this world who could make their profit of this land if they only had a leader to bring them thither."[12]

Why the humble came is only a guess, for they could not express themselves in writing. Roberval in the previous century had had an order on the prisons—that was one way of getting men to come. The men who accompanied de Monts and the others were not secured in that way: they seem to have included a good supply of honest craftsmen, men for almost every necessary task. Of course romantic notions of freedom appeal to this class of men—we have abundant testimony to that effect from later ages—as well as to 'their betters,' and among the early colonists of all nations, notions of freedom were strong. Commendable as they were, they were also the cause of a great deal of trouble. Conspiracies and incipient rebellions seem to have been endless. Disobedience seemed almost the rule: when five of de Poutrincourt's young men refused to leave their camp and come aboard his vessel for the night, two of them as a result were killed by the Indians, two died from the wounds they had received, and the fifth was the man Duval whom Champlain later had hanged at Quebec. As Lescarbot says, "the disaster was caused by the folly and disobedience of one whom I will not name, for he died there: he was wont to play the braggart among young fellows . . . and because they would not let him get drunk, he had sworn . . . that he would not return to the long-boat, nor did he. . . ." (being one of the slain).[13]

Freedom seemed to go to everyone's head! And anyone who has ever been out of civilization knows how unavoidable that is. Once away from their familiar surroundings, men become hard to handle. Separated from families and friends, they become restless and like armies on foreign soil, they feel free from restraint. Starting over again in a new country beyond the law (except such law as the leader can by moral authority supply) is no simple business. And so the French, like the English, were to find that colonization was no mere parading about in the bush, firing off your gun at a moose or a savage (not much difference between them, really), no mere giving the Indian a bead for a beaver skin. Lescarbot puts it well: "Many who are ignorant of navigation think that the establishment of a plantation in an unexplored country is an easy matter, but by the history of these voyages they will see that it is much easier said than done. . . . In vain does one run and weary himself in search of havens wherein fate is kind!"[14]

Some of these early adventurers, considering their difficulties, did very well, De Monts especially. He kept on for several years despite financial losses and despite the infinite number of perplexities and disappointments prepared for him at home —there were still many there who thought 'colonizing' could pay and so wished to grab some of its profits—and if he did not found a colony, that was his bad luck, for in his case it does not seem true to make the customary declaration and say that as a fur-trader he was indifferent to settlement. The truth was that colonizing is always prodigiously expensive and that settlers of a genuine kind were as hard to find in France as diamonds. The proof of the statement is obvious: these early ships' companies did not contain a single woman!

Quebec, 'founded' though it was in 1608, for years remained merely a fur post, its men a rude garrison liable to be withdrawn at any time. But when Louis Hébert secured a grant of land on 'The Plains of Abraham' and brought his family out to live on it, which was not until fourteen years after Champlain had first visited the St. Lawrence, then indeed, something had happened. The presence of women meant that the French had married themselves to the new world and the guarantee of the future lay in the new sounds that were shortly to be heard about the post—the voices of children to whom Canada was native land.

Notes to Chapter 2.

1. For example see Gabriel Sagard, *The Long Journey to the Country of the Hurons* (Paris, 1632) (Champlain Society Edition), Vol. XXV, 118.
2. See Sagard, op. cit., p. 134, where he specifically accuses his fellow-countrymen of demoralizing the Indian women.
3. According to an article in the *Bulletin des Recherches Historiques,* Vol. 34, p. 634, in the entire period 1608-1667 only three marriages were recorded at Quebec between Frenchmen and Indian women. Marriages, of course, did not have too immediate a bearing on the situation.
4. *The Works of Samuel de Champlain* (Champlain Society Edition), Vol II, p. 101.
5. For contrast and for pioneering at the other end of the period, our end, see the interesting account of the attack on, and conquest of, the Peace River country in the nineeteen-hundreds by A. M. Bezanson, *Sod-Busters Invade the Peace* (Toronto, 1954).
6. Marc Lescarbot, *The History of New France* (1615) (Champlain Society Edition), Vol. II, p. 348.
7. Ibid., Vol. II, p. 321.
8. Champlain, op. cit., Vol. III, p. 98.
9. Lescarbot, op. cit., Vol. III, p. 164.
10. Sagard, op. cit., p. 102.
11. Ibid, p. 62.
12. Lescarbot, op. cit., Vol. II, p. 312.
13. Ibid, p. 334.
14. Ibid, p. 278.

3: The foundation stones of New France

NEW FRANCE AS A COLONY, as distinct from a mere trading post, dates from after the first English occupation, under the Kirke brothers, which ended in 1632. As a trading post, there is little reason to think that Quebec would have advanced much beyond the later English posts on Hudson Bay. It is true that it was surrounded by a fair amount of arable land and had a not impossible climate, but a mere trading post, whatever the nature of the country around it, is unlikely by itself to change into a community. The parallel in the Hudson's Bay territories to what was to happen at Quebec after 1632 is to be found in Red River in 1812, when at last there appeared a man, Lord Selkirk, to whom the founding of a colony was all in all.

Here again we come to Champlain. No Champlain, no Quebec. Few men in the face of the dissipation of his life's work which the Kirkes' occupation accomplished, would have had the heart to begin all over again. That, however, is what he did. Without his insistence, France probably would not have persisted in her stipulations for the return of the colony, and when it was returned, it took him to nurse it back to life again. This task he had just nicely begun when death overtook him (1635), and it was left to his successors to carry on. The line he had struck out had apparently become plain, for after this there was no turning back: France was on the St. Lawrence to stay.

To one other man must go a large share also for the survival of French power in North America. This was the great Cardinal Richelieu. It was Richelieu who put behind colonization projects, and for the first time, the official power of France. Until his death in 1642, his aid and support continued to be given to the colony. Richelieu, though a cardinal, was not primarily interested in the missionary side of French colonial activity. He was a secular statesman, far-seeing and Machiavellian in his attitudes, and he was apparently determined to secure for France her footing in the new world.

Richelieu's concern with the economic side of statecraft and its reflections in colonial policy was so close as to evoke the assertion that he, not Colbert, was the father of 'Colbertisme', that is, the system whereby the power of the state was applied directly to the economic side of life.[1] This is what writers in the English language usually call 'mercantilism'. Mercantilism in some form or other is much older than either Richelieu or Colbert, but it was Richelieu's mercantilism by which New France was first affected, not Colbert's, and that for the simple fact that Richelieu preceded his disciple by some thirty years.

Richelieu's idea seems to have been to extend French overseas commerce and dominion by taking a leaf out of the Dutchmen's book: he accordingly organized several monopolistic trading companies, some for one part of the world, some for others, and to these he gave large powers. Although not one of them was successful, the fault was not altogether his, and the particular company by which he intended to make Canada a true colony may be called the least unsuccessful. This company was the famous 'Hundred Associates.' It was little more than a reshaping of the similar ventures permitted by the king before its organization in 1627, the difference being that whereas its predecessors had been private ventures, it had the active support of the State.

The 'Hundred Associates', though mercantile in objectives, was not composed principally of merchants: in fact, among its members, there were only twenty merchants. An inspection of names gives the strong impression that Richelieu filled out the one hundred associates by conscripting his own officials. At any rate, there was enough influence and wealth among them to enable a fleet to be raised, with plans for taking a number of colonists to Canada. Unfortunately, as all this was coming to fruition, the comic-opera war of 1629-1632 broke out, and among its incidents was the arrival at Quebec of three privateering brothers who had been born and brought up in France and who now proceeded to take Quebec on behalf of an English king who did not want it. These were the Kirkes, sons of an English Protestant merchant of Dieppe, a man probably burning with resentment at the prospect of being debarred from the trade of the St. Lawrence. Their capture of the company's fleet virtually bankrupted it and prevented it from playing its intended role.

After the war was over, England returned Quebec to France

in return for the French king's promise this time really to pay a debt which he should have paid some years before. It was during this second phase of the company's régime, in the decade 1633-1643, that the scales were turned and Canada, from being merely a fur post, became a colony.

The colony begun: the sixteen-thirties

The company, which operated by passing on to others through grants the primary work of settlement, had the good luck to find several superior applicants coming forward. When these persons had committed themselves to New France, the job was virtually done. It was in 1633 that Dr. Robert Gifford was given one of the first seigneurial grants in Canada, just to the east of Quebec itself, on the Beauport River:

> "En toute justice et seigneurie, à perpétuité, une lieue de terre à prendre le long de la côte du fleuve Saint-Laurent, sur une lieue et demi de profondeur, à l'endroit où la rivière appelée Notre-Dame-de-Beauport entre dans la dit fleuve, icelle rivière comprise."[2]

It was in June 1634 that Gifford, bringing along with him perhaps as many as forty others, some of them afterwards of famous name in French Canada such as the Juchereaux and the Bouchers, disembarked at Quebec. Thus began the well-known Beauport countryside, the heart and centre of French Canada.

Various statistics have been collected to show the number of inhabitants at given times and the immigration year by year, but it is not an easy matter to find agreement among them. Salone[3] thinks that there may have been 90 or 100 persons around Quebec by 1636. By that year, he says, Quebec, Beauport, Beaupré, and Trois Rivières had acquired a settled French population, " 'des Français habitués' comme on dit couramment."[4] Lanctot gives a table of "young female immigrants,"[5] beginning in 1634. He manages to find just 11 in the crucial decade, 1634-1643, and only 47 in the decade following, 1644-1653 inclusive. Down to as late as 1662, his total is no higher than 228, so that the colony was limited in a fundamental fashion during this period. Benjamin Sulte says that "en 1640, nous ne dépassions guère deux cents âmes."[6] Another inquiry produces 296 immigrants between 1608 and 1640.[7] Still another gives a table of population for Quebec from 1608 to 1631. We begin with 31 individuals in 1608[8] and reach a crest of 85 in 1621 and 1622, after which we gradually sag down to 55 on the eve of the English occupation.

Such figures are not impressive. They are overshadowed by

a much simpler concrete fact, namely that it was not until 1644 that there was landed at Quebec the first horse in Canada![9]

While Englishmen in thousands were flocking to New England (something like fifteen or twenty thousand to Massachusetts Bay alone, in the sixteen-thirties), it was only by ones and twos that Frenchmen were being coaxed out to New France. An impartial observer of, say, 1650, looking at what had occurred in the English colonies as contrasted with New France, would have had little hesitation at predicting the ultimate outcome.

For the time, nevertheless, the sixteen-thirties saw the corner turned: New France had become the abode of Frenchmen overseas, to more and more of whom it was becoming 'home'. This was the first great point which the passage of the years decided. The second was decided not by time but by specific act, but it had scarcely less to do with the colony's fate than did the first: this was the decision not to admit Huguenots. Of this decision, much could be written, for it brings into juxtaposition all the tremendous questions posed for that age, and for our own, by the existence side by side of two religions, two philosophies, two ways of life. Nearly five generations later, at the English Conquest, the questions posed and apparently decided in 1628, had all to be faced again, and once more the two religions would stand in jarring contrast, their antagonisms, now reinforced by race, providing much of the stuff of Canadian history.

In 1628, when Richelieu resolved to exclude the Huguenots, the decision was necessarily made on circumstances as they then were. There is no reason to think that Richelieu, left to himself, would have made it as he did. It is true that he was a cardinal of the Church, but religious zeal did not play much part in that cold and opportunist heart. Primarily he was a statesman, playing the statesman's game of power, and since considerations of power made it wise for him to favour Protestant countries, favour them he did. Hence his nickname, "The Cardinal of the Huguenots."

Much pressure was put on Richelieu by pietists such as Bérulle to[10] secure the exclusion. Two considerations seem to have decided the matter. The first and perhaps less important was religion. In 1628, the very year of the exclusion, Richelieu and his master Louis XIII were in the camp before the Protestant city of La Rochelle, which later had to yield to them. Yet they do not seem to have been much affected by fanaticism. But other important people were, including some close to the fate of Canada.

The second and more important consideration was the simple point that Canada had been left for over twenty-five years to a succession of Protestant merchants, all of whom had been expected to make a start in colonizing it and, with the possible exception of de Monts, none of whom did. The Huguenots had simply thrown their prospects away. Was it that like other Calvinists, they were so occupied with the main chance that they could not 'see the distant scene?' It does not seem improbable. "A man's reach must exceed his grasp," says Robert Browning, "or what's a Heaven for?" The Calvinist's reach has seldom exceeded his grasp and consequently there has been no heaven for him. Betting on a sure thing does not found empires: that interesting occupation has been left to the vain and frivolous Catholics and Anglicans, romantics whom dull sobriety has not inhibited from indulging in grandiose dreams.

So the French empire in America was to be a Catholic empire. In romantic daring, it would be none the worse for that: in solid accomplishment, perhaps much the worse. If the Calvinist cannot found far-flung empires, he is a good hand at consolidating the ground. Huguenots unwanted in France might have come to Canada in numbers more or less comparable to those of their fellow outcasts, the Puritans in New England. Then the whole history of the continent would have been different. As it was, New France was to be Catholic, Catholic of the Counter-Reformation. Zeal, piety, strict morality, stern conformity, the humanitarian spirit, and a simplicity which opened the doors to an over-production of miracles, were to mark the new community's life. Implicit in the decision was the theocracy shortly to appear, the all-powerful rule of a priestly class which held on with little modification until the English Conquest, and in some respects, still holds on. Here, along the St. Lawrence, was to be placed a little corner of North America that should preserve, perhaps more faithfully than any corner of Europe itself, those medieval centuries that had been so completely dominated by the great Church of which New France was to prove one of the most devoted provinces.

'Upon this rock—'

The conditions which made possible this preservation and extension of medievalism resulted from the circumstances of New France's growth. These were such as to mark the new colony from the first with a strong individuality, and were easy and encouraging from some points of view, so severe from others as to render at times its continuance doubtful. They may have constituted that 'optimum challenge' of which

Arnold Toynbee in his study of civilization makes so much.

What were these conditions?

Among the encouraging elements, the transfer to America must be placed high. Here we have—and this applies to all the new-world peoples—clear as crystal, the beneficent effects arising from the challenge of a new environment. From the very first landfall on American soil down to the present day, the wilderness has called forth resourcefulness, adaptability, ingenuity, hardihood, and a host of similar qualities. It has been the largest visible stimulant of both the French-Canadian and the English-Canadian peoples. The fact is so obvious that it does not need enlarging upon—except in that this book as a whole is an enlargement upon it.

The French found in the new world unlimited scope for their sense of adventure and for their sense of freedom, both of which were cramped at home. Those at the top, such as a Champlain or a La Salle, instead of taking part in the king's wars and campaigning on the Rhine, could cross the ocean under the king's flag and find for the king new rivers such as the Mississippi, and new routes through the 'trackless wilderness.' The author can testify from modest personal experience that no more attractive occupation exists. Pathfinding brings with it as tangible a sense of accomplishment as man can well have. Its effect is a tonic to his whole being, a challenge to perform other feats of pathfinding in other and more complex spheres: it thus spills over into accomplishment in Church and State and culture.[11]

A second formative experience grew directly out of the first: this was the challenge of the Iroquois. New France was not occupied easily. The early brushes along the seacoast, with the occasional Frenchman killed in ambush, were only what explorers everywhere have had to anticipate. But after the colony had been founded, its very existence had to be fought for, fought for long and continuously, and often it hung by a thread. For half a century the Iroquois were at the gates of the colony. Dollard des Ormeaux saved it in 1660,[12] the Marquis de Tracy in 1665. Nor was that the end, for years later, the Iroquois were still at it, and in 1689 the dreadful massacre of Lachine carried fire and slaughter to the gates of Montreal. It was not until the beginning of the eighteenth century, when in Queen Anne's War (1703-1714) the Iroquois were forced into neutrality, that New France could feel free of the danger. Other colonies had their Indian wars but for none was the struggle so long or so bitter as for Canada. These long years of travail were years of purgation—those who could not 'stand the gaff,' *les fuyards*, went back to France. The French who remained fought long and hard and valiantly for every inch of soil they won.

Closely related to the fight for existence in the colony were the forest experiences in which the Hurons were overwhelmed and many a Jesuit missionary sent to his martyrdom. It is impossible to overpaint the effect of the Jesuit martyrdoms on French Canada's history—an effect which has steadily increased as time has rolled on. Here was heroism, stark, fearless heroism, heroism purged of all the dross of worldliness. No wonder that a great Catholic church this day adorns the site of the martyrdoms or that a Protestant and English Canadian poet should put the martyr's faith in moving words:—

> "There is no gain but this—that what you suffer
> Shall be of God: your loneliness in travel
> Will be relieved by angels overhead;
> Your silence will be sweet, for you will learn
> How to commune with God; rapids and rocks
> Are easier than the steps of Calvary.
> There is a consolation in your hunger
> And in abandonment upon the road,
> For once there was a greater loneliness
> And deeper hunger."[13]

Here at the very base of French Canada's story lies that firm foundation, saints of the Lord. Could there be a firmer! Latimer and Ridley, we English think of, Hampden, Florence Nightingale, David Livingstone, and the long roll of secular heroes: we have nothing that shines more brightly than do names like Brébeuf and Lallemant. For their like, perhaps we must look to old France itself and St. Joan.

But for St. Joan there are more direct comparisons. Prominent almost from the first were the women in New France's story. Marie Hébert, wife of Louis Hébert, the first settler in 1617, has left a memory of pioneer endurance which is still green. In another generation came the famous trio, Marie de l'Incarnation, Jeanne Mance, and Marguèrite Bourgeois. These women founded the schooling and nursing callings of New France and several of the actual institutions in which they were concerned still exist: Marie de l'Incarnation, a combination of mystic and practical person, was the foundress of the Ursuline Convent of Quebec. Marguèrite Bourgeois instituted the primary education of girls in the Montreal district, and her efforts eventually echoed throughout the colony. Jeanne Mance was the nurse *par excellence*: her monuments are found today throughout the land in the innumerable Catholic nurses' residences which bear her name. Much more significant than the specific tasks these women performed was their example and inspiration: their bravery, their constancy, their kindness and faithfulness have set the pattern for Quebec womanhood ever since.

The century appropriately closes with a secular heroine, Madeleine de Verchères, the youngster who, as every school child knows, beat off the Iroquois and saved the people of her household. It is all a remarkable record, set down here in a word only and with many good names omitted. Any country with such a roster may call itself fortunate. It would be strange if a heritage of this type had not influenced the intimate life of French Canada, giving to woman a place and importance little affected by her legal disabilities. After all, the Roman law was kinder to her in matters of property than was English common law. New France, from many angles, was a woman-fashioned society.[14]

Women were not the only remarkable personages to be found in New France. The words are pretentious perhaps, but they should nevertheless be used—the colony abounded in great souls! For we have to add to the marytrs and the women the men of action: they form a list whose names have been familiar to all Canadians, French and English, from earliest childhood. As long as men retain their interest in geographical exploration, such names as those of La Salle, Joliet, and La Vérendrye, to select only three from a score, will continue on their lips.

All in all, it is something not often encountered in history for a few hundred people to provide the locus and origin of so long a list of distinguished names.

It is no wonder, in view of the foregoing, that the French in America were filled with a sense of magnificent accomplishment. As the seventeenth century drew to a close, they could contemplate a colony stretching along the St. Lawrence for a couple of hundred miles, and other, though smaller, settlements in Acadia, Cape Breton, Isle St. Jean and Terre-Neuve. They had captured all the English posts in Hudson's Bay and had worsted the English in fair fight. Later on, Englishmen were to boast that one Englishman was worth three Frenchmen, but to judge from the encounters in America during the seventeenth century, which invariably ended (before they had really begun) with the pusillanimous surrender of the English, at that period one Frenchman was easily worth three Englishmen. When that Frenchman was a Lemoyne d'Iberville,[15] he was worth whole garrisons of Englishmen, especially if they happened to be Hudson's Bay men. And in addition to proved valour, the French had penetrated into the distant recesses of the continent, writing a chapter in exploration that ranks with the greatest. In comparison with the wealth and the number of inhabitants of the English colonies, the accomplishments of the French may seem small. That is not the comparison French Canadians have been accustomed to make. They have thought of the inequalities they faced and of the valour with which they faced them. To whom, they might have asked, has history given the glory of Thermopylae, to the Persians or to the Greeks?

It is easy to see what all this comes to when added up. Most people at some time or other in their history think of themselves as uniquely favoured by fortune. The step to the idea of the chosen people is a short one. French Canada holds this view of itself today and has long held it. It has furnished the main psychological drive for her survival and has become the well-worn myth of her history. Here were God's chosen few. Here on the soil of North America were once more being displayed the *gesta Dei per Francos*. Here were God's martyred saints, their blood shed vicariously for their race. Could there have been a better set of foundation stones for a people?

Notes to Chapter 3.

1. Henri Hausser, *La Pensée et l'Action Economique du Cardinal de Richelieu* (Paris, 1944).
2. "In full justice and seigniory, in perpetuity, a league of land taken along the side of the River St. Lawrence, by a league and a half in depth, at the place where the river called Notre-Dame-de-Beauport enters the said river, that river included."
3. Emile Salone, *La Colonisation de la Nouvelle France* (Paris, c. 1910), p. 58.
4. Ibid., p. 62.
5. Gustave Lanctot, *Filles de Joie ou Filles de Roi?* (Montreal, 1952). p. 76.
6. *Mélanges Historiques* (Montreal, 1918), Vol. II, p. 16.
7. *Bulletin des Recherches Historiques,* Vol. 46, p. 179.
8. Ibid., Vol. 37, pp. 321, 386.
9. *Canada and Its Provinces,* Vol. 23, p. 289.
10. Pierre de Bérulle, 1575-1629, founder of the Congregation of the Oratory and later Cardinal.
11. For example, the Jesuit pathfinders produced the Jesuit *Relations,* a splendid literary monument in early Canadian history.
12. This has been disputed by Professor Adair, but he has not affected the myth.
13. E. J. Pratt, *Brebeuf and His Brethren* (Toronto, 1940), p. 24.
14. See for more of this p. 51.
15. See Nellis M. Crouse, *Lemoyne d'Iberville, Soldier of New France* (Ithaca, N.Y., 1954).

4: A community formed

NOT LONG AFTER THE YOUNG KING LOUIS XIV came of age, New France was given the institutions of a province of France (1663)—governor, intendant and Sovereign Council, with deputy governors and intendants at Montreal and Trois Rivières. The current legal code of the metropolitan capital, the Custom of Paris, hitherto informally used, now became the official code, and as such began its evolution into 'the law of Canada.'

The new turn brought not only institutions but a new vigour embodied in new and able men, conspicuously the Intendant Jean Talon. Talon may have been only a subordinate of the great administrator Colbert, but the energy with which he went at getting the settlements on their feet was his own. His measures are well known—the valiant attempts to set up industries such as shipbuilding and brewing, the new villages he founded back inland from Quebec, his gallant efforts to find wives for men who otherwise would have had indefinitely to face the rigours of celibacy. Under this tide of initiative, the old bad days of 'free enterprise' were left behind and the settlements, thanks to public initiative, began to fuse into something like a community. The worst of the pioneering stage was over and men could now think of themselves not merely as Frenchmen overseas, but as colonials; that is, as people who, remaining just as French as ever, were probably in the new world to stay. During the generation after the establishment of the royal province of New France, all the big things that mark a people's life got some kind of permanent form given to them: government, law, landholding, the kind and amount of education deemed necessary, the relations between Church and State— all such big matters took on the shape they were to maintain until the English Conquest.

What is to be said of the big things can also be said of the little, for in little things as in big, every new group of people strives for a norm of behaviour. When this is achieved, a way of life has been created, and in it, certain types come to be regarded as representative. Any such 'norm' becomes surrounded with ritual behaviour, behaviour which is in a quite indisputable way 'correct'. In New France, a type was ready to hand, in the Catholic priesthood. Here was a group which led a stylized, ritualistic life, the ideal of those to whom it gave leadership. Among the forces that made the French society of Canada, gave it its tone and its day-to-day ways, the habits and manners of the priesthood were to be foremost.

But new societies must begin at the beginning. Every life situation has to be worked out and surrounded with rules, for when people are precipitated into new environments, the old rules often will not apply. "Is it proper?" becomes one of the major questions in life (hence our North American spate of 'etiquette books', with ready-made rules for people who face new situations for which they do not know the rules, and for which there may be no rules). Was it proper for a man owning a seigneury to work with his own hands? Not in France, certainly. But in France seigneurs were of seigneurial rank, whereas in Canada almost anyone might be a seigneur. Many peasants were to become seigneurs in Canada. Must they no longer work with their hands? Since the usual alternative was to starve, the rules got changed.

Most things did get changed in the new world. They got changed while remaining the same, and that has been the mark of its life, whether English or French: Canadians have brought their civilization across the sea with them but have adapted it to fit their new environment; *'plus ça change, plus c'est la même chose.'*

Our objective here must be to try to discover how the French genius got changed in transplantation to Canada; the French genius, that tough, resilient spirit which for century after century had been forming itself in the most fertile land in Europe, constituting itself the centre of civilization, of culture, of wealth, and of power. To English Canadians, immersed in their own rich heritage, it rarely occurs to reflect that their French fellow-citizens brought with them the proudest and most distinguished tradition of Europe. It has never been forgotten. It is this background of two proud cultures, utterly different, that gives to modern Canada its own especial character.

New France not a replica of old

New France, however, did not become a mere replica of old France either in people or in ways of life. Culturally, it was a colony and only slowly did it get past that stage of development. Only slowly was mere imitation succeeded by something with elements of originality and it is hardly until our own day that the French genius in North America has begun to show sure signs of creating a new French culture, as French as that of France, and quite unlike it.[1]

The people of New France were drawn from limited areas within France: mainly from Normandy and neighbouring provinces and from Paris. With few exceptions, they were northerners. This meant that they were people of *la coutume* rather than of the *lex scripta* or Roman law; beer drinkers rather than wine drinkers; people in whose background the tradition of the *pays d'états* with their provincial assemblies was partially present; people from the prosperous parts of France. To know anything about France of the old régime is to know that it was a kingdom of infinite divisions. Law, custom, way of life, language, differed enormously over this huge country. This diversity was not to be reflected in New France. Just as the English colonies represented not all of English society but segments of it, so New France was drawn from a part only of old France. From the beginning, therefore, it had greater uniformity than the old. Its people within a generation or two had become a new blood group. Its laws, customs and institutions were virtually uniform from the beginning. As time went on, its history was to reflect no significant internal partitions, divisions, or schisms. If variety is the word for old France, homogeneity is that for New.

Uniformity, system, comes out strongly in matters of government. Some authority there must be. All the colonizing peoples agreed in accepting their traditional authority and for all except the Dutch, this lay in a crown. Colonial institutions emanated from the various crowns under whose protection the settlements lay. Most historians have contented themselves with describing the crown of seventeenth century France as an 'absolute monarchy'. The statement is hardly correct even in theory and it is far removed from reality in practice. Between the king's will and the ordinary citizen, there were interposed a dozen different degrees of authority: estates (that is, representative bodies), *parlements*, provincial governors, the self-governing municipalities, ancient feudal authority, and the tenacious, all-pervading web of custom. Even at the centre, while ultimate decision lay with the king, there was much devolution of authority in the shapes of ministers, councils, and vast arrays of officials, each with his carefully guarded sphere of power. The great apologist of divine-right monarchy,

Bossuet, put the situation neatly when he said: ". . . many writers have tried to confound absolute government with arbitrary government. But no two things could be more unlike. . . ."[2] In the seventeenth century, there seems to have been little or no suspicion on the part of the French that they were not free men: that was reserved for the later eighteenth, when the shadow of revolution was beginning to appear; and it was not until that period that the free institutions of England came to be the standard of comparison. Compared with a modern totalitarian régime, such as that of Russia, old France was liberty itself.[3]

Relatively little metropolitan complexity was introduced into New France. Despite the importance and even the semi-representative character of the *Conseil Souverain*, there never was a *Parlement*, still less provincial 'estates'. There were no *communes* (self-governing municipalities). The bureaucratic structure itself was quite simple, with everything in strict subordination to governor or intendant. In France, the citizen was seldom confronted with the actual power of the State: in New France, it was rarely absent from his life. Nor would he have wished it otherwise. Government in a country where nature responds readily is normally a nuisance: of this, the supreme example has been the United States and the British colonies from which it was constituted. But in a hard land where every blade of wheat has to be fought for, men need all the assistance they can get. Hence government was no less welcome in New France than it has been in the later Canada. All Canadians know instinctively that for the big jobs, they have to get together and lend their united weight. For building transcontinental railways, they have never been able to rely on private initiative. The decided difference in attitude towards government in Canada from that in the United States is the result.

The primary duty of government is protection from the external enemy; the second, almost as important, is the maintenance of law and order. In a struggling colony with an Iroquois behind every tree, the first duty needed no emphasis, and the second was little less apparent. It is not hard to understand how, when New France became a province, everyone welcomed the governor, the representative of the king himself. As for the intendant, though his office had never been a popular one in France, he was welcome too, for he would have the ear of the minister. Few foresaw the endless see-saw of bickerings and accusations which would grow up between the two great officials. It is a far cry from the sycophantic words of the intendant Duchesneau, writing in 1679, and the strident resistance of a Dupuy, just a half-century later. *"Je n'ai jamais eu non plus présomption de prétendre aucun égalité avec Monsieur le Gouverneur,"* exclaims Duchesneau.[4] Dupuy in contrast roundly reminds Governor Beauharnois that the king never transmits his whole authority to anyone and that he had better keep within his own bounds. Governors invariably tried to reduce these royal maids-of-all-work, the intendants, these official king's busybodies, to 'the status of superior clerk'. As a result, every despatch from Canada carried complaints, accusations and intrigues.

> *"Pour lui avoir représenté ces choses, je me suis attiré des paroles si pleines de mépris et d'outrage que je fus contraint de sortir de son cabinet, pour apaiser sa colère."*[5]

It was the intendant's business to carry on the day-to-day administration of the colony. In a parliamentary system, it is the public process of discussion and decision which gets attention. This not being present in the old French régime, the administrative side of government—the making of regulations, their enforcement, their evasion, the claims of individuals—bulked proportionately larger. Interminable are the despatches which flow across the ocean, giving explanations and comment on every aspect of the colony's life. From them it is possible to form some idea of how carefully tended the new plant was and, incidentally, of the round of the intendant's duties. A constant stream of ordinances, edicts, decrees and other forms of executive act came from the intendant and also from the governor. "Ordinance of M. Talon which condemns Jacques Bigeon . . . to ten livres fine for swearing and blasphemy." "Ordinance of M. Talon on the subject of a land grant in Côte Sainte-Geneviève." "Ordinance on a petition of the Jesuits. . . ." "Ordinance which decides that certain acts registered in the Sovereign Council shall be expunged." "Ordinance on the demands of the Agent-General of the West Indies Company." "Ordinance establishing justice at Montreal under the terms of the titles, etc., of the Sulpicians." "Ordinance for making records of titles to land for the seigneury of Montreal." "Ordinance restoring to liberty Jacques Prevost and Rémy Dupille. . . ."[6] "Decree on the subject of Millers," "Gifts between living persons declared to have their full and entire effect," "Decree limiting grist mill charges to one fourteenth," "Decree ordering those having thistles on their land to cut them each year," "Decree giving to a contract of marriage its full force, although not signed on the testimony of witnesses. . . ."[7] All these, the small change of a community's life, from the years 1666 and 1667 alone; many others are lost. While the fundamentals of the old French law could be used, infinite minor adaptations to local circumstances had to be made. These, mounting up year after year until the fall of New France, formed the major content of those 'laws of Canada' which were re-enacted into force by the Quebec Act of 1774 and which still remain at the core of the legal system of Quebec.

The French brought to the new world all their sense of possessiveness, linked to their sense of family. Property, its disposition, and the rights of survivors, these were the big things. Few men could be so humble as not to leave a few possessions to form the contents of a list carefully drawn up by the local notary, with values duly entered. The notary himself became from the first a characteristic figure, his records a transcript of the ever-flowing life about him: from marriage contracts to 'cessions', 'quittances', 'obligations', notations of sales and inventories of goods. Naturally the lists of these notations grew steadily longer as the colony became established: Jean de Lespinasse's 'repertory' of 1637 has only three 'pieces' in it, but already in 1663 Guillaume de Saint Germain in his had sixty-four. Notaries at first were seigneurial officers, but gradually, thanks to the centralizing instincts of the intendants, they were drawn into the orbit of Quebec and became *notaires royaux*.[8]

The notaries' registers are typical of French legal methods in that every last detail is scrupulously noted in a written minute—the *procès-verbal*; this, duly witnessed, seems to have been as much the cornerstone of French law as was the writ of English. Formality marked all legal processes and it must not be forgotten that the law twined itself around the life of the people in as intimate and constant a fashion as any natural creeper. "Viewed by the Court the Letters Patent of the King in the form of Edict given at Saint Germaine-en-Laye in the month of June last, signed *Louis* and lower down *By the King*, *Colbert*, and at the side is written *visa Le Tellier* to serve as the Edict instituting rules for the procedures of the Sovereign Council of Quebec; signed *Colbert*, and sealed with the Great Seal in green wax upon red and green silk tape and countersealed upon the same wax and tape, by which His Majesty wills that his officers of the said Council . . ." etc., etc. All this jargon may be mere antiquarianism now but it represented the experience of centuries and had as its objective the performance of public and private business properly and in due order. A king surrounded with such rigid formalism in action, however powerful he might be, must have found it difficult, save on exceptional occasions, to cut through it: again, French absolutism, on inspection, appears to be a singularly 'limited' absolutism.

Reproductive valour in New France

Not only had the routine of daily life to be established but the great measures which were to turn a barely surviving fur post and mission into a colony had also to be undertaken. On most of these, the changes have been rung to the point of boredom. They include Talon's public enterprises, which were reflections of his master Colbert's ideas of state action in the field of economic life.[9] In an effort to get away from the detached riverside homestead and, under the king's orders, to group the people in villages, as in Europe, Talon laid out some model sites north of Quebec. Details of these were lost until, a few years ago, air photography revealed them.[10]

The best known of all the big public measures was the bringing over of people, particularly of the young women who came to be termed *les filles du roi*. Like all new countries, New France desperately lacked people, and like them all, its sex balance was far overweighted on the male side. This balance was tipped still further when many of the soldiers of the Carignan-Salières regiment decided to stay in the colony. To redress the situation, the authorities persuaded young French women to come out, offering the greatest of all inducements —husbands. A good many were sent and nearly all married off at the ship's side. Efforts ever since have been made to traduce their characters but these have not been convincing. The simple fact that the colony from the first had been wrapped in the swaddling clothes of priestly concern and that its morals were regulated in the strictest conceivable manner would render it impossible that the sweeping of the streets should be gathered up and sent off to Canada. The girls sent were average young women of the lower classes, or more desirably, peasant girls, and their morals no doubt were just those of most women—in the safety of marriage, perfectly reliable.[11]

Every new country is in this sense a paradise for women. "All girls become wives, all widows remarry," says one author. In New France, no girl needed a dowry to buy her a husband —it was her brother who needed one to help him get a wife. It is only as the balance rights itself that woman's position becomes less favourable. When we get to our own era of crowded cities to which young women flock, woman's scarcity value having fallen, her market price falls too.[12] To paraphrase Macaulay, "as civilization advances, woman inevitably declines." But on this continent, her scarcity value, having lasted well over three centuries, has secured for her a place which has left a vast mark on North America, colouring its culture and its affairs, making it still the woman's continent *par excellence*.

To populate New France there could be only two sources of people, immigration and the cradle. Of the two, immigration was the less important. Only a few thousand all told crossed the seas during the entire French period and the bulk of these came in the ten years or so after the province was founded. They comprised several distinct groups: *les filles du roi*, the disbanded soldiers, government and fur-company officials and employees, various individuals who came on their own (the latter, the smallest group of all) and the indentured servants or *engagés*.[13] The *engagé* served for three years and then was free. (In the English colonies, the term was seven.) The proportions of the various groups in the total immigration have been given as: 3,900 *engagés*, 3,500 soldiers, 1,100 *filles du roi*, 1,000 deportees, and 500 persons coming freely at their own expense.[14]

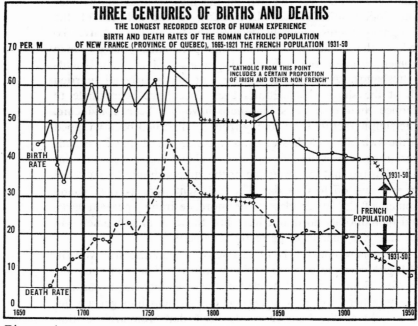

THREE CENTURIES OF BIRTHS AND DEATHS
THE LONGEST RECORDED SECTOR OF HUMAN EXPERIENCE
BIRTH AND DEATH RATES OF THE ROMAN CATHOLIC POPULATION OF NEW FRANCE (PROVINCE OF QUEBEC), 1665-1921 THE FRENCH POPULATION 1931-50

Diagram 1

Among the settlers, there was no conspicuous preponderance of country people, though probably many had a rural background. Many also put themselves down as artisans. Among the 'gentlemen,' there were few of noble birth—why should a man of any prospects come to the wilderness? Retired officers as a rule were not a success, any more than their English counterparts two centuries later. Both came into their own when there was fighting to be done and at other times often lived in a poverty that was something more than genteel. The country did not lack good leaders in the arts of peace as well as in scalp-raiding and exploring, but most of these, men like Dr. Robert Gifford, Pierre Boucher, and the founder of the famous house of Lemoine, came of humble stock. They were the class of man who has made North America: good, solid lower middle class, on the way up.

In human interest, however, all other aspects of population take second place to the astounding stock-breeding programme of the colony.[15] Not only were young women sent out and married off *instanter*, but also every possible encouragement was given to early marriages and to remarriages. Girls habitually married at puberty, and some were contracted for before reaching it. Young men waited until sixteen, but not to encourage them in sloth, penalties were imposed on those who did not take the plunge soon enough.

"Marie Denot . . ., lost her husband, probably in 1652. She had two daughters, Marie, thirteen years old, and Marie-Madeleine, a baby of two. The elder became the wife of Jean Lanqueteau a short time before her mother's second marriage to Mathieu Labat, in the beginning of 1653. Both mother and daughter were soon widowed. . . . The twice-widowed Marie Denot with two daughters and an imminent grandchild chose a protector and third husband in Louis Ozanne. She also found a husband for her widowed daughter who had recently been delivered of a son, François. On January 26, 1655, there was a double wedding: Louis Ozanne became the mother's third husband and Philippe Etienne the second husband of the daughter."[16]

Yet until the end of the seventeenth century, the numerical disparity of the sexes doomed a considerable number of men to batchelorhood. This helps to account for the unprecedented speed with which widows were remarried. Dollier de Casson relates a case of a woman remarrying before her first husband had been buried. The result of all this was one of the fastest increases of population known, an increase even faster than in polygamous Egypt, present holder of the world's record, where also every last ounce of reproductive power is exacted from a woman. In the first decade of the colony, 1661-1670, the birth rate, despite the scarcity of women, was about fifty per thousand of the entire population and it rose from that level steadily, attaining sixty per thousand at the time of the Conquest. *"Les femmes y portent presque tous le ans."* The marriage rate was about thirty-five in this first decade, compared to a modern rate of eight or nine.[17] Since living conditions, apart from the Indian danger, were also quite good, with little plague or famine, it is no wonder the colony shot ahead in its home-produced population. Of course, since the starting base was so small—it did not pass 10,000 until about 1685—the total was not, in absolute figures, high. At the Conquest, after a century of unremitting reproductive valour, it reached only 65,000.

The Canadian 'gentleman'

Government, population, seigneurialism, the Church, these are the well-worn topics of all the history books. Law, to which some attention has been given above, is as a rule passed by. The seigneurial system and the Church are topics so all-pervading that they come in everywhere. Here only a few general remarks can be made on them.[18] With respect to seigneurialism, two or three big facts stand out: the French brought to North America the system of landholding to which they were accustomed and the circumstances of the new world wrested this system into their own shape. Remarkably few Frenchmen of the seigneurial class became seigneurs in Canada: as pointed out above, the Canadian seigneur was home-grown. By far the most successful specimens were not men at all, but religious corporations—the Jesuits, the Sulpicians, the Ursulines. By 1706, the Jesuits had almost 2,000 *censitaires*, and about the same date the Sulpicians, on the Island of Montreal, had 3,000.[19] In addition to them, there were from the first a few outstanding and successful men or families like the de la Bouteilleries at the River Ouelle, the Lemoines opposite Montreal at Longueuil, the absentee Berthelot, a rich man in France, possibly a farmer-general of taxes, who put a good deal of money into the Island of Orleans and in 1676 got it erected into a 'county' (Le Comté de St. Laurent), plus the patriarch Pierre Boucher of Boucherville, *"une des seigneuries les plus peuplées, les plus riches de la colonie."* While the plain men were flourishing in this way, the ex-officers, the Varennes, the Chamblys, the Perrots, and others, were next door to starvation and besetting the authorities for petty little jobs to keep them alive. Simon Denis, for example, who had a fief opposite Montreal, went off to take the lease of the sedentary fishery at Canso, neglecting his seigneury.[20] The families which had come first (in the sixteen-thirties) such as the D'Ailleboust and the Répentigny, did no better. By 1679, they were sinking into misery. "They have too many children," said Frontenac.[21]

Most accounts have overstressed the picturesque side of French-Canadian seigneurialism, the ceremonies of homage, the annual jollification at the seigneur's expense into which the rent-paying days were turned, the effective ways in which simple men turned forced labour (la corvée in France) into the 'bee' (la corvée in Canada). All this is well enough, but what was more frequent was the usual colonial condition of land-grabbing and absenteeism, combined with hard, unsentimental attitudes on both sides. There is no limit to the detail with which seigneurialism may be explored but despite the sentimentalism of certain French-speaking historians who talk of the loss of 'our nobles'[22] and seem to wish the old feudalism back again, seigneurialism in New France was for the most part a makeshift, doomed to disappear before the circumstances of the new country. 'The nobles', on examination, turn out to be a rather shabby lot.[23]

Yet seigneurialism seems to have worked as well as any other method of landholding would have done and when it is examined in detail, it is not completely different from the English colonial land system of the time, which also had plenty of room for the great estate and the conditional grant. Where it was joined to an intelligent paternalism, it probably was helpful to the settler; where it was not, it was disregarded. Everything was on the side of the settler, almost nothing on that of his 'betters.' The major social heritages that seigneurialism has left to modern French Canada are two: one of them being a few charming old manor houses and the other and more important, recognition of a hierarchical class structure which, if it no longer provides for a class of gentleman landlords, still admits an élite of culture and of occupation.

In the second half of the seventeenth century, the little settlements of the sixteen-forties and fifties, which had just emerged from the trading posts and missions of the earliest period, changed definitely into an established colony. To this colony, a settled and certain government was given. Satisfactory methods for the distribution and holding of land were devised. A social system emerged. Some educational services were established. The Church as it was to exist until the English Conquest was put on a firm foundation, controlled by the king but with enormous influence and the strong corporate sense infused into it by the weighty personality of its first bishop. A legal system which, despite its excess of paternalism, gave a maximum of justice at a minimum of cost was worked out. If all this was within the context of small numbers, the foundation laid was good honest work, and it would take the building that would be placed upon it.

Notes to Chapter 4

1. See pp. 441, 442.
2. Quoted in J. B. Robinson, *Readings in European History* (New York, 1934), II, p. 275. To Bossuet, the words *absolute power* apparently carried something of the meaning of the word *sovereignty* to us.
3. For studies of the constitution and institutions, see, among others, Max Beloff, *The Age of Absolutism* (University Library Series, 1954); P. R. Doolin, *The Fronde* (Cambridge, Mass., 1935); R. Doucet, *Les Institutions de la France au XVIe Siécle* (Paris, 1948); Henri Hausser, *La Pensée et l'Action Economique du Cardinal Richelieu* (Paris, 1944); Philippe de Sagnac et A. de Saint-Léger, "Louis XIV, 1661-1715" in *Peuples et Civilizations, Histoire Générale,* (Paris, 1949): C. V. Wedgwood, *Richelieu and the French Monarchy* (London, 1949); W. F. Church, *Constitutional Thought in 16th Century France* (Cambridge, Mass., 1941); G. Zeller, *Les Institutions de la France au XVIe Siècle* (Paris, 1949).
4. Public Archives of Canada, *Correspondence Générale, Série* C[11] A, Vol. 5, p. 31, *Duchesneau au Ministre,* Nov. 17th, 1679.
5. Ibid., p. 40, referring to Frontenac, Nov. 10th, 1679: "For having placed things before him thus, I drew upon myself words so full of scorn and so outrageous that I was forced to leave his office in order to appease his wrath."
6. See *Archives de la Province de Québec—Ordonnances, Commissions, etc. des Gouverneurs et Intendants . . .* (ed., Pierre Georges Roy, 1924).
7. From the *Ordonnances des Intendants et Arrêts du Conseil Supérieur* (Quebec, 1806), II, pp. 128 ff.
8. See Pierre Georges Roy et Antoine Roy, *Inventaire des Greffes des Notaires du Régime Français* (Quebec, 1942). As can be imagined, the lists of possessions give valuable information on household goods and their values.
9. C. W. Cole, *French Mercantilism, 1683-1700* (New York, 1943).
10. The present writer, after flying above Quebec, bears witness to the clearness with which they can be seen. They are carefully planned in the form of a square, with a public common at the centre, radial roads to the corners, and each homestead running more or less wedge-shaped from the common to the outer boundaries.
11. See Gustave Lanctot, *Filles de Joie ou Filles du Roi?* (Montreal, 1952).
12. There is always a 'bulge' in the female age group of 15-25 years in large cities: this represents country girls for whom there is no longer a place at home.
13. In the eighteenth century, another group was added — those who had broken the anti-smuggling laws, especially smuggling in contraband salt, the *faux-sauniers;* these were minor criminals, just like moderns who get caught smuggling in cigarettes from the United States.
14. Pierre Georges Roy, *"La Paroisse et l'Habitant Canadien sous le Régime Français"* in the *Catholic Historical Review,* April 1932.
15. For graphic details, and on the position of women generally, see Isabel Foulché-Delbosc, "Women of New France" in the *Canadian Historical Review,* June 1940.
16. Ibid.

17. Jacques Henripin, *La Population Canadienne au début du XVIII*e *Siècle* (Paris, 1954), p. 121. See also Paul Veyret, *La Population du Canada* (Paris, 1953).
19. Emile Salone, *La Colonisation de la Nouvelle France,* (Paris, c. 1910), Chapter IV.
20. Salone, op. cit., p. 234.
21. Ibid.
22. Canon Lionel Groulx, for example. An older historian, Benjamin Sulte, is much more realistic; see his *Mélanges Historiques* (Montreal, 1918), Vol. I, pp. 80 ff. Sulte says quite bluntly: *"Le seigneur n'était qu'un agent de colonisation agissant sans salaire."*
23. Sulte says: *"Un petit nombre de seigneurs appartenaient à la noblesse, et de plus, ils étaient presque tous des habitants anoblis pour leur services en ce pays."*

5: The community established: a description of New France about 1700

THE MOST SOLEMN MOMENT OF THE MASS HAS come, the moment of the elevation of the host. The church is crowded with neighbours and townsmen, intent on the ancient rite, with its assertion of the continuing existence of Frenchmen and Catholics in the new environment, this harsh new world where so many old ways of life have to yield to necessity.

Two hands go up, clasped together, a man's and a woman's. Eyes stray from the altar at the sacred moment and stare at them. Everyone knows to whom the hands belong and what their being raised at such a moment signifies. For a marriage has just taken place, irregular and frowned on by the clergy, but a marriage nevertheless, the well-known folk ceremony of the *mariage au gaumine*. There has been a church full of witnesses, but two friends close by are ready formally to attest the act. The marriage will endure. And irate parent, jilted fiancé or the bishop himself will not be able to break it. For the people hold it to be a marriage 'in the sight of God' and girls resort to it when obstacles present themselves to the regular ceremony.

By the turn of the century, 1700, New France, as the folk marriage indicates, was working out its way of life. While still very much of a colony it could consider itself there to stay.

Of one phase, very specific in nature, of the people's accommodation to the new environment, a unique account exists in the almost yearly census tabulations. These provide a record such as no other country possesses, for they begin practically at the beginning, 1666, and go on almost year by year until the last great wars. They give the population (by localities, by age, sex, and occupation) and the agricultural situation (acres cleared, amounts of the various crops, numbers of domestic animals).[1] A continuous picture emerges, complete for nearly three centuries.

By the census of 1698 (the tabulation closest to the end of the century), there were 13,815 French people in the country, and 1,540 neighbouring Indians. As was to be expected in a new country, females were still in a minority—6,424 to 7,391. There were 6,400 children under fifteen years of age, or nearly 50 per cent of the total.

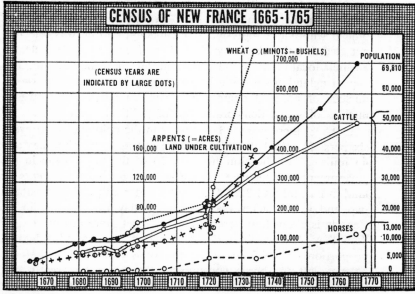

Diagram 2

This little handful of people was sprinkled all the way from Malbaie (Murray Bay) to the upper end of the Island of Montreal, but it had a strong concentration in the neighbourhood of Quebec, with both ends tailing out to nothing. On the south shore, Rivière du Loup marked the eastward extension, Chateauguay, opposite the upper end of the Island of Montreal, the western, but on this shore there were still quite large stretches with no inhabitants. On the north shore, settlements were more numerous, though the picture of 'the continuous village' given in most of the books is overdone, 'continuous villages' with houses within shouting distance of each other existing only here and there. Only in the neighbourhood of Quebec was settlement close.

The population of Quebec itself was just under two thousand, that of Montreal just under twelve hundred. Trois Rivières had just a few score. No other centres of importance existed. Yet the people could hardly be considered scattered, for each little settlement was grouped about a church: the French word côte (e.g., Côte St. Antoine, Côte des Neiges, etc.) nicely describes these little knots of people; it would stand the translation 'neighbourhood'. A *côte*, formalized, became a parish, the vital cell upon which the organization of French Canada is based. The Canadian parish resembled the New England town: each was a communal settlement organized around a church. The difference between them lay in the weakness of political organization marking the parish and its strength in New England. New France developed only one official who had a representative capacity, and he was selected, not elected—the *Capitaine de Milice*. New Englanders elected all their local officials and their ministers into the bargain. The New England town with its free-for-all town meeting was a nucleus of political democracy. The Canadian parish was a nucleus of social democracy, but of political authority.

In 1698, there were 2,310 houses in the colony (one to every six persons, well below the modern average), 62 churches and 43 mills, 37 of the churches and 26 of the mills being in the government of Quebec.[2] There were some 6,000 *arpents* of land in pasture and 32,000 *arpents*[3] under cultivation, or about two and a half acres per person. Today the average in all Canada is about four acres, though we get more out of an acre than they did two centuries and a half ago. A considerable proportion of the food raised to-day is exported so that the balance left for home consumption may not be greatly different. Two commodities enable this to be checked—wheat and cattle. In 1698, the wheat crop was 160,978 *minots* or just about twelve and a half bushels per head. Modern domestic consumption is usually taken as about ten bushels per head, or less. Allowing for less variety in foodstuffs, and remembering that little wheat was then exported, we can agree that the Canadian of 1698 had enough to eat. In addition to breadstuffs, he had his animals—among them, ten thousand 'horned cattle'. This gave him .77 of a cow per person. In 1951, Canadians possessed .59 of a cow per person: the Canadian of two hundred and fifty years ago thus had a little more cow than modern man.[5]

New-world contributions to agriculture were first recorded by the census takers in 1692, when Indian corn appeared— 4,597 bushels of it. In Acadia (for which an almost equal amount of statistical material is available) the Annapolis Valley, as it now is, had already begun to produce the apples for which it is still famous, 1,584 fruit trees being listed for Port Royal in 1698, or about fifteen for each family. In the words of a contemporary, Acadia was regarded as "a little Normandy for apples."[6]

By the end of the seventeenth century, New France had already become more than a mere 'settlement.' Yet abundant testimony to its recent origins still remained. The physical evidences of newness were everywhere—lack of roads, stumps ringing the cleared fields, with the unbroken forest never far away, inadequte dwelling houses, makeshift wooden churches. More subtle were the marks being made on man's mentality by the fight with the forest. The Canadian settler had all the ingenuity which new conditions bring out: he could literally 'turn his hand to anything,' from Indian-fighting to furniture-making. He was, in fact, putting out attractive work in the whole compass of the domestic arts, not in furniture-making merely, but in the more sophisticated areas, such as the art of the silversmith. It was frequently noted that the women seemed to excel the men in intelligence and liveliness. Was this the favoured place of woman in a new society already reflecting itself?

Labour even more than woman continued to have a scarcity value. Hence the yearly appeals to France for contingents of *faux-sauniers* (salt smugglers), for soldiers who might marry and settle, for almost anyone. The appeals produced few results. Proposals were not lacking to enlist forced Indian labour (*les panis*). It has always, however, proved impossible to enslave the Indian: he prefers death. Negro slavery was also discussed, but few negroes were brought in. There seems to have been no moral objection to slavery but the country was not suited to it and so Canada escaped the curse of the Southern States. Negro slavery in both French and English periods was limited to a few domestics.

Frontier aberrations

A society in the making never fails to throw up strongly marked personalities. Two good groups of examples come from Acadia. One of them consisted in the four brothers Damours, who had come out from France and settled on the St. John River. According to de Villebon "they have been so given to libertinism and independent action that they cannot submit to authority. . . . They have natures which have been entirely spoiled by long freedom and habits acquired from the Indians.'[7] De Villebon had even worse luck with some of his priests, especially a certain Abbé Baudoin, who had begun life as a soldier and then had entered the priesthood. As a priest, he seems to have had difficulty in forgetting his army ways. After he had been provided with a year's subsistence in advance, so said the inhabitants, Baudoin "abandoned them for six months in order to range the woods with ten or twelve savages." He had refused to administer the sacraments. In an affair over which Indian should have which woman, "when M. Baudoin found that neither the Indian nor his concubine would exchange mates, he threw himself on him, and, having kicked him in the stomach . . . left him covered with blood and returned to the village to boast of his martial exploit."[8] And much more of the same. Fortunately there were not many priests of that kind. But everyone who has been on the edge of settlement knows that strange types, whether lay or clerical, are apt to drift there.[9]

In another respect, the colony showed itself close to its pioneer origins and that was in its poor agricultural methods. Where hands are few, land and wood plenty, and knowledge scarce, farming methods must be crude. In the new settlement "the only good farming," it has been said, "is poor farming"— get the trees down, get the soil open, get the seed in. Hence the complaints by officialdom in New France of the way in which the trees were slashed down and burned up, of the waste of manure, the dirty seed. It is when men get crowded together that they have to caress Mother Earth for her bounty. When they first unveil her, they rape her.[10]

In the late sixteen hundreds, men were not yet crowded in New France. New areas for settlement were constantly being spied out as, for example, that along the rivière Sainte-Anne, near Quebec, later to become the parish of Saint Ferréol. Canon Soumande and four experienced men, going on a short exploring trip, "ont trouvés deux côtes, chacune le long d'une rivière. Dans le première il y a de quoi placer cinquante habitants . . . et dans la seconde il y a du terrain pour en mettre au moins quarante. Le plus beau pays du monde . . .!"[11]

It was this easy outlet which made feudalism in the new world farcical. No doubt there had been a time in Europe, before the forest primeval had been conquered, when men had felt as free as they were to do in New France. But freedom is invariably lost through the negligence of those possessing it and this probably would have been the case in New France too, except for an event that still lay in the unsuspected future, the English Conquest. For the time, however, the weight of those above sat lightly on the shoulders of those below, and these latter had an easy road to the heights beyond them. By the period of this survey, around 1700, many of the original seigneurial families, confessing failure, had been dispersed and quite often their successors were not persons of seigneurial rank at all, but successful peasants. Some middle class seigneurs had also thriven. The Longueuils had built a fine stone fortress-manor house; the Bouchers, with Pierre Boucher, now a patriarch and still the head of the clan with over two hundred descendants, had successfully developed their property, and a few others had done the same. Such men might be considered not nobles, but 'squires,' substantial men in the countryside and its natural leaders.[12]

By 1700, the basis had been laid for the legend of the rural age of gold which bulks so large in French Canada. There was a time when all had plenty, when the mornings were brighter and the birds sang sweeter, so its literary expression often runs, when all men were honest fellows and all the girls were beautiful.[13] The legend appears soon after the Conquest and continues down the present day. However over-idealized this traditional picture may be, the countryside of Canada, when land was plentiful, seems to have enjoyed a good share of well-being, free from most of the plagues and afflictions, human and material, that affected its counterpart in France.

That the peasantry had their pride—and their surplus for 'conspicuous consumption'—seems evident from 'the horse question,' as it emerged at the time. The despatches of the intendants are full of the evils resulting from the peasants' horse-owning proclivities: they have far more horses than they need, these horses eat their heads off, they lead to idleness, softness and display. Home authorities reply in kind. The intendant "will see to the reduction of the number of horses. The settlers have no need of them except to till their land and haul their wood and their grain. It is not natural for the settlers to use them in winter to travel from place to place, instead of going on snowshoes, as they should do." Horses "lead to a life of effeminacy, diminishing bodily strength and wholly destroying manliness and courage. . . ."[14] Despite official thundering, the peasants persisted in risking the dangers of the softness incurred through riding behind horses and continued to conduct themselves like what must have seemed to their betters as 'gentlemen.' "Fancy a peasant riding a horse," we can hear the great men of Versailles saying. As the modern Canadian workman has his car, the eighteenth century Canadian peasant had his horse. He had gained that much by moving to the new world, at any rate.[15]

It is pleasant, for the present author at any rate, to include with horses the other faithful friend of man. In addition to William Kirby's shop-sign image of *The Golden Dog*,[16] three real dogs have reached the pages of history. One was *Pilote*, famous in his day, who lived at Montreal in the sixteen-fifties and who won his spurs, if a dog could win spurs, by detecting lurking Iroquois.[17] The other was a dog named *Vingt Sols* (Twenty Cents) who served in the same capacity at Niagara in 1688. The third was the son of *Vingt Sols*, unfortunately nameless. He carried garrison letters the fifteen miles from Chambly to La Prairie and back, scouting out Iroquois incidentally, and making the journey, so we are told, about as fast as the trams of a later age could do it. He was put on the strength and drew rations. In fact, he drew them for many years after his death![18]

Seventeenth-century town planning

The French Canada of our period was largely rural[19] but both Quebec and Montreal were already quite distinctly cities, though small ones, possessing the self-consciousness of cities and with that concentration of social development which marks the urban area.

"Nothing seems so beautiful and magnificent to me as the situation of the City of Quebec. . . ." Thus the great Frontenac, shortly after his arrival.[20] But he goes on to criticize the lack of order and symmetry in the buildings and their disposition; in such matters "one ought to think not only of the present state of affairs but of the future," for Quebec may "one day be the capital of a great empire." It is interesting to find the fighting governor turning up as Canada's first town planner.[21]

Frontenac's advice got as much heed as that of other town planners with long views. Quebec straggled around the base of its cliffs and up the hill, and on. The upper town from the first held the official buildings and the big churches. The road down in the sixteen-sixties was flanked by Indian huts (*cabanes*) surrounded by a palisade. The lower town in the seventeenth century seems to have been the more considerable of the two.[22] In 1667, the upper town already had several churches and two convents, the latter of stone. By the beginning of the eighteenth century, the Cathedral had been fiinished but according to Charlevoix in 1720, "it would not be worthy of a good parish in one of the smallest towns of France."[23] In the lower town, stood Notre Dame-des-Victoires (1688). Its architect Baillef also built the Episcopal Palace (1693-1697), "the most elaborate building of seventeenth century New France."[24] There was also the Jesuit Church (to be pretty well destroyed in the siege of 1759). Altogether, by the eighteenth century, Quebec could boast of more and finer public buildings than could any other colonial capital north of Mexico City.

Montreal from the first was frontier and self-willed. It was the 'jumping-off point' for the *pays d'en haut*, the starting point of the canoe route that built Canada. As befitted a frontier town, until well down in its history it was crude and rude and dirty, as some would say it still is. Innumerable are the testimonies to this in the countless ordinances made to clean it up. In 1676, property owners were to clean daily the space in front of their establishments and put the sweepings out of the way. In 1679, they were not to empty the winter's refuse in the streets. In 1680, they were to fill in the wheel-ruts. In 1706, they were to build latrines as alternatives to using the streets, and not to keep pigs in their houses. In 1715, they must not put garbage on the streets and in 1716, again they must not. In 1725, they would be fined if they did. In 1741, they had to put their winter's dirt on the river ice. In 1711, carters were not to run horse races through the streets, and in 1749 drunken drivers galloping horses would be fined three livres.[25] No streets were paved during the eighteenth century, though in 1721 an ordinance ordered the building of wooden walks, eight inches high, one foot wide, two feet out from the sides of the houses. This does not mean that they were built.[26]

As a certain compensation for dirt underfoot, the city, in efforts to prevent the fires that have been so frequent and so catastrophic in all our wooden towns, gradually covered the roofs with tin (*fer-blanc*); travellers used to note the 'luminous' aspect of the town and it came to be called *la cité d'argent*.[27]

Both in Montreal and Quebec, the ordinary house must have been uncomfortable, for the first mention of glass in the windows is 1689. By the eighteenth century, good town houses had glass windows but as late as 1749, farmers' houses still used paper. Even at the end of the century, the Upper Canadian pioneers had very few glass window panes.[28] Furniture, in contrast, rapidly became available. The well-to-do imported a good deal from France and local craftsmen made the rest. It was varied, substantial, and often of artistic merit. The supply of tableware and its usage seems to have been about on a level with middle and lower class circles in France. Knives were personal. As late as 1749, they were not set, each guest bringing his own.[29] The date of the introduction of forks is uncertain though in the higher circles they were known as early as 1662. But even in 1700, the custom of cutting off a hunk of meat with your pocket knife and then eating it in your fingers must have still been not more than just a little old-fashioned.[30] Most plates, cups, and so on were wooden, but vessels of silver and earthenware were well enough known.

Heating was most commonly by fireplace, though the stove gets a mention as early as 1693.[31] After the *Forges de St. Maurice* were opened in 1733, stoves became common. The stove and the frying-pan, two objects that to-day are sufficiently dissimilar, in those days were not too far apart, as their identical name in French indicates, *poêle* (though of different genders). If we go far enough back in time, we possibly arrive at a pot with a handle, which could hold coals or be used for cooking, indifferently. Taking a slightly different shape, this adaptable vessel could become a *bed-warmer* or, as the French affectionately and significantly called it, *une demoiselle*.[32]

Food seems to have been plentiful, but must have lacked variety, and towards the end of winter, colonists everywhere might be cursed with scurvy if their home-made beer and imported wine ran out. During the French period, tea and coffee were rare, and tea, for long after the Conquest, was looked upon as an effeminate English drink.

A surprising amount of energy, based on religious zeal, went into hospitals, and into homes for the aged, for the insane, and for 'fallen women.' Doctors were present from the first, but in strictly limited supply. The only species of professional man not found in the French period was the *avocat*, or lawyer. All colonies, English as well as French, made efforts to get along without this pestiferous breed but all were equally unsuccessful, and eventually they got in everywhere.[33] New France from the first seems to have been well supplied with artisans. It is naive to think of the average Canadian of the seventeenth century as a *coureur-de-bois*. He was far more likely to be farmer, artisan, or townsman, not much different in his standards of civilization from his contemporaries in France but, on the average, better off.

The spirit of New France

It is much easier to describe the physical and corporate conditions of a society than its spirit. The description here given hangs largely on such big hooks as social class, the position of women, the question of provincialism, crime, punishment, race and faith. It leads up to the principal point—whether or not a new society, a Canadian one, was evolving by the eighteenth century.

New France from the first was a society of ranks and classes. That is why Quebec City was always described by the travellers as having the air of a little capital. At the apex were the governor and the bishop, with the intendant just half a step down, followed in order by the hierarchy of officials, cathedral and monastic clergy. A perusal of the mountains of despatches they sent off to France gives the impression that nearly all intendants were fussy old maids and that one of their chief jobs was tattling on the governor. De Champigny, for example, writes to the minister, November 5th, 1699,[34] that M. de Callières in his opinion "has begun with so much *hauteur* and with a manner so unco-operative, that I had never before seen anything to equal it!"

As for the governor, he brought into the colony a reflection of majesty itself. And while he represented the aloofness, the arrogance of the throne, he combined that with its paternal interest in the humble efforts of its subjects to be good citizens. On one occasion, the minister himself, the king's immediate representative, enclosed a letter for Madame de Repentigny. The king had read with pleasure her remarks on her discovery of dye-wood and some blue clay near Montreal that would make pottery, to say nothing of her account of the increase in the number of linen looms.[35] With what pride Madame de Repentigny's bosom must have swelled on receiving such a message as that!

Around the governor, as military leader, were grouped the soldiers. Regular officers of the king were 'somebodies'. Unfortunately Canadian gentlemen found it difficult to get very far up in the ranks of the 'somebodies' unless they were men of prowess such as Lemoyne d'Iberville.[36] The 'somebodies' themselves regularly seem to have got into the usual trouble of soldiers stationed abroad—getting married![37] And frequently to Canadian girls of low, or at least, lower degree, without dowries to sustain officers in that estate to which they were accustomed. Prohibitions of the practice were frequent.[38] The trouble reached its climax when a nephew of the great Marquis de Vaudreuil married far, far beneath him—his wife's mother had been a domestic in the governor's establishment![39] But what was the governor to do when the bishop himself had married them? Off went a despatch which might be condensed into a shriek of agony—'For Heaven's sake, stop this marrying bishop! He is marrying off all the able-bodied soldiers, and it is impossible to keep the forces together!'[40] The Council at Versailles thereupon drew up a memorandum. "It is necessary to write emphatically to the bishop recommending him not to perform this kind of marriage."[41] Meanwhile, two things occurred: Vaudreuil got permission to pack his nephew off to Isle Royale, and the bishop went on performing the marriages!

Beneath officialdom stood the *bourgeoisie* of the two towns. They were important people. Some of them sat on the Supreme Council and if occasion warranted it, they knew how to talk to both governor and intendant.[42] It was this group of men, some of whom had a certain wealth, conductors of the fur trade and of the import business, who, when they were not among those who returned to France, were to be dispersed by the Conquest, robbing French Canada of its past share in *le grand commerce*, reducing its business side to minor retail trade. Under conditions of competition dependent on London connections, they were to prove no match for the colonial and Scottish merchants who crowded in. Their survivals still exist in the many pleasant and valuable pieces of furniture and silver to be found in modern museums.

The lower classes of the towns do not come in for as much attention as do those mainstays of the colony, the sturdy *habitants*, but they must have consisted in the usual grouping of occupations, with the usual new-world shortages in the skilled trades and the more specialized crafts. In the third quarter of the seventeenth century, Quebec was filled with undesirable crowds of beggars. "In 1676, the Sovereign Council enjoined three hundred beggars to return to their (land) grants."[43] Here were the defeated: it is never difficult to recruit for any city the appropriate submerged classes, the proletariat, the broken.

In attempting to convey the general tone of French society, one at once comes upon the French conception of liberty. The historical constitution of France knew no such notion of liberty as did that of England. There was private right in plenty, but it was mainly property right. In France the absolute rights of the free citizen, his right to justice, to a fair trial before his equals, his right to participate in the business of the realm, either did not exist, or if they had existed, had decayed. The king, nevertheless, was far from all-powerful. One of the best checks on his power was the simple stubbornness of his people. In Canada in 1664, a revenue duty of 10 per cent had been fixed by royal authority. Many and loud were the objections registered with the local authorities, who made their representations to the Court. In 1670, these were successful, and the duty was reduced to 5 per cent.[44] Here was a good picture of the processes of French government and of the way in which the absolute power of the king came into harmony with the will—or, more usually, the 'won't'—of the community.

For the private ventures of private people, the old régime provided considerable elbow room. Here again, theory and practice might be at variance. In theory, every subject must submit to the authority of the crown's representative. In practice, constant are the complaints from him that Canadians are too independent and cannot be controlled. "The spirit of independence that rules here . . . that kind of independence which has stepped in."[45] Such phrases are frequent. And then there was the authoritarian dictum on women. Women have no rights to honours, but they may sit in their husbands' pews. They have a right to holy water and to the sacramental bread but they may only walk in procession after all those who have recognized rank.[46] Despite this laying down of the law, no colony surely boasted as many prominent women as New France. Most of these were in religion, it is true, but there were also a number who were not. There was Madame de Repentigny, whose industrial inventiveness has already been noted. And there was Mademoiselle Louise de Ramezay, born 1705, daughter of the governor of Montreal. The governor having died, mother and daughter carried on the management of his property, and the daughter, who did not marry, continued after her mother's death. In 1745, she built a flour and sawmill. In 1749, she built a school. By 1756, she was making single purchases of lumber of up to sixty thousand livres. She remained a successful business woman until her death in 1776.[47]

The harsh French law

In any seventeenth-century society, punishments were severe and to modern minds, cruel. New France was no exception. While there was no outbreak of frenzy such as the witch-burning at Salem, torture was used to procure confessions, and under the harsh French law,[48] accusation was almost tantamount to conviction. Still, a good deal of latitude was allowed for human failings if they did not involve religious dogma (and none did) or what was almost worse, sexual deviation. An example occurring at Montreal involved the explorer of the west, Duluth. In March, 1678, one of the watch, wending his way homeward, heard two women screaming that they were being murdered. He rushed into the café from which the cries came, one of dubious reputation kept by a Mme de Folleville. Here he found, seated eating, the great Sieur Duluth. Rather than antagonize him, the officer withdrew, asking Mme de Folleville if she did not know that curfew has sounded. She replied haughtily that she had not heard the bell. A year or two later, the same café was again the scene of disturbance. André Hachin, bailiff, and Denis Marsaut, jailer, were making their rounds at ten o'clock. Again a row in de Folleville's café. They entered to find some men quarrelling over their cups. In trying to enforce the law, the officers angered the drinkers, who fell on them and chased them down the street. The two officers took refuge in another inn and secured two men to accompany them on their rounds. Hardly had they got outside when they were attacked by one of their pursuers and one of the reinforcements was hurt by a stone. So many complaints were laid against de Folleville's café that the seminary, in whose jurisdiction it was, decided to suppress it. But Mme de Folleville was a woman of powerful connections and it took all the power of the seminary to close up her café.

Hangings were public and were infinitely more gruesome in those days than to-day, though they do not seem to have been overly common. One of the difficulties was to find a hangman. They all turned out alike—thieves, drunkards, the lowest of the low—all except a respectable negro slave purchased from the south in 1731 and "treated with great consideration by the authorities."

In 1690, one Jean Haude-Coeur was brought to Montreal on a charge of murder. He was found guilty and sentenced. His right hand was to be chopped off in front of the home of the victim and on the scaffold he was to receive six breaking blows on the legs, thighs, and arms. Then he was to be broken on the wheel. Luckily for the accused, while the Sovereign Council was debating an appeal, word arrived that without benefit of the trimmings, he had already been hanged!

Less macabre than this was the case of François Quintal, who disappeared for a few days and was later put into prison on suspicion of private trading with the Indians. The constable, Guillaume Vanier, and the jailer, went one day to see him. Vanier ordered wine for all hands (who included some women companions). All became merry and Vanier began to brag that he had been the only one able to lay hands on Quintal. The prisoner disagreed and, one thing leading to another, stabbed the policeman with the jailer's knife, which he had borrowed to cut tobacco with. Punishment—pay costs and a fine![49]

All in all, for those who do not feel the lack of intellectual liberty, the 'right to speak the thing you will,' who will accept subordination and the cramping restraints of a small community (the vast majority of mankind) New France must have provided quite a good life. "Wrong doers cannot live in Canada" said Pierre Boucher, "they get too close a watch kept on them."[50] Everyone accepted things as they were without rebellion. Why not? They were all Frenchmen together, they were all Catholics together, and by the end of the seventeenth century, they were pretty well all (in the French sense) *parents* together. It is true there was some friction between French grandees, lay or clerical, and the native-born, but there were no Huguenots and no English to trouble the peace.

Perhaps the most significant point of inquiry is the last one here to be made, whether anything like *la nation Canadienne* had developed by 1700. Of this there are at least some indications. When Louisiana was founded, Frenchmen rapidly worked up the Mississippi and in Illinois came into contact with 'Canadians' from Quebec. Jealousy between the two rapidly developed and, it is said, the 'Canadians' incited the Indians to pillage the 'Louisianians.'[51] Then there is the quotation used a good deal by French-speaking historians[52] which in making a protest to the authorities for going against the interests of the inhabitants, speaks of those who have lived in Canada, "their fathers, grandfathers, great-grandfathers, great-great-grandfathers before them." Here is one of the earliest and clearest stirrings of native self-consciousness. From the first, the people of the new land had been called *Canadiens*, but that was only a manner of speaking: they had merely been Canadians because they lived in Canada. And now, after most of a century, they had their ancestors behind them, three and four generations of them. They were beginning to *feel* themselves Canadians.

Already there had been a good many attempts to describe their characteristics and nearly all these had combined in the view that *Canadiens* were both independent and docile: they could not be driven but, managed adroitly, they took leadership and were unswerving in their loyalty and obedience. Physically they were well formed. The French they spoke was uniform, and it was good French. They were one in race and faith. There was already a line between them and the French. "Good workers, who apply themselves with assiduity to the soil, not only do they live decently and are without comparison happier than those that in France are called 'good countrymen' but also, since the spirit of this country is to take life easily and because they have much of the Indian humour, which is light, inconstant and tires quickly of application to work, seeing the liberty which they take so boldly to run the woods. . . ." so rambled on the Intendant Duchesneau in a despatch of 1679 to the minister.[53] Other descriptions, mostly later, are numerous, and contradictory. A people can be described in as many ways as there are persons to describe it. The point is that descriptions cannot be made of something that does not exist, even in the imagination. The Canadians of 1700 existed. A new French people, not yet conscious of their separation from the metropolitan French, had come into being.

The community established / 53

Notes to Chapter 5.

1. See Diagram No. 2 embodying some of the principal items, 1665-1765.
2. i.e., the governmental district based on Quebec.
3. An *arpent* may be taken as, roughly, an acre.
4. The *minot* equalled 1.07 bushels.
5. Though cattle then were not as large or as efficient as they are to-day.
6. Joseph Robineau de Villebon, *Memoir on the Present Condition of Port Royal, October 27th, 1699,* as given in J. C. Webster, *Acadia at the End of the Seventeenth Century* (New Brunswick Museum Monographic Series No. 1, Saint John, 1934). De Villebon was governor of Acadia.
7. Ibid., pp. 85, 87, quoting de Villebon on Oct. 1st, 1695.
8. Ibid., p. 50.
9. See Chapter 23.
10. Well-known frontier types such as the *coureurs des bois* and the explorers are not dealt with here.
11. *Bulletin des Recherches Historiques,* Vol. 7, p. 5, "have found two neighbourhoods, each along a river. In the first there is enough to locate fifty settlers . . . and in the second there is land to put at least forty on. The most beautiful country on earth. . . .*"
12. Emile Salone, *La Colonisation de la Nouvelle France* (Paris, c. 1910), pp. 23, 314; W. B. Munro, *The Seigneurial System in Canada* (New York, 1907), p. 172.
13. see pp. 224, 225.
14. Public Archives of Canada, *Série B,* Vol. 34, *Royal Memorial to Vaudreuil and Bégon,* June 15th, 1712.
15. The actual number of horses returned for 1698 was 684 among 13,000 people. The next return was for 1720, a total of 5,274. This for a population of 24,000, practically all rural, does not seem excessive. See diagram No. 2.
16. See his novel *The Golden Dog (Le Chien d'Or),* published in 1878.
17. See Dollier de Casson, *History of Montreal, 1640-1672,* translated by R. Flenley (London & Toronto, 1928).
18. Benjamin Sulte, *Mélanges Historiques* (Montreal, 1918), Vol. IX, p. 16.
19. About 77 per cent, at which figure it remained until 1881.
20. Public Archives, *Série C^{11} A,* Vol. 3, *Au Ministre,* Nov. 2nd, 1672.
21. *Recherches Historiques,* Vol. 32, p. 16.
22. See Jesuit *Relations,* 1664-1667, *Letter of Father Beschefer,* Oct. 4th, 1666, describing Quebec.
23. Alan Gowans, *Church Architecture in New France* (Toronto, 1955), p. 48.
24. Ibid., p. 82
25. About 60c or say $5.00 in 1958.
26. Details gathered from *Recherches Historiques,* Vol. 44, pp. 133-136, article by E. Z. Massicote, *"Par les Rues de Montréal au Bon Vieux Temps".* Also Vol. 21, p. 25; Vol. 55, p. 194 etc.
27. Ibid., Vol. 30, p. 281.
28. Ibid., Vol. 38, pp. 56-57.
29. Ibid., Vol. 35, p. 265, citing Peter Kalm.
30. Ibid., pp. 263-267.
31. Ibid., Vol. 22, p. 334.
32. Ibid., Vol. 48, pp. 34-42.
33. Ibid., Vol. 4, p. 18, quotes La Hontan: "This vermin does not infest Canada."
34. Public Archives, *Série C^{11} A,* Vol. 17, pp. 81 ff.
35. Ibid., Calendar to *Série B,* p. 417, June 6th, 1708.
36. Ibid., p. 290, *The Minister to Frontenac,* April 7th, 1691.

37. See, *inter alia, Recherches Historiques,* Vol. 2, p. 86 *A Letter of Dénonville to the Minister,* Aug. 20th, 1688.
38. Ibid., p. 290.
39. And later on was causing scandal by living with a man not her husband. See Public Archives, *Série* B, Vol. 47, p. 51, May 30th, 1724.
40. Public Archives, *Série* C[11]A, Vol. 43, p. 55, *Vaudreuil to the Minister,* Oct. 20th, 1720.
41. Ibid.
42. See Chapter 7.
43. Salone, op. cit, p. 251.
44. Ibid., p. 217.
45. Public Archives, C[11]A, Vol. 52, p. 3, *Beauharnois and Hocquart to the Minister,* Oct. 15th, 1730.
46. Ibid., *Série* B, Vol. 48, *Memorandum of the King,* May 15th, 1725.
47. *Recherches Historiques,* Vol. 37, p. 30.
48. " . . . L'accusé n'a pas connaissance du dossier qu'on établit contre lui. Il n'est pas interrogé qu'à huis clos. . . . Les témoins sont entendus hors de sa présence. . . . Le jour du jugement, il ne comparait devant le tribunal que si sa présence est expressément réclamée. . . . Enfin la question, c'est-à-dire la torture, peut lui être infligée, soit pour lui arracher des aveux, soit pour lui faire dénoncer des complices." G. Zeller, *Les Institutions de la France au XVIe siècle* (Paris, 1949), Chapter IV.
49. Details gathered from *Recherches Historiques,* especially E. Z. Massicote's *"Couvre-feu et Rondes de Nuit",* Vol. 36, pp. 266-269.
50. Salone, op. cit., p. 134.
51. Nellis M. Crouse, *Lemoyne d'Iberville, Soldier of New France* (Ithaca, N. Y., 1954).
52. Salone, op. cit., p. 438; Guy Frégault, *La Civilisation de la Nouvelle France* (Montreal, 1944), p. 268.
53. Public Archives, *Série* C[11]A, Vol. 5, Nov. 10th, 1679.

6: New France
and Roman Catholicism

No branch of the Roman Catholic Church
has more faithfully preserved the spirit of the high Middle
Ages than has that of French Canada. Naturally nothing stands
still and to-day French Canada is in flux, but in the years when
the country was being established, the aim to preserve unchanged the spiritual past was almost realized. On the religious
and ecclesiastical side, New France came close to the cleric's
dream, the perfect society which only the Church can provide.

He who would understand the intellectual system upon which
a Catholic community turns, must understand its philosophical foundations. Yet, however clearly the external student may
observe this intellectual foliage, he will not feel the intricacy
and intimacy of the root system out of which it springs and
which springs from it: one can see the worshippers at the shrine
but he cannot see the spirit which animates them. The best,
therefore, the non-Catholic can do is to describe as objectively
as he can, well knowing that whereas he may comprehend
those areas which the two branches of the Christian faith have
in common, he cannot penetrate the inner mysteries of the
other, its nuances, the puzzles which make what seems irrational or erroneous to him, rational and holy for another. And
yet, what historian of Canada worthy of his salt can fail to
make this effort? The two peoples for nearly two centuries now
have been yoked in partnership and surely those who would
analyze their common life must try to understand both. A
word, then, on the medieval background.

The medieval church was not in the same sure position on
all points of doctrine and knowledge as it was to be later. It
was to be the outstanding contribution of those great centuries
of philosophic and theological discussion which run from about
1100 to 1300, to clear up much of the confusion. The papacy
itself, great as had been the advance made under Gregory VII

(1073-1085), had not reached the authoritative position it later was to arrive at. "There is no need that the Pope should expound to us the will of God", said a twelfth century Archbishop of York, "have we not the Scriptures to instruct us?"[1] In the schools of Paris during the late twelfth century, many were the rival theological views put forward. The variety of opinion can be estimated from the collection of intellectual brain teasers set out in the celebrated Abelard's *Yea and Nay* (*Sic et Non*): "Is God the author of evil, or not?" "Is God all-powerful, or not?" etc., etc. With the vigorous growth of intellectualism, (reflected in the founding of the first universities, 1150-1200), theological and philosophical diversity, based on the individualism of able scholars, proceeded apace. The persons who got things back on an even keel were certain great doctors of the Church, among whom St. Albert and Thomas Aquinas stand out pre-eminent. The vast compendium of St. Thomas was knit together by an inner logic: it had "a place for everything and everything in its place." The result was a system that for centuries stood the heaviest intellectual assaults. Its revival in the form of "Neo-Thomism," of which the centres are Louvain, Belgium, Laval University, Quebec, and the Medieval Institutes in the University of Montreal and St. Michael's College, Toronto, is an evidence of its vitality. It was this co-ordinated structure as interpreted by the Spanish commentators of the sixteenth-seventeenth century, especially the Jesuits Suarez and Bellarmine, which was introduced into New France by its earliest ecclesiastics (who naturally knew no other), and which in truncated form has continued to flourish there down to this day.[2]

The central point in St. Thomas's teaching was that faith and reason are not antagonistic but may be reconciled. By 'faith' he meant the Christian faith. It was his task to elucidate that faith and to seek to understand it by hard, rational examination—"to justify God's ways to man." St. Thomas could take many points for granted which our age cannot—the literal inspiration of Holy Writ, for example. Nor was he encumbered with the embarrassing amount of knowledge that we now possess, though he had a far greater store than we moderns suspect. His method was to take the fixed points and reason out others from them.[3] By this means, St. Thomas in the course of his volumes ranges the whole scale of divine qualities and human existence.

The *Summa*, as compendiums of it quickly make clear, nicely illustrates how far the Catholic and the Protestant mind have moved away from each other in the centuries since the Reformation. Here on the one hand is this splendidly logical collection of categories, each neatly discussed, and on the other the pragmatic, testing experimentalism of later Protestantism; a quality not so evident in the earlier days but now that Protestantism has proved so hospitable to free inquiry, more and more fashioning the minds of those whose tradition it is.

Behind St. Thomas at almost every point, the great shadow of Aristotle is discernible. Through St. Thomas, Aristotle lived again and Greek thought once more poured into the western world. For each of them all things were arranged, in increasing order of complexity, from the most minute up to the highest point, God. Each order of things, therefore, was peculiar to itself. Each thing, or being, was an individual, distinct and separate from other individuals, existing in its own right. Here is one of the roots of our own democratic creed of equality, and of equal rights.

For St. Thomas, and for Catholics down to this day, individual could not merge with individual. It would have been hard, presumably, for St. Thomas to follow the modern scientist down into those dim recesses of life where it cannot be clearly asserted that the organism under discussion is either plant or animal. To St. Thomas, an animal is an animal, fixed and determined, with clear bounds marking it off from plants on the one side and from humans on the other. To moderns, the line is less certain, the deductions that may be made from the formal definition less secure. We compare the psychologies of man and the higher apes without prejudice about the soul, that is, without much concern for hard-and-fast categories. Every discussion in St. Thomas by contrast leads up to the highest point or category, God. On the way, everything, category by category, gets systematic exposition. What Protestant can systematically discuss, say, the 'cardinal virtues,' name them and enumerate the qualities of each? Yet when St. Thomas discusses *prudence* as one of them, he does it logically, sanely, and in admirably orderly fashion. It would do no one any harm to put his ideas together about prudence. This to Roman Catholics, especially to the educated French Canadian, has been the stuff of instruction for centuries.

The picture has its shades as well as its lights. It is not difficult to discern in St. Thomas's discussion of animals, which by definition cannot have rational souls, certain aspects of most Catholic societies, especially the so-called *Latin* societies. If animals do not have rational souls, they are placed here for the good of man, who stands above them in the hierarchy of things. The step is not great to the exploitation of animals, possibly to their cruel treatment.[4] "Societies for the Prevention of Cruelty to Animals" would not be likely to arise in Catholic countries: something mildly pantheistic has entered into the Protestant mentality which prevents it from concurring too heartily with St. John, when he proclaims of heaven, "without are dogs."[5] Much the same kind of remark could be made about St. Thomas's discussion of women.[6] The 'woman's rights' movement would not have arisen in a Latin Catholic society. Quebec, in whose founding woman had such a high place and which has always assigned to her a unique importance, nevertheless was the last of the Canadian provinces to yield to 'votes for women.' This does not mean that woman does not have an honourable place in such societies, though it becomes more and more conditioned by the fear of her dreadful attractions as one goes south in Europe, but they do not find much place for the conception of equality and the frank acceptance of it which has arisen in the Protestant north.

To non-Catholics, much of the *Summa* to this day makes good sense. But if it has to be taken or left as a whole, there are regions into which it is impossible to follow it. With the discussion, for example, of 'The Pure Spirits',[7] it takes on the Alice-in-Wonderlandish atmosphere of an especially clearly remembered dream. Everything about the 'Pure Spirits' is logical but with the sensible foolish logic of Alice.

Then turn from the 'Pure Spirits' to the discussion of a great topic like *justice*, and see the difference. With such topics as *justice*, we are at the entrance to much that lay behind the development of our own English system of law, and through it, our other public institutions. The modern English-speaking world finds underneath itself an embarrassing amount of Thomist foundation, and woe to it if it ever discards that for sheer expediency, for its liberties will disappear with its absolutes.

French Canada has been schooled in these absolutes too, schooled much more strictly and self-consciously than has English Canada. The difference seems to be that French Canada has had the whole Thomistic structure, 'Pure Spirits' and all, while for English communities, the Reformation set up a screening process that has sloughed off much in the Thomistic system.

Here, then, in this great theology and philosophy French Canada was cradled: hardly one of her educated sons is not steeped in it. For any understanding of 'how the other half lives,' whether as of the seventeenth, the eighteenth, the nineteenth, or the twentieth centuries, some passing acquaintance with Thomism seems imperative.

The various aspects of French Catholicism

Equally imperative for study of the colonial Church is it to know a little about the major forces that at that time were affecting Catholic life, mainly, of course, in the motherland. Four of these stand out: the French Counter-Reformation, Jesuitism, Jansenism, Gallicanism.[8] Of these, Jansenism alone, except possibly in the spirit which marked it, did not cross the seas. The Counter-Reformation in France set in on Henry IV's turning Catholic in 1593. It reached its apex in spiritual zeal about 1640 and then tailed off to end with such easy exhibitions of righteousness as the persecution of the Huguenots under Louis XIV and the revocation in 1685 of their charter of toleration, the Edict of Nantes. In a memorial to Governor Dénonville of New France, 1686, Louis (one could think, shamefacedly) explains his reasons for the revocation: there is such a large number of conversions to the Catholic religion that revocation has become necessary! Dénonville is exhorted to labour for a like result in Canada. If any are obstinate, he might billet troops on them or imprison them.[9] In the New France of 1686, Huguenots must have been as rare as palm trees. But well before Louis's death, the fire was going out of the Counter-Reformation: the age of the Enlightenment was at hand, the age of Montesquieu, Voltaire, and the *philosophes*. Scepticism was replacing religious zeal. This wave from France, however, took nearly a century to roll across the Atlantic: the French Enlightenment did not reach New France until the nineteenth century.[10]

While the French Counter-Reformation was at its height, it gave rise to that magnificent zeal, that burning faith, which sent the Jesuits to the Indian villages and to their horrid martyrdoms (1635-1649). It inspired such heroism as the founding of Montreal (1642). Down to the sixteen-sixties, it was a piercing light of piety and evangelism. Then with the destruction of the missions and the retreat to the colony,[11] all this devotion, thus concentrated on one small colony with a dominating and ascetic ecclesiastical politician at its head (Laval), turned a bit sour: it turned into a French Catholic puritanism which has had few parallels in its pressure upon the allegiance and the personal conduct of its adherents.

It was natural that Catholic puritanism should be primarily concerned with the dangerous qualities of sex. The conduct of women, eternal Eves, came in for constant ecclesiastical censure. Mgr. de Laval found it necessary to launch a famous *mandement* against behaviour of a kind not entirely unknown to our own generation. It was directed "against the luxury and vanity of women and girls in church."

"Of what crimes do they not make themselves guilty, and what punishment is to await those who carry this showy apparel into our churches, appearing in these places consecrated to prayer and penitence with indecent clothing, making visible the scandalous nakedness of arms, shoulders and throat, covering them only with transparent drapery, which serves often only to give more lustre to these shameless nudities. . . ."[12]

"The last thing man will civilize is woman," the good bishop might have echoed if he had been capable of so drastic a *mot*. Woman, on her part, might have defended herself in her usual way—she was not responsible for man's own nature! And of that, the church was equally fearful. "The brothers D'Auteuil . . . one lives publicly with the Réaume woman, whose husband is in the Upper Country and the other with the Berloger woman, whose husband is in the West Indies." The bishop complained to the king himself and the king said the intendant must do something about it![13] The king being Louis XV, he surely must have sent his injunction, if he ever saw it, with his tongue in his cheek! An unmarried woman is retained by a widower for the education of his daughter and the care of his household and he quickly gets a letter from the minister himself about it, thanks to what he calls "calumnies set on foot by Père Joseph."[14] Despite all this watchfulness, nature apparently would out, for in 1744 a house "for the restraint of girls of a bad reputation" was under consideration.[15] By 1744, it is possible that the climate had become a little milder than in Laval's time. Surely something of the sort must have been occurring when it could turn out that a priest, ordered back from Quebec to Acadia, had taken with him as servant, a woman disguised as a man![16]

Bishop Laval, and after him Saint-Vallier, made every effort to prevent balls and plays. *Le Tartuffe* of Molière came in for special animosity. In 1694, a certain de Manereuille, an unlucky producer of plays who had strayed to New France, planned a performance of *Tartuffe*. Saint-Vallier published a *mandement* against the theatre in general and then a second against de Manereuille in particular, forbidding him to enter the church "because of his impieties, blasphemies, etc." The poor producer could only claim that he was a good parishioner who performed his religious duties.[17] The recitation could go on, but it gets into minor areas and there is discernible as the eighteenth century wears on, considerable resistance on the part of the secular authorities to the more unreasonable type of pressure—the nuns in Quebec failed in trying to get all the second story windows in the houses around their property boarded up and in preventing any more being built that could overlook them.[18] Yet the old current continued to run, for as late as 1757, a royal ordinance was procured prohibiting games of chance.[19] Among the games prohibited were *le passe-dix, le dupe, le quinze*, etc. This in a time of war, with the land full of soldiers!

The struggle for dominance in and over the Catholic Church of French Canada

It is impossible to write about the Canadian Church, whether from the spiritual or the administrative angle, without referring to the man who was in most respects its founder, Bishop Laval. Laval had been a pupil of the Jesuits for ten years and he became their successful candidate for the bishopric. His relations with the Order were close and, like many other Catholic *dévots*, he is said to have had yearnings to become one of its members. Jesuit influence coloured the church life of the colony.

When the liberties of the Church (a wide term) were involved, Laval fought intendant and governor alike, not hesitating to use his influence at Paris against them. He was austere and narrow, zealous for the kingdom of God as he saw it, for education and for the moral good of the colony, an ecclesiastical[20] statesman of not unusual type.

One of his major contests centred round his determination to have a clergy entirely dependent upon himself, with no *curés fixes*, that is, no parish priests with permanent tenure. In a thinly populated colony this policy was sensible, although it was vigorously opposed by the lay authorities. In the struggle, victory went to Laval and his successor, Saint-Vallier, and the parish priest became and has remained an appointee of the bishop, who shifts him about as he sees proper.

When Laval arrived, he found only three parishes all told— Quebec, Montreal, and Chateau Richer—and he promptly reduced Quebec to humble status by making himself its curé. He set up fifteen parishes in 1681 and in 1683 he claimed twenty-five residing priests,[21] but there is something not firm about this figure, for as late as 1708, only fifteen fixed charges were reported, and by 1720 the number had grown only to twenty.[22]

Sedentary curés were all the more necessary in that most of the seigneurs were failures in their local duties: thanks to absenteeism, poverty, the wrong attitude (some were mere business men playing at being squires), or simple expanse of forest, the seigneurs, with exceptions, failed to stand to the settlers *in loco parentis*. This cast the greater burden on the curés, who therefore needed the support that a fixed charge could possibly give. And yet there was Abbé Morel in the sixteen-sixties with some thirteen districts under his care! This, of course, was a normal frontier experience that nothing could remedy but time. Thanks to the breeding power of the *habitant*, time came to the rescue with remarkable celerity and by the end of the seventeenth century, the 'continuous village' aspect of the St. Lawrence was beginning to take shape.

Ecclesiastical centralizing tendencies displayed themselves in many spheres. Laval provided a standardized plan for church buildings: he seems to have hoped that by imposing his own uniform (and severe) designs in architecture, he would aid himself in maintaining uniformity in other directions.[23] His influence in architecture, which in turn rested upon Jesuit notions inspired by the same type of thinking, being exerted in the malleable days of the colony, was formative, and the tradition of church building which he set going left and leaves permanent marks upon the appearance of the countryside of the St. Lawrence.

Laval, the bishop, the man primarily responsible for setting up the provincial form of government, was unlikely to accept rivals to his power. Yet two sets of rivals appeared and both managed to make good their existence: these were the Sulpicians and the Recollets. The Recollets had been first to come to New France but had to abandon their mission because of their poverty.[24] They returned in 1674, unwelcome visitors. In the course of a quarter-century they found a place for themselves, since their simplicity took them close to the people. They built churches in Quebec and Trois Rivières. Governors and other officials, finding in them a certain foil against the bishop and the Jesuits, supported them, and four governors, including Frontenac, were buried in their church.

The Sulpicians came to Montreal. They too represented opposition to the powers-that-were, especially in that they were off by themselves, nearly two hundred miles away. Under a versatile superior with many elements of greatness, Dollier de Casson, who not only wrote the very readable *History of Montreal* (1673), but discussed a project for a canal at Lachine and designed the Montreal parish church, they flourished, their prosperity based on their rich seigneurial lands. Good feeling between them and the bishops was conspicuous by its absence. The Montrealers rallied round them. Rivalry between two such cities as Montreal and Quebec is clearly inevitable, but the ecclesiastical gulf accentuated it and built it into one of the major aspects of French-Canadian society. The bitter battles of the eighteen-seventies over the establishment of a university at Montreal were in logical sequence, as is the marked, though reversed, difference in atmosphere between the Universities of Laval and Montreal today. Both in the Church and out of it, Montreal manifested a spirit of independence not pleasing to the authorities. Its society was freer (and its churches more ornate) than those of Quebec.

In the *ancien régime*, Church and State were twisted up together. If at a given moment one appeared dominant, this reflected the accident of personalities: there was no thought of revolutionary change in their relationships. It is not possible to make a simple statement to the effect that as the power of the Church fell, that of the State rose.

The nearest French Catholicism (before 1789) came to experiencing revolution was in the period from about 1665 to 1695 when the Gallican movement was at its peak. Gallicanism was an old story in the Church of France, going back to the Conciliar struggle of the fifteenth century. In its broadest aspects, it simply was a phase of the universal and unending struggle between Church and State. What were the spheres of each? In contentious cases, which authority should prevail? As the centuries passed, this large question of principle was rendered still more difficult by the rise of the nation states. In France, the king, as the symbol of all Frenchmen, could hardly accept a rival authority.

Sometimes the king's attempt to control the Church is termed 'political Gallicanism,' while the efforts of the Church of France to free itself from too much Roman control are known as 'ecclesiastical Gallicanism.' They both came out to the same thing, a national church, with the king as its secular head, just as in England. In the seventeenth century, only by the narrowest margins did Gallicanism miss being a repetition of Anglicanism. Louis XIV went a considerable distance in the footsteps of Henry VIII but by the chance of circumstances and a pious wife, he did not go the whole. With both monarchs it was much more a matter of political advantage than of religion.

The relations of the Church in France with the Crown rested on the Concordat of Bologna of 1516. This document regulated such matters as the appointment of bishops, appeals to Rome and ecclesiastical taxation. It superseded the earlier, unilateral declaration of the French Church known as the Pragmatic Sanction (1436) which had declared against the universal power of the pope and in favour of a General Council as the supreme governing body of the Church: this had been the central issue in the great Conciliar struggle. The issue had slumbered in France and had apparently been effectively buried by the Catholic zeal generated out of the Huguenot wars. Then as *le grand monarque, le roi soleil,* progressed from splendour to splendour, nationalism returned to the Church of France, and in 1682 there appeared *The Four Articles of the Clergy.* These went right back to the position of 1436, denied the temporal power of the pope, proclaimed Conciliar Supremacy, and declared the decisions of the popes, even in matters of faith, to be subject to revision. These articles put Louis XIV into a position similar to that which had been assumed by Henry VIII in the Act of Supremacy, 1534—"Supreme Head of the Church on earth."

The popes had their own methods of reply and in the end they won a tactical victory. In 1693, Louis abandoned *The Four Articles* (which he had had proceed from the clergy themselves) and in 1695 a royal edict set forth the relations that were to obtain between Church and State until the Revolution. The Gallican claims touching jurisdiction over doctrine were abandoned but the Church lost its remaining authority in law over secular matters. And since coercive authority was left with the State, the secular courts had an entry into the examination of ecclesiastical decisions in the spiritual realm. The contest as a whole rested upon the widely held seventeenth-century view of divine-right monarchy. The pope might be the pilot of the vessel but the king was its captain. The king was 'elected and chosen of God,' a semi-priestly character himself, a 'bishop from without,' as the term went.

Louis XIV was the most Catholic of monarchs, just as Henry VIII had been, but the Church, if not the faith, was to suffer from its two defenders. While France did not go as far as England and no national church out of communion with Rome resulted, the struggle in securing the triumph of 'political' Gallicanism had its effect in bringing about the more tolerant, easy-going eighteenth century, which in turn was father of the Revolution.

Into Canada, 'ecclesiastical Gallicanism' did not enter: there were no disputes in the colony as to where lay the ultimate power to shape Catholic doctrine; in fact, there were no doctrinal disputes whatever. Thanks to Laval and the Jesuits, a completely orthodox, wholly ultramontane Catholicism was nurtured in New France and to this day there have been no departures from it. How genuinely ultramontane the Church of Canada was is another question. The impression is strong that Canadian ultramontanism has been primarily the resort to a distant power which cannot interfere much: the way to mastery in your own house lies through Rome. Rome is a rod to be kept in pickle. In nineteenth-century English Canada, the same tactics were often resorted to by 'Imperialists' who, on examination, appear mainly as parties anxious to serve their own interests. In both cases, the external loyalties have seemed genuine to those holding them.

In 'political Gallicanism' the State eventually won a large victory. Despite a Laval, the king, acting through governor, intendant, and law courts, came to control the ecclesiastical authorities at every point. But the road to victory ever rang with the noise of battle. Despatches to France constantly advise that it is time to institute a secular clergy.[25] Logical arguments are put forth: if men are not given the spiritual sustenance afforded by a resident priest, they are not liable to pay the tithe (which ecclesiastics were always trying to extend, and *habitants*, with pertinacity and success, plus the support of the government, were always trying to whittle down). There are too many priests—"useless ecclesiastics who, for want of employment, are beginning to engage in worldly play, feasting, and dissipations."[26] There are not enough priests . . . ! Priests are starving and the tithe must be paid! And so on.

In the end, church jurisdiction over lay persons was cut down to the lowest point, the civil power having the last word in every case. Although taxes on all were negligible, the Church and the clergy were taxed along with the rest. The State regulated the tithe. It regulated the *dots* or 'dowries' that girls becoming nuns had to pay.[27] It forbade the formation of new religious orders and prohibited some that had been formed from taking vows and wearing special habits.[28] It bade—though in this it failed—the clergy to stick to "the word of God and evangelical religion" in their sermons. It chose the bishop. As Lanctot says, *"l'Eglise canadienne était l'absolue prisonnière de l'Etat."*[29] Of course, as he makes clear, it was a benevolent captivity, and the statement is more typical of the eighteenth century than the seventeenth, yet "it was only the British Conquest which freed the Canadian church, so much so indeed that ever since the beginning of the English régime, it has found itself freer than under the kings of France."[30]

The Catholicism of the humble

Contest in these lofty areas passed over the heads of simple people, who had been brought up to regard king and clergy as the twin pillars of their temple. For such people—the vast majority—contests could go on about every aspect of Church and State without in any way touching the central mysteries.

As M. Ives Thériault puts it in his novel *Les Vendeurs du Temple*[31] one may differ from the Church authorities on every subject under the sun except one and vigorously maintain his own opinion: that one subject is dogma or as a contumacious priest of the eighteen-seventies stated it, "I have expressed opinions which are not yours, my Lord, but the opinions of a bishop bind no one—And how could they bind anyone when those even of the Sovereign Pontiff do not make law? Note that I say *opinions*, not *decisions*."[32]

Religion for the masses was what it always had been and always will be: a consolation, an explanation of death, a mode of escaping from a sense of sin. Though the rival creeds probably would not agree, on this basis there may not be a great deal of difference between them. For Roman Catholics, religion provided the support of immemorial usage and in the curé a strong shoulder to lean upon. To Protestants, a sacramental religion of rites and ceremonies must seem mainly formality and therefore vain, but when a sincere Catholic performs, shall we say, the stations of the cross, or engages in the mass, *for him* something precious and mystical occurs. For the Roman Catholic, all the critical occasions of life are sacramentalized—being born, adolescence, marriage, death. In this sense, it is a religion as old as the yearnings of humanity itself, which it reflects. Toynbee talks about "the ever latent *worship of a Mother and her Son* who started on their travels along the King's Highway under the names of Ishtar and Tammuz."[33] In his *The Evolution of the French People*,[34] C. V. Seignobos tells how in the twelfth and thirteenth centuries, virtually a new religion arose in Europe—the devotion to the mother idea, under the name of Mary. It transformed and made gentler the severities of the preceding age. Something of the sort seems to have occurred again in New France.[35] The eighteenth century was not as close to bloodshed and martyrdom as was the seventeenth. It, too, was gentler, and the cult of Mother and Son as a result, become if possible, more prominent.[36]

The intense spirit of piety that had been brought across to New France was reflected not only in devotion to Mary but in the vogue of countless saints, who sprang up in every locality, any one of them, apparently, more or less effective as an intervener between God and man.[37].

It is this ready anthropomorphism of Catholicism which mystifies, and usually antagonizes, Protestants. To them, Roman Catholicism is not a monotheistic religion. However, for the people of eighteenth-century New France, and probably for simple people everywhere, this aspect of it seemed to present no difficulties. The saints became like Greek heroes if not Greek gods, mingling intimately in everyday life and possessing large, though uncertain, powers which might be got on your side by the appropriate ritual.

The puzzling mixture of spiritual and material with which Roman Catholicism confronts the Protestant is exemplified in the brawl which occurred on the Island of Orleans in the middle of the eighteenth century.[38] In the year 1703, the curé of St. Laurent gave to the curé of St. Pierre a precious relic belonging to his parish, nothing less than the *arm-bone of St. Paul!* The gift, made without the consent of the parishioners of St. Laurent, rankled. It rankled even though the people of St. Pierre had the arm-bone done up in a silver monstrance made in Quebec. It rankled for twenty-eight years, in fact. (*"Ils ont toujours murmuré de cet échange."*) Then in 1731, a raid was made at dark of night on the church of St. Pierre. The relic was 'liberated', and carried in triumph to its original site. Only the personal intervention of the bishop, and that with difficulty, plus suitable apology, secured the restoration of the relic to St. Pierre. In such an incident it is hard to distinguish piety from local pride, credulity from the tribal spirit. Yet quite possibly for many 'the arm-bone of St. Paul' worked miracles!

The fervent piety of French Canada has always been well attested and it remains to-day unabated. It manifested itself in dozens of forms—not only through churches and church attendance, but in the formation of orders, the founding of hospitals, the setting up of charities, the opening up of schools.[39] There must have been scores of devoted people in the little colony.

This unrelenting, buzzing activity, some of it intolerant and harsh, most of it Christian and kindly, in the area broadly called religious, is neatly characterized by the riddle which some French Catholic clerics, friends of the writer's, bandied about one day in his presence. "What are the three things that God alone knows?" Answer: "Where the Jesuits get their money, what the Franciscans live upon, and the number of religious orders in the province of Quebec!" Quebec remains to-day, as it has always been, the land of religious orders and of Catholicism.

Notes to Chapter 6.
1. Quoted in H. W. C. Davis, *England under the Normans and Angevins* (London, 1909), p. 126.
2. The best explanation of Thomist (or Scholastic) philosophy and theology which the writer knows is *The Philosophy of St. Thomas Aquinas* by Hans Meyer (St. Louis, Missouri, 1946).

3. This is perhaps a little unfair to St. Thomas as it is really a description of the method of the Jesuit commentators. This latter method has come down little changed in the classical colleges of French Canada, where it still forms the basis of instruction. *"Probat quod Deus sit"* (Prove that God exists), an actual examination question, illustrates the type. In answer, each candidate writes down his version (in Latin) of a carefully worked out syllogism.
4. Something of this lingers in French Canada, probably not much. Yet the present writer himself remembers seeing in rural Quebec a large man being drawn along in a tiny cart by a not very big dog, an unusual spectacle for North America.
5. Revelations, xxii, 15.
6. See Meyer, op. cit., p. 207.
7. Ibid., p. 221.
8. For preliminary remarks on the Church in New France, see Chapter 3.
9. Public Archives of Canada, Calendar to *Série B*, p. 274, *Versailles,* May 31st, 1686.
10. See Marcel Trudel, *L'Influence de Voltaire au Canada* (Quebec, 1945). Also Paul Hazard, *La Pensée Européenne au XVIIIe Siècle: de Montesquieu à Lessing* (2 Vols., Paris, 1946).
11. After the destruction of Huronia, missions continued but on a relatively small scale.
12. *Mandements, Lettres Pastorales et Circulaires des Evêques de Québec;* ed. H. Têtu et C.-O. Gagnon (4 Vols., Quebec, 1888) Vol. 1, p. 106.
13. Public Archives, Calendar to *Série B*, p. 51, *Memorandum of the King to M. Robert,* May 30th, 1724.
14. Public Archives, *Série B*, Vol. 36, *The Minister to de Gallifet,* Mar. 21st, 1714; *de Gallifet to the Minister,* Mar. 21st, 1714.
15. Ibid., Vol. 78, *President of the Navy Board to Curé of Montreal. M. Déat,* Apr. 17th, 1744.
16. Public Archives, *Série C¹¹A*, Vol. 68, *Bishop Dosquet to the Minister concerning the priest St. Vincent,* Apr. 30th, 1737.
17. Benjamin Sulte, *Mélanges Historiques* (Montreal, 1918), Vol. X, p. 16.
18. Public Archives, *Série B*, Vol. 50, *Navy Board to de Beauharnois and*
19. Ibid., Vol. 105, Mar. 6th, 1757.
20. As an offset to narrow puritanism, the gallant struggle of the Church to prevent the debauchery of the Indians by the white man's firewater, which went on under every bishop, but never with more determination than under Laval, should be noted. It has often been described.
21. Public Archives, *Report*, 1900, p. 196.
22. *Bulletin des Recherches Historiques,* Vol. 40, p. 648, *"La vie religieuse dans les paroisses rurales Canadiennes au XVIIIe siècle"* by Claude de Bonnault.
23. Alan Gowans, *Church Architecture in New France* (Toronto, 1955), Chapter III.
24. They were a branch of the Franciscans who rigidly adhered to the conceptions of St. Francis of Assisi, the founder, and embraced poverty as a good.
25. See, for example, Public Archives, *Série C¹¹ A*, Vol. 11, p. 81, *Intendant Champigny to the Minister,* May 25th, 1699.
26. Ibid., Vol. 106, *de Beauharnois and Hocquart,* Oct. 25th, 1730.
27. Ibid., Vol. 43, pp. 237 ff., Dec. 19th, 1721. Governor Vaudreuil succeeded in getting these reduced, whereupon the bishop proclaimed that this was because he had two daughters of his own who wanted to become nuns!
28. Ibid., Calendar, p. 204, *Pontchartrain to Raudot,* June 10th, 1706.
29. Gustave Lanctot, *Une Nouvelle France Inconnue* (Montreal, 1955), essay on *"Servitude de l'Eglise sous le régime français",* p. 170.
30. Ibid., p. 171.

31. Quebec, *c.* 1950
32. Thomas Charland, *"Un Gaumiste Canadien: l'Abbé Alexis Pelletier",* *Revue d'Histoire de l'Amérique Française* (Montreal), Sept. et Dec., 1947).
33. See p. 423 for more on this.
34. New York, 1932, p. 141.
35. Lanctot, op. cit., essay on *"Le Culte Mariale en Nouvelle France".*
36. Ibid., quoting Kalm (1749), "The Virgin Mary seems more honoured in Canada than God himself", p. 52.
37. Including St. Abrossepoil who, according to a clerical friend of the present writer, originated from the phrase for stroking a dog's hair backward *"(c'est à brosse-poil")* and had no other existence!
38. Marius Barbeau, *"L'Ile d'Orleans"* in the *Queen's Quarterly,* 1942, p. 374.
39. For example, the efforts of people like the brothers Charron at the beginning of the eighteenth century and of the nuns throughout.

7: New France reaches the provincial stage

THE OPENING YEARS of the eighteenth century in New France saw a local man, the Marquis de Vaudreuil, appointed governor; he remained the king's representative from his appointment in 1705 until his death in 1725. Vaudreuil had come to Canada in 1687 and had risen through the various ranks of officialdom to the governorship of Montreal: from this place he was appointed to the chief command. He had married a Canadian wife and had come to be regarded by Canadians as one of themselves. His term coincides with a marked heightening of local self-consciousness. To this there is abundant testimony. The quotation referring to the various generations which have already been born on Canadian soil has been given in Chapter 5.[1] The concomitant of this succession of the generations is a close-knit community, bound by neighbourhood blood ties: three generations go far to establish this. Then there are the first indications of tension between natives and metropolitan French, the first stirrings of that son-father antagonism which marks the growth of communities as it does that of individuals. By the time that Vaudreuil's native-born son had been appointed to the command previously held by his father, 1755, there could be no doubt: New France had attained the provincial stage in its social evolution and in that stage was, through the medium of the English Conquest, to pass out of history.

In both New France and New England, the provincial stage was probably hastened by the good times that followed the great wars of Louis XIV. There was peace between England and France from the signing of the Treaty of Utrecht, 1713, to the outbreak of King George's War, 1743; thirty years' freedom from border raids and Indian warfare, freedom to grow and to expand the economy. This was the period which saw New France establish and strengthen its lines of communications from Louisbourg on the Atlantic, on through to New Orleans on the Gulf of Mexico. It saw the opening up of the great West by La Vérendrye. It witnessed a thriving *entrepôt* trade develop with the New Englanders in Cape Breton, and connections established with the French West Indies. Within the colony shipbuilding and iron works *(Les Forges du St. Maurice)* were set going, in addition to various minor branches of industry. Population increased rapidly, the seigneurial area was extended, and new lands brought under cultivation. For the one and only time in the colony's history, exports exceeded imports. All the indexes show the period to have been one of prosperity.[2] Prosperity extended the arts of peace, made men more contented with their lot, prompted them to think of the community in which they lived as stable and assured. With assurance of permanence and well-being came love; love for the immediate home, the house, the barns, the trees, the fields —*le petit pays*; then for the totality of it, which, men being what they are, quickly becomes an abstraction, the *patria, la patrie.* In some such way, the French in the new world become New French, Canadians; Canada becomes their world, it becomes more than men, animals, and land; it becomes a spiritual possession.

Cultural growth

One of the major indications of social evolution is surely to be found in education, for people concerned with their community naturally wish to have their children initiated into the 'customs of the tribe'. Education is much more than this, but this it is fundamentally: the effort to preserve and perpetuate that way of life which seems good to the people following it. It has usually been the practice among English Canadians to disparage French-Canadian education and to think of Roman Catholicism as synonymous with ignorance. It must be agreed that it has been Protestants, more particularly Calvinists, who have displayed the greatest zeal for universal education, for Calvinism, being a religion of 'The Book,' has everywhere insisted on the ability of its people to read 'The Book': Scotland, Holland, and New England are evidence enough of that. Judged by Calvinistic standards, Catholicism has not measured up in schooling for everybody. Neither has Anglicanism, which occupies a midway position. In the eighteenth century, it is probable that most Scots and New Englanders could read and, after a fashion, write.[3] Most French Canadians (and most Englishmen) could not. Yet New France was not entirely devoid of elementary instruction. The Ursulines provided it for a number of young girls and there were also a few schools for boys, such as those instituted by the brothers Charron, in the second decade of the eighteenth century. In addition, there were well-known technical schools instituted in the seventeenth century: in them there were taught navigation, surveying, some agriculture, carving, gilding, and various other skilled trades. While such schools touched only a few people, they were centres. But everything considered, primary instruction was weak.

In secondary and higher education New France's record was quite good. A school was established by the Jesuits in Quebec in the sixteen-thirties, and in 1663 there was begun the *Grand Séminaire* ('Big Seminary') of Quebec, whose existence has been continuous down to to-day. The studies conducted in it were much on a level, in their Catholic version, with those of Protestant Harvard College. *Le Grand Séminaire* (which turned into Laval University only in 1852) can therefore claim to be the second institution of higher learning in North America (Mexico City excepted). In 1668, the *Petit Séminaire,* which has also had a continuous existence, was added to the *Grand*: its functions were those of a secondary or preparatory school. Both institutions gave the typical education of the day: much Latin, much scholastic philosophy, much theology, mathematics, and some gestures in the direction of literature. Despite the rather repellent nature of the curriculum, it turned out men who could speak and write and who had good manners, as it has continued to do down to this day.[4] How many of them it turned out, it is hard to determine. It is said that between 1693 and 1703, there were 130 students, but as late as 1730 Bishop Dosquet was complaining that not enough native-born priests were being trained to meet the demand. One authority says that 843 students entered the Seminary during the French régime, that is, in a century, a little over eight per year, and only some 120 of these became priests.

At Quebec, there was also the Jesuit College, which was established in 1635 and lasted until the Conquest. Its classical course was organized in 1655 and at that time four instructors were employed. By 1676, this had increased to six, but by 1732, it had declined to three. In 1669, there were about 100 students, but around 1720 this number had shrunk to about 50. Incidentally, students rose at 5:15 a.m. The complete course at the Jesuit school took five years.

It is evident that middle and higher education on a modest scale was not neglected in New France. There was no element of originality about it. Much the same remarks could be made about New England.

Salone summarizes the position succinctly: "At Quebec: the Jesuit College, the Seminary of Quebec, the Ursulines, the technical schools. At Trois Rivières: the Recollet College. At Montreal: the Ursulines, the Seminary of St. Sulpice, the Daughters of the Congregation of Notre Dame. In the country: the Sisters of the Congregation, with fifty mistresses; the Charron schools of 1711-1720, with ten teachers brought over in 1719. The Charron schools collapsed. Beyond the above, nothing!"[5]

In addition to education, we get glimpses from time to time of other aspects of cultural growth. Of these, easily the most prominent was in architecture, especially in church architecture, a topic to which further reference is made in Chapter 15. In 1750, there were a hundred and ten churches scattered up and down the St. Lawrence, of which thirty-seven each were in the Montreal and the Quebec districts.[6] There were twenty-nine between these two districts and seven below Isle aux Coudres. Of these, there survive in whole or in part, mainly in part, some twenty-three. To-day, according to Gowans, there would seem to be seven seventeenth-century church buildings left in Quebec, and some of these only in the form of a wall or other remnant. This leaves sixteen others for the period down to the Conquest, all of which have been much restored. Of them all, the most complete in their seventeenth-century form seem to be the present chapel of the General Hospital in Quebec, once the Recollet church there, which goes back to 1671, and the church of Notre Dame des Victoires in Quebec's Lower Town, which was built in 1688. To the writer, the most impressive survival is the church at Beaumont, 1725, for there, posted in the vestibule for all to read every Sunday, is Wolfe's stern order to the countryside to submit, or take the consequences—the burning of its houses and the destruction of its farms!

Other evidences of cultural growth were present, though apart from handicraft, not impressive. There was some religious painting and one of the artists, Frère Luc, French-born, is described as "a painter of some merit." In wood-carving, extending into sculpture, accomplishment was greater and of much artistic merit. Of the literary arts, there appears not to have been a trace, though that is not to be taken as meaning that there was no appreciation of the written word. Several private libraries are known to have existed. In 1758, Joseph Nouchet of the Superior Council had two hundred and twenty-three books, among them two volumes of Voltaire.[7] It is even asserted that towards the close of the régime, a literary society was formed in Quebec. Yet during the whole period, no printing press existed in the colony. Surely if there had been much demand for one, officialdom, despite the dangers it might have fancied from it, would have yielded.

There were a few indications that scientific interest was awakening. In 1734, a rain of ashes fell at Quebec. Samples were sent over to France for analysis and proved to be ordinary wood ash from forest fires.[8] In 1744, four thermometers, "the invention of M. de Réaumur," were sent out with instructions for observations to be taken.[9] There was also the work of Dr. Sarrazin, a good botanist, discoverer of the Canadian 'pitcher plant.'

It is evident that New France was developing as a typical Catholic colony, with an *élite* of informed and intelligent people who, in turn, would have built up an appropriate local culture which would not, however, have been widely diffused.

Eighteenth-century government

Government also moved slowly onward, and by the Conquest many of the officials, including the governor general, were native-born. But the spirit of government remained overwhelmingly paternalistic. This involved a trans-Atlantic level of interest which is hardly to be imagined to-day. Despatches never ceased to pass across the ocean about the most trivial matters: chimney sweeps, the provision of an additional midwife, whether the citizens of Quebec should keep their wood piles away from their houses to avoid fire, and the difficulties of the government in replacing the two donkeys previously sent out.[10]

The despatches also allow of close description of government at more important levels. A woman who has concealed her pregnancy is taught a lesson that will prevent her doing it again—she is hanged! Torture is occasionally still used. *Lettres de cachet* are not unknown but when the bishop asks for a supply, he is emphatically refused. One despatch illustrates in detail the French method of promulgating new law. In 1725 it was decided that only two *cabarets* (taverns) should be allowed in each parish. First of all the agreement of the bishop to the measure is secured. Then an *Arrêt du Conseil d'Etat du Roi* is drawn up. The *arrêt* is registered in the Superior Council (November 13th, 1724). Under it the intendant issues his ordinance proclaiming the law (January 18th, 1725). Copies are then sent into all the *côtes*, to be published and posted up by the captains of militia. Letters are sent to every parish curé advising him of the legal steps taken and asking the names of 'honest parishioners' to whom permission 'to hold cabaret' may be given.

A still more interesting 'play by play' account of the way in which French government worked is afforded by a dispute which arose over the fur-trade post on Lake Temiskaming.[11] The post had been allocated by Intendant Bégon apparently without proper notice. According to Vaudreuil, the governor, this alienated some of the merchants of Montreal to such a degree that they would not pay their taxes. The intendant counter-attacked by asserting that those who had petitioned against the allocation of the post were unimportant nobodies and that the governor had probably put them up to it anyway in order to 'wangle' the post for one of his favourites. At last a meeting of those concerned was held in Quebec and there, after long debate, a new allocation was made. During the debate, the threat not to pay taxes came up again. Vaudreuil in his despatch says he passed over "this seditious speech" because he wanted to prevent disunion in the colony! On the boundaries of the post coming up for discussion, Vaudreuil said he did not know what they were, whereupon a certain Sieur des Musseaux "told him that no one knew better than himself (Vaudreuil), since he had drawn them in the first place." This at least was Bégon's report. The governor apparently accepted this bit of plain speaking, too. After that, they managed to get the limits of the post redrawn by mutual agreement (thus upsetting in part the intendant's arrangements), and finally the intendant issued his covering ordinance.

We can picture the scene: the principal merchants of Montreal and Quebec assembled in the intendant's palace, the governor and intendant both present in person, the tables covered with papers and maps, the defiant assertion that if this sort of things is to go on "*Le Roi ne devoient plus compter sur les secours qu'il luy demandoit*"—"the king would no longer be able to count on the aid [e.g., taxes] he had asked of Montreal"—and a little later one of the gentlemen as good as telling the governor to his face that he was lying! This is hardly the sort of thing that can be called 'absolute government.' Neither is it in the English sense self-government. It is government with large but irregular amounts of liberty within it. No wonder Vaudreuil could go on to write that "it is not in the inhabitants of the cities only that one remarks this spirit of mutiny and of independence: it spreads through all the inhabitants of the country, who are at their ease, rendering them less submissive and less prompt to carry out the orders they receive for his Majesty's service." The conclusion of a governor of the old régime is not far off—if prosperity leads to such results as this, then means must be found for rendering the inhabitants less prosperous.

French soldiers and Canadian morals

In the eighteenth century as in the seventeenth, endless concern was shown over the morals of the colonists, new threats to which were arising with the complexities of the times. Good fathers in France were discovering the virtues of distant Canada as a place of deposit for their worthless sons, whose morals on arrival in the colony seem to have been as loose as their purse-strings. Bad as these eighteenth-century 'remittance men' were, they were nothing compared to a threat to religion itself. And was this not actually present? Had not the bishop discovered the presence in the colony—during the summer only —of nine Huguenots? Was he not justified in calling loudly for their expulsion?[12]

The threat of threats descended towards the middle of the century with the arrival of the gaudy intendant Bigot and of several battalions of regular troops, whose unfortunate infant results followed in logical sequence. Bigot's gold-plated dinners, his balls and general jollifications have often been commented on. Few have been as plain speaking as a curé of the time. "M. le curé preached a sermon this morning on balls. . . . He said that all 'assemblies, balls and country parties' were infamous, that mothers who brought their daughters to them were adulteresses, that they only availed themselves of these nocturnal pleasures to put a veil over their shamelessness and over fornication. . . ."

It looks as if, despite the valiant resistance of the clergy, the moral and social life of the capital was, by the last decade of New France's existence, becoming 'sophisticated' to an unpleasant degree.

An interesting example of the new type of person appearing with the growing complexity and maturity of the colony was the woman who reported the above sermon—Marie Elizabeth Bégon, née Rocbert de la Morandière, daughter of a man who rose to be *sous-délégué* of Montreal.[13] In 1718 she was married to Michel Bégon, a younger brother of the intendant, who seems to have resented the marriage as one beneath his family's status. There was the further difficulty that the governor had refused the husband, a soldier, permission to marry, and it was alleged that the couple had been wed *au gaumine*.[14] Madame Bégon evidently was a person of some education for she taught her daughter some history, geography, and Latin. She evidently could read English, for she is reported as translating an English letter for Governor La Galissonnière, who was married to her niece. The goings-on of high society, despite her quotation from the curé's sermon, do not appear to have been too offensive to her, provided she was herself within the charmed circle.

In 1749 Madame Bégon went to France, where she was bitterly disappointed with her reception. Like many another colonial before and since, she had gone as to a shrine and had found, not the warm welcome that she had anticipated for one who had helped to hold the far-flung line of Empire, but indifference at best, and often ridicule. "It seems that here I don't know how people ought to live and that I am nothing but an Iroquois . . . if I can once get home, I shall be happy indeed."[15] The French are particularly skilful to this day in alienating their cousins from overseas, and this unhappy skill has turned more than one Frenchman from Canada into a French Canadian, just as similar receptions in England have, though less frequently, similarly affected English Canadians. Here is one root of nationalism.

Madame Bégon's case may give the answer to the final query —whether on the eve of the Conquest there had come into being in Canada a new people, aware of their own existence. Madame Bégon apparently did not rise to such heights of abstract thought—she simply went back to Canada hating the French. There must have been many like her.

The French authorities themselves recognized the existence of a new type in Canada. In 1737, the Intendant Hocquart gave a lengthy description of it. The Canadians were of good physique. They were adaptable,—"they were all skilled in the use of the axe," the universal tool of the pioneer. They loved attention, were independent, reserved, vindictive, constantly on the move, without the rustic appearance of French peasants. Their women were keen-witted and intelligent. "The peasants never undertake any matter of importance without their advice and approval." All the women were fond of dress—no new discovery, surely! And "in that respect there is no difference between the wife of a little shopkeeper and the wife of a gentleman."[16] All visitors from the old world, incidentally, at whatever period in history, have remarked upon the overdressed condition of the North American female and the absence of any class line in woman's dress. They have also remarked on her quick intelligence, product, perhaps, of a society where little is forbidden to her, as compared with her traditional domestic seclusion in the old world. Freedom has so marked her manners that the European observer often believes her morals to be free too. Peter Kalm, the Swedish traveller, made an observation to this effect when he visited Canada in 1749 and for good measure he remarked upon the idle frivolity of the young ladies of Quebec. But then he moved in fashionable society, and there too, as well as in the country, his disparaging remarks did not render it less probable that the men were not undertaking "matters of importance without their women's advice and approval."

The not overly flattering description sent home by Hocquart could not have been far out, for it was echoed by Kalm and by other writers and in the despatches of other officials. "The Canadians are touchy and vain," one of 1730 reads, "but they must be treated according to their temper and with gentleness." In 1757, Montcalm was warned that "mildness, patience and moderation are often necessary with these people. . . . The valour of the Canadians may be counted on with certainty, as well as their zeal and willingness, as long as they are not treated in a distasteful manner. . . ." In other words, no metropolitan *hauteur*, please! Across the lakes, the same resentments were at the same time being set up in the breasts of mere colonials like Washington by other imperial officers of another tongue.[17]

Analyses such as the foregoing do not confirm the existence of nationalism. It is too much to assume the existence of nationalism in Canada before the Conquest. What can be safely assumed is that stage of social evolution which it has been the business of this chapter to examine—provincialism, the consciousness of separateness in sameness, the adolescent's independence in dependence, the loyalties, antagonisms, and resentments that plague adolescence.

Notes to Chapter 7.

1. See p. 53.
2. The results are obvious in the statistics: population in 1706, 16,500 approximately; in 1739, 42,500. Cattle in 1706, 14,000; in 1734, 32,000. Land under cultivation in 1706, 42,000 *arpents;* in 1734, 163,000 *arpents.* See Diagram No. 2.
3. See Samuel Eliot Morison, *A Puritan Pronaos* (London, 1936).
4. Laval University professors of to-day say they get many American post-graduate students and that the first thing they have to do is to teach them to write—English!
5. The chief secondary authorities on education during the French régime are: Emile Salone, *La Colonisation de la Nouvelle France* (Paris, *c.* 1910), pp. 405 ff; Abbé A Gosselin, *L'Instruction au Canada sous le régime français* (Quebec, 1911); L. P. Audet, *Le Système Scolaire de la Province de Quebec* (Laval University, 1950-1952). See also Abbé Maheux, "The Origins of Laval Uni-

versity" (CHA Report, 1952). See among others Public Archives, *Série C¹¹A*, Vol. 7, *Dénonville to the Minister*, Oct. 13th, 1685, and the Calendar to Vol. 106 as well as the Calendars to *Série B*, Vols. 60, 61, 68, etc. These entries confirm the shrinkage of the seventeen-thirties and indicate incidentally that the study of law was being established at the same time.

6. Alan Gowans, *Church Architecture in New France* (Toronto, 1955), map. 4.

7. *Bulletin des Recherches Historiques,* Vol. 24, p. 285; Vol. 32, p. 129. It is interesting to find a Montreal merchant in 1742 asking his correspondent "not to forget the *'livre de Robinson'* " which was presumably *Robinson Crusoe* (see J.-E. Roy, *Histoire de la Seigneurie de Lauzon* Chapter IV, p. 213).

8. Public Archives of Canada, *Série B*, Vol. 61, Apr. 13th, 1734.

9. Ibid., Vol. 78.

10. All examples from Public Archives Calendars to *Série C¹¹ A*.

11. Public Archives, *Série C¹¹ A*, Vol. 47, pp. 72-154.

12. Ibid., Vol. 89, Sept. 18th, 1741, and Oct. 8th, 1747; Salone, op. cit., p. 457.

13. A lesser version of the Intendant, whose representative he was. On Madame Bégon, see J. N. Rouleau, *"La Société Canadienne au XVIIIᵉ Siècle"* (M.A. thesis, *Université de Montréal*, 1952).

14. See Chapter 5.

15. Letter of January 20th, 1750.

16. Public Archives, *Série C¹¹ A*, Vol. 67, *de Beauharnois and Hocquart to the Minister*, Oct. 30th, 1737.

17. For an elaborate analysis of French-Canadian characteristics past and present, see Georges Vattier, *Essai sur la mentalité canadienne-française* (Paris, 1938). Vattier collects many observations from the seventeenth and eighteenth centuries on the character of French Canadians. Many others are easily traced down through the Calendars to the dispatches in the Public Archives of Canada.

8: The lilies come down!

"The 8th of September, 1760, at eight o'clock in the morning, the Marquis de Vaudreuil, last governor of New France, signed at Montreal the capitulation which put an end to French rule in our country. The prolongation of the heroic struggle . . . had become impossible. The English general, Sir Jeffrey Amherst, surrounded the city . . . with twenty thousand men, to meet whom there were hardly twenty-four hundred soldiers. Food, artillery, munitions, everything was lacking. No more help could be expected from France. . . . The fatal hour had sounded and it was necessary to bow before the inevitable. . . ."

IN THESE SIMPLE, moving words Thomas Chapais opens his *History of Canada*.[1] Writing almost one hundred and sixty years after those days, the author is sad, yet proud; sad when he lets his imagination play over the events, proud when he recalls the strides made by his people since they occurred. After some paragraphs of description of the first moments of conquest, he turns to the scene of a hundred years later when the first legislative session in the new Province of Quebec, consequent upon Confederation, is about to open. "Look here, upon this picture and on this!" he exclaims. In 1760, the situation of the French Canadians "was dolorous and justified every feeling of alarm. An abyss had opened under their feet and thenceforth was to separate their past from their future. The present was desolate and that future sinister." Then he asks his readers to turn their thoughts forward a century. The old city of Quebec is *en fête*. The crowds throng about the ancient sites, whose scars have long been healed. A royal salute is fired as the governor comes to open the session of the representative body charged to pass upon the laws, the education, the public domain, the institutions of the province.[2] "And that governor, escorted by English troops, who present arms to him as to a sovereign . . . is a man of the French race and language, he comes to preside over the inauguration of a

French legislature, created by an act of the Parliament of England, to administer freely a French province."

Chapais' two pictures outline in classic simplicity the epic of his people, and few writers in French, before or since, have failed to celebrate it along with him. Here was a little handful of people, forced to descend into the valley of despair and yet, after a time, winning through, coming to terms with their conqueror, turning the edge of his sword and ending up by gaining their freedom. In humanity's troubled story, it is a familiar theme; but one that never loses its poignancy for those who have experienced its realities. No study of Canada is worth the name that does not seek to explore it and to bring out its full meaning, both for those who passed under the English yoke and for those who, later on, were to form themselves into another people within the former dominions of the king of France.

What would the course of events have been if the Conquest had not occurred? The 'ifs' of history are legion and no answer can be provided for them. "The moving finger writes, and having writ, moves on." Only speculation remains. Would New France have gone on a generation later to revolt against its mother country as did Spanish America? Would a new and independent French America have arisen, forming its own pattern, neither republican and democratic like English America, nor monarchic and aristocratic in the old-world sense? Would such a new France have displayed the instabilities and the injustices of Spanish American 'republics' or would it have reflected in greater or lesser degree the self-governing pattern of its neighbours? Such questions are vain. New France ceased to exist. The lilies came down!

We are forced, therefore, to deal with an uncompleted evolution. A society that had reached the provincial stage was arrested in its development and did not reach the national life to which, possibly, it might have attained. All began over again, and the New French had to learn to relive their lives as 'new subjects' of the British king. Their story from that day onward was to consist in a patient rescue of themselves from the débâcle that came upon them, a piecing together again of their communal life and a reluctant sharing of portions of that life with their new fellow-subjects. Eventually, perhaps, it would mean a frank and free partnership of both peoples in something greater than either, something that in our own age is slowly taking shape, a Canadian nation.

Reflections of this sort were impossible in the day of conquest. At that time, only the din and smoke of war occupied men's minds. Campaign after campaign had been fought, along the coasts, in the wilderness, up and down the long corridor between Montreal and New York. In most of them the French had been successful. Braddock and his men had been annihilated in the forests of western Pennsylvania. Oswego, that English window on the lakes, had been taken. Loudon and Abercrombie had been discomfitted in the tangle of mountain and lake where the northward-flowing waters separate from those that go down the Hudson. Gallant victories these, achieved by those regiments of the king whose battle colours still may be seen on display in the ancient city through whose streets they once had been proudly carried, and by the native Canadian militia, who had fought gallantly after their fashion.

At last the tide of war had turned. A far-away individual named Pitt had decided that France must be humbled, not across the Channel but across the Atlantic.[3] Like a modern Churchill, he had rallied the English nation and had found ships, admirals, new generals, new battalions. With his coming, war took on grimmer aspects. In 1758, Louisbourg fell. The year following, 1759, the great amphibious expedition was prepared which was to result in the fall of Quebec. After its long agony of the summer of 1759, cut off from the ocean, bombarded by day and by night till it was little more than a ruin, the fate of the city had been determined by the short decisive engagement known in history as the Battle of the Plains of Abraham (September 13th, 1759). Quebec had been surrendered and the British flag had been hoisted over its walls. "Yesterday a vessel arrived at this place from Quebec, which contains the agreeable news of the capture of that place on the 17th of last month", says the *New York Mercury*, Oct. 15th, 1759.

Then, in the spring of 1760, a last ray of hope dawned for the French. If Lévis from Montreal could but bring the English commander Murray to action and defeat him, the city might once more be his. The impossible almost happened! Lévis did bring Murray to battle just outside the walls and there occurred an almost exact replica of what had happened the previous September: Murray was defeated and retired within the fortifications. He had a two weeks' supply of ammunition. But unlike Montcalm's successor, he hung grimly on, well knowing that the issue would be determined by the ensign worn by the first ship to round the corner of the Island of Orleans:

"Nul étendard ne flotte à son mât d'artimon

Est-il contre ou pour nous? Est-il ange ou démon? . . .
Tout à coup, du vaisseau qui présente son flanc. . . .
Et les guerriers saxons du haut des parapets
Et les soldats français penchés sur les falaises
Voient monter au vent les trois couleurs anglaises!
Le sort avait parlé, notre astre s'éclipsait. . . ."[4]

The ship which carried "*les trois couleurs anglaises*" proved to be the vanguard of a fleet. Lévis, realizing the game was up, broke up his camp and retired for his last-ditch stand at Montreal. After the Battle of the Plains, the British had left Murray behind at Quebec in an almost impossible position and only great determination and good luck avoided the dissipation of all the vast efforts of the previous campaigns, the death of Wolfe included. Amherst, the commander-in-chief, does not stand up overly well in the light of history: a cautious, heavy man, he had afforded little aid to Wolfe and the next spring, 1760, does not seem to have made any effort of moment to rescue Murray from his predicament. The British won Canada by the gallantry of individual officers such as Wolfe, the courage of the rank and file, sea power, and, perhaps above all, by the organizing ability of William Pitt.

The various meanings of the Conquest

The Conquest had as many receptions as there were interests concerned: old England, New England, old France, New France, to each of these it meant something different. Possibly the only point of agreement was as to the might of England's sea power and the decisive nature of sea power in the world-wide struggle of which the Canadian campaigns formed only one phase.

For the American colonies, the fall of New France was the signal for unlimited rejoicing: the old northern enemy, the enemy who for generations had been used to burst unheralded out of the bush to slay and scalp and burn, had at last been put out of harm's way. The forts that had been barring American western egress from the mountain passes would henceforth act as guardians to the advancing trains of settlers—Fort Duquesne would become Fort Pitt, then Pittsburg. Colonial loyalties, as someone has said, "slopped over." A statue was erected to George III (later to be melted down for bullets to fire against his soldiers). Never had the English race seemed more firmly united. Americans had borne an honourable share in the campaigns and American soldiers had rejoiced to see the territories of their ancient enemies ravaged. It had been mainly Boston pressure which had led to the expulsion of the Acadians in 1755,[5] and it was colonial troops who got most satisfaction from the destruction wrought on the St. Lawrence: as one of them put it at the time, "We burned and destroyed upward of fourteen hundred fine farm-houses, for we, during the siege, were masters of a great part of the country along the shore, and parties were almost continuously kept out ravaging the country, so that 'tis thought, 'twill take them half a century to recover the damage."[6] A New York bard termed the French

> "That savage, treacherous Race, which to subdue
> Required no less a Conqueror than you. . . ."[7]

Thus spoke the English colonists!

In old England, the news of victory was naturally received with rejoicing. William Pitt's fame rose higher than ever; if that was possible in a day when every ship brought news of fresh victories. Pitt, the navy, the soldiers of the king, the discomfiture of both France and Spain, all these combined to make 1759, as it was promptly called, the year of victories, *annus mirabilis*. Yet, very soon, the utility of the victory began to be questioned. What use was Canada, anyway? "We did not enter into the present war with a design to conquer Canada," said a pamphleteer of the day,[8] "but only to secure our colonies. . . . Canada produces nothing that can ever possibly make a colony flourish. . . . But how different a country is Louisiana: capable of bearing almost anything, from the temper of the sky, the goodness of the soil, and from the multitude of long, deep and beautiful rivers with which it is everywhere enriched and adorned." Louisiana, he continues, has forty times the importance of Canada, which has only the fur trade, a very inconsiderable thing![9] The anonymous pamphleteer was not the only one to deride the retention of Canada: in an age which measured everything by its cash value, there were plenty of more valuable colonies. Why then retain it? This attitude was to confuse British colonial policy for another century. It had a great deal to do with losing the first Empire and it came close to losing the second.

In France, few tears were shed for the loss of Canada. The king had fortified both Louisbourg and Quebec at vast expense and to fight the Seven Years' War he had sent some good officers and some thousands of troops. But the heart of France had never been in colonizing ventures. Louis XIV himself had exclaimed that "to people Canada, it would be necessary to depopulate France," and thereby he had made the great refusal, deciding to keep his subjects at home.[10] About the same time, the Jesuits had ceased publishing their annual volume of *Relations* (1673), so that Canada gradually ceased to be known in

France, except in official circles. In such circles, what was chiefly known about it was that it was costing the government about five hundred thousand livres a year: if we take the livre as equal to about a dollar of our money, half a million a year seems a small price to pay for a foothold in America. But it seemed large to the French government, too large. No wonder that when an appeal for more force came from Canada, at the height of her agony, the French minister, mindful of his country's perils on the battlegrounds of Europe, could answer: "When the house is on fire, we cannot bother about the stable." Canada, moreover, had to suffer the same comparisons with Louisiana as were voiced by the English pamphleteer. It would never amount to anything. It never had amounted to anything, compared to the West Indies. And, in case of war, it must inevitably fall to the English. The war was probably half lost before it was begun, and the wonder is that the French held out so long.

Then, when the news of the Conquest came and in the interval before the peace was made, tongues were loosed, and all the voices seemed unfavourable to efforts to get the country back. The greatest of the voices was that of Voltaire and that sharp-tongued man did not spare poor Canada. "In truth you should drive home with the Duke de Choiseul (the chief minister of the time) my taste for Louisiana. I have never been able to understand how they came to choose the most detestable country in the North, only to be kept by ruinous wars, and abandon the finest climate on earth."[11] "We had the inclination to establish ourselves in Canada upon the snows, between the bears and the beavers."[12] And again, in his *Candide*, the well-known: "You know that these two nations are at war for a few acres of snow (*quelques arpents de neige*) and that they are spending for that war far more than Canada is worth." Finally, after he had heard of the loss of Canada: "In one day . . . 1500 leagues of land had been lost. These 1500 leagues, being glacial deserts, were not, perhaps, really a loss. Canada cost much and brought in very little. . . ."[13] Voltaire was only the most extreme of many. Just as a century later many 'little Englanders' tried to throw away the British Empire, so in the eighteenth, many 'little Frenchmen' were not moved when the French empire, if not thrown away, was lost. It passed the imagination of either set to see the future.

What the Conquest meant for the Canadians

For New France, conquest meant conquest: it had meant first the rushing to arms of all the menfolk down to boys of thirteen; next the burning of your home and my home, the destruction of the little provincial capital, the ravaging of the countryside, the appropriation of the crops by those who had not sown them (when they did not burn them), the carrying off of the cattle. It meant the enemy's ships in the river before your eyes, the sound of his bugle calls in your ears, the alternative to you, simple countryman, of submitting to him in your own person, or of taking to the bush and seeing from afar your farmstead go up in flames. All conquests go deep—they are among the deepest of human experiences.[14] None went deeper than that of New France. It was the reversal of reversals— *Les Bastonnois* (the Canadian name for the New Englanders) triumphing over those who had so frequently triumphed over them, the English over the French, the disorderly, anarchic, crude English over the soldiers of the most cultured country in Europe, over a king who stood, not for huckstering, but for order and glory. Worst of all, it was the triumph of Protestantism over Catholicism: that preserve of the Church, that precious jewel in the Madonna's crown, New France, which had refused to admit even a fellow-Frenchman if his faith were suspect, handed over to the profane, to the foreigner and the heretic!

Contemporary accounts naturally do not pause for philosophical reflection: they remain in the area of the specific— property destroyed, casualties, the horrible prospect of a famine winter, care of the wounded. The official and military stories are matter of fact and succinct: it is from the clerical side, the more feminine side, that we learn something of the emotions that reigned. The very titles of the bishop's *mandements* (his pastoral letters) give us an index of the times and their stresses. In 1753, a year of peace, he prescribes prayers for recovery of the Dauphin. Two years later comes the first note of apprehension, with appeals for prayers on behalf of the exiled Acadians. Then in the early years of the war, the various successes call each for the singing of a *Te Deum*: "Fort Bull taken: the naval victory on Lake Ontario: the repeated blows on Lac St. Sacrement (Lake George): desolation carried into the provinces of Virginia, Pennsylvania, Maryland." In 1757, more thanksgiving—"The precious marks that Heaven has been giving for a year past of Its protection over the Kingdom and over the sacred person of His Majesty." Again in 1758: Mandement ordering a *Te Deum* for the victory of the 8th July. But with 1759, the note changes: "From all sides, dear brothers, the enemy is making immense preparations, his forces at least six times greater than ours. . . ." No more *Te Deums*. The curés are ordered to sing the psalm *Miserere mei Deus*. By April, public prayers of contrition are called for, and by October, with Quebec in enemy hands, a *mandement* goes out on "the sad situation of the colony," among the last issued by the bishop, who within a few months was dead. The people are to mend their ways, repent of their sins, lest God punish them still further. Join to this the bishop's stark description of the ruined colony, as set forth in his letter to the Minister in France; the almost total destruction of Quebec, the desolation of the countryside, upward and downward; the flight of the inhabitants—surely he would be dull of soul who could not comprehend the apprehension, the anxiety, the deep tragedy, which conquest involves.

Another and still more intimate glimpse of what conquest means comes through the pages of the Ursulines' Annals.[15] "Around the citadel, groups of French officers are seen in consultation; their gloomy countenances tell of indecision, weariness, and despondency. . . ." The nuns after the surrender of the city, styled themselves 'prisoners of war.' And after the second siege, by Lévis, "it was then, more than ever, that our convent became a hospital . . . how depict the horrors we have had to see and hear . . . the cries of the dying and the lamentations of the onlookers. . . . After having dressed more than five hundred patients . . . there still remained others unprovided for. Our barns and sheds were full of the wounded. We had in our infirmary seventy-two officers, of whom thirty-three died. The amputation of legs and arms was going on everywhere." And then, on the final surrender of Canada, "we could not persuade ourselves that Canada would be so easily given up. Nothing is left for us but to adore with submission the impenetrable decrees of the Almighty."

Only as the years receded did the full measure of things become evident and only, too, with their passage, did the conquered find words in which to picture it. English Canadians, whose communities have arisen long after the event, as a rule approach this passage in their history with cool detachment: they feel the triumph of Wolfe and of British arms and identify themselves with it, but it is, after two hundred years, a cool triumph, with not much exultation in it, not much emotion brought to bear upon it. Two great wars have shrunk these eighteenth-century engagements almost to the level of minor skirmishes. For French Canadians, the case is quite other. Seventeen-sixty was the year in which the French flag came down, never to go up again. Before that year lay generations of glorious accomplishment when they were masters in their own house, subjects of the greatest king in Christendom. After it, the generations of tribulation have been strung out. Would their race and faith perish, or could it in some measure survive? No wonder then that Chapais opens his *History* with the contrasting pictures placed at the beginning of this chapter. In the interval between them, for him and for every other French Canadian, a miracle had occurred: the miracle of *survivance*, survival. French-Canadian writers have never ceased to celebrate that miracle; for all of them it takes the same form and most of them it inspires with eloquent words.

The story of the Conquest received its first classic expression in the pages of Garneau's *Histoire du Canada*.[16] Garneau wrote in an age in which history was confined to narration, so that to appreciate the effect his book had on his countrymen, the reader must peruse it at length until its spirit makes itself felt. The pages on the Conquest make no general observations, but there arises from them an exhalation, as it were, of patriotism and of tragedy: here was a little broken people, left alone with its masters. His book as a whole is a celebration of survival and despite its many inaccuracies and sometimes its unfairness, it has been accepted by the educated public of French Canada as the classical exposition of the story. A generation after Garneau, the Abbé H. R. Casgrain could write:

"During the hard years which followed the cession of the country to the foreigner, the little people on the shores of the St. Lawrence, ruined and completely abandoned, had only one thought, saw only one way of salvation: make themselves forgotten, bend back on themselves, live apart and in a sense ask pardon for existing. They had struggled valiantly. But finally, they had been conquered by the masters who governed them. Was it prudent to awake their suspicions? We were entirely disarmed and at their mercy . . . Wait and be silent, seemed the surest tactic."[17]

He then speaks of the sudden enthusiasm for Canadian history which swept over his community when he was a youth and of how the first volume of Garneau was put into his hands and those of his classmates. Here was the formulation of the first part of the canon of Canadian history which has ever since been accepted in French Canada: a people who had come through deep waters.

The second part of the canon is exemplified in the passages of Chapais (writing nearly two generations later still than Casgrain, or about 1920) referred to at the beginning of this chapter. Not only had the little people come through deep waters, but they had survived and, by Chapais' generation, they had more than survived: they had once more become masters in their own house!

The pattern thus set has been redrawn at frequent intervals with little change. Jules Léger in his *Le Canada français et son expression littéraire*[18] speaks of "les années terribles," followed by the slow revival of freedom, won by hardy French Canadians from their tyrannical masters. Benjamin Sulte had already sounded the note[19] of self-confidence and self-congratulation: "The royal troops, few in number, accomplished nothing without our participation. . . . It was our militiamen who decided the day at Carillon. . . . Every French Canadian has the right to be proud of those glorious times!" Nothing of the hang-dog conquered about this writer, certainly.

Coming down to our day, Canon Groulx, examining the question of whether, as French Canadians have themselves often stated, the Conquest was a "providential benefit" in that it saved Canada from the atheism of the French Revolution, will have none of such providential benefits. He refuses, by inference, to see any good in it. The Conquest was unmitigated disaster. If it was providential, "to what ends did God permit the expulsion from America of the Catholic nations, France and Spain? Why this half of the hemisphere delivered to all-powerful Protestantism? Why the extraordinary expansion of the Anglo-Saxon across the world?" A peculiar Providence, indeed. God seems to have become badly confused over the matter, we almost hear the good Canon saying.[20] In his *History of French Canada*[21] Groulx appears to swing back some distance to the providential school:

> "A little folk, this little people of sixty-five thousand conquered souls. But a redoubtable people, thanks to its geographical position, and its extent of territory, and by its ethnic and social genius so different from the rest of the Empire. . . . Here was a handful of colonists . . . abandoned in a corner of America. Let it yield, let it be snapped up by the stronger and who would dare to reproach it. . . . But we have spoken of the vigour of soul of this little people of pioneers, its impatience of every yoke, its passions for liberty. And we are at the morrow of 1760. . . . In America, strange airs are blowing about the continent. . . . What probability then is sketched out for a French Canada rivetted to a will to survive, in its energetic refusal of assimilation. . . . All of a sudden a history starts up, takes on austere grandeur, a tragic beauty."

If this is not providentialism, it is at least the heroic interpretation of history, which must be close to providentialism—unless it is good Catholic doctrine to view man as sheer will defying fate.

With Gustave Lanctot,[22] one of the latest writers on the subject, the old view is once more expressed, and movingly.

"Hostilities continued, Great Britain throwing eighteen thousand against a colony of seventy thousand souls. The supreme decree was inscribed in history, a decree by which New France became a British province. In that dreadful hour, grouped around their altars, the people refused to lose the valiance of their days of colonization and of heroism. Kneeling at the feet of their Divine Protectress, they sent up from all their churches and from all their hearths, the filial prayer of the catechism: 'Remember, O most gracious Virgin Mary, that never was it known, that anyone who fled to thy protection, implored thy help or sought thine intercession was left unaided. . . .' This invocation from the whole of a people reflected but one hope, to safeguard its French spirit and its Catholic heart. Sent out on the wings of prayer, generation after generation, this moving plea, the Virgin Protectress of New France heard and granted. She granted it so effectually that the seventy thousand suppliants have become four millions of faithful, who, across the width of Canada, in this Marian year, before the Immaculate Virgin . . . kneel and pray to Her and glorify Her with Catholic souls and French words."

These are eloquent words; they are all eloquent words, all these words that affirm the survival of a small people whose history has been one long record of the determination to survive. Survival had been difficult enough in the seventeenth century under Iroquois attacks: it was to become, apparently, still more so in the eighteenth, under the weight of defeat, invasion and, finally, conquest. Is it any wonder that since those days for most of French Canada history has become something of a mystique, a national myth in almost set terms, believed in, to be affirmed and hardly to be investigated, the guarantee of the miracle of survival?

With the Conquest, had the lilies in fact come down? Or, if they had come down, would they some day be rehoisted? Or if not the lilies, would some day some other flag, symbolizing the same faith and the same heroism, the flag of a people new minted in the crucible of adversity, be hoisted in their stead? In 1760, who was to say?

Notes to Chapter 8.

1. *Cours d'Histoire du Canada* (Montreal, 1919)—to the present writer's mind, the fairest and most authentic piece of historic analysis to come out of French Canada. Many historical works in the French language

are marred by their writers' prepossession with the misfortunes of their own people. Emotional depth is understandable and to be sympathized with, but it may easily get in the way of objectivity; with Chapais this is never the case.

2. Chapais puts it: *"Nos lois, nos institutions nationales,* etc." English Canadians find themselves chilled by the exclusiveness of the first person plural and they would probably bridle at *"nos institutions nationales"*, but *"nation"* and *"nationale"* carry a more limited sense in French than in English.

3. The ministry which Pitt was to dominate was formed in the spring of 1757.

4. Louis Frechette, *"La fin du régime français à Québec"*. This may be translated as follows:

> "No standard floats at her mizzen
> Is she for us or against? Is she angel or demon?
> All at once from the vessel as she comes about
> Both the English warriors from the tops of the parapets
> And the French soldiers leaning over the cliffs
> See streaming to the wind . . . the tri-coloured English flag!
> Fate has spoken, our star is eclipsed!"

5. Though within a century the Puritans, thanks to the sentimentalities of their poet Longfellow, had succeeded in getting rid of all sense of sin for that affair.

6 *New York Mercury,* Dec. 31st, 1759, "Journal of the Expedition up the St. Lawrence".

7. Ibid., Oct. 29th, 1759, "On the Death of General Wolfe".

8. *Sentiments Relating to the Late Negotiations* (London, 1761), Anon.

9. French administration apparently separated Canada from Louisiana somewhere in the present States of Indiana and Illinois. By Louisiana, the pamphleteer meant everything across the Alleghanies, north almost to the lakes. He assailed Pitt for being ready to treat without stipulating for the surrender of this area, but when the Treaty of Paris was finally signed, it turned out that England had everything, right west to the Mississippi; that is, she had Canada and the best of Louisiana too.

10. How could an English king have "kept his subjects at home"? The defeat of the French was written in every aspect of their institutions.

11. *Voltaire to Le Comte d'Argental,* Nov. 1st, 1760.

12. *To Mme du Deffand,* Oct. 13th, 1759

13. *Précis du règne de Louis XV.* (These quotations collected from Emile Salone, *La Colonisation de la Nouvelle France* [Paris c. 1910], pp. 428-429.)

14. The present writer has tried to analyze *conquest* as a historical and psychological phenomenon in his *Colony to Nation* (Toronto and London, 1957).

15. See *Glimpses of the Monastery: Scenes from the History of the Ursulines of Quebec during Two Hundred Years, 1639-1839* (2nd ed., Quebec, 1897) by a Member of the Community.

16. This book first appeared in three volumes from 1845 to 1848 and it has run through many editions. The Conquest is described in Book 10.

17. *Oeuvres Complètes* (Quebec, 1873), I, *Le Mouvement Littéraire au Canada.*

18. Paris, 1938.

19. *Histoire des Canadiens-Français* (Montreal, 1887), Vol. VII, pp. 89 ff.

20. *Notre Maître le Passé* (Montreal, 1944), pp. 125 ff.

21. Montreal, 1952, Vol. III.

22. Gustave Lanctot, *Une Nouvelle France Inconnue* (Montreal, 1955), the essay on *"Le Culte Mariale en Nouvelle France".*

Part II
British North America

9: Aftermath of conquest: two worlds in one

WHEN THE LAST FRENCH TROOPS and the last French officials had disappeared down the river, Canadians must have felt much like the prisoner in his cell when he hears the bolt shot on the door, the unfriendly guard outside. Yet even between guard and prisoner there springs up sooner or later a species of intimacy—they at least come to know each other's shortcomings. So with a conquered and a conquering people. At first suspicion, sullen looks from the one, arrogance from the other. Gradually, little acts of accommodation, such as everywhere pass between humans thrown together. Then, here and there some knowledge, individual friendships like that between John Fraser and Dr. Badelart, the Highlander the patient of the French doctor on the actual field of battle that fateful September day of 1759, the French doctor the prisoner of the Highlander, close friends for forty years thereafter.[1]

It was not, however, merely a matter of individuals meeting, but of two societies totally different from each other and neither uniform within itself. Both had their ranks and classes. French society was uniform in religion and in outlook, but from the top of its 'gentry' to the bottom of its peasantry, the distance was great. English society was hardly uniform in a single particular, for not only was there the traditional gulf between the aristocrat and his 'inferiors,' but there was also a wide, vocal and powerful layer inserted between the 'gentleman' and 'the lower orders.' This middle class was powerful and constantly challenged the ruling class. Moreover, its members were often pitted against the ruling class by denominational differences.

The English ruling class

The English ruling class, in which were comprised practically all military officers and governmental officials, was Tory and feudal. In England the great Whig nobles, whose tradition stemmed from the 'Glorious Revolution' (1688), might wield the power of government, but the squire and parson occupied their immemorial place in the countryside. The difference in outlook between William Pitt, Earl of Chatham, and the men who officered his armies and governed the colonies his genius had conquered was vast. Read the debates on the Quebec Act![2] Burke, Fox, Barré, all these traditional Whigs, speak out for free government. But when Guy Carleton was examined before the House, a different note obtruded, the note of military arrogance, coupled with a severe consciousness of class distinction.[3]

The typical eighteenth-century British 'officer and gentleman' was a man with a family behind him, a family with property, which meant servants in the house, and property in land, which meant tenant farmers outside it, touching their caps. His military education had been thorough, though not liberal, and if it were joined to a good mind, it could produce a good specimen. He probably spoke French reasonably well, an important asset in Canada. His training had been in the habit of command, than which nothing could have been more necessary in armies consisting of officers from the top and men from the bottom of English society. In religion the eighteenth-century officer was a member of the established Church of England, and in politics a Tory. If left to manage a situation by himself in a society which accepted something like his own class distinctions, he was capable, through his paternalistic traditions, of doing a good job. Challenged, as wherever there was an English population they necessarily have been challenged, such men often turned ugly and displayed their worst side. Specimens can be gathered by the score from every corner of empire. Such men were adepts at conquering an empire, some of them very fair at governing it (providing it consisted of 'natives') when conquered, and almost just as good at losing it again, for if at one stage of the conquered country's development, they could win respect through paternalism, at another, through their exclusiveness and arrogance, they could incur only hatred. It was not until the weight of the 'sahib' was removed from the British North American colonies, and the political genius of Revolution Whigs substituted for it (beginning with Durham in 1837) that the continued existence of the second empire became assured.

The Whig governing class was just as aristocratic as the lesser Tories. But it gathered about it those groups which inherited the Puritan tradition—commercial men, rising industrialists, 'dissenters' of many sorts. The terms 'dissenter' and 'merchant' often coincided, and among 'dissenters' were to be reckoned Scottish Presbyterians. Such men found their opposite numbers in the Puritans of the new world, for Puritanism meant a strong carry-over of the seventeenth-century Roundhead tradition, and antagonism to the officers and gentlemen, who were equally representative of the seventeenth-century Cavalier tradition. In this way, the American Revolution was a continuation of the seventeenth-century civil war, that is, of the religious and social clash between the two types of British subjects.[4]

The English Tory aristocrat carried with him many vestigial remnants of medievalism. His religion enabled him to understand and appreciate Roman Catholicism better than Non-Conformism. His objection to Catholicism was mainly political: he did not object to its doctrines or to its ritual so much as to the fact that at its head was a foreign potentate, the pope, allegiance to whom conflicted with allegiance to the king. His attitude towards trade and traders was similarly medieval: trade and gentility would not go together. The fighting, sporting feudal baron had despised the trader: so did his eighteenth-century representative. The medieval Church had distrusted the trader. Trade, to the Church, was at best a neutral occupation, at worst an immoral one. Trade with its emphasis on gain, had been base and demoralizing. The eighteenth-century Tory shared this attitude too.[5]

The Calvinistic doctrine of the calling produced an entirely different attitude towards trade and gain, endowing them with virtue. The Calvinist had already built up Great Britain into a commercial state and was rapidly building it up into an industrial state. He could not feel limited by the medievalism which still frowned on unlimited grasping of 'opportunities', and on 'charging what the traffic would bear'. Calvinistic traders could display arrogance and a sense of importance quite equal to the aristocrats. Whatever their occupation, whether clergyman or tinker, were they not called of God to their work and were they then not engaged in God's work just as much as any other men, those who had the power of government included? "Whatsoever thy hand findeth to do, do it with thy might." Were they not of God's elect? As the rhyme attributed to Dean Swift had it:—

> "We are God's chosen few,
> All others will be damned.
> There is no place in heaven for you;
> We can't have heaven crammed!"

The two ways of life, those of the Tory Anglican aristocrat and of the middle-class Calvinist, form complete contrasts. Long before Durham penned his famous phrase, they were "two nations warring in the bosom of a single state" and two nations not in the sense that Durham meant, but two sections of the English-speaking peoples. In the American colonies, it was noted that the most pertinacious and stubborn of all the opponents of the king during the Revolution were the Presbyterians. In the English Civil War of the previous century, the same had been said of 'the middling sort of people'. The battle, fought to an approximate draw in England, was in the thirteen colonies to result in victory for the 'dissenters'. In Canada it was only by the narrowest margin that the 'dissenters', in the persons of the rebels, or Americans, failed to triumph too. Historically the main line of division in the English-speaking world has been incidentally national, basically denominational, that is, Anglicans against other Protestants.

To introduce these two elements at once into the small conquered colony, where from the first they had to deal with each other at arm's length, was to call for trouble. It is not surprising that for some years after the Conquest, the conflict in Canada was not so much between English and French as it was between one set of Englishman and another set, with whom the leaders of the French were in alliance.

Representative figures for the two groups abound. The best-known of them were the two governors, James Murray and Guy Carleton. These men from the beginning were sympathetic with the plight of the French and did all they could to ameliorate it. They displayed towards them—'the New Subjects'—qualities of kindness, magnanimity and justice. For the vexing question of the laws they sought a settlement which would restore to the French the régime that they had formerly known. They worked for the widest toleration and the most secure privileges for the Roman Catholic religion. They assumed that the colony would continue to be French, its language and institutions French, and that the English traders were interlopers, whose presence could be barely condoned. As a result, they earned the affections of the French. "Sir Guy Carleton is justly beloved of all classes of people," writes the annalist of the Ursuline nuns.[6] "His mild and paternal administration, his prudence and benevolence, his personal merits and kindness have rendered him dear to all ranks. . . ." Carleton had suffered a head wound during the Battle of the Plains and had been nursed for months by the kindly sisters,[7] an experience that may have determined his attitude. When he left the province in 1778, he took with him, as tutor to his young children, a Catholic priest, the Abbé Bailly, whose selection as coadjutor bishop of Quebec he was later to secure. His wife was a particular friend of the Ursulines. Between the Carletons and the 'New Subjects' the harmony could hardly have been closer. This harmony could be expressed in the same strong terms for the first governor, Murray, and in terms almost as strong for Lieutenant Governor Hope in 1785. It was to be broken only with the appearance of the Francophobe Sir James Craig in 1807.

Middle- and lower-class British

The English trading community, for its part, cast up strong, if not distinquished, characters. Until the nineteenth century this community was not large, and in the first difficult period after the Conquest, it was very small. Murray and Carleton never lost an opportunity of belittling its members. They were inconsiderable persons, ex-soldiers who had turned tavern-keepers, fly-by-night traders and such like. "A set of licentious fanatics," Murray called them. Carleton insisted that although they made high claims for English law and an assembly, they had little property among them, were men of no account, except in the making of trouble, men seeking to turn their personal grievances into a cry for public rights.

> ". . . lately one John McCord, who . . . formerly kept a small Ale House in the poor Suburbs of a little country town in the North of Ireland, appearing zealous for the Presbiterian Faith, and having made a little Money, has gained some Credit among People of his Sort; this person purchased some spots of Ground, and procured Grants of more, close to the Barracks, where he run up Sheds, and placed poor people to sell his Spirits to the Soldiers, finding that his lucrative Trade has lately been checked . . . he has commenced Patriot, and with the Assistance of the Attorney-General, and three or four more, egged on by Letters from Home, are at work again for an Assembly."[8]

Imagine the aristocratic North of Ireland Anglican, Carleton, confronted by the equally North of Ireland Presbyterian Mc-Cord, seller of cheap spirits to the troops, multiply the situation, both in Canada and in other colonies, and you get one facet, not an unimportant one, of the dissensions of the next decade.

Carleton had already foreseen those troubles. Soon after his arrival in the colony (1766), he had written to the Secretary of State, estimating the military and strategic situation

(Feb. 15th, 1767). The province as it was, was indefensible: its fortifications should be put in repair—"no pains, address nor expense too great to root out faction or party . . . to establish that security and strength as can properly curb and overawe, should such ever arise, [those] who by the ties of loyal subjects and honest men are not thoroughly bound to their duty." Other letters in a similar strain followed.   In 1767, Carleton was already preparing for the American Revolution: as the sequel will show, he must bear some responsibility for producing it.

Another of the thorns in Carleton's side was one Walker, a resident of Montreal, one of those "adventurers in trade, or such as could not remain at home, who set out to mend their fortunes at the opening of this new channel for commerce."[9] Walker had already caused trouble in Montreal by his antagonism to the military and had been the victim of a notorious incident, when, one night a number of disguised men, presumably officers, to whom his 'radicalism' had made him obnoxious, had entered his dwelling, terrifying him and, before leaving, clipping off one of his ears. The town had seethed with hatred between the two groups of Englishmen,[10] and Walker had been furnished with a grievance that was to last him the rest of his life. He takes his place among the trinity of famous ears, along with John Prynne, who had his struck off by order of Charles I, and thereby helped Charles to the loss of his entire head, and the obscure Captain Jenkins, whose similar fate at the hands of the Spaniards precipitated the war with Spain in 1739 that signalled the opening of the last acts in the great duel for empire.

Walker was a typical English, or New English[11], troubler in Israel, a man with an over-acute sense of his rights, whose semi-martyrdom, though having something of the ridiculous about it, was to build another brick into an unlooked-for wall, that of English liberty. But the mercantile group as a whole could not have been as black as men like Carleton painted it. In the first years, its members were mostly the queer lot that always gathers in colonial backwaters, but in a decade their increase in solid substance was rapid. After the war was over, not even Carleton any longer belittled the merchants, however much he may have disliked them.

French and Catholic conceptions of society

With what amazement the French must have looked at these goings-on among their conquerors! To the Calvinist, opposition to authority was part of the air he breathed—hence the maledictions of aristocratic governors. To the French, submission was the law of life. "The powers that be are ordained of God," "Render obedience unto the power": these were the great texts upon which Catholic political thought had always been based and still is, together with the equally significant and correlative "Render therefore unto Caesar the things which are Caesar's; *and* unto God the things that are God's". Obedience had been preached from every pulpit, obedience political as well as religious. On the occasion of the coronation and marriage of George III (1762), the Vicar-General of Montreal wrote to his clergy: "Sovereign arbiter of the fate of all men, He disposes to His liking of thrones and empires, and He gives crowns to whom He pleases. Happy the peoples to whom in His mercy, He reserves princes born for the welfare of their subjects. . . ." He then enjoined his brethren to contemplate their good fortune in having had given to them a good king and a governor "who seem to have nothing more at heart than to cause to disappear from our eyes the horrors of the war. . . ." The Vicar-General of Quebec, Briand, afterwards bishop, expressed the same sentiments and then added:

"The religion that we profess especially instructs us in this duty taught by Jesus Christ Himself, and which His disciples so strongly recommended to the first Christians. St. Peter, Prince of the Apostles, . . . orders submission to the king and to all those who share in his authority: 'Be subject . . . both to the king and to the officials sent by him.' He enjoins us to render him all honour and respect, *regem honorificate*. The Apostle Paul goes into further detail on these duties. 'I conjure you', he says, in his First Epistle to Timothy, 'above all things, to make supplication, prayer and petition for kings and all those who are raised in dignity, to render to the Sovereign Master of the universe who has given us them, deeds of grace, in order that under their protection we may lead a contented and a peaceful life.' . . . After orders so clear and authority so formal, would we not be most condemnable, Our dear Brethren, . . . if we did not acknowledge with all the fidelity and zeal possible, an obligation which Jesus Christ has taken so much care to make known to those who worship Him?"

He then orders prayers for George III.[12]

It is important, at the beginning of the troubled history of a double civilization, to grasp the full significance of these words: in French thinking there was no more room for disobedience to the new king and his representatives than there had been for disobedience to the old. In a day before the sense of nationalism had gone far, the conquered people's sentiments of loyalty were transferred to the king who had conquered them. Today the Church continues to preach, as it did two centuries ago, submission to the secular power. It will preach this duty as long as it exists and, as long as they are Catholics, French Canadians will obey. That is one reason why one of their number could proclaim that the last shot fired in defence of the British connection in Canada would be fired by a French Canadian. Further, it is an explanation of the determined fight made by French Canadians against the terrors of self-government, when the subject came to be mooted. "A growing colony . . . ought not inconsiderately to ask laws and customs unknown to it: it ought, on the contrary, and such is the opinion of your petitioners, place itself wholly under the benevolence of its August Sovereign, who best knows the government suitable to his subjects and the means most proper for making them happy."[13] No understanding of the role of French Canada in Canadian history can be secured without some grasp of Roman Catholic political thought, and almost the beginning and end of this is subjection to legitimate authority in the State, as in the Church.[14]

The ordered and authoritarian nature of Catholic doctrine avoided for French society the extravagant diversities of English: violent personal quarrels could occur, and quarrels about status or personal rights, but not the high (and low) debates on the nature of the State itself, which the English apparently never got settled. On public affairs, in both Church and State, all Frenchmen tended to speak with the same voice. All, that is, except the men on the bottom, who spoke with no voice at all, but simply acted, and acted sometimes in a way contrary to the admonitions of their superiors: if we could only have a few good letters from the simple farmers of Quebec on such subjects as the Conquest, the Quebec Act, and the American invasion, how different our conceptions might be!

Church and clergy

In this small society of ranks and classes, the clergy stood at the top of the scale. They were the guardians of the religious, moral and cultural springs of the race. At the time of the Conquest, according to Benjamin Sulte,[5] there were present in Canada 164 clergy, parish priests and monks both included, or about 1 to 427 people. Sulte divides his total into 112 born in France and 52 born in Canada. Of those born in France, 28 had been in the country over thirty-five years. There were also in Quebec, according to Governor Murray, 111 nuns.

Twenty-four years later, in 1784, the census returned only 126 priests, all told, but 234 nuns. In 1788, the bishop stated that there were 140 priests in his diocese. By 1794, there were 160, or about 1 to 1000. Such numbers do not seem excessive. The pre-Conquest Church had had vast grants of land—all told, over two million acres[16]—but its revenues, with the possible exception of the Jesuits', do not seem to have been impressively large: Murray reports the Bishop of Quebec as in humble circumstances.[17]

Power, influence and respect did not depend upon wealth, but upon the qualities of leadership and of humanity possessed by the clergy, upon tradition and upon the spiritual mysteries which they guarded. The Conquest greatly strengthened their position, destroying the secular side of French authority but for practical purposes leaving the spiritual untouched. The main difficulties the English found in allowing the French, as the Treaty of Paris ambiguously ordained, the freedom of their religion, concerned the recognition of a Roman Catholic bishop in an empire which had long since proscribed 'popery', and the question mark over the loyalty of those priests who were born in France. Time would solve this latter problem; that of the bishopric was more thorny. A typical, untidy English arrangement was at length arrived at: a private suggestion was made to the logical candidate while in England that he slip across the Channel and get himself consecrated, go back to Canada, where to his own people he would be the Bishop of Quebec and where to the government he would be, as before, 'Superintendent of the Romish Church.' He continued to lead this double life for many years and it was not until the nineteenth century that the government gave him legal recognition as *Roman Catholic Bishop of Quebec.*

Much turned on the personality of the individual holding this office. The first incumbent, Briand, was ideal, in that he was zealous for the interests of his communicants, of unquestioned loyalty to the British crown and on extremely good personal terms with the governors. It was he who was the principal agent in establishing that tacit alliance between Church and State which has ever since been so effective in keeping French-speaking Canadians within their two traditional allegiances. His adaptive skill was great but at times it would seem to have bordered on the servile: "You know the impetuous and ardent spirit of the French and the character of the Canadian too well to disapprove of my policy. He is accustomed to being decided by his superiors. He speaks out at times, but he submits and subjects himself to the yoke, and soon falls silent. . . ."[18]

A vivid idea of the kind of society that was being rebuilt in Canada after the Conquest, in which the Church was to have such a vast place, is to be obtained from the *Mandements* of the Bishops of Quebec.[19] Evidently, it was to be one in which relations between Church and State were to be close, if not as close as previously. The English governors distrusted Catholicism but they liked Catholics when these latter were gentlemen. There was not the slightest disposition to curtail freedom of worship. "Religion is perfectly free at present: if any depart from their duty, it is their own fault."[20] But something like the old medieval investiture conflict developed between the two institutions: how much share should the State have in naming the bishop, determining what priests were sent where, and so on? The result of the skilful fencing of Bishop Briand and his successors was that the State was left on one side.

Yet on two occasions during the period a section of the populace conducted itself as it never would have done in the previous régime, and defied the authority of its church. The first was during the American invasion of 1775, the second during the war with the French Republic.[21]

During the period, the parish priests, as the natural leaders of their communities, gained in prestige. "For almost half a century, the presbyteries were the rendezvous for Canadians occupied with the future. Hence proceeded a new class, the men of politics."[22] This is a most important statement, for it indicates the revolution in the class structure of French Canada that was enormously to influence its future. Its implications will be further considered below.

It would be a fair inference from the *Mandements* of the first fifteen years or so that the 'lower orders of people' had rather got out of hand, for not only were there the repeated injunctions to loyalty already mentioned, but also thundering denunciations of *habitant* conduct. In 1774, in the course of a lengthy excoriation of the sins of the countryside, the bishop became specific on the subjects of "adulteries and public concubinages, drunkenness among the poor and among females." The next year he had to declaim against the continuation of this, especially sexual deviations of every description, which, he claimed, had become more common.[23] After the American war these fulminations stopped, but since Briand died in 1784, it is impossible to decide whether it was his personal zeal which inspired them or objective conditions.[24]

By the close of the century the Church seems to have re-acquired its old measure of control, and the *habitants* were once more taking their direction from it (though the virus of the Enlightenment was already at work upon the small new middle class). A new era of expansion had begun for it, which is reflected in its growing strength in education. In the seventeen-nineties, the bishop had stood off the dire threat from the government to establish a *université mixte*, partly by pointing to the three hundred students at the Montreal seminary, for what room did such a number leave for a new institution? He had denied the allegation of the English authorities that the country-side was virtually illiterate by claiming that an average of as high as thirty persons per parish could read and write! And then, as the new century began, two new seminaries had been instituted, both of which flourished: "the new Little Seminary in Montreal" and the Seminary of Nicolet, in which Latin classes began in 1803 and where in 1805, there were already fifty students.[25] All in all, the Roman Catholic Church in French Canada seems by 1800 to have recovered its lost ground, and since it did not have to deal with a Catholic government, to have gained an autonomy that it could never have possessed under the kings of France.

The Canadian upper classes

The seigneurial class had traditionally stood next to the clergy in status. Contrary to the impression often conveyed, relatively few of this class went back to France at the Conquest and some of those who did, like Pièrre-Paul Margane de Lavaltrie (1743-1810), afterwards returned. When the legislative council provided for by the Quebec Act was formed, the seigneurial class was prominent in it, almost dominant. Some seigneurs were of considerable means—if we are to judge by the dowries which they gave to their daughters.[26] They were often charming people. "Old M. d'Ailleboust, an accomplished example of the French gentlemen of the last (eighteenth) century, a model of taste and elegance, gallant towards the ladies, of an agreeable and flexible spirit, a great card-player, quite indispensable for the embellishment of parties and choice little suppers. . . ."[27]

As long as non-representative government continued, the seigneurs held their place well, but their prestige and influence declined as the assembly rose, and after the turn of the century they no longer call for separate study. While there were a number of them in the first assemblies, they had to compete with the new men whom the times were bringing to the front, and they could maintain only the place which their natural

talents gave them. As Lieutenant-Governor Milnes put it:—
"The Aristocracy is daily being lessened in power and prestige"
(1800). Yet "I conceive the foundation of it (the new constitution) must rest upon a due proportion being maintained
between the Aristocracy and the Lower Orders of the People,
without which it will become a dangerous weapon in the hands
of the latter"![28]

It was among the seigneurs that the English of the governing
classes and the rising merchants found their friends. So pronounced was the alliance that for the first generation or so
after the Conquest, it looked as if a new ruling class might be
forged, both through mutual interest and also by intermarriage.[29] Inter-racial marriages were legion, and carried with
them a minimum of consciousness of race and faith. Thomas
Coffin, of a well-known New England family, who arrived in
Quebec from Boston in 1776, married Marie-Marguerite,
daughter of Godfrey de Tonnancour. She brought him some
seigneurial lands and "£66,902 5sh. 3d." as a dower (if these
were French *livres*, divide by five to get it into dollars but no
small sum at the time in any reckoning.) The marriage
ceremony, 1786, was performed by an Anglican minister, and
repeated by a Catholic priest. Coffin built a church for the
Catholics of his seigneury but remained a Protestant himself
until the last year of his life (1841). Eleven of his children
grew up, at least one of whom, W. C. H. Coffin, became a
Roman Catholic and, marrying a French wife, founded a
French branch of the family.

Pierre Guèrout (1751-1800), of Huguenot parentage, in
1793 married Josephe-Marie Woolsey, daughter of John Woolsey and Marie-Josephe Rottot. In this case it was the wife with
the English name, Woolsey, who was French and Catholic.
The couple had eight children, all baptized Roman Catholics.
From one of them, Julie, descended the English Protestant Le
Mesuriers of Montreal; from another, Narcisse, who became
an Anglican minister, the late Colonel William Wood of Quebec, the historian.

The best-known of all these inter-racial alliances were those
of the Grants, William (1744-1805) and his nephew, David
Alexander. William married in 1770, Marie Catherine
Deschambault, Dowager Baroness of Longueuil, the Anglican
minister performing the ceremony. They had no children. He
died a Protestant. His nephew married, 1781, the daughter
of this lady by a previous marriage, and it was this daughter
who carried with her the title of Baroness de Longueuil. The
barony, eventually recognized as a valid colonial title, thus

passed into a Scottish and Protestant line, where it remains.

The Grants form excellent examples of the post-Conquest middle class. Like most Scots, they had coats of arms somewhere in their family background, though not much but assurance in the foreground. William Grant, in Quebec by 1763, set up as a general merchant, speculated in paper money, bought the Chateau de Ramezay for this trash in 1764, took advantage of his legal status as a minor to wiggle out of certain contracts, became the "conceited boy" denounced by Murray as one of the men demanding an assembly[30] and bought his first seigneury in 1768. Two years later he bought his seigneuress. Years later, 1799, he subdivided his seigneury, which lay on the outskirts of Quebec, quite in the modern manner. He served against the Americans in 1775—along with many of the other old countrymen. He was caught up in the financial crisis of the last years of the war, but recovered himself and became a leading and useful citizen, prominent in the first Agricultural Society, 1789, in the founding of the Quebec Library the same year, President of the Constitutional Club in 1792, and so on. It is evident that the 'licentious fanatics' of the seventeen-sixties had evolved into something more than licentiousness or fanaticism. Many of these men, perhaps a majority, married French-Canadian wives of the seigneurial class, and thus secured a kind of back-door entrance into the ranks of the 'gentlemen'. Until the grant of an assembly, 1791, they continued to be thorns in starchy governors' sides, though they could no longer be thrust down as easily as when their ascent was just beginning. It was to be their ironical fate to become the chief victims of the representative government for which they themselves had contended.

The impact of the English and Scots upon the life of New France has a close, if distant, historical counterpart: the Norman Conquest of England in the eleventh century.[31] In the century after Hastings, the upper classes of the two races had rapidly intermarried, forming an amalgam that was neither Norman nor English and whose members probably spoke both tongues. But Norman England was isolated behind its sea barriers, and so at long last the Normans were absorbed into the native population and their language, after half-conquering English, died out. Quebec was destined not to be isolated. More British kept coming, and Montreal, standing as their eastern outpost, was to become a city of two languages. The English who intermarried did not have to abandon their racial identity or their language.[32] On the top layer of society families arose which maintained French and English, Catholic and

Protestant branches. While the children of inter-racial marriages tended to fall back into one of the two groups, thus preventing a genuinely bicultural society from emerging, they did not, in so doing, lose all contact with the opposite race: French Coffins probably remember their origins and recognize their blood-relationship with the English Coffins. Mere names no longer are entirely safe guides to racial origin, or to religion.[33] Something close to a new society came into existence, especially in Montreal, an Anglo-French society. And the English language penetrated the French as Norman French had English. English often carried back into French old French words no longer used—for example, *jury*.

The seigneurial class had to undergo an attack on two fronts. Scots and English on the make married its daughters and their dowries. And most of the seigneurs were not fitted for the hurly-burly of competition which was to beset them from their own people. No better evidence of their dismay at the onrush of new men is needed than the shriek of agony in their Petition of 1766: "We [have been] accustomed to respect our superiors, and to obey the orders of our Sovereign, to which we are turned by our education, as well as by our religion. . . ." And now— "A crowd of people have come in, in the wake of the army, who as clerks and managers for London merchants, merit no preference, either by their conduct or by their lack of education . . . and some of our own compatriots, people of no birth, without education, incapable of proper feelings, soldiers demobilized from the French army, barbers, serving-men, . . . even Jews . . . who have not hesitated to raise themselves above the new subjects, to whom this species of man was hitherto unknown!"[34]

The seigneurs significantly mention new types coming forward among their own people. As opportunity opened up, these would steadily increase in numbers and in weight. The grand gesture of paternal beneficence made by Pierre-Paul de Lavaltrie on the occasion of the election of 1792 must surely have been among the last of its kind. After his election had been declared, he "made, on the spur of the moment, a most generous gift to his *censitaires*. 'My dear children', he said to them, 'I abandon to you the *Lods et Ventes*, the right of pre-emption, the forced labour (*corvée*), etc., etc. . . . .'"[35] How long is it, one wonders, since, even in the Province of Quebec, a landlord has addressed his (perpetual) tenants as "My dear children"!

The new French middle class

The new types represented various layers of a new French

middle class (not Lavaltrie's "dear children", though possibly their offspring gone to town). This class was professional rather than commercial, for the commercial side of French-Canadian life, thanks to the Catholic outlook, remained weak. It was the product of the ancient seminaries, and it consisted first of all in the men of law, who were to be joined later by the doctors and by journalists. It seems to have had two sections, one old, one new. The older group consisted in families whose members had held office under the kings of France and who had successfully accommodated themselves to the new régime. Such were the Panets and the Taschereaux. Jean-Claude Panet (1728-1778) arrived in Canada in 1740 and later became a French official. After the Conquest, he at once became an English official. In 1767, he became an advocate, and in 1776 a Judge of Common Pleas. His son, Jean-Antoine Panet (b. 1751), became an advocate in 1773, and in 1792 the first Speaker of the new House of Assembly. His brother, P.-M. Panet (b. 1731), was also first a French and then an English official, and in 1778, he, too, became a judge of Common Pleas.[36] Among the Taschereaux, Gabriel-Elzéar (b. 1745) became active in the politics of the old province of Quebec and later sat as member for Dorchester, 1792-1796. He was made a legislative councillor in 1798, and a judge a little later.[37] In all, there were some nine French-speaking judges in the eighteenth century, most of them born before the Conquest. Here was the nucleus of a kind of Canadian *noblesse du robe*.

The judges formed the top layer of the rising classes. Behind them, but still of dignified status, were men who filled minor civic positions such as Louis Joseph Le Proux of Trois Rivières, who died in 1817, "after having made himself into one of the most useful citizens of his time as merchant, church warden, justice of the peace, captain, then major, of militia, clerk of the markets, inspector of chimneys, high constable, and part seigneur of the fief of Cournoyer."[38]

Somewhere midway between English and French were the various French-speaking Protestants who came into the little province after the Conquest—the Haldimands, Cramahés, Monnets, Gugys, Guérouts and others. Many of them were Swiss. They were readily accepted as individuals by French Canadians, but regarded with suspicion as a class, on the assumption that they were 'borers from within': the epithet *un Suisse* is still used in Quebec with this derogatory meaning.[39]

In New France there had been no *avocats* (barristers), only the less formidable brand of 'law-man' known as *notaire* (solicitor), but after the Conquest, the *avocat* promptly put in his appearance. In 1765, nineteen commissions as advocate were given, nine to English, ten to French. In succeeding years, the number each year seems to have been small (in 1790, for example, only three).[40] Nevertheless, the *avocat* turned up in sizeable numbers in the first legislative assembly of the province (1792) and thereafter had far more than his numerical share in its political life. He was the man Sir James Craig had in mind when he referred contemptuously to the assembly: the French were now officially provided with "an orator in every parish".[41]

The rise of the lawyer was accompanied by that of other men who had little in common with the old official and professional classes, men of humble parentage who found their occupations arising out of the steady growth of the province, both rural and urban. Such a one was Benjamin Cherrier (1757-1836) who, having gone part way through the Collège Saint-Raphael at Montreal, returned to the Richelieu countryside and earned his living as a land-surveyor. His grandson became a court clerk in Montreal, and one of his great-grandsons a banker in Montreal. This family pattern is identical with that of innumerable middle-class English-Canadian families.

Cherrier had as a colleague in the first Assembly of Lower Canada another surveyor, also of humble origins, Joseph Papineau, the father of the more famous Louis-Joseph. Joseph Papineau was "the first who by his education . . . pulled his family up out of the mediocrity which is the lot of honest farmers."[42] Apparently land-surveying was a useful social ladder in this way: Sir Wilfrid Laurier's father was a surveyor. The Papineaux became seigneurs by purchase and stood at the head of a long line of professional descendants, of whom Henri Bourassa was one. In the first assembly, what might be termed the 'upper rural and urban bourgeoisie' seem to have comprised the largest single group, not counting the advocates in with them. The urban members of this group were mostly comfortably off wholesalers and importers.

The anonymous mass

In the same assembly there was also a good 'sprinkling' of genuine men of the people and with them we come to our last class division, the anonymous mass. Jean Boudreau (1747-1827), M.L.A., was the son of an Acadian refugee. He himself was a sailor. Jean Digé (1736-1813), M.L.A., was born in France, came to Canada and became a sailor and codfisherman. In his marriage contract of 1763 he declares that he can neither read or write. When the first assembly was formed, he was projected into a brief fame as M.L.A. for Kamouraska and then subsided into his former role of honest, humble citizen. Another member similar to him was Joseph Dufour from the Isle aux Coudres. Joseph, it appears, soon got too much of the grand company he had to keep at Quebec. "Endless speeches from 'big guns' who used such long words that I could not understand them. Always being compelled to compromise my conscience by giving my voice on questions that I couldn't understand! . . ."[43]" Under such stress Joseph had the good sense not to stand a second time. He appears to have been a six-foot-seven-inch innocent! Perhaps his height explains his election.

The vast majority of people in French Canada throughout its history have been 'lower class', if this term be considered appropriate for the salt of the Quebec earth, the farmer or *habitant*. The *habitant* himself has ranged all the way down from the successful people who turned themselves into seigneurs by purchase, an achievement common early in the eighteenth century, to simple hewers of wood. Yet among the members of the first assembly, there seem to have been none described simply as *habitant* or *cultivateur*. And the province was overwhelmingly rural: at the Conquest, neither Quebec nor Montreal were towns of more than a few thousand inhabitants and at the end of the century, together they still possessed no more than 15,000 people, out of a total of about 200,000.[44]

The number of composite portraits of the people of Canada painted by travellers and sojourners would fill a good-sized library.[45] According to French officials like the Intendant Hocquart, the native Canadians had been vain, lazy, resentful of authority but relatively easily brought to heel[46] and had had a good many other unflattering qualities. The first English officials, on the other hand, had been quite ecstatic in praising them: ". . . perhaps the bravest and best race upon the Globe".[47] Private observers tended to go back part way to the Hocquart estimate. "The Canadians are simple and hospitable, yet extremely attentive to interest, where it does not interfere with that laziness which is their governing passion . . . they are excessively vain . . . there is something in the climate which strongly inclines both the body and mind, especially the latter, to indolence. . . . The Canadians are devout rather than virtuous, have religion without morality, and a sense of honour without very strict honesty." Thus the author of *Emily Montague*, the first novel about Canada,[48] mingling honey and vinegar. It is doubtful if the peasantry deserved all these strictures, though it is to be noted that years before the Conquest, the inordinate number of saint's days—that is, holidays—had worried the authorities, and the bishop had managed to curtail the list of *fêtes* by amalgamating nineteen of them with Sundays.[49]

The peasant has never been able to speak for himself. He has, however, been able to act, and in the period being considered, his actions came close to deciding the fate of the province. He soon began to discover the freedom of the English régime and, when the American Revolution came along, if he was not for it, he was not against it. His refusal to serve against the invaders provoked an abrupt change of tune on the part of the authorities: to Guy Carleton the 'lower orders' now became "the most ungratefullest wretches . . .!" The *habitant* seems to have dropped his memories of the king of France and the old régime like a hot potato and to have devoted himself to being himself, quite glad to get out of his obligations to priest and seigneur, either English or French, King George meaning as much, and as little, to him as King Louis. Actions spoke louder than words.

The Canadian peasant was not a political animal: high matters passed far above his head. "They'll be happy under any well-regulated government, and perfectly contented whilst they remain exempted from taxes, providing no alarm shall be sounded to rouse apprehensions touching the safety of their religion."[50] The writer might have added "provided no attempt is made to subject them to the old *corvée* or to compulsory military service"; both of which attempts were, in fact, made, provoking stormy results.

By 1800, officialdom had got back to the Murray view. Lieutenant Governor Milnes observed that "the Canadian *habitants* are, I verily believe, an industrious, peaceable and well disposed people," and then he added, penetratingly, "but they are, from their want of education and extreme simplicity, liable to be misled by artful and designing men. . . ."[51]

Milnes went on to praise the virtues of the *habitants'* own leaders, the captains of militia. The *capitaine de milice* was an old French office which, in attenuated importance, had continued. He was the link between government and the locality; he was chosen, as Milnes says, "from amongst the most respectable of the Canadian *habitants*." He served with no pay, took much of his private time for public tasks and altogether was a most useful citizen. Here was a nucleus around which local government might have become a training ground for self-government. That was not to be.

The characteristics of the *habitant* probably have not changed much from those days to our own. Those who know him 'on his native heath' invariably like him. They find his manners good, his hospitality ready, and consider as simple or admirable, according to their own point of view, his relative freedom from the commercial ethic. It is this which leads those who must 'work, for the night is coming' to see in him an idle man. Whatever may be said about him, he is not likely to be much affected by it.

That the *habitant* suffered no great harm from the Conquest, one type of evidence makes clear, namely, his biological behaviour. In the conquered province of Quebec, the people multiplied with astonishing celerity. In 1760, their numbers were approximately 60,000, and in 1790, 160,000; an increase in one generation of about 166 per cent, about five per cent annually. The birth rate after the Conquest seems to have been higher than before it:[52] in 1770, it had reached the astronomical figure of 65 per 1000.[53] After all, there was land and food for all, and the English 'conqueror' was rarely seen. No wonder that an English governor could say, while deploring what he had to say, that "there cannot be a more independent Race of people nor do I believe there is in any part of the world a country in which equality of situation is so nearly established."[54] People in such a situation were not groaning beneath a tyrant's yoke.

Analysis of the class situation in the generation after the Conquest makes it clear that the impact of the one people upon the other was not a simple matter and that, while there was a great deal of accommodation between the two, the process was varied and irregular. The flux of time alters every situation. For better or for worse, the generation after the Conquest saw a new society come into existence, both French and English in its nature, yet in some of its characteristics neither French nor English. Perhaps it would not be too bold to call it Canadian!

Notes to Chapter 9

1. Abbé H. R. Casgrain, *Oeuvre Complètes* (Montreal, 1895), II, p. 174.
2. *Debates of the House of Commons in the Year 1774 on the Bill for making more effectual Provision for the Government of the Province of Quebec*, drawn up from the notes of Sir Henry Cavendish (London, 1839)—usually referred to as *The Cavendish Debates*.
3. A cursory examination of Carleton's correspondence at once confirms the point. See especially his letter of Oct. 25th, 1766, to Shelburne, Secretary of State, and the two following documents given in Shortt and Doughty, *Documents relating to the Constitutional History of Canada, 1759-1791* (2nd ed. Ottawa, 1918), Vol. I, p. 276.
4. See for a good specific illustration the career of William Knox, Under Secretary of State during the crucial years, especially as commented on by Chester Martin, *Foundations of Canadian Nationhood*

(Toronto, 1955). Martin gives Knox and Carleton the dubious honour of being the principal authors of the American Revolution.

5. But where are we to put Major (later General) Gabriel Christie, who from 1764 to 1794 had acquired by purchase nine seigneuries, together with a brood of bastard sons to whom he left them? (*Bulletin des Recherches Historiques*, Vol. 51, p. 71).

6. *Glimpses of the Monastery, 1639-1839* (2nd ed., Quebec, 1897) by a Member of the Community, p. 311.

7. Abbé Auguste Gosselin, *L'Eglise et l'Etat au Canada* (Evreux, 1916).

8. Shortt and Doughty, op. cit., p. 294, *Carleton to Shelburne*, Jan. 20th, 1768. McCord became a 'rebel' during the Revolution.

9. Shortt and Doughty, op. cit., p. 284.

10. See for this and for the period generally, the basic study by A. L. Burt, *The Old Province of Quebec, 1763-1791* (Toronto, 1933).

11. Born in England, went to New England, thence to Canada; became a 'rebel'.

12. The above passages of scripture are translated from the French and Latin.

13. Shortt and Doughty, op. cit., Vol. II, p. 763, *Address of the Roman Catholic Citizens to the King* (*c*. 1778).

14. An excellent discussion of this subject is contained in H. A. Rommen, *The State in Catholic Thought* (London, 1947). Note the elusive nature of the word *legitimate*.

15. *Histoire des Canadiens-Français* (Montreal, 1887), Vol. VII, p. 73.

16. Public Archives of Canada, *Report* 1892, p. 14.

17. Shortt and Doughty, op. cit., Vol. I, p. 47.

18. Gosselin, op. cit., p. 11, *Briand to Carleton*, 1773.

19. *Mandements, Lettres Pastorales et Circulaires des Evêques de Québec*, ed. H. Têtu et C.-O. Gagnon (4 Vols., Quebec, 1888).

20. *Glimpses of the Monastery*, op. cit., p. 296.

21. See next Chapter.

22. Sulte, op. cit. (footnote[15]), p. 92.

23. *Mandements etc.*, op. cit., Vol. II, pp. 250, 260.

24. It is curious to find in Abbé Auguste Gosselin's *L'Eglise du du Canada après la Conquête* (Quebec, 1916), private letters from Briand written at just this time stating that everything is normal, with people behaving themselves well.

25. The above from the *Mandements etc.*, op. cit., Vol. II.

26. For many interesting *minutiae* on this subject and for the pages which follow, see F. J. Audet and F. Surveyer, *Les Députés au Premier Parlement du Bas-Canada, 1792-1806* (Montreal, 1946).

27. Benjamin Sulte, *Pages d'Histoire du Canada* (Montreal, 1891), p. 412.

28. Public Archives, Series Q, Vol. 85, p. 228. *Milnes to the Duke of Portland, Colonial Secretary*, Nov. 1st, 1800.

29. On intermarriage see *Bulletin des Recherches Historique*, Vol. 21, pp. 84-86 which lists 985 marriages in Montreal Protestant churches, 1766-1800, in 285 of which the names of the parties were one English and one French.

30. Public Archives, Series Q, Vol. 2, p. 233.

31. For an intimate picture of this 'Anglo-Norman' society see the snobbish, over-jocose, and charming *Mémoires* of Aubert de Gaspé (Quebec, 1886); de Gaspé married *une anglaise* and two of his daughters married English husbands.

32. It is possible that we have a sign-post to this semi-amalgamation in the appearance of a new saint's day; on Mar. 17th, 1765, there was celebrated in Quebec city for the first time the feast of—St. Patrick! (*Recherches Historiques*, Vol. 24, p. 63).

33. See the remarkable list of English-French families given in J. C. Bracq, *Evolution of French Canada* (New York, 1924), p. 173.

34. Public Archives, Series Q, Vol. 4, p. 23.
35. Audet et Surveyer, op. cit., s.n. Lavaltrie, p. 310.
36. Five Panets, in all, became judges.
37. Taschereaux in the official life of Church and State are innumerable. There were Cardinal Taschereau, Sir Henri Taschereau, Chief Justice of Canada, Mr. L. A. Taschereau, the late Premier of Quebec, and many others, generation after generation. The Taschereaux are one of the few *well-defined* families of Canada. See P.-G. Roy, *Les Juges de la Province de Québec* (Quebec, 1933).
38. Gerard Malchelosse, *Les Cahiers des Dix* (Montreal, 1953), p. 218.
39. Note its effective use in this way by Roger Lemelin in his novel, *Pierre le Magnifique* (Quebec, 1952).
40. *Recherches Historiques*, Vol. 39, p. 577.
41. Public Archives, Doughty and McArthur, *Canadian Constitutional Documents, 1791-1818*, Mar. 3rd, 1810, p. 373.
42. F. Ouellet, *"Joseph Papineau et le Régime Parlementaire, 1791"* in *Recherches Historiques*, Vol. 61, p. 71, quoting a letter of L.-J. Papineau.
43. Audet et Surveyer, op. cit., quoting the de Gaspé *Mémoires*.
44. Population of Quebec City in 1805, 7,838.
45. See Gerald M. Craig, *Early Travellers in the Canadas, 1791-1867* (Toronto, 1956) and William Earl, "The Canadas in the Writings of British Travellers and Immigrants, 1791-1841" (unpublished thesis, Queen's University, 1956).
46. See p. 78.
47. *Murray*, Oct. 29th, 1764.
48. Originally published in London in 1769.
49. *Mandements etc.* op. cit., Vol. I, p. 42.
50. *Finlay to Nepean*, Feb. 9th 1789 in Shortt and Doughty, op. cit.
51. Public Archives, Series Q, Vol. 85, p. 278, *Milnes to Portland*, Nov. 1st, 1800.
52. See Jacques Henripin, *La Population Canadienne au début du XVIIIe Siecle* (Paris, 1954), pp. 119, 121.
53. Compared with the Canadian figure for 1956 of about 27.
54. Public Archives, Series Q, Vol. 85, p. 728, *Milnes to Portland*, Nov. 1st, 1800.

10: The first attempt at living together

WHEN TWO PEOPLES DIFFERENT IN EVERY aspect of their lives are forced to share the same house, it cannot be expected that everything will go smoothly. When the one people has 'muscled in' on the other, the original occupants can hardly be blamed for not accepting its presence with gratitude. In Canadian history, which is largely the working out of this problem, the wonder is, not that things have gone badly, but that they have gone so well. It was the formative years after the Conquest which largely determined the course they would take.

On the French, the Conquest with its long aftermath has had approximately the same effect as a revolution: a people who had never had to make revaluation of their way of life, now had to pull themselves together and find within themselves the resources to meet a totally new situation. The mere struggle for survival can in itself be of revolutionary effect: join this to learning to work a new set of institutions, and the result must have within it something of that release of energy which marks revolutions.

The thesis must not be exaggerated. After the Conquest religious institutions remained little changed. And changes in the secular institutions did not come all at once, nor did they affect all alike. At first, they must have appeared small, merely the substitution of one monarchy for another. But the eighteenth century was to end in the greatest change of all, representative government, and that was to prove the instrument of something close to revolution itself.

On the morrow of Conquest, two tasks presented themselves to the 'New Subjects': how to remain alive and, for those who thought about such matters, how to remain themselves. The first was to prove the easier, with all hands rallying to it and the conqueror proving unexpectedly helpful. The second has engaged French-speaking Canadians from that day to this, and on it has been built the great historic creed of *la survivance*: the survival of race and faith under hostile circumstances. Freedom in the English sense has never much interested French Canada. Survival of race, faith and language is its compendium of inalienable rights!

The battle has been waged on many fronts. Sometimes it has been against some of the English, with the aid of others of them. Sometimes it has divided the race itself. It has centred round well-worn topics: religion, everywhere and always; its various sub-aspects, such as the religious orders, the Catholic episcopate, the right of tithe; law, with its innumerable ramifications; language; education; economic conceptions; social usage and to some degree morals (e.g. divorce). In the period of this chapter, from the Conquest to the War of 1812, all these come conspicuously into play.

The period falls into four divisions: between the Conquest and the American invasion of 1775-1776; from that episode to the point at which the French Revolution began to make itself felt, say to 1794; the period of the Revolution; and the subsequent period of Napoleon.

The period of racial myth-making, 1760-1775

The first period has become the ground for racial myth-making. It is hard to say when this process had its beginning. The English naturally thought well of their own magnanimity as conquerors but the French must have had their own views on that. The English-Canadian school child has always been told about the way in which the Highlanders, that first hard winter, cut firewood for the nuns and the nuns knitted long stockings for the Highlanders; but French school children have probably had the seamier side of conquest carefully explained to them, and many French historians have stressed it. Tales of the ravaging and burning that accompanied the last campaigns are said to be still repeated round the winter fire and conscious nationalist myth-making was begun with Garneau. Garneau gives the impression that the conquered people were subjected to considered and cruel oppression. He rather spoils his effect by going on to tell of what the Spaniards did to their French co-religionists when they took over Louisiana. In that province, without provocation of conquest, the Spanish officials treacherously seized twelve of the people's representatives, sending six "to rot in the dungeons of Cuba and summarily executing the other six". There may have been much blundering on the part of officialdom in Canada and there were many private pieces of sharp business practice, but there was no arbitrary shedding of blood, no overt and considered tyranny. *"L'Angleterre commença par nous traiter mieux que la France n'avait fait en aucun temps."*[1]

Many French-Canadian historians make a distinction between the soldiers' rule—the *régime militaire*, 1760-63—and the civil government that followed it, agreeing that things went well in the first period, when the ultimate fate of the colony was still not decided, but not so well under civil government. Insofar as intention went, the civil governors continued the *régime militaire*, one of them, Murray, being common to both. But the first period of civil government was a much more severe test, for during it permanent institutions had to be set going and some attempt made to fuse two very different outlooks.

Contrasting points of view came out in every area and in every rank:—"The French ladies never walk, but at night . . . they saunter slowly, after supper . . . they have no idea of walking in the country, nor the least feeling of the lovely scene around them. . . . They seem born without the smallest portion of curiosity, or any idea of the pleasures of the imagination, or indeed any pleasures but that of being admired; love, or rather coquetry, dress and devotion, seem to share all their hours. . . ."[2] The writer of these lines, an active English woman, thought she was recording in objective fashion the habits of the French ladies she met in Quebec: that she met many of them, liked them and was liked by them, her book makes plain. How popular she would be when they read it, if ever (for she adds, just to rub it in, that none of them can read)! Yet what she thought, her menfolk would think (except in that they found the French ladies *chic* and attractive, which would be a further offence in feminine eyes) and as a man thinketh, so is he. Mixing oil and water is easy compared with mixing French and English.

In a more masculine area, that of the law, the limitless confusion caused by the long-range edicts purporting to establish the new legal position has often been commented on. Was the old law abrogated by conquest? Had English law been set up in its place by the Proclamation of October 7th, 1763? Should there be juries? Could Roman Catholics serve on them? Should lands still be granted in seigneury? Should land and other property be divided among heirs according to the 'laws of Canada' or by the common law of England? Could Frenchmen who could not take the Test hold any civic positions, even the humblest? Should courts reflect French absolutism (cheap law continuously dispensed) or English self-government (dear law, dispensed infrequently)? It is only necessary to ask these questions to see how difficult it was to answer them. Nearly all of them led into the area of religion.

In practice what happened was that English judicial officers were rummaged up, attorneys from both religions admitted, and some practical compromise made in the customs with which the inhabitants were familiar. But the judicial officers were a queer lot of legal riff-raff for the most part, well got rid of by exile to an unimportant distant colony; the attorneys did not understand each other, and no one knew for sure what were the old customs, 'the laws of Canada'. The opportunities were perfect for the rogue or sharp business man, and he duly took advantage of them, getting poor *habitants* snarled up in legal tangles which led to the loss of their property, and buying up their old paper money for a song.[3] This period of plunder left a lasting impression on the French mind. It was not counter-balanced by the known sympathies of the governors.

Even the governors' sympathies took on less substantial proportions when their unfriendly attitudes towards the religious orders and their attempts to keep the ecclesiastical heads sub-ordinate to the civil power became known. There were also various suspicious characters about the province, former priests turned Protestants, who got too much encouragement from officialdom. Canadians cannot be blamed for remembering that English officials, however sympathetic, were first of all Protes-tants. The British government shilly-shallied over religion, as over everything else, but its representatives could hardly have been other than glad to see Canadians drawn away from their church. This, however, did not mean that there was anything approaching coercion.

One of the major difficulties was that the English code of the time deprived Roman Catholic British subjects of civil rights. French Canadians had liberty, according to the Treaty of Paris, to practise their religion "so far as the laws of England do per-mit" but no one knew how far that was. To hold and attend services was one thing, to be able to take a seat on the council without taking the Test oath abjuring popery, was another. To have a bishop, dependent on Rome, was still another.

The form of government was as much under debate as were the laws. The proclamation had promised an assembly. Five hun-dred Protestant incomers claimed the sole right to constitute it. The situation being impossible, nothing was done and although an assembly was recommended once more in 1769, Guy Carle-ton got home in time to stop any nonsense like that. Hence, Que-bec dragged on under a conciliar form of government, and in

1774 this form was consecrated by Act of Parliament and was to endure until 1791. It did not offend the French: the *habitants* knew nothing about representative government and cared less; seigneurs and priests, conservative to a degree beyond the imagination of the most reactionary of English Tories, dreaded it.

The Quebec Act of 1774 put a formal end to the confusion by giving priest and seigneur what they wanted: the right to collect the tithe again, the seigneurial tenure (in matters of property and civil rights, "resort shall be had to the laws of Canada") and the modified oath of office which allowed of conciliar government including Catholic subjects. As the new period wore on, French became the language of discussion, some English gravitated towards the French group and for the next sixteen years, the seigneurs exercised more influence in government than ever before or after.

One piece of progress was made, the institution of English criminal law. George III's reactionary ministers had this much of English freedom in them that they were unwilling to restore the old French system of secret trials, torture and the other benighted accompaniments of Roman law. A magistrate of Paris as late as 1781 could argue that "public trials would only injure the reputation of the defendant, lead to intimidation of judges, and permit the escape of accomplices."[4] English criminal law, with judge and jury, public trial, counsel for the defendant, cross-examination of witnesses, presumption of innocence, took its permanent place in the province. Its effect has been continuous and incalculable: if an agency of Anglicization be sought (even as object of execration), here surely is one of the most prominent, for decade by decade it has bent French minds into English ways of looking at the liberties of the subject.[5]

The Quebec Act announced that the English criminal law would be used "because of its greater lenity". In the light of some of the executions of the era, one wonders what severity would have been. David McLane, tried and condemned for high treason (1797) "was brought through the city, back tied to a sled . . . an axe and block poised in front of him. His calm and assured air and his good looks won the hearts of the crowd. . . . After the ladder was kicked away the body swung, hitting the sides of the gibbet. After twenty-five minutes, Dr. Duvert pronounced him dead, saying 'Il est bien mort! . . .' All had been under the impression that McLane was to be disembowelled and his entrails burned while he was still living, but he was dead when the hangman opened his breast, took out his heart and entrails, and burned them on a chafing dish. Ward, the executioner, then cut off the head, and showed it to the mob!"[6]

Public hangings continued in Canada until 1869, the last one being held in Ottawa, the culprit the assassin of D'Arcy McGee. What ended them and similar barbarities was not a mode of trial but the gradual softening of manners which has marked modern times. Yet English criminal law while it reflected its times in the horror and severity of its punishments, also gave the accused a sporting chance: this was particularly important in political trials, where so much depends upon the individual's constitutional right to take his own stand, offensive to the authorities though it may be.

From the American Revolution to the French Revolution

The American Revolution divided inhabitants of the province not so much by race and religion as by social class. Among the English, the official class remained loyal. Merchants were divided: some attempted to ride two horses, some cautiously waited to see what was going to happen, some became ardent rebels while others remained loyal. Most of the men who afterwards rose to wealth and prominence in the community rallied to Carleton in that dark winter of 1775 and helped to save the city from the foe: the natural conservatives, apt to be the naturally prosperous, remained loyal and there was a purge of the type that is always against authority. Merchants whose loyalty survived the first campaign began to find fat pickings in the supply of the British armies: this did nothing to cool their attachment to the British cause. The Revolution strengthened the conservatism of a business community that found politics contributing to its prosperity.

Similar but more pronounced class differences manifested themselves among the French. The bishop, as all bishops must, denounced rebellion. Seigneurs and priests were loyal to a man. The townsmen of Quebec were loyal. But the *habitants* dismayed the authorities by welcoming the Americans.[7] Though Carleton could hardly raise a soldier among them, Congress recruited several battalions.[8] What animated the *habitants* has ever since been in dispute. Is it not reasonable to believe that while the mass would be indifferent to this private English quarrel, there would be quite a number who could catch a glimpse of what was at stake? Simple peasantry can hear the call of freedom. And for those who could not, there was the weight of the government's hand in the shape of the *corvées* and the attempts at forced military service,[9] these in addition to the rumours that must have spread to the effect that the rule of priest and seigneur was to be re-established.

The war of the American Revolution was for French Canada, as for English America, a civil war. In the United States, one element of society triumphed; in Quebec another. Those who fought shoulder to shoulder with Carleton during that gloomy winter of 1776 were just as much 'United Empire Loyalists' as those a little later to be formally termed such. The directing classes of French Canada by supporting the authorities removed from themselves all suggestion of a conquered status, associating themselves with the Crown of Great Britain and government from above, rather than from the people. For the clergy, their stand during the war sealed the alliance between the two authorities, secular and spiritual.

After the War of the Revolution, the English and French who had stayed loyal settled down to run the truncated province of Quebec. They mingled but were not united. The old problems immediately erupted again. The English men of business were dismayed at the legal cesspool which the province had become, at the inadequacies of the antiquated 'laws of Canada' and at the fantastic incompetence of the judges.[10] The French seigneurs were determined to keep things exactly as they had been—or to push them back still further! They began to match the phrase 'New Subjects' with the term 'New Canadians'. They opposed what to English merchants seemed elementary securities of justice, the habeas corpus writ and trial by jury, and in this they were vigorously supported by the aristocratic wing of the English, under the leadership of Judge Dr. Adam Mabane and Lieutenant Governor Hope. The business men's attacks were not much aided by the bankruptcy into which peace, bringing the first of her long succession of calamities to Canada, had precipitated nearly all of them.

For eight or ten years the province was to be torn by this factional strife, when once more the British Parliament was to intervene in an attempt to end it, with the Constitutional Act of 1791 as its device for the purpose. But representative government, as accorded by the Act, was to make more problems than it solved. The English had apparently thought that it would automatically bring the spirit of commercial progress along with it: the French used it to assert their rights and to claim a greater share in the administration of their own province. Thus the clash of the seventeen-eighties was merely postponed and intensified, until eventually it broke out in the bloodshed of 1837.

The story was not to end there, though this is to anticipate.

Still, since Canadian history is in a measure written round this little band of English in Quebec—these 'Anglo-Normans'—their continuing place in the country's life is large. The rebellion of 1837 seemed to mean their triumph, since it put an end for a time to representative government. When in the late eighteen-forties, representative government was changing into Responsible Government, once more the English, who had never ceased to battle and intermarry with the French, attempted to break out of their prison, this time through rioting, burning and declaring in favour of Annexation. Failing, they fought the old fights over again, and in the eighteen-sixties made still another attempt at escape, this time with more of compromise in it than previously. The result was Confederation, to which one of their number, Alexander Tilloch Galt, significantly contributed first by proposing it (1858), next by securing for its English Protestant minority protection within the new province of Quebec and again by opening to them vistas of new hinterlands in the Hudson's Bay Company's territories. The vistas were turned into realities. The Canadian Pacific Railway was built. Montreal's capitalists extended their hegemony to the shores of the Pacific. At that point in time we may perhaps leave them, snugly ensconced in their mansions on Mount Royal, growing richer and richer—and less and less important, a minority within a minority. They had come to Canada for the main chance, hoping incidentally to dominate the French. They have continued to pursue the main chance but now the French dominate them.

The period of the French Revolution

In the second test, that imposed by the wars with revolutionary France and Napoleon, the English of Lower Canada did not face the temptations which confronted them in the American Revolution. For the French, the situation presented itself differently. The old mother country, of which they could never cease to be the loving children (*"il resta dans la coeur des Canadiens un amour vivace . . . nous aimerions toujours la France!"*)[11] was in tumult and her agents were pressing up through the United States, crossing the border and spreading their propaganda everywhere.

The bishop felt it necessary to remind his priests that attachments to France had been entirely broken by the Capitulations of 1759 and 1760.[12] This official attitude of unshaken loyalty to the crown has never since been varied. It reduced the scope of the rebellion of 1837, it toned down frenzy over Riel in 1885 and it was an influence in moderating the storms that raged over the issue of conscription in both world wars.[13]

"Recall that you were born French. . . . Count upon the support of your neighbours and of the French. . . . Canada should be a free and independent state, *corvées* and seigneurial dues abolished; all religions should be of free choice and the Catholic priests named by the people, as in the primitive church. . . ."[14] appealed the French agents. It was heady stuff, especially for a people who less than twenty years before had proved ready to welcome a set of invaders with similar doctrines. The wonder is it had as little effect as it did. It did have some, though mostly indirectly. There were riots and tumults on the island of Montreal, some refusal of civil obedience in Quebec City, and among the country people refusal to accept a militia act (1794) entailing a limited degree of compulsory service, and the law requiring compulsory work on the roads (1796). Just as in 1775, the *habitant* was refusing to serve in causes that did not seem to him to concern him.

Joined to lack of concern, the ordinary man must have found many things, such as seigneurial dues (the new seigneurs often 'put the screws on')[15] and the tithe, which helped to alienate him. There were the long peasant memories of the paper-money business and the English sharpers (the good gold *louis* that the French Crown had sent out in its last campaigns had promptly disappeared into peasant stockings and had not yet reappeared: they did not do so for another generation). And there was that disgrace to English institutions, the press-gang. In 1804, a son of Judge Panet, being in London, was 'pressed' and served in the Mediterranean for two years as a common sailor aboard H.M.S. *Excellent*. His father's influence secured his discharge.[16] Others were not so fortunate. In 1807, Simon Latresse, aged twenty-five, was seized by a press-gang under Lieutenant Andrel of H.M.S. *Blossom*: the gang forcibly entered a place of public entertainment where the young man was. He tried to escape but was so severely mauled that he died. The people of Quebec were reported as up in arms over the incident.[17] It is only fair to the civil authorities to remember that the navy seemed to be a law unto itself in the matter. Still, kidnapping young men or beating them to death if they put up too much of a fight was not good advertisement for the British régime. These abductions were to turn up just over a century later, when, in the celebrated election of 1911, Nationalist agents sent men around the countryside disguised as British naval officers and inquiring how many sons were in the house. The memories of country people are long: Quebec's attitude towards conscription in 1917 was much the same as it had been in 1794, and in this opposition to compulsory service the old memories of the press-gang played no inconsiderable part.

As during the American invasion, it is impossible to believe in a widespread grasp of issues; but without revolutionary appeals and the favourable reaction of individuals here and there the symptoms of resistance would not have made themselves evident.[18] The two occasions put together, with 1837, 1896 and 1917 added to them, render it evident that the ordinary people of French Canada have sentiments of their own which are apt not to coincide with those of their ruling classes, even though eventually they make their submission.

As the struggle in France went on, its anti-clerical, anti-religious side became more and more useful in strengthening the ancestral faith and church in Quebec. The English Conquest represents the physical severance from France, the French Revolution the spiritual. The later severance did not throw the French-Canadian people on to their own resources as much as the earlier one had done, but it was a strong reinforcement, and nationalism, signs of which begin to be evident within the period, was related to it. After the Revolution, the French of Quebec could no longer think of themselves as mere severed members of a larger community: they had become, willy-nilly, a community which could not look beyond itself, except to an international church, for its own spiritual sustenance. Thus once more, the conservative side of Canadian life was strengthened: Canada was becoming the home of lost causes.

Physical evidence of the lost cause appeared in the province after 1789 with the arrival of *émigré* French priests.[19] The British authorities did not like this but the addition to conservative and monarchical forces could hardly be spurned. A suggestion made a few years before for priests from the British Isles had not proved welcome to the bishop: as he confessed, British priests were too much accustomed to political liberty and "we have required from the Canadians exact obedience".[20] The *émigré* priests were to prove invaluable recruits and it is said that much of the subsequent argument against the proposals for public secular education was furnished by them. They also became objects of distrust to governors who were not as pro-Catholic as Dorchester had been: Milnes and more especially Craig. But some distrust might be forgiven officials who were harassed with the possibilities of war and invasion, and who found important posts, such as that of Superior of the Seminary of St. Sulpice, being held by French-born priests.[21]

In retrospect, the seventeen-nineties now appears as one of those rare periods when the relations between the two races were relatively good. Representative government produced debate over the language to be used in the assembly, but when the French refused to accept the priority of English, little feeling resulted, especially as it became evident that the English were willing to work for the general good. In those days, as contrasted with our own, the English spoke French but the French did not speak English. This was also the period when the Bishop of Quebec was offering one of his churches to the Anglicans as a place of worship. The leaders of both groups had a good deal in common, there had been considerable intermarriage among them, and now that the English had come up in the scale and were many of them seigneurs themselves, there was less than at first to keep them apart. It was to be the next decade which would see incipient nationalism among the French and the retreat of the English to that position of defence which they have never since ceased to occupy in Quebec.

Meantime the English were increasing rapidly in numbers, and, as the age would have put it, in 'respectability'. An interesting census of Quebec City and suburbs taken in 1792 returned a total population of 6,163, of whom 662 were either *anglais* or Protestants—say 10 per cent. In 1805, corresponding figures were 7,838, of whom 1,530 were Protestants, an increase to just under 20 per cent.[22]

What was engaging the attention of these groups of French and English at this time, the seventeen-nineties? The war with France, of course. The new assembly and its work, naturally. Beyond that? Some notes from 1795, apparently by Dorchester, mention, as leading topics of the day, a general government for British North America, the militia problem, the tenure of land—a perpetual problem in the Canadas—the desirability of opening a university and instituting schools, the Jesuit Estates, the claims of the Sulpicians, whether Montreal should have a separate customs house, what to do with the old town walls of that city, how to secure the growing of hemp in the province, together with the "judicature, the boundaries of the province and the Indian trade."[23] The old walls of Montreal, which had never deterred an enemy, were eventually pulled down, though Montreal did not get the advantage from that act which so many European cities have secured—a fine belt of public parks—and a separate customs house was established there. The other points were mostly to remain long on the list. The Jesuit Estates quandary was not cleared up until the eighteen-eighties: it is interesting to find a group of French citizens contending at the time that these lands, and others given to the Church by the king of France, were not the private property of the Orders holding them but public trusts, to be used for the good of all, preferably for education.[24]

As an indication that the province was now getting somewhere, it was the seventeen-nineties which saw the founding of the *Quebec Agricultural Society* and appointment by the government of a Provincial Naturalist! The first French book had been printed in Canada (by Fleury Mesplet) in the late seventeen-seventies. A newspaper was begun in Montreal about the same time, though it did not continue, the present Montreal *Gazette*, its successor, dating from 1785. In 1792, the first assembly gave the French their great chance, the opportunity to act in a corporate way. In general, in the seventeen-nineties prosperity reigned, the numbers of the people were increasing rapidly and many new settlements were being made. There could be only one outcome to such conditions, namely an awakening to self-consciousness on the part of those people who already had five or six native generations behind them. With that awakening would come the tensions of the nineteenth century, bringing the nationalistic movement with its new men and its new leaders.

In 1797, David McLane, the man so barbarously executed, was reported, correctly or incorrectly, to have said that he "wished to know how the Dorions, and Mr. Papineau . . . were affected, and that this deponent informed him he believed them Friends, very inimical to the British government."[25] Around these well-known families there was already gathering the nucleus of the later *parti rouge*, with its nationalism and its fondness for Voltairean ideas. As Trudel shows,[26] the 'Enlightenment' with its scepticism, its philosophical reflections on the nature of the State and of religion, its Rousseaux and Voltaires, had begun to cross the ocean about the time of the Conquest and by the end of the century, when many a man had Voltaire's writings in his collections, was in vigorous flow. It is a great mistake to believe that the 'Enlightenment', which so strongly put its mark on eighteenth-century France (and the rest of Europe), did not reach French Canada. It did not have conspicuous effects in the eighteenth century, but by the middle third of the nineteenth it was in full spate, colouring not only men's thoughts, but their actions, political, religious, literary. Canada had its 'eighteenth century', and French Canada had far more of it than English, but for Canada the 'eighteenth century' lay mainly in the nineteenth!

The early nineteenth century

To the doctrines of liberty and equality which were blowing

out of France, there must be added British constitutional experience. French Canadians at the turn of the century were being subjected to the same type of experience later undergone by British Indians: both peoples heard a great deal about the glories of the British constitution and about its essence consisting in freedom. It is not to be wondered at that some of this talk was taken seriously. The editor of Le Canadien, Pierre Bédard, put at his journal's 'masthead' a significant excerpt from the Bill of Rights of 1689. He contended for 'Ministerial' (that is, Responsible) government: this sprang from his constitutional lore. Demands of this sort for freedom were dismaying to British governors, especially to stiff old army officers like Sir James Craig.

Le Canadien was suppressed by Sir James Craig in 1810, under a severe and panicky war-time law against sedition. At the same time the governor imprisoned Bédard and two others without accusation or trial. Bédard demanded to be brought to trial and would not take his release when to avoid the consequences of his own arbitrary action the governor ordered it. Bédard's demand to be tried, Craig found more than a little embarrassing. A touch of humour is lent to this otherwise sour period in Lower Canadian history by the duel between the choleric governor and the recalcitrant little assemblyman. Craig sends orders that Bédard is to be released. Bédard, not having had his trial, refuses to be released! Craig sends orders to expel him, forcibly if necessary. Bédard, plunged in a mathematical problem, his diversion, refuses to be interrupted. After he has finished, he condescends to hear what the gaoler has to say to him. He is to leave the jail or be put out of it by force. He reluctantly consents to go.[27] Not many men can claim the honour of having been thrown *out* of jail!

For the period down to about 1805, all the testimony is towards growing harmony: the two races coming to work together at the top, the religious question slumbering. Then suddenly animosities flare. Why?

One explanation, perhaps too easy, is the establishment in that year of a new English newspaper in Quebec, the Quebec Mercury, edited by Thomas Cary. Mr. Cary had too facile a pen for the good of the country, and when he began making aspersions against the French, his shafts went home. Every subjugated people is sensitive and French Canadians, who laboured under the impression that the fact of subjugation had been erased by the status of British subject, and were dowered with hereditary Gallic egotism, were as they have remained, a people without a skin. Yet before the Mercury's aspersions began, tension seems to have been mounting up as the French assemblymen found their strength, as issues emerged and as the assembly's membership changed from a seigneurial to a legal caste. To these latter members, representative government was a new toy as well as a medium of self-importance: only on some such basis can there be explained the assembly's prickly assertions of its rights in incidents like its causing the editor of the Montreal *Gazette* to be arrested on a charge of "false, scandalous and malicious libel" for publishing trivial and bibulous banqueting toasts critical of certain measures carried by the majority.[28]

On the English side, it was in the official area that alienation had proceeded farthest. English-speaking merchants working daily with French employees (especially the Nor'Westers in and out of Montreal) and often married to French wives could now furnish somewhat the same cushion between the two racial extremes as had been furnished by officialdom at the beginning of the English occupation. For this reversal of the roles of the two groups, officials and merchants, a handful of men must bear the responsibility. Among these the major offender was the more or less perpetual governor's secretary, Herman Witsius Ryland. The Anglican bishop of Quebec, Jacob Mountain; the editor of the *Mercury*, Thomas Cary; the attorney-General Sewell, all played leading parts, while the climax was capped by the governor who arrived in 1807, Sir James Craig. In various shadings this group of men represented the quintessence of eighteenth-century English Toryism in all the depth of its intolerance, its lack of imagination, its devotion to a narrow fixed range of ideas and institutions, its total inability to see how the world looked to other people. These men and their fellow senior officials enjoyed the fruits of conquest in a hard, literal sense. From his various appointments, Ryland in 1807 was in receipt of £1,300 per annum, Halifax currency (at $4.00 to the pound), while Sewell from one source or another derived £3,172. These sums in terms of the dollar of our own day, would be something of the order of $30,000 and $70,000,[29] very nice stipends to come from a small colony. Even though some of the annual budget still was paid from Great Britain, these figures combined with others like them represented a considerable levy on the inhabitants. The mere knowledge that English functionaries were being given such sums, the sight of them swelling about, the arrogance of their attitudes, these were enough in themselves to provoke intense resentment on the part of Canadians of standing, but whose standing, as members of a minority and one without much economic prowess, was always more or less precarious. The wonder is that they stood it as long as they did.

Herman Witsius Ryland had been Dorchester's secretary. He has been described as very much of an Englishman in the sturdiness of his prejudices, but his name points to a non-English origin. Dorchester had evidently given him more sympathy for the French than he could absorb, for under later governors his anti-French and anti-Catholic prejudices quickly appeared and they became more and more violent. In a small community such views cannot fail to become known; he did not trouble to conceal them and he sought to influence subsequent governors with them, especially Craig, a man after his own heart. His place in the little colony was large and his responsibility for creating hostile sentiment direct.

Jonathan Sewell, New England born, was not so extreme. A lawyer who had mastered the old French law, complete with its Gallican tendencies, his analysis of the then current situation was acute and much the same as many an English Canadian of Montreal would make to-day, mainly turning on the incompatibility of the two races. He comes down in the French canon of Canadian history as an enemy of French Canada, more subtle and less intemperate than Ryland.

Mountain entertained views common to almost every Anglican clergyman of the day: the degradation of the 'established church' in finding itself so unfavourably situated in comparison with the Catholics; the mortification of having to endure a rival bishop—"How can there be two bishops of one city?" he inquires—and the dangers to faith and State of having masses of people who put allegiance to a foreign potentate, the pope, ahead of their allegiance to their rightful sovereign.

Craig, in French-Canadian eyes, was simply a monster, his governorship termed then, and still, the 'reign of terror'. Had he not deprived loyal subjects of their militia commissions, suppressed the first French newspaper, *Le Canadien*, and imprisoned three assemblymen? True, he did all this by virtue of an Act of the legislature, but what cause had he shown?[30] Craig seemed to think that every gesture of opposition to his will was treasonable, little realizing that it was his intolerances which most tried the loyalty of French-speaking British subjects. He was an intensely suspicious man, it would appear, and at all times egged on by Ryland. When a young barrister of Quebec went abroad on private travels, Craig wrote to Ryland, then in England: "There is a young man of the name of Christie . . . who has just received his commission as a barrister. This young man is going home immediately, and without one possible motive personal to himself. . . . He has prevaricated

in giving his reasons two or three times. . . . He now makes
an appearance for which he certainly has not the means, and
seems to be at no loss for his subsistence while at home. He is
very intimate with Plessis (the bishop), and we strongly suspect
is going home as an agent of his. . . ."[31] It gave Christie wry
amusement years afterward, when this correspondence had been
put into his hands, to discover the motives which had actuated
him at the time, theretofore unknown to himself. Suspicion of
everyone is a marked feature of all dictatorial régimes, and
in Craig's eyes, circumstances warranted suspicion. The country
was filled with French, Napoleon was preparing to conquer
Russia, Wellington was locked up in Portugal, the pope had
made his peace with the emperor, and the Americans were
making trouble and probably soon would make war. So what
was a governor, in bad health and with little military support,
to do?

Win the inhabitants, most of us would say to-day. "The inhabitants! An untrustworthy crowd of papists, all waiting to
stab His Majesty in the back," Craig probably would have
replied. "Trust them? Let them rather know who is master!"
And so the sorry farce played itself out. It is the never-failing
recipe for the loss of empires followed by 'the sahib' the world
over from that day to this.

Yet treasonable attitudes, and practices still more, were conspicuous by their absence during this last of our periods preceding the War of 1812. Nothing is more evident than the
change from the old disturbed days of the seventeen-seventies
and nineties. Napoleon evoked only passing interest in Lower
Canada: the old sentiment for France had been so weakened
by the Revolution that the enticing prospect of a new French
régime under a dictator and *parvenu* seduced no one. French
Canadians were to prove all that by their valour in the war.
Craig might have saved his ammunition for the real enemies
at hand, those south of the border. As *Le Canadien* said, against
them the French language and the Catholic religion were the
best of defences: the real danger appeared to be in the community of interest between the Americans and His Majesty's
English subjects.

Whatever the niceties of the situation—and it is impossible
to say unreservedly on which side the blame for it lay, though
the heavier portion would appear to rest on some of the English
—the racial quarrel, heightened by the transfer of power from
the seigneurial to the middle class, evoked the first burst of
French-Canadian nationalism. No blows were struck and
nothing worse occurred than the arrest of the assemblymen
and the temporary suppression of *Le Canadien*, but such inci-

dents were sufficient to set a tradition. Much allowance must
be made for the smallness of a community where every incident
tended to be personal and news of every incident hurtled about
with the speed of lightning. Moreover, the function of opposition was not as yet well understood. Craig was like the Tudor
sovereigns in equating opposition with disloyalty. *Le Canadien*
impresses the modern reader not with its violence but its tepid-
ness. It kept on talking about 'the ministry', using a term from
British parliamentary life in application to the local executive,
much to the annoyance of Sir James. It made play with two
party names—*le parti Canadien, le parti-anti-Canadien*—and
this invention of 'parties' was in itself a pretension hardly to
be condoned in colonial life. And it filled its columns with
squibs and 'take-offs' which to-day are notable mainly for their
dullness:—

> "Sickle in hand, on the field of Fortune
> The Englishman and the Canadian venture forth.
> Both active and both together eager
> To acquire that which people call wealth,
> But the Englishman having his place in front.
> Happy reaper, he can mow undisturbed.
> The other humbly follows in his track,
> Works as much and can only glean."[32]

However terrible such sentiments were, nothing is surer than
that the best way to provoke them had been that taken by the
Mercury—a direct attack on the Canadians. No people worthy
of their salt would have withstood this goading without retort:
"that animal is dangerous; when one attacks him, he defends
himself." Self-consciousness would in any case have come to
French Canada and the sense of tribalism being what it is,
whatever the circumstances it would have brought antagonisms. But the Rylands, Sewells, Mountains and Craigs, with
all their pretentious magnificence, their hatreds and their repressive efforts, ensured its coming in virulent form. The whole
course of the relationship between the two races may be predicted from the events of the first decade of the nineteenth
century, and this must be the excuse for the inordinate length
taken here to describe the period. Henceforth, for many years
Canada was to follow the path of many other societies towards
misunderstanding and civil strife. It was to be her great good
luck, however, that both peoples eventually came to see that
endless quarrelling was an unprofitable and uncomfortable way
of living together, and in the effort to find a better, to stumble
on ways of putting up with each other.

Notes to Chapter 10

1. Benjamin Sulte, *Histoire des Canadiens-Français*, Vol. VII, p. 90 —"England began by treating us better than France had ever done".
2. *Emily Montague* (London, 1769), p. 46.
3. See Public Archives of Canada, Series Q, Vol. 7, p. 7, *Carleton to Hillsborough*, Mar. 28th, 1770, with enclosures from a *capitaine de milice* giving details. See also pp. 99, 100.
4. Frances Acomb, *Anglophobia in France* (Durham, N.C., 1950), pp. 92-93, quoting A. J. Boucher d'Argis, *Observations sur les lois criminelles de France* (Paris, 1781), p. 63 ff. This position is virtually the same as that of Chartier de Lotbinière, speaking for the Canadians against the proposed Quebec Act. De Lotbinière makes the usual non-English case against the jury system, and claims that guilt had to be meticulously established under the old French law. Moreover, how would it be possible to mingle two systems of law simply by using the terms 'civil' and 'criminal'? See Shortt and Doughty, *Documents relating to the Constitutional History of Canada, 1759-1791* (2nd ed., Ottawa, 1918), Vol. I, p. 562.
5. Admittedly, there are still few spheres in which the attitudes of the two peoples as a whole are more in contrast. Yet liberalism in Quebec has in great part proceeded from the continuous influence of these legal processes on the lawyers. A criminal trial as conducted in Quebec to-day does not differ, except in language, from one conducted elsewhere in Canada.
6. Aubert de Gaspé, *Mémoires*, (Québec, 1886), p. 144.
7. *Mandements, Lettres Pastorales et Circulaires des Evêques de Québec*, ed. H. Têtu et C.-O. Gagnon (4 Vols., Quebec, 1888), Vol. II, p. 269.
8. Whose members as 'American Loyalists' were afterwards assigned lands in the neighbourhood of modern Columbus, Ohio, where the name *Popineau* is still to be found. A review of the whole subject is in V. Coffin's *The Province of Quebec and the Early American Revolution* (Madison, Wis., 1896), especially in Chapter VI.
9. The facts are not in dispute; the official documents are full of them.
10. For these two topics, see Hilda Neatby, *The Administration of Justice under the Quebec Act* (Minneapolis, Minn., 1937).
11. Sulte, loc. cit., pp. 89-90.
12. *Mandement etc.*, op. cit., p. 471.
13. See the dramatic scene depicted in Roger Lemelin's novel, *Les Plouffe* (Quebec, 1948), p. 432 ff.
14. Quoted in Thomas Chapais, *Cours d'Histoire du Canada* (Montreal, 1919), II, p. 112.
15. Public Archives, Doughty and McArthur, *Canadian Constitutional Documents; 1791-1818*, p. 120, *Monk to Dundas*, June 6th, 1794.
16. Public Archives, *Report*, 1892, XXV.
17. *Le Canadien*, Sept. 19th, 1807.
18. With this Chapais seems to agree — see loc. cit.
19. By 1795, 22 had come; *Mandements*, op. cit., p. 483.
20. Ibid., p. 429.
21. Doughty and McArthur, op. cit., p. 396, *Sir James Craig*, Oct. 1st, 1810.
22. A good many English turn out to have German names: where these Germans in Quebec came from is not evident—their presence is remarked on by more than one reporter. Were they ex-Hessian mercenaries?
23. Public Archives, Series Q, Vol. 57, pt. 2, p. 323.
24. Public Archives, *Report*, 1892, XIV, *Dorchester to Sydney*, Jan 9th, 1789: "It must have been a mistake when it was said that the estates and buildings of the College for education belonged to the

Jesuits, who were no more than rectors and professors and managers".

25. Public Archives, Series Q, Vol. 79, pt. 1, p. 7, May 10th, 1797.
26. *L'Influence de Voltaire au Canada* (Quebec, 1945).
27. Aubert de Gaspé, *Memoires*, p. 341.
28. See Robert Christie, *A History of the Late Province of Lower Canada* (Quebec, 1848), Vol. I, pp. 238 ff. One of the toasts: "The Honourable Members of the Legislative Council, who were friendly to constitutional taxation. . . ."
29. It is difficult to strike an exact equivalent but in those days beef was about 8c a pound, and a labouring man did well to earn $1.00 a day.
30. The Act (37 Geo. III, c.vi) providing for detention without trial of persons committed for high treason, suspicion of high treason, or treasonable practices, and prohibiting bail or the benefit of habeas corpus to them. This Act was renewable annually and was so renewed until 1812 (when it might really have been needed), in which year it lapsed. It was a forecast of Regulation 21 of the Defense of Canada Regulations, 1939, issued under the War Measures Act: this Act, which can be used to abrogate all civil freedom, is still (1958) on our statute books.
31. Christie, op. cit, Vol. VI, p. 165.
32. *Le Canadien*, Dec. 27th, 1806. The above translation, made by the present writer, is guaranteed no worse poetry than the original.

11: The private quarrel
of the English

TWO OF THE GREAT FORMATIVE EXPERIENCES of English Canadians have been the English Conquest of French Canada and the American Revolution. While the great events constituting them were unfolding, English Canadians hardly existed, but as they came into existence, they found the two experiences there ready-made, waiting for them. The English Canadians were the heirs of the Conquest, and they were only too much aware of what it entailed in the way of fancied racial superiority. As for the American Revolution, it split the English race: that is its major significance in English Canada. For Americans, the Revolution did what revolutions always do, unloosed new springs of energy, opened new horizons, changed the direction of the stream of history. It gave them shining new gospels, which fitted their circumstances and have been their chart and compass ever since.[1] It gave them the necessary enemy. It gave them the pride of equality with the former mother country, whose measure they had so decisively taken. It changed them from adolescents to men.

What the American Revolution meant for Canada

The Revolution did none of these things for Canadians. As an English population slowly gathered north of the line, it inherited, not the benefits, but the bitterness of the Revolution. It got no shining scriptures out of it. It got little release of energy and no new horizons of the spirit were opened up. It had been a calamity, pure and simple. And to take the place of the internal fire that was urging Americans westward across the continent there was only melancholy contemplation of things as they might have been and dingy reflection of that ineffably glorious world across the stormy Atlantic. English

Canada started its life with as powerful a nostalgic shove backward into the past as the Conquest had given to French Canada: two little peoples officially devoted to counter-revolution, to lost causes, to the tawdry ideals of a society of men and masters, not to the self-reliant freedom alongside of them.

The life of the mother country had always sat rather lightly on the thirteen colonies: they had from the first been eclectic in their attitudes and had grown so rapidly that any effectual domination from across the ocean had been impracticable. In what was left of British North America after the Revolution, the little colonies were weak and the mother country strong. Great Britain 'governed' them to a degree unknown in the old colonies.[2] And yet those in power in Great Britain never displayed much intelligent knowledge of the local situation: how could they, when virtually none of them had ever crossed the Atlantic? The situation was one which hindered the free energies of the colonists from surging forward. Again, for Americans the American Revolution meant liberation, for British North Americans, frustration. It was no accident that for generations afterwards, contrasts continued to be drawn by observers (mainly British) between the spirit of confidence on the republican side of the line and the sluggishness and sloppiness of the colonial scene.

Attempts to arrest the flight of time are rarely successful. They have been more successful in French Canada than in most other societies, but even there they have led to the frictions centreing around such names as Papineau and Laurier. In English Canada, they could not be successful or even prolonged, for the whole genius of the people was against them. But they could disturb the peace, and it was the meeting of the two currents, past and future, which cast up the Howes, Mackenzies and Baldwins, and finally Canada as we know it to-day. The special qualities of Canadian life arise from this fact, that it is both in spirit and in institutions, a mixture of that which was left behind across the ocean (and that was not modern Great Britain, but eighteenth-century Great Britain) and that which was being built in North America, namely, equalitarian democracy.[3] Great Britain seems to have been more the home of starchy privilege in the eighteenth century than it was in the seventeenth. But North America represented escape, opportunity, and therefore equality. "His English blood almost boiled in his veins when he was placed at table with two servant women," said Lieutenant Coke.[4] "He never expected," he went on, "to have found the levelling system introduced into the British provinces to such an extent." The little scene puts the situation in a nutshell: officer and gentle-man sitting at table with two servants in a British colony—a world had crashed!

It is the worst qualities of a people, not its best, that are usually exported, and so the emphasis on rank and privilege which fills the pages of every British traveller and writer of official despatches seemed more extreme in the colonies that it was in Great Britain itself, where other and newer forces were at work. Still, in Great Britain the half century from the Amer-ican Revolution to the reforms of the later eighteen-twenties was decidedly reactionary, with its suspensions of habeas corpus and its 'Peterloo Massacres': the British governing class had been puzzled at the American Revolution, shaken by the French and terrified by Napoleon. When, therefore, its rep-resentative encountered the American Revolution rearing its head in Britain overseas, in the form of equality, their exclama-tions are understandable.

The American Revolution, as noted in Chapter 12, was not so much a national war as it was a civil war.[5] With appropriate exceptions made, it could even be considered a class war, a war between the top layers of society and those down just under-neath them. With additional provisos, it could, as suggested, be held to be a continuation of the unfinished English civil wars of the seventeenth century. Does this make it a war be-tween Cavalier and Roundhead, Churchman and Puritan? In many respects, yes.

The heritage of ritualism

If the American Revolution was, in many respects, a war between Churchman and Puritan,[6] inquiry must be made into the attitudes generated by the two groups and the ways of life centring round them. First Anglicanism must be dealt with, for Anglicanism was the focus of the lost cause which had to retreat from the new American nation to the Canadian bush. This is not to say that every Loyalist was a member of the Church of England but that the significant Loyalists were, the leaders, and that it was taken for granted that the Church of old England would be the Church of new British America. Anglicanism was officially transported to the new soil as was the British flag; in fact, flag and church were hardly distin-guishable.

When the Church of England was cut off from Rome, the necessary effect of the separation was the increase in the signi-ficance of the external act. The Roman Catholic priest could possibly afford to be careless in his ritual, convinced that he could work a miracle. When miracle-working ceased to be an attribute of the priesthood, the gorgeous sheath of ritual remained.[7] Hence an increasing emphasis on it, both in the church and in the way of life of that dominant group in the nation of which the church was the reflection. Among the governing classes of England, every last detail of life and conduct tended to become a ritual act, performed in appropriate manner. Field sports, especially hunting, table manners, deportment, the social observances (the elaborate nineteenth-century ceremonial of visiting cards, for example), the wearing of clothing—the whole range of conduct in matters great and small was embedded in a ritual of cast-iron stiffness.[8] And if ritual clothed the minor aspects of life, how much more did it embrace the major—the occasions of state, the life of majesty, the hierarchical arrangement of ranks, the ceremonial of army life, war, and death in battle.[9]

In the later eighteenth and the nineteenth centuries, the ritualistic attitude towards life could hardly have been more prominent. It is surely not necessary to labour the point, for no one with any range of reading in English literature or any acquaintance with England can have failed to be familiar with it.[10] It is closely associated with the romantic attitude, which is also marked among the upper classes of England. A ruling class, many of whose members have had experience in the fighting services all over the world, infuses throughout its own membership, and far beyond it, a sense of glamour, of exotic coloration, of the heroic. The romantic attitude sees life and things with some distortion—it is the reverse of the matter-of-fact. It provides soil for the growth of myth. Modern English and American life are in marked contrast in these two attitudes, from big things to little.[11] American myth is synthetic—it can do little better than invent hatchets for George Washington. There are no fairies in American woods.

Canadians are somewhere in between. There is not in Canada the complete informality that characterizes so much of American life (one has only to think of the opening of Parliament as compared with that of Congress), neither is there the devotion to romanticism and ritual found so ubiquitously in England (think of the very title, redolent with sentimental romanticism, 'Captain of the King's Flight'; contrast the overtones in the two phrases, the English 'Admiral of the Fleet' and the American 'Fleet Admiral'). As a plain people, Canadians test things by whether they will work or not, just as do Americans, yet keep a small door open to the mysterious past. But that is a point that has been reached not without friction. For a considerable share of Canadian history, the two currents fought each other. It was English upper-class romanticism, its feelings for the ritualized, stylized life ('it is not done') versus the democracy that had emerged from the forest, with its empiric tests of utility and its lack of restraint. It was the unfailing buttress of upper-class romanticism —Anglicanism—against the plain puritanism of a world in the making, its conscious Bible simplicity, and the emotionalism of a religion made on the spot.

The necessary consequence of ritualized life is a society of ranks and classes: a viscount is no more to be allowed precedence over an earl than is a layman to be allowed to get up in the midst of morning prayer and 'testify'. And between 'well-born' and 'base-born', the hierarchical gulf in eighteenth- and nineteenth-century England yawned wide. In the metropolis it was always in some measure under fire, and the road to 'respectability' there was not overly long; just one generation, in fact, if supplemented with education and money, which might mean preferment and the opening of innumerable doors. The road to 'respectability', if not to the entirety of 'belonging'! "A hundred years ago (1855) Emily Eden noted that there was something about Gladstone's tone of voice and 'his way of coming into a room' which was definitely 'not aristocratic'."[12]

From whatever angle the cleft in English society is viewed, in whatever part of the world it is encountered, the great divide seems to have been associated with the state church. If a man were not a 'churchman' most doors were closed to him. In the non-revolutionary colonies, every attempt was made to render this equally true. In England, membership in the state church was a *sine qua non* for membership in the governing class, that extraordinary amalgam of birth, wealth and blood (old and new) which had ruled England since the Norman Conquest, and which had survived, relatively unchanged, the upsetting events of the seventeenth century.[13] In the colonies, the fear that others would step into the sacred circle added weight to the arm of the state church and its lay representatives. In the former colonies, all this had been weak and even in Virginia, where the Church of England was the official church, its power had been small.[14] But those who had fought against rebels were a select band and practically all their leaders were of the official religion. Their consciousness of difference from Yankees and Puritans rose with the struggle. Consequently if a new start were to be made in the northern bush, the bad old sectarianism must be left behind: the new colonies must be of pure religion and undefiled, that is, they must be Anglican.

Here is the fundamental point in British North American

history after the American Revolution. We have all heard *ad nauseam* of Clergy Reserves and Family Compacts, and of the limitations on the performance of the marriage ceremony by non-conformist 'ministers': such points remind us that the major line of division in all the colonies was between 'the established order' in Church and State and those who were products of their North American surroundings.[15] In other words, the American Revolution was in a sense transferred from the United States to linger on in British North America. But in British North America, neither side was to win. The logical concomitants of the two streams' meeting and mingling were the high points of tension in Canadian life such as the rebellion of 1837, the attainment of Responsible Government and of the kind of independence which Canada has to-day achieved for itself.

All this is only saying again that Canada, as much a child of revolution as the United States, though on the wrong side of the blanket, differed from the United States in that it represented the compromise of English traditionalism and of North Americanism and was a mixture of the two—'and the mixture as before', rather more American than English. Or English at the top, and American at the bottom.

But what was it to be 'American'? First of all, it was to have been a member of a society at most a century and a half old, one still living in the shadow of the forest, still affected in every nook and cranny of its being with the consequences of newness and new conditions: flexibility, adaptability, impermanence, formlessness, a society whose natural surroundings produced in it a genius diametrically the opposite of the English governing class's feeling for stability, discipline, order. Private Stephen Jarvis, member of a Connecticut family afterwards well known in Upper Canada as Loyalists, "joined the regiment called Stark's Corps. . . . I was at a loss as to what I should do for arms and accoutrements and applied to my commanding officer from whom I got no information . . . I . . . again applied to my officer stating the necessity of procuring Clothing and arms. . . . Not getting any satisfaction, I got very angry and told him that instead of commanding soldiers he wasn't fit to drive an English wagon. . . ."[16] This sturdy (and mutinous) assertion of equality was in 'the British Army', not that of the rebels, albeit an American ('Tory') portion of it. What the situation frequently was in the ranks of the 'free-born republicans' can well be imagined. But again, is it necessary to elaborate? Everyone knows what the spirit of North America has been, its disregard for the ornamental side of life (its contempt for it, indeed), its feeling that 'anything that will work will do', its hostility to distinctions in rank and status. ". . . In a new country there is more liberty and less culture (than in England). The framework of society is more flexible, but society itself is a cruder thing. Everything is in the making. There are no Mighty Memorials of the Past to abash and inspire the mind, and men seem to depend on themselves alone. The independence is, of course, mainly unreal, but it affects them none the less. It follows that there is a lack of reverence in colonials, a self-assertiveness and a disposition to boast, which are not pleasing. . . ."[17] The reference is to South Africa, but it will do for all 'new countries', from the founding of 'Newtown', Naples, by the Greeks in Italy millenia ago, to the latest settlement on the Alaska Highway. It is only because the two attitudes, the old world and the new, are so utterly different that it has been thought necessary to describe them as fully as is here done.

They have not been without many variations, some of which have already appeared in our story. The merchants who came in the generation after the Conquest represented a kind of half-way house, old world and Calvinist as many of them were. Merchants always aspire to 'thrive to thegn-right', as the picturesque old Saxon phrase has it, that is, to become 'gentlemen', and so begin the class situation all over again. In a country like the United States, which swept out its past, this is exactly what happened—a new and native class structure grew up on the ruins of the old. This new structure[18] had no official place for 'established' Anglicanism and English aristocracy.[19] But it gave honour to the 'merchant princes' and to-day the great industrialists are major upper-class components in a country still passionately attached to equalitarian conceptions. In British North America, the old ghosts of class did not vanish, but remained as a focus of social and political tension—a repetition, again be it said, of the struggle between upper and middle classes which had divided seventeenth-century England —and one of the two chief elements of dramatic relief which the earlier period of Canada's colonial history possesses.[20]

Notes to Chapter 11.

1. Notably the summary of the eighteenth-century views on natural right contained in the Declaration of Independence and in the first ten amendments to the American Constitution. This phrase from the Declaration of Independence is more than a form of words: it is a great text of scripture which has rung down the ages . . . "that all men are created equal; that they are endowed by their Creator with certain unalienable rights; that among these are life, liberty, and the pursuit of happiness".
2. See Mrs. H. T. Manning, *British Colonial Government after the American Revolution, 1782-1820* (London, 1933).

3. See also Chapter 28.
4. Quoted in Gerald M. Craig, *Early Travellers in the Canadas, 1791-1867* (Toronto, 1956), p. xxxiii.
5. See also p. 152.
6. Rev. Charles Inglis, later the first colonial bishop (of Nova Scotia), seems to have seen it in exactly this light, though to him all non-Anglicans were 'dissenters'. He assumed the identity of the cause of King and Church, though he seems to have had some doubts about the colonies from Virginia southward which he did not know at first hand. See J. W. Lydekker, *The Life and Letters of Charles Inglis* (London and New York, 1936).
7. That a still deeper mystery can surround any religious service, most would agree, but it is not often that the edge of things spiritual is touched; hence ritual as a vacuum-filling device.
8. Every aristocracy, of course, ritualizes its life, whatever its religion. In this sense, the Church of England was an aspect of the ritualized life of the ruling classes. A variant of nineteenth century description of it was "the Tory party at prayer".
9. See West's well-known picture, "The Death of Wolfe".
10. The explanation of the psychology inspiring the ritualistic way of life, the present writer suggests, rests upon the fact that the English people, having ceased to celebrate and participate in the 'miracle of the mass', turned to celebrating that which struck them in its turn as most evident and desirable in life, their own existence! English ritualism, in Church and State and ordinary life, is a perpetual affirmation of English existence and its excellence. The altars of the Middle Ages had been decorated and venerated in a faith. The home, the poetry, the institutions, the expansion of England, constituted the new altars, consecrated to the new faith — *Englishism*!
11. "I always keep my bedroom window open in the winter, day and night, and the heat turned off", said a young Englishman, "keeps me from getting soft." The American would say that making yourself uncomfortable reduces your physical efficiency. Infinite concrete examples of the two attitudes come to mind.
12. G. D. H. Cole, *Studies in Class Structure* (London, 1955).
13. See also p. 96.
14. Most of the clergy of Virginia were Scots Episcopalians. They were held in low esteem. The 'Old Dominion' was run by the wealthy planters who could 'take their religion or leave it alone'.
15. To the latter should be added Presbyterian Scots, who from the seventeenth century on may be equated to North American Puritans. Minor variations are numerous, and some will be examined later.
16. J. J. Talman, *Loyalist Narratives* (Champlain Society Edition), p. 159 in "The Narrative of Stephen Jarvis".
17. E. F. Braley, *More Letters of (Bishop) Herbert Hansley Henson* (London, 1954).
18. See, for analysis of it in wearisome detail, the sociological series known as *Yankee City* (Yale, 1945), and for amusing, yet penetrating, variations on the theme, J. P. Marquand's novel, *Point of No Return* (New York, 1949).
19. 'Episcopalianism', a private creed, Anglicanism without teeth, was another matter. Its ritualistic appeal to the classes representing stability, order and the *status quo* in the United States has been strong.
20. The other, of course, being the racial clash.

12: The first wave
of English settlement

To go from French Canada to English-speaking British North America, is to plunge into complexities unknown earlier. New provinces—Nova Scotia, Prince Edward Island, Cape Breton, Newfoundland, New Brunswick, Upper Canada —come into view. New peoples appear; the racial and linguistic variations of the British Isles, Germans of several types, Dutch, some Negroes, and those drawn from the new amalgam to the south. New communities grow up, with their focal city points, each with its character. And these are scattered from Cape Race to the Strait of Detroit, and, with a jump, to mid-continent on the banks of the Red River. All this within a single lifetime.[1] To compress the details of the process into a few thousand words is a task the historian can accomplish only if he attempts to paint, not the literal, crowded canvas of a Brueghel, but the impressionistic picture of a Corot.

New groups of settlers must be followed to their clearings in the northern forests, and there surrounded with their means of livelihood, their daily habits and the appurtenances of their daily life. More intricate than these, their institutional environment—their churches, their schools, their laws, their government—demands explanation. Most subtle of all, their sentiments and their allegiances must be discovered. In such tasks, the observer is faced with the individualism of the Anglo-Saxon, the apparent anarchy of Protestantism. And all of these, geographical dispersion, racial particularism, sectarian atomization, work themselves out against a counterpoint of old-world conceptions of law, order and privilege. As one contemplates the scene, he falls to wondering at the marvel by which it was all gradually transposed to the more or less integrated national community which is Canada to-day, especially when he sees every decade adding to the geographical complexities and to the allurements of the establishment next door.

The Maritime Provinces: Newfoundland,
Prince Edward Island, Cape Breton

To establish the point of departure, the beginnings of English Canada, can we, as if from some infinitely high aeroplane, picture the scene which would have presented itself in that formative quarter of a century between the Revolutionary War and the War of 1812? If so, towards the east, far out in the entrance to the Gulf, our eyes must rest on the oldest and the newest of the Canadian provinces, Newfoundland. In the period here discussed, Newfoundland was still hardly more than a series of fishing stations, and was in the second stage of development, pioneer settlement. Yet its urban nuclei, especially St. John's, were discernible, though small, and the breed of Newfoundlanders was becoming recognizable. The Royal Newfoundland Regiment, which did signal service in Upper Canada during the War of 1812, so testifies.

Closer in towards the continent lies another island province, Cape Breton: an island anchored at the point where Gulf and Atlantic meet and bobbing about like a buoy, as it were, between the two currents, open to both of the rival worlds, the one associated with the giant river and its great lakes, the other with "the deep-voiced neighbouring ocean". A little knot of Loyalist refugees is discernible around what was to become the chief city of the island, Sydney, and, pressing up from the nearby peninsula, persons of Gaelic speech and the Catholic religion. In Cape Breton, they will shortly be joined by ship-loads of their fellows direct from Scotland (1802), until by the end of the immigration (1828) some twenty-five thousand Highlanders, both Catholic and Presbyterian, will have come to the island. These Highland settlers were to bring with them not only their language and their faith but a poetic strain rarely found elsewhere in the colonies. Their poetry rose beyond mere balladry; it was a native literature, albeit because in a little-understood tongue, unknown.

"Thig criogh air an t-saoghal
   Ach mairidh ceol agus gaol."

"An end will come to the world,
   but music and love will endure."

The poetry of the Cape Breton Gael was not to be a thing of the moment: it continued to be written all during the nineteenth century and into the twentieth—as a modern bard illustrates, with his (trans) "It wasn't Eaton's we depended upon to keep us supplied with clothing, but industrious mothers with their knitting needles in the winter."

It may be suspected that most of the poets came from the Catholic faith. Not much of a welcome to idle verses could be expected from Presbyterian divines who registered their resentments at the replacement of the "good, old psalm tunes" by "the frivolous music" of Isaac Watts! Isaac Watts frivolous! But then, he was English. With such Sassenach threats descending on them no wonder Presbyterian divines saw in the insular situation a rampart for race and faith; as one of them was wont to say in his prayers, "And more especially do we thank Thee, O Lord, for the Gut of Canso, Thine own body of water, which separateth us from the wickedness that lieth on the other side thereof."

Presbyterian severity could not be maintained twenty-four hours a day. People came for miles to the communion services, occasions of high spiritual dignity and sometimes spread out over several days. But on the margins of the services were to be seen frolicking youth and courting couples, and sometimes, a little further removed, on the edge of the surrounding bush, traders with illicit strong drink. Thus did the new world break down the old, until Presbyterian communion service in Cape Breton came within hailing distance of Methodist camp-meeting in Upper Canada.[2]

Cape Breton is only one of the "right-little, tight-little islands" found in Canada: each one, to its proud inhabitants, whether Cape Breton, Newfoundland, Prince Edward, Manitoulin or Vancouver, is 'the Island'. All are distinctive; it is only lack of space which prevents more extensive description.

Prince Edward Island (*Isle St. Jean*) is a more productive Cape Breton, but without the latter's minerals. It did not lose its French population after the English conquest, but it rapidly gained another, one of those composites which were to mark nearly all the colonies: a few miscellaneous American English, Highland and Lowland Scots, some Loyalists. Small as it is, Prince Edward Island is still a community of communities, with the original lines of distinction not yet broken down.[3] Not only not broken down but persisting in a dozen usages and life habits, the origin of which is lost to those possessing them. And yet, so strong is the sense of Prince Edward Island against the world that up to a few years ago, it was possible in Charlottetown to go down and watch 'the foreign mail' coming in—from Nova Scotia!

Nova Scotia

When we cross to Nova Scotia, the scene becomes more complex still, for every part of the peninsula has people of differing backgrounds. On the east, Presbyterian Highland Scots began to come in as early as 1772, the year of the arrival of the now famous first ship, the *Hector*, to be followed by Catholic compatriots up Antigonish way in the seventeen-nineties. This literal *Nova Scotia* extended down westward and eventually linked up with Scots Irish around Truro, Yorkshire Methodists on the Isthmus of Chignecto, and the New Englanders of the Annapolis Valley. There was also the mixed population of the capital, Halifax, which contained elements from all along the Atlantic coast and from Ireland, to say nothing of the leavings of British garrisons; and there were the Rhinelanders and Hanoverians of Lunenburg; occasional French Protestants, some of whom came with the English armies (Martels, Dauphinies and the like); the scattering of New Englanders farther down, along through Liverpool to Yarmouth; and during and after the Revolutionary War, the throngs of refugees, soldiers, officials and ordinary settlers whom history knows as United Empire Loyalists.

Many another Loyalist family suffered blows from fate similar to those of one which may stand as typical, the Farish family. The Farishes took part in the pathetic failure at Shelburne.[4] Then after some years' struggle on that infertile soil, they left and went to Virginia, where they received a friendly reception. A son, Greggs, who went to sea on a British ship, swung once more into the English orbit. He lived for a time in London, where he obtained some medical training. After the Treaty of Amiens, 1802, chance brought him back to Nova Scotia, this time to Yarmouth, where he began to practise medicine. A long-lost younger brother was discovered in the United States and the family in some measure reconstituted. When Doctor Farish died, his son succeeded him as a family doctor, and then a grandson.[5] The family evinced a deep piety, tending to puritanism but not a harsh puritanism—an Anglican version of Wesleyanism. In this, they were perhaps typical for their time and locality.

The mass of Loyalists did not stay in Nova Scotia, which is not a Loyalist province, though many a Nova Scotian has been absorbed into the Loyalist tradition by osmosis. At the time the Loyalists' mark on the province was divisive, for their presence created two parties in the assembly, the 'Old Comers' and the 'New Comers': the distinction remained for many years.[6]

Nova Scotia was first of all New England—*New England's Outpost*, as it has well been called[7]—New England projected eastward across the Gulf of Maine, with its self-confidence, self-reliance, orderliness, neatness. All these marks are visible as soon as one gets off the Digby ferry and drives up through Annapolis. Not visible to the eye, but still easily found, is the New England attitude towards State and Church. Most New Englanders in Nova Scotia at the Revolution had been ready to join with friends and relatives in rebellion, and all of them shared New England's views on self-government. Their politics were powerfully reinforced by their religion. While nearly all came as nominal Congregationalists, they were simple people and the heady appeals of the 'New Lights' under such preachers as Henry Alline reduced stiff New England Congregationalism into something warmer and cruder, whence in turn it swung round into a little more stability in that successful frontier denomination, the Baptist.[8] As Congregationalists or Baptists, Nova Scotian New Englanders had no place for the ornamental side of life, whether in Church or State: the ritualism of the established church and the ritualism of a monarchical society were alike objectionable to them. When Loyalist Episcopalian clergy came among them, they could make little impression. As one of them, from his lonely post on Handley Mountain, whence the sapping away of various flocks by his enemies had driven him, well put it:—

"I would sooner prevail on His Holiness at Rome to throw aside his mitre for a red cloak and a white wig, and bid a last farewell to the luxuries of the Vatican—to solicit the Bostonians to elect him deacon of the Old South meeting-house, and chant the edifying version of the Psalms to the tune of 'Hush my dear, lie still and slumber,' than I could prevail on a Whig Oliverian, [Cromwellian] a friend to the American Congress and Boston town meetings, to become a good churchman."[9]

The percipience of the author of the quotation did not, however, prevent his indulging in derogatory descriptions of these stiff-necked Puritans, although they were his own people and he was a 'dissenter' turned 'churchman'.[10] Their ministers were "ignorant shoemakers", or "strolling, fanatical teachers". Since he 'had the law on them' and took away some glebe lands claimed by them, his failure to bring the people over to his denomination can be understood. His was the invariable failure of a clergy representative of an upper class—a failure which has occurred over and over again on innumerable frontiers.[11]

These 'dissenting' preachers often were fanatical. But they reached the people on their own level and were sincere, however simple. They could afford to leave sophistication to their successors—and would have been shocked at the suggestion that they would ever have acquired it.

After a series of 'hot and strong' religious meetings, a woman in 'the Valley' wrote back to her aunt in Rhode Island—this was towards the end of the century—about the wondrous experience which had been vouchsafed to her during the course of the meetings. Having had occasion to step out of the house after dark, what should happen to her? In her own words, in their faded, yellowed writing, "I saw Jesus". There appeared to be no doubt about it: there He was, plainly visible, just outside the house.[12] Of such is pioneer Protestantism wherever it is found, perennially reborn out of the simplicity of the ordinary man, but never completely departing from its roots in Holy Writ. By and by its raptures cool; instead of the old log meeting houses, it builds neat churches, and in another generation or two, when the small frame church has been replaced by a fine stone edifice and gentlemen in frock coats solemnly take up the collection, decorum and dignity return once more: the sect has become a church, and the church itself, whatever its denomination, finds it just as difficult to retain the humble as did its Anglican predecessors.[13]

The settlement of Nova Scotia occupied about a century, from the old Annapolis days[14] to the completion of the Scottish occupation of Cape Breton. But Halifax was founded, formally and with a flourish, as a town and capital, in 1749. Thenceforward, there was a centre in which life went on with due pomp and ceremony. Generals reviewed their troops on the Parade and admirals were rowed ashore in their gigs. Gentlemen drank their port and madeira—much of both. Courts of law, judges complete with wigs, sat in all solemnity. Army offenders ritually received their three hundred lashes, and marine malefactors were duly hanged at yard arms. A theatre was built and in 1789 the *Beaux Stratagem* was performed. "It is particularly requested that ladies will dress their heads as low as possible," ran the announcement, "otherwise the persons sitting behind cannot have a view of the stage."[15] Sedan chairs appeared for rent, charge one shilling up, the 'chair-park' being at the Courthouse.[16] Ladies, however their heads were dressed, in little Halifax as elsewhere, were up to their usual tricks: "Some of the females who have lately arrived at this place from London, seem to exert all their talents to daub and finify those parts which require no ornament and to expose to view such other parts as nature seems to intend that every modest woman shall conceal."[17]

While fine ladies watched theatricals indoors, press-gangs stalked the streets outside and if their man would not come peaceably, they took him violently.[18]

And to cap it all, in the first sixty-six years of the city's existence or until 1815, there were thirty-three of glorious and highly profitable war, with all the fighting somewhere else. In each of these, privateers were fitted out in the port of Halifax. Partial lists show eighteen letters of marque for the Seven Years' War (1756-63) and forty-four for the War of 1812-1814. During this latter contest, no less than two hundred and one prizes, mostly American, were brought into port. Their cargoes laid the foundation of many a snug fortune. The most famous of the privateers, the little sixty-seven-ton schooner *Liverpool Packet*, took forty-four prizes during the War of 1812. One of her owners was Enos Collins, in his youth himself a privateer officer. Later, in the eighteen-twenties, he became—and no wonder—the richest man in Halifax, one of its leading rulers and Episcopalians, its first banker.

A tang of the salty, lusty atmosphere of the period, this time that of the American Revolutionary War, is blown across the generations by the following notice, which appeared in the *Nova Scotia Gazette*, January 12th, 1779:—

THE REVENGE

Captain James Gandy, who has been on several cruises, has met with great success.

All gentlemen volunteers:

Seamen and able-bodied landsmen who wish to acquire riches and honour are invited to repair on board the *Revenge*, private ship of war, now lying in Halifax Harbor, mounting 30 carriage guns, with cohorns, swivels, etc., bound for a cruise to the southward for four months, vs. the French and all H.M. enemies, and then to return to this Harbour.

All Volunteers will be received on board the said ship, or by Captain James Gandy, at his rendez-vous at Mr. Proud's Tavern near the Market House, where they will meet with all due encouragement, and the best treatment.

Proper advances will be given.

God save the King.

N.B. As it is expected that many of the Loyal inhabitants of this province will try their fortunes by entering on board so good a ship at a favourable time, a protection will be given to their being impressed on board Men-of-War. . . ."

Shortly thereafter the *Revenge* sailed, in company with the *Halifax Bob*, and in May, "both vessels returned with richly laden prizes."

Some idea of the profits made out of war may be arrived at from the case of Philip Marchington, "who followed the British Army during the American Revolutionary War, and came here from New York with about £35,000 of money. He bought property which increased in value, and left a large sum for his two children."[19] The surprising but not untypical pioneer sequel was that "He built a church in which he was preacher."

What a mixture of war, booty, piety and sin the old *Warden of the North*[20] has always been! As Enos Collins is reported to have remarked, in his older days, "You will observe, sir, that there were many things happened then we don't care to talk about." Regular soldiers being fully occupied with Napoleon, "the London prisons were emptied of felons to get men who would enlist for the forces here. I can remember that women refrained hanging out their clothes on a washing-day because they saw a soldier about. . . . In 1716, Captain Westmacott, of the Royal Engineers was going his rounds of duty at night [as a citizen member of a volunteer police patrol], when he met two soldiers whom he attempted to arrest. They had stolen goods in their possession and fell upon him and murdered him, for which they were hanged."[21] "In the so-called 'good old times', there was no Infants' Home, and bodies of these were not unfrequently found where they had been exposed to perish."[22]

Nova Scotia is nearly everywhere open from the sea: this has meant rapid acquisition of the appurtenances of civilized life. Halifax, particularly, with ships of war never absent from its harbour or red-coats from its citadel, quickly became a little capital, and the air of local metropolis, not mere provincial city, then acquired, has never been lost. Attention to the arts of life followed close on satisfaction of material wants. It was in the late eighteenth century that a species of semi-artist known as 'silhouettist' turned up for the first time in the city. For those who were not able to go abroad and have 'miniatures' painted, the silhouettist filled a need: he cut out the shadowed likeness of your side face from a piece of paper and there you were! The equivalent of a modern photograph.

In 1808, a real artist came to Halifax, took up residence and began to paint the portraits of the notabilities. This was Robert Field, an Englishman, a man not too proud to do not only oils, but water-colours, engravings, and miniatures. Much of his work remains. His *Bishop Inglis* is now in the National Portrait Gallery, London, his *Prevost* and *Sherbrooke* (the two governors) are, or were, in the Halifax Club, to which resting place, it was once strongly hinted, they had been taken after having been 'lifted' from the Province Building. Field has been considered the best portrait painter ever to reside in Nova

Scotia. The little city must have been rapidly taking on polite airs if for the ten years he passed there such a man could earn his living by painting its *haut monde*. Of course, money for portraits came easily in the roaring days of war: Field left three years after peace had descended on the town.[23] From such a source, too, probably came the impulses which led to the province equipping itself with a good piece of architecture— Government House, 1805. The total population of Halifax in 1801 was only 8,532.[24]

At the turn of the century the Nova Scotians, hardened in the fires of war and sharpened by seafaring, were on the verge of self-consciousness, travelling along the same road to the status of *a people* as their fellow-provincials of the French tongue up the great river.

New Brunswick

Across the Bay of Fundy, quite another scene presented itself. Nova Scotia is practically an island, and insularity promotes independence. But across the Bay is 'the continent', that vastness which prior to the American Revolution had been divided between the two old foes and the aborigines. And now a third group had somehow or other to wedge itself in. The Loyalists had been brought up to Halifax and thence within a few months they were given their second chance in 'the continent', which for practical purposes meant the valley of the St. John River and contiguous areas.

Most of the men who were to make the new province of New Brunswick had been under arms in the Revolution and had no option about leaving their old homes. Like their brethren whom they had fought, they were Americans, children of the new world, with its attitudes, its excellences and its shortcomings. They were from all the colonies, though mostly from the north, and of all ranks and classes. Conspicuous among them was the little group of 'gentlemen' who had been commissioned officers. Most of these men had occupied the places in society which make men cleave to things as they are. They had been officials, or 'land proprietors', or both, or simply educated men. Harvard graduates among them were numerous. As the right wing of American society, they suffered the universal fate of right wings in successful revolution, and those who would not conform were expelled. Just as after the Russian Revolution of 1917, grand dukes had to take to driving taxi-cabs in Paris, so after 1783, the former American upper classes were to be found scattered about the world living similar hard existences. Some went to London. Others, equally resolute, still leaders, still with men under them, albeit these men were now civilians, came to the northern bush. There, leaders and men all enlisted in that permanent North American war, the war against the wilderness.

Since the New Brunswick Loyalists comprised many educated men, they were the most self-conscious of all the exiles, and they have left behind them a considerable literary monument in the papers of the Winslow family, the editing of which by the late Canon Raymond constitutes one of the major accomplishments of Canadian nineteenth-century scholarship. In the countless letters of these pages, from son to father, from husband to wife, from one intimate friend to another, the epic of upper-class Loyalists has been set down: their joys and sorrows, their exaltations, their blighted hopes, their shortcomings and their successes. Out of it all, one point emerges clearly: whatever the explanation of their original decision, they were all convinced that it had been taken out of principle. They were sufferers in a cause, exiles for righteousness' sake; the only group of settlers Canada has ever had (with minor exceptions such as Hutterities and Doukhobors) who have come "seeking a faith's pure shrine", rather than merely to worship "the Goddess of Getting on."

Loyalist leaders had been under no illusions about the British military with whom they worked. Edward Winslow, direct descendant of the old pilgrim of the *Mayflower*, was not the only one among them to see through the Clintons and the Howes, with their incompetences, their indecisions and their mistresses. If Loyalists such as he could have found a Washington among themselves the result of the war might have been different. That was not to be, and when exile came for these men, they took the old monarchical system with them as a matter of course. As time passed and republicanism pressed, they found their convictions strengthened. In this way in New Brunswick was to be preserved the empire as it once had been, a blend of old world and new, of status and democracy. Those who left their native land behind never ceased to be Americans—they simply refused to be republican Americans.

Most of them left more than possessions or political sentiments. Stephen Jarvis, who came first to New Brunswick and later went to Upper Canada, left behind him in Connecticut, father, mother, brothers and sisters. After the storm had passed, the old connections were resumed and relations visited back and forth—as they have never ceased to do.

Edward Winslow at first was enthusiastic about the St. John, its lands, its climate. Everything seemed to promise well. He himself had a large part in the arduous tasks of accommodating the fourteen thousand people transferring to the river from Nova Scotia (where they had spent the winter), victualling them and getting them on the land. Despite the bush, the Loyalists seem to have been glad to get out of Nova Scotia—away from 'the rebels', as they termed the previous inhabitants of that province.

Occupation of the valley, everywhere accessible by navigable waters, was no great problem—it was easier to clear the forest than to clear land titles encumbered with jungles of red-tape and previous vague claims, and at a city, Halifax, some hundreds of miles distant. Difficulties of this type at once produced agitation for a separate province and within a year *New Brunswick* was the result.[25] The men of status naturally secured whatever public posts there were. Initial progress was rapid and enthusiasm grew with the crops. The little cities of Saint John and Fredericton sprang up.

Within ten years something had gone wrong. In the seventeen-nineties many families removed to Upper Canada, both those with status and those without.[26] Edward Winslow thought the exodus grave enough to write a discouraging piece about it for the newspaper and allowed such words as 'deserters' to cross his kindly lips. New Brunswick was good enough for him, he said. Yet a few years later he himself was beginning to complain of his disabilities. He had never had a major public post, but he did have eleven children and feared that to support them he would have to go and beg great men's favours in London and be sent, perhaps, to the ends of the earth. His old friend, Ward Chipman, was equally discontented. There seemed to be no future of importance for him. And yet he had given his best years to his new homeland, in the thankless and unpaid post of Solicitor-General.

Explanations for the despondent attitudes of so many excellent men come out bit by bit. For lack of a local college Chipman has to send his son back among the old enemies, back to his own old college, Harvard. There the boy does brilliantly, but what is there in New Brunswick for him to return to? Winslow sends off his oldest boy, aged nine, to school in England. For the others, as they come along, he begs commissions in the army—and has to enjoin on them to behave themselves and live on their pay, strange conduct for an eighteenth-century British officer! One, thanks to 'influence,' becomes a purser on an East Indiaman. The father's sisters, spirited young women when they came up to Halifax in 1783, gradually wither on the bough. The New Brunswick stage was too small. There were too many men 'of family' after too few places.

And yet, what a charming and intelligent group of people these outcasts were! Winslows and Chipmans, Uphams, Blisses, Leonards, walk through the pages of the Winslow *Papers*, carrying with them the good manners, intelligence and class consciousness of the generations of Harvard that lay behind them. No wonder that a little later, in this remote northern forest, there was built, on a foundation of white-pine logs but with Anglican and old-world superstructure, the first shrine of Canadian poetry.[27]

A province of contradictions, such was New Brunswick; of old-world nostalgias, new-world attitudes, of lost causes and new hopes, of Harvard refinement and lumberjack crudity, a province with wings not quite strong enough to take it off the ground.

Quebec—Lower Canada

Across the Témiscouata portage from the St. John lay the foreign world of the St. Lawrence. By the end of the eighteenth century it, too, like Nova Scotia, was developing a life of its own with the opportunity to share in the English culture then being carried by the winds across all the seas. Its growth was securing it certain amenities. Hotels and restaurants, assembly rooms, were making their appearance and there was even a modest attention to the cleanliness of the public streets.[28] In 1801, a public water company was formed in Montreal; water was to be brought down from the Mountain in wooden pipes, at seven dollars per service semi-annually; there were sixty-three takers.[29]

A few years before, in 1791, a theatre group of young French-speaking Canadians in Quebec City had begun to give plays, opening with Beaumarchais' *Barber of Seville*: as evidence that the puritanism of the old régime was not yet dead, the Church did all it could to prevent the undertaking.[30] The clerics did not prevent the venture from having a fitful success: at least, plays continued to be given and the players acquired a hall in an upper story to play them in. It must have been primitive—"It would be a libel to give the name of theatre to the present wretched hole"[31]—but it did duty for many years. Plays in French, which predominated at first, gradually receded in numbers, and the *Théâtre du Marché à foin* became mainly English. Plays were given at irregular intervals, usually by amateurs but on occasion by travelling companies. Possibly of more interest to the average citizen was the exhibition in 1798, undoubtedly for the first time on record, of—a giraffe! Quebec City was fertilized by the tide of shipping which in the seventeen-nineties began to carry away Canadian produce to England, where the demands of war were in the usual way opening insatiable markets. The middleman got the largest share of the profits. The new trades in wheat or timber multiplied his numbers in the old city and elevated his status.

Montreal, in contrast to Quebec, continued to live off its fur-trade hinterland. These were the great days of the Nor'Westers, with the fur brigades leaving Lachine every spring, bound for the illimitable West. In 1786 and again in 1793, when Alexander Mackenzie scored his two bull's-eyes and got to the Arctic and the Pacific oceans, every Montrealer must have raised a cheer, for exploits like that meant money in the pocket and new estates on the Mountain. The second English chapter in the life of Montreal was being written. Its conclusion, an ironic conclusion, the downfall of the Nor'-Westers and their absorption by the Hudson's Bay Company, lies just outside our present period (1821). Meanwhile, the city flourished on the humble beaver as it had never flourished on it in the days when Canada had been New France.

Upper Canada

Montreal did not flourish alone on the humble beaver. For up river, men who had had a similar experience to the makers of New Brunswick were taking up the axe against the forest. Up river, bound to Montreal by the great waterway, there was to grow what would prove to be the largest colony of them all, Upper Canada. It was to take its colour, in part, from the people with whom it began, the western inland Loyalists, and to owe its material progress to the gifts of nature. In winter the snow lies lighter every foot of the way from Montreal to Toronto and in the west at Windsor, it may disappear. A good climate and more fertile soil than the other colonies, these factors were to explain Upper Canada's size and wealth, just as its remote situation and its distances from the sea were to explain the slowness with which at first wealth and settlement grew.

Upper Canada's first wave of settlement, like New Brunswick's, consisted in the defeated remnants from the south. Many simple men among them would have been hard put to it to explain how they happened to have got where they were. In western New York, failure to sign 'The Articles of Association' automatically made a man guilty of treason to the Revolution. How many people would neglect to sign, it is easy to imagine, for political decision must have been prompted by any one of a score of reasons, and perhaps most frequently of all, indecision was decision. The point is that once a man got lined up with one side, he was usually there to stay.[32] Hence the terrors of the northern bush for those that were with the losers.

Every Canadian knows the traditions they brought up with them: not only memories of homes confiscated or destroyed, but of personal suffering, the separation of families,[33] the cruelties of the republican mobs. These can all be documented: whatever a Loyalist's views on political theory, his views on the treatment he and his had received at the hands of former countrymen were clear-cut. These views, reinforced by the War of 1812 and extending to successive waves of newcomers, were the psychological foundation stones of Upper Canada—Ontario—determining in as great a measure as they did in New Brunswick, its basic outlook down to our own day.

The Upper Canadian Loyalists were of many racial stocks, but of much the same social and economic level—a humble one. There were exceptions, naturally—a few leaders, such as Sir John Johnson, son of Sir William, whose tenantry in the valley of the Mohawk had furnished many of the rank and file —but it was not until the wave of immigration from New Brunswick in the seventeen-nineties that the new province received what might be termed a Loyalist *élite*. At that time, families like the Robinsons, the Jarvis's, the Ryersons, all made their way westward, bringing both qualities of leadership and the invidious claims of status.

As for the ordinary man, whether his name was Van der Voort or Macdonnell or just plain Smith,[34] all his ambition was to get some land and settle down where the wicked would cease from troubling. "Me, I'm the eighth on my father's farm,"[35] said one modern representative of the species. "Rightly, we're Dutch, you know. Yes," he added, "we come up here from New York State"—and then, reminiscently—"after the war." For him there had been only one war.

In Upper Canada, the Loyalists had a clear field. There was no one to push aside, neither previous English of dubious loyalty as in New Brunswick, nor previous French—just the trees. The only French in the area, those along the Detroit River, became Loyalists themselves, for they crossed from the American to the Canadian side because they preferred British rule. Since most of the new arrivals had come from the edges of settlement, they just went on with the task of pioneering, and while they had their hardships, they were little different in quality or intensity from those of other pioneers. The result was that the new settlements got on their feet fairly quickly, and after the province of Upper Canada was formed in 1791, quite quickly. The string of towns along 'The Front' right through to the Detroit river is one proof of this, the rapid increase in population (around one hundred thousand by about 1812) another. The substantial and even elegant houses built during the period, a number of which survive, constitute still another. And the sturdy resistance made to the Americans in 1812 is perhaps the best of all.

Why, then, is modern Ontario not a 'Loyalist' province like New Brunswick? The simple answer is that the province offered too many attractions to be left to six or seven thousand people and their descendants. Others crowded in at once, practically all of them from across the border, and since they had been born subjects of King George, who was to read the political secrets of their hearts? The various attempts that have been made to classify the post-Revolution American immigrants have not been successful—the so-called 'Late Loyalists', 'ordinary Americans', and the like. The telling point was that down until the eighteen-twenties, the people of Upper Canada and also those of the Eastern Townships of Lower Canada were overwhelmingly of the continent: they were North Americans. And as North Americans, they were democrats, and monarchists or republicans as occasion required.

No chapter in Canadian history has been so frequently rewritten—and over-written—as that of pioneer days in Upper Canada. There is little new to be said about those days, except by way of fresh illustration. Pioneer qualities have often been described: the rawness, the crudity, the conceit, the ignorance, the superstitiousness, the intemperance—all that decline of civilization which 'beginning life over again' entails;[36] the good spirits, the neighborliness, the hospitality, the simplicity, the sense of accomplishment, the sense of freedom, the self-reliance. Writers tend to go in one of two directions, to idealize or to denigrate. And yet it should not be difficult to understand the life of those days, and that for the plain reason that our attitudes of to-day are little different from those of our predecessors of one hundred and twenty years ago. It takes more than substituting Cadillacs for oxen to change attitudes.[37]

Our first wave of pioneers, then, was American, body and soul, but pre-Revolutionary American. Yet wherever the post-Revolutionary American life of settlement impinged with especial sharpness upon the new provinces it too can still be seen: St. Stephen, New Brunswick, Stanstead, Quebec, and Niagara-on-the-Lake, Ontario, all three places, in the width of their streets and the style of their houses, tell us that here the

American frontier (using less and less paint as it worked northward) crossed the border into British America. Niagara-on-the-Lake is a little wedge of eighteenth-century classicalism, with all its good proportions and good taste, driven into our Canadian ugliness and colonial small-mindedness. The same influence, but in different materials, can be seen in the old Loyalist settlements along 'The Front'. Below the Bay of Quinte, the building material was local limestone, but shape and proportions were often similar to the clapboard colonial houses of New England. Above the Napanee River and along the lake, the more ambitious houses echo Sir William Johnson's 'new' house at Johnstown, New York (about 1765), and his older one farther down the Mohawk,[38] but they are built in brick. The first wave of settlers, especially those in the eastern part of the province, came closer to instituting an English-Canadian style of domestic architecture than has any later generation.

Ten miles west of Kingston, on the shores of the Bay of Quinte, lies 'The White House', the oldest dwelling along the Bath Road: it was built in 1793, a distinguished house then and distinguished to-day. With characteristic Canadian vulgarity, someone has jammed in between it and the lake, a dirty little 'soft-drinks' roadside stand (a typical pioneer attitude). The house itself is clapboard over grouting. It is rectangular and of excellent proportions. Some of its original furniture, still in daily use, was brought up from Vermont by the family that built the house and still lives in it. Up the road a few miles, in the village of Bath, is another house of similar type, also on the edge of the water, built by and still occupied by other members of the same family. Here is stability, here is beauty. It all came out of the hard work of Loyalist pioneers in the seventeen-nineties; and the smart 'progressive' fellows of our own times, if they saw a dollar in it, would sweep it away in a twinkling.[39]

In contrast to such houses were the public stopping-places of the day, which all travellers saw and which they fully reported upon, for in them went on communal life. As reflections of pioneer days, the sedate houses and the gracious lives they enshrined were just as representative and no more representative than the promiscuity, drunkenness and filth of the public stopping-places, the rapacity and vulgarity of those who kept them.

From the first the shape the new province should take was a subject for many conflicting ideas and ideals. Plain pioneers, Loyalist and otherwise, simply wanted to get on with the immemorial job of building a countryside. The new natural leaders among them, such as the Cartwrights and the Rankins of Kingston neighbourhood, or the Hamilton who founded Hamilton, Ontario, did not get far beyond looking after the interests of their own localities. The little provincial capital (first Newark, then York) attracted men of larger ambitions. There, where favours were to be dispensed or good places secured, arose a group similar to that which had been found in all older colonies, the 'insiders' who, in the case of Upper Canada, came to be called 'The Family Compact'. They were compact from the first, and, as their young people inter-married, time duly turned them into more or less of a family.[40] Some of them were Loyalists, most of them were not. Many were the usual ubiquitous Scotsmen on the make.

"I found the . . . lieutenant-governor surrounded with the same scotch Pedlars, that had insinuated themselves into favour with General Hunter, & that have so long irritated & oppressed the people; there is a chain of them linked from Halifax to Quebec, Montreal, Kingston, York, Niagara & so on to Detroit—this Shopkeeper Aristocracy has stunted the prosperity of the Province & goaded the people until they have turned from the greatest loyalty to the utmost dis-affection. . . ."[41]

A traveller of the time noted as the most descriptive phrase the pioneer mind could evoke for sheer acquisitive ingenuity, the term 'Scotch Yankee.' As everywhere else, many such 'Scotsmen' found it useful to become zealous members of the Church of England, for there lay the ready instrument of power.

It was the alloy formed from melting together personal inter-est, professional concern, the state religion of England, political tradition, and family relationship, which was to govern, or rather, misgovern, Upper Canada for half a century after its founding, just as similar, if not precisely identical, alloys were doing the same job, with a similar mixture of capacity and incapacity, in all the other provinces. Some members of these 'family compacts' had small ideas, some large, some good, some bad. Few were poor at looking after their own interests. The first lieutenant-governor, John Graves Simcoe, is not unrepresen-tative of this early governing group, though untypically dis-interested. As an old soldier of the War of the Revolution, he was well acquainted with the continent and its people. He was keen on his job of setting up a new province—we find him asking Winslow in New Brunswick to place at his disposal his experience in getting New Brunswick started. He welcomed American immigrants—in this respect he was almost a typical

North American 'promoter'—and in building through roads like Dundas Street and Yonge Street, he sketched out a physical basis for the future. But he was a man of his class, very much an English squire, and he could not understand an ungraded, non-hierarchical society. And so in his new province the old world and the new were once more mingled; privilege and unprivilege, aristocracy and democracy.

The unprivileged found their voices in what to-day would be called 'the sects'. 'Dissenters', as they were called in those days, were all who could be comprised, in the words of Bishop Mountain of Quebec, under the heading of "a set of ignorant enthusiasts". As long as ignorant enthusiasts wished merely to make themselves ridiculous at their camp-meetings and their conversions, with their roarings, their speaking with tongues and their rollings on the ground, they were left alone; but when it came to giving them legal privilege, authority rallied and 'ignorant enthusiasts' became 'licentious fanatics'. When Elder Reuben Crandall, a Baptist, married a couple outside of the district for which he had a license, he was sentenced to fourteen years banishment. Only with difficulty did he get out of his predicament. The man whose attitude towards him was hardest was himself a Loyalist—John Beverley Robinson,[42] afterwards Chief Justice Robinson. Robinson was the descendant of a long line of Virginia and New York squires who had lost their lands at the hands of just such ones as Crandall. Such men as Robinson were not going to have the experiment repeated on Canadian soil, if they could help it.[43]

The principal 'dissenting' groups were the Methodists, the Presbyterians, the Baptists, the Lutherans, the Quakers and the Mennonites. Each one of these had its special characteristics and each left its enduring mark on Canadian society. Methodists, thanks to Wesley's Arminian theology and to the doctrine of conversion, strengthened a new community's natural feeling for free will. If God could change a man, surely he could change society. Much of our zeal for 'reform' comes from the crusading spirit of early Methodism.[44]

Presbyterians, whose pride in their historic church and in their fatherland made the efforts of Anglicans to include them in the ranks of 'dissenters' particularly invidious, brought with them to Canada everything we associate with the term Calvinism, its good and its evil, its strength and its weakness. Calvinism in one way or another covers most of our heritage.[45] Its dourness has suited sombre Canadians and it has greatly reinforced the individualism, the energy, the utilitarianism and the short-sightedness of a people who even without it would have been constrained by their situation to view life in materialistic colours. As the century wore on, Calvinism wore down—before 1820, for example, there were no non-Calvinist Baptists; after that date, their numbers increased. It was this erosion of Calvinism which, a century and a quarter further on, was to permit the union of Presbyterian and Methodist in the United Church of Canada. But in the period of this chapter, Presbyterianism had not yet made its full impact on Canadian life; that had to await the large Scottish immigration of the post-war era.

"And it appeared if I would make ready and go immediately to the westward, the Lord would make way for me to settle in the wilderness where no others were settled and that both me and my children might settle there, and that it would open a door for a Meeting of Friends in that place."

Thus a Quaker in 1800. Quakers felt led by the hand of God in establishing their settlements (of which that near Newmarket, Ontario, was the chief), though it may be surmised that their reasons for "going immediately to the westward" were not very different from those of that group in Boston which, in 1636, made the first of America's innumerable pilgrimages towards the setting sun, when, in petitioning the General Court of Massachusetts Bay for permission, they alleged as their reason "the strong bent of their spirits." The Quakers were quiet people, the salt of the earth, who avoided trouble. Not all 'dissenters' were. Most, in fact, had a sturdy sense of their rights and this was reflected in the long duel with the Anglicans which began shortly after the province was set up, over the Clergy Reserves, the marriage question and in general, the fundamental issue of whether the Church of England was to make good its claim to being an established church.

No body of men could have conducted themselves in a way more calculated to defeat their own ends than did the Anglicans, more especially the Anglican clergy. The major example of this, Archdeacon Strachan's unhappy feud with Egerton Ryerson, is too well known to need further reference. A minor one is furnished by the Rev. John Langhorne at Ernestown (Bath), who announced that "as marriages performed by ministers other than those of the Church of England were illegal, persons so married were free to marry someone else. Two Lutheran couples took him at his word and came to him to be married—with a switch in partners!"[46] Langhorne was at frequent feud with the Rev. Robert McDowell, the nearby Presbyterian minister. Pioneer Scots, whose own state church did not spring from a royal matrimonial scandal, could hardly have been expected to take superior Anglican airs lying down.

The Rev. George Okill Stuart, Archdeacon of Kingston from 1812, was another stormy Anglican petrel, whose quarrels with his Presbyterian colleague, Barclay, whatever the fine points of right involved, did nothing to advance Christian harmony. Stuart was a successful real-estate promoter who obtained large grants of land about Kingston, on one of which Queen's University is built.[47] One good thing at least was not "interred with his bones": the huge house he built—in Anglican good taste, if also in grandiosity—which to-day provides for Queen's the most distinguished Principal's residence in Canada.

Stuart, son of a Loyalist, was educated at Harvard. That was the difficulty with Anglicans—they stuck to an educated ministry. Educated people having educated taste, they found little attraction in coming to a colony to starve on pittances. The primitive zeal, lamented the Bishop of Quebec, which led men to sacrifice all for a cause, was no longer to be encountered. But he could have encountered it easily enough—in places where its existence was unwelcome to him, among the Roman Catholic clergy and among the 'dissenters'. It was primitive zeal, living on a pittance, which drove the Methodist circuit-riders and Baptist preachers; and it was they as much as bishops or governors who were determining the future of Upper Canada. Nor can the charge against them of untutored ignorance be too successfully maintained. Most of them did not have much book-learning, that may be granted. Most of them were ready to accept and abet an undue emotionalism in their service, that too may be granted. But many of the Baptists had been trained at colleges such as Colgate or Dartmouth, and no man who wrote as well as Egerton Ryerson need bother about charges of lack of education. Even in theology, their departures from orthodoxy were not as wide as might be supposed. Their bedrock was Scripture, and none of them thought of themselves as severed from 'the general body of Christ' and from His 'universal Catholic Church'.

The plain truth was that plain people then, as now (when members of these very denominations grown older make much the same charges against the newer sects as were made by the Anglicans against themselves) demanded a plain unsophisticated religion and that educated gentlemen enmeshed in the English web of class interest were unable to supply it. They lost the pioneers, as the leading modern denominations are losing the labouring man, and for much the same reasons. The wonder is that the Anglican church, as a rural church, survived at all.[48]

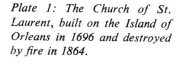

Redpath Library, McGill University

Plate 1: The Church of St. Laurent, built on the Island of Orleans in 1696 and destroyed by fire in 1864.

Plate 2: St. Andrew's Presbyterian Church, Niagara-on-the-Lake, built in 1831, restored 1937 and still in use.

Plate 3: The White House on the Bath Road, Ontario, built in 1793 by William Fairfield, U.E.L., and still occupied by his descendants.

Plate 4: Chief Justice Sir William Campbell's house built on Duke Street in Toronto in 1822, now used as an office.

The 'climate' of the times

Into the area of government a book like this cannot penetrate far: it must limit itself to a glance at the general directions in which old-world methods and institutions were modified by the new environment. Many of these are obvious, and have often been commented on. They include: the clash between ideas of status and ideas of equality, particularly as embodied in legislative council and assembly; the amalgam gradually formed between monarchy, with its overtones of mysticism, ritual and divine right, and self-government, which gives us our present Canadian polity;[49] the running fight between ritualism and informality (e.g. Sergeants-at-arms and the panoply of monarchical splendour on the opening of the legislature, plus homespun members, some barely literate); the difficulties of translating local experience into law and action when filtered through a Colonial Office some thousands of miles away and that by sailing ship; the opportunities for jobbery and favouritism which such a situation presented; the contrast between the relative efficiency and intelligence of public-service traditions obtaining in Great Britain and the slipshod methods and second-rate personnel which had to be accepted in the colonies; the regrets which this contrast often provoked over the lack of an aristocracy; and the queer fish who often turned up in public places of importance. As an early governor said, referring to such situations:—"It was with difficulty that persons could be obtained to accept the office of Judge. In the Eastern District, the duty was discharged by Country Gentlemen. In the Western, as characters of this description were not to be obtained, the appointment was offered to some respectable Merchants, but they excused themselves. . . ."[50] "Gentlemen came out much obliged to their friends at home for good Places."[51]

This mixture of traditional attachment and circumscribed but independent localism often boiled over:—

"Cheniquy got enraged, asked Mr. Jackson, 'if he was not ashamed to call the Governor a damned Rascal?' 'Recollect,' said he,' 'that you are speaking of the King's Representative.' 'Damn the King and him too, what have we to expect from either of them? I have asked for no favours since I have been here, nor do I intend to ask for any.' 'If you make use of such language,' said Mr. Cheniquy, 'I will leave the room.' 'Leave it and be damned,' said Mr. Jackson, 'I care as little for you as I do for the Governor or his master.' Mr. Cheniquy left the room."[52]

In those times the punitive functions of government were

conducted in the spirit of the dark days of old, scarcely touched by modern humanitarianism. Jails were public horrors, criminals were still exposed in the stocks and many were the offences for which death could be and was imposed—one of the amateur judges referred to above sentenced a poor fellow to death for having stolen a watch (the man proved innocent, but since he was already hanged, that was small consolation to him).[53] Executions were public and they were public shows. As late as 1859, there were still eleven capital offences.[54] Yet there are a few signs of severity slowly being mitigated. It is true that since provincial courts did not have recourse to the convenient sentence of transportation the infamous banishment statute was passed instead,[55] but on the other hand, by the same Act, the penalty of branding was, except for manslaughter, abolished. The most horrible of all punishments, the medley of mutilations reserved for traitors, continued on the books but the rigour of the law, authorities agree, was more terrifying on paper than in practice. In the treason trials of 1812, symbolical nicks were made in the limbs of those about to be hanged, drawn and quartered, but the judge was graciously pleased to direct that the victim's entrails be not burned before their still living eyes, so something had been gained.

The climate of the times also comes out clearly in other matters. Take the two relatively minor points of slavery and duelling. When an attempt was made in 1804 to abolish slavery (of which there had never been much and which had not gone beyond domestic slavery), familiar Southern lines of argument were resorted to. A compromise had to be made, "securing the property already obtained upon condition that an immediate stop should be put to importation and that slavery should be gradually abolished."[56] Duels, too, were still accepted as a matter of course among 'men of honour'. The Clerk of the Council, Mr. Small, killed the Attorney-General of the Province, Mr. White, in a duel, January 1800, "having reason to suspect that the Attorney-General had propagated a report reflecting in the strongest manner on the character of Mrs. Small."[57] Mr. Small, probably because he was a 'gentleman', was acquitted, justice still having fairly close linkage to class.[58] Duelling lingered on in Upper Canada, becoming less and less frequent, until mid-century.

There is an easy, perhaps too easy, explanation of pioneer crudity and harshness, in whatever rank of society — the lack of education. To this, there is abundant testimony. "Throughout all Canada, there is no public library, except in Quebec, and this is small and consists mostly of French books. . . ."[59]

A university "is very much wanted in Canada, where education is at a low ebb. . . ."[60] For the few, a partial solution was to be found in John Strachan's famous 'school for the sons of gentlemen' opened in Cornwall in 1804. Strachan, a Scottish Episcopalian by paternal descent and a Presbyterian by usage, had come to Canada in 1799 and in Kingston, where for a time he conducted a private school for the Cartwrights, had sized things up. Result: Presbyterian doctrine "not much in demand while the Church of England, on the contrary, has good prizes in possession, and splendid ones in remainder."[61] Secondary result: Strachan strikes for the prizes and becomes an Anglican clergyman. His percipience duly found its reward: pupils, many of whom were destined to become important public men; ecclesiastical advancement; life one long, highly enjoyable battle with 'non-conformist' opponents; and a permanent place, if a somewhat peculiar reputation, in Canadian History.

It was to be many years before even the 'sons of gentle-man' were adequately supplied with schools and longer still before ordinary people had any at all of consequence. "The lack of schools and other privileges . . . was felt most keenly by them as their children were of an age to require schooling and society. . . . My father always thought that his father made a mistake in moving into this country."[62] The Hinman family, of whom the remarks are made, were a type quite common in early Upper Canada. They migrated from New England in 1799 and settled near Colborne, where they were neighbours of another American family one day to be prominent in Canadian life, the Masseys. They were specimens of those self-respecting, self-reliant immigrants of pure English stock who came in from the old colonies, not because they were loyalists, but because they were settlers who found political allegiance as between Congress and King largely a matter of indifference: were they not all the same people? "Few emigrants bent their course this way, till they were convinced of the civil government being well established, and upon a constitution happily adapted to the minds of the people, since which numbers of respectable inhabitants have come in from the different States. Some of whom have come in their waggons quite from North Carolina. . . ."[63] Such settlers, accustomed to the schools and books of their native provinces, found it hard to accept prevailing Canadian conditions of ignorance. Yet testimony to these is endless. The inhabitants say "that the rising generation is returning to barbarism" laments Governor Simcoe in urging the case for the establishment of local educational institutions. The school followed in the wake of the American pioneer:

was it not to be supplied to the King's subjects?[64] In Simcoe's time, the day on which democratic education would be available for British North America and acceptable to all its people was still distant.

How backward could a backward province be? One rough test lies in 'the fashions'. Here is Kingston high society putting its best foot forward at a ball in 1804:—

"Among the ladies, that is, the young ones, the present exaggerated Grecian costume was further exaggerated, with the addition of cropped heads, and waists between the shoulders. Some of their elders . . . rejoiced in imitation court dresses of half a century before: long waisted stiff silk gowns, open in front, with lace . . . aprons; high-heeled shoes, and their powdered hair rolled over huge toupees stuffed with wool. . . . Some of the younger men were cropped, and wore no powder; some of the elders wore bob-wigs, most of them had their hair tied in long queues. . . . Some beaux had large bunches of black ribbons at the knees of their small clothes, others buckles; their upper garments were no less dissimilar, some had swallow-tailed coats, others the broad skirts of the days of William III."[65]

The broad skirts of the days of King William III, 1689-1703, just over a century previous! Fancy even an 'elder' of to-day wearing clothes one hundred years 'behind the times'! But then, the same elders, we are told, "at an early lunch given on the launch of a vessel . . . with our leading men present, all got furiously drunk before noon." Drunk or sober, they knew the difference between class and class and how to keep 'their inferiors' in their places:— "It now appears strange (1869) to look back on smart evening parties given in the attics of one-story houses, or second stories over shops little better. . . . Public balls or 'assemblies' were select, and the families of those who sold at retail . . . were blackballed if presented."[66]

The backwardness, ignorance and snobbishness make a disagreeable picture but it was not entirely unrelieved. Newspapers began to spring up as soon as the province was constituted. In the rising centres a few people managed to give their children some education. The 'circuit-riders', however derided they might be, impressed on the people who heard them, after the manner of Protestantism everywhere, the necessity of enough learning for Bible reading. Inherited energy, with its concomitant of prosperity, brought in similar influences; thus in 1806, there was organized at York "The Upper Canada Agricultural and Commercial Society."[67] The best proof that things were on the mend and that the province was not to become a land of peasants is the testimony to its rapid improvement. ". . . Round the whole Bay (of Quinte) [it is] so thick settled that their improvements already meet, and form the appearance of a beautiful, old-settled country." This, for ten years of work, was impressive. "Orchards are in great forwardness for the age of the settlement, some of which already bear fruit—peaches, cherries and currants are plenty among all the first settlers."[68]

Not only that: when they were clearing along the Niagara River banks, about two miles above the falls, they discovered a well which emitted "a gas of inflammable air, which when confined in a pipe and a flame applied to it will boil water of a tea-kettle in 15 minutes."[69]

Still further proof of the march of 'civilization' is supplied by the rapid rate at which the gifts of nature were being destroyed. The carrier pigeon at first 'darkened the sky', but the pioneer soon put a stop to that. When the province was first instituted, the Atlantic salmon was still migrating in vast numbers and spawning in every stream below Niagara Falls. But trees recklessly slashed down allowed the soil to be eroded into the streams so that spawning grounds and salmon began to grow fewer. Extinction of pigeon and salmon proved beyond the powers of the first generation of pioneers[70] but their successors in due course accomplished it. The last salmon, once, according to some reports, as plentiful as in British Columbia, were caught just after Confederation.

In this first generation of the new province, everyone had the optimism of the pioneer, which not even sordid jobbery and other aspects of misgovernment could dampen. Everyone had the optimism of the pioneer and also his cupidity and his shortsightedness. For both qualities the little capital, York, offered a display counter. One of the major occupations of its leading citizens was 'land-grabbing'. Chief Justices Elmsley and Powell and Solicitor General Grey accumulated from twenty to fifty thousand acres of the public lands each.[71] An executive councillor named Shaw received not only the 6,000 acres granted to all councillors but 1,200 each for all the members of his family, eight persons, or a grand total of 15,600 acres.[72]

Such expansive views of private interests were not reflected in concern for the public good. A plan made for York in 1789, before it was chosen as the capital, provided a public square with eight principal streets leading off it, each ninety-six feet wide. This plan, which would have given the metropolis of Toronto streets as wide as those enjoyed by most American

towns,[73] disappeared, to be replaced by a dismal rectangular
cluttering: it was considered 'too ambitious'. In 1818, provision was made for a broad promenade along the whole water-
front. The trustees of the scheme were John Beverley Robinson, William Allen and other leading citizens. "The trustees
failed to hold and (eventually) the railways succeeded in
acquiring." The same lack of vision has marked most of the
subsequent period down to the present. In 1852, a plan was
made for a "Road or Esplanade 100 feet wide, along Toronto's
harbour front." "This design seems too ornamental" is scrawled
across the face of the plan. Nothing was done about it and it
was at this period that "the railways succeeded in acquiring."
"The civic negative was assuming the virtues of habit." In
1911, the city boggled at the plan for drives and boulevards
along the Humber. In 1955, it was busily filling up its remaining ravines. Thus a site which originally had many assets of
natural beauty was turned into a vast sprawling mass of self-
strangulation, with little distinctive about it but its noise. And
hardly a man among its 'up and coming' citizens would not
call this century and three-quarters of narrow-mindedness
'progress'.[74]

Red River

'Little York' was immensely 'far west' in those days, while
Amherstburg and the Detroit River settlements were on the
outer edge. But there was a 'West' still further west, one quite
beyond the horizon of all but a tiny handful of people: this
was the little knot of French, half-breeds, Indians and fur-
traders clinging to the banks of the Red River in what is
now Manitoba. In the early nineteenth century it was to be
reinforced—and divided—by Lord Selkirk's Scots. Until they
came, the fur-trader was king of the castle. To the Nor'Westers' contempt, the Hudson's Bay Company had settled establishments—in one of them "the chief building two storeys high
and covered with lead." Lead, in the bush, five hundred miles
from the coast! "All their chimneys are deep narrow holes,
and . . . the heat goes principally up the chimneys, there is
neither a Canadian or Swedish stove used in all the country."[75]
Once more, apparently, old-countrymen were demonstrating
that art in which the world over they have been adept, the art
of making themselves uncomfortable.

The Nor'Westers were after furs, not establishments, and
by any method. "Jan. 1, 1802, I treated my people with two
gallons of high wine . . . and before sunrise both sexes . . .
were intoxicated. . . . Feb. 16, 1804: (after more 'high wine')

Grand Gueule stabbed Perdrix Blanc with a knife in six places; the latter in fighting with his wife, fell in the fire and was almost roasted, but had strength enough left, despite his wounds, to bite her nose off. . . ." Thus Alexander Henry,[76] as respectable a citizen as most other Montrealers when he was at home.

The route from Newfoundland to the Red River is three thousand miles long. In the period of our present chapter, all along that vast length of water at whose opposite ends these two regions lay, spots and dots of humanity were assailing the bush. Down on the Atlantic, the codfish were hauled into the dories. In Upper Canada the trees were falling. On the prairies, the guns blazed in the buffalo hunt. At some points, as in Nova Scotia and Lower Canada, the forest had been pushed back and discernible local communities had sprung up. At others, the process had not much more than begun. But everywhere there was energy and on the part of some, a glimpse of a vision—a new British North America to take the place of the old, a new home in an abundant land.

Notes to Chapter 12.
1. Halifax was founded in 1749. The Red River settlements of the Earl of Selkirk began just over sixty years later.
2. For Cape Breton see especially Mrs. Charles Archibald, *Early Scottish Settlers in Cape Breton* (Nova Scotia Historical Society Collections, 1914), p. xviii, and Charles W. Dunn, *Highland Settler: A Portrait of the Scottish Gael in Nova Scotia* (Toronto, 1953) from which book the Gaelic verse given above is taken. My acknowledgements to Col. L. F. Grant of Kingston for the anecdote about the Gut of Canso.
3. My informant is Professor Andrew Clark, of 'Island' descent and a student of the Island.
4. Information and documents furnished by Mr. H. G. Farish of Montreal.
5. The last printed account available, about 1930, stated that the Farishes had contributed 127 years of doctoring to Yarmouth.
6. See Beamish Murdoch, *History of Nova Scotia* (Halifax, 1867), Vol. III, p. 61.
7. J. B. Brebner, *New England's Outpost* (New York, 1927).
8. Henry Alline's seductions of the faithful are still remembered in 'the Valley'. A correspondent writes: "Out of the heat engendered by quarrels, comes the unbalanced and fantastic movement led by Henry Alline. . . The first Baptist ordination took place in Yarmouth county in a back country kitchen when two or three fanatical believers in immersion as necessary to salvation set apart one of their own number as a preacher of their perverted gospel" . . . . "the harm caused by the insane fanaticism of these New Light preachers. . . . "
9. E. M. Saunders, *The Life and Times of the Rev. John Wiswall, M.A., a Loyalist Clergyman, 1731-1821* (N.S.H.S. Collections, 1908), p. 52.
10. A not uncommon phenomenon in the old colonies during the eighteenth century, where a kind of colonial 'Oxford Movement'

carried some of the Puritan clergy into the ranks of the Church of England.

11. And which appears to be no more understood by some of its British followers to-day than it was in the eighteenth century. For example, Mr. Lydekker of the S.P.G., the author of the biography of Bishop Inglis, speculated as to whether an American bishopric would not have prevented the Revolution; in other words, put out the fire by pouring oil on it.

12. Private family correspondence shown to the present writer.

13. See for this type of social analysis the various books of Professor S. D. Clark of Toronto; also William E. Mann, *Sect, Cult and Church in Alberta* (Toronto, 1955).

14. The French Port Royal became Annapolis in 1710, and the Highland pioneers had taken up most of Cape Breton by 1828; settlement was at its height well within these dates.

15. Murdoch, op. cit., Vol. III, p. 78.

16. Ibid., p. 132.

17. *Winslow Papers, 1776-1826*, ed. Rev. W. O. Raymond (Saint John, 1901), p. 226: *Edward Winslow to his Wife*, Halifax, Sept. 20th, 1784.

18. For the press-gang in Nova Scotia, see Murdoch, op. cit., Vol. III, pp. 241, 244, etc. Press warrants were granted by the provincial authorities under provincial statute of 32 Geo. II and were only for a limited time. It took a good deal, however, to restrain British naval officers from arbitrary seizures.

19. W. M. Brown, *Recollections of Old Halifax* (N.S.H.S. Collections, 1908), read before the Society in 1895, p. 75.

20. The title of the liveliest portrait of a Canadian city so far drawn—by Thomas Raddall (Toronto, 1948).

21. Brown, loc. cit.

22. Ibid., p. 19.

23. Harry Piers, *Artists in Nova Scotia* (N.S.H.S. Collections, 1914). p. 101.

24. Murdoch, op. cit., Vol. III, p. 215. In 1819 the even better Province House was occupied.

25. This was the standard explanation for the new province until 1933 when Marion Gilroy published "The Partition of Nova Scotia, 1784" in the December issue of the *Canadian Historical Review* and undertook to show that the separate government was a reflection of the British post-Revolutionary policy of 'divide and rule'. Chester Martin has given the weight of his authority to this and in his *Foundations of Canadian Nationhood* (Toronto, 1955) makes William Knox, who he thinks did so much to provoke the Revolution, the author of this policy. But Knox became provincial agent for New Brunswick, so the two influences met. There is no doubt about the anxiety of the new settlers for a separate government.

26. The Bayham Baptist Church, near Port Burwell, Ontario, was founded about the turn of the century by people from the Maritimes among whom was numbered the ancestor of Thomas Edison, a man who had been sentenced by the republicans to be hanged; Stuart Ivison and Fred Rosser, *The Baptists in Upper and Lower Canada* (Toronto, 1956), p. 119. This Loyalist Edison's grandson, Sam, father of Thomas, was on the rebel side in 1837. He fled and, as a result, Thomas Edison was born an American.

27. See p. 243.

28. The hotels, which sometimes began with a flourish as accommodation for 'the gentry', gradually sagged down to the ordinary continental norm, overwhelmed, as often as not, by the vulgarities of democracy.

29. *Bulletin des Recherches Historiques*, Vol. 38, p. 263.

30. Ibid., Vol. 43, p. 33.
31. Quebec *Mercury,* Aug. 18th, 1818.
32. For an example of how indecision determines allegiance, see Michael Smith, *A Geographical View of the Province of Upper Canada* (Hartford, Conn., 1813) as quoted in Gerald M. Craig, *Early Travellers in the Canadas, 1791-1867* (Toronto, 1956), pp. 50 ff. The passage describes Americans in Canada during the War of 1812.
33. Roger Stevens of Attsford, Vt., who later settled in Upper Canada, in joining the King's Forces had his property confiscated "with the full knowledge of Roger, Sr. (his father), who actually received a fee for assisting the American authorities"—Ivison and Rosser, op. cit. p. 145. See also p. 152 for another family separation.
34. Some names from a Prince Edward County graveyard: De Wate, Vangesen, Ackerman, Minacher, Vandusen.
35. The eighth generation.
36. See p. 202.
37. The average English-speaking Canadian of to-day would be more at home with the people of his great-great-grandfather's day than he would, or is, with his contemporary fellow-citizens whose mother tongue is French. See also pp. 443, 444.
38. Both delightfully preserved to-day by New York State.
39. Americans avidly buy up Canadian antique furniture, a newspaper dispatch tells us: Canadians themselves evince no interest in it.
40. A brother of Sir John Beverley Robinson married one of the Jarvis girls. Every group of any permanence tends to become 'a family'.
41. Public Archives of Canada, Series Q, Vol. 305, p. 189, *Judge Thorpe,* Dec. 1st, 1806.
42. It is only fair to state that Robinson afterward learned a tolerant respect for the merits of the sectaries. See Maj.-Gen. C. W. Robinson, *The Life of Sir John Beverley Robinson* (London, 1904), p. 178, where the Chief Justice pays a handsome compliment to the services of "the dissenters' preachers" in inculcating "the doctrines and truths common to most Christian denominations".
43. Ivison and Rosser, op. cit.; Julia Jarvis, *Three Generations of Robinsons* (privately printed, 1953).
44. See the present writer's *Colony to Nation* (Toronto and London, 1957), for fuller reference to Methodism.
45. See also pp. 97 ff, and Chapter 28.
46. R. A. Preston, *A Clash in St. Paul's Churchyard, Historic Kingston* (Kingston Historical Society, October 1956), p. 33.
47. And on a minor portion of another in the neighbouring countryside the present writer now lives. The area is designated locally as 'The Mile Square'. Years ago it was divided into farms and nowadays some of these are being covered with ordinary suburban houses. To the occupants of these the rural Loyalist civilization that preceded them is as dead as that of the Indian.
48. It would not have done had it not been for the coming in the next period (after 1820) of thousands of immigrants from England and Northern Ireland who had never lost their connection with it.
49. See pp. 282 and 291, 292.
50. Public Archives, Series Q, Vol. 280, pt. 1, p. 250, *Simcoe-Dundas* Apr. 2nd, 1794.
51. Ibid.
52. Public Archives, *Report,* 1892, *Affidavit of Titus Simons,* Feb. 2nd, 1807.
53. James A. Roy, *Kingston, The King's Town* (Toronto, 1952), p. 32.
54. J. E. Jones, *Pioneer Crimes and Punishments in Toronto and the Home District* (Toronto, 1924), p. 7.
55. 40 Geo. II, c. 1, 1800: it was under this Act that Robert Gourlay

was later banished. It is said that of all others, banishment was the sentence most dreaded. The penalty for unlawful return was death.

56. Public Archives, Series Q, Vol. 279, pt. 2, pp. 335, 49.
57. Ibid., Vol. 287, pt. 1, p. 104.
58. Sir John Beverley Robinson, C.J., later said that the practice was to acquit "when all was fair".
59. Duke de la Rochefoucault-Liancourt, *Travels through the United States of North America, the Country of the Iroquois, Upper Canada, in the Years 1795, 1796, 1797; with an Authentic Account of Lower Canada* (London, 1799).
60. Public Archives, *Report*, 1890, Note 9.
61. Roy, op. cit., p. 5.
62. Smith Hinman "Biography and Sketch of the Hinman Family, 1649-1905" (private MSS.)
63. *The Correspondence of Lieutenant Governor John Graves Simcoe* (ed. Brig.-Gen. E. A. Cruikshank, Ontario Historical Society, 1925), Vol. III, p. 193, "A Letter from a Gentleman in New York", Nov. 20th, 1794.
64. Ibid., p. 350, to the Bishop of Quebec, Apr. 30th, 1795. Simcoe very penetratingly points out to the bishop how unlikely it is that clergymen brought from England will fit into a pioneer environment and urges a university in order that men may be trained on the spot.
65. George Storrow Brown, "Montreal Fifty Years Ago" in *The New Dominion Monthly*, 1869-1870.
66. Ibid.
67. Public Archives, Series Q, Vol. 305, p. 96.
68. *Simcoe Correspondence*, op. cit., Vol. III, p. 191.
69. Ibid.
70. The first conservation measures date from 1807. They were quite ineffectual.
71. *Durham's Report* (London, 1902), p. 160.
72. G. C. Paterson, *Land Settlement in Upper Canada, 1783-1848* (Toronto, 1921), p. 63.
73. London is the only Ontario city that has streets of these American dimensions.
74. Details from K. M. Lizars, *The Valley of the Humber, 1615-1913* (Toronto, 1913).
75. Public Archives, *Report*, 1886, Miles Macdonell, the Glengarry (Upper Canada) man in charge of Selkirk's settlers at the Nelson Encampment, 1812.
76. *Journals of Alexander Henry and of David Thompson, 1797-1814* (ed. E. Coues, London, 1892).

13: The War of 1812,
constructive conflict

WAR, SURELY, IS THE DEEPEST EXPERIENCE a society can have. While most Canadian wars have been fought
on other people's soil and far away from home, yet in the view
of the English branch of the Canadian people, whatever others
may have thought, they have always been wars of high moral
purpose. From the defeat of the Armada in 1588 to the defeat
of the Communists in Korea, the tradition has been continuous.
Philip of Spain was succeeded as the threat to liberty by
Louis XIV, Louis XIV by Napoleon, Napoleon by the German Empire and Hitler, and Hitler by the present Russian
autocracy. The average English Canadian does not know his
history well, but he invariably feels that he fights, not for any
interested motive but for ultimate objectives, of which the
clearest to him is "freedom." In this respect, he would, if
informed only slightly beyond the average, probably draw a
contrast between the wars mentioned and the great mid-
eighteenth century wars with France which made Canada British, for the Conquest in which they resulted might cause him
certain twinges of conscience.[1]

There is one war which gathers up all the moral fervour of
other conflicts, all the convictions of justification, and unites
to it the vast sense of the heroic, the tide of passion, which
arises from the attempt to defend one's own hearth and home
against a would-be conqueror, and that is the War of 1812.
The place of this contest in Canadian history goes far beyond
the military events involved: it goes to the roots of Canadian
life. As a factor in the building of the Canadian nation, it is
hard to see how it can be outranked by other experiences. For
two years and a half Canadians of both races struggled with all
the power that they possessed against an enemy who seemed
to them determined to possess himself of their soil, who landed
on their shores, carried off their animals, burned their houses,

destroyed their towns and caused their young men to perish in battle.

The American attempt to conquer Canada

While the American effort to conquer Canada is not to be compared with the European wars of conquest either in scale, in destructiveness or in ferocity, yet it was of the same species, an attempt at conquest, and an attempt at the conquest of a peaceful people, most of whom considered the invaders blood of their blood and flesh of their flesh and who were therefore in double anguish at the unnaturalness of the onslaught. The War of 1812, turning the people of the republic into foes, completed the separation which the War of the Revolution had begun, and confirmed Canadians in that determination on which their separate nationhood more than anything else has been built, the determination not to be 'Americans'. Without it, the long decades of peace might have served to heal the breach which the Revolution had created and to have made even Loyalists look with favour on the new state their old countrymen were building. With it, Canadians were confirmed in their separate allegiance; it had furnished them with an enemy and ever afterward they were quick to detect hostility in his glance. An event which goes far to explain the existence of two English-speaking peoples side by side cannot, therefore, be lightly passed over.[2]

The two and a half years of war had their setting in a much longer period of disturbed relations. From the end of the Seven Years' War in 1763, there had only been a few years of good relationships between mother country and colonies until the revolutionary troubles began. The first blood was split in 1775 and peace was not made until 1783. Thereafter there were the bickerings arising out of the peace. Great Britain's retention of the 'western posts' and the difficult adjustment of the relations between Americans, British and Indians kept the western frontier uneasy. Everybody expected that the American expedition against the Indians which culminated in the Battle of Fallen Timbers, 1794, would lead to war.[3] After Jay's Treaty settled the problem of the West, the French wars drove fresh wedges in between Great Britain and her old colonies; and from their commencement until the Americans took the plunge and declared war in June 1812 there were few periods in which responsible people were not predicting the outbreak of an American war. The war was, therefore, but the military expression of a state of hostilities which had long existed.

Despite the imminence of war between the two English peoples, there was much going and coming across the boundary and communications north and south rapidly improved. On the American side, settlement caught up with and passed settlement on the Canadian side, and as a result of the rush westward, a stream of American immigrants entered Canada. People from New Hampshire and Vermont came into the Eastern Townships. At first these were men whose sympathies had been on the British side and who now took the opportunity to reforge their old allegiance;[4] but within a few years, political considerations apparently ceased to have much bearing and the major point became good, cheap land. The story was the same in Upper Canada. Simcoe's attempts to ensure that the people who came in would have their hearts in the right place did not avail much in the rush for the fine lands of the western peninsula and in the face of his own anxiety for settlers, so that in a short time the original Loyalist element there consisted of little more than a fringe along Lake Erie. Egerton Ryerson estimated the population of Upper Canada in 1792 as about 12,000,[5] at about 50,000 in 1800 and about 75,000 in 1812. The original 6,000 or 8,000 Loyalists could not in a single generation have accounted for more than, say, 20,000 of this total. Authorities concur with the estimate of a contemporary who considered that in 1812 about one-fifth of the whole population, whatever it was (and his estimate went up to 136,000 for this),[6] were of old-country origin, one-fifth Loyalist, and the remaining three-fifths ordinary Americans. Yet to call people who might come from almost any state, be of any creed and range the whole spectrum of political belief 'ordinary Americans' does not get us far, for the type had not yet hardened and probably most of them had been born into the British allegiance, which they accepted with little difference in their attitude from that of the Loyalists themselves.

This American immigration was one of the commonest topics of comment at the time. Nearly everyone in the governing class (and in the little colony the term was a reality) viewed it with misgivings, many with alarm. War with the old colonies seemed inevitable and here was the province of Upper Canada being filled up with American citizens who were bringing their society, their religion, and presumably their political allegiance, along with them. Here was 'infiltration' on a grand scale. However, in characteristic frontier fashion, while everybody talked about the problem, no one did anything about it, especially since there were those among the governing class who had lands to sell to the infiltrators.

A cool view of the situation would have forecast what actually happened, namely, that only a small minority of the newcomers would be actively disaffected. Cruikshank[7] publishes a list of three hundred and twenty-two names of persons "who did voluntarily withdraw from the province without license during the late war." He also gives numerous citations from the military of both sides during the war which indicate that the people of a given district were, or were not, loyal. But these simply add up to this, that ordinary plain people were desperately afraid of incurring the wrath of the armed men who came among them. Moreover, the unprovoked aggression with its accompaniments of suffering and destruction must have turned many a former American into an Upper Canadian. "About thirteen years after Moses Hinman came to Canada the war between England and the United States began, when he cast in his lot with his adopted country against his old home, sending two of his three sons to help defend Canada. . . ."[8]

The declaration of war must have caused thousands of Moses Hinmans to examine their political consciences; and the two facts that no large-scale acts of treason occurred and that the war was prosecuted to a victorious conclusion show that American origin was not the danger that it had been supposed to be. It was not the American tradition that was destined to prevail in British North America but the Loyalist American tradition.

French Canada and the war

Another group of people, to judge from the past, might also have been expected to contain persons who would give aid and comfort to the enemy, the French-Canadian *habitants*. There were many such found among them in 1775 and again in 1795: why should they not be present in 1812?

And yet they were not. Governor Craig and Mr. Rylands had assumed that the French would be disloyal, as had many another Englishman. If Craig and Rylands had been allowed to carry on indefinitely, their methods probably would have created disloyalty, but on Craig's recall and Ryland's supersession, it was loyalty, not disloyalty, that made itself evident. Craig had warred against the classes that probably would have been loyal despite him: men who are the heirs of their society, as the rising intelligentsia were, are not likely to wish to see it conquered by strangers, and in this case by strangers whose resemblance to the original conquerors was more than skin deep. If trouble were to be expected, the place to look for it in 1812 would be among the country people, for that is where it had occurred before.

It did not occur there again. The *habitants* did not welcome the Americans as liberators. They did not give them aid and comfort. On the contrary, when summoned to arms, they answered readily, a sharp contrast to 1775, and fought bravely against the invader. Why the difference?

One explanation lies in mere time. In thirty-seven years even simple country people had been able to work out the situation. They could see that not all *les anglais* were the same *anglais* and they were quite capable of sizing up the two groups and of deciding that they were better off with the devil they knew than with the devil they knew not. Again, the Americans were friends of French revolutionaries, tarred with their atheistic brush, and the clergy had made sure of attitudes on that point. Further, there had been many years of prosperity under the British during which the settlements had multiplied and re-multiplied, thus giving content to everyone, removing the incentive towards change.[9] Possibly still another reason lay in the appointment of Sir George Prevost as governor: his healing personality had already begun to make itself felt by the time war was declared.

Whatever the explanation, French Canada's attitude in the War of 1812 was entirely different from what it had been previously. It is true that there was no affectionate coming together of the races in the face of the common peril and that the racial strife, at least as it was reflected by the bickerings in the Legislature, went on uninterruptedly, but that did not alter the fact that French Canadians fought, and fought well. Everyone has heard of Colonel de Salaberry and of the victories at Lacolle and Chateauguay won by him and the French Canadians under him. These feats of arms have come down in memory and have coloured the mentality of French-speaking Canadians from that day to this. As Chapais well puts it:—

"It was the day of Chateauguay, a day which shines with so much lustre in our history. It would no doubt be excessive to attribute to it the proportions of a grand battle but its strategic results give it a capital importance. By the tactics of the commander and the intrepidity of the soldiers, it rightfully marks a glorious date for our race. For it was essentially a French-Canadian victory. It is ours and no one can deprive us of it. Chateauguay was our reply to the imputations of Craig, of Ryland and of Sewell. Chateauguay was our revenge. Chateauguay was the affirmation of our undeniable loyalty and of our ardent patriotism. Chateauguay was the heroic illustration of the national mentality which was being slowly formed."[10]

For both Canadas the war was essentially defensive. No one in his right mind ever thought of any significant invasion of American territory, still less of conquest.[11] This same sense of the justice of the war lent power to the defenders' arm, while the opposite, the uneasy prickings of conscience which came to so many Americans, correspondingly weakened the American effort. The war party in the republic was frequently assailed not only for fighting an unnecessary war but for the afflictions it brought to an unoffending people of the same race and blood. No people can fight at its best under these circumstances, certainly not Anglo-Saxons. This psychological handicap must have counted in the extraordinary ineptitude shown by the Americans. Not only lost battle after lost battle, but generalship abysmally low in quality, poor supply arrangements, utter lack of intelligent over-all plan, inefficiency, desertion, cowardice, marked all but the closing months of the war.

The present author has written elsewhere, half in jest, that the War of 1812 was the most satisfactory of wars in that both sides won it. Both sides have ever after claimed to win it, it is true, but on further review, the writer can come to no other conclusion than that the Americans did not win it. It is true that the peace represented a draw, none of the issues for which the war was fought being settled—none even mentioned —but if attempting to conquer another country and failing ("conquest would be a mere matter of marching," Jefferson is reputed to have said) is victory, then the Americans were victorious. If invading the soil of a peaceful neighbour some eleven times and being ignominiously thrown out just as many, be victory, then again the Americans were victorious. But since Canadians, of both races, were as the modern phrase goes, 'on the receiving end' of these eleven invasions and since they fought with all their might to expel the invader, and fought successfully, since to them the war represented a gigantic American failure to conquer them, they can hardly be blamed for considering it a smashing American defeat.

That, at least, is what French-speaking militiamen seemed to think with their parody of "Yankee Doodle":—

> "Les premiers coups que je tirai
> Sur ces pauvres rebelles
> Cinque cents de leurs amis
> Ont perdu la cervelle.
> Yankee Doodle, tiens-toi bien
> Entends bien la musique
> C'est la gigue du Canadien
> Qui surprende l'Amérique."[12]

The war turns Loyalists into Canadians

In its details, the war was like other border wars and it has left behind it the border tradition of warfare. Those who have written about it have, until recently, not been much interested in its large aspects, more particularly in its over-all strategy, so much as in the day-to-day events, the battles, invasions, raids, burnings, and at sea, the two-ship duels (which had as little naval significance as such events very well could). Interest seems to have been similar to that of the small boy in a scuffle: "How many times did he hit you? How many times did you hit him?" When neighbours fight each other across an arbitrary boundary line, some such attitude necessarily develops—it received its expression once and for all in the medieval Welsh border warfare, when Taffy was discovered to be a Welshman and (therefore) a thief, who came over to 'our' side of the border merely to steal a leg of beef! Most of the books on the War of 1812 are careful to explain that while in this engagement or in that 'we' lost so many men, 'they' lost so many more, as if victory rested on the mere arithmetic of casualty lists. The apparent lack of plan in each American campaign joined to the repeated raids destructive of little else than private property accentuated this scalp-taking aspect of war. And since the weight of the raiding fell on the Loyalist settlements, the earlier fund of hatred was multiplied, providing sufficient store to last for many generations.

Consider the following Loyalist experiences, for example, the one from the Revolutionary War, the other from the War of 1812:—

"My grandfather, Jacob Bowman . . . was surprised at night, while his wife was sick, by a party of rebels, and . . . taken prisoner; his house was pillaged of every article, except the bed on which his sick wife lay, and that they stripped of all but one blanket. Half an hour after my grandfather was marched off, his youngest child was born. . . . Their cattle and grain were all taken away. My father, Peter Bowman, . . . was only eleven years old. As the pillage was at night, he had neither coat nor shoes; he had to cut and draw his firewood half a mile on a hand-sleigh to keep his sick mother from freezing; this he did barefooted. . . ."

This particular family escaped to the British lines, along with Nellises, Secords and others, all well-known Canadian names.

The other narrative is that of Mrs. Amelia Harris, daughter of Samuel Ryerse (or Ryerson), the uncle of Egerton Ryerson and founder of Port Ryerse on Lake Erie. Mrs. Harris was then a girl of twelve and her mother lately a widow:—

"On the following morning, the 15th of May [1814], as my
Mother and myself were at breakfast, the dogs made an unusual barking. I went to the door to discover the cause.
When I looked up I saw the hillside and the fields as far as
the eye could reach covered with American soldiers. They
had landed at Patterson's Creek, burned the Mills and village
of Port Dover, and then marched to Ryerse. Two men
stepped from the ranks, selected some large chips, came into
the room where we were standing, and took the coals from
the hearth, without speaking. My mother knew instinctively
what they were going to do. She went out and asked to see
the commanding officer. A gentleman rode up to her and
said he was the person she asked for. She entreated him to
spare her property and said that she was a widow with a
young family. He answered her civilly and respectfully and
regretted that his orders were to burn, but that he would
spare the house, which he did, and said in justification that
the Buildings were used as barracks and the mill furnished
flour for British troops. Very soon we saw [a] column of
dark smoke arise from every building and of what at early
morn had been a prosperous homestead, at noon there remained only smouldering ruins."[13]

Mrs. Harris's mother was from New York City. After the
war it is not surprising that she reconciled herself to the country
of her exile—"her husband's grave was there". Put the two
stories together and multiply them and it is not hard to see
on what foundation the Province of Ontario was built.[14]

Nor is it from this angle difficult to appreciate why the military virtues of the Canadian militia, in both provinces, so much
excelled those of the American. American militiamen were
exhorted through the media of some of the most grotesque
proclamations that surely have ever been issued by generals
to their troops, in most of which overtones of bad conscience
make themselves heard,[15] while Canadian militiamen were
defending their hearths and homes. As a result they took their
place on honourable terms alongside the British regulars and
the regular 'provincial corps' formed in the colonies, though
it was the latter two categories of soldiers who did the serious
fighting.[16] The war could not have been conducted without
the professional experience which the British forces contributed
and especially without the supplies that Great Britain furnished.
It would be quite wrong, therefore, to think of it in terms of a
national Canadian effort. In Lower Canada, where one might
assume a repetition of the old French feeling against *les Bastonnois*, those who fought seem to have regarded themselves as
British subjects, rather than *Canadiens*—Colonel de Salaberry

was a British officer—fighting a British war. In Upper Canada, people were barely beginning to think of themselves as Canadians. They were fighting against 'the republicans'. Canadian nationalism came after the war, not before it.

Effects of the war

The effects generally of the war may be thought of as 'short range' and 'long range' in nature. Both are easily traceable. Save in the actual areas of combat and destruction, the most immediate and surprising effect was a considerable access of well-being. It was the same story as has since become familiar in Canadian history: much money poured out to pay for war supplies acted as a powerful propellant to the economy. In Nova Scotia there was prize money and the receipts from the customs duties collected in occupied American territory; these later on helped to build Dalhousie University, as that institution, speaking in stone and bronze, proudly informs the visitor to its campus. In New Brunswick, the shelves of the merchants were "swept clean by the neighbours" in Maine, who became so short of goods, thanks to the British naval blockade, that they came over the line and bought whatever was available. New Brunswick and Maine came as close to being neutral in this strange war as two official combatants could be. Communication does not seem to have been interrupted and there was no suspicion of hostilities on the border. As a result, the New Brunswick Loyalist tradition, not being renewed in blood, is somewhat different from that of Upper Canada: wistful, rather than belligerent. In Lower Canada, there was the immense expenditure of army and navy in Quebec, and the active trading with the enemy which did so much for Montreal. Quebec, like Halifax, has always flourished on war, never more so than in the early nineteenth century. In Montreal there were shrewd rising capitalists like John Molson, who felt no sense of sin in combining patriotism and profits; Molson's second steamboat, the *Swiftsure*, was used as a troop transport as soon as she was launched. "During 1813 and 1814, the Molson vessel made fifty-eight round trips between Montreal and Quebec, mostly under charter to the Quarter-Master General's department."[17] She transported over 8,000 troops. It is possible that this forced draft greatly increased the rate at which steam navigation was developing in Canada.[18]

Montreal was half in the war and half out. It was the professed object of the American campaigns to take it, but only one side of Lake Champlain co-operated in this, the other, the easterly or Vermont side, maintaining the same kind of relationship with Lower Canada as did Maine with New Brunswick, though on a better basis of reciprocity. British troops fighting the Americans on the west or New York side of the lake were fed on food supplied by Americans living on the east side. In return, Montreal middlemen supplied the Vermonters with their necessary imports of manufactured goods. As one American paper observed at the close of the war, Montreal should have erected a monument to President Madison: by making war, he also made Montreal.

Even in Upper Canada, the tale was not too dissimilar, though in that province only one belligerent, not both of them, lent a helping hand. British money touched every point as far west as Michilimackinac. York recovered from its burning, while as for Kingston, the troops and the naval headquarters made it much more prosperous than it had any prospect of being once peace descended upon it. The great ship under construction at the war's end, H.M.S. *St. Lawrence*, 104 guns, is said to have cost over £300,000. Even after peace, the Kingston dockyard was costing £25,000 per year and employing 1,200 labourers.[19] A further bit of evidence of what was going on comes from local tradition. Along the Bath Road between Kingston and Adolphustown are many fine old farm houses, some of them well and truly built of cut stone. A number of them are still occupied by the descendants of the original families,[20] most of whom will tell the inquirer that "this house was built about a hundred and forty years ago": this takes them back close enough to the war to indicate that they represent the war-time prosperity of the farmers adjacent to the great depot, Kingston. Like all other Canadian wars, then, the War of 1812, though fought on Canadian soil, turns out to have been 'a good thing'.

The intermediate effects of the war were plainly visible in the fifteen years following its conclusion. The hostility towards everything American, becoming associated with one group or another, embittered nearly every local problem, more especially in Upper Canada. Three of these problems rose to acute heights—the Methodist question, the marriage question, and the alien problem.

Methodism had come into Upper Canada from the United States and its older ministers were nearly all American born. While none of them had had his loyalty impugned (and one Methodist, James Richardson, afterwards a minister, had served valiantly as Master of H.M.S. *Montreal*, being seriously wounded at Oswego, 1814), it was always easy—and popular—for ultra-loyalists to raise against such men the cry of treason and republicanism. The Methodists, clergy and laity, lay under these malicious imputations for many years, and it was often other clergymen who were foremost in making them. Since the Methodists constituted the largest single denominational sector of the population, it is easy to understand the currents of unrest that such accusations would put into motion all over the province.

The controversy came to two heads, one in 1827 and the other in 1833-1834. The first was occasioned by the publication of Archdeacon Strachan's celebrated "Ecclesiastical Chart" and the accompanying letter, which contained the statement that "the teachers of the different denominations . . . are for the most part from the United States, where they gather their knowledge and form their sentiments; indeed the Methodist teachers are subject to the orders of the Conference of the United States of America, and it is manifest that the Colonial Government [cannot] . . . prevent them from gradually rendering a large portion of the population . . . hostile to our institutions, both civil and religious. . . ." This charge was taken up by a committee of the assembly, which vigorously refuted it.[21] The controversy continued to rage until the Canadian Methodists severed themselves from the American Conference and accepted the oversight of the British, on terms not devoid of humiliation to themselves. Until the Methodists went to these lengths, thousands of loyal subjects lived in the shadow of disloyalty which, in the temper of the time, could mean something close to excommunication.

The question of what ministers had the right to solemnize marriage was an old one. In makeshift British fashion, the right apparently inherent in Anglican clergymen and Catholic priests had been extended as a legislative grant to 'Calvinists': in practice 'Calvinists' were those who held licences to solemnize marriage in a particular locality. But Methodist preachers could not possibly be dubbed 'Calvinists' and so were unable to perform the marriage ceremony. This was another grievance, and one of magnitude. Not until 1831 did a satisfactory Marriage Act become law in Upper Canada. With it may be coupled the "Act for the Relief of Religious Societies," 9 Geo. IV, c. 2, which allowed 'dissenting' groups to form themselves into corporations for the purpose of acquiring and holding property. Arrogance in Church and State being what it was, none of these measures might have been passed any sooner if there had been no war. Yet the spirit engendered by the war so embittered the ultrapatriots of Family Compact and Anglican Church, and the perils of the war so frightened them, including as they did the dreadful vista of democracy and loss of privilege, that it is reasonable to assume their opposition prolonged the period of unsettlement.

The same spirit comes out over the last of these questions, the Alien Question. Were persons born in the colonies before 1783 and who had migrated to British North America after that date still British subjects? Were their children British subjects (a) if born in the United States, (b) if born in British North America? Could any such people hold land, vote, be elected to the Assembly? The embarrassing fact was that tens of thousands of people in Upper Canada found themselves in such a position. It was raised in discussion through a celebrated British court case which appeared to make all those entering the provinces from the United States after 1783 'aliens' and therefore, under the law of the day, to invalidate their titles to their land. If there is any social threat more disturbing than the threat to a man's ownership of his own property, it is hard to imagine what it is, yet thousands of people who had been in the province for over thirty-five years now found themselves under it. Many an original grantee must have died, with his son or even grandson living on the family property. Were all such people to find their titles of dubious value? Efforts were made by the authorities to get the question settled and a despatch from the Colonial Secretary, 1825, specified the terms of an Act which the local assembly should pass and promised its acceptance if it were kept to these terms. Unfortunately the Act was to demand an oath of allegiance. "The whole American population raised their voices in wrath at the insinuation that they were foreigners who required an act of grace to be confirmed in the possession of their property and their privileges."[22] The consequence was that no Act was approved until 1828: for three years the province was in agitation, the Loyalists, whose titles were not involved, against the later Americans. Here was as divisive an issue as could well arise; it arose directly out of the War of 1812 and it had a good deal to do with preparing the soil out of which grew the rebellion of 1837.[23]

The long-range effects of the war are what might be expected: a transmutation of the passions of the day into permanent emotional attitudes. French Canadians found themselves not only accepting their status as British subjects, but asserting it. Upper Canada, and it was on Upper Canada that the war had the most telling effects, found its identity as a community. It entered the war as a string of pioneer settlements along the lakes and it emerged from it as a colony with some cohesion and some feeling of community: thence from 'colony' to 'province' (in the social sense) was to be for it a short step. The anti-republicanism on which it had been founded was confirmed and deepened, changing from dislike of a particular form of government to dislike of the people who lived under it, to anti-Americanism.

In few other parts of Canada did this sentiment of hostility persist so long (except in New Brunswick, where it was nostalgic rather than bitter). It was the informing sentiment of Ontario society a short half-century ago, and it may still be reawakened, though now overlaid with other interests, and with other emotional alignments. For Upper Canada, the War of 1812 provided the common basis of nationhood—hatred and fear of the external foe. The structure built on these emotions remains, and through Upper Canada, become Ontario, it has been extended (diminishing in force with distance) to all the provinces lying to the westward. It is possible that there would have been a Canadian nation without the War of 1812, but it would have been a less self-conscious one, one less securely based emotionally, one whose continued existence would have been less certain. It therefore does not seem too far out to say that the War of 1812 is one of the massive foundation stones of modern Canada.

Notes to Chapter 13

1. These he is conscious of feeling with regard to the expulsion of the Acadians, even though he has no historic responsibility for it.
2. If any further testimony were needed to its influence over the generations it could be supplied by simply opening the pages of such books as James Hannay, *The War of 1812* (Toronto, 1905) or Egerton Ryerson, *The Loyalists of America and Their Times* (Toronto, 1880). Both of these preserve, virtually unchanged, the emotional tone of the war period after a lapse of almost a century.
3. War measures fill the four large volumes of *The Correspondence of Lieutenant Governor John Graves Simcoe* (ed. Brig.-Gen. E. A. Cruikshank, Ontario Historical Society, 1925).
4. See Mrs. C. M. Day, *History of the Eastern Townships* (Montreal, 1869), for numerous specific examples.
5. Ryerson, op. cit., Vol. II, pp. 309 ff.
6. Michael Smith, *A Geographical View of the Province of Upper Canada* (Hartford, 1813), p. 62.
7. *A Study of Disaffection in Upper Canada, 1812-1815*, Tr. Royal Society of Canada, 1912.
8. Smith Hinman, "Biography and Sketch of the Hinman Family, 1649-1905" (private MSS.)
9. One of the best indexes of economic well-being surely is the speed at which the next generation is produced. In 1814 there were in Lower Canada 13,317 baptisms in a population of about 250,000 or a rate of about 53 per thousand (English included). There is no record on earth of a higher birth rate than this. Death rates, of course, were also very high: 7,895 deaths, or a rate of about 31 per thousand. Data from Robert Christie, *A History of the Late Province of Lower Canada* (Quebec, 1848). Modern rates for Que-

bec are about 30 and 10, natural increase in favour of the earlier period.

10. *Cours d'Histoire du Canada* (Montreal, 1919), Vol. II, p. 268.

11. The British campaign which resulted in the burning of Washington was in part retaliatory for the burning of York, U.C., but mainly to put pressure on the Americans to conclude peace. The man who, of all others, saw the war as defensive was the Duke of Wellington.

12. *Bulletin des Recherches Historiques*, Vol. 31, p. 414. First sung, it is supposed, in the American invasion of 1775. Translation is approximately as follows:

"The first shots that I fired
On those poor rebels
Five hundred of their friends
Had their brains blown out.
Yankee Doodle, watch out!
Hear the music clearly
It's the Canadian dance
Which surprises the American."

13. Both incidents from J. J. Talman, *Loyalist Narratives* (Champlain Society Edition), pp. 316, 147.

14. It is only fair to report that there are many references to the good manners and humanity of many American officers in their attitude towards the unfortunate Canadian people during the war. See *inter alia* Major John Richardson, *War of 1812* (Brockville, Ont., 1842), p. 125.

15. An example: General Smyth's exhortation of Nov. 17th, 1812, when preparing for the third invasion of Upper Canada (see Christie, op. cit., Vol. II, p. 55). The proclamation is too long to quote but the following paragraph gives its flavour: "Companions in Arms! The time is at hand when you will cross the streams of Niagara to conquer Canada. . . . Rewards and honours await the brave. Infamy and contempt are reserved for cowards. Companions in Arms! You came to vanquish a valiant foe, I know the choice you will make. Come on, my heroes! And when you attack the enemy's batteries, let your rallying word be 'The Cannon lost at Detroit or Death!' " American militiamen sometimes found alternatives to both the cannon and death by refusing to fight out of their own country or (not unlike other militiamen) taking to their heels!

16. The provincial troops consisted of three categories—the regular 'provincial corps', the 'embodied militia' and the ordinary militia. The latter did no serious fighting. Col. William Wood, *Documents of the War of 1812* (Champlain Society Edition).

17. Merrill Denison, *The Barley and the Stream* (Toronto, 1955), p. 105.

18. Despite the usefulness of the steamer *Swiftsure* it never seems to have occurrd to any naval officer to experiment with steam in a fighting ship.

19. R. A. Preston, *The Fate of Kingston's Warships* (Kingston Historical Society, October 1952).

20. This is rapidly ceasing to be true as "progress" displaces simple farmers by suburbanites.

21. Public Archives of Canada, Doughty and Story, *Documents Relating to Constitutional History of Canada, 1818-1828* (Ottawa, 1935), pp. 371, 377.

22. Aileen Dunham, *Political Unrest in Upper Canada, 1815-1836* (New York, 1937), p. 72.

23. The famous controverted election of Barnabas Bidwell in 1821 had precipitated the whole issue and Bidwell's son, Marshall, became one of the leading radicals in the eighteen-thirties.

14: The great days of settlement, 1820-1850

CANADA HAS GROWN TO ITS PRESENT SIZE in a series of spurts. Its course has been like that of one of its own Laurentian rivers: a long quiet lake, then a quickening of the stream and a hurried tumbling over the rapids, then again a quiet, if larger, stream. After Jacques Cartier, nearly a century of almost nothing, then the first pulsation of growth with the coming of the French population. Then the quiet consolidation of the eighteenth century, followed by the second major migration, that of the Loyalists and their successors. Once more a stretch of 'slack water' until after the wars, and then, beginning about 1820, a rush over the rapids from 1820 to 1850, a generation whose end sees a completely altered picture. Again, the pace slackens and it is not until the very close of the nineteenth century that it begins again. This time, from 1900 to 1930, it widens out into a flood, filling up the West and vastly stimulating the East. Again, a period of rest, followed by the frantic expansion of the post-war period from 1946 on, which has once more created a new country and a new society. Thus from the refounding of Quebec in 1632 to our own day, we have had five cycles of growth and expansion, each one accompanied by an inpouring of new people who altered the shape of things in some fundamental fashion. The period of the present chapter, 1820-1850, is the middle one and like the others, it is in high colours.

After more or less peaceful relations with the United States had been assured by the Treaty of Ghent and the Rush-Bagot Agreement,[1] the British North American colonies could settle down to what most of their people would have regarded as their real business, and that was not war, but growth. Few English colonists there were who did not look forward to growth in population, in productivity, in urban life, industry, education, even in self-government. Few would have wished a colonial level in and for itself; nearly all would have assumed that at some distant day, their own little community would be great and important.

Many, perhaps most, of the French-speaking people of Lower Canada would not have accepted this view of life. French Canada's imagination was for the past, rather than for the future. It had little sympathy with the mobile, Anglo-Saxon way of life. It sighed after stability, the perpetual Eden which some present-day exponents of the theme seem to hold as having existed before the Conquest, without any English-speaking snakes to whisper in Eve's ear. Naturally there were exceptions, and some of these were to make their presence evident before the end of the period—Georges Cartier, railroad lawyer, conspicuously so—but, in general, French society, even when not looking to the past, was of the Latin Catholic world, and as such interested in the family, in religion and in intellectual concepts—especially in the concept of nationalism which bestowed such welcome oratorical prominence—rather than in agricultural and industrial revolutions. This difference in basic outlook has formed the largest difficulty in the associations of the two races, causing misunderstanding at every turn. It was a major factor in the Rebellion of 1837, and it lay at the root of the quarrels over immigration, the settlement of the Eastern Townships and the St. Lawrence Canal question. It is because of their outlook that Professor Creighton can say that the French-Canadian radicals and rebels were the real Conservatives.[2]

English Canadians responded every year more and more whole-heartedly to the norm of the continent, to *development*. If, as an American author was later to observe,[3] 'progress' (that is, material development) was not quite so dominant a deity in Canada as in the United States and the golden calf not worshipped quite so assiduously, that was mainly because there was less gold. Such words as 'progress,' 'growth,' 'development,' in the hands of the philosopher may be slippery, but their practical implications are plain enough. It was difficult for Catholicism with its static conceptions to accept these latter. The Protestant can always claim that his Mammon is not really Mammon, but a means to a more satisfactory society —and sometimes his societies warrant the claim—but 'progress' and Protestantism are never far apart. Nor are the concepts contained in 'progress,' even when vulgar, identical with those in 'capitalism.' 'Capitalism' is the narrower word. There is a real sense in which the Massey family, who in the period of this chapter were just getting into the production of agricultural implements, were making them 'to the glory of God.'[4]

At the close of the war, none of the colonies was impressive, either in population or in wealth. A decade later, evidences of new life were abundant. A generation later, they had grown beyond recognition. This was the period, 1820-1850, in which a new staple product, wood, was building a new economy along the St. Lawrence and its tributaries, especially the Ottawa, and along the rivers of New Brunswick. The stream of immigration was flowing. The forest was being pushed back before the fields. The fertilizing influence of these basic economic factors was to turn pioneer settlements into colonial areas, and colonies into provinces. Upper and Lower Canada, despite their differences, were linked in uneasy partnership by the St. Lawrence. And though to Lower Canadians the new English settlements up river did not have much reality,[5] Quebec and Montreal were never far from the minds of Upper Canadians, and many of them had seen the two cities. As yet, however, with this important exception of the two Canadas, the only connection between the various British North American colonies lay in the word 'British.' In nearly all particulars of their life, they lived in separate worlds with no intercommunication; and as late as the eighteen-thirties, when the steamship *Royal William* attempted to pioneer a passenger run between Quebec and Halifax, she failed dismally. Given this local isolation, the task of the historian remains as it was before—how to keep half a dozen separate stories marching abreast. The only feasible solution seems that already adopted, the rapid *coup d'oeil*.

Growth in numbers

The basic datum line must be population, for this book is a study of people in society, that is, of how the human animal behaves. As previous chapters have indicated, our census data are extraordinarily rich, so that even for the limited period of a few nineteenth-century decades, there is a great deal known about the growth of the Canadian population. There is also much information on religions and ages. Racial origin is not as satisfactory, but the broad division into 'French' and 'others' may be worked out with tolerable accuracy, and towards mid-century finer subdivisions appear. Emigration figures from the British Isles to British North America exist from 1815.[6] There is also statistical material on agriculture and on the economic side generally.

In 1821, British North America contained about three-quarters of a million people. In 1851, this number had increased to 2,300,000. Thus in thirty years the population had tripled. A comparison may be made with the growth of the Canadian West in the twentieth century. In 1901, the three prairie provinces contained 419,000 people and in 1931, when their first great wave of immigration stopped, 2,354,000. During this period of exactly a generation, Canada as a whole received 4,571,000 immigrants. How many of these went to the three western provinces, the writer does not know; but if they be allowed half, they received about two and a quarter million immigrants in the thirty years. In the thirty years here under discussion, 1820-1850, the eastern provinces received a maximum immigration from overseas of 995,981. And yet they grew little less rapidly than the three western provinces in the present century.

Our century has provided immensely greater technical facilities for settlement than did the early nineteenth. To remind ourselves of that, we have only to think of the railroad, the telephone, canned food, medical science and so on, and contrast these abundant auxiliaries to life with what was the sole major piece of power equipment possessed by our ancestors of a century and a quarter ago—the steamboat. To lack of technical equipment must be added the difficulty of bringing the forest under cultivation: this stands in contrast to the open prairie. And yet the earlier period saw almost as rapid an expansion of humanity as did the later.

Anyone who remembers the 'boom days' of the period around 1910, based on western settlement, or recalls the hectic atmosphere of the nineteen-fifties knows what a rapid expansion of population does to the psychology of the society experiencing it. It catches humanity in one of its most baffling moods—a mood of exhilaration and exuberance, compounded of the constructiveness, the arrogance and the lunacy which are so marked in our species.

The expansion of the period 1820-1850 was not uniform throughout the colonies. In those days, as in our own, the Maritimes did not share the sky-rocket ascents of the inland provinces: thus in 1817,[7] there were some 80,000 people in Nova Scotia and in 1851, about 275,000. This was a creditable multiplication by a little over three, but in Upper Canada the multiplier was ten—from 95,000 in 1814 to 952,000 in 1851. New Brunswick was peopled at a slightly lower rate than Nova Scotia, while Lower Canada increased from about a quarter of a million in 1806 to 890,000 in 1851. From 1822 to 1851 its population doubled, but that of Upper Canada in the shorter period from 1825 to 1851 was multiplied by about six.

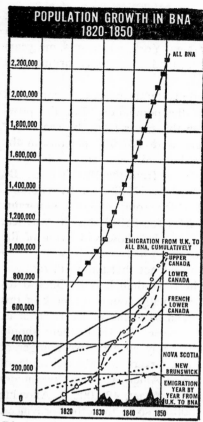

POPULATION GROWTH IN BNA 1820-1850

2,200,000
2,000,000
1,800,000
1,600,000
1,400,000
1,200,000
1,000,000
800,000
600,000
400,000
200,000
0

ALL BNA

EMIGRATION FROM U.K. TO ALL BNA, CUMULATIVELY

UPPER CANADA

LOWER CANADA

FRENCH LOWER CANADA

NOVA SCOTIA

NEW BRUNSWICK

EMIGRATION YEAR BY YEAR FROM U.K. TO BNA

1820   1830   1840   1850

Diagram 3

An interesting question for the period concerns the way in which the population of the colonies was altered by the tide of immigration. The observer has only to go about the provinces to-day to see that it was altered, and drastically altered, for there are still innumerable 'colonies' descended from the newcomers of the time. North of Ireland Protestants, South of Ireland Catholics, Highland Scots of both religions, Lowland Scots, Lutheran Germans, all of whom came in this generation, are still with us, and still conscious of their origins. How far did they swamp the previous deposit of population and thus change the nature of the society that had begun to form?

An examination province by province and in detail would be tedious and beyond the space available. The Maritime provinces were least affected by the new inrush, though the period added new groups to all of them, such as the Northern Irish in the Upper St. John Valley of New Brunswick, or the rearguard of the Highland immigration into Cape Breton. Still, in most particulars, these older communities remained what they had been. It was Upper Canada which was the most radically altered. But the exact way in which the million new arrivals of the period were distributed over the various provinces we have to come at indirectly. Most of them landed at Quebec, we are sure of that. For a typical five-year period (1830-1834 inclusive), of the emigrants that left the British Isles for British North America, 81 per cent turned up at the port of Quebec, and from thence scattered over the two Canadas (if they did not find their way to the United States!) This statistical finding is in accordance with the opinion of the day. Further, relatively few of those arriving at Quebec remained in Lower Canada. Other elements in the sum consist in the number of deaths on the ocean voyage or shortly after landing (not inconsiderable), and in immigration into Upper Canada from Great Britain by way of New York, which in some years may have reached several thousand. No exact arithmetical balance sheet is possible.

The distribution of immigrants by provinces is confirmed by data on the birthplaces of the population. For the province of Canada, information on this exists from the year 1842 to the present. In 1842, there were 242,000 persons in the united province who had been born abroad,[8] all of whom except a few thousand Germans were from the British Isles. By 1851, this number had increased to 428,000 or by 186,000. During the same period 1842-1851 some 433,000 emigrants had set out from the British Isles for British North America. To this number there are to be added those still living of the 562,000 who according to Johnson[9] had come between 1815 and 1842. Since there is some evidence that the death rate was no higher in Upper Canada in 1851 than it is in Ontario to-day,[10] and since immigrants are usually young, the bulk of this half million should have still been surviving in 1851. That is, somewhere in British North America in 1851, there should have been, allowing what is probably an excessive number of deaths, something like three-quarters of a million people of British birthplace in British North America. In the two major provinces there were, as a matter of fact, 428,000.[11] Allowing (generously) for another 75,000 or so in the other provinces, we get a total of half a million. A minimum of about one-third of the emigrants was missing: they had either died *en route*, returned, or emigrated again to the United States. Every Canadian knows which channel would take off the largest number.[12] The net result of re-emigration and a heavy local birth rate, nevertheless, was that the provinces rapidly secured a native-born population.

The statement made above, that the death rate in Upper Canada in 1851 may have been no higher than it is to-day,[13] may seem surprising, given our modern advantages, but the usual impression of the period as one of enormous infant mortality, epidemic diseases, short lives and numerous deaths may need some revision. Certain causes of death carried off large numbers, but others fewer than to-day. Thus while 20 per cent of all deaths were returned as from contagious diseases, not including 'consumption' (which accounted for just under 10 per cent of the total deaths, or about 79 per hundred thousand, as compared with a modern rate of 30), there were only fifty deaths reported in the whole province from cancer.

And of course, however numerous deaths may have been, they were outbalanced by a birth rate higher than the modern. Ontario in the early nineteen-fifties had a birth rate ranging around 25 per thousand, but Upper Canada in the early eighteen-fifties had one of about 34 per thousand.[14] Impressive, therefore, as has been the reproductive prowess of our people in the nineteen-fifties, it was more so still in the eighteen-fifties. Nevertheless, natural increase could not have been great enough to increase the population of the new inland province as rapidly as actually occurred. Despite inability to retain all immigrants, immigration added a significant quota, as it must in a fertile, empty land—which seems to be the only case in which it does greatly affect the rate at which population grows.[15]

How completely the immigration of the generation dominated many areas of Upper Canada is evident from a little further statistical information. In Grey, which was then a frontier county with a total population of 13,000 in 1851, just about half had been born in the United Kingdom (and many of the balance would be their young children born in Canada). In Peel, the situation was the same, with natives of Ireland vastly exceeding others from the United Kingdom. A detailed examination would show progressively increasing proportions of old-country-born (and their children) from the Quebec border westward to the head of Lake Ontario, thence north-westerly to the Upper Lakes. As might be expected, the older counties on the St. Lawrence and on Lake Erie were the most 'native'. In the cities, the concentration of immigrants was much higher than in the counties, each place separately reported showing an actual majority of overseas-born. In Toronto in 1851, among its 30,000 people, only 10,000 would plead guilty to having been born in Canada.

Lower Canada also presented interesting features in its growth. In 1822 it contained 427,000 people, far more than Upper Canada's 150,000, but by 1851, the upper province had the greater population of the two—a situation which gave rise to George Brown's furious "Rep. by Pop." crusade and the eventual destruction of the provincial union. In the earlier year, 1822, it was estimated that of the 427,000 about 327,000 were French-speaking, 100,000 (22 per cent), English. In 1851, there were 670,000 French and 220,000 'English', the latter being about 25 per cent of the total. In 1951, the percentage of 'non-French' was eighteen. Montreal and Quebec by mid-century had become far more English in racial origin than in the period preceding the War of 1812. In 1851, 54 per cent of the people in Montreal were of non-French origin, and in Quebec 43 per cent; compare this with the microscopic percentage of English Canadians in Quebec City to-day. At mid-century Montreal was as close to being an English city as it was to become: after that period, the proportion of English steadily declined.[16]

In 1844, there were some 70,000 people in Lower Canada who were born overseas (practically all in the United Kingdom) and although there was a large immigration through the port of Quebec in the following seven years, only some 83,000 in 1851. Thus relatively few immigrants remained in Lower Canada. Then, as always, Lower Canada kept abreast of Upper by its own extraordinary fertility, maintained from the beginnings of its history: in 1851, its birth rate (both races) was nearly 41 per thousand (1951, 29.8) and its death rate 13.1 (1951, 8.6), both being substantially higher than those of Upper Canada.[17] The causes of death in Lower Canada in 1851 were not satisfactorily ascertained, but the census reported infant mortality as being twice as high as in Upper Canada.

The immigrant British

Here, then, lay the great revolution of the generation after the War of 1812: the flooding into Upper Canada of an entirely new population which in some localities constituted the pioneering stock, in others came in among people who already had a long North American experience behind them. Sometimes this new population gave its characteristics to the community (as when North of Irelanders persuaded Loyalists to become Orangemen),[18] and sometimes it merely added a new element to those already there; but everywhere it brought with it new customs and attitudes which had to be adjusted to those of the people already present.

On the whole, the revolution was accomplished with relatively little disturbance, though there is one considerable exception to the statement, namely the gross violence of the Irish, particularly of the Orange Irish, at elections and other times.[19] In Lafontaine's Terrebonne election of 1841, his Reformer constituents "found Dr. McCulloch's supporters (many of whom were canal labourers and navvies who were not entitled to exercise the franchise at all) armed and ready for them, and as the latter had contrived to secure an advantageous position for a hand-to-hand fight, the French Canadians adopted the better part of valour and withdrew from the field without recording their votes."[20] An even more striking instance of the divisions worked in the new country by the Irish immigrants

THE NEW STYLE AND THE OLD:
GOTHIC REVIVAL AND CLASSICAL

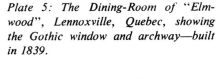

Plate 5: The Dining-Room of "Elmwood", Lennoxville, Quebec, showing the Gothic window and archway—built in 1839.

Plate 6: The City Hall at Kingston, Ontario, built in 1843; a fine example of the late classical style.

Plate 7: Bishop Strachan's Funeral, November 5th, 1867, passing the corner of King and Yonge Street in Toronto along a route lined by the 13th Hussars.

lay in the prolonged disturbances on the Ottawa, especially at Bytown, precipitated by the so-called 'Shiners'—Irish labourers in the lumber camps. For a number of years 'Shiner' shindigs were so serious as to disturb the peace of the entire community. The Irish just seemed to require a dog to kick, and the French Catholics, among whom they were thrown, naturally provided it. "Of this place (Bytown) I am pretty sick. What between treacherous Papists and truculent Orangemen, it is hardly safe to walk the streets even in daylight. . . . A greater set of ruffians than the whole population of Bytown, it would be hard to find out of Tipperary".[21]

No wonder the Irish dominated the local scene in Upper Canadian elections, practically ruling Ontario for the rest of the century: there were twice as many of them as either English or Scots![22] In Lower Canada, the French were quick to take over their tactics, with the result that the major points of election disorder to-day are not the Orange districts of Ontario but certain areas of Montreal.

In contrast with the Irish, the Scots quietly consolidated themselves, and quickly rose in the scale. The Scottish mercantile community of Montreal was an old story with its wealthy bourgeois aristocracy, but as a result of the post-1815 influx other Scots rose to prominence on every hand. We have merely to recall the endless list of 'Macs' in our political annals, of whom the great Sir John, an immigrant of 1820, was only the most prominent, to remind ourselves of that fact. Or we can contemplate the blessed lot of those lucky enough to be born with the name of Mackenzie—Sir Alexander Mackenzie the explorer, William Lyon Mackenzie the "little rebel", Alexander Mackenzie the second prime minister of the Dominion, Sir William Mackenzie of the railway combination Mackenzie and Mann, President Norman Mackenzie of the University of British Columbia, Robert Mackenzie, native British Columbian and later distinguished English political scientist, and, disregarding hyphenated Mackenzie King, so on *ad infinitum*. As the peers put it in *Iolanthe*, "Bow, bow, ye lower middle classes!"

While Scots, Highland or Lowland, or mixtures of the two, were not the sole architects of Confederation, they contributed a disproportionately large number of the founding fathers— Macdonald, Brown, Mowat, Galt, among others. They built our railroads and founded our banks. They occupied most of the prominent Protestant pulpits and many of the university chairs, when these came to be founded. Their original colonies retain much of their identity: they are invariably marked by the prominence of the school and the number of professional men who have come out of them. Does this century-old exodus of ability mean that there is now nothing much left to come out of them? There is some evidence for this view: no one would contend that the Scot is as conspicuous in our affairs as he once was. In the universities he founded he no longer has his former prominence and instead of interminable 'Macs' in class lists, there are chiefly the ordinary collections of Smiths and Joneses. Few if any Queen's students of to-day could from their knowledge of Gaelic translate Queen's Gaelic 'yell'. Yet Gaelic is still spoken in outlying districts and proudly clung to, especially in Cape Breton, as a badge of an honourable past.

The Scots have been too successful for their own good. Success has moved them up the scale and perilously close to off the map. It is the humble who will be exalted, and what Scot was ever humble? Disturbances such as the rebellions removed large numbers of the Scottish people, for with their good sense, many of them saw no reason for remaining in a disturbed country when there was a peaceful one alongside. Yet in the long run, it is not necessarily the people of common sense who survive, but those who stubbornly, blindly and often against their immediate individual interests dig their heels in and stick it. So Canada, to her loss, is not so Scottish as she was once, though still very Scottish, infinitely more so than the United States.

Compared with either Scots or Irish, the middle- and lower-class English, as a racial group, are almost without feature and untraceable. English people have little clan sense and while those born in England stick stubbornly to English ways, constantly talk of 'home' and refuse to their dying day to become Canadian, their children blend with their surroundings and become part of their community, whatever it may be. There are still remains in Canada of 'the Scottish vote' or 'the Irish vote', but who has ever heard of 'the English vote'? Irish and Scottish settlements may be found all over eastern Canada and in some districts an Irish or a Scottish accent is still discernible,[23] but nowhere in the country, except, curiously enough, among the Lunenburg Germans, are there traces of English accent,[24] and practically nowhere are there to be found 'English' settlements recognized as such. The only one of which the author knows is to be found along the Penetang Road, north of Barrie, Ontario. Here about 1819 came a group of English families, settling around Crown Hill. Among them was the grandfather of Charles Drury, first Minister of Agriculture of Ontario and great-grandfather of Ernest, later premier of the province.[25] Of the nineteen families who settled that fertile strip of country, eleven remained in the neighbourhood in 1955. Their farms flourish and are still marked by an English neatness, but there is little or no consciousness of origin.

The officer and gentleman

Apart from the ordinary settlers of middle-class and yeoman stock, there were two groups of English who became conspicuous—some would say all too conspicuous: these were the members of 'the classes' and the individuals at the other end of the social scale. The subject, necessarily often referred to in these pages, involves nothing short of the migration of the English social system, complete with ruling class and official church. 'Ruling class' includes not only governors and high officials, but local magistracy and officialdom, army officers, most professional men and that rather numerous group of private persons who thought of themselves as 'gentry'. As long as the old colonial system lasted, before Responsible Government won the day, the members of this traditional English 'ruling class' cut a wide swath in all the provinces.. It was always possible for an old countryman 'of good connections' to secure letters of introduction to a governor and these, if his personality found favour, might be transmuted into an official place or a favourable land grant.[26] We have only to think of Colonel Talbot and his acres, to understand the situation.[27]

Land grants were available as of right to all ex-officers and many of these men—the 'half-pay officers' as they were called —took advantage of them. Mrs. Jameson (whose husband, as Attorney-General of Upper Canada, was himself an example of the export of the English social system) on her route westward from Toronto discovered an ex-admiral on a pioneer farm. Ex-admirals among the stumps were rare, but half-pay officers of lesser rank abounded. They built houses with the money they had brought with them, and left behind them descendants who carried on a colonial as opposed to a Canadian tradition—in some cases, for generations. Their presence in a district introduced a class consciousness which cut across the natural democracy of North America and which further divided a province already weakened by heterogeneity of origin.

Perhaps the best-known concentration of officers and gentlemen was in the Kawartha lakes region: at least it has subsequently became well known because of the literary proclivities of some of its members, for it was to it that the famous Strickland family belonged, with the two sisters, Mrs. Moodie and Mrs. Traill, as well as the not quite so well-known brother Samuel.[28] Of recent years, we have had further information about the district in the form of John Langton's *Early Days in Upper Canada* and his sister Anne's *Journals*.[29] Mrs. Moodie's principal book *Roughing it in the Bush*[30] has become a Canadian classic, and deservedly so. The Langton books are equally illuminating. They may be put together with that other enormous collection of literary material, the travellers' tales and advice to emigrants, of both of which there are scores and scores of examples.

Some of them are of considerable literary merit and since practically all of them were written by persons who were, or considered themselves to be, 'gentlemen', the literary presentation of the Canadian scene during the first half of the nineteenth century, to the average modern Canadian, seems foreign and alien. Yet there can be no question of its interest and of the immense amount of light it throws on conditions of pioneer settlement. It also explains quite satisfactorily why the 'gentleman' so seldom succeeded as a settler, and beyond that, it indicates the source of much of the class division that has marked not inconsiderable areas of Canadian life. The trans-Atlantic migration of the English social structure put a brake on the emergence of native forces (Mr. St. Laurent, the son of humble parents, whose brother kept a grocery store, would have been a subject for condescension less than a hundred years ago, as, to some degree, was Alexander Mackenzie, our stone-mason prime minister of the eighteen-seventies) and prevented their having the free run in Canada which they had in the United States. A recent American observer summed this up by saying that "Canada does not have the same 'free-wheeling' democracy that we have in the U.S."

An interesting reminder from the days of 'gentry' settlement is to be seen on the Ottawa River, about twenty-five miles above the capital. There, on a delightful site looking across the valley to the northern mountains, was built, it is said by a family of the name of Pinhey, a large stone house, with a spacious ballroom in the upper story.[31] Nor only a private ballroom, but on a neighbouring slope, a private church! When the writer last saw it, the church was deserted and the walls of the churchyard broken, but gravestones indicated the ranks of the ancestors buried there. At the time the original family had shrunk to an elderly brother and sister, who lived in part of the big house. The whole property was in bad repair. A similar yet dissimilar situation may be found, again in a most picturesque location, on the south-eastern shores of Lake

Simcoe, where a family named Sibbald settled. They, too, built a private church, but it is in good repair still and its own churchyard is filled up with admirals and generals who served all over the world.[32]

Still another example of 'gentry' settlement comes from the opposite side of Lake Simcoe, around Barrie. Here a considerable number of people from the lesser squirearchy found their way to the beautiful shores of Kempenfeldt Bay, and secured generous grants at strategic points along it. Among them were Senator Sir James Gowan, Dalton McCarthy's family, and that of Colonel O'Brien of 'Noble Thirteen' fame. Shanty Bay, now a pleasant summer place and the site of an interesting Anglican church with a distinct old-world air, was the home of O'Brien. Within the town of Barrie itself, a dozen or more families of this description, indifferently English or Irish, gathered—Ardaghs, Boys, Gowans, Stratheys, Creswicks, Lallys, Morgans, Stewarts, and others—and as early as the eighteen-sixties, their large many-chimneyed brick houses in their park-like grounds with their wide views over the lake, crowned the ridge along the northern edge of the town. They soon became a local 'Family Compact', not only by their intermarriages but by their firm hold on the good things of the county. All of these men were zealous Anglicans of the low-church variety, and none of them were wasters of the remittance-man type, as their long monopoly of the professions, the bench and local parliamentary representation well indicates.[33] Yet their presence gave the town an unmistakably non-North-American air in that the class line was apparent, and rigid.[34]

On one occasion, when a meeting of the townsmen had been called to make a local decision, Senator Gowan, himself a lifelong resident, appeared before it. He did not speak as one man to another, but as a kindly father cautioning his inexperienced children: "Be careful what you do: think well before you act", such were the words he used. The townsmen were untutored small business men at the best and they probably needed the leadership of a disinterested, educated man of larger experience, but the patrician detachment of Sir James (as he later became) was hardly what we think of as 'new world'. No calling *him* by his first name! To-day, with the weakening or removal of the old families, their houses turned into apartments, the adjacent lands built over, the old-world class lines have disappeared and this particular place seems to be much the same as any other Canadian town, with everybody calling everybody else by his first name and the little lower-middle-class business man happily making his usual mess of things.

Though they influenced it and described it, the English emigrés never dominated Canadian life. One of the situations they most frequently described (in whatever period is being considered) and the point of friction which hurt them the most was the upsetting of the class line.[35] All of them bewail the difficulty of getting servants and deplore the independence of those they do get. They are forced into a reluctant self-dependence in which they take some furtive pride: "Our neighbours the Dunsfords have been living without a servant most of the summer, and the ladies have done all their own washing. They gain great credit for their exertions, and are not a little pleased with them."[36]

Not only servants but all old-countrymen not of the 'gentry' apparently made themselves obnoxious. The pages of Mrs. Moodie and her fellow-settlers are full of the independent, objectionable immigrant, far worse in his swaggering offensiveness, his ability to spot and bait a 'gentleman', than the native Canadian. ". . . A young farmer from my own county in England . . . had evidently turned all his attention . . . to the study of Yankee manners and idioms, which, disagreeable as they are, he certainly managed to render more offensive by his unpleasant caricature; cool impertinence he mistook for independence; and a swaggering, jaunty air for an easy manner. . . . The Anglo-Canadian copies the worst and the most prominent features of the American character, and the British settler in his turn caricatures the copy. . . ."[37]

The 'Anglo' or native Canadian, like all those who are 'on the outside looking in', in copying the American, as he has done throughout his existence, necessarily copies the latter's worst traits: he is like the traditional savage who imitates the superior white man by putting on his hat and his shoes with nothing in between. Americans themselves have seldom regarded this imitation as a sincere form of flattery. It has merely buttressed them in the opinion that Canada is just a blurred tag-end of their own country. This opinion seems to have been rather generally held in our present period, 1820-1850. The usual American image of Canada was somewhat like that of the 'wild West' a generation later; a region of escape, a gathering point for the refuse of society who could not make a go of life elsewhere. This is a view of the frontiersman not usually put into the idealistic theses on him: the present writer from his observations on our northern frontier, can testify that there is a good deal of truth in it.

Still, with all his faults, the native Canadian was born to equalitarianism and carried it about with him among all conditions of people without offence: the English lower-class immigrant was experiencing a release from prison and taking it out on his former gaolers. The 'gaolers'—gentry—moreover, were often in a worse estate than himself because of the difficulty of descending to the labourer's status: the pioneer farm was no situation for a gentleman, any more than it is to-day. Only the very few who had large resources[38] or who could link a professional career to a country life remained in the countryside, and they became not yeomen farmers but a species of country gentleman. Nothing is plainer than that, in the difficult conditions of pioneer Canada, it was impossible to introduce the traditional English type of society. It is only to-day, a century and more later, when the forest has been conquered and much urban wealth accumulated, that native capitalists are doing what has been done immemorially in England, taking up farming as merely a pleasant form of country life, a relief from the monotony of attending directors' meetings. Even so, the richest of them is not successful at making himself into a feudal lord, for time and circumstances have not yet pressed heavily enough to make men ready to accept a new feudalism, and so would-be feudal lords have to be content with bossing a minimum number of employees and a maximum amount of glittering new machinery. Thanks to the rapid production of wealth, new social classes are arising in Canada but their crystallization in a form resembling anything like the traditional society of the old world is still a long way off.

The 'gentry', taken in the mass, were not much more than people with some education and a good upbringing (Anne Langton's family was of the business world). There was still another class of English, than which few less useful immigrants could have been found. These were the paupers, the 'commuted pensioners' sent out from Chelsea Hospital and other similar types gathered up from city back streets and exported mainly to help England get rid of what was called her 'redundancy of population'. They were probably not as offensive as the men who were 'transported' to Australia, but they filled the Canadian cities with beggars and petty malefactors, and furnished one of the essential ingredients of a 'lower class'.

"I regret to state that many of the Pensioners who arrived last season, having commuted their Pensions, are in great distress. They have squandered away their commutation allowance and cannot, without further assistance, remain on their land, and are either too indolent or unable to labour with energy sufficient to provide for their families."[39]

The shortcomings of the pioneer

Almost every English book about Upper Canada had a long list of grievances, objections and criticisms and not many commendations. The books by Scots tended to be interested more in the economic side, and they were perhaps a shade less critical. The few written by Americans or Europeans saw the frontier scene with more detachment and lacked the supercilious tone of so many of the English.

The list of grievances and criticisms must be headed by the point already touched on, the class question. Nothing seems to have pricked the English writer so emphatically on the quick as the discovery that the English hierarchy of classes did not exist. He invariably cried out "Republicanism", the invasion of American attitudes, and rarely realized that equality was in the very essence of pioneer life. In England itself, class relationships, their clash and particularly their alteration, in new economic and political circumstances, have provided one of the principal themes of a literature. In Canada, this has not been the case, and that because class consciousness has been slight. Its place has been taken by consciousness of religious and racial difference.

Criticism was directed, secondly, to the many specific shortcomings of pioneer communities. Among these were the inconvenience, discomfort, hardship and dirt of travel and accommodation, than which nothing apparently could have been worse. The present writer, having had experience of all this (except dirt) in out-of-the-way areas, believes that these writers do not exaggerate. Their constant encounters with disobliging or uncivil hosts, however, probably spring from old country *hauteur*, which was quickly resented by highly independent natives. When the steamer service from Quebec upward was developed, conditions afloat rapidly improved and by mid-century, this method of travelling received general praise. But before railroad days, a journey by sleigh from Montreal into the remote recesses of the upper provinces, even with the ordinary courtesies of the road, must always have been a difficult experience.

The general casualness and carelessness of the backwoods were another principal target for observers. A minor example:— "The first thing I saw on coming downstairs this morning was Sally Jordan milking the cows—where do you think? Exactly at the step of the front door; this is to enlighten you as to Canadian ideas of tidiness. I have seen all the sweepings from the up-stairs' rooms ornamenting the snow before the front door."[40]

Pioneering does not make for the domestic proprieties. First things must come first, hence the dirt, the rough-hewn attitudes, the vulgarity. The educated among the English folk could seldom accept these conditions—unless, as some among them did, they 'went the whole hog' and outprimitived the primitive —and the simple men among them accepted them only with reluctance. It was for this reason that Southern Irish and Highland Scots took to pioneering (though they did not make the best of bushmen[41]) with less difficulty than others from the British Isles. They came from one primitive set of conditions to another and apparently could the more easily put up with hard food, heat and cold, smoke in the eyes, mosquitoes, flies, lice.[42]

Primitive conditions have left their mark on all of us, and subsequent generations have had hard work freeing themselves from their effects. This freeing a society from the effects of immersion in the primitive is what is called building a civilization, and anyone knows how frantically we have worked at exactly that task all along the line, not only in primary personal attributes such as cleanliness, but in social movements (temperance, efforts against gambling, prostitution, etc.), religion and above all education. The cult of the hygienic so prominently displayed in modern America—"Have you got a silky skin?" "Do you smell sweet?" "Are you quite safe from feminine embarrassments?"— hammered home with all the vulgarity of the advertising man, himself merely a backwoodsman in city clothes, is a reflex from pioneering days when baths, being superfluous luxuries, only to be taken under conditions of difficulty, were resorted to sparingly. Modern abhorrence of the bearded man possibly arises from the feeling that beards mean unwashed faces.

Per contra, the female of the pioneer species in America has always delighted far beyond her old-country cousins to adorn her outward person. Bishop Laval's shocked denunciations of the ladies who came to mass with their flesh just nicely showing through their bodices has already been quoted.[43] Peter Kalm, among his nasty remarks about the belles of Quebec, alleges that they do nothing all day long but deck themselves out and sit at the window to attract suitors.[44] Then comes the turn of the fair neighbours of *les Canadiennes*, the American girls. The German soldiers in the Revolutionary War were attracted by their handsomeness but cooled down by their lack of feminine mystery and overplus of finery: "This petticoat rule is spread throughout America, but in quite different type from in Canada, where it aims at the welfare of the man, while here (e.g. in New England), it seeks his ruin. The wives and daughters make a display beyond the income of most of the men. . . . The daughters simply must put on style, for that is the mother's will. . . ."[45]

This was not to be the last time that American women were to be accused of such attitudes. As an old Scot said of them "They'll take a man frae the plough to fetch them a skeel (pail) of water." Their cousins north of the border were reported as not much different. "Among the women, the love of dress exceeds all other passions", says Mrs. Moodie. "In public, they dress in silks and satins, and wear the most expensive ornaments, and they display considerable taste in the arrangement and choice of colours. The wife of a man in moderate circumstances . . . does not hesitate in expending ten or fifteen pounds upon one article of outside finery, while often her inner garments are not worth as many sous."[46] Yet American women sometimes say that Canadians are not as 'smart' as themselves, so we are thrown back to the Hessian officer's verdict, which was also Ernest Hemingway's, and the American woman emerges the worst offender of the lot, albeit the most highly sanitized.

To describe fully the great days of settlement would be to fill a separate and a large volume. Fortunately there is no need to do so, for no period of our past has been more fully investigated.[47] Until recently the generation that followed the War of 1812 seemed to constitute the basic datum line of settlement for most Canadians of Ontario origin. It was from it that the folk-lore figure of the pioneer was projected into all our schoolrooms—that hero who, shouldering his sack of grain, trudged uncomplainingly through the forest the sixty miles (or was it a hundred?) to the nearest mill, carrying back again the meagre ration of flour that was to result from it and with which his wife (engaged in the interval in fending off the wolves from her sick baby) and children would be sustained during the fierce winter.

If it be Mrs. Moodie's classics that we depend on for our picture of the times, the result will not be too different from the above. Mrs. Moodie may be taken (at her own words) as an example of that class of English people whose device seems to be "trouble and how to get into it". Her pioneer experience was bitter. She seems to have fallen among a group of American 'hillbillies' who were not typical of the average backwoodsman, either native or immigrant.

"Imagine a girl of seventeen or eighteen years of age, with sharp, knowing-looking features, a forward, impudent carriage, and a pert, flippant voice, standing upon one of the trunks, and surveying all our proceedings in the most impertinent manner. The creature was dressed in a ragged dirty purple stuff gown, cut very low in the neck, with an old cotton handkerchief tied over her head; her uncombed, tangled locks, falling over her thin, inquisitive face, in a state of perfect nature. Her legs and feet were bare, and, in her coarse, dirty red hands, she swung to and fro an empty glass decanter."[48]

No better picture of the 'poor white' could be drawn! Such people were to prove thorns in the English gentlewoman's flesh until the bush drove her out to the 'Front' and she settled at Belleville. The Langtons and their friends a little farther in had hardships to contend with, as must anyone in the bush, but their experiences were not bitter: Anne Langton even managed to capture and retain servants, while Mrs. Moodie's books are one long cry of agony about the insufferable insolence of 'the lower classes.' Yet in the end, the bush defeated the Langtons too. As one of Mrs. Moodie's low-class neighbours said to her "I've never know'd an English gentleman to get on in the bush." She was completely right, and the proof of it lies in the thousands of times they have failed at it, all the way across to Vancouver Island.

The solid citizens

How would Mrs. Moodie have written, one wonders, if instead of a bush farm in what was then the farthest back of the backwoods, her husband and she had tried their luck among people like the Hinmans (to whom this book has already referred)? Moses Hinman built his spacious house near Colborne, Upper Canada, in 1812. (It was still in use by the family in 1902.) He had come from Connecticut in 1799. He regretted the lack of schools, and like all his neighbours, sighed for reading matter. "At one time, I (his son) bought a number of old newspapers, and read them with the greatest of pleasure, such as I could not be hired to read now." But the worst that resulted from this communal ignorance was that the neighbours seemed to get petty in their attitudes, and in their churches were always accusing each other of deviations from the creed and staging diverting, long-drawn-out church trials: in these trials orations could be made, witnesses badgered and the most intriguing kind of confession extorted—all in the name of God. Few exercises could have been so rewarding.

Another result, according to Mr. Hinman, was that when the Mormons appeared in the settlement in 1837, they carried off a number of followers to their many-wived paradises. "A preacher by the name of Savage, formerly a Methodist preacher, preached for them around here who had quite a number of followers, who were mostly of the ignorant class." Mr. Moses Hinman and family definitely were not "of the ignorant class." "Mrs. Moses Hinman would sing counter with her daughter Esther, and Mrs. Truman Hinman and others would sing treble. Aaron, my father, and Truman, would sing bass and tenor and my grandfather would direct and criticize. She (Mrs. Moses) thought that they were all able to read music and to know when it was well rendered. . . ."

Moses had got converted "at a meeting held in Samuel Waite's barn in the township of Haldimand in 1819, held by the Methodists. . . . In about 1824, my parents left the Baptist Church and joined the Methodist Church, owing to a change of belief caused by reading Fletcher's *Checks on Antinomianism and Election and Predestination*". And a little later, "Mr. Daniel Massey, the father of the late H. A. Massey, undertook to raise a barn without liquor, which proved a failure on the first day, but he rallied his temperance friends (my grandfather amongst them, who went about four miles) and they put the building up on the second trial without whiskey."

What would Mrs. Moodie have said about those who would have had nothing to do with her church, who could not have been 'gentry' in her definition of the term, yet who were as self-respecting people as ever were made, the most valuable type of citizens this country could have received? Was she able, as a matter of course, to read music? Would she have had capacity or patience enough to read Fletcher's *Checks on Antinomianism and Election and Predestination*? Yet the Hinmans and their neighbours were Yankees, too; chips from that indomitable old Puritan block whose origins went back beyond New England to the old England of the Roundheads. Their blood runs still in modern Canada and it is no accident that the family of one of them, Daniel Massey, has risen to fame.

From atoms to community

The story could go on and on of those fascinating days, when all the provinces were finding their feet and when what was destined to be the most successful of them, Upper Canada, was having its second birth. The tale has merely skipped about, sampling the life here and there, nowhere painting it out in full, and everywhere leaving large blank spaces in the canvas. What a stirring time it must have been! Everything at a beginning, everything in seeming disorder—disorderly piles of windfalls, disorderly and ugly fields of stumps, still more disorderly and ugly men among them, many of them as uprooted as they hoped to see their stumps.

That was the word: uprooted! There was, of course, a native generation, which already felt Upper Canada as home, but as we have seen, it was almost flooded out by new-comers. Any moving uproots a man, but a moving from across the seas to what was very literally a new world must have been a shattering experience, even though supported by hope. Migration involved reconstruction of a man's entire life pattern. Those who had been brought up with the shadow of 'their betters' constantly across them found release that could hardly have resulted otherwise than in independence, insolence, and assertive conduct. Yet it is on the better among these qualities that the new world has been built: self-reliance and independence, these are among the qualities it draws out of men. They just have to be left to time to soften.

Migration also brought together under new conditions men who had not before been aware of each other's existence. An Englishman, a Highlander, an Irishman, perhaps a German or even a Negro, might all be dumped down in the same bit of bushland, where the need for mutual aid would gradually force them into some kind of working relationships. But how infinite the possibilities of misunderstanding between them, how slender the basis of concerted action![49]

The new associations into which individuals were forced were paralleled by those of the settlements they formed—the great tapestry of sub-communities stretching across the country. In the Ontario county which the writer knows best, there are Highland townships, North of Ireland townships, Catholic Irish settlements, a French township and other minor French settlements, one or two German communities, many miscellaneous English, a few Negroes, and various odds and ends. Modern means of communication, plus the developing spirit of Canadianism, have tended to blur the outline of the original groups, but they are still there, still marked by their own habits, still with their traditional associations in church, political party and attitude towards the State, still to a large extent intermarrying with their own kind.[50] The writer has in mind a little community of Irish Catholics whose geographical and religious boundaries have held unchanged ever since the first days of settlement. Its members still form an 'island' in the larger Scottish and Northern Irish townships about them. There are no longer fights on the Twelfth of July, and when they meet the people of this particular countryside are good friends. Still, the original framework of this separate community is there, and intact. Multiply this by the hundred and by the intangible coefficients of strange habits and bitter traditional hatreds such as they were a century and more ago, throw in an unknown tongue, which would have been necessary wherever there were Gaelic-speaking men about (and almost as necessary for some 'English'-speaking Irish), and you get some idea of the welter that must have been Upper Canada.

It is no wonder that the English writers could not bring themselves to admit the existence of anything that could reasonably be termed a society.

"Canada is a colony, not a country, it is not yet identified with the dearest affections and associations, remembrances, and hopes of its inhabitants: it is to them an adopted, not a real mother."[51]

"I do not feel at home here yet: my former life, my sea voyage, and travelling some seven hundred miles through a new country, appear more like a dream than reality; my very existence in these drowsy woods appears doubtful, till I rouse myself by thinking on my College friends, my hunting days, the animating hounds, the green open fields and the scarlet coats."[52]

It has taken the intervening century and a quarter not only for 'gentlemen' like Mr. Radcliff to feel at home but also for the 'yeomen' of whom he speaks and who, so he says, when travelling bought themselves meals just as expensive as those of 'their betters'. "A fine country for the labouring man", said Mrs. Moodie, repeating a sentiment expressed over and over again. But the labouring man, too, had difficulty forgetting. The green hills far away rose for him too. And his children, though they had never seen them, heard of them and marvelled. Gradually that sentimental attitude for 'the old country' became a staple of Canadian life, with personal memories changing into second-hand nostalgias and what were once the ties of home fraying into mere political association—the whole complex mounting up to 'patriotism' as Canadians knew it. Only in our own time has the love of the land, "the dearest affections and associations" of which Mrs. Jameson spoke, begun to take place of this hankering after the past and given Canada at last the chance to become "not a colony but a country." Nevertheless, at the end of the period, by 1850 a new British North America had come into existence, larger, wealthier, with wide stretches of quiet comfortable farm land, with more cities, more amenities, working itself towards the point where it could clothe these things with "dear affections . . . remembrances . . . hopes".

Notes to Chapter 14

1. Removing armed vessels from the Great Lakes.
2. *The Commercial Empire of the St. Lawrence* (Toronto, 1937).
3. See Charles Dudley Warner, "Studies in the South and West, with Comments on Canada, 1889" in *Complete Writings* (Hartford, 1904), Vol. III, p. 484.
4. It would have been more difficult for the Molsons of Montreal or Gooderham and Worts of Toronto to have made such claims for their products.
5. Nor have some succeeded in acquiring it: in a conference held in the University of Montreal, 1956, at least two members were given badges of identification reading "Queen's University, Toronto" and "McMaster University, Toronto". Possibly his colleagues at the University of Montreal were not aware of the burden put upon a Queen's man who is made to proclaim that Queen's is in—of all places—Toronto!
6. The first complete census of the Province of Canada was made in 1851, the beginning of our decennial censuses. The other provinces also began this practice in the same year. This census has some retrospective material.
7. The censuses were taken at varying dates in the different provinces and at irregular intervals.
8. But that term does not include the United States.
9. S. C. Johnson, *A History of Emigration from the United Kingdom to North America, 1763-1912* (London, 1913).
10. Census, 1851, Vol. 1, pp. 562, 574.
11. The censuses of the Maritime Provinces do not give birthplace.
12. How difficult it is to decide from available statistics exactly what the situation was may be gathered from the following trial balance for the population of Upper Canada during the 27 years, 1824-1851. For these years we have (1) frequent provincial censuses and (2) yearly returns of emigrants leaving the United Kingdom bound for British North America (collected in Johnson, op. cit., p. 344). We may assume that 90 per cent of the 80 per cent which landed in Quebec proceeded to Upper Canada, or say 70 per cent of the total leaving the United Kingdom. The returns of births and deaths in the census of 1851 and previous incomplete returns indicate an annual natural increase of about 25 per thousand. Keeping the calculation, which must be rough, to round thousands, it works out as follows:

1	2	3	4	5	6	7
	Population by Census	Probable Natural Increase	Immigration via the St. Lawrence	Expected population	Actual Population	Difference
	151,000					
-1851		273,000	585,000			
	952,000			1,009,000	952,000	57,000

a Col. 5 = 2 + 3 + 4.

b In the original and more elaborate table of which this is a summary the "expected Population" was calculated afresh as from each of the fifteen census returns.

c This table would indicate that the province retained all but 57,000 of the total of its natural increase and immigrants too. This finding by no means coincides with the disparity mentioned above between immigrant arrivals and actual population born abroad. A means of reconciliation may perhaps be found in predicating a large annual immigration from the United States across the land frontier.

13. Total deaths returned: 7,775; population, 952,000; rate 8.06.
14. Census, 1851, Vol. II, p. 5: births, Upper Canada, 32,681; rate, 34.
15. See also Chapter 24.
16. But the total number of English (that is, 'non-French') in Quebec is not declining: there were in 1951 almost as many people of 'non-French' origin in the province as the total population of the province a hundred years before.
17. The semi-frontier county of Rimouski in 1851 had a birth rate of 47 per thousand!
18. See p. 397.
19. Instances abound: see Fred Landon, *Western Ontario and the American Frontier* (Toronto, 1941), pp. 159 ff.
20. J. C. Dent, *The Last Forty Years* (Toronto, 1881), p. 49.
21. Frank N. Walker, *Daylight Through the Mountain: the Life and Letters of Walter and Francis Shanly* (Toronto, 1957).
22. In 1851, 176,000 Irish by place of birth (religions not distinguished) as against 82,000 English and 75,000 Scots. Native-born were not distinguished by racial origin. In 1951, the racial origins of native-born included, there were more people of English origin than of Scottish and Irish combined.
23. Notably the Ottawa valley.
24. An addition must now be made for that blend of western England and Southern Ireland which Newfoundlanders carry on their tongues.
25. The sons, grandsons and great-grandsons of Charles Drury now carry on the family farm (as of 1956). One of them, the former Premier of Ontario, is Sheriff of Simcoe County and his courtesy supplies this information.
26. See, *inter alia*, Isaac Fidler, *Observations on Professions, Literature, Manners and Emigration in the United States and Canada made during a Residence There in 1832* (New York, 1933), p. 133.
27. Col. Talbot's status has not been sufficient to prevent his original homestead and house taking the usual melancholy Canadian turn— it is now (1958) the summer place of a family from Detroit!
28. Author of *Twenty-Seven Years in Canada West* (London, 1953).
29. Both edited by H. H. Langton, the latter under the title *A Gentlewoman in Upper Canada* (Toronto, 1950).
30. London, 1854, and Toronto, 1926.
31. Hamnet Kirkes Pinhey was one of the original settlers of the Township of Marsh in which there were numerous 'half-pay officer' settlers. See A. S. D. Ross, *Ottawa, Past and Present* (Toronto, 1927), pp. 38, 40.
32. This family may be the prototype of the family of Mazo de la Roche's novels. The estate is now a public park but Sibbalds still live in one of the original houses on it.
33. They supplied the rectors of the Anglican church, staffed the medical and legal professions, and found at least three places on the Bench. Their participation in municipal politics, while it did occur, was not prominent.
34. One lady, on the fringes of the group, being unfortunately a Presbyterian, observed to her minister that "one had to be most careful on one's 'days' (reception days) to avoid getting the wrong people in the drawing-room together for so-and-so could hardly be expected to remain in the room if so-and-so entered!" The situation corresponded to Mrs. Jameson's well-known "petty colonial oligarchy, a self-constituted aristocracy. . . . "
35. Anne Langton, *A Gentlewoman etc.*, op. cit., p. 131.
36. Ibid.
37. Thomas Reed, *Six Years in the Bush, or Extracts from the Journals of a Settler in Upper Canada, 1832-1838* (London, 1838).

38. For example the Radcliffs of Adelaide Township. See *Authentic Letters from Upper Canada* (Dublin, 1833, reprinted Toronto, 1953).

39. Public Archives of Canada, Series Q. Vol. 377, pt. 1, p. 1, *Colborne to Goderich, 1833.*

40. Anne Langton, op. cit., p. 88.

41. Public Archives, *Report*, 1889; "Having observed on our march that the Highlanders lose themselves in the Woods as soon as they go out of the road. . . . " *Col. Henry Bouquet to Gen. Amherst,* July 26th, 1763.

42. "When a Methodist itinerant asked a Glengarry Highland woman with a pail of water in her hand for a drink from her cup, she not only gave him to drink but strained the water through her soiled handkerchief to remove the wigglers." See John Carroll, *Case and His Contemporaries* (5 Vols. Toronto, 1867-1877), Vol. I, p. 44.

43. See also p. 61.

44. See also p. 78.

45. *Letters from America, 1767-1779: Brunswick, Hessian and Waldeck Officers with the British Armies* (ed. Pettengill, Boston, 1924), p. 118.

46. Susanna Moodie, *Roughing it in the Bush or Life in Canada* (London, 1854, and Toronto, 1926), p. 221.

47. Some of the local histories are very good, such as A. F. Hunter's *History of Simcoe County* (Barrie, 1948), or Mrs. C. M. Day's *History of the Eastern Townships* (Montreal, 1869). See also such writers as E. C. Guillet, *Early Life in Upper Canada* (Toronto, 1933) and his *The Great Migration: the Atlantic Crossing by Sailing Ship since 1770* (Toronto, 1937). For special groups see G. H. Needler, *Otonabee Pioneers: the Story of the Stewarts, the Stricklands, the Traills and the Moodies* (Toronto, 1953), and for historical romancing, such novels as Patrick Slater, *The Yellow Briar* (Toronto 1934) and Grace Campbell, *The Thorn-Apple Tree* (Toronto, 1942) among many others.

48. Moodie op, cit., p. 88.

49. This point is well brought out in Robertson Davies' play, *At My Heart's Core* (Toronto, 1950).

50. There is still a strong tendency to marry within the group: that is, Scots still marry Scots, etc. This is particularly marked in the Maritime provinces, where in each case the largest single group of children is born of parents of the same origin. In Ontario and Quebec, intermarriage has proceeded farther and in some cases there are more children of, say, Irish father and Scottish mother than of two parents of either origin. To take an example from 1946, the year before the post-war immigration began: in Ontario in 1946, there were 4,097 children born to mothers of German origin (most of them probably of several generations' Canadian residence). Of these 1,658 had fathers of the same origin, the next largest group of fathers being English, with 837, though the total number of "British" fathers was 1,845. Taking it the other way round, there were 4,020 children born to fathers of German origin. Of these 1,658 had mothers of the same origin, again the next largest group being English, with 912. The same results would come out with any of the other origins that go back to the great days of settlement, but not with the more recent groups. Since intermarriage must occur chiefly in towns and cities, it follows that rural districts still are pretty much what they were when originally settled.

51. Mrs. Jameson, *Winter Studies and Summer Rambles* (London, 1838).

52. *Authentic Letters* etc. op. cit., p. 110, William Radcliff to Arthur Radcliff, December 1832.

15: Victoria Regina

1 8 3 7. YEAR OF BLOODSHED AND PORTENT! Armed
rebellions in the Canadas! Louis Joseph Papineau scuttling
over the American border and William Lyon Mackenzie fleeing for his life! Old King William dead and a new monarch
on the throne—a young girl, a queen. "The twenty-fourth of
May, the Queen's birthday," the children shouted lustily. The
role that the day has played indicates the vast place the reign
was to have in Canadian life. In Canada "the twenty-fourth of
May" (or the nearest Monday) is still a public holiday, marked
by fireworks—the only fireworks day of our national year; and
now its relationship to monarchy has been weakened by
time, duly and properly made over by the children, those unfailing realists, into "firecracker day". For their elders "the
twenty-fourth of May" brings back other images—of the
Queen's head on coins and stamps, of the great long summer
of peace that her reign constituted for Canadians, and of the
way in which time and history seemed to stop for a moment at
her death.

Under Victoria, Canada, as we know it to-day, grew up. The
long period of nearly sixty-five years that was her reign com-
prehended such a huge sector of our brief history! It saw
the scattered colonies come together into the Dominion and
slowly learn to face the world as one. It saw them grow and
mature in a dozen different ways. And simply because it was
so long and had upon it the unity of this single name and single
life, men came to think of it as part of the perpetual order of
things: there had always been a Queen upon the throne and
her name had always been Victoria. It had been Victoria in
her girlhood when old grandfathers had been boys, Victoria
in her widowhood when their sons were fathers, and Victoria,
the revered old grandmother, when grandsons—the grandsons
of the men who had built this country—were setting off their
rockets and Roman candles on the anniversary of her birth.
It had always been Victoria, it seemed as if it always would

be Victoria. Canada was Victorian in nearly every fibre of its being.

So much so that to-day, when many monarchs have intervened, it comes with something of surprise to find survivals —and there are survivals, if few of them—of that older world that existed here before Victoria. Could there be anything before Victoria? The English-Canadian folk memory is so coloured by Victorianism that it is hard to imagine what it could be. Were there aspects of a more masculine time then? To a continent devoted to the feminine principle, Victoria, The Queen, the gracious queen, the mother of nine, the grandmother of her people, as she at last came to be, capped the climax, rounded off the feminine order of things. Only in dim corners did the old bass growls from the eighteenth century continue to be heard: gruff, salty voices by the sea, as they downed their rum, and thought of the blood that used to run in scuppers. And others, the tenor tones of intellectuals speaking in the old-fashioned accents of Voltairean France. A few such eighteenth-century voices there were, and small survivals of their appropriate surroundings—an old-world deportment, an old-world sense of status, odd bits of furniture, old stone houses, one or two public buildings, some churches, and here and there in Halifax or Quebec or Kingston, a street or square. These pre-Victorian evidences of our history must be sought for, but they exist, and they serve to remind us that we are not wholly of recent vintage.

From the eighteenth to the nineteenth century

In Europe the great changes which mark the transition from the older world of 'gentlemen' and aristocrats that we conveniently dub 'eighteenth century', began well before the end of the calendar year 1800: that event which marked the turn in history's page, the French Revolution, was only the most dramatic of them. But even in Europe the Napoleonic Wars kept everything in suspense until after Waterloo, and the new world of the nineteenth century, with its bustling business men, its aggressive Protestantism, its multitude of good causes and great dreams, is not dominant until the second or third decade of that century. This means, given the usual time-lag, that in the colonies the currents of history do not set in their new courses for still another decade or two. British North America's 'nineteenth century' therefore begins in the first years of Victoria's reign, and anything colonial prior to 1837 may be regarded as 'eighteenth century'. To English Canadians (neglecting the educated minority that knows of it through books) the eighteenth century, except in the few visible remains referred to, is almost non-existent, for it was blotted out by the Atlantic crossing. That vast break in tradition, accomplished principally in the nineteenth century, bruised the past if it did not destroy it, and made it easy to believe that history began yesterday. This was the normal experience for new communities—the world began with themselves! And for most modern Canadians of English speech, that means it began under Victoria.

In European civilization (of which that of England is a subsection) the eighteenth century, as marked by its literature, its art and architecture, the structure of its society, its religion, was dispassionate and detached, unsentimental, intellectual rather than emotional; above all, as it so often itself proclaimed, *rational*.[1] There could hardly be a collection of qualities that would recommend it less to the lower- and middle-class people who flocked to British North America during the great post-Napoleonic emigration. The 'historical climate' of the nineteenth century, especially the middle third of it, was marked in contrast by warm emotions, by passionate concern, sentiment descending to sentimentality, by causes, movements, crusades —everything that appeals to the ordinary man, especially to the ordinary man on the way up. The rear-guard action fought by the old world of privilege provided not only reactionary politics but also much of the stuff of what is loosely called 'romanticism'. This word is most frequently used with literary connotations but it also denotes a spirit that applies to all areas of life. While exploration of the vast historical swing which underlies the contrast between such phrases as 'the Age of Enlightenment' (*l'éclaircissement*) and 'the Romantic Movement' is impossible here, some of the major points in the transition from the one to the other can be noted.

Romanticism

With the loss of the rear-guard battle imminent, the conservative elements of society began to turn for consolation to that distant medieval past in which their supremacy had not been challenged. This yearning after the colour and mystery of a dim past is a principal mark of what is usually termed 'romanticism'. In this sense, 'romanticism' is nostalgia. By an easy transition it can also get an application to space as well as time (far-off fields look green), in which cases we are apt to dub it 'escapism' and call its political expression 'imperialism'. The transition from 'eighteenth century' to 'nineteenth century' is marked at every step by one aspect or another of what might be called 'the romanticism of nostalgia'. The by-products of this attitude are to be seen in literature, music, architecture, the graphic arts, in religion, politics—in the whole range of society. But there was also another kind of romanticism, easily understood by those who had caught a gleam of hope, as every colonist had, one that might be called the romanticism of accomplishment. It was equally under the spell of the mystery of life, if not of the mystery of medieval life, and equally convinced that things are bigger than they seem. It was logical for persons with this kind of dream to turn to the giant task of creating a 'brave new world'. The romanticism of accomplishment also affected the whole range of society.

A third aspect of nineteenth-century English attitudes was a direct descendant of the eighteenth-century 'Age of Reason': the intellectual grouping known as 'utilitarianism', *'laissez-faire'* or 'philosophical radicalism' whose central tenet was 'enlightened self-interest' as the most useful social principle. This school served England well in helping to bring about that institutional house cleaning in the generation after Waterloo which enabled her to play her role as industrial and liberal leader of the nations, but it was too much of the intellect to influence trends of opinion in backwoods colonies. J. A. Roebuck, long a colonial agent in London and a prominent philosophical radical, in discussing the union proposed for Upper and Lower Canada in 1822,[2] calmly proclaimed that in comparison with *interest*—the direct interest of the individual in his own concerns—such frivolities as religion and race were nothing. "What nonsense!" would have replied any Canadian, then and now, caught as we all are in the passions that arise from race and religion. The eighteenth-century Enlightenment deeply affected American thought through such men as Benjamin Franklin and Thomas Jefferson and through the natural-rights philosophy. But in this respect, English Canada is in contrast to the United States, whose older areas were intellectually more mature. The current of thought stemming from 'philosophical radicalism' could not be of major influence in British North America.

Romanticism in religion

In religion, largest single sub-division of a period's phases, romanticism's rear-guard battle was fought in the British world by the ritualists of the Church of England, the Anglo-Catholics associated with the Oxford Movement. In France, the same battle was fought, with much greater prospects of success, by a variety of Monarchist factions and by a group of Catholic intellectuals whose impact on the whole Catholic world was to be of vast proportions. This was the group which inspired the Catholic revival of the nineteenth century, a phenomenon which turned the papacy of Pius IX (1846-1878) into a pivot of history for the Roman Church. Both English and French movements had direct repercussions in the colonies.

The ritualistic movement in the Church of England found its echo in English Canada not so much through the cultivation of high-church practices, as in insistence on the exclusive view taken of 'The Church'. The divisive nature of exclusive pretensions is evident. In Upper Canada it prompted the classic controversy between Strachan and Ryerson, was at the heart of the Clergy Reserves struggle, and resulted in the bitter fight over the University of Toronto, Trinity College being founded as a high-church institution after the non-sectarian provincial university had been set up. This high-church wing of the Anglican Church was constantly assailed by the Toronto *Globe*, the 'Puseyite' (the name coming from one of its leading exponents in England) and the Roman Catholic looking very much alike to it. In this attitude it had some measure of justification, for in England 'Puseyite-ism' was leading many men to Rome. In Canada a consequence for which high-churchism was partially responsible was the strange alliance between English-speaking high tories and French-speaking Cartier 'Reformers'. The high tories in Macdonald's Liberal-Conservative coalition had no great objections to granting the Roman Catholics of Upper Canada separate schools (and would have willingly accepted the same for their own denomination). They were consistently successful in maintaining this policy of separate schools against George Brown's ultra-Protestant attacks. Brown himself regretted that low-church Orangemen should be betrayed by their leaders into supporting policies favouring the Catholics. Since it would have been impossible to set up a public separate-school system in Upper Canada without Conservative support, and since the Orangemen were one of the major components of the Conservative party of the times (the eighteen-forties and fifties), it follows that one of the gifts of the Orange Order to Ontario has been separate schools.[3]

Canadian high-churchism does not seem to have led any considerable number of persons into Catholicism, though the Hon. John Elmsley, Catholic protagonist of separate schools in the eighteen-forties, had been an Anglican. High-churchism is, however, taking a belated revenge to-day in unexpected quarters, to wit, in the old 'non-conformist' denominations. Now well-fed and complacent, as they emphasize more and more the stylistic, the formal, the ritualistic aspects of devotion, surrounding themselves with 'chancel style' church buildings and other aids to piety, they hardly seem to be aware that they are treading 'where the saints have trod' and groping for the pre-Reformation path.

Romanticism in its other aspect, that of accomplishment, or 'executive romanticism', as it might be termed, fitted the Canadian Protestant bodies like hand to glove.[4] Here was a new country with 'fields white unto harvest', a new world to be built morally and spiritually as well as physically and politically. Observers of the time are in agreement that conditions in the new settlements were often deplorable. Sexual laxity,[5] intemperance, ignorance, of all these were the settlers accused. Religious services among them at first were rare. The new settlements were thus made to order for the efforts of those who burned to better the world about them.

After the fires of the seventeenth century had cooled, religious zeal (in both Catholic and Protestant countries) had fallen to a low temperature. Its renewal in England was marked by the Wesleyan movement[6] and in North America by the frontier revival known as 'The Great Awakening': it was this latter movement which, spreading into the British colonies, was to establish the strength of the simpler denominations, especially the Baptists and the Methodists. In the nineteenth century these 'hot and strong' varieties of religion made contact with the evangelical zeal that was spreading out from England and which was of a more sophisticated type.

The very centre of the Evangelical Movement, as the new wave of old-country fervour came to be called, was the little group of men gathered around the well-known figures of William Wilberforce, Zachary Macaulay (father of the historian) and James Stephen, adviser to the Colonial Office—the members of the so-called 'Clapham Sect'. To them the modern world owes not only the initiative in the abolition of slavery but leadership in a dozen other humanitarian directions.[7] In particular they typified the immense interest that the period was to take in the extension of Christianity. Within a little over a generation, 1790-1840, Christian missionaries had penetrated the world, 'from Greenland's icy mountains to India's coral strand'. In the missionary movement, British North Americans, as soon as they reached some degree of maturity, were to take their place, and a large place it was to be. As early as 1846, there went out from Nova Scotia the first British American missionary, the Rev. John Geddie, a studious, well-equipped man, sent by the Presbyterian Church to the distant New Hebrides. Thus the colonies early began to share in the work of expanding British civilization through the missionary. Nothing comparable could have occurred in the eighteenth century.

The repercussions of this vast movement communicated to the colonies the spirit which initiated it at home, a spirit steeped in the romanticism of accomplishment, one which convinced its participants that a better world lay ahead. The effect of energetic Victorian convictions in making Christianity a creed for the here and the now hardly needs demonstration, for the evangelical wing of every great denomination, the Church of England included, stressed practical social improvement. The social gospel of modern Protestantism traces back to the evangelical revival of the early nineteenth century.

The class structure of the evangelical movement hastened this transmutation of religious zeal into social service, for it was based, not on 'hell-fire and damnation' sectarianism but on the participation of sensitive, educated men. When such men came to the colonies, or were born there, the orderly and intellectual elements in Protestantism received strong reinforcement. The change in tone in all the denominations coincident with the large post-Napoleonic immigration is evident and expresses itself in several directions. Within a generation of the beginning of this new immigration both Presbyterians and Methodists had established colleges. In Upper Canada they were putting up some church buildings of architectural merit. In Nova Scotia, the same transition is reflected in the work of men like Dr. McCulloch, founder of Pictou Academy and first President of Dalhousie University.

One interesting group of men much influenced by the nineteenth-century religious revival and who in their turn greatly influenced Canadian life was the southern Irish Protestants of whom the Baldwins, the Blakes, and Judge Gowan of Simcoe County were outstanding representatives. These men had lived in a Catholic society. They were members of the 'Ascendency' (as the Anglican church was dubbed in Ireland); and as with their brethren in the north, association with Catholics had reinforced their Protestantism, which had retained much of the crusading Puritanism of the seventeenth century. But unlike the North of Ireland Anglicans, they realized that the Irish society they knew could never become Protestant, and like the earlier Anglo-Norman Irish, they had associated themselves with their surroundings. When these families came to Canada, although their social status would have given them secure membership in Family Compact circles, they espoused the popular cause. It has been of immeasurable importance to this country that Robert Baldwin and Edward Blake were South of Ireland Anglican Protestants. In Canada, their Irish experience transmuted itself into low-churchism, liberalism and nationalism.

When Senator (later Sir James) Gowan's astonished eyes saw a cross displayed on the altar of Trinity Church, Barrie, he shook the dust of the accursed spot from his feet in anger, and built his own church across the way: it was something to be remembered to see Sir James, ostentatiously ignoring the abode of 'popishness', stalking into his private church every Sunday morning followed by his little train of semi-feudal retainers. Low-church Anglicanism, offshoot of Ireland and the Evangelical movement in England, was in some respects closer to Methodism than to high church. Through the Blakes and Baldwins, the low-church wing of Anglicanism built Wycliffe College in Toronto and this institution has mothered a long succession of religious achievements.

In France, the heightening of piety in the eighteen-thirties which eventually conducted the Roman Catholic Church to the Lateran Council and the doctrine of papal infallibility (July 18th, 1870) may be thought of as an aspect of nostalgic romanticism closely linked to the Bourbon restoration (1815-1830) and thus in itself an effort to cancel out the Enlightenment and Revolution (the same effort was to be made by Marshal Pétain after France's defeat in 1940). Since it came to involve the whole Catholic world it was an aspect of romanticism more significant for history that the corresponding English Oxford Movement (even if that movement did wear, as one of the trophies at its belt, John Henry, Cardinal Newman). In that it caught up into itself the same revival of zeal which marked the Protestantism of the period (including foreign missions), it was 'in the spirit of the age'. But it was also moved forward by the talents of as keen a group of Catholic intellectuals as the Church had possessed for some centuries. These men saw the necessity for a reply to 'rationalism', and their efforts were directed to refounding Catholicism on a philosophic basis that could meet the new scientific world views: few of them would have met liberalism, child of eighteenth-century rationalism, with a frontal attack, as Pius IX was to do in his Syllabus of Errors (1864), which document anathematized with bell, book and candle the modern world's whole current of thought. Despite it, in Europe keen minds in the Church have been able to produce a working compromise with new knowledge which has prevented its entire desertion by the intellectual. But in French Canada, the Church, fortified by the revival of seventeenth-century zeal which was signalized by the return of the Jesuits in the eighteenth-forties and the appointment of the extremely stiff and old-fashioned Catholic, Bourget, to the bishopric of Montreal in 1840, welcomed the Syllabus and, save for individual exceptions of no great importance, conquered the intellectual, thus ending 'the eighteenth century'. Strewn over the Quebec battlefield were such corpses as *le parti rouge* and *l'Institut Canadien*. In English Canada, in contrast with French, the intellectual was destined to win, and the Protestant churches have had to accommodate themselves to his triumph. It remains for later ages to see what the eventual result will be.

Romanticism, imperialism, nationalism

Religion romanticized time. But there was also the powerful romanticism of space, one of the main roots of what was later to be called 'imperialism'. Many are the prayers and poems addressed to the gods of distant places,[8] and countless times have the 'voices' been answered. Long before Canadian military establishments had taken on bone and sinew, sons of the 'well-born', drawn by these and the dozen other attractions of the military life in an expanding, world-wide empire, were apt to find their way into the British army. Such a one was General Williams, the Nova Scotian hero of the defence of Kars during the Crimean War. Just as conspicuous was young Dunn, son of the Hon. John Henry Dunn, Receiver-General of Upper Canada. The elder Dunn had migrated from England in 1820 and after making a fortune from channels not unrelated to his office, he returned there, an excellent example both of Family Compactism and of the English colonial exile. He took his son back with him and the latter, under circumstances of great gallantry in the Charge of the Light Brigade, gained the first Victoria Cross. An adventurous life and violent death followed. "A fearless, headstrong youth who wanted to be a soldier almost as soon as he was able to express a wish." Here was a perfect pattern for the romanticism of empire. It was followed by many whose family names are well known in 'upper-class' Canadian circles — Robinsons, Denisons and others.[9] All of them shouted in the voice of the schoolboy rallying the ranks, or clashed with their fiery few and won. All of them were setting wider and wider the bounds of the 'Land of Hope and Glory' (which was not Canada). Here was colonialism, pure and undefiled, an attitude transmuted by romanticism into imperialism, a sentiment maintained longest and most determinedly everywhere in dependencies by an upper class. Here was the background for the emotional words of English Canada, those uttered with the chin up, words like 'British' or 'far flung'.

British-born immigrants to British North America in the nineteenth century brought with them empire in their hearts. It was at its least a form of home-sickness. But their act of settlement was in itself an affirmation of faith—if they did not like British institutions, they were free to continue on to the United States, as many of them did. This negative selection strengthened the colonial spirit of attachment to the mother country, which was further reinforced by the proximity of the giant that in discarding empire had come to hate 'The Empire'. As a result, in few places has the romantic aspect of empire made as strong an appeal as in English Canada. The direct effect of the nineteenth-century romanticism of nostalgia is, in this particular, abundantly evident: the older elements in English Canada will long remain romantic about the empire on which the sun never used to set and about the good queen under whom the bounds of empire were set at their widest point.

The idea of empire impeded the growth in British North America of another semi-romantic sentiment,[10] that of nationalism. Nationalism is collective self-realization. Often, as in the case of the adolescent boy, self-realization sets up psychological disturbances such as inward unsureness and its outward corrective gestures of assertiveness: these do not make for peace in the family. The modern world has reason to fear nationalism, which has been among the chief causes of its wars. But parents have reason to fear adolescence. In older countries which have been under foreign domination the intensity of feeling that self-realization induces can be understood: it is no wonder that it produces its prophets and its poets. Nationalism both creates the myth and appeals to the myth it has created: in this way it is essentially romantic. The eighteenth century could cry with Pope

"For forms of government let fools contest;
    Whate'er is best administer'd is best."

but it was the nineteenth that flung out by the score such poems as *England, My England* or *Deutschland über Alles*.

In new countries, nationalism has not as a rule had to contend with repressive forces of the same strength as in old, and it has therefore had a lower temperature. This is true even where the rule of the mother country has been terminated by revolutions, as in South America and in the United States. Yet American nationalism, thanks to its revolutionary origin, is more intense than Canadian. Canadian nationalism constitutes almost an exact parallel to the approach of a youth to manhood: the same stages can be traced in the life courses of both, and with a good deal of specific detail. In a normal family the tension between the generations does not result in disruption; an equilibrium is reached. Canadian (along with Australian and New Zealand) nationalism has not provided the high dramatic moments, the ringing speeches, the heroic deeds, of the more intense movements. It has been, therefore, less tinged with romanticism than these have, more of an indigenous natural process. In this way in the field of nationalism the change from the eighteenth to the nineteenth century in the white colonies of English speech was not emphatically marked.

There was one white colony, not of English speech, of which this statement could not be made—French Canada. As a previous chapter has shown, the Conquest was for it a species of revolution, and the struggle to widen the area of self-government continued the psychological storm thus begun. Influences, as a rule not stressed by French-speaking writers, also came in from the French Revolution. The result was the nationalistic movement of the early nineteenth century, begun under the auspices of *Le Canadien* and continued by Louis Joseph Papineau until it reached a crest in the Rebellion of 1837. This movement took a shape similar to movements of the sort in other Catholic countries of the Latin tradition. There was the same absence of social reform in its program, the same cleverness in manipulating existing institutions, the same heady eloquence, and there was the same divergence between the leaders and the Church, the leaders finding in freedom an absolute that tempted them away from traditional doctrine. Nationalism has always divided Catholic countries, because it implies enshrining of a rival god. Hence, although it has had support from individual clerics, the official church, which from its very nature cannot be 'national', has walked warily. In this attitude, in Lower Canada as elsewhere, its introduction to the phenomenon could hardly fail to confirm it, for the little band that gathered about Papineau was composed of people of dubious Catholic orthodoxy.

It has often been assumed that French Canada has continued on into the twentieth century, a mere hold-over from the seventeenth, the unaltering product of the Church's purest age of missionary zeal. '*Je me souviens*'. Every society presents many aspects, and one of French Canada's is this seventeenth-century survival. It may be its most prominent. There are necessarily others, for even in Quebec it never has been true, Louis Hémon's day-dreaming to the contrary, that nothing changes. And among these other aspects of French Canada is a reflection of the French eighteenth century. That this reflection came in by the back door does not lessen its significance. The Catholic revival of the nineteenth century tended to bury and to discredit the eighteenth-century Age of Enlightenment, associating it with 'free-thought', atheism, secularism, and other such horrors, all summed up in the word *liberalism*. But it does not take much to discover what a source of ferment in French Canada was this intellectualism of the previous century.[11]

It is now known that shortly after the English Conquest, the works of Voltaire began to make their appearance in Canada. They found their way into numerous private libraries—and there were private libraries at this early date in French Canada—and were read, apparently by a considerable circle among the *élite*. Along with Voltaire's writings, other less tangible influences from 'The Enlightenment' also penetrated the province, where they took the shape so much dreaded by a clergy of rigid orthodoxy: the young Louis Joseph Papineau, for example, is said to have lost his faith while at school in the Grand Seminary at Quebec, and he never afterward regained it. To men like him, the French Revolution was something to give rise to mixed feelings. They rejoiced in the spirit of liberation which it seemed to embody but they realized that it was taking their former country one step away from themselves, leaving them lonelier than before. To the French-Canadian intellectual growing up in the early nineteenth century, the barrenness of the rapidly expanding English commercial civilization must have been just as uninviting as the obscurantism of the gloomy and dictatorial seventeenth-century past from which he was escaping. He must have found the croakings of the classical economists about rent and wages just as repellent as the doctrines, still being taught in his schools, of absolute monarchy as the ultimate perfection of human government. Conflicting influences of this type would drive the intellectual along the road towards nationalism, that is, towards the creation of a society conceived in his own image.

Such men could not fail to be powerfully influenced by the currents of nationalism running out of the French Revolution. *Le Canadien's* 'masthead' slogan—*notre langue, nos institutions, nos lois*—was not much more than a version in local terms of *liberté, égalité, fraternité*.[12] French-Canadian nationalism was to have much more in common with European nationalism than with English-Canadian in that it was to be a struggle for liberation.

After the Rebellion of 1837, Papineau found his way from the United States to France, where his tenets were reinforced by his associations with the republicans of the day. He returned to Canada in 1845, bringing with him his old ideas strengthened by this period of his exile. The party which grew out of his career, *le parti rouge*, was suspect from the first, and eventually the differences between it and the hierarchy flared up into open strife. When in the eighteen-sixties many French-Canadians of unimpeachable orthodoxy rushed to Italy to help defend the Pope against the Garibaldian legions, at least one of their compatriots, Arthur Buies, was to be found on the opposite side. At home, after Bishop Bourget had succeeded in virtually destroying *l'Institut Canadien*[13] of Montreal, the body of principles represented by *les rouges*, which closely resembled European liberalism, became less and less effective politically, and at last it was formally abandoned in the great speech on political liberalism made by Wilfrid Laurier in 1877. This was the speech in which Laurier proclaimed himself a Liberal in the English, or Gladstonian sense, and repudiated anything that savoured of lack of orthodoxy in religion. Nevertheless, the persecutions of the clergy pursued Laurier until well after he had become prime minister of Canada, and even to this day there are groups among them who distrust, as synonymous with, if not atheism, at least with secularism, the word *liberal*.

It could never be claimed that the 'eighteenth century' touched a large proportion of the people of French Canada: they leapt, were forced to leap, almost directly from the seventeenth century to the modern world, passive under the alien forces round about them. That is why a French-speaking literary historian, Jules Léger,[14] referring to the more formal aspects of literature, can remark that romanticism as such was not much known before 1855 or so, that before that the French classical period (say 1630-1690) had dominated French-Canadian writing and reading: Corneille and Racine, he says, were still the reigning favourites of serious readers. But was M. Léger not aware of the strong eighteenth-century influences on both French-Canadian writing and thought of mid-nineteenth century which Trudel has since depicted?

M. Léger's description of that period as a sudden leap from classicism to romanticism, is right enough for what might be called popular literature, the literature that appealed to the heart, except in that the romanticism of nostalgia began on the very morrow of the Conquest. The experience having driven them in on themselves, it is natural that French-speaking Canadians should ever since have looked back to their own past, before the English troublers came, to find a place of spiritual content. This attitude opens the gates wide to the romantic attitude, which in French Canada is virtually synonymous with the nostalgic. The twin sentiments find constant expression. Not a generation has passed since the Conquest without someone painting the glories of *les bons vieux temps*,[15] when every sturdy farmer's table groaned with food and every fireplace blazed with cheerful warmth. The golden age has moved up in date, but has always kept a fixed distance behind the writer, like his shadow. Gérin-Lajoie in *Jean Rivard* (1862) rhapsodizes over *les vieilles terres transmises de père en fils depuis des générations*. Aubert de la Gaspé in his *Anciens Canadiens* (1866) harks back to the generation previous to his own birth (1786), the post-Conquest period. P. J. O. Chauveau ends his *Charles Guérin* (1852) by bringing his hero back to his native fields, after the bitter deceits of 'the world', where he marries the girl who had ever been waiting for him.

Another pleasant little book from this lost world is *Laurentian Heritage* by C. B. Rouleau, which relates to the childhood of the writer in the eighteen-seventies. A couple of chapter headings give some idea of its atmosphere: "When Heaven Smiled on Our World"; "Homespun Idyll: How one woman queened it on a Quebec farm."

The very classic of romantic nostalgia for the past is Adjutor Rivard's *Chez Nous* which, though of our own century (the W. H. Blake translation is 1924) carries us back once more to 'the good old days'. It is consecrated to nostalgia, nostalgia for the childhood of the writer, nostalgia for the happy, happy days—of the race! Every page is redolent with sentiment for the blissful existence of the simple countryside (never a mosquito in sight), where every man was strong and every woman's eyes "shone with loving kindness," where good curés sauntered through quiet village streets, giving kindly greetings to the urchins and good advice to everyone. Even the beggars and pedlars bathe in the soft light of idyllic pastoralism. The story of Quebec shines out so vividly from such pages: "Here, on our land, we are *chez nous* and masters of our fate. Beaten on the battlefield, forced to admit the stranger to our national home, here on our farms, we still lead our own lives. These we will barricade, shutting out the intruding world. . . . Not a moment of that past (which is ours, as the future is not) must be lost."[16]

Romanticism in architecture

In both French and English Canada no other phase of the change from 'eighteenth century' to 'nineteenth' is so conspicuous to the eye as that which manifests itself in architectural style.

In Nova Scotia, the eighteenth century survives in a few public buildings and in a considerable range of domestic architecture. St. Paul's Church, Halifax, was built about a decade after the founding of the city. It is thus (1958) about two centuries old: this is its chief merit. Its style is vaguely New England. Its frame construction has outlasted scores of the solidly built stone churches of the St. Lawrence Valley. Two other public buildings in Halifax have much greater distinction of style than has this ancient church, namely, Government House and the Province Building. Both of these are nineteenth century in actual date of construction, but eighteenth in style, proportions, and restraint. Outside of Halifax, apart from the ruins at Louisbourg, perhaps the most interesting site in the province is Annapolis. Here the eighteenth century may still be seen and, with imagination, felt. Official Annapolis was 'old country' with its fine stone fort and barracks: humble Annapolis, in its graveyard, was Massachusetts over again. Nova Scotia is New England all through 'The Valley'[17] and in the western part of the province generally—New England in the design, proportions and material of its domestic architecture, New England, too, in its social and religious attitudes, but pre-Revolutionary, eighteenth-century New England. Of its 'nineteenth-century', or 'romantic', architecture, possibly the less said the better.

In Quebec, the architectural dimensions of the past rise to larger proportions, too large for adequate discussion here. There is not a great deal left of the seventeenth century, though there is some; but more important than actual physical remains, there has been sufficient time and isolation for a native tradition to develop. Experts agree that in Quebec we have a distinctive style, both for ecclesiastical and domestic buildings, based on French prototypes but not merely derivative. "There were regions in France, like the Ile-de-France, where a fusion of tradition similar to that which produces the parish church of Quebec took place but nowhere was the combination of elements exactly the same. The parish church tradition of Quebec is in this sense entirely indigenous, entirely unique: one of which French Canada can justly be proud."[18] Similar remarks could be made for dwellings. Few observant persons can have failed to notice the pleasant old farm-houses along the St. Lawrence. Below Quebec, they are surrounded by verandas supported from the foundation walls, usually with entrances underneath to the basement, giving an effect that calls to mind a ship's bridge. Above Quebec, the flaring bell eave appears, and extends as far west as the French language. There are also the distinguished old manor houses, some of them actually of seventeenth-century construction: these would be masterpieces anywhere.[19] In Quebec city, there are plenty of houses, indeed whole blocks and streets, which are eighteenth century in appearance, though often nineteenth in actual date of construction. They give to the town that old-world appearance which makes it unique on the continent, but possibly they are more pleasing to the tourist than to those who have to live in them.

The most interesting specimens of eighteenth-century style in the Province of Quebec, and in the opinion of the writer, the most distinguished architecture the century has produced are the churches on the south shore of the St. Lawrence below Quebec City. Among them, those of Beaumont (1727), St. Jean Port Joli (1756), Kamouraska (1791), stand out, though all altered much since their first construction. All of them are entirely different from anything to be found in English Canada, typically French but just as typically Canadian. Each one with its characteristic roof and walls, its simple yet striking white-and-gold interior, its well-kept grounds, is a gem.[20]

The result of unbroken, indigenous tradition was splendid —as long as tradition remained unbroken. But when the nineteenth century, with its pervading romanticism, descended upon Quebec, disaster followed. Montreal led. In the eighteen-twenties the old parish church, whose origins went back to 1672, having become too small, it was decided to build another. The result was the present Notre Dame, 1824-1829.[21] The main points about Notre Dame are that it is 285 feet long, 134 feet wide, and will seat over ten thousand people. It was built at a time when admiration for the Gothic past was not equalled by knowledge of it. Hence grandiosity and imitative ugliness replaced the earlier grace, which was ruthlessly pulled down. The architect was an Irishman, James O'Donnell, who fittingly was buried under the church he built. As was said of Vanbrugh, the architect of Blenheim House, could it not be said of him:

"Lie heavy on him, Earth, for he
   Laid many heavy loads on thee!"

The worst consequences of the Gothic revival in French Canada were not in the parish church of Montreal, whose very size and pretentiousness possibly made it supportable, but in its innumerable blurred copies up and down the river: "as bizarre an assemblage of edifices as could be found anywhere."[22] It is hard to understand why a people who have prided themselves on the heroic maintenance of their past should not have hesitated to destroy one of the most significant aspects of that past, their splendid heritage of architecture. During the nineteenth century, church after church from the previous great age of building was either pulled down completely or disastrously reconstructed. The ugly new edifices which replaced them, it might be argued, are indigenous style, too. Quite true: their like could not possibly be found elsewhere. No doubt they testify to the reality of French Canada's existence and buttress *l'amour-propre* but why do they not exhibit some of the artistry of the preceding age?

Their social explanation probably lies in the conjuncture of an awakening group consciousness (to which *la survivance* was supreme among miracles) with the romantic spirit of the age. 'Gothic' reminded simple souls of the great days of the medieval past, grandiosity was a testimonial not only to *la survivance* but to the general excellence of *la race canadienne*. Yet it would be a very peculiar God who could take any pleasure in having them erected to His glory.

In Upper Canada, people did not pull down their architectural inheritance, for a very good reason: there was none. Or, rather, there was little. Some specimens of that little survive, standing out like aristocrats among a crowd of parvenus. A few districts may be singled out. Among these the provincial capital need not be included, unless it is to be considered as redeemed through Osgoode Hall. This building, begun in 1829, was added to and renovated down to 1859. The changes appear to have been for the worse. As planned "the Osgoode Hall of that date [1829] must have ranked with some of the finest monuments of the eighteenth century in North America."[23] "The drastic changes of 1857" were all nineteenth-century in spirit as well as in date, according to Armstrong, and completely eclectic—you just reach over and pick a toy off the counter, saying "this would look nice" and then put it into your building. If pictures are to be trusted, Toronto once had some good buildings but it made short work of them, so it may be left to rejoice in its skyscrapers.

It is not the capital, but Niagara-on-the-Lake, Kingston, and, for rural domestic construction, eastern Ontario,[24] which deserve inspection. Niagara-on-the-Lake is pre-romantic, and it looks it, a delightful bit of the eighteenth century (reflected through American eyes, of course), with its churches and many of its houses. It is questionable if these will much longer be allowed to impede that modern 'progress' which is burying the neighbouring fruit lands under industrial construction, for who is there to give the love and pride that would protect them? Beyond Niagara along the Lake Erie shore, there are some good farm-houses, notably a few in the neighbourhood of Colonel Talbot's dwelling (which itself is interesting but not remarkable). Apart from a few oases such as these, Ontario west of Cobourg is mostly 'nineteenth century', an architectural desert, scene for the operations of an invading army.

Kingston is unique. It may be compared with Halifax and Quebec, but it is not as crowded as Quebec and not quite as slummy as Halifax. And some sections of it preserve the eighteenth century better than either of the others. Its market square has two sides (though one of them is disfigured by the pseudo-Greek temple of a bank) which the architect must find sheer delight. One of these is composed of the city hall (built 1843), the most dignified city hall in Canada. The satisfaction which the citizens of Kingston take in it, their pride in their past, and their acumen in discerning what makes their city attractive are illustrated by the way in which in the eighteen-eighties the battery park out in front of it was turned into a railway freight yard. Men of our own generation have "shamed the boast that they are wiser than their sires" by tearing off the great hand-cut entrance pillars and grinding them up for road-metal. In a genuinely civilized country those responsible for such a deed would have been regarded as criminals: it seems accident, not intelligence, which has secured us any public amenities we happen to have in Canada.

Kingston has not only the remains of its city hall, but also its court-house and its Anglican cathedral, all in the same pre-Gothic, semi-classical style. There is also a pair of federal buildings close by, with a little park between them, the whole making a pleasing *ensemble*. King Street, which runs off the city-hall square, has many examples of the attractive old stone residences which are only now, a century and a half after their building, becoming appreciated. To take a walk through some of the old streets of this town is a delight, and there is hardly a man among its old inhabitants who would not tear them all down to-morrow. The town has many buildings which exemplify not only Upper Canada's 'eighteenth century', but also its transition to the 'nineteenth', such as the two churches which were built just about at the half-century mark, the Roman Catholic St. Mary's Cathedral and the Methodist Sydenham Street. Of these, St. Mary's is the more impressive in sheer bulk, and it is a better example of the revived Gothic than its counterpart in Montreal. It has not, however, the grace of

Sydenham Street, which, while not 'medieval' in its shape and seating arrangements, scores through an effective arrangement of spire and roof. Both these churches, particularly Sydenham, and the town as a whole, triumph over mere period by the beauty of their stonework.

If Canadians were Americans, with comparable pride, Kingston, which Bruce Hutchison has described as "a symphony in stone", might get treatment similar to that which Williamsburg, Virginia, has received, and, as it were, be 'put under glass' (as has been done with nearby Fort Henry) for the delight of the future and the strengthening of Canadian social bonds. No such danger, however, seems to confront it.[25]

Despite the occasional successful edifice, English Canada suffered just as dismally in its public architecture from the Gothic revival as did French. In Upper Canada, it could hardly be termed as 'revival' for, as indicated, there was not much to precede it, and therefore the first major wave of construction had to be Gothic. In all English Canada there can only be a handful of pre-Gothic churches still in existence, and there never were many of them, at least, many of any importance. English Canada architecturally is hopelessly of the nineteenth century, a product of a period in which taste was at a low ebb. For illustration, one has only to look around—at the three big churches on Church Street, Toronto, all built about 1850, at the federal and Ontario Parliament Buildings—in fact at almost any public building. For real grotesques, the derivatives from the derivatives which adorn the city of Winnipeg 'take the cake'—especially the old Manitoba College (now St. Paul's) and the city hall. So deeply did the revival bite into Canadian mentality that probably down to this day, few can think of a church as other than a building with pointed windows (and the more bad stained glass the better).

Yet the Gothic style could go so far that its very grotesquery could win it a certain charm. There is a house in Kingston built at the very zenith of revival: the spindly, open-work veranda supports of this structure, its innumerable little points and projections, make it attractive. Another comes to mind in Lennoxville, Quebec. Built in 1839, it does not have two rooms on the same level. Wooden flowers and fruits dart out at you as you climb the staircase. Fretwork ('carpenters' Gothic') riots everywhere. Windows are divided and subdivided, each pane with a point to it. It was probably intended to carry the romantic, mysterious airs of an old castle on the Rhine. To get such airs imprisoned in Canadian white pine was no slight task (and a still greater task to keep it all dusted).

The difficulty involved in the architectural swing from the one century to the other lay in the fact that no true Victorian could leave a straight line alone. Straight, simple lines, severity of outline, are the mark of an aristocratic society. Efflorescence, embellishment, the surrender to 'niceness' come in, in architecture as in everything else, when the climate changes from aristocratic to bourgeois, in other words, when the 'eighteenth century' is succeeded by the 'nineteenth', or Georgianism by Victorianism. It was characteristic of British North America that this change should have come to it about a generation after it had got well under way abroad, roughly coincident with the middle-class civilization that was growing up in the shade of the post-Napoleonic mass immigration. Such change forms a deep ground swell of history. It affects every aspect of life.

In the lesser household arts, one of which was well developed in the colonies, the change was as conspicuous as in architecture. Colonials from the first made their own furniture. A considerable quantity of it survives from the eighteenth century. The writer knows of at least one eighteenth-century house (1793) which still has the same furniture that was put into it when it was built. Chairs, tables, beds, thanks to the goodness of the wood used and the simplicity imposed by limited facilities, are all aristocrats. Then when the 'climate' changed, bunches of grapes, sprays of leaves, carved in beautiful native walnut, began to gallop along the undulating backs of settees. Chair legs developed seductive curves. One of the major contributors to this Victorian exuberance was the well-known furniture-making house of Jaques and Hay, Toronto, whose pieces to-day to the uninitiate are minor prizes. Everyone at the time said "how nice"; just as the ladies did over the ever-swelling circumferences of their rioting, romantic Victorian crinolines.

Romanticism and colonial literature

The next field of illustration is that of writing. It may be contended that in mid-nineteenth-century British North America there was not much writing. On the contrary, there was a good deal. There was not much literature, but of writing in the form of newspapers, and of a considerable number of literary periodicals, there was much. Until well on in the nineteenth century, the literary periodicals bore the marks of the eighteenth century: they were characterized by a certain formality and a ceremoniousness that we would find strange to-day. They were keenly aware of the gradations in society. As the century went on, formality was often replaced by fulsome grandiosity: "The Turkish room contained 'repose-inviting couches' . . . and in the centre 'a most luxurious-looking ottoman. Long festoons of verdant wreaths hung in graceful sweeps, and, lighted by one handsome chandelier, the room was the beau idéal of a temple prepared for Love and Beauty'."[26]

Generally speaking, the literary magazines were run by expatriates. Well-educated, they brought with them contemporary British culture, then totally immersed in the later romanticism.[27] They wrote for a select group—people like themselves. The motherland was invoked and allegiance strengthened by patriotic poetry. Much of this writing was marked by a self-confidence and worldly assurance which even to-day many of our Canadian writers lack. Attempts to penetrate the native Canadian scene usually took the form of nature worship, for to the British immigrant this country meant Indians, lakes, animals, not communities of people. Often there was a patronizing tone about such writing, as if the authors were seeking to enlighten. This was understandable, if irritating, for the writers were people of wider experience of life than the locals: many, for instance, were military people who had lived in odd corners of the globe that were barely names to colonials. Hence such articles as "Sketches of Syrian Manners," "Alligators and their Roar," "Marching in India". Romanticism comes out in the subjects: the pages were full of Arab sheiks or feudal castles or of impossibly beautiful and virginal maidens. Homesickness was often in evidence.

"Blest isle of the Free! I shall view thee no more,
My fortunes are cast on this far-distant shore
In the depths of dark forests my soul droops her wings,
In the tall boughs above me no merry bird sings . . .
In dreams, lovely England, my spirit still hails
Thy rich daisied meadows—they green sunny vales."

This was from Mrs. Moodie's *Literary Garland*.[28] In literary quality Mrs. Moodie's verse was a far cry from the equally nostalgic *Lone Shieling*.[29] The *Literary Garland* deserves a chapter to itself, but for it the brief remark must suffice that it reflected its editress and her circle, as remarkable a group of exiles as we have had.

Another interesting example comes from Toronto: *The Maple Leaf or Canadian Annual*, 1847-1849. This publication was the first fruit of higher learning in that city, its editress being the wife of Principal McCaul. It was therefore the progenitor of many succeeding attempts by academic exiles to obscure to themselves the calamitous fact that they were now on the wrong side of the Atlantic, and probably 'for keeps'. The three volumes of this periodical are filled with fine engravings—much too good to have been executed in Toronto —full-page scenes of Greece and Rome, or serene and lovely women dressed in the exotic garb of the East or the fanciful draperies of classical times. They reflect a longing for the unreal (itself a prominent trait of romanticism), a hankering after the sophistication that could not be found in 'Muddy York'. "In the present publication, an attempt has been made to introduce among us that combination of Pen and Pencil Sketches which has been so eminently successful in the mother country." The editors desired to spread "the soft influence of refined taste." They stated that they had determined to accept only Canadian contributions, or as they put it, "when we formed the idea of offering to Canada a literary wreath, we determined that the only hands which should weave the garland should be those of her Children by birth or adoption." Most of them seem to have been by adoption, for it is hard to conceive of any of those by birth writing on "Val d'Ossola," "The Maid of Saragoza" or "The Destruction of Cambyses' Army."

Maple Leaves suffered the same fate as all the other literary journals of the time, lapsing after a short life. Not all were so colonial or so high-flown, and after the turn of the half-century a much more down-to-earth tone prevailed. But that had no avail in saving the periodicals exhibiting it, such as *The British American Magazine*, 1863-1864. All alike went under, wrecked on the intellectual barrenness of colonial life.

Books, had there been any, would have met the same fate. When poor John Richardson, a Canadian who had actually written a book, came back home in the eighteen-forties,[30] he carried with him hopes that his production might make some appeal to his countrymen. "I actually obtained," he says, "among a population exceeding a million of persons, not less than two hundred and fifty subscribers. . . ." "At Detroit, and its immediate vicinity, was [*sic*] laid the chief scenes of my Indian tale of 'Wacoustah', and as the Americans are essentially a reading people, there was scarcely an individual in the place who was not familiar with the events described in it, while, on the contrary, not more than one twentieth of the Canadian people were aware of the existence of the book, and of that twentieth not one third cared a straw whether the author was a Canadian or a Turk."[31] We may comfort Major Richardson, in whatever Elysium he may be resting, by assuring him that he would not find things impressively changed if he were to return to his native country to-day, one hundred and ten years later: there was no national pride in English Canada in 1847 (but plenty of dislike of 'the damned Yankees') and, except in limited circles, there is not much more to-day.[32] Thomas Chandler Haliburton, who in Nova Scotia at the same time was writing his immortal *Sam Slick* papers, would have had a thin living out of those he sold in his native province: it was only after his acceptance in the two senior countries and after the lapse of a century that his native province canonized him. He deserves canonization, too. But there is none of the romantic about him: he is the earthy, matter-of-fact North American, neither 'eighteenth' nor 'nineteenth' century in the European sense, just himself in his homespun surroundings.

The story of indifference to native production was exactly the same in French Canada: a hopeful year or two, and then extinction. But the French periodicals were different in tone from most of the English. They were from the first open to the implications of nationalism. They had a sense of native history not found in the English. They were more aware than the English of the native scene and understood that what gives it significance is not its pine forests and lakes but its people. This may arise from their religion, which has always been severe in its anthropomorphism and has never shown any tendency to let 'nature' get the edge over 'man'. But the French periodicals bit the dust, too, victims to the same lack of interested readers, few in any colony, fewer still in those which, like ours, had left so many of their traditions somewhere else.

The coming of the nineteenth century in politics

One other field cannot be neglected, the largest and most intricate of all, if it could be adequately explored, namely the political form of society and its political ideals. If the eighteenth century was the century of aristocracy and good taste, it was also, and logically, the century during which 'the lower orders' were supposed to know their place, which was a long way below that of 'the quality'. It was the century of prescriptive rights in which no idea was so sacred as that of property. The attempt of those who benefited from these attitudes to keep them going formed the major source of social tension in colonial life. Legislative Councils liked to think of themselves as 'The Lords', colonial dignitaries were insistent on the right style of address, and visiting old-country players, seeking patronage, addressed themselves humbly "To the nobility of. . . ." The native-born of ordinary condition and the recently arrived immigrant with land at his back did not appreciate all this as much as did "the nobility of. . . ." The old-country immigrant himself is invariably described as an individual who immediately upon acquiring land acquired the airs that went with it and often became as Tory as the governor.

His 'betters', the men at the top, were in an old-world sense, gentlemen, courteous in manner, dignified, suave. Their surroundings were similar. Life for many of them was a matter of servants, of considerable leisure, of punctilio (duels were an aspect of punctilio). It mounted to heights of distinction on special social occasions. "While in Toronto, I had the pleasure of attending a very brilliant ball given by the Chief Justice Robinson, whose *savoir vivre* not less than whose *savoir faire* ever render his parties the most agreeable that are given by any private gentleman in Canada. . . ."[33] Even if some of their members had had to climb up the ladder to eminence, the ruling group clearly possessed many of the attributes of an aristocracy. This was most pronounced in York, the inland, backwoods capital. In Kingston *hauteur* was less marked and people were closer together. In Montreal, the big merchants were the dominant group, and wealth gave them the same standard of life as the gentlemen in York. But how could they really compete when so many of them had come over the route of old John Molson, who still, after he had attained wealth, could be seen standing of a morning at his brewery door, chaffering with the farmers for their barley?[34] In Quebec, while officialdom was associated with race, yet, as earlier chapters have shown, there was considerable coming and going among the *élite* of both groups, and more disposition on the part of the general populace to accept 'the quality' than there would have been in an English-speaking city. And in Halifax—and nowhere was dignified status more prized—they were all Nova Scotians together, with relations among themselves which did not differ much from those between rich and poor over in Boston. One is forced back to York as the centre of gentility and of tension.

An indication of the sort of thing that provided daily grievance, and daily evidence of privilege, is furnished by William Allan, founder of a well-known Toronto family. According to the *York Almanac* for 1823, Mr. William Allan was a Trustee of the General Hospital of Upper Canada. He was a Commissioner under the Alien Property Act. He was the President of the Bank of Upper Canada. He was Treasurer of the Home District, Collector of Customs for York, Commissioner of the Peace for the Home District, a colonel of militia, Inspector of Shop, Still and Tavern Licenses for the Home District and, lastly, Postmaster of York. This would seem almost enough for one man. Allan was a family compact all in himself. But in addition to him, as one goes through the lists of officials of the time, great and small, one finds the same names over and over: Baby, Strachan, Dunn, Powell, Boulton, Robinson, Jarvis, Ridout and various others. Of Ridouts, Thomas was Surveyor-General, a member of the Clergy Reserves Corporation and a trustee of the central school. Samuel was second clerk in the office of the Surveyor-General and Sheriff of the Home District. George was a barrister and a director of the Bank of Upper Canada. Thomas G. was a cashier in the Bank of Upper Canada. Much of this was and is inevitable in any community, for family influence will always tell. But until mid-century, York (Toronto) was a small community and monopoly was too visible to the naked eye. Sharp reaction against it was unavoidable, and this took the form of the Rebellion of 1837. As armed outbreaks go, the rebellion seemed relatively minor at the time but as it recedes into the past, its place in Canadian history gets larger. Its legacies in the form of differing conceptions of society are still with us.

In most countries of the western world, the great historical swing from the gilded, privileged world of the past that we conjure up with the words 'eighteenth century' to the more workaday existence which we dub 'nineteenth century' was accomplished amid the storms of civil conflict. France had its revolutions, one great and two small. England in 1832 came close to hers. On the continent of Europe, the year 1848 was 'the year of revolutions'. The Canadian rebellion and the ensuing disturbances, down to the Montreal riots over the Rebellion Losses Bill and the Annexation Manifesto (1849) are the parallels to these disturbances, the parents of a new age.

For that age, the word 'democratic' rises too easily to our lips. If there is one thing we can be sure of, it is that while in politics as in all else, the period saw the swing from oligarchic privilege to another order of things, that other order was not democracy. Democracy as a creed prior to Confederation was rather less approved by the vocal classes than is Communism to-day. Democracy was "the red, fool fury of the Seine." Worse still, it was what the Americans had! Liberty? Yes! Equality? Certainly! Fraternity? Of course! But no democracy! The birth of the 'nineteenth century' did not make the British North American colonies into 'democracies'. What it did was to broaden power down, from colonial grandees to people on the way up, from the John Henry Dunns to the John A. Macdonalds, that is, to a fairly wide middle class.

As the old eighteenth-century world gave place to the nineteenth, life as designed for the few, for meeting their tastes and satisfying their wants, was rearranging itself. More people had more substance, more technological changes provided more wealth, and as a result, new men came to the front. There was more education available. In the year 1800, it is probable that the average man in British North America was illiterate or nearly so: by 1850, illiteracy was already beginning to be not the normal but the exceptional condition. Monopoly was disappearing: the hold of the Church of England over colonial life had been broken and even Methodists became accepted, if not acceptable. The bad taste of mid-century may be related to the change. New people, new notions, and not always notions that have much basis: taste is possibly like butter—if spread out, it has to be spread thin. Whatever the figure used, one fact stands out clearly—during the second quarter of the nineteenth century, the British American provinces were moving out of their old historical environment, which was a reflection of Europe's eighteenth century, into a new one. And in the very middle of this second quarter, in 1837, there had begun the reign of good Queen Victoria. In the spirit which her name seemed to designate so well, our national life was to unfold.

Notes to Chapter 15.
1. 'Age of Reason', 'eighteenth century', 'The Enlightenment' are phrases often used with a rough identity.
2. *Remarks on the Proposed Union of the Canadas* (London, 1823).
3. See the quotations from *The Globe* of 1855-1856 in F. A. Walker, *Catholic Education and Politics in Upper Canada* (Toronto, 1955), pp. 224 ff.
4. And the American too. It is to the romanticism of accomplishment that the American can most readily surrender himself, in envisioning some big task to be done (whether 'lend-lease' or the bridge over San Francisco harbour!)
5. E. A. Talbot, *Five Years Residence in the Canadas; and Including a Tour Through Part of the United States of America* (2 Vols., London, 1823).
6. John Wesley experienced his conversion in 1738.
7. For the 'Clapham Sect' see Ernest M. Howse, *Saints in Politics, the 'Clapham Sect' and the Growth of Freedom* (Toronto, 1952).
8. "For the Red Gods call me out and I must go!" says Rudyard Kipling while John Masefield cries that he must go down to the seas again, and longs for "a tall ship"!
9. One of Sir John Beverley Robinson's sons became a British general. Another example would be Capt. Harold Denison, R.N. (1878-1953); born in Toronto, educated at Upper Canada College, he served during his active life with the British Navy and thence retired (1920) to Toronto and 'the old homestead' (*Globe and Mail*, Dec. 24th, 1953).

plex of many factors.

10. 'Semi' because nationalism, like all these large attitudes, is a com-

11. The subject as a whole is too large and too complex for definitive treatment here: the best work on it in English, and almost the only work, is to be found in O. D. Skelton's *Life and Letters of Sir Wilfrid Laurier* (Toronto, 1921) Vol. I, Chapters 2 and 3. For those who read French, new light has been thrown on the subject by the work of Professor Marcel Trudel of Laval University in his *L'Influence de Voltaire au Canada* (Quebec, 1945), and still more may be expected from the forthcoming biography of Louis Joseph Papineau by M. Fernand Ouellet.

12. This is in agreement with the findings of M. Fernand Ouellet in *"Mgr. Plessis et la Naissance d'une Bourgeoisie Canadienne (1791-1810),"* a manuscript shown to me after the above passage was written.

13. The celebrated club which took in the European books and journals that Pius IX was to condemn in his Syllabus of Errors.

14. Jules Léger, *Le Canada Français et son Expression Littéraire* (Paris, 1936).

15. See p. 45.

16. Another rural idyll of this type is Abbé H. R. Casgrain's *Le Tableau de la Riviere-Oulle* (c. 1863).

17. 'The Valley' is the Annapolis Valley running up towards the Isthmus of Chignecto.

18. Alan Gowans, *Church Architecture in New France* (Toronto, 1955), p. 97.

19. See Pierre Georges Roy, *Vieux Manoirs, Vieilles Maisons* (Quebec 1927).

20. See p. 46 and Gowans, op. cit., also Ramsay Traquhair, *The Old Architecture of Quebec* (Toronto, 1947).

21. See Olivier Maurlaunt, *La Paroisse, Histoire de l'Eglise Notre Dame de Montréal* (Montreal, 1957).

22. Gowans, op. cit., p. 6.

23. C. H. A. Armstrong, *The Honourable Society of Osgoode Hall* (Toronto, 1952), pp. 49 ff.

24. For something on this, see p. 157 ff.

25. For notes on the earlier architecture of Ontario, see E. R. Arthur, *Early Buildings of Ontario* (Toronto, 1938) and Dorothy Dumbrille, *Up and Down the Glens* (Toronto, 1954) which has some good remarks on buildings in Glengarry County. That a certain interest in such matters is now stirring is attested to by the existence of *The Ontario Architectural Conservancy Committee* which at least gets as far as making lists of buildings of interest.

26. Description of the ball in honour of the Governor General, Apr. 22nd, 1840, as quoted in E. C. Guillet, *Toronto from Trading Post to Great City* (Toronto, 1934), p. 428.

27. The later phases of romanticism were still nostalgic, but nostalgic for times and places everyone knew never had existed—"unsubstantial faery place that is fit home for thee" said Wordsworth; and Tennyson could still talk about "the horns of Elfland faintly blowing" though he was painfully aware that there was no Elfland and there were no horns.

28. 1841, p. 347.

29. "From the lone shieling and the misty island
   Mountains divide us and the waste of seas,
   Yet still the blood is strong, the heart is Highland
   And we in dreams behold the Hebrides. . . . "

30. Major John Richardson, author of *Wacoustah, Tecumseh,* etc. A native of the present Windsor region, he had served with distinction in the War of 1812. His story of his return is given in his *Eight Years in Canada* (Montreal, 1847).
31. Richardson, *Eight Years,* op. cit., pp. 108, 92.
32. Though it may be agreed that these circles are widening.
33. Richardson, *Eight Years,* op. cit. p. 122.
34. Merrill Denison, *The Barley and the Stream* (Toronto, 1955).

16: Mid-century

BY MID-CENTURY THE TERM 'British North America' is beginning to take on observably collective meaning. The historian can feel the various colonial streams converging: the most difficult of his problems, tracing a number of separate watercourses, is being eased. But it is eased only to be immediately increased, for once the scattered colonies have come together into Canada, the scene becomes so wide and so varied that it requires the utmost effort to make a single picture. This chapter is concerned with ascertaining whether each individual colony (in the political sense) had grown through the level of 'colony' (in the social sense) to that of 'province' (in the same sense) and whether any of them had advanced beyond the 'provincial' level to the next one, that of independent community or nationality. By approximately mid-century, all the eastern colonies had been given Responsible Government.[1] There could have been no more distinct milepost in their march than that: as self-governing entities, they must have been more than mere collections of newly arrived individuals. Yet they were nearly all in different stages of social evolution.

The Maritimes

Until as late as 1817, in the eyes of the Colonial Office Newfoundland had been merely a fishing station, and its governors had come and gone with the fishing fleet. About the same time provision was made for titles to land, for regulation of the marriage ceremony and for other fundamentals. In 1832, representative government was introduced and then in 1855 Responsible Government. Newfoundland is traditionally 'Britain's oldest colony', but while the tradition is a pleasant one, it has little significance, for the mainland colonies were all ahead of it in actual development. Newfoundland at mid-century had passed beyond the mere fishing station, its people were there to stay, that is true, but the island had not reached the provincial stage.

Across the Cabot Straits in Nova Scotia, there was a different situation. While the original racial strains had not faded out, the magic of 'Nova Scotian-ness' subordinated them all. Right down to to-day, Cape Breton Scots may be just as staunchly 'Highlanders' as were their ancestors of a century and a half ago, but they are also just as much 'Nova Scotians'. The late Premier Angus L. Macdonald's[2] people had been in Cape Breton for generations, he spoke Gaelic, and when he became premier, he dressed up the Clerk of the Assembly in kilt and tartan, but the moment he got out of Nova Scotia he was very much a 'Nova Scotian'. Between him and his colleague, Colonel Ralston (1885-1948), who came from the old New England settlements in Nova Scotia, but who was even more of a 'Bluenose' than was 'Angus L.' himself, Nova Scotianism was an unbreakable bond.

This consciousness of oneness within Nova Scotia had already been established by mid-century. The proof of the statement can be found simply by turning up the files of the newspapers of the period and noting the local patriotism which they exhale. And further evidence is forthcoming from two conspicuous directions: one of them, the personality of the most prominent Nova Scotian, Joseph Howe, and the other, the literary productions of Judge Haliburton, known usually simply as *Sam Slick*.[3] Those who read Haliburton will know their Nova Scotians, not as scattered individuals, or as little groups lost in the wilderness, but as a people.

Nova Scotia received its due share of attention from the reporting traveller. Three classes of observation stand out. One is the abundant testimony of the adaptability of the 'Bluenose', who could take his axe in hand after having got in his crops, and literally hew a ship out of the forest. He could then put his crops on board of her, sail her to Boston, or farther, and sell his produce there. The second observation was on the poor opinion that all Maritimers, Bluenoses included, had of their community. "Nothing succeeds here," said one man reported by J. F. W. Johnston in his *Notes on North America*.[4] To succeed, one had to go to Boston, as did Donald Mackay, the supreme master of the art of clipper shipbuilding. And the third observation was also on the minus side, namely, the province was marked by an easy-going sloppiness. Lumber, for example, instead of being piled neatly, was left lying in untidy heaps almost as it came from the saw, and therefore failed to command the available markets on the best terms. This slackness, it is evident, was itself a concomitant of pioneer versatility.

By mid-century Nova Scotia's great age of sail was at its height and Nova Scotians were to be found in every port in the world, often in command of their own Nova Scotian-built ships. There seems to be no warrant for carrying the negative observations into this area, which represented commercial enterprise of a range well beyond farmer-bushman-sailor adaptiveness. Everyone, then and now, acknowledged the Nova Scotian's virtues as a sailor and admired the vast maritime industry (for so small a province) his port merchants had built up. Here was the very heart of the Nova Scotian tradition as it has come down to modern times: the great days of sail, *Wooden Ships and Iron Men,*[5] as one writer has entitled his book about them. Here was "Nova Scotia against the world," for there is nothing to make a man recognize his identity so quickly as getting away among foreigners. The old salts who year after year retired from the sea and came home to live in the little 'outports' of the province would be very much aware of the fact that they were Nova Scotians (a few still exist!), and this attitude would permeate the general population, especially through grandsons and other small boys.

There are a dozen other angles from which the state of the province as of about 1850 can be canvassed. The city of Halifax, about which something has already been said, though small[6] had some well-defined metropolitan characteristics. It was the political and military capital. It was a naval base of importance, which fact gave to all its citizens a wider view of men and affairs than an inland city of the same size could have. It was in command of its own hinterland. Just as London, through the colonial policy of the British government and its control of finance, kept a world in fee, so Halifax, through the provincial government and by its control of the province's financial structure, kept its hinterland subordinated. And this may account for the relatively steeply graded class structure in the capital. From great dignitaries at the top, bishops or British admirals, on down through wealthy merchants into the lower middle classes and the slum dwellers, Halifax contained almost the whole range of society. Its social conscience was not lively, and the top ranks, though charitable enough in a distant way, did not worry about the misery that lay not far away from them. The slum dwellers they probably looked on much as hard-bitten old sea-captains regarded fo'c's'le hands.

Halifax was the commercial, military, political and religious capital. But its position did not go unchallenged, although the only area in the province which was unit enough to make its weight felt, the Annapolis Valley, was not strong enough to produce a rival centre. The Valley people, being mostly Baptists, resented the Anglican group in Halifax which seemed in such firm control—to them, Halifax was, opprobriously, 'the garrison'—but while their resentment could express itself in the support which many of them gave to the great tribune of the people, Joseph Howe, they never succeeded in wresting control from the capital.

The sense of power enduring over generations breeds that confidence which marks the people of the successful capitals. At mid-century, Halifax had had just over a century behind it, and a pretty good century. It had put the marks of metropolitanism upon its citizens. To this day, the Haligonian, although no longer (thanks to modern transportation) sure of his metropolitan position, retains some of this air of quiet self-assurance.

There can be little hesitation, then, in according Nova Scotia the rank of 'province'. In fact, the question arises whether that rank was not already too low for it and whether it should not have been promoted to the next, that of 'nationality'.

With New Brunswick, the case is different. The province, being spread over several river systems, does not possess the physical unity of Nova Scotia and this markedly affects its nature. It was only in the lower St. John Valley that Loyalist stock gave cohesiveness. The people on the Miramichi and the Bay of Chaleur were out of touch with those on the Bay of Fundy, a fact which came out strongly in the battle over the railway question. Should Saint John have its way and link itself by rail with the American seaboard, or should the 'North Shore' win and swing the province into the orbit of Montreal? This battle was at last won by the North Shore, with the Intercolonial the expression of victory, and the result was the famous reversal of decisions about Confederation (1866). That, however, is to anticipate. At mid-century, for practical purposes New Brunswick still was the St. John, with its two Loyalist cities, Saint John and Fredericton.

As a previous chapter has stated,[7] in these towns a pleasant society controlling the economic and political life of the valley had grown up, a society which knew so few dissensions that it was indifferent to the issue of Responsible Government itself. This society, thanks to the riches in its pine forests and to the maritime enterprise of Saint John merchants, had acquired a little leisure, possessed its university and produced in Fredericton a charming group of people among whom a genuine poetic movement was to arise. It was out of its midst that the later

Roberts and Carmens were to come. Men such as these were not rebels: their creative efforts did not run away in political declamation, as did Joseph Howe's, nor were they much concerned with the society about them, as was Haliburton. They turned, almost of necessity, as did the exiles who were writing in Upper Canada, to the natural world, revelling in the delights of woods and streams. Masters in their own house, content within the British colonial framework, without the sense of responsibility for their own fate, still less the desire to quarrel with it, which marked the active groups in the other provinces, they force the verdict that New Brunswick at mid-century was not a political community, not a 'province', but a 'colony'.

Lower Canada—the English

With Lower Canada, or 'Canada East',[8] the situation was quite different. The British conquest had destroyed 'New France', but created 'The Province of Quebec'. When in 1791, the Province of Quebec became 'Lower Canada', partial self-government soon made its hybrid nature plain. In extreme terms, it became Durham's "two nations warring in the bosom of a single state." That was its tragedy. And yet as we have seen the two nations were not as completely separated as Durham's phrase suggests: they had their relationships and between them there was an intangible something in common. If there had not been, the Papineau rebellion would have been drawn out into a long racial war. It was not. There were English-speaking rebels among the French, and there were French-speaking loyalists among the English. With the worst of the abuses corrected, as a result of the ten years of remarkable political achievement that succeeded the rebellions, the two races did not find it impossible to live together. We can, therefore, hardly equate 'Lower Canada' with 'French Canada'. By mid-century was Lower Canada a 'province' and were the French Canadians what Durham termed them, 'a nation'? If not, what were they?

If to be a political entity, possessing its own ways of doing things, worked out over a considerable period, was to be a 'province', then Lower Canada was such. It had its own legal system—and law is sometimes said to be 'the science of society'—and its own special *cachet* derived from the presence of the two races. If these had not taken each other to their hearts, at least they were not at each other's throats: they had achieved a *modus vivendi* which the bloodshed of the rebellion had failed to destroy. To-day, as in the past, only a casual visit is needed to the Province of Quebec to establish the existence of this unique society, which has come down for nearly two centuries without much basic alteration: not "two nations warring in the bosom of a single state," but rather, two peoples misunderstanding each other at every point, yet grumblingly going along together and, in spite of themselves, building some kind of common structure over their heads.

Yet since there was too little in common for the two peoples to build anything close knit, there could be no possibility of Lower Canada passing out of the 'provincial' stage. It would have been impossible for the English to have abandoned their ties with the rest of their race and equally impossible for the French to agree on a significant range of common objectives with them. There therefore was no possibility of Lower Canada realizing itself as Nova Scotia was doing, and passing into another stage of social development.

Within the province, however, the two races each present a separate problem. The English at mid-century were still a powerful and a relatively numerous group.[9] They were in a majority in the city of Montreal, the counties of Bonaventure, Missisquoi, Ottawa, Shefford, Sherbrooke, Stanstead, and formed large minorities in several other counties. In the city of Quebec, they were three-sevenths of the total. An energetic minority of these dimensions, comprising a high proportion of the wealthy, could hardly have failed to put its special stamp upon its community, though in return to have the community's features impressed upon it. Every minority is marked by the same broad psychology: it fears the majority; it anticipates attacks on its privileges or rights; it attributes to the majority undesirable characteristics and it blames the majority for everything that goes wrong. To these and similar attributes of a minority group, the English of Lower Canada were no exception: their fears of the majority were so great that in 1849, their leaders came out with their famous 'Annexation Manifesto' which, if successful, would have led to their inclusion with their fellow English and Protestants in the United States. This was not to be: the English of Lower Canada were destined to remain in their minority position and were to have to make what they could of it. It is anticipating the march of history, but stating something that everyone knows, to say that many of them, rather than accept the minority position, got out, as their descendants have continued to get out, thus shrinking the English minority everywhere but in the city of Montreal and its suburbs to a ratio far below that at which it stood in 1850.[10]

Numbers, energy and wealth did not suffice to endow the English of Lower Canada with a strong corporate character. For one thing, they were divided religiously, there being 143,000 of them Protestant and the rest, 77,000, Roman Catholic. They were also divided in the other customary directions. Over half were native-born, but of various recent origins. Some 50,000 had been born in Ireland, 14,000 in Scotland, 11,000 in England and 12,000 in the United States. Add to this diversity of origin, the diversity of Protestant denomination (then a much more divisive factor than today), the division between the city dwellers in Montreal and Quebec and the farmers, and the class structure of the English population of the cities with its commercial grandees at the top and its dock labourers or teamsters at the bottom, and we can understand that the 'English' of Lower Canada could not have been expected to form an integrated community. It is true that among them there were a number of sub-communities with some age and tradition behind them, such as the old mercantile families of Montreal, or the farmers of the Eastern Townships, but these did not focus the aims and aspirations of everyone.

The English of Lower Canada at mid-nineteenth-century were, in truth, still colonists, still thinking of themselves as severed fragments of the great group in the homeland to which they belonged. Many of them have not to this day advanced beyond this position. In his book *The Barley and the Stream*, Mr. Merrill Denison says of one of the members of the Molson family that "he was more British than the British." This is the precise description of the colonist: the man who, separated from his motherland, perhaps for generations, magnifies its attractions, allows his imagination to play over this land from which he is 'temporarily' cut off, and dreams of some day returning 'home'.

Perhaps it is wrong to think of such men even as colonists: they represent an earlier stage of society. In both Montreal and Quebec were numbers of families whose progenitors had come to Lower Canada precisely as they would have gone to India or to Hong Kong. Some of them had made fortunes and returned.[11] Others had stayed on, like Sir Hugh Allan (1810-1882) of steamship and Canadian Pacific Railway fame, to found families and large commercial undertakings. Such men had become the important individuals in that vast attack on its hinterland—a hinterland that had extended and was to extend again, right through to the Pacific Coast—which made Montreal the capital of 'The Commercial Empire of the

St. Lawrence', to use Creighton's phrase. Their relations with 'the natives' might be cordial, but they could never be on a footing of equality. These men were 'sahibs'. There is a world of difference between coming to a country to begin a new life and throw one's energies into building a new society, and coming to it merely to exploit what opportunities it offers, and then return. Every port in the world has seen this latter kind of white intruder. He has been a product of trade and mainly of the staple trade, such as that in fur, fish, lumber, or, farther afield, tobacco, sugar, cotton and opium. Quebec and Montreal were, as it were, Canadian Shanghais.

In Canada, the fur trade had been a dress rehearsal for the later trades in wood. It had brought many a Scot into the wilderness. The more fortunate had eventually got back to Scotland: the less fortunate had found themselves anchored to Indian wives and their children reverting to the Indian side. Those half-way between had often ended their days in Montreal. Similarly the 'square timber' and 'deal' trade brought many an English and Scottish merchant to the ports of British North America, either as agent of an old-country firm or as middleman between the lumbermen up river and the old-country importing houses. Some of these men passed years in the country, to return home on retirement. Others founded firms on the Canadian side of the water and on their retirement, their sons succeeded them.

Of the timber firms, that of Price Brothers is among the most interesting. The original William Price came to Lower Canada early in the nineteenth century, as an immigrant rather than a merchant, but soon got into timber and land speculations, and thence into the timber export trade. He built mills and developed a large all-round lumber business. When he died, his sons and then a grand-nephew carried on the firm, which from the first bestrode the Atlantic, with members constantly scurrying back and forth between Quebec and Liverpool. A branch of the family re-rooted itself in England and in the twentieth century a completely separate English timber firm arose, trading not with North America, but the Baltic.[12] The Quebec family of Prices is still intimately associated with the trade in wood, and for many years has been in pulp and paper manufacturing, in addition to ordinary sawmilling. Its officers continue to be English, its ordinary employees, French.

Another family of this type was Pollock, Gilmour and Company which began in Glasgow as ship-owners and Baltic timber importers. After the Napoleonic wars, it transferred to Liverpool and the colonial trade, establishing branches known as 'the foreign houses' in all the principal shipping ports. One branch of the family became Canadian, and a power in the Canadian timber industry. Other branches criss-crossed the Atlantic; Sir John Gilmour, a member of the British Macdonald and Baldwin governments, belonged to one of them.

Members of these mercantile families have been marginally Canadian: that is, their old-country associations have been so close that they themselves hardly have known which side of the ocean has claimed their ultimate allegiance—they would probably assert that there is no problem, they being loyal subjects of the queen. That is not an attitude that similarly situated families could take in, say, Buenos Aires. Men of this type until recent years used still to be common among the English group in Quebec city—the Garrison Club was full of them—and they lent to their group an atmosphere found infrequently in this country. A somewhat similar situation exists in Victoria, B.C., where the Union Club has provided relatively the same atmosphere. In Quebec, this was maritime, redolent of ships and shipping, embracing both sides of the ocean at once.

In a foreign port (such as Riga) such men and such families would have remained British in word, deed and dress down through the generations, but a British 'garrison' or 'colony' has been hard to maintain on the soil of a self-governing country of the same allegiance and partly of the same official language. These old staple trade families have thus tended to become absorbed and their members, by migration to other parts of the country, to become ordinary Canadians. The Dobells, for example, sent out representatives from England just after mid-century, and established a large business in Quebec. One of the family remained and eventually sat in the House of Commons (Hon. R. R. Dobell, a minister from 1896-1902). The writer remembers meeting another in Quebec, a son of this gentleman, who had lived 'half-way across' the Atlantic and still, as a very old man, spoke with an English accent. A few years before the time of writing, he met a member of a younger generation of the family who was a graduate of McGill and in every way a Canadian among others.

Such families, which after the fur trade was taken away from Montreal in 1821 formed the mercantile aristocracy, could hardly constitute themselves leaders of the Lower Canadian English community, for they were too unrepresentative: there was too much of the transient about them and they were not in touch with the rural English. Nor could they co-operate politically or socially with the French, for they normally thought of the French in terms of bushwhackers and logdrivers, of babbling intellectuals with silly agitations about political rights, or of almost equally troublesome clergy, who had to be propitiated by suitable gifts, if lumbermen and timber exporters were to get on with the job. Here was the deepest sense in which there were "two nations warring in the bosom of a single state": it is the one written on every page of Canadian history —the clash over two ways of life, the English concept of 'progress',[13] and the French and Catholic desire for stability and the unchanging rural life. For the situation in Lower Canada the parallel is again, say, India. The English merchant adventurer (with some exceptions) descends on a territory for what he can get out of it, makes what he can out of it, and then departs. The American industrialist who owns much of Canada to-day is not very different in his attitude, though thanks to Canadian public opinion, not quite so irresponsible. But no group of merchants sitting in foreign ports ever made a nation (except inversely by the pressures they aroused against themselves and their home counrty): for that, it requires the man who comes to stay. In Lower Canada, it was the many English who had come to stay, those on the land, who at mid-century looked like the centre around which a Lower Canadian English society would gather.

That was not to be: it is one of the ironies of history that the great trading city of Montreal, focus from its beginning for the exploitation of the hinterland and stronghold of all that we associate with the brittle urban in life, has emerged as the centre of English society in the modern province of Quebec, while the country communities blessed with fertile soil and beautiful terrain, with industrious settlers and reasonably good markets, have shrunk away and in the English scale of things in Canada, have become of minor importance. Again, the explanation is obvious, and as before: the English Protestant attitude towards life, that attitude which puts success in living before living.[14]

'Trade follows the flag' it is said. In British expansion, in the persons of merchants and officials, they have as often as not gone together. At mid-century, English officialdom in British North America was in retreat before self-government, but it still carried much weight and its military sub-layer was conspicuous as a component of urban society. Nowhere was this more so than in Lower Canada, where was the ancient capital, the seat not of a mere provincial governor but of vice-royalty.[15] The military were present in small detachments in almost every little urban centre and wherever they were, there was the ceremonial side of empire along with them. At mid-century officers still were drawn from the nobility and gentry of Great Britain, and they brought with them the type of life in which they had been brought up. Their influence on the classes with whom they came in contact socially was vast: every prominent professional man and every rich merchant hoped to marry his daughter to a British officer and gentleman (or at least his wife did) and a surprising number succeeded. The older descriptions of colonial life invariably have much to say of the balls, the jolly parties (skating, tobogganing and cutter-riding were the great favourites), the amateur theatricals, which centred round the local garrison.[16] Through such channels the officer class exercised a subtle influence on Canadian life, both for better and for worse. It kept currents of snobbishness in constant flow. Yet it never imbued Canadian youth with much love of the soldier's life as such. It allowed the leading people in every town to see a way of life that was not middle class and commercial. Canadian commercialism for years was modified by the presence of the 'gentleman', and possibly, as contrasted with the United States, is still mildly affected by the ideals the word embodies.

Many are the anecdotes which illustrate the contrast between the practical business man of straight common sense and the semi-playboy character of the officer and gentleman.

"On one occasion when the dining room [of the Donegani Hotel, Montreal, a favourite stopping place for American men of business] was well filled with guests, Lord Mark Kerr, an eccentric officer, thought it was time to create a little excitement. He rode his horse straight into the dining room and round the table. The guests sat in their chairs stunned. The manager rushed in, but the scene was over. Lord Mark Kerr was waiting for him outside, and the manager exclaimed:— 'Oh, my Lord, this will ruin me!'

'How much will the damage be? Will that do?' handing him a cheque for a hundred dollars.

The manager returned smiling, and explained to the guests, when they all thought it was very funny. . . .

The play was a ball on the stage. They danced a polka. The names of the officers were:— The Earl of Erroll, Lord Lascelles, Lord Melgund and the Hon. Arthur Egerton. . . ."[17]

Fancy 'going to a show' and seeing such lions as that on the stage, especially when one was only an ex-fur-trader's wife! But as the authoress of the little book from which these lines are drawn sadly says:

"With the departure of the Garrison (after Montreal ceased to be the capital), the character of Montreal society life entirely changed. The people about whom I have written the foregoing imperfect snatches of reminiscence have been replaced by another society which has gradually developed itself, but on totally different lines, not united as in the old days, but broken into numerous sets, who scarcely meet each other. . . ."[18]

The remark could have been made of any other town where Imperial officers had been stationed. With their departure, the British North American colonies moved one step farther out of the aristocratic parental orbit, one step closer to forging their own middle-class pattern of life.

Lower Canada—the French

If the English of Lower Canada remained colonials, what is to be said of the French? The Conquest had relegated New France, which had been a province of the French Empire in much the same sense as Virginia had been a province of the British, to a condition more familiar elsewhere in the world than in North America; but, as in most of these other cases, it did not destroy the conquered. In the short space of half a century, and thanks to the free genius of English institutions, they found their feet again and came to realize that the events of that period had made them a people: it had been for them a kind of incubating statge. There can be no doubt about this: French-speaking Canadians early in the nineteenth century had come to be aware that they were a people, alone and self-dependent in a potentially hostile continent. They were, as they always referred to themselves, not 'French' but 'Canadiens', as much a new-world type, and a new type, as their neighbours. In 1834 Ludger Duvernay succeeded in instituting their 'national' day, that of St. Jean-Baptiste. In 1836, Etienne Parent placed a beaver and a maple leaf at the masthead of his journal, *Le Canadien*,[19] symbols afterwards taken over by the rest of the country.

By mid-century French Canadians had possessed themselves of most of the apparatus of a people's existence. Schools, rising to collegiate status, were, for the few among them, an old story; for all, their church was their focus of existence. They had taken up their relative weight in the professions. They had a lively newspaper press.[20] Literary culture had had its beginnings, if not much more, for by mid-century Garneau's *History* had already appeared, and there had been some lesser works. Yet, in a passage parallel to that of Major John Richardson's already quoted on Upper Canada, Michel Bibaud could write:—

"Serait-on bien compris au pays canadien,
Ou les arts, le savoir, sont encore dans l'enfance
Ou règne, en souverain, une crasse ignorance?
Peut-on dire, en vers, rien de beau, rien de grand?
Non. L'ignorance oppose un obstacle puissant. . . ."[21]

Garneau (1809-1860) and Crémazie the poet (1827-1869) have been called 'Two Precursors'.[22] Crémazie put his finger neatly on one point that always retards literary development in provincial society—the competition that comes from the metropolis: "If we only spoke Iroquois!" he exclaimed, as the editions from Paris poured in in a drowning flood.

The major evidence that French-speaking Canadians were a people did not, however, lie in a local culture, but in politics.

The apex of the political evolution, the Rebellion of 1837, represented no such minority movement as its counterpart in Upper Canada. Relatively few people took an active part in it, but there could not have been many who did not sympathize with its general aim—more elbow-room for the aspirations and ambitions of French-speaking Canadians and a larger place for them in the government of their own province. Although the rebellion failed, it embodied the protest of a people and after it, French Canada could not have been governed for long without its own consent. Yet the union of the two provinces (1840) was imposed on Lower Canada by imperial ukase. Its terms were harsh and could easily have been interpreted as a second conquest: the device of equal representation was a direct attempt to secure an English majority, and in addition to this, there was the proscription of the French language in the legislature. Then there were the memories—and what peoples have longer memories than the French?—of the repressions and the executions following the risings. The painful histories of other countries where rising nationalism was being crushed at that period by armed might—Poland, the Italian provinces of Austria, Ireland—must make us wonder how peace and mutual acceptance could ever have returned to the two societies of Lower Canada.

Peace never would have returned and Lower Canada would have slid off into the abyss of endemic civil war if it had not been for the extraordinary concatenation of events and extraordinary men of the eighteen-forties which led to our Canadian miracle, Responsible Government—that is to say, self-government. But the self-government of two peoples in partnership: the Union of 1840 was not broken down into its constituent elements, the experiment went on and, though it appeared to fail at last, it was glorious failure for it led to something much greater than itself, Confederation. And was it a failure? For twenty-seven years, 1840-1867, two antagonistic peoples and two provinces had been learning to live together. Naturally all was not sheer harmony. But in the light of the innumerable cases the world over where such experiences have meant hatred and bloodshed, those are entitled, it would appear, to some congratulation who have merely kept the peace. The twenty-seven years of the Province of Canada went beyond merely keeping the peace: they included some of the most prosperous times the country has known, they were marked by great material achievement and, biggest thing of all, they taught many men in public life that others, following a way of life in complete contrast to their own, must be accepted, could be co-operated with on the basis of agreeing to differ, could become good friends. This fragile yet immensely strong federation of ours, bridging so many 'unbridgeable' chasms, had its foundations laid in the uneasy period of the Union.

When Lafontaine and Baldwin discovered each other and found they could work together, they were instrumental in burying the biggest hatchet in Canadian history. The partnership thus formed represents the biggest decision ever taken in Canadian history, for it was a pledge that efforts would be concentrated on building a political and social house to shelter both races and based on co-operation and compromise. This surely meant, if it meant anything, that each gave up its separate national aspirations, whatever they were, and agreed to find a common aspiration. If there had been another hand than Lafontaine's at the helm of French Canada in those fateful days of the eighteen-forties, there might have been in Canada the assassinations and the murders by night which normally mark the course of a people struggling to be free. There were none of these: the two peoples continued to have much the same relations with each other as before and the path was found through negotiation and debate.

For French Canada, Lafontaine's decision to co-operate with Baldwin in working the Act of Union and in securing Responsible Government logically meant the abandonment of the notion of *la nation canadienne*[23] and the acceptance of something else, which at the time was not clear, but has since evidently become partnership in a bicultural nation. It is no wonder that the decision has never ceased to divide opinion in French Canada and to provide much of the tension in Canadian life. To accept the partnership, or reject it? To risk all the dangers of association with the dynamic and materialistic English Protestant world, or to fight for isolation and a separate French Catholic state? These have been the questions confronting every fresh generation of French-speaking Canadians, and possibly with increasing emphasis.

When the decision was made, nationalism, as the modern world knows it, was not as strong a passion as it is to-day, and a century under the British Crown and English institutions, which had entered deeper into their way of life than many would have cared to admit, had habituated most French Canadians to their situation as British subjects: even in the midst of rebellion, it is to be doubted if many of them had wished more than local self-government. Once this was achieved, there were too many conservative forces to permit of a revolutionary path to the abstractions of nationalism and democracy. The proof lies in the failure of Papineau's disciples, *les rouges*. These men, standing for the liberalism of the Enlightenment and of the French Revolution (which included freedom from all yokes, the religious included) received an unexpected degree of tolerance and encouragement from a fervently Catholic people, but there was no chance of their dominating the province and later on Laurier had to make the great formal retreat of 1877 before his own Liberal party could find much acceptance from his people. French Canada, given its antecedents, could never have been anything else than French, Catholic and conservative, and this combination in itself was a guarantee of a long period of provincialism. Whether the prospect was pleasant or not, that meant that its nature compelled it to remain under the British Crown and become a partner in the developing Canadian experiment. As in other Catholic countries, its intellectuals, especially those whose Catholicism has worn thin, have often been separatists. But the conservative masses, led by their conservative church, when it has come to the point, as it did over the conscription issue in 1917, have not gone far along that road. Better to keep the ills they had. . . .! "The Canadian speaks out at times, but he submits. . . ."[24] And so French Canada is not likely to work out its destiny as a nation, but as a partner within a nation.

Upper Canada

After Lower Canada, Upper Canada. And what is to be said of Upper Canada at mid-century? 'Colony' or 'province'? Running his mental eye over that large tract from the Ottawa to the Upper Lakes, which even in 1850 was reaching up northward to the edges of the Canadian Shield,[25] the observer can only remark on the variety and difference of the scene from locality to locality, and he is hard put to it to pick out threads of the same colour running through it all. Upper Canadians in 1850 were not a people in the sense in which Nova Scotians and French Canadians were. They had no national aspirations, as did sections of French Canada. They had no common attitude towards any of the large questions of the day, religious or secular. They were mostly Protestants, but among Protestants there were religious divisions as bitter and almost as deep as those which separated Protestant and Catholic. They were, with relatively few exceptions, loyal British subjects, but some of them were for a paternal monarchy such as that of George III, others for something much like an eighteenth-century Whig oligarchy, and others again for a democracy on the American pattern: there was as little political agreement among them as religious. On the great social questions of the day, they were divided almost as deeply: in the eighteen-fifties many a meeting was held in Toronto to protest American Negro slavery. Yet most Upper Canadians of the possessing classes were sympathizers with the South. On a social question then reaching towards the huge development it afterward attained, temperance, the divisions were equally sharp. In politics, during the eighteen-fifties half a dozen distinct 'splinter groups' can be traced, each with its own programme and representing its own sector of the province. Underlying all of them, affecting every man in them, were the deep divisions which had rent the province in the Mackenzie rebellion, divisions in turn inherited in large part from the class structure and social concepts of the eighteenth century.

In stage of development, the province varied all the way from the comfortable old agricultural counties of the east to the frontier areas of Huron and Bruce, from the relatively high civilization of Toronto and Kingston to the hillbilly colonist with whom Mrs. Moodie apparently had more than her share of acquaintance.[26] What was Upper Canada? Was there an Upper Canada?

There is one point of view from which an affirmative answer could be made: Upper Canada, like Ontario to-day, afforded the means of a common life for its inhabitants, simply by floating in the constituents of the whole continent's way of life, for it was primarily North American. Nothing made it more emphatically American than the frequent declarations heard in it that it was 'British'. If it kept a little private ribbon of its own in its button-hole, it wore clothes of the prevailing continental cut. When British travellers, coming across New York State to Niagara Falls, saw a Union Jack flying across the river, they invariably said they somehow or other felt more 'at home' than on the American side. They then fell to telling their readers how exactly like the Americans were the people of Upper Canada, especially in all their objectionable traits. Only one exception to the prevailing identity as a rule was made—in Upper Canada everything was meaner and dirtier than across the line![27]

Travellers' tales are not always to be taken at their full value. Upper Canada had resources and a climate which were comparable to some of the neighbouring states, and these, too, drew it into the norm of the continent. Every statistical piece of evidence indicates a rapid rate of growth. There are also many other corroborations, such as the long-continued attempt by the commercial class of Montreal after the War of 1812 to get their city shifted into the upper province. The spirit of the province's leaders, especially after about 1845, was quite similar to that of their neighbours. Both were 'go ahead', though the Upper Canadians did not 'go ahead' quite so fast as the Americans.

Similarities to neighbouring American areas extended into many other aspects of life. In Upper Canada after the Rebellion of 1837, and to a considerable extent before it, free (and noisy) debate was taken for granted. Maritimers looking upon the spectacle found the Donnybrook atmosphere of Upper Canada distasteful. The atmosphere of its politics approximated that of the 'Yankee democrats'. All this is another way of saying, in more bookish language, that Upper Canada at mid-century was an aspect of the American frontier. As such it was hardly a 'province', for a mixture is not a chemical substance: it was a 'colony' whose different areas varied all the way from an advanced 'provincial' stage to mere outposts of settlement. What it was not, it seems to the writer, was an integrated community.

At mid-century British North America, it is evident, presented a mass of differing characteristics, both province by province and regionally within the provinces. It is a well-worn truism to say that whatever unity it had was supplied by the English language and the British allegiance yet, truism or not, the statement has to be made. Immediately it is made, a large exception is claimed from it for the French language and the tepid allegiance to the British Crown of the people of French speech. For mid-century the exception was more apparent than real. French Canada had accepted English public institutions and its leading men were working them in partnership with men of English speech. Once the proscription of the French language ended (1846), the language question ceased to be of foremost importance. And since both races were serving their apprenticeship in the art of self-government, the situation had not developed far enough for questions of ultimate allegiance to have much importance. The Union of 1840-1867 was a compromise of the usual sort—each side proclaiming that the other had got the better of it. In reality it was a strategic phase in the two-centuries-old partnership of the races.

Looming just over the horizon was the railway age, and when it came, consolidation and expansion had to come with it. Collectively, British North America at mid-century was 'provincial', but the forces were there which in a few years more would change its outward shape and possibly its inward attitudes.

Notes to Chapter 16

1. Only the new distant foundlings of the Pacific Coast remained as 'Crown Colonies'.
2. 1904-1954.
3. There were various Sam Slick books: the first appeared under the title of *The Clockmaker; or the Sayings and Doings of Samuel Slick of Slickville* (Halifax, 1836). The series of this and other Sam Slick books kept coming out until 1853.
4. Edinburgh, 1857.
5. F. W. Wallace, London, 1924.
6. Population in 1851, 20,749.
7. See p. 154.
8. As it became after the Act of Union, 1840.
9. For figures, see p. 193.
10. 1951 one to about 4.5 for the whole province.
11. This was more marked among the Quebec timber firms than among the Montreal merchants, most of whom began in a small way and worked up.
12. Sir Keith Price and Sons.
13. See p. 188.
14. See the present writer's *Colony to Nation* (Toronto, 1957), pp. 66 ff.
15. See also pp. 296, 297.
16. Charles Dickens has left us in his *American Notes* a record of his participation in a set of garrison plays in Montreal.
17. Adèle Clarke, *Old Montreal: John Clarke, His Adventures, Friends and Family* (Montreal, 1906), p. 34.
18. Ibid.
19. *Bulletin des Recherches Historiques,* Vol. 43
20. Ibid., Vol. 38, pp. 472-474, a list of 76 newspapers and periodicals begun (and mostly ended) before 1840. Of these, 32 were French, 44 English. In the decade 1830-1839, 25 English 'papers' were begun, 14 French. During the eighteen-thirties *Le Canadien* and *La Minerve* were the main newspapers in French.
21. Quoted in Jules Léger, *Le Canada Française et son Expression Littéraire,* (Paris, 1936):
    > Would one be understood in the Canadian land
    > Where arts, knowledge, are still in their infancy,
    > Where, above all, a crass ignorance reigns;
    > Can one say, in verse, nothing beautiful, nothing great?
    > No! Ignorance imposes too powerful an obstacle. . . .
22. Léger, op. cit.

23. Though it should be noted that the French word *nation* cannot be translated by the English word 'nation'. *Nation* means almost any blood group, for example, *la nation métisse*, the French-Indian half-breeds of Red River. 'Nation' minimizes the element of blood relationship or race and stresses the political community.
24. *Bishop Briand*, 1773. See pp. 103, 104.
25. The line of settlement ran from about Renfrew through Perth to just north of Kingston, thence along the edges of the Shield just north of Peterborough, Lindsay and Orillia to Penetang. On the west shore of Georgian Bay it had not yet reached Owen Sound. It came out on Lake Huron somewhere near Kincardine.
26. See pp. 200, 204.
27. This point more fully discussed above, p. 202.

17: The height of prosperity: British North America during the eighteen-fifties

THE EIGHTEEN-FIFTIES were to provide the most prosperous decade the colonies enjoyed down to the settlement of the West in the early twentieth century. There were several explanations, and as many consequences. The decade began with depression but by 1853 recovery was well under way, and by 1855 the country was 'booming'. Like all nineteenth-century 'booms', that of the eighteen-fifties ended in a 'bang' and the depression of 1857-1858 ensued. But things quickly picked up again and some of the eighteen-sixties were almost as 'succulent' as were the eighteen-fifties.

In general terms it was the upswing of the business cycle which explained the eighteen-fifties, but a number of specific factors may be easily identified. Great Britain's war with Russia drew wheat and timber abroad in vast quantities. A second gift fell off the Christmas tree in the form of many millions of pounds of British capital dumped into the country to build railroads. A third was provided by the Reciprocity Treaty of 1854, which made British North America for twelve years an associate member of the United States *Zollverein*.

The consequences of all these big matters were a continuing rapid growth in population, the occupation of most of the remaining good crown lands, an increase in the size of cities and the complexities of their life, the emergence of new social classes, and most important of all, an observable gain in confidence that led people out a little beyond the timidities of the colonial state. Much of all this is to be set down to the credit side of the new regime in politics with its union of the two provinces and its internal self-government.

In 1851, the population of all British North America was 2,313,000. In 1861 it was 3,174,000. This was an increase of 37 per cent in the ten years, a rate not yet again attained. Upper Canada alone added nearly half a million people to its population, Lower Canada just under one quarter of a million. It was this disparity in growth which produced George

Brown's intemperate crusade for 'Rep. by Pop.' and wrecked the old union. Not only the two large provinces grew, but every province: Nova Scotia increased by 20 per cent, New Brunswick by just over 30. There is nothing like the rapid increase of the race to make men feel confident, so, with numerous children sprawling in every yard and some money in their pockets at last, British North Americans in the eighteen-fifties began to get rid of some of that self-distrust that previously had made them so different from their neighbours.

A healthy local rural culture

We are everywhere faced to-day with the shrinkage of the countryside. Townships that once were populous are stationary or in decline. Many are deserted. Yet as foolish man battens down under bricks and mortar the earth he lives by, his ingenuity coaxes more and more produce out of it, so that his numbers are by that fact once more increased. But increased almost entirely on an urban basis. Districts scarcely more than pioneer areas, such as many in the West, are now caught in the rural retreat and few new pioneer districts remain to be opened up. The contrast with a century ago is decided. At that time, the trees were still falling, the pioneer settler was

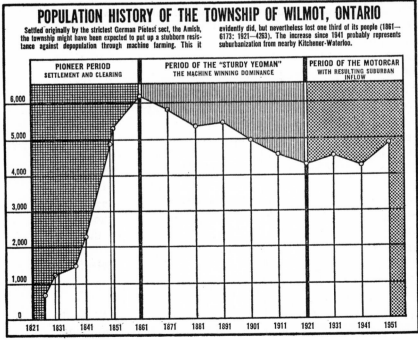

POPULATION HISTORY OF THE TOWNSHIP OF WILMOT, ONTARIO

Settled originally by the strictest German Pietest sect, the Amish, the township might have been expected to put up a stubborn resistance against depopulation through machine farming. This it evidently did, but nevertheless lost one third of its people (1861—6173: 1921—4263). The increase since 1941 probably represents suburbanization from nearby Kitchener-Waterloo.

| PIONEER PERIOD SETTLEMENT AND CLEARING | PERIOD OF THE "STURDY YEOMAN" THE MACHINE WINNING DOMINANCE | PERIOD OF THE MOTORCAR WITH RESULTING SUBURBAN INFLOW |

Diagram 4

the characteristic figure, and all hopes were anchored to the extension of the fields. Townships increased in population decade after decade,[1] farm houses were never large enough and country schools were crammed to the doors with three times as many children as they were ever again to contain. The buoyancy of life, the rapid improvements being effected in standards of living, these things were noted by many observers, especially in the Upper Canada of mid-century. The grim days were over: ". . . What a change has come over all this region of country! The logs and trees in the 'highways' are gone! Thousands of great patches of forest are gone—and most spacious farms are opened out to the sun. The shanties and the ancient log houses are gone, and beautiful framed dwellings, stone and brick mansions, are dotting this whole territory of enterprise. . . ."[2]

A healthy, reasonably prosperous, though not affluent, rural life marked all the provinces. Above all, it was a self-sufficient rural life. People found their satisfaction in their work and their recreation within their own neighbourhood. Those were the great days of barn raisings, husking and quilting bees, and other such combinations of work and fun—when 'from Aunt Dinah's quilting party, I was seeing Nelly home.' Each country district, centred round its cross-roads hamlet, tended to be a unit of its own. Within it, people worked together, played together, lived together. The complex blood relationships that mark the rural clan had already been set up in the older provinces, and in the eighteen-fifties they were fast developing all over Upper Canada.[3] The settlers brought with them a portion of their old-world heritage of music and dance —though much was lost on the ocean crossing—and this provided the staple of their folk culture. As wealth increased and the fiddle gave way to the parlour organ, the folk heritage was supplemented by intrusions from the towns and from farther afield: thus after the American Civil War, Stephen Foster's plantation melodies became popular, and they continued to hold a prominent place in Ontario country life until the twentieth century—there must be few of the old people whose voices have not rolled out 'My Old Kentucky Home'. The 'home' remained in Kentucky: there were not many original productions. This local way of life which, thanks to Protestantism, was a stage or two beyond a peasant folk culture, remained intact until the outer world's pressure grew too great for it, somewhere in the first quarter of the twentieth century. Until then, Canada was literally in the horse-and-buggy age (buggies were just coming in, in the eighteen-fifties) and a good age it was: simple, parochial, limited, but healthy, contented, marked by a wisdom close to the soil.

This rural and native British North American culture took the other ingredients of life as they came along and incorporated them. A case in point is associated with the railroad. Here was the major technical novelty of the period, perhaps of any period. "No other mechanical invention ever was received with such universal respect, admiration and glamour as was the iron horse. It rapidly became almost as much a friend to man as had the real horse before, and when it panted while climbing a hill, he sympathized, encouraged and commended its successful efforts. The cranks on its wheels, while moving up and down but at the same time forward, resembled the knees of a sturdy Clydesdale horse and there was a rhythm that led to poetry and song."[4] On the occasion of the opening of the Northern Railway (1853), 'song' was duly supplied, genuine new-world folk material: the engine apparently was called *The Josephine* and some immortal 'Cye' was her driver:—

> "I dressed myself from top to toe,
> And from Toronto I did go
> My hair all combed so slick and fine,
> I looked as prim as The Josephine.
>
> . . . . . .
>
> "At Bradford station next we run
> Where Downie with his dog and gun,
> To keep the girls from off the line
> Looking at Cye of The Josephine". . .[5]

The writer himself in his youth was told by an old man that when a schoolboy, he was taken down one morning with the class to stand at the station and greet the first train ever to steam through the woods—the same run celebrated in the verses, October 6th, 1853, the year the railway joined Lake Simcoe to Lake Ontario. It had been the great occasion of his childhood and one of his vivid memories.

To French Canada the timeless life of the countryside was well suited, and it was commended by religious leaders. English Canadians were too much attracted by the 'spirit of the age'—too fond of railroads—to be entirely happy with it. The farmer did not expect to remain a simple peasant; he did expect to settle his sons around him and see them all thrive. Nor could he fail to be touched with the stir of the world, and particularly the feverish activity involved in building a new continent. So then, as now, some of the country folk went off to greener fields across the line and got caught up in the growing urban industrialism.

The end of good land: the perpetual frontier of the North

The limits of good land in all the provinces were soon reached: Canada was no second United States, and by the end of the eighteen-fifties, men were beginning to perceive that if they wished to remain on the land, they had only two alternatives—the rock and muskeg of the Canadian Shield or the fertile fields of the Western States. Many chose the latter. Today, as one drives west from Port Huron in Michigan, for some miles he can literally see the Canadian frontier projected westward across the boundary: the same brick houses he has left behind him in Ontario, the same general layout of the farms, and, it must be confessed, the same departures from the usual American standards of neatness.

At home, as the frontier turned northward, it rapidly advanced across the last considerable areas of tillable soil: these lay up on the Georgian Bay and the present city of Owen Sound is their nucleus. Not far from it the bony shelves of limestone began to stick through the soil; they were to preserve the Bruce Peninsula for another sixty years as the refuge of the lumberman. Farther east, the edges of the Shield had long since been reached but in the eighteen-fifties, government, with an energy not previously associated with government in Canada, had begun to drive pioneer roads back into it—the Ottawa and Opeongo, the Perth, the Addington, the Hastings, the Bobcaygeon, and others both in Upper and Lower Canada. The native-born knew the country too well to condemn themselves to it, and the immigrants who were placed on these roads promptly got into the usual tenderfoot difficulties, burning off the pine and leaving the sand and rock exposed. Though here and there 'oases' within the Shield gave opportunity for reasonably successful farming, the first assault on this rock-ribbed old fortress, which everywhere bars the way to the north, failed, leaving as its major results, charred stumps, abandoned fields and a thin deposit of 'poor whites', whose descendants in some cases remain a social problem to this day. People of energy, after skimming off the cream in the shape of the pine, got out.

What the environmental conditions do to people was beautifully illustrated by the chatty remarks made by a descendant of one of these families in the writer's presence. A frivolous, tiresome woman, nearing sixty, with hair dyed red, she talked of her old uncles, who lived in a western American city. She herself lived near New York. Her son was in the American Air Force. She kept adverting to the upper-class British stock to which she belonged, but she herself had no observable resemblance to an English woman of the upper classes. "My grandfather," she said, "came out to this country eighty or ninety years ago (i.e. about 1860). He was a retired British Army officer and suggestions were made to him in England that he could get lots of land for himself in Canada. He bought seven or eight hundred acres around a place called . . . in Ontario. It's all rock. So his boys stayed there for a while and then they lit out. I went back there once years ago and one of the girls was still there, seventy years old, still looking English and still playing the organ every Sunday in the little church." This woman was clinging tightly to the shreds of British aristocratic tradition in her family background, though in every way— demeanour, freedom of manner, flashy appearance—she was very much a middle-class American of the less stable type and proud of it. If her father had stayed in Ontario, poverty would have reduced her to something like the 'poor whites' around her in all except the pride of tradition and a demeanour which would probably have been more acceptable than that which she possessed.

The rising cities and their life

Once the land is conquered, people have no alternative but to congregate in town and city, where they may find new means of livelihood. In the late eighteen-fifties the British provinces, just reaching this parting of the ways, had not yet gone very far towards urban life. By the census of 1861, there were only nine 'cities' in the United Province: Montreal, Quebec, Trois Rivières, and Sherbrooke in Canada East; and Toronto, Hamilton, Ottawa, London and Kingston in Canada West. In the other provinces, there were Halifax, Saint John, Fredericton and St. John's. Other than these there were just a few towns of from 1,000 to 6,000 people each. Of the nine Canadian 'cities' only three, Montreal, Quebec and Toronto, were of any size. Sherbrooke and Trois Rivières were under 7,000, the others ran from about 11,000 to 19,000. The city which had lately been chosen the capital, Ottawa, the former Bytown, was under 15,000, still a rough sawmill and lumberjack town. Later to be immortalized by Goldwin Smith as a 'sub-arctic lumber-camp', it was described as "scarcely having a British look about it"[6]—this because of the presence there of between 3,000 and 4,000 Canadians of French origin. It was chosen capital because it was well away from the American frontier (sixty miles!) but to many an Upper Canadian that failure to have a British look made it more of a foreign town than, shall we say, Pittsburgh.

The only remark that seems justified about the other small

places is the complete lack about them of anything that justifies remark. Always excepting Kingston, and Kingston has already been dealt with.

Montreal, Quebec, and Halifax are also old and familiar stories. During the decade Montreal began to inch forward towards that suggestion of cosmopolitan metropolis which it has since acquired in larger degree and which, as a city of two cultures and a great port, it always will possess. In 1860 it had nearly reached 100,000 in population and was thus already one of the larger towns of the continent. It still was predominantly a city of English speech, though not an English city. How could it be when so many of its citizens had been born in Ireland and professed the Roman Catholic religion?[7] "We have three populations in Lower Canada, the French Canadians, the Irish Catholics and the British Protestants," exclaimed a public man of the day.[8]

In Upper Canada, Toronto was moving into its proud, self-claimed position of 'Queen City of the West' (and it is seldom realized to-day how far 'west' western Upper Canada seemed to those who still carried an Atlantic scale of longitude in their minds). It was also 'Toronto the Good' and that because so many of its inhabitants were zealous Protestants and had so many churches which they zealously attended. Its population was just under 45,000 and its principal constituent, as with Montreal, was Irish. But a very different kind of Irish, for they were mostly Protestants from 'the black north'. But it also found room to shelter some 12,000 Catholics of various stripes, the majority, presumably, also Irish. It was an explosive mixture, and the resultant bangs and thumps would shock us to-day. Turbulence, as we have seen, had marked elections from the beginning of the Irish immigration in the eighteen-twenties and turbulence marked the celebrations of the great Irish occasions, July 12th and March 17th. On March 17, 1858,

"On returning from the House to his hotel, (D'Arcy) McGee's carriage was besieged and stones and brickbats filled the air. His driver was knocked from the seat, but held to his way. On finally reaching the hotel, they found a large mob making very offensive demonstrations and the lower storey of the house sacked and gutted. That morning, as the Saint Patrick's procession was moving along the street, one of the participants, Matthew Sheady, had been stabbed and mortally wounded by a two-pronged pitchfork. Another man 'got hold of a neck-yoke' according to the newspaper account and was looked upon as quite a hero, since he had been able to knock down three or four other 'papists' with it. All these acts were committed in the open and before many witnesses, yet in such sympathy with the evildoers were the city police force generally that no arrests were made and justice could be had neither for the murder of Matthew Sheady nor for the sack of the National Hotel. . . . the police force of Toronto was 'one vast Orange Lodge, the chief was an Orange official and the recorder a past Grand Master and the gaoler a present Grand Master'. . . ."[9]

When a whole vast organization was devoted to fanaticism —in the legislature of 1857 there were no less than twenty members of Upper Canada's sixty-five who were either Orange-men or represented the Orange interest[10]—and with two such provocative individuals about as George Brown, forever riding the Protestant horse, and the Roman Catholic Bishop Charbonnel, with his extreme and European attitudes on the relations of Church and State, it is no wonder that the city crowd occasionally got a chance to enjoy a little heart-warming head cracking.

Old men and new

Browns, Charbonnels and mobs did not make up the whole of Toronto. There were still the old families, ensconced in their great mansions close to the water,[11] and there were also many new men making their appearance and their bid for importance. Everywhere else in the colonies the story was much the same. The English timber exporters of the seaports have already been mentioned. These men for the most part conformed to the old pattern and, as Anglicans, took their places easily within the ruling hierarchy. They were similar in this respect to the great brewing and distilling families that were coming into prominence, such as the Molsons of Montreal, the Gooderhams of Toronto, the Labatts and Carlings of London. None of these clashed with the older Tories but quickly became almost indistinguishable from them. They could not fail to be Anglicans, for it was not in the genius of Catholicism to cast up large-scale capitalists and there was no place for brewers and distillers among the 'non-conformists', or 'evangelical denominations' (as it is preferable to call them after mid-century).[12]

The Ottawa Valley produced a prominent group of new men, who rose to great wealth on the basis of lumber. Among them were American immigrants, such as the Eddys and Bronsons, but towering above them all was John R. Booth, a native Canadian, who was already well known at the time of Confederation and later was to become the unchallenged 'King of the Ottawa'. There were many others, whose families have continued to be prominent in the life of the Ottawa, such as the Edwards, Gilmours, Frasers, MacLarens and Gillieses. In Toronto, where the 'non-conformism' of the new men was one of the most shocking features of their appearance, there were, to name only a few, John Macdonald, the Methodist merchant, William McMaster, the Baptist banker, later a senator and the man after whom McMaster University was named, the Methodist Massey family, who were to become the most conspicuous and representative of all such men, and William Davies, founder of the industry which grew into the modern firm Canada Packers.

William Davies may serve as an example. He was an English immigrant, of poor but sturdy origin. In Toronto he began humbly but diligently, studied the conditions of his trade and gradually branched out, in the process helping signally to fit the Canadian packing business, especially in pork, into the requirements of the overseas markets (which he largely created) and to teach the Ontario farmer the job of raising the most suitable products in the most suitable way. He was a devout Baptist, which meant that he was a strong individualist. A simple man from a simple background, he was not indifferent to larger aspects of life, both aesthetic and intellectual. He was described as "a man of stern integrity, indomitable will and unflinching courage"—the very kind who must have filled the ranks of Cromwell's Ironsides. No wonder his business got larger and larger and his residences graduated from the humbler areas of Toronto to the most fashionable. Like so many men of his type, as he prospered he became increasingly interested in charities, but he was never 'overcome with the world' and never ceased to protest at the extravagance and sophistication accompanying his denomination's growth in wealth.

"There has been built in this city recently a large Baptist Chapel, Gothic, brown stone, spire pointing upward, if not heavenward, marble baptistry, etc., cost $100,000 and odd, and the organ $7,000 besides, and I believe it has been paid for, but it has been built regardless of the needs of the city. One of the members, a M.L.C., say a Senator, very wealthy, married an American, natural result they soon had an American minister, then this new building also American, then the Lady and the minister lay their heads together, and they get a professional singer a sort of prima donna and she is paid $300.00 per year and many are very much hurt about it. . . ."[13]

Davies was strict, but not narrowly intolerant. While he frowned on alcohol, he confessed he was not completely 'T.T.' himself, and when Sunday band concerts were abolished in the parks, while he could not help concurring, he felt that perhaps it would have been better to listen to bands than "to be playing at skittles" in places where liquor was obtainable. He mingles his religion and his pork-packing in good Calvinistic fashion ("whatsoever thou doest, that do to the glory of God!"). He takes part in the inevitable Baptist brawls but seems to stay pretty well in the centre, not forsaking the church, as many others do when a melodeon is brought in, but contenting himself by referring contemptuously to it! As befits a stubborn nonconformist, he is suspicious of 'these French' and while not liking the Orangemen, is still less a lover of Catholicism or anything that looks like it: even melodeons may be papistical, the thin edge of the wedge, while as for the ordination he attended in 1855 "during the ordination, [they] laid their hands on his head. Tell me in your next if that is usual in Baptist Churches in the Old Country. It occurred to me and others that it savoured of Anti-Christ."[14]

Hostile to French and Catholics, he is equally against Tories and Anglicans. "I do not know anything about his [Sir Edmund Head's] character but he is very thick with the old Tory School, viz Allan McNab and others". And then he goes on to illustrate how close non-conformism must always be to republicanism. "He (the governor, the Queen's representative) must not assume too much, for the people here, tho' very loyal, go in strongly for the principle 'The Queen, her rights and no more, the People their rights and no less' ".[15] Again when the Prince of Wales came out in 1860, he took a cool view of the visit and when the Prince began visiting convents in Lower Canada and shunning Orangemen's arches in Upper, then "I do not think his tour is found a success. . . . I certainly think that the people are less loyal than before he came."[16]

Davies's successive domestic 'moves' reflect the march of Toronto away from the lake and his personal march up the social scale. First a couple of rooms on Agnes Street, long since swallowed up in slum and business. Then to Alice Street for a short time, then out to a farm north of Danforth Road. Back again by 1857 to Davenport Place in the suburb of Yorkville and then in 1865 to a more pretentious neighborhood— Wellesley Street between Church and Jarvis—until overtaken there by 'a lacrosse ground'—"and it was an abominable nuisance". Thence the final move—to the new fashionable suburb of Rosedale, where in 1876, he bought three acres and built a fine house between Park Road and Huntley Street.

With the move to Rosedale, William Davies had arrived. He had long since become wealthy and respected in his own communion, and among business men. Now he had mingled with the 'select few' and his sons and grandsons could go on to take their place with the first of the land.[17] Throughout this far from untypical career, Davies remained the same industrious, honest man, too independent in his attitudes to be lovable, with no 'side' but much honest pride, and respected by all. A typical Baptist, a typical lower-middle-class man on the way up, a typical 'success story' and a typical illustration of the reshuffling of social classes that has gone on in Canada.

The first provincial university

William Davies says nothing in his letters about what we can now see was the most significant of all the occurrences in Toronto during the decade or, for that matter, in all British North America—the establishment of the University of Toronto, the provincial university. This non-sectarian college aroused bitter controversy at the time and was assailed by all the denominations with the vehemence that only the times could supply, for as non-sectarian it must be 'godless'. But the University was a portent of things to come and began at once to acquire a life of its own and to put its mark upon students. The year 1854, for example, saw the establishment of its *'Literary and Athletic Society'* which is still in active existence.[18] As good professors everywhere should, its staff soon began to get into trouble for the objective views they took of other people's 'sacred cows'. In 1853, at a meeting of the then 'youthful institution' which was growing up in the University's shadow, the Royal Canadian Institute, Rev. Dr. McCaul, first president of the University, speaking on "The Genuineness of Some of the Ancient Classics" had occasion to advert to an article in the Institute's *Canadian Journal*, published by one of his staff, which gave "the impression (unfounded) that parties denying the inspiration of the sacred Scripture are permitted to publish their erroneous opinions through the columns of its organ."[19] Evidently the charges of 'atheism' constantly made against the institution could not apply to its president. Neither, apparently could solicitude for freedom of thought.

The University's academic standards seem to have been respectable from the first, though not severe. In a fourth-year paper set for candidates for honours, 1856, there were twenty-three questions, all relating to the history of the ancient world, and calling only for brief factual replies: "What Greek and Roman historians have specially devoted their attention to national distinction and characteristics of race? Name their works". "Name the principal authorities, in chronological order, for the geography and history of Britain from the earliest times to the close of Roman Occupation, with the names of their works". Such papers had strong ethnological content, as might be expected from their setter, Sir Daniel Wilson, whose major field was archaeology. No department of history would use this type of question to-day, students being expected to show ability in analysis rather than in mere memory.

Unfortunately, the provincial university began with the wrong colours hoisted—Toronto, rather than Upper Canada (Ontario) and so has never had the same recognition of its place in the province as have the great sister institutions of the West.

In one particular, the University could not fail to make an immediate impact upon the public, that is, in its building, the present University College. It is well known that every effort was made to have this erected on an ambitious scale, in order to 'anchor' the University's land-grant resources and prevent the politicians of the day nibbling them away, but the result was a building considered pretentious at the time and somewhat on the grandiose side. University College after a century of use is softened and humanized and those who have thronged its halls can never think of it without affection, so they are probably not well qualified to pass on its architectural merits. That it is frankly imitative is clear: it does its best to look like a Norman fortress (with some touches of a cathedral) and with its stone face and brick rear it may merit the old jibe of having 'a Queen Anne front and a Sally Anne back'. But somehow, despite Norman keep, flaunting itself proudly against no possible enemy, it is impressive. Perhaps one reason for that is the excellence of its workmanship and the infinite detail of ornament in the stonework. From another point of view, the building illustrates delightfully the swing from the earlier, eighteenth-century style to late romanticism—Tennyson at the time, not to speak of the pre-Raphaelites, was filling his poetry with Marianas in their moted granges, literary equivalents of University College, Toronto.

The remarkable thing about University College was, like Dr. Johnson's dog walking on its hind legs, not that it could be built well but that it could be built at all. The establishment of a provincial university argued a slowly growing sense of community in Upper Canada. There were many other 'arguments' of the same kind which had their crystallization at the

time: the Toronto Industrial Exhibition (1851), the incorpora-
tion of the medical profession of Upper Canada (1851), the
first professional theatrical performance[20] in Toronto (1836),
the original unit of the Toronto Stock Exchange (1852),
the Toronto Normal School, and many others, both in the
provincial capital and lesser places. All this growth came from
the subjugation of the forest. What was going on in Upper
Canada is this bright and cheerful decade—for so it was, despite
the roars of rage that resounded from political platforms on
the hated nature of the Union—was going on in the other
provinces, if at a slower rate. Each one was beginning to be
more aware of itself and aware of the place of the group to
which it belonged in North America. British North America
was a phrase which had begun to possess some discernible
content and reality. There were prophetic overtones about it
and it cast before it the shadows of coming events.

Notes to Chapter 17

1. Take the Township of Wilmot, Wellington district, as an example:
   population in 1825, 720; in 1829, 1,272; in 1837, 1,454; in 1841,
   2,220; in 1851, 5,297; in 1861, 6,173.
2. Letter in the *Christian Guardian*, July 31st, 1850.
3. Anyone who knows the Ontario country-side knows of the dominance in this locality or that of certain family names, all members
   related in a degree of complexity that baffles the outsider. For
   example, in Simcoe County practically everyone by the name of
   Arnold, Black, Banting, Jennett or Lennox can claim kinship.
4. Frank N. Walker, *Four Whistles to Wood Up* (Upper Canada Railway Society, 1953), p. 22.
5. Ibid.
6. W. H. Smith, *Canada, Past, Present and Future* (2 Vols., Toronto,
   1851), Vol. II, p. 359.
7. 14,179 Irish-born, the majority Irish Catholic: this does not include
   children born in Canada.
8. Christopher Dunkin, speaking in the debate on Confederation, 1865.
9. Isabel Skelton, *The Life of Thomas D'Arcy McGee* (Gardenville,
   P.Q., 1925), p. 336.
10. Toronto *Globe*, Jan. 9th, 1857.
11. Bishop Strachan's palace on the bay shore, 1818-1900, occupied
    the block west of the present Royal York Hotel. Sir John Beverley
    Robinson's house was a little further west.
12. Presbyterianism was marginal in this respect: probably the Church
    of Scotland would have tolerated distillers but the branches probably
    not. Sir John Carling was brought up a Methodist but his brewery
    drove the family into Anglicanism! See the present writer's *Colony
    to Nation* (London and Toronto, 1957), p. 368.
13. *The Letters of William Davies* (ed. W. S. Fox, Toronto, 1945),
    p. 135: William Davies to a friend, June 15th, 1876. The church
    was Jarvis Street Baptist Church, almost the only one of numerous
    near-by "Gothic, brown stone churches" which has been able to
    hold out against encroaching slums and industrialism—because it
    reverted to the hell-fire and damnation 'fundamentalism' which
    seems to appeal to the city proletariat as it did to the simple
    pioneer. Another bit of the irony of history!

The height of prosperity / 271

14. Ibid., p. 45.
15. Ibid., p. 56.
16. Ibid., pp. 123-124.
17. One of the grandsons edited the letters, W. S. Fox, late President of the University of Western Ontario, another was a prominent Canadian banker. The family remained sturdily Baptist and did not promote itself to Anglicanism.
18. As an alumnus the writer may perhaps be pardoned for stating that in 1954 he had the pleasure of addressing the hundredth annual meeting of this society in which he had once taken an active part. He was able to tell his hearers that at his own graduation dinner he had heard a description of the formation of the society from a graduate who had actually been present at the occasion. This represents a fair degree of continuity for a young community.
19. Toronto *Globe*, Mar. 18th, 1853.
20. As noted in the unpublished diary of Henry Rowsell, then a Toronto bookseller, under the date of Monday, Feb. 22nd, 1836.

18: The period of Confederation

IN THE YEAR OF CONFEDERATION, 1867, one man's long life still spanned back to the end of the American Revolution, the destruction of the first British Empire and the beginning of the second American experiment. During that time, not long as history goes, an immense amount of work had been done in the isolated northern wilderness. Clearings had been made, the clearings had been expanded into the open countryside, roads had been built, houses had been built, towns and cities had been built: all this mainly on a basis of hand labour. It was immensely more than had been accomplished in New France in its whole history and almost as much as in the thirteen colonies prior to the Revolution. British Americans of those days, like ourselves, were always comparing themselves to the Americans, to their own disadvantage, and while the colonial condition had hampered energy and acted like a brake, nevertheless they perhaps did not have to feel as inferior as they did. After all, it was a thousand miles from the sea to the St. Clair river: this river penetration inland was like an arrow's flight, whereas the thirteen colonies had attacked the wilderness on a wide front and at many points.

The conditions of the accomplishment had been onerous enough to leave their permanent mark on the British North American. Climate was hard, communications difficult, soil in many districts poor or non-existent, and next door the heathen raged. All this meant unsureness, prosaicness, a taciturnity easily running into pessimism, a conservatism not common south of the border. Many of these qualities remain: Canadians are not as optimistic, as volatile, as imaginative, as experimental, as assertive, as egotistic or as energetic as are Americans. Those among them who have possessed such qualities have often become Americans.

When one considers the lions in the path, the wonder is that Canadians have ever been able to form a big country of their own, still less something that is slowly becoming visible as a national character. "Two nations warring in the bosom of a single state" is a phrase that can never be far from any Canadian's mind. It indicates, however, only one out of a dozen forces that were pulling them apart. Yet, possibly because of the very dissonances that made for so much discomfort in life, a better day lay ahead. Possibly it was natural, after nearly a century of growth, that a period of consolidation should ensue. At any rate, everyone knows that in the eighteen-sixties came the great miracle which turned scattered provinces into the Dominion of Canada, thus opening the way for the future that Canada is now achieving.

Hatred as a virtue: Canada as a melting-pot of belief and prejudice

Few of us nowadays would welcome the social tension that must have characterized the years just before Confederation. In English Canada to-day, while the old spirit can be reawakened, the day has gone when every valiant Protestant soul could flame with anti-French and anti-papal zeal. Mr. St. Laurent when chosen Liberal leader in 1948, speaking in French, said "You would be astonished at the good will that exists towards us everywhere throughout the country. It exists, and we must meet it half-way". French Canada, being the smaller, has been slower in dropping its guard but it, too, has visibly moved. To-day no responsible federal statesman of any party would ground his policies on inflammatory appeals to race and religion: in the eighteen-fifties he would, and did. The major example is George Brown, a man of whom the pure crusader may approve but in whom it is hard for the average middle-of-the-roader to see much more than the fierce intolerance of hatred; that, and the sublime faith in his creed and his race which, when identified with 'the right', has always made so strong and disturbing a force in history.

While Brown was thundering in covenanting appeals against pope and priest (and that, of course, was just it—the Scottish Reformation over again, the saints against the scarlet woman, the whore of Babylon), dissent from Catholic orthodoxy was having more support in French Canada than it had ever had before or ever was to have again.[1] If the Reformation rose to a belated climax in Upper Canada with George Brown, the Enlightenment shone again with *les rouges* in Lower. These men, as followers of Papineau, were nationalistic and more or less anti-British, although they had not got as far on in these attitudes as the more extreme groups of our own day. They urged the rationalism of the eighteenth century with a French combination of fervour and intelligence. The Catholicism of some of them wore thin and a few left the church altogether. They represented the only strong anti-clerical movement in the history of French Canada. If they had triumphed, they would presumably have made Quebec what France is to-day (except in that they would have had different material to work with). They did not triumph, mainly because they were never more than a small minority and because the church rallied its forces and delivered against them one of its most ferocious assaults.

If Louis Joseph Papineau had been a good Catholic, the Rebellion of 1837 would have been far more formidable, and an 'Ireland' might have appeared in Canada, never to disappear. Before the outbreak, his heterodoxy had half discredited him but when he returned to Canada after his exile in France, it was as if the prestige of liberal France returned with him. Or of that atheistic, immoral, republican France which had sprung out of the Revolution, the clergy would have said. And his disciples, writing in journals of which *L'Avenir* (1847-1851) was the chief, would have given them plenty of reason for their opinion. *L'Avenir* was edited by J. B. E. Dorion, the so-called *enfant terrible* of the time. His contributors included his brother, A. A. Dorion (as Sir Antoine, Minister of Justice, 1873-1874), J. Doutre, M. Dessaulles, various other Dorions, several Papineaux and others. Nearly all these men were at one time or another 'bad actors' in the eyes of the clergy and orthodox laymen of Lower Canada. No wonder! *L'Avenir* of January 18th, 1850, declared that "The Catholic clergy of Canada is much too rich: the tithe gives it an undue influence, which it has greatly abused, to the misfortune of the country". For good measure, the journal advocated annexation to the American republic largely because "a democratic republic has no need of priests". And then, just to rub things in, it added "the reading of the Gospel is without any doubt the especial cause of the superiority of the Protestant nations over the Catholic". *L'Avenir* could end a long essay against religion and the Inquisition with: "The Catholic clergy to-day, no more than other false devotees, cannot burn its adversaries, thanks, not to the progress which their reason has made, but to philosophy which has extinguished the faggots. However, the spirit is always the same and if the clergy could, the arguments of which it would make use would be the same". This was just what George Brown was saying in Upper Canada.

L'Avenir was the most extreme of the *rouge* papers but its successor, *Le Pays*, was not far behind it. Both represented the same group as *L'Institut Canadien*. Destroyed though they all were by Bishop Bourget, the surprising phenomenon surely is that such a party, anti-clerical, apparently anti-Catholic and anti-Christian, should have had any support in Lower Canada at all, let alone getting some of its members chosen for parliament. English Canadians holding similar views would have had no chance of election in the Upper Canada of the time! Of course, the tenets of *rouge* members took some time to become known. As long as they confined themselves to joining with Montreal English Tories in advocating annexation, they could be endured, though not liked. But as George Brown's intolerant philippics against popery and the priests, Catholicism, Catholic schools, and 'the French' became known throughout the province, it must have been with a good deal of annoyance that good Catholics and Frenchmen saw a group of their own people reaching out for an alliance with such a man. Brown through his newspaper *The Globe* was forever calling on Canadians to "warn off the foreign priest who dares to dictate to them through his Lower Canadian slaves".[2] When the two extremist groups got together in the abortive attempt to form a government in 1858 (the Brown-Dorion four-day ministry), success for them was evidently impossible. In time these groups were to grow together to become the Liberal party, but that was to be the work of years.

A society ranged against itself in such ways could not have been comfortable to live in. On its English side, it was as bitterly divided by denominationalism as was French Canada by belief and unbelief. There could be no community at all between high-church Anglicans and Methodists, and there were no warm relationships—there was not much more than a wary toleration—between two groups apparently so close as Presbyterian and Methodist. Even within what might have been expected to be a homogeneous group—a small Protestant religious denomination, like the Baptists—differences were conspicuous and difficult. William Davies warns off a certain individual from coming to a post in a Baptist church in Toronto: he does not have sufficient gifts of reconciliation for these difficult people: "The churches here are composed of Yankees, English, Irish, Scotch, Welsh and Canadian, rather irreconcilable elements. . . ."[3] 'Canadians', who seem to have been thought of as merely one element among others in Canada, were themselves as divided as the rest. When the coalition of 1854 was in prospect, the old Tory, Sir Allan MacNabb, a native, had declared that he would support anyone or anything that would hamper the Clear Grits, also natives.[4] In his eyes, 'Clear Grittism' represented Mackenzie-ism; the rebels of 1837 were still the rebels in 1854. This deep rift in Upper Canada, based on the rebellion, has continued to be evident almost down to the present day. At the Conservative Convention of 1943 in Winnipeg, Hon. Earl Rowe in a speech of exhortation, in which he made the conventional jibes against the opponents, the Liberals, remarked parenthetically: "Liberals? . . . Reformers as they once were—*rebels*, my father used to call them!" To the onlooker, it appeared as if Mr. Rowe still thought of them as *rebels*.

To ensure Protestant and English ascendancy, George Brown campaigned for 'Rep. by Pop.' or home rule for Upper Canada. From this point of view—'Rep. by Pop.'—Confederation itself may be regarded as the consequence of the ardent effort of each province to get away from the other, a genuine divorce. If so, little did they foresee that such a divorce in the years to come was to marry them more tightly. It may, however, be questioned whether the desire for divorce was as ardent as 'home-rulers' thought. Something was growing up between the two halves of the province of Canada, and at the top levels of government, and probably to a distance down, understanding was penetrating: how could it be otherwise when men had to work together? The ties of blood and language are not the only ties, important as they are: mutual interest is also important, especially if there is nothing much more than general background ideas to disturb it. The accusation has always been levelled that there was much more—that Upper Canada paid the taxes and Lower Canada spent them or that separate schools were foisted on Upper Canada by Lower Canadian votes. While such charges as these were valid up to a point, they were not what has served as the basis of separatism abroad—the use of the law as an engine of coercion, arbitrary government with its accompaniment of arrest and imprisonment, judicial murder and military repression. No one could doubt that Canada in the eighteen-fifties was a free country: in fact, to judge by the amount of freedom of speech that was indulged in, no one could imagine a freer. It is therefore logical to conclude that if there had been enough statesmanship, the disruptions of the eighteen-sixties need not have occurred. The historian keeps coming back to George Brown as the force which destroyed the old Union: and—it must at once be added—thereby summoned up the necessity for another solution, which in happy retrospect, was Confederation.

The Southern threat

Few modern Canadians, except those brought up in Europe, can understand what it must mean to have a volcano erupt in the back yard of the house next door. And yet that is exactly what happened in 1861 with the outbreak of the American Civil War. For four years this horrid struggle raged, giving to Americans a blood-bath that was to constitute for them a deep spiritual experience. It drew them in, it almost drew England and France in, it came within a fraction of spilling over across our border, and finally it drew in thousands of our most adventurous youth, who rushed off to join Northern armies. Though British North Americans did not, as did Americans, have "to stand up and be counted", yet the great debate on slavery and its bloody decision raged at their doors, and, as with everything else of a great nature in the United States, they heard nearly every word of it. They could not help becoming emotionally engaged when Americans fell to fighting each other.

The number of those who would have favoured slavery in 1860 was probably microscopic. Persons, however, who took their cue from official England and who felt themselves to be aristocrats, tended to think of Southerners as 'gentlemen' and consequently at first to find their sympathies on the side of the South. It was easy for French Canada to see the South as a minority fighting the oppressions of the majority, and allow its emotions to verge towards the Southern side. Neither of these attitudes was important, for the mass of Canadians soon seized on slavery versus freedom as the issue and came down on the side of freedom. Many an indication of this had already been given, especially in the sympathies and help extended to the 'Underground Railway', which relayed escaping slaves from the South to a haven on Canadian soil. Canadians were proud of the asylum they could extend, and colour discrimination, even in the spots where the slaves settled, was, until recent years, hardly known. In fairness to Americans, it must be added that there was in this Canadian attitude some of the 'holier-than-thou' strain, which always shows up in Canadians when their neighbours fumble a moral problem—their well-intentioned, honourable Pharisaism over the McCarthy attack on liberty in the nineteen-fifties was another example.

Few peoples can retain their complete sanity while fighting, and a volatile people like the Americans are perhaps particularly prone to hit out hard at a real or imagined enemy. The British colonies were lucky to escape. In Canada everyone recalled the War of 1812 and the guerrilla invasions of 1838-

1839, each of them an unprovoked assault on a people who were weak and who considered themselves good friends and neighbours. Was the experience to be repeated now for a third time and on a huge scale? More impressed by their neighbours' plight than by their own danger, British North Americans, with the school boy's malicious satisfaction in seeing a big boy who has bullied him get into trouble of his own, waxed sarcastic at their neighbour's fate. The *Acadian Recorder* of Halifax, perhaps merely through the fortunate deficiencies of its type-setter, came out with an issue or two in which its column of American news was headed 'UNTIED STATES'. Later on this was 'corrected' and there was substituted for it the equally revealing 'DISUNITED STATES'.

Luckily for the colonists, the Civil War did not boil over: all they got was the much less formidable aftermath—the irruptions of irresponsible Irish Fenians. The Fenians actually did them an enormous service, and the blood of those militia-men who fell fighting them at Ridgeway was shed for a cause greater than they knew, for the fear of the threat (which could easily have mounted up to drag in the American nation) drew British North Americans together and was important in bring-ing about Confederation.

Yet not even the apprehension of the eighteen-sixties shifted Canadians far in the direction of the military life. They would not embark on a big scheme of military preparation during the Civil War[5] and when it and its concomitants were over, they turned their backs on organized service in arms. The attitude was characteristic of a pioneer people: fight willingly when the enemy actually appears, but refuse to prepare for him and to believe that it can ever happen again. There are so many other things to be done. The sense of community is so weak. And the number of unemployed gentlemen whose only career is arms is small. Societies in the bud are not fighting machines.

One prominent effect of the American Civil War on Canada was a setback in the advance of democracy. It was, according to British Tories, democracy which had occasioned the Revolu-tion in the first place, and now, after eighty years, democracy was proving, as they had contended all along, an impossible social attitude. It resulted not only in coarseness (and every Tory knew how coarse Americans were, even those who, like Lord Ashburton, married them) but in a liberty which amounted only to anarchy. 'Uncle Sam' was a loud, tobacco-chewing individual who bolted his food, ' 'lowed' and 'guessed' and had absolutely no regard for distinctions of rank. His system of government, if system it could be called, was loose and weak, and now war was proving that the so-called union was little more than a league of states.

Most true-blue Canadians took their cue from this kind of estimate, no matter how much better they knew their American neighbours than did their English superiors. And many who were not true-blue shared these anti-democratic sentiments, especially in French Canada, where traditional instruction stressed the view that the king was the Lord's Anointed and that next to one's spiritual head, one must give obedience and respect to one's sovereign. This teaching still leaves its traces in modern Quebec. It has also been a counter to nationalism: even an English and a Protestant sovereign is, after all, appointed by God to rule and as such commands more allegiance than a French Revolutionary principle like the sovereignty of the people. In 1864 a counter-blast to *rougisme*, speaking of a lecture on democracy by M. Dessaulles, exclaimed:—

> "There you see, there's *vox populi, vox dei* . . . that's what our *rouges* are putting out, ideas quite new in Canada . . . where we indulged ourselves in thinking that Her Britannic Majesty was our august sovereign and that we were her subjects. M. Dessaulles has said, and all the democratic hierarchy has repeated it after him, that the roles are interchanged: we are the sovereigns and our gracious sovereign is our humble servant. . . . As to me, . . . I shall retire to the Antipodes rather than be the subject of a democratic kingdom. The *rouge* axiom, *vox populi, vox dei,* which M. Dessaulles translates: 'kings are subjects and subjects are kings', saps at its base all respect for authority and seeks to destroy the equilibrium of the social scale. . . ."[6]

The consequence of the retreat from democracy (or rather the retreat from the advance towards democracy) was that when the plan for Confederation was worked out, no voices were raised for democratic principles. The zenith of democracy has been reached, thanks to the left-wing pressure, in the measure which made the Legislative Councillors elective (19 Victoria, 14-15, 1856). This measure had been accepted by the Assembly in the previous year but rejected by the appointive Council. In 1856, however, it passed: current members would remain life appointees, but vacancies would be filled by election. There were to be twenty-four electoral divisions for each province (which later became the number of their senators), and Councillors would be elected for eight years, a dozen each two years. This brought the Council into resemblance to the American senate. But there was to be a property qualification. The leader of the opposition to the measure was

George Brown, who, though leader of the democrats, was no democrat. He correctly foresaw confusion when both chambers could claim to represent the people. After this experiment, which lasted too short a time to show conclusive results, the popular principle went into retreat and in the Confederation debates few there were to stand up for it—virtually no one except that valiant *rouge*, A. A. Dorion. The result was our present appoitive senate, our property qualifications and, generally, an attempt to strengthen the executive side of the government.

The long-range effects of this tendency, accentuated by what appeared to be the failure of the American democratic experiment, have been important in differentiating Canadian society from American. The government of the United States is much more one of participation by the individual citizen than is the Canadian. It calls for constant expression of the individual's opinion, and lends itself directly to the pressure of public opinion (legislators have no need to follow party lines in Congress or state legislature). In Canada the citizen registers his vote once in four years and then may go to sleep again, secure in the knowledge that 'they' will look after things. Since 'they' becomes increasingly the cabinet, what he does is to give full power of attorney to a small committee each four years or so, well knowing that virtually nothing he can do in the interval will have much effect on the group to whom he has given his blank cheque.

That this absence of republican responsibility suited the average colonist at the time would be the impression from an examination of the royal visit of 1860. The Prince of Wales was enthusiastically received as the heir apparent of a monarch who was genuinely a sovereign, and as the young father of everyone, with power at his disposal. The visit gave a new lease of life to the old class pretensions which, after the winning of Responsible Government, had begun to slumber. The psychology of English Canadians then or now on the subject of the monarchy is impenetrable. How, it might be asked, could people adhere to two such incompatible ideas as rule from above and rule from below, warmly in each case and without sense of their incompatibility? A partial explanation lies in the old-country birth of many leading citizens, who brought with them to the new world the ideas of the old. Yet native Canadians, too, rested with complete ease in monarchical institutions, and when the monarch sent her first-born son unto them, they responded in generous demonstration: those who would have dared to respond in any other way would probably have been hit over the head by an Orange shillelagh, and the fact that the Orangemen acted so badly as to bar the Prince from landing at Kingston is no refutation of this, for Orangemen were their own best judges of 'loyalty', and if others did not accord with their ideas on such subjects, they were *ipso facto* 'disloyal'. Since those days both the Orange Order and old-country attitudes have weakened in Canada and to-day when royalty comes among us, the impression is that it is regarded mainly as providing an exotic spectacle.[7]

In 1860, the most democratic of Clear Grits could advocate popular institutions without any feeling of disloyalty towards the Crown. This lack of consistency was, after all, the very essence of English institutions. Among the French, more need was felt for getting the theory right, and *rouge* attempts to do so gave splendid opportunity for right-wing sniping.

"It is evident, they (*les rouges*) say, that to claim in Canada that we are subjects of Her Britannic Majesty is to express a fiction and even a falsity, if one takes these words in their absolute sense. The Queen of England being sovereign only nominally, we cannot be her *subjects* in a positive way. The Queen of England is for us but the symbol of the English people, we are therefore only symbolical subjects. From the moment that it is admitted that her sovereignty over us is a pure theory, a constitutional fiction, it must also be admitted that the loyalty we owe to her also cannot be a reality."[8]

L'Observateur, commenting on the above, with French logic, adds "But they are all perjurers when they take the oath to the Queen." In 1860 few English Canadians would have cared to commit themselves on symbolical sovereignty and from that day to this, few would have been interested in getting the theories squared away. But who will contend that the *rouge* attitude of a hundred years ago has not become, for practical purposes, our general attitude—symbolical 'subjects' of a symbolical 'monarch'? Of course, few English-speaking Canadians have the slightest difficulty in talking all in the same breath about these completely contradictory concepts, democracy and monarchy, the rule of the people and loyalty to the Queen. Logic in such matters may be left to lesser breeds.

Dissension in retreat before political union

"It is perfectly reasonable and natural that those who come to our shores from the old world, should look back with lingering affection and veneration to the land of their fathers . . . but that an intense national prejudice amounting to bitterness and leading to discord and strife, should usurp the place of those holier feelings, is greatly to be deplored. And yet such is often the case. These people (immigrants) seem to think their only duty in the land of their adoption, is to point out defects, and appear not to think of having assumed any obligation, or that they are at all identified with its interests."⁹

The quotation lights up another phase of this relationship between old country and new, which does not consist only in the common institutions of state but also in the sentiments of ordinary people. This book has already referred to the difficulty with which the immigrant lays aside his past and to the dissonances in colonial society arising from its conglomeration of new elements. Both these points the author quoted also mentions:— "that so many elements are combined in our population, has been considered Canada's greatest weakness. . . ." By 1860, if the inrush from Great Britain and Ireland of the period 1820-1850 had not occurred, the original English-speaking population would have arrived at enough knowledge of itself to be considered a community:¹⁰ this is what happened in Nova Scotia, where immigration was small. But on the St. Lawrence and the Lakes, as a result of the Great Immigration nearly everything had to be begun over again, and so the process of building up a community was retarded for between a quarter and a half a century. Notwithstanding this, by 1860 the forces of internal cohesion were once again in the ascendant, and British North Americans by that time were groping for something better than mere colonial existence. Out of the churning about of the late eighteen-fifties and the eighteen-sixties Confederation eventually came, and along with it that arrangement by which within three years one of the most remarkable geographical expansions on record took place—the peaceful extension of the new Dominion through to the Pacific.

There were plenty of straws in the wind. About 1860, J. A. Macdonald, in answer to George Brown's campaign for dissolution of the Union, maintained that it would be impossible to go back to the old arrangement, that the old provinces of Upper and Lower Canada had disappeared and that if the Union were dissolved, there would have to be at least three new provinces created—one to the west, one to the east and one, running from about the Bay of Quinte to Montreal, in the centre. He went on to say, on another occasion, that Canada was now something more than a province, that it was fast becoming not a colony but an ally of Great Britain. Here was the shrewdest man of the day with a vision in his eye, the vision of nationhood. Put this kind of sentiment alongside that expressed by the Rev. Wellington Jeffers, an Irishman by birth: "Every person expecting to stay in Canada and expecting his children to have their inheritance here, whether he was born in England, Ireland or Scotland, ought to feel himself to be a Canadian; he ought to feel for the character and glory of Canada, and to be devoted to its interests."[11]

The major obstacle to further nationalism lay in the perversity of many of the English Canadians themselves. It was not only old-country immigrants who decried the Canadian scene, but also many a Canadian born, especially among the 'better' classes. This attitude has lasted until our own day: "Can there any good thing come out of Nazareth?" In contrast, could any bad thing come out of the distant Jerusalem across the ocean, the scene of glory, the fount of honour?[12] In another direction, another type of division was produced by the insensate racial and religious cries of one man and his group. This was George Brown, already referred to several times. It must be admitted he was ably seconded and, had it not been for the unbridgeable gulf between one class of papist hunters and the rest, something like a holy war might have descended on the French. Luckily the Orange higher command stood aloof: indirectly through it the Catholics of Upper Canada had secured their separate schools, and it was able to combine politically with Catholics in Lower Canada to keep extreme Protestantism from breaking the Union. "God moves in a mysterious way, His wonders to perform."

The more zealous members of the evangelical churches were all George Browns. No evangelical church can approve of Rome and evangelicals always have felt it their duty to deplore Rome's unfortunate dupes. The French were "not entirely destitute of the forms of Christian worship," but "the system of Popery" was "but one form of heathenism, with just enough of Christianity to assign it a name and a place among the churches of Christendom."[13]

What a splendid basis for racial understanding and national unity such public pronunciamentos as these must have created! "Not entirely destitute of the forms of Christian worship"— this to the spiritual descendants of the Jesuit martyrs! "The ignorance and debasement of the French Romish population of eastern Canada."[14] Very possibly equal condescension could be found on the opposite side, just as it still can be found on both sides to-day: it may be closer to the average attitude than is understanding and tolerance—one place where it can at once be 'tapped' is among civil servants on either side of the racial barrier in the city of Ottawa; if there, probably elsewhere. One sometimes wonders by what miracle two such peoples have continued to live together without flying at each other's throats.

Possibly it was because among each of them were those who were having their glimpses of better days. The necessity of becoming something in oneself is strong in every man and in every society. In English Canada, despite much intolerant condescension, more people of a native cast of mind than elsewhere were probably found in the ranks of the only considerable native Protestant church—the Methodist. Anglicans might hark back to England and Presbyterians to Scotland, but Methodists from the beginning had been North Americans and as their co-religionists came in from the mother country, they fitted not into a colonial but a native church. The Methodist church had more than a little to do with making Canada.

> "The time will come when the vast solitudes which extend far away to the great Pacific shall be thickly populated by our conquering race. We cherish the belief that when that period shall arrive . . . the Wesleyan matin song of the holy Sabbath . . . raised aloft by the tuneful voices of the Methodists of Cape Canseau, following the golden pathway of the sun, shall float from spire to spire, from city to town, from town to hamlet, from hill to vale, from river to lake, across the whole continent, never ceasing, until the dying strains shall be lost in the grand chorus which shall swell up from the far-sounding waves of the measureless sea."[15]

That time has come!

Methodism's *Christian Guardian* had for years been among the most prominent and the most national of Upper Canadian papers—the only good paper in Upper Canada, a visitor once said of it. As the denomination grew stronger, other periodicals were established; and each, as it looked into the situation from a native point of view, seemed to develop the same aim —the stimulation, by all proper devices, of a national spirit. Thus in 1860, the *Wesleyan Repository and Literary Record* tackled the subject of literature: "Even if unexceptionable literature could be obtained from other lands, it is nevertheless highly desirable that we should cultivate a national literature of our own." Methodism's deed was as good as its word, for its church papers and periodicals, of a surprisingly high level for the day, led the way, and the books of history and of reminiscence contributed by its clergy, which went into thousands of homes, form to this day thrilling chapters in Canada's story.[16] Methodism never ceased to be a literary church and one of its brightest lights was the controversialist, the educationist, the preacher and writer, Egerton Ryerson.[17]

Yet Methodism was but one of several forces pushing British North Americans closer together. The truth is that time was doing its work, building something new three generations after the great catastrophe of the race, demanding that that something clothe itself in appropriate forms and, if good luck supervene, be imbued with its own appropriate genius. The spirit of the years to come was moving in the eighteen-sixties and the result was to be the Dominion of Canada.

Notes to Chapter 18.

1. See pp. 222 ff.
2. Toronto *Globe*, June 15th, 1855.
3. *The Letters of William Davies* (ed. W. S. Fox, Toronto, 1945), p. 112.
4. Thomas Chapais, *Cours d'Histoire du Canada*, Vol. VII, p. 93.
5. The Militia Bill of 1862, which proposed a considerable local force, was defeated in the Assembly.
6. *Le Rougisme en Canada* by *L'Observateur* (Quebec, 1864), p. 43.
7. See pp. 163, 281, 282.
8. Extracted from the *Lectures* by M. Dessaulles at the *Institut Canadien* and quoted by *L'Observateur*, op. cit., p. 57.
9. Quoted by Mrs. C. M. Day, *History of the Eastern Townships* (Montreal, 1869).
10. See Chapter 14.
11. *Christian Guardian*, Aug. 29th, 1860.
12. The author knows whereof he speaks. As late as the nineteen-thirties, efforts to establish Canada as a concern in her own right and not a mere appendage of Great Britain earned the bitter hostility of large sections of the native-born. The situation is happier today, now that there is more equality in status.
13. *Christian Guardian*, Apr. 16th, 1856.
14. Wesleyan Methodist Church, *Minutes of Conference for 1865*, Vol. II, p. 372.
15. Rev. J. R. Narroway, representative of the Wesleyan Conference in the eastern Provinces to the conference at Kingston, 1860, in the *Christian Guardian*, June 20th, 1860. My thanks for these quotations to Mr. Malcolm Finlay, M.A.
16. There were many of these: e.g. John Carroll, *Case and His Contemporaries* (5 Vols., 1867-1877); Rev. Robt. Cooney, *The Autobiography of a Wesleyan Methodist Missionary* (Montreal, 1856); Anson Green, *The Life and Times of Anson Green*, written by himself (Toronto, 1877); Geo. F. Playter, *History of Methodism in Canada* (Toronto, 1867); and Abel Stevens, *Life and Times of Nathan Bangs, D.D.* (New York, 1863).
17. See his *Loyalist of Canada and Their Times, The Story of My Life*, etc., etc.

Part III: Canada

19: A nation begun

WHEN IN 1867 CONFEDERATION was at last achieved, thoughtful people must have pondered the meaning of the accomplishment. The question had been under debate for a number of years, but in not much more than an academic way right down to the last. It is true that many Nova Scotians had taken alarm, and that a government had been defeated in New Brunswick, presumably on the issue. But the impression is strong that, with the exception of Nova Scotia, it was more an affair of governments than of people, that the temperature of the movement was not high, that the British North American provinces eventually were carpentered together, not smelted. If they had been smelted, as the American states had been, the 'climate' of the years succeeding their confederation would have been altogether different and Canadians would be different people to-day, with much greater consciousness of themselves and much more mutual readiness to accept and understand the other cultural group and the several sections. This was not to be: the pressure was weak, and the composing elements did not flow together.

Carpentering or smelting?

The pressure was weak, yes. Confederation was arrived at through rational channels, not emotional. On emotion over the movement the opposition had almost a monopoly: the case for the affirmative was put mostly on grounds of reason, good substantial reason. For any student of Canadian history this is familiar territory; one instance may, however, be cited to show how far from the emotional the average discussion was. Writing in *La Revue Canadienne*, 1865, Joseph Royal, highly conscious of the volcano erupting next door, considers the proposed union largely for the sake of defence. He comes out for a regular army, as against volunteer and militia. "The volunteer and the militia are worth something only as auxiliaries. Never can they replace regular troops. . . . We lack soldiers and fortifications, that is, everything; our duty is then to find out what the political regime is which will give us both, without hindering the march of material progress. . . . The neighbouring American republic suffocates us because it is great and powerful, and we are to-day isolated, feeble and poor. . . ." If Royal was representative of his people—and he was not without prominence—the type of consideration which recommended Confederation to French Canada may be inferred: it was put upon rational grounds. Practically every speaker in the Confederation Debates of 1865 put it upon rational grounds, and the chief of these was that of Royal—defence against the United States. Virtually the only emotional voice raised for it was that of D'Arcy McGee. McGee's speeches are splendid and they have the vision which the stolid native could not summon, but it is probable that the man most inspired by them was the man who made them. Confederation was not made by emotional appeal and while there have been plenty of hot (but few lofty) passages in Canadian life since, it has been the common-sense tone which, with some prominent exceptions, has marked it.

Still, carpentered is not quite the exact word, and, of course, no metaphor can be exact. Confederation opened the way for the elements to flow together, and during the succeeding years they have done this to some extent, so that it is more than a mere hammer-and-saw job we we are dealing with. In 1867, some slight chemical combination was effected, so that things could never again be as they had been: this much at least happened.

Many people would contend that not much more than this happened in the making of the American union and that the Civil War proved it. The South had to be conquered into union: this does not look a case of smelting. The assertion will not stand. The American Revolution had been an intense spiritual experience in which all the states, and practically all the citizens of all the states, had shared. The links then forged could never be cast off—and so the Civil War was to prove. The author once remarked to an intelligent Southern woman that it was difficult to understand how the South could have submitted, why the North had not had a perpetual *Ireland* on its hands. "We submitted, it was bitter, but we wanted to save our union," she replied.[1] The prospect of dissolution meant grim necessity, not glorious vision, for Southern minds.

For the British North Americans, there was nothing in common but the label, and for Lower Canada, one word of that was not very acceptable. Maritimers knew as much of Upper

Notman Collection, courtesy McCord Museum, McGill University and Maclean's Magazine.

Plate 8: *Andrew Allen and his Family in the Drawing-Room of their house in Montreal in 1871.*

UPPER CLASS VICTORIAN DOMESTICITY

E3-1401. "Made in Canada" Tweeds, good Winter weight, neat patterns and overplaid, as cut E3-1400

32	33	34 35
6.00	6.25	6.50

EI-5657

8914
$2.75

3109
$3.00

5410
75°

LADY RUBY
$1.25

5405
$1.75

4409
$1.25

5745
$5.00

6987
$22.50

K2-64/25. Rococo Couch, very soft and luxurious, spring seat and edge, deep tufted top on heavy duck, 8 rows of double clinched buttons, upholstered in fancy figured velour, fancy scroll frame and heavy turned feet, golden oak, 78 ins. long and 27 ins. wide, castored complete, making the best value on the market **13.75**

K2-32/49. Hall Rack, solid oak, golden finish, hand carved and well made, 36 inches wide, 80 inches high, fitted with 12 x 20 inch shaped British bevel plate mirror, box seat, four neat brass hat and coat hooks **10.00**

K2-28/142. Bent Post Iron Bedstead, finished in white enamel, gilt chills, 1 inch posts, heavy scroll fittings, size 4 ft. 6 in. only. The best value we have ever offered. Can be supplied also in nile green. Price......... .... **5.25**

Plate 9: From the catalogue of the T. Eaton Company for the year 1905-1906.

THE FAMILIAR SURROUNDINGS OF OUR FATHERS

Canada as they did of other parts of the wild West, which was not much; Lower Canadians cared nothing for it, and the Upper province reciprocated both attitudes. For George Brown and his followers, Confederation meant 'home rule for Upper Canada', freedom from French and popish domination, and not much more. For the Lower Canadians, it meant much the same thing in reverse. The Maritimers were dragged in as make-weights. The whole performance looked artificial. Artificial, until we remember the strength of the label, both 'British' and 'North American'. The colonists were colonists, the majority of them devoted to 'the parent state', and all of them, French included, were afraid of Americans who did not use the geographical adjective: the colonists were British *North* Americans, as American as the Americans, and many of them rather more British than the British. While such a foundation could never be as secure as bonds formed from within, it was the only one available, and as such, it strengthened and broadened, until it became what we have to-day.

In the opinion of many, it may be agreed, the colonists in 1867 did no more than form a league of provinces, just as their neighbours had formed a league of states. Time was to prove the view wrong, though not before politicians of small calibre had done their best to make it come true. It is singular how small and short-sighted those having large places in the public eye can be, even in the greatest of situations. For many years George Brown's figure loomed colossal over Upper Canada, yet the man never developed more than parish vision. Mackenzie and Mowat were no better. Given its extent plus its complexities, in no country in the world should the saying be more constantly taken to heart than in Canada that "where there is no vision, the people perish," and at no other time of Canadian history than in the generation after Confederation was there more necessity of its being taken to heart. Yet vision has always been in short supply in Canada, and that is one reason why it remains "a precarious creation". The charge of narrowness extends far beyond these men: it extends to whole provinces and to whole classes of men. Was it, then, merely a league of provinces that had been created?

There was some opinion on the other side and one convincing argument. The opinion warmed up to become the first expression of nationalism, but the convincing argument lay in a document and with those who had put it together—the British North America Act and its framers, of whom John A. Macdonald was without question the chief. It is hard to resist the conviction that Macdonald knew very well what he was doing

—creating a nation—and it seems clear that he had a pattern before him. That pattern was Alexander Hamilton's plan for the American union as introduced at the Constitutional Convention of 1787: our constitution is not far from being Hamilton's American proposals of eighty years before.[2] It is a fairly close adaptation of the monarchical system to the republican form of government—or if the reader wishes to turn the phrases around, that will do just as well. Canada is an actual republic, a *pro forma* monarchy, and John A. Macdonald was the man who made her so.

Confederation, then, implied nationalism. There can be no mistake about that, for the opinion was frequently voiced: the provinces were moving out of their narrow parochial orbits into the sunlight of national life. Provincial politicians were, Macdonald hoped, about to turn into national statesmen. Nothing was clearer than the intent of the Confederation project, the creation of a new nation. Creation, however, is a complex process whose results cannot be gauged in advance, and the created, being endowed with separate life, must take its own way. The offspring of the founding Fathers was perhaps not so entirely in their own image as they might have wished. For one thing, after an encouraging infantile cry or two, it did not evince much vitality. A sickly child, it had to be nursed along, until most of its parents were dead, and only after a long adolescence did it begin to exhibit manly vigour.

The roots of Confederation

What might be termed the psychological roots of Confederation are in plain evidence long before the event occurred. They consist mainly in the effects of growth and development, which almost necessarily bring a larger sense of community with them. Accounts of how things were 'in the youth of the author', which abound in the publications of the eighteen-sixties, invariably remark on the amazing rate of advance in Canada. In all the provinces this strengthened localism, but it also broke down parochialism and, with the growth of cities and towns, provided the classes of people who could lead towards the larger project. The literary periodicals of the day evince this in many ways. The *British-American Magazine* (Toronto, 1863-1864) is of an altogether different order from its predecessors. Its contents are mature, its tone intellectual and matter-of-fact: the romantic sentimentalism of the previous period has disappeared. Here were men facing their world with clear eyes, men not long likely to be content with the poorer when the richer vision appeared before them.

Most of the periodicals published in the late eighteen-sixties reflect a good deal of conscious nationalism. There are many references to such topics as a 'national' literature. The *Saturday Reader* (Montreal) remarks on the lack of national ballads (in which it was wrong, for it had simply not discovered them) and deplores the lack of attention given by Canadians to Canadian writers. "The intellectual classes of Canada," it contends, "are like the Italian who preferred to go to the galleys rather than read an Italian book."[3] This may have been just a little unfair, but there have always been Canadian readers to whom it could be applied. Our intellectuals, or semi-intellectuals, have been under the tutelage of the guardians of a superior culture, whom institutions of learning have always brought in— partly in the conscious intent of keeping that culture safe—and these exiled guardians have found it difficult not to be contemptuous of colonial products. This attitude has been almost as considerable a negative factor in the appearance of a native literature as the competition of the metropolitan products themselves.

The New Dominion Monthly celebrated Confederation with some national songs. If other Canadian poetry of the day was not better than these (and some of it was) the 'intellectual classes' may be forgiven for fleeing it:—

> "Hark the bells are gaily ringing, Hark the bells are gaily ringing,
> Hark the bells are gaily ringing, Songs for our Dominion singing,
> Glorious songs of Canada. Hear them ringing, gaily ringing,
> Gaily, loudly, proudly ringing, Glorious songs of Canada.
> Hip Hurrah for Canada!"

The tune was down on the same level. *The Dominion Monthly* professed to be all for native talent. "The number of Canadian writers of ability who have already contributed. . . ." it found most encouraging. "We are astonished at the multitude of manuscripts which keep pouring in upon us from almost every corner of the Dominion and still more are we surprised at the large proportion of them which display real talent. . . ." But how were they to be rewarded? *The Monthly*'s subscription list was sixteen hundred, a figure on which it congratulated itself but not one which would bring a native literature into being. The consequence was that most of its material came from abroad, presumably at bargain rates.[4] Possibly, however, local talent was not as abundant as *The Monthly* had declared. ". . . The publishers offered . . . a prize of twenty dollars for the best suitable New Year's tale; but we did not receive one, answering the conditions. . . ."

Such periodicals as the *Saturday Reader* and *The Dominion Monthly* present a new phase in Canadian social development. They are chatty and easy, and addressed not only to old gentlemen who know their classics. The deduction is that at the period of Confederation, society was moving towards a wider basis. These periodicals probably went into substantial urban homes, not necessarily into the homes of the rich but into those of persons who might be described as 'solid citizens'. We come back by another route to one of the familiar processes in the growth of self-government, the widening of the economic base and the widening of interests.

Later observers confirmed what a glance at these literary periodicals has indicated: Confederation was marked by the appearance of national feeling. No one would suggest that this was general, deep or fervent—it was just a mild thrill of patriotism and pride in the great accomplishment, founded on a realization that at last colonials were getting a homeland of their own, something beyond their father's house in which their love and interest could be rooted. "The *Canadian Monthly* owed its existence to the short-lived glow of national feeling which passed through the veins of the community on the morrow of Confederation."[5] Note the word *short-lived*: the same article which contains it also employs the phrases *transient enthusiasm*, and *flagging movement*. "I can call spirits from the vasty deep," boasted the Welshman Glendower in Shakespeare's *Henry IV*. "Why so can I, or so can any man; but will they come when you do call for them?" queries the annoying Hotspur.[6] So literary monthlies and others could call for the spirit of nationalism to come out of the vasty deep of English Canada but when called, come it would not.

From French Canadians, there is no evidence that anyone tried to summon it. They were already a people, with their own traditions and objects of devotion, and Confederation for them was not the making of a new nationality but the safeguard of an old. No visions of the broad future of the new Dominion seem to have come down in the French language. Nevertheless the narrow nationalism which can at times be not more than parochialism was not much in evidence. Confederation might be simply an expedient, but it apparently was worth an honest trial. And when a French lieutenant governor occupied Spencerwood, a thrill of pride went over the new province of Quebec at the thought that the representative of the queen was of French blood, spoke in the name of the queen in French, and had a royal salute accorded him by English troops. All this meant, not the triumph of the old race over the new, but the burying of the hatchet, a new start, with one large sphere of action, the historic province, reserved to French-speaking North Americans to administer mainly by themselves and for themselves. They could afford to look with complaisance on the presence of an English minority in the province, for they had numbers on their side. The Constitutional Act of 1791 had condemned the English of Lower Canada to a minority position, and now Confederation which, through their spokesman Galt, that minority had also urged, condemned it to perpetual minority. This position the English, thanks to a long indoctrination in majority rule, accepted with remarkably little difficulty. As the years have passed, they have become increasingly impotent politically and, conspicuously in the city of Quebec, have abandoned whatever claims they may have had to representation (even municipal). Their situation disproves any 'inevitable' or 'unbreakable' connection between English stock and self-government—for the English of the province of Quebec, Confederation, in a sense, was the Conquest in reverse. They have been no worse off under it than were the French under the first Conquest, and possibly not much better: at any rate, they have accepted it, and, everything considered, accepted it meekly.

French Canadians might be a people, but French Canada was still provincial, still having its centre of reference outside itself. London had become one, Paris had always been one. So had Rome. And, as the years rolled by, the proportions of Rome had grown: it became and remained the major metropolitan centre, and French Canada was its province. It was to defend Rome against the hordes of atheistic Garibaldians that the Papal Zouaves set out. It was to Rome that all ears were attuned in the denunciation of the errors of the modern world. It was to Rome that all eyes turned to contemplate the splendours of the great General Council of the Church which was to lay the coping stone of papal absolutism in the form of the doctrine of Papal Infallibility.[7] "*Rome encore, oui, toujours Rome comme point-capital de toutes les grandes questions qui peuvent agiter la société, parce qu'elle est la ville maîtresse des nations. . . . Rien de ce qui concerne Rome ne saurait donc indifférent.*"[8] Such an orientation at least tended to exclude the narrower aspects of racialism, so foreign to the genius of a worldwide religion and yet so often, through those whose Catholic attachments have weakened, flowing out of it.[9]

The most self-conscious nationalism of the Confederation

period, on either side of the racial fence, was that which centred around the Toronto movement known as *Canada First* and its journal *The Nation* (1874-1876).[10] The range of *The Nation*'s interests indicates the nature of the movement. It desired to foster budding Canadian culture, particularly on its literary side. Art, it felt, was already receiving reasonable recognition. On colonialism, its attitude was not much different from that of those who everywhere wish to see communities standing on their own feet, though it did not mark out with any precision the various areas of colonialism, as, for example, the political, the psychological and the cultural. It wanted increased Canadian autonomy and was pleased to see the Imperial garrison withdrawn because this removed a source of social colonialism, but it strongly disavowed desire for 'severance'. This, however, was the charge made against it by *The Globe*; it was "disloyal to England."[11] Until very recent days such a charge, as powerful as denunciations by the Church in Quebec, has always been sufficient to wreck anyone or anything against whom it has been made in English Canada. Neither *The Nation* nor the movement it represented were to prove exceptions to the rule, and by 1876 both had come to an end. *The Globe*, in its avowed and aggressive colonialism, was probably more representative of the age: "Canada," it proclaimed, "except by a mere play on words, is not a nation."

A few years later, 1883, *The Bystander* was to say: "When *Canada First* came into existence, the very utterance of the name 'Canadian Nation' was denounced as treason."[12] It then added: "Who denounces it now?" *Canada First* as a movement had begun in 1871 with W. A. Foster's pamphlet *Canada First*.[13] The twelve years' interval apparently had not been without its trend, a trend toward nationalism. But *The Bystander* had also talked of "the short-lived glow of national feeling": this glow must have been short indeed if by the early eighteen-seventies it was once again treason to talk of a Canadian nation.[14] It is always hard to estimate subjective states. The general point, however, is clear—Confederation was not born of any emotional surge.

Ottawa, symbol of nationalism

One unexpected by-product of Confederation turned out to be a national capital. Everyone knows how little Bytown in the bush had ambitiously turned itself into Ottawa and then, by a series of almost ludicrous attempts on the part of the politicians to avoid the unpleasant task of making up their minds, had emerged from its obscurity to find Quebec, Montreal and

Toronto all shoved aside in its favour. When Confederation was at last effected, the provincial capital moved up into the position of capital of the Dominion. As such it became the gathering place, not only of the politicians but of civil servants and of all interested in the machine of government. All the other cities, Quebec, the ancient capital, included, found themselves reduced in rank—some to mere commercial centres, like Montreal, others to mere provincial capitals. Ottawa thus came to have especial significance in Canadian life as a symbol.[15]

To Ottawa, as capital, came all elected persons, French and English, Catholic and Protestant, Maritimers, central-province men, and within a few years, members from all across Canada to the Pacific. At Ottawa, they had to work together, and the atmosphere of 'the best club in the country' was favourable to congeniality: friendships could hardly be prevented from crossing lines of division. The role of Parliament itself in teaching Canadians to work together, as Canadians, can hardly be overestimated, for no group of men can go on year after year addressing themselves to the problems of a common body politic without themselves giving to that body something of reality. To a considerable degree also the Civil Service played this same role of forcing-house of nationalism,[16] for its job was to run the business, not of a province, but of the country as a whole. To put words in the enemy's mouth, it constitutes a vested interest in nationalism. A third agency of liaison arose directly as a consequence of the national capital, though not centred there, namely all those country-wide services and organizations, which radiate out from the political structure. To name only two or three of these is to clinch the point: the Canadian Pacific Railway, the Bank of Montreal, any of the national Protestant churches, not to mention the post office, the coinage or the customs houses.

A fourth formative factor arising out of there being a national capital, could, if there had been a strong national spirit, have been the most important of all, namely the growth of a literacy intelligentsia in the national capital. This growth was not evident until the eighteen-eighties (with Archibald Lampman as its first example), but thereafter it strengthened and others were added to Lampman. Such men could have only a Canadian outlook: a provincial vision from the capital of Canada is not consonant with good sense. But a civil service alone is not a good supporting structure and so the growth of a nucleus at the capital did not go far and Ottawa never became the cultural capital of the country—to the country's great loss!

At first Ottawa was symbol only, a symbol of the future apparent to the eyes of the few. But vision slowly descends. Slowly, hesitatingly, a new spirit reaches out from Ottawa. A description of it would produce an infant likeness of 'The Canadian' for, with Confederation accomplished, almost for the first time 'The Canadian' begins to take on shape and composite form (composite because he swallowed several sub-images of himself). In 1870, or thereabouts, everywhere else but in Ottawa we find 'Ontarians', 'Nova Scotians' and others such. Even those who, like the *Canada Firsters*, longed for a national state, looked for one in their own image: only at Ottawa, among the politicians and their associates, was it imperative to think— to feel—in new terms, in terms applicable to all of the new Dominion. As Cavour was saying about Italy, so men like Macdonald and McGee could say of their work, "We have made Canada; now we must make Canadians!" In 1867, if the species *homo sapiens canadensis* existed, it existed as an idea only, an idea in the minds of a limited number of men. As the years passed, the mere classification was by some mysterious process to come alive, or more or less alive. "In the beginning was the Word."

Notes to Chapter 19.

1. She was not the only Southerner who has given him this reply.
2. The Hamilton scheme is given in James Madison, *The Federalist* (Chicago, 1893), p. 185. See also W. B. Munro, *American Influence on Canadian Government* (Toronto, 1929).
3. Dec. 30th, 1865.
4. Which is also a current situation, though to-day's editors 'buy goods' from the United States rather than from Great Britain.
5. *The Bystander,* Toronto, January, 1883.
6. I *Henry IV*, III, i.
7. July, 1870.
8. *Revue Canadienne,* September, 1865, p. 535.
9. To both Fascism and Nazism former Catholics contributed heavily. Extreme nationalism seems to proceed out of the universal Church by a kind of ricochet.
10. Examined in greater detail in the present writer's *Canada, Nation and Neighbour* (Toronto, 1952].
11. See *The Nation*, Oct. 22nd, 1874.
12. *The Bystander,* loc. cit.
13. Foster was its leading spirit throughout.
14. The strength of colonialism in the post-Confederation period probably rests upon the heavy 'old country' immigration of 1820-1850. While the proportion of native-born increased rapidly after 1861, many, perhaps most, of them must have had old country parents. They would therefore, still be colonists and, in contrast to those of Loyalist descent, would not have reached the provincial stage.
15. The symbol rather than the city. Ottawa city without the Canadian government is unimportant and provincial. See also p. 249.
16. Yet, as noted above, civil servants have never been able to transcend racial jealousies.

20: The new nation:
the critical years

AFTER THE NEW DOMINION had been laboriously brought into existence, both men and circumstances seemed to combine in an effort to destroy it. The first scheme for a transcontinental railway failed dismally. Economic depression descended, and clung to the country year after year. As a result, people emigrated in their tens of thousands and the total population grew only at a snail's pace. In the new West, instead of rapid settlement, the curse of racialism descended and its two armed outbreaks disturbed the peace of the entire country. Canada's tragic *leit-motiv*, which for a few years seemed to have been left behind, once more made itself evident, and rose to new heights.

Twenty years after Confederation, few would have cared to risk a large wager on the continued existence of the Dominion. "The Separatist policy—that is, the policy of trying to form a nationality of the disjointed and scattered provinces of British North America cut off from the rest of the continent—is a palpable failure. . . . I declare for Commercial Union with the United States as a substitute for the National Policy." Thus spoke J. W. Longley, Attorney-General of Nova Scotia.[1] The *Manitoba Free Press*, commenting upon a suggestion that Newfoundland might enter Confederation, put the same point of view with the true western brusqueness: "If the people of Newfoundland know when they are well off, they will give the Dominion a wide berth. There are few provinces, if any, in it to-day that would not rejoice to be out of it, and that would not forever stay out if they were."[2]

The Week, a journal for the thoughtful, put its finger on several of the spots causing the difficulty. They are all almost equally familiar to us to-day—geographical dispersion at the bottom of it all, with sectionalism and racial division thrown in for good measure. The greatest curse was racial division.

"All the important disintegrating causes . . . fade into utter insignificance when brought into contrast with the forces at work in Ontario and Quebec. . . . Ontario, rapidly advancing in wealth, population, education and political enfranchisement. . . . Quebec, bankrupt, uneducated, a century behind in civilization and freedom. . . . The French of Quebec are to-day the great barrier in the way of a real living union of the British North American Colonies."[3] These were harsh words. *The Week* stood for the national idea, which it urged, however, in high, thin, over-cerebral notes and with none of the understanding for the other side of the house that intellectualism of a sufficient calibre should have been able to display. Other organs of opinion had none of its modest degree of restraint, nor were its own columns entirely closed to extreme expression:—

> "[The people of Ontario] see the French language, French history, French sentiment and French philosophy instilled into the minds of Canadian children in the schools of Quebec, while allegiance to Rome and Pontifical infallibility are steadily inculcated in the churches and homes.
> "Can the people of Ontario submit any longer in silence? Could but the heroes who rose that glorious September morning long ago on the Plains of Abraham before the astonished gaze of Montcalm and his troops return for one brief day to the scene of their brilliant achievements, with what thunder tones would they arouse to united thought and action the men of Ontario? Let Ontario's sons view with shame the position their Province holds in Confederation. . . ."[4]

Such was the spirit abroad while both English- and French-Canadian militiamen were hurrying westward to put down the Riel rebellion.[5] A national effort? The approach to civil war, rather. And why? Because French-speaking Canadian Catholics would not turn themselves into English-speaking Canadian Protestants. No wonder the execution of Riel provoked a fury of resentment in Quebec and built for Honoré Mercier that nationalist party which in one form or another has ever since devoted itself to widening the gulf.

The French were accused of lack of sympathy for English-speaking Canadians, of lack of patriotic aspiration for Canada as a whole.[6] They were accused mainly of trying to be themselves and preserve their identity. Being French, they returned their accusers' vituperations with interest.

To English Canadians then and to English Canadians now, it is the words of the poet which are to be recommended:

> O, it is excellent
> To have a giant's strength; but it is tyrannous
> To use it like a giant.

For there have not been many years in the long association when English Canadians have not been ready to use their strength upon their weaker partners. To-day at long last, some content for the term *Canada* is emerging, and some love for it. It is only as love replaces hate (whenever that distant day shall be) that Canada's tragedy will be resolved. To be a good Canadian it is necessary first to be, in heart if not in form, a good Christian, with tolerance and forgiveness in one's soul. Few on either side have been able to measure up to that vast ideal.

Could the vision of the future have been caught, as to-day it has in some measure been, that, too, would have resolved our racial passions. But in the generation after Confederation, Canada, after a little gasp of national vitality, seems to have relapsed into its old gloomy colonialism.

> "At dinner, they spent the intervals of the courses in guessing the nationality of the different persons, and in wondering if the Canadians did not make it a matter of conscientious loyalty to out-English the English even in the matter of pale-ale and sherry. . . . Our friends began to detect something servile in it all. . . . They did not suffer . . . any . . . advantage of the colonial relation to divert them from the opinion to which their observation was gradually bringing them,—that its overweening loyalty placed a great country like Canada in a very silly attitude, the attitude of an overgrown, unmanly boy, clinging to the maternal skirts, and though spoilt and wilful, without any character of his own. The constant reference of local hopes to that remote centre beyond the seas, the test of success by the criterions of a necessarily different civilization . . . gave an effect of meanness to the whole fabric."

This is Canada seen through not very friendly eyes, those of the American author, W. D. Howells,[7] but it strikes home, for we are still at it, still afraid to be ourselves, though as often as not to-day the reference to the distant scene is to the United States, rather than to England. We have still many miles to go before we become ourselves, and a people in that sorry position will always from time to time turn on each other.

Why did the Dominion survive?

If the Dominion survived, why did it survive? And why did it survive without bloodshed? Its survival is one of the minor miracles of history, one of the major miracles of Canadian history, and, like other miracles, it is hard to explain. In the second half-century after his death, we have not yet realized the debt we owe to Sir John Macdonald, that ribald, bibulous nationalist. As these lines are written, the cult of Macdonald is rapidly rising and before long we may may find in him something that we have hitherto lacked, a national hero. The humble people who extended the fields and built their houses and who, before Macdonald's death, had begun to flock out onto the western plains, would not have had his vision but neither did they have thought of defeat. Blind coral polyps, if you like, they kept plodding on, building the new land. Some day that land will find its poets to celebrate them, and to reveal it to itself.[8]

Mr. Howells himself may be called upon as witness to the excellence of this colonial people whose ideals he derided:—
". . . He could not conceive of the American steamboat clerk who would use the politeness towards a waiting crowd that the Canadian purser showed . . . Basil made a point of speaking him fair, when his turn came, and the purser did not trample on him for a base truckler, as an American jack-in-office would have done."[9] An old-world air of good manners may have still been clinging to Canadian transportation officials in the eighteen-seventies but the winds of democracy, American style, were to blow most of it effectually away before the twentieth century was reached. What could not have been anticipated was the surprising deterioration of such virility into the courtesies of our own day!

Howells pays a graceful tribute to our womanhood: [The young girl's] "beauty was of the most bewitching Canadian type. [She] was redeemed by her New World birth from the English heaviness; a more delicate bloom lighted her cheeks; a softer grace dwelt in her movements; yet she was round and full, and she was in the perfect flower of youth. She was not so ethereal in her loveliness as an American girl, but she was not so nervous and had none of the painful fragility of the latter. Her expression was just a little vacant, it must l e owned; but so far as she went, she was faultless. She looked like the most tractable of daughters, and as if she would be the most obedient of wives." In addition, her taste in dress was faultless and her costume, though conveying the effect of modishness, was made of inexpensive materials. Canadians will recognize the type: it has been contributing the best of daughters and wives ever since. And since the young beauty got on the boat at Kingston, she probably was of Loyalist stock and just as American as Mr. Howells. It has been a peculiar delusion among Americans that to be a Canadian is to be English: they have not made allowance for the mixture that has been made here and for the effect of the surroundings. As another American writer put it a few years ago: "I had been told that the Canadians are second-hand Englishmen. No estimate could convey a more erroneous impression. . . . One can mark already with tolerable distinctness a Canadian type which is neither English nor American. . . ."[10] These words reveal the secret of survival.

Mr. Warner might find the difference between Americans and English Canadians nowadays not as great as when he wrote. On the other hand, both authors might still be inclined to concur with the writer in *The Wesleyan Repository* who contended that the Canadian type was "half-way between the light Yankee and the heavy Englishman".[11] Modern Canadians will at least accept the adjectives.

Canada in 1871—the cities

In 1871, Canada contained just under 3,500,000 people.[12] Their distribution among the four new divisions of the country—Ontario, Quebec, Nova Scotia and New Brunswick—was not very different from to-day nor were the proportions of their religious denominations. In racial origin, there were few in the country other than 'British' and 'French', with those of French origin constituting about the same proportion of the total then as now—about 30 per cent. Collectively, the people were younger than they are to-day. The birth rate, though dropping, still was high—with nearly 29 children under one year of age per thousand of population in Ontario and nearly 34 in Quebec.[13] The death rate was proportionately high, it being 20 per thousand for the Catholic population of Quebec: in the Protestant communities, it would be lower. But 43 young Catholics per thousand of the Catholic population were being born, as against a possible 26 young Protestants.[14]

Since of the 3,500,000, only some 400,000 odd (12 per cent) were to be found in the cities and towns (only twenty places had a population of more than 5,000), the typical Canadian of 1871 must have been a country dweller: for every person in towns (giving a liberal interpretation to that term, to take in small places that were still closely related to the countryside about them), there were about eight in the country, along the seacoast, or in the bush. The data bear out the view: they tell us that the 'average man' was a farmer. So large a place did the farmer play in the country's life that he must have a chapter, the next, to himself; here we look at the condition of towns and cities.

The city, Lewis Mumford says, is a work of art: he calls it man's supreme work of art. He is thinking of those great metropolitan centres over which the centuries have cast their sheen and which continue to command the pick of mankind's brains and energies. In 1871 Canadians would have had no reason to think of their cities in such exalted terms as that. Most of them were small and, by old-world standards, the oldest among them was recent. Three of them must get some individual attention, Montreal (107,000), Quebec (60,000) and Toronto (57,000).

Montreal, then as now, was luxurious, frowzy and enticing, a go-as-you-please place where millionaires' mansions overlooked dirty, disease-ridden slums—in 1885, its smallpox outbreak caused it to be feared and shunned. Yet at that very moment it was in process of stealing priority from Quebec as a port and rapidly becoming the commercial metropolis of the country. The old city of Quebec has played many roles: first as the gay little capital of New France, then as the rising metropolis of British Canada, with acres and acres of square timber lying in her timber coves to assure her prosperity, then as part-time capital of the Province of Canada. After Confederation, with the capital moved to Ottawa, Quebec had to accept provincial rank. Then came the decline of the timber trade. As a result, the city remained stationary in population for decades. and it was not until the new wave of local industry began to mount in the twentieth century that her present cycle of growth began. This has moved Quebec upward, though within the second group of Canadian cities, not, as in the old days, in the first. But her historic past and her role as capital of the French province will always carry Quebec beyond the status of mere provincial capital.

Toronto was still the rising western star. The pleasant old estates along the bay shore were rapidly being destroyed as the railroads turned that area into the mixture of steel, smoke, industry and slum that most people think of as 'progress'. In their place, new streets were being opened up farther in, complete with new mansions, new brick and iron-work fences and new trees. The trees had hardly grown up enough to make the new districts pleasant to live in, before the new mansions had become old and degenerated into 'institutions', rooming-houses, slums and brothels: plenty of all can still be seen along that once great and shining avenue, Jarvis Street. Meanwhile owners or their heirs had moved off, to start the process over again in another 'development'. This perpetual leap-frog marks any North American city. White humanity, like the Indians before it, soils its surroundings and solves its problems by getting out and starting over again. The Indians left nothing behind, but the whites leave slums.

Next to the larger places there was in 1871 a group of four cities each having over 20,000 people: Halifax, Saint John, Hamilton and Ottawa. The national capital in 1871 had 21,000 people in it. Since then it has increased sixteen fold. Its only buildings of note were the recently completed Houses of Parliament. The magnificent series of parks and drives with which the federal government has endowed it were, of course, completely lacking. Its streets were seas of mud, its public accommodation of the scantiest. Around the 'stopping places' of 'Lower Town', during the rafting season, congregated hundreds of river drivers, each ashore for no good purposes, glorying in the amount of liquor they could hold and the amount of punishment they could endure in a fight. It is no wonder that the rollicking French folk song honouring them should be entitled *Laissez-passer les raf'mans*. It would have been bad luck for anyone who had tried to stop them 'passing'.

The other towns ranged down from London, with 15,000 people, to Brockville with just over 5,000. All but four—Trois Rivières, Lévis, Fredericton and Sorel—were in Ontario, and of these all but Guelph and Brantford lay along the line of the St. Lawrence and the lakes. Among them, Kingston, the largest, had long since given up the race with Toronto and was sinking from its dreams of metropolitanism into a provincial town which, nevertheless, was tepidly proud of its buildings and its men—there must have been some special character about a place which in a single generation could produce a Mowat, a Cartwright, an Alexander Campbell, and a Macdonald. The rest, St. Catharine's, Guelph (another stone city), Chatham, Belleville and Port Hope, were simply pleasant country towns and lake ports.

The Dominion as a whole was well into its railway age, with rail transportation available from Rivière du Loup to Sarnia and from Toronto north to several Lake Huron ports. The Intercolonial to Saint John and Halifax was just over the horizon. Farther afield were speculations about the possibility of a connection with the British territories in the West, speculations which, by 1885, John A. Macdonald was to bring down out of the clouds and make into a reality. With the so-called rebellion of 1870 on the Red River, eastern Canadian minds increased overnight several times in size and thrust: thenceforth it was to be the illimitable stretches of the interior which were to provide the chief field for imagination. When in 1885, the 65th Regiment of Canadian militia, sent to aid in quelling the North West Rebellion, arrived at Calgary on the recently laid rails of the Canadian Pacific, a Toronto paper reported that:

"Before the arrival of the troops, the Canadian Government was freely sworn at. Many did not know there was a Government. . . . The officers and men were not mercenaries either, but volunteers, and they came to protect. . . . A great number of the inhabitants of Alberta are not Canadians, and until recently they had a very faint conception of what the Canadian Government and Canadian people could do. . . . It was not the Snider rifles of the Canadian Volunteer Militia which wrought this change [from hostility to respect] so much as the gentlemanly bearing of the officers, the patriotic devotion of the men and the complete organization of the Alberta field forces by . . . Major-General Strange. . . ."[15]

Canada was thus carried westward into her new territories by the new railway and the Canadian militia, the French-Canadian 65th from Montreal (at the very time that the bitterest of racial and religious insults were being hurled against 'the French' back home). It took provincial eastern Canadians many years to grow up to both large conceptions, the biracial nation and the vast transcontinental expanse which was to cradle it, and many, even of the educated among them, have not grown up to them yet. But a silent expansion of mind has gone on and the idea *Canada* is much vaster now than in the sad days of the eighteen-eighties.

The excellence of Toronto

The period was not all gloom: despite its discouragements, its alarums and excursions, civic life went forward and the landmarks which usually herald the growth of a culture appeared. Many a non-Torontonian among the readers will regret to hear that in all of these Toronto easily led. There was good reason for it: Montreal was two cities, and not a community at all (it is not a community to-day), the rest were too small. Toronto was western, new, energetic, optimistic and equipped with all the talents which it has pleased God to place in the Anglo-Saxon's keeping. It wrung reluctant testimonial from the very Americans themselves: "Toronto . . . one of the most orderly, well-governed, moral, highly civilized towns on the continent —in fact almost unique in the active elements of a high Christian civilization. The notable fact is that the high concentration here of business enterprise is equalled by the concentration of religious and educational activity."[16]   Few Torontonians, even of to-day, when the city has altered somewhat, can fail to blush, surely, on reading the above; to blush, and to reflect on what good judgement the man had!

If those from outer darkness are inclined to doubt, let them look into such a book as *Toronto, Old and New*[17] and be convinced. Here in page after page of photographs, the city's glories are unrolled. Public buildings, private residences, men of all the professions, and churches, churches, churches. Few cities can have invested more money in church buildings than has Toronto. For architecture, it is unfortunate that the apex of religious zeal coincided with the apex of poor taste. Churches, one would think, should be permanent, as they are in the old world, buildings which over the centuries gather about them the hopes and the traditions of their people. Not so in the new world: the most lavish church building may no more be there to stay than a collection of Indian wigwams. Up to-day, down to-morrow, in this ceaselessly mobile society of ours. Exceptions there are, it is true. In Toronto, there are still a number of downtown churches which fend off the results of dispersing congregations, and possibly the traditional central churches of the various denominations— St. James and St. Michael's Cathedrals, the Metropolitan Church and St. Andrew's Presbyterian—will maintain themselves against the centuries. Public buildings, too, may stand against time: no one has yet suggested pulling down University College or Osgoode Hall (though that may come).

Mr. Adam's pages testify to the sumptuousness of the residences and the emptiness of the streets: this was the age of the horse-car, shortly to be superseded, and except for its infrequent clatter, cities were still full of quiet streets, with real homes (not real-estate 'homes') on them. The book impresses one with the quiet solidity of Toronto residential life. The impression is reinforced by the endless portraits of leading citizens. Quiet, grave men, scores of them. None of the smart aggressiveness such a collection exhibits to-day. Gravity, of course, was tremendously reinforced by hairy faces (it was an age when men were not afraid to accept the logic of their manhood), but the faces that look out from behind the endless varieties of beards are not those of 'smart alecks'. These men respected themselves: they had characters, not merely reputations, and fixed places in the society they themselves had built. Nor was there any nonsense about status; first things came first. The Premier of the province, Oliver Mowat, leads, and others take their appropriate place in dignified order: provincial cabinet ministers, the judiciary and the mayor follow. The mayor receives an official bow: in a municipal administration where, the author alleges (despite the eulogy quoted above), "the strings of the civic administration in many of the departments, unhappily, still 'hang loose' ", the mayor, "justice requires it to be said, has proved an honest and efficient administrator". Aldermen as such are not admitted to the gallery of worthies. Next come the clergy, lawyers, doctors and the various branches of the teaching profession, including the musicians. Lastly, at the back of the book, in what evidently was deemed the proper place for them, the business men.

Toronto was representative of English Canada: it still gave honour where honour was due, and an eloquent clergyman or distinguished lawyer had a rating many times as high as the man of business, to say nothing of the mere money-maker. The photographs in Adam's book reflect and perhaps explain this social gradation: the calmness and intellectuality of many of the professional men, the real ability stamped upon them, their sense of assuredness, as compared with the lack of these qualities in the faces of most of the business men who rated a photograph. Between these men of the eighteen-eighties and ourselves there lies a social revolution, "the transvaluation of all values". In those days, the brash new Anglo-Saxon world of North America still had its connections with an older order of things, with a way of life that rested on a vigorous and dynamic Protestant faith, a faith that kept its spiritual values well to the front.

It had its connections, too, with a society in which rank and class were accepted without question. If the top layers had been left back beyond the ocean, the ideas of a graded society had not and every little town and city in the country attempted to reconstitute it as soon as it came into existence. Sometimes this attempt was made by meretricious, or merely ridiculous means, such as the building of houses trying to look like feudal castles, or the flaunting of dubious coats of arms.[18] More often, it just represented the natural forces of differentiation—ability, family tradition, professional skill and the dignity with which everyone endowed such things. For social status by no means depended upon money alone: if that had been so, the clergy would not have had the place of honour which there was no question of their holding. Leading lawyers did well, it is true, and their establishments were often large and pretentious, much more so than those of the doctors, for the medical priesthood had not then risen to the height it was afterwards to attain. But all the professions, whether their members were rich or poor, seemed to share in the esteem society accorded them. To-day, money speaks in much louder tones, and learning in much humbler, while both law and medicine have cut down their own status by leaning too far towards the cash.

The aggressive business man was not absent from these pages: he has never been absent from our story. In the Canada of the eighteen-eighties many of these men were already wealthy. Their mansions rose around the mountain at Montreal or along the crest of the hill behind Toronto. In these favoured situations were to be found what were still virtually country estates, such as 'Oaklands', the residence of Senator John Macdonald, the home of S. Nordheimer or, perhaps grandest of all, that of S. H. Janes, a real-estate speculator who had made a large fortune. This house was built of white limestone and stood on the hill just to the westward of the present Avenue Road. It was the last word in magnificence.

> "The walls of the spacious hall are wood-panelled for eight feet from the floor, with embossed leather carried up to the ceiling. The dining-room will be hung with rare tapestries, the spoils of old Italian palaces; and many costly treasures from the cities of the ancient Florentine Republic will adorn this modern Toronto mansion. Among the latter are a Roman sarcophagus, statuettes in marble. . . . The drawing-room will be treated after the manner of Louis Seize. . . ."

This was the house that later on passed into the possession of Sir William Mackenzie, the railroader. In it, just before the outbreak of the First World War, Sir William entertained the Governor General, the Duke of Connaught, the son of Queen Victoria herself, and his lovely daughter Princess Patricia. Alas, this solid limestone castle—"the style of the architecture is pure Norman"—proved too weak to resist the buffetings of the depression of the nineteen-thirties and was ignominiously torn down, its site to-day, after long standing empty, being covered by apartments. Some forty years of life, and it vanished. It served its builder and a few others, then gave place to the smart, crowded, conventional buildings of the 'middle-middle' many. It is a commentary on the movement of our society, a society each and every one of whose inner forces seems to render impossible the emergence either of permanence or of distinction.

As with houses, so with families. George A. Cox was born in Northumberland County, Ontario, in 1840. He worked his way up from telegraph operator to manager of the Midland Railway, 1878. He then got into finance and by 1890, at fifty, was President of the Bank of Commerce. Mr. Cox was a highly respected citizen of Toronto and, as became his eminence, a senator. What was almost more, he was a prominent member of Sherbourne Street Methodist Church. His imposing home on Sherbourne Street, 'Sherbourne House', remains little altered, though it has long since ceased to house his family.[19] One of Senator Cox's sons, Harold, became the leading man in the Canada Life Assurance Company. He is referred to in rather depreciative fashion by C. L. Burton in his interesting auto-biography, *A Sense of Urgency*,[20] as not being the kind of man who would 'stay on the job'. Harold was always running off to England where his money had made him 'M.F.H.' ('Master of the Fox Hounds'), an honorific that would have meant nothing in Canada but in England indicated acceptance into the gentry: it was almost as good as a peerage. So much for the son of the late telegraph operator at Peterborough. He had perhaps realized his ideal, and what seemed to be the ideal of so many Toronto business men, and had converted himself into an English gentleman. Success could go no further. When he died, childless, he and his wife meritoriously left their wealth for the benefit of the employees of the Canada Life, but this sensible bequest was put to an end by the courts, and the property dissipated. How familiar the story is! 'Families' no more flourish in this new world of rampant equality and whirling change than do baronial mansions.

One name conspicuous by its absence from the portrait gallery of the business men in the eighteen-eighties was that of Timothy Eaton. Yet by the year in which his first 'Mail Order Catalogue' was sent out, 1884, he had been some fifteen years in business and had had a major share in establishing that which we have long since taken for granted, the cash-over-the-counter, one-price, no-bargaining system of selling goods, thus rescuing retail shop-keeping from the vestiges of the oriental bazaar which had clung to it throughout the ages.

Since 1884 Eaton's catalogues have become a national insti-tution. The first one, of thirty-two pages, had no illustrations. There were thirty-five departments represented, nearly all textiles. Few ready-made goods were offered. Two years later, a picture of the store appeared and it was announced that it was in possession of a telephone—one telephone—No. 370. These first catalogues underline the fact that in the eighteen-eighties we are standing between two worlds, an old and a new. There is still some Victorian dignity even about a mail-order catalogue. There is no high-pressure salesman-ship, rather a desire to inform: the letter-press is instructive and logical. The class distinctions of the day are recognizable and recognized: 'Housemaids' Aprons' are plainly labelled such. There is no modern flamboyance: when the first illustrations appear they show some men's ties, a massive, ugly pickle jar or cruet, and a baby carriage with a parasol over it; these are repeated unchanged in the following years. The Victorian reticences were properly observed. Bustles and corsets were advertised from the first, and you could buy them from one dollar up, but ladies' dresses were modelled with sour dowagers inside them, and night clothes, far from gracing some youthful female sprite, were exhibited in wrapped-up form: there were none of those alluring figures which are alleged to make the modern mail-order catalogue favourite reading—or, rather, inspection—for rude youths in regions remote from city sophistication.

Eaton's shared with the age its universal feeling for self-respect. There was an intangible note of honest pride about its catalogues, the mark of a strong individuality with strong convictions. To-day's impersonality was absent. The feeling of 'manifest destiny' hovered everywhere. Time has proved the presumption correct. It might almost be said that Toronto rose to national fame on Eaton's catalogues and on that other institution which was forging ahead parallel with Eaton's, the Canadian National Exhibition.[21]

While 'wealth' and 'civilization' are not synonymous terms, they are related: no wealth, no civilization. And, perhaps, the converse: too much wealth, little civilization. Canada in the eighteen-eighties was in a happy midway position. Whereas to-day change is so rapid that no matter how effective or beautiful anything may be, it no sooner appears than it is hurried off by something else with a new appeal,[22] the country as a whole was developing but slowly. This gave an opportunity for consolidation. As a result, at least in the more favoured centres, something like a native civilization was beginning to appear, with its own phenomena, its own problems, its own zest. If problems and phenomena were reflections of those of the great world without, that was but natural, for any new civilization must be imitative at first. In the first generation of the Dominion, distance and the difficulties of transportation, while they did not screen out the best from the outside world, did serve to prevent that world overwhelming us, as with our extreme ease of communication it tends to do to-day. To put it another way, metropolitanism still had its limits and there were parts of the continent which were not yet suburbs of New York.

Dawn of a local urban culture?

Before they were overwhelmed by syndicated news despatches, by the 'boiler-plate' copy sold for the inside pages of the newspapers, by the American branch plant, by American sport, by the American 'movies', by the later radio and by a thousand other metropolitan products, Canadian cities had their brief flicker of independence. Mr. Eaton's store grew up out of itself, with little reference to New York, as did the 'Toronto Ex.' So did the newspapers of the period, though to a lesser degree. Though higher education was much influenced by England and Scotland, little by American examples, the Canadian school was being fashioned in its own image. The spirit of most Canadian churches was responding to native conditions. Canadians originated their own games, such as lacrosse and hockey. In that area more strictly labelled 'cultural'—the theatre, music and the arts—the picture was mixed. The theatre had been dependent from the first and this dependence was not to cease until the theatre disappeared: it is only in our own day that a native theatre is showing any promise of growth.

In music, Montreal and Toronto from an early day had enjoyed the visits of the reigning celebrities, and in Toronto particularly a vigorous local musical life had grown up. The first opera had been given as long before as 1853: this was Bellini's *Norma*, conducted by a Signor Arditi. It had been well received. But as early as 1845 Toronto had had its own concerts and choral groups, one of the first having been organized in that year by Rev. John McCaul, President of King's College. By the eighteen-eighties music had long since passed the tentative stage.

"One of the most pleasant musical reunions which have taken place this season was that held last Friday evening in the Theatre of the Toronto Normal School. . . . The unusual and gratifying spectacle was presented of an audience of seven hundred listening with evident and appreciative enjoyment for two hours and a half to the performance of classical chamber music interpreted by artists who, save one exception, are resident musicians of this city. . . ."[23]

At the end of the decade, the astonishing statement was made that "during the season of 1889-1890, no fewer than fifty-six operatic performances were given, while the number of different operas presented was twenty-six":[24] these included such well-known classics as Rossini's *William Tell* and even Wagner's *Lohengrin*. Nowhere in Canada has vocal music touched such peaks in the present century.

Despite this local vigour nearly every leading musician was

a native of Great Britain, except Mr. and Mrs. Clarence Lucas who "in September last accepted a position at the Conservatory of Music, Utica, N.Y." In this matter of English coming to Canada and English Canadians going to the United States the facts are clear—each generation, not only in music but in higher education, is largely a new generation, and the formation of a native intelligentsia is thereby that much delayed. It may be that the greener fields of the United States attract able young Canadians and that the gaps are filled with imports, or it may be that the imports come as low wage earners and thus drive out those who have been accustomed to higher. At any rate, the flow through the country—in by the St. Lawrence and out over the border—never ceases. There are few aspects of Canadian life on which it does not cast light.

It would be only tedious to chronicle the internal history of each of the arts, but a word or two on painting may be permitted, as the development of this art defines sharply the boundaries between a merely provincial culture and national culture of some originality. There had been desultory art movements years before the period of this chapter, and religious painting in the province of Quebec had had a long history, but art in any organized way had to wait until after Confederation before it got its chance. In 1872, the Ontario Society of Artists was organized but the results were apparently not very satisfactory for in 1874, *The Nation* could write of its annual exhibition that while there were "some large paintings which prove that bold and picteresque scenery may be found without crossing either the Atlantic or the Lakes for it. . . ." yet "Mr. Miller has been to Wales this year, an old and favourite land, with whose mists and brooding storms he is more at home than with the blue skies of Canada".[25]

In subsequent years, little improvement took place, and when one knows the sort of reception native efforts got, one can easily understand why.

> "Mr. O'Brien affords his friends a great pleasure by allowing them to visit his studio every Saturday afternoon. Of whatever beauty and poetry there is in Canadian scenery, he has made himself the master, and . . . if there is not more —if our lakes have flat shores; if we have not as yet, in addition to the beauty of the wilderness, that of cultivation and finish; if our cities, villages and churches are not ancient and picturesque—the defect is in the subject, not the painter. Mr. O'Brien's 'Windsor Castle' proves that he could find the power of treatment if we could find him the themes."[26]

Here was colonialism with a vengeance and in a place least expected—the professedly nationalistic journal *The Week*. But then *The Week* had too close a connection with the exile of The Grange[27] for its own good and his eyes never lost their English and Oxford focus. Still, it is somewhat surprising to find *The Week*'s 'no-nonsense, let-us-be-sensible and understand everything' attitudes hiding a streak of tawdry Victorian romanticism: 'Windsor Castle' was picturesque—"the splendour falls on castle walls". When an exhibition from Scotland came along, showing among other things the engraving of "A Scotch Lassie", it warmed up at once.[28] Surprisingly enough, despite accusations about "this being a young country" and the usual declarations that art would have to wait, there appears to have been among the prosperous bourgeoisie, which covered its walls with far more paintings than would be thought appropriate to-day, a considerable picture-buying public. Dutch windmills and English cows were still the favourites but several natives seem to have done reasonably well from their paintings: Robert Harris, Homer Watson, F. M. Bell-Smith, "fared very well indeed".[29] Still, reckoning in the work of these men, Canadian artists in the eighteen-eighties had not yet penetratingly adjusted their eyes to the Canadian scene. Much less had they persuaded their fellow-citizens to see what they looked at or that what they saw was true and beautiful. The vision remained for another generation to capture, and the man who is given the credit of the pioneer in it is Charles W. Jeffreys, who with his "intense Canadian spirit", was "one of the first to preach the doctrine of the pine and the spruce as themes fit for the Canadian painter."[30]

The talk of the times

Civilization never advances on all fronts at once: it was too much to hope that, in a young community such as the Dominion in its first generation, the advance on these difficult fronts of the arts would be impressive. There were plenty of other directions in which to move. Of these, material progress was, and remains, the most obvious and that which interests the most people. Men being what they are, it must always be so and for one person interested in a new play or painting there will always be a thousand to admire a new make of car or feel elation at the sight of poor old mother earth being imprisoned under fresh bricks and mortar. But there is an intermediate area, one in which the average intelligent person of some education normally lives: that area concerned with the day-to-day questions that affect society. This is an area that usually provides the stuff of most of our intelligent conversation. We are lucky in that in the eighteen-seventies we had several journals of opinion which mirrored what was being talked about, that is, what the social interests of the day were. Unfortunately little more than a list can be made of them here, and since politics, which assuredly provided the major staple of conversation among the men, takes us into reasonably familiar ground, it is omitted.

In 1874, somebody wanted one of the queen's sons as governor general. This precipitated the kind of discussion that one might expect, dividing the imperialists from the nationalists much as it would to-day. The snobbery which was set going as a by-prdouct of the institution of the governor generalship came under fire. Closely related to this topic was the question of 'loyalty'. 'Loyalty' in those days meant 'loyalty to England'. One journal was at pains to point out that a distinction was to be made between 'loyalty' and patriotism and that it was time to put the emphasis on the latter quality. It can be inferred that good minds were getting a little tired of that "reference to a centre outside themselves" which Howells had found so depressing in Canada. Yet, in the middle eighteen-seventies there was already talk of some kind of imperial consolidation. In the next decade, the objective had become more closely defined as 'Imperial Federation' and this topic, therefore, divided people in much the same way as nationalism had done. In the latter eighteen-eighties it was reported as the most lively of all: this is understandable when we remember that these were the days when 'Commercial Union' with the United States was also being advocated. The two policies quickly became identified with the two parties, and the election of 1891, with Sir John A.'s "A British subject I was born, a British subject I will die" as Conservative slogan, turned upon them. In characteristic Canadian fashion, the two extremes simply averaged themselves out. Sir John succeeded in dying a British subject, commercial union with the United States did not take place, but the Canadian personality slowly growing from within, brought closer the day of formal loosening of the imperial tie.

In the earlier eighteen-seventies even the most enlightened journal of the day, *The Nation*, was outspoken against 'the French' and harsh in its attitude towards Roman Catholicism, especially towards 'separate schools'. A slight softening of this extremism may be present in its successors *The Bystander* and *The Week*, though as the quotations given in Chapter 20 indicate, even in this latter periodical uncompromising offensiveness was common. While 'the French' are still reprehensible, for being everything which an Englishman is not, yet on balance, they have a right to exist. Specific points about their society earn drastic criticism, such as the casual, even antagonistic attitude towards vaccination during the great Montreal smallpox outbreak of 1885. Yet men were not wanting who came to their defence, such as P. D. Ross of Ottawa, who pilloried British intolerance and misunderstanding. Race, it would seem, was even more divisive than religion. If no casual gathering of Protestants was ever happy until its members, by various indirections, had ascertained whether there were Catholics present or not, still Catholics who spoke English, while they were misguided and unfortunate, were friends and neighbours (and as a rule good ones) whereas no one could understand the 'gibberish' the French talked: they were mostly away off there in Quebec by themselves, and no one was able to find out what they were up to. Luckily for the country, it was only now and again, at the moments of crisis, such as the two Riel episodes, that their existence was brought to the attention of the average man in English Canada, though it remained true that a large fraternal organization continued to devote itself to the task of keeping the flame of hatred alive and that many men of prominence belonged to it. The Prime Minister himself was one of them, but perhaps that was just another of his ways of fighting the devil with fire!

Another range of topics testified to the increasing awareness of itself that was marking Canadian society. It was beginning to examine its social attitudes, the niceties of conduct and the religious and moral questions of the day. In the eighteen-eighties co-education, then a novelty, received a good going over. There was much concern for the purity of the female, and some apprehension that to put her into a class-room with a male teacher and male students would lead to her downfall. A bill was actually introduced into Parliament by John Charlton, M.P., proposing to make seduction of female students by their teachers a crime. As *The Bystander*[31] very sensibly said:

> "The framer himself had expressed his willingness to abandon the clause which not only set a gratuitous brand on the profession of the teacher but was calculated to put mischief in the heads of female pupils. . . . A teacher has to come down from his desk to flirt, whereas between male and female flirting is made as easy as possible. . . . Seduction is a term which, when applied indiscriminately to the

illicit intercourse of the sexes covers a serious fallacy—it implies that the criminal advances are always on the side of the male. . . ."

To-day, with woman fully emancipated, we know a good deal more about her than the legislator of 1883 but not, apparently, more than *The Bystander*. As the paper went on to say "all sins are not crimes, or amenable to criminal law." Mr. Charlton's bill failed in 1884, but in 1885 he introduced the first *Sunday Observance* bill at Ottawa. It failed there, being adjudged *ultra vires*, but was introduced and passed in the Ontario House. Next year, 1886, his Seduction Bill came up once more and this time *The Week* assaulted it in much the same terms as had *The Bystander*. In the meantime, the number of innocent young lady pupils seduced by their teachers remains unrecorded. The danger they stood in at least did not prevent the ladies from taking their courage in their hands and proceeding resolutely on, not only to co-education, but into every other sphere where they stood in the same danger, even into that indescribably filthy quagmire which, *The Week* protested, would irretrievably besmirch them, politics. But then, the girls of the eighteen-eighties were different from their granddaughters, as the following proves:—

"Freckles, it is said, have this summer been all the rage . . . and of course means have been devised for enabling fair faces to display the coveted beauty spots. To rub the visage with . . . fine sand seems to have been an early device for producing them; and . . . a considerable trade has been doing in 'freckle sand'. This probably did not always produce the desired result, and was found to have an unpleasant effect on tender skins. Artists have therefore come forward, and any lady may now have her beauty enhanced by any number of freckles she chooses to pay for. . . ."[32]

Freckles made to order may have been new: dress was as old as Eve, occasioning the same old reactions. In the eighteen-eighties these did not have the fiery ring of Bishop Laval's day,[33] but they sprang from the familiar source. In Quebec, a priest forbade a mixed tobogganing party—the sexes, in these forays, got too much mixed up! In Toronto, *The Week* reduced it all to a matter of good manners:—

"Just now we are in the midst of our usual equinoctial about *décolleté* dressing. We have received the usual unpleasant reminder about its origin, and the customary uncomfortable warning as to its unhealthfulness, while references to its frequent phase of immodesty have been many and broad. . . . The evil disposed go to reformatories, and the criminals to prisons but the vulgar we have ever with us, and vulgarity is a law unto itself. . . ."[34]

For us moderns *décoletté* dress combined with bustles and 'buns' is rather hard to imagine, but daring woman can accomplish anything, though it is probable that in this particular case we would be inclined to agree with *The Week* and find the results in not very good taste. Taste was a major province of this rather 'high-brow' journal: it undertook to act as a guide and censor of the finer points of manners—in other words, a large new mass of people required bringing up to the standards of the few who in a previous generation had constituted colonial 'society'.

What *The Week* was against—and it was against most things —would give us a fair idea of where the centre of social opinion rested in these days of our grandfathers. It was against 'hot and strong' religion, which included the evangelists Moody and Sankey and particularly those incomprehensible, lower-middle-class hot-gospellers then just getting under way, the Salvation Army. It was against French ultramontanism and Protestant bigotry, the Quebec theocracy and the Bible in the schools. It was against Sabbatarianism pushed to an extreme, but it was also against secularism and militant free-thinkers, though it admitted their right to be militant. It was against French-Canadian religious *naïveté* and separate schools in Ontario but not against either of them with the ferocity of the Orange Order and the late George Brown. It was against democracy in education and the abandonment of standards because of democracy. It was for—one of the few things it was positively *for*—a bilingual country. It was against racialism. It was against imperial federation. It was "against prohibition and for temperance." *The Week* was clearly a middle-of-the-road liberal and intellectual periodical. Small wonder that its readers were limited and its life not very long. In that day of fierce partizanship, the majority of men, and especially the majority of the educated group, would probably have quoted at its editor the Biblical verse to the effect that the Laodiceans, neither hot or cold, God would "spue" out of his mouth. Put in equally inelegant modern language, this has been translated into the joke against the liberal as "one who gets out five minutes before the fighting starts". The Canada of the eighteen-eighties afforded no hospitable niche for the civilized person who is all for maintenance repairs but finds that the world does not need turning upside down.

Crusaders and sceptics

No topic stirred society so violently as did 'prohibition'. The debate had been going on for half a century, at first languidly, but as the uglinesses taken in its stride by a frontier society came to be seen for what they were, with rising temperature. When the small town began to spring up and the habits that may have been tolerable in the backwoods roadside tavern began to obtrude on the consciousness of prim Methodist and Baptist shopkeepers, many of them fresh from the respectabilities of urban lower-middle-class England, the vulgarity, the disorder, the economic wastefulness of drunkenness became joined to humanitarian concern for its victims—the unfortunate wives and children—and was wrapped up in religious emotionalism.

How close frontier life and the temperance movement were to each other is illustrated from a report of the meeting of a women's temperance society in the eighteen-seventies, which passed a resolution to pray for "the two wickedest places in Canada." What and where were they? Barrie—at 'end of steel' on the Northern Railway, and Winnipeg, in a similar position on the Red River. The writer, a native of one and long a resident of the other, has heard many a tale from 'old hands' about both places that would justify the concern. Both were, in the language of the North, 'jumping-off points', where civilization and the wilderness met, where strong men delighted to show how much swearing they could do, how many fights they could sustain, how much liquor they could hold and how many of the 'ladies' who hovered round such places, could be made susceptible to what they imagined to be their charms but to what in reality was their loosely guarded cash.

One interesting topic that could never have been far from discussion among thoughtful people was religion. Not the hymn-singing, shouting religion of left-wing Protestantism, but the vast debate that was then gathering strength over the very nature of man and the world. In Europe, 'science' and 'religion' had been battling it out for a generation, but hitherto in Canada little had been heard of the grand discussion which was to go to the very roots of life. Canadians had lived in a simple world and the faith of their fathers had come down to them little changed. It was not before the eighteen-eighties that even the few sophisticates were ready to be swept into the wider intellectual currents of the outer world, though by that period a good deal of talk about agnosticism was to be heard, and an agnostic journal had even made its appearance in Toronto, under the title *Secular Thoughts*.[35] The celebrated Robert Ingersoll had come and had made his atheistic orations. But all this was in the old style, including, as it did, ingenious argument about the real meaning of 'eternal' in the Biblical phrase 'eternal punishment'—not 'everlasting', said the classical scholars but 'for an age', *aeternitas* (duration uncertain). Such discussions had been at the heights; only slowly did they shift into the scientific area and there, too, they were still too rarified to cause explosions.

A letter which appeared in *The Week* of April 25th, 1886, could contain the following passages:— "In these days of scientific naturalism and critical historical research no unification of the conflicting creeds . . . will be possible on any basis which retains one vestige of the supernatural part of Christianity. True, an esoteric belief in God and immortality, even the divinity of Christ, might be retained . . . but it could never be successfully made obligatory, or enjoined authoritatively. . . ." This was plain language for 1886, but it did not raise a storm. While the writer was penning it, people in every hamlet, town and city, people of every rank and condition of life, were streaming to church, never more of them, and there they heard sermons suited to their particular mentalities, but virtually all of them orthodox, though many of them liberal. In the eighteen-eighties we were still in the age of faith and had not yet begun that process of sliding out of it without thinking or talking about it which has been so conspicuous in our own day.[36]

The zeal and vehemence that went into the life of the nineteenth century, as compared with our own day, especially into such areas as politics and religion (and these two fields contained most of the others, in particular the racial and linguistic controversies, separate schools, temperance) is accounted for in part by the fact that there were not nearly as many avenues for the dispersion of energies or the sublimation of hates. To-day most young people have weekly doses of soporific in the 'movies' (nightly doses of it, now, with television) and every ordinary man in the country is glued to his television set watching baseball or hockey. There are also a dozen and one other lightning rods, such as rushing up one highway and down another in a car. During some seventy or eighty years, we (not only Canada, but the continent) have moved, as it were, from mid-seventeenth century back into the second or third century of the Roman Empire: from the stern Puritanism, self-sacrifice and sense of duty of our grandfathers, or that minority of them which determined social attitudes, to the gay insouciance, the craving for cheap excitement, of the city mob, which determines them to-day. A backlog of solidity remains, of course, for the city mob, with its 'bread and circuses' attitude, is not in entire control—but a backlog of solidity remained in the later Empire too.

Sport, organized and unorganized

In no surer way does our present period mark this turn—this historical retrocession, if the reader desires to call it that—than in the emphasis it begins to place on sports. The word is *sports*, in the plural, not *sport*, not games and not *amusements*. *Sport* is an old, yet always current, conception, ranging all the way from the conception Gloucester in *King Lear*[37] had of it to the most massive of diverting spectacles, such as war. *Games* are games. *Amusement* is what *sports* have become in our own days. The ideas behind such words are protean —they change as they are examined. They all relate, more or less vaguely, to the lighter side of life. The Puritan—and he was dominant among our ancestors—felt that life was real and life was earnest and the grave was not its goal. Thus, through the gate of sport, we come also to this end of an age, this change in the course of history, which we have encountered just above in the field of religion. The dignity and gravity which marked the Canadian town and city at its highest, when every respectable citizen walked to church on Sunday morning in plug hat and cut-away coat, followed by his numerous family, and decorously returned to eat his Sunday dinner of roast beef, was no sooner won (over the rowdyism of frontier days) than it began to be sapped by the irresponsibles of society. The irresponsibles occur at the top, where they are few, but conspicuous, and at the bottom, where they are many and sordid. The developing city brings along both types, and both demand amusement. The growth of organized sports is therefore a good indicator of the turn from rural values to urban, from grave to gay, from Puritan to pagan.

The word *sport* conjures up a whole sociology and volumes could be written exploring it. Every people has always had some kind of physical diversion that might be given the term: years ago the author used to watch Cree Indians at Hudson's Bay posts playing what they called *football*. The ball was launched and the whole encampment joined in kicking it. There were no *sides*, and no goal posts, just vague ends. Men, women and children scrambled for a kick at the ball. Everybody enjoyed themselves and nobody won. Medieval football has been described as just such a game. At the other end of its scale, there were the clashes of knights in armour, either in the tournament or on the battlefield. War for 'the gentleman' has

The new nation / 321

been the ultimate sport and he always has sought an approach to it in his games: when he began to organize himself, he naturally created two rival 'teams' to do battle. This is the major form of his legacy to our time, though we also have one which comes partially from the gentleman's duel, partly from the same roots as the gladiatorial show of ancient Rome, namely boxing. it in his games: when he began to organize himself, he naturally Boxing was originally 'the manly art of self-defence', but when it was taken up by the crowd (few members of which would be able to defend themselves with their fists), excitement, vicarious punishment, and blood were demanded. Boxing became the equivalent of the gladiatorial show or the Spanish bull-fight.

In the eighteen-eighties, Toronto ('the Good') was just becoming large enough to support professional gladiators.

> "It is natural for such a form of athletic exercises to be popular among Anglo-Saxons . . . a kind of safety-valve to pugnacious instincts. . . . Boxing is valuable as developing self-command, caution, watchfulness, calculation, not to say every muscle in the human body. . . ."

Here was 'the gentleman' speaking.

> "But there is a danger . . . a recent 'glove fight' in the Albert Hall, Toronto, was nothing less than a prize fight for the 'gate-money' . . . The contestants fought fourteen rounds, and the features of one at least were scarcely recognizable when the sponge was thrown up. . . ."[38]

Here was 'the gentleman' deploring! Deploring the attitudes of the mob. To-day we simply call it 'democracy' After all, we do as yet draw the line at slaughter.

Horse-racing, traditional preoccupation for top and bottom of society, was also beginning to be prominent in Toronto:

> "The Canadian Turf has not yet formed for itself such a train of blacklegging rowdyism, and general blackguardism as that which now graces by its presence every English race-course. Still, the gambling-table was there, and sharpers' tricks were evidently practised. . . . We have no social magnates . . . [such as those] who . . . still rule through the English Jockey Club, and make its voice, in some degree, that of honour. That the leaders of Canadian Society are among the company on the race-course is a belief that requires limitation[39]. . . . Still, it is to be hoped that honourable men on the Canadian Turf will do all possible to preserve their sport from stain. . . ."[40]

'The sport of kings' was not the only device for indentifying oneself with 'quality'. There was that relatively new game lawn-tennis, which had been introduced into Toronto in 1874.

Plate 10: St. Paul's College, Winnipeg, built as Manitoba College about 1880.

THE IMITATIONS OF THE IMITATIONS

Plate 11: Casa Loma built as a residence by Sir Henry Pellatt in Toronto about 1914.

Plate 12: "Goddesses of Liberty, 1898" (including "The Lady who's known as Lu").

ASPECTS OF THE FRONTIER

In 1886, it continued to hold its own as a fashionable and exclusive pastime,[41] nor had it become the hard-slugging exhibition of pure athletic skill it now is:—

> "The present grounds of the Toronto Lawn Tennis Club are on the north side of Front Street, between York and Simcoe Streets[42]. . . . The entrance fee in its early days was placed at a high figure, and even at the present time is far from a low one, $25.00 . . . with a yearly subscription of $5.00. The members are all elected by ballot. . . ."

No doubt about the class line here!

> "Invitations for the 'Monday Afternoons' are issued by the committee. . . . On these occasions there is often a gathering of the representative beauty and fashion of Toronto, who meet, some to play but the majority, we must confess, to look on and talk. . . The grounds of the Lawn Tennis Club present quite a brilliant appearance on a fine afternoon, with a number of ladies and gentlemen, either seated on the raised benches which command the courts, or grouped about the arbor, while various young men and maidens flit over the grassy sward—many arrayed in the effective colours of the Club, crimson, blue and brown. . . ."[43]

What a delightful picture of well-bred young people at play! And what a wonder that it remained accurate for so long! Not until after the First World War, when the gravel court came in, did the emphasis turn to speed and the 'maidens' or 'ladies' into 'girls', with legs!

Tennis held on longer than that other English game, cricket. To-day cricket in Canada has virtually ceased to exist (except, possibly, in Toronto and on Vancouver Island). In the eighteen-eighties, it still hung on, though rapidly declining, and it still was heavy with class connotations. "Cricket is so intricate that few ladies can understand it [as with modern baseball]. . . . Besides which, cricket is too slow for the average Canadian. . . . Further, the number of Canadians with means and without vocations, from whom to draft the 'gentlemen players' who are the backbone of cricket in England . . . is very small. . . ."[44] The writer clearly had his "centre of reference elsewhere," looking over his shoulder to see if Daddie was approving.[45]

The team games are plainly sublimated warfare. Each team represents a tribe, or nation. The colleges furnished ideal fighting tribes, as they still do, and some of the first of our national games recorded were between colleges. These also formed the first international: there seems to have been an early connection between McGill and Harvard, for football games between the two were recorded and photographed as early as 1875.[46]

Tribalism was slow in filtering down from the universities to the towns, but when it did, it found a territorial base, and the new game hockey developed as much as inter-town warfare as it was athletic performance. Camp-followers, or spectators, appeared in due course. Since all's fair in love and war, professionalism soon made its appearance, disguised in the various well-worn forms at first but becoming gradually more open, until in hockey it has now almost put an end to the amateur. But by our own time, we have passed city-state warfare, and are engaged in the strife of great provincial regions: to-day, if 'The West' loses the Grey (football) Cup, it has lost its regional honour. And as professionalism has become more and more accepted, tribalism and gladiatorialism have mingled: many 'fans' still manage to combine the two. For some, professional hockey satisfies the fighting instinct and provides the hope of blood. For others, it is an artistic performance, an incredibly swift and violent ballet rather than a game. For still others, it is purely tribal—the racial struggle fought out in another medium, as witness the disturbances in Montreal in 1955 arising from the disqualification of 'Rocket' Richard, the famous member of *Les Canadiens.*

Racial friction in both amusement and sport has been present from the first. One of the great winter spectacles of Montreal used to be the 'Ice Palace', which was the central piece in a winter carnival consisting of fancy-dress skating, torchlight parades by snow-shoe, illumination of the ice palace and its 'storming', with fireworks to match.

On the second night of the carnival, the Frenchmen invited their sister snow-shoe clubs to join their procession. Out of a thousand members of the Montreal Club, four attended. Next night, at the storming of the ice-palace, the few scores of French snow-shoe-ers who took part refused to join the serpentine tramp over Mount Royal. . . . This whole matter shows Montreal is becoming two separate cities. . . . Differences of race prevent the sympathy which either in the small field of civil life, or the larger one of country, is required for real union."[47]

And so we come back, by an unlooked-for path, to Canada's cancer of racial hatred. Nothing is too small to be seared by it, nothing too large. If quiescent one moment, it breaks forth the next. In no period, not even at the Conscription crisis of 1917, was it more constantly in play than in the generation following Confederation. That it did not ruin us we may owe to the fact mentioned by Adam Smith that "there is a lot of ruin in a nation." There must have been a lot of ruin, even in the youthful Dominion of the seventies and eighties, or it surely would have been destroyed. And that it was not was perhaps owing in part to men's attentions being drawn away from the central issue by the other interests and other occupations of the period pictured here.[48]

Notes to Chapter 20

1. *The Week*, Toronto, Nov. 12th, 1885.
2. Quoted in *The Week*, Jan. 15th, 1885
3. *The Week*, June 11th, 1885.
4. "Carlos" in *The Week*, July 16th, 1885.
5. See below, pp. 302, 306.
6. *The Week*, May 28th, 1885
7. William Dean Howells, *Their Wedding Journey* (Boston, 1874), p. 218.
8. The present *outhouse* school of poets is not very helpful in this respect.
9. Howells, op. cit., p. 173.
10. Charles Dudley Warner, "Studies in the South and West, with Comments on Canada, 1889" in *Complete Writings* (Hartford, 1904).
11. February 1861, p. 164.
12. The first Dominion census is a fundamental source. It reprints the statistical material of the French régime (see p. 41). Also, the first census, in contrast with those of the Province of Canada, assumes the familiar bilingual form to which anyone who uses public documents has long since grown accustomed.
13. For Canada as a whole the figure was 30.6; for New Brunswick, 29.9; for Nova Scotia, 27.9.
14. See Diagram No. 1.
15. *The Week*, July 23rd, 1885, article initialled G.B.E.
16. Warner, op. cit., p. 506.
17. G. Mercer Adam, *Toronto, Old and New* (Toronto, 1891). This book reflects the Toronto of the eighteen-eighties.
18. See such books as E. M. Chadwick, *Ontarian Families* (2 Vols., Toronto, 1894) or, down a stage, *The Toronto and Hamilton Blue Book* (Toronto, 1902).
19. It was bought in 1916 by the Robert Simpson Company and made into a residence for women employees.
20. Toronto, 1952.
21. The Agricultural Association of Upper Canada held a fair in 1847. It evolved into the Toronto Electoral Agricultural Society and this in turn into Toronto Industrial Exhibition, 1879. Much later this became the Canadian National Exhibition.
22. Take the illustrations in our periodicals: they come out in an immense range of colours and some of them, such as reproductions of paintings or photographs of landscapes, are beautiful beyond the dreams of our fathers. Yet after a hasty glance we throw them aside—more of the same to-morrow!
23. *The Week*, Apr. 30th, 1885.
24. Adam, op. cit., p. 132.
25. *The Nation*, June 12th, 1874. See William Colgate, *The Toronto Art Students' League* (Toronto, 1954), for quotations from *The Canadian Monthly*, 1873, to the same effect.
26. *The Week*, Mar. 5th, 1885.
27. Goldwin Smith.

28. *The Week,* Apr. 29th, 1886. *The Week's* intellectualism must have been distinctly trying to what was still in some respects a frontier city. Thus in reporting the exhibition of the Canadian Society of Etchers, which it warmly commends, it exclaims: "The recognition of true Art as it is presented here, devoid of the meretricious illusions of colour, and in many cases rather indicating the artist's idea than working it with laborious finish, is one of the best tests of a true feeling for Art." (Apr. 2nd, 1885.) Here surely was intellectual puritanism as its bleakest.
29. Colgate, op. cit.
30. Colgate, op. cit., p. 28.
31. July, 1883.
32. *The Week,* Oct. 30th, 1884.
33. See pp. 60, 61.
34. *The Week,* Feb. 10th, 1887.
35. *The Week,* Jan. 13th, 1887.
36. There are signs that we may slide back into faith in the same slipshod way.
37. *King Lear,* I, i.
38. *The Week,* Feb. 21st, 1884.
39. e.g. 'will not stand up to examination'.
40. *The Week,* June 5th, 1884.
41. *The Week,* June 17th, 1886.
42. This would place them in the shadow of Bishop Strachan's palace, just down the street from the present Royal York Hotel.
43. *The Week,* June 17th, 1886.
44. Ibid., June 5th, 1884.
45. Like a certain college principal in much more recent days who used to put up the English football scores on the bulletin board although he was Canadian-born and could hardly distinguish one English team from another.
46. See *Weekend Magazine,* Vol. 3, No. 52, 1953.
47. *The Week,* Feb. 2nd, 1885.
48. Several pages should also have been devoted to the struggle waged in French Canada against the forces of reaction, both in Church and State. The struggle destroyed the old *rouge* party but it brought forth Laurier and the Liberal party, and it gave French Canada a training in popular government and political philosophy complementary to that supplied by the Rebellion period. No more gallant set of men has ever graced the Canadian stage than those who in the eighteen-seventies fought political and religious bigotry in Quebec and at the cost of ostracism and of innumerable legal and political battles established the right of their countrymen to vote as they liked without clerical *influence indue* (the classic phrase) being exerted upon them.

21: A sturdy yeomanry: Canada in the 'horse and buggy' age

'THE HORSE AND BUGGY AGE' is a belittling phrase. To the smart modern city dweller, it conjures up a picture of old men with beards poking along country roads and using queer words, which they enunciate (over the radio) in still queerer voices. It is especially hard for the modern city dweller, with his ant-like ways, to imagine another mode of life, different from his own and with different values. It always has been hard for the city dweller to appreciate rural values (especially when so many city dwellers are escapees from the country). During most of history the countryman's fortunes have answered to the derisive terms the city dweller applies to him, for he usually gets the worst of it, and sooner or later is depressed to the level of either a peasant, a serf, or a slave. More rarely, he is elevated to that of gentleman or feudal nobleman—in which case he earns the citizens' equally hearty contempt for different reasons.

There have been, however, rare periods when the country has provided a way of life that was good and neither depressed nor elevated, whereby large numbers of men attained to substantial heights of well-being. These have been the 'yeoman' periods, when sturdy, independent men owned their own land and lived their own lives, with no consciousness of inferiority to others. The 'franklin' of the English Danelagh appears to have been such a man, as was the English yeoman of the seventeenth century and early eighteenth century—the man who took the measure of Charles I and his cavaliers. We read of the same type in more distant times, in both Greece and Rome, and we also read sad poetry about their decline.—

"But a bold peasantry, their country's pride
When once destroyed, can never be supplied. . . ."

It has been North America's boast that her soils could provide the foundation for such a yeomanry as no other land in the world had ever previously been blessed with. The boast has not been idle, for if there has been anything more distinctive about the continent than its millions of 'sturdy yeomen' who called no man master, it is hard to say what it has been.

To-day our 'bold peasantry', assailed by the machine, by over-supply and by the impossibility of getting help, is changing its nature. Some of it is turning itself into a cross between capitalist *entrepreneur* and country gentleman. Some of it is sinking into 'small-peasant' status. It is leaving the land in increasing numbers and experts tell us that the exodus will have to go on, the farm people's proportion to the whole of the population steadily declining. The situation has gone farthest in the United States, but Canada must follow the same path. This chapter, therefore, is concerned with an era that probably has already passed.

What era? That era before the opening of the West had introduced pure commercial agriculture, before modern power had been applied directly to the farm, before the process of suburbanization had begun, but after the hardships and the crudities of the pioneering age had been overcome. That era of hearty work in the fields, man with man, of simple yet abundant fare, of good housing and substantial comfort, which was briefly interposed between the days of settlement and the sweeping over the countryside of the industrial revolution and its urban values. The era when the countryside was following its own way of life, and not looking over its shoulder on the fashionable pace-setting of the city. It was the era which in New England claimed its poetic voices to preserve it for posterity: the era of "The One-Horse Shay," of "The Barefoot Boy" and the smithie standing "Under the Spreading Chestnut Tree." In English Canada, it found few poetic voices to sound its praises but to-day many are the retrospective testimonies which appear to its excellence.[1] As befits Canadian reticence, all of these are in prose and most of them hide their sentiment behind a bantering humour.

Such an era, thanks to the mobility of things in Canada, was necessarily fleeting. A solid, settled rural life had no sooner emerged than it began to be eroded. No social situation is ever completely neat, so that different regions meet their fate at different times, but a rough average would give us the first generation after Confederation, down to the first decade of the new century, for the period wherein 'the horse and buggy age' reached its characteristic expression, its high point. The age, it is now clear, was in itself an aspect of the industrial revolution of the nineteenth century, for it depended upon gravel

roads, machine craftsmanship in conveyances and field implements, and to some degree on long-distance haulage by railroads. It is the enquivalent of the 'coaching era' in Great
Britain, or of the clipper ship, which latter was in itself perfection but the kind of perfection that has to be pushed aside
when entirely new conceptions come in to play, as they did
with steam power. The 'horse and buggy age' is merely an
interval, a delicious hesitation or hovering, between the old
saddle-horse and ox-cart era, civilized man's best previous
effort, and the high-speed technique of our own times.

The Canadian country-side

In the eighteen-seventies all over Ontario, the fine com-
modious brick houses were rising that still dot the countryside.
In most other provinces, building was in frame, and in the
better parts, as the Annapolis Valley, the frame house, like
its prototype in New England, got some paint. Big barns were
going up too but these rarely got paint, whatever province
they were in. About 1878, there appeared that series of *County
Atlases* of Ontario which depicted the houses and farms by
name, both in drawings and on maps. They add vastly to our
knowledge of the countryside at that time. While presumably
only the best places are shown in the cuts, enough are shown
to convince us that the older districts were becoming not only
comfortable but wealthy. Inside those houses, there was plenty
of furniture—of varying excellence—plenty of warmth and food.
Warmth came from stoves, the fireplaces having been either
closed up or not having been installed in the newer houses,
and from wood cut on the occupants' own farm by their own
hands, with no obligations to a power saw: it "warmed them
twice". Goldwin Smith, in his astringent way, bade the people
of the day remember that "the stove is as debilitating as the
tropics". He was wrong: it did not carry tropical diseases and
it was a good ventilator. Nothing more cheery than a good
maple fire in a big iron stove, with the men sitting about it
smoking their pipes and telling tales of winters that really had
been winters! Nothing, except the tinkle of the bells on the
'cutter' as it rolled along in the moonlight over the snow, with
plenty of 'buffalo robes', a good horse, and, if you were lucky,
your best girl beside you. It is distressing to reflect that the
children of to-day have never heard the most distinctive of
all Canadian sounds—the merry jingle of the sleigh-bells!
At every farmhouse in those days, winter and summer, there
was hospitality and seldom was the stranger turned away. On
every table there was plenty, sometimes "a rude plenty," which

is what Lord Durham alleged the French-Canadian peasantry possessed, sometimes a well-served plenty. And if a countryside was anywhere near average, cleanliness could be depended on —the women saw to that. If a family fell below the line, it soon got a reputation. There had been plenty of filth among the immigrants; where had it gone to? That is hard to say, but in thirty or forty years, gone, for the most part, it had.

The country-side had become not only clean but, with exceptions, god-fearing and law-abiding. When one man, in too much of a hurry, attempted to take in his grain of a fine Sunday, "the neighbours soon stopped that," an old lady who had been one of them exclaimed. Church-going became the rule and in most districts those not associated with a church would have been regarded as 'queer'. It was around Confederation that the innumerable little brick churches which dot the country-side of Ontario began to appear: the brave days of the circuit rider were already far away. Nearly all those country churches were plain, and many of them ugly, though to this statement Anglican churches were sometimes an exception, and these latter often attempted to keep their grounds attractive, a sin against Puritan unworldliness which Methodists and Presbyterians rarely committed. Whatever the denomination, when the community turned out on some public occasion, such as a local funeral, everyone participated. In some districts children were given half holidays for funerals (theoretically, to enable them to attend), and at the service 'the connection' sat in the centre of the church. But already, so intricate were blood ties becoming that at most funerals approximately the same people—that is, most of the district—sat in the centre.

Except in certain 'hard-rock' areas, denomination—within Protestantism—was already becoming of secondary importance. It was the local community and the blood group which counted. Differences remained, of course. Methodists maintained and extended their formidable list of taboos—taboos against alcohol and tobacco, against the theatre and card-playing, against dancing, against all sin whatsoever. Their 'camp-meetings' had pretty well disappeared, but they still carried on their 'love-feasts' and revival meetings. Such practices staid Scottish Presbyterians could not abide. When a Glengarry Scot paused awhile to hear a Methodist revivalist exhorting, his comment was "Yon man talks to God as if he were a sma' boy, and he was telling him to come down out of his apple tree!" Methodists were themselves to become decreasingly effervescent as the century were on, so that less and less was to separate them and the Presbyterians. The years after church union (1925)—mooted for long before—were to make it clear, indeed, that it was not Methodists who had swallowed Presbyterians, but Presbyterians who had swallowed Methodists.[2]

Not every countryside was idyllic: frontier roughness struck through many of them, and in some, cases of severe disorder have been recorded. There was what has been pictured as the reign of terror conducted about 1875 by the 'Black Donnellys' in the township of Biddulph, Ontario. The story has it that for years the Donnelly pair and their seven sons terrorized the countryside, carrying highway robbery, arson, assault, destruction of property and even murder to all who opposed their will.[3] If half the legend they left behind is true, some modifications need to be made in the traditional picture of British law and order. Transfer this story of local bad men to another age and put in a public authority much weaker than the weak authority of the law in the countryside of 1875, and you get an explanation of medieval feudalism. Centuries before, the terrorizing Donnellys could have defied authority and, by building castles, could have turned themselves into feudal barons.

Ontario in 1875 was, however, not Europe in 1075. With little towns and villages springing up everywhere, authority was never far away and there was not opportunity for many Black Donnellys. Disorder in town and village rapidly came down into one of two forms, either local rowdiness interspersed with the occasional but not frequent crime of violence, or the scrimmages conducted by the rank and file of the Orange lodges.

"In Coldwater, there is neither law nor order. The place has a number of toughs, and people are afraid to come to town at night for fear of being pounced upon by some of these night owls. People have had their horses beaten and their rigs overturned or broken."[4] Coldwater, a little village near Midland, Ontario, was at that time a frontier sawmill town, and the situation described, which is much the same as in the contemporary 'wild west' (except for the absence of six-shooters) may be considered normal for a frontier community of the time. In the neighbouring settlement of Orillia, which was a little larger, matters did not go quite as far, and the case of the half-drunk lumberjack whose arrest was attempted (unsuccessfully) by the wholly drunk constable[5] suggests one stage away from frontier conditions: there was at least a constable present on the streets of Orillia in 1875, even if a drunken one.

Rural disorder was still annually translated into urban by the Irish, either as migrants from the country-side or direct.

The only recorded reading of the Riot Act in the city of Toronto occurred on July 23rd, 1874, when a Roman Catholic procession began moving down Church Street. "Crowds of anti-Catholics began stoning it. The procession, which was going to a service at St. Mary's Church at Bathurst and Adelaide Streets, kept moving. When it reached Bay Street, Mayor Francis H. Medcalf appeared to read the Riot Act. . . ."[6] But as compared with the conditions of a generation before, already referred to, those of the post-Confederation period were tapering off into their subsequent peacefulness. Rural disorder in Canada has been a wave following the frontier.

The typical Canadian farmer

Just after Confederation, if we may judge by statistics,[7] the typical Canadian farmer was the owner of between fifty and one hundred acres. In Ontario, he had some twenty-two acres under crop and in Quebec, about seventeen. In the upper province the typical farmer grew some seventy-two bushels of wheat, for this was the great wheat period, and in the lower, twenty. In Ontario, he possessed about eight head of cattle and in Quebec, just over six. His farm had two or three horses in Ontario and one or two in Quebec. The Quebec discrepancy

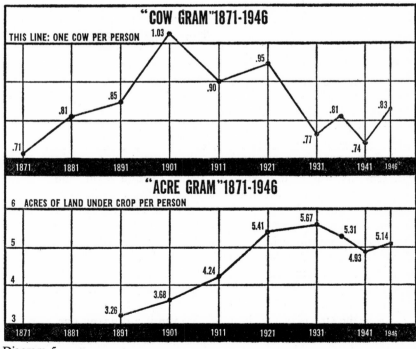

Diagram 5

in horses was made up in oxen, of which there were about two to every five farms.

In both provinces the average family was large, though it was getting smaller. In 1851 it had been between six and seven persons, but by 1871, it had come down to under six in Ontario and about six and a half in Quebec. In both, each farm family apparently possessed one or two 'light carriages' (though the average was higher in Ontario than in Quebec). 'Light carriage' may have been the general term for the various passenger 'rigs' that had been coming in since the eighteen-fifties, of which the buggy was the most important, numerically and socially, with the democrat (a 'rig' with two or three cross benches accommodating the entire family) not far behind.

The average farm already had a fair amount of machinery on it. In each case, the Ontario farm was more fully mechanized than was that of Quebec.[8] But it also still produced many of the traditional commodities whose manufacture has long since been transferred to factories. Thus the Ontario farmers each made twenty pounds of home-made cheese. Even in homespun cloth, the Ontario farm women turned in a respectable total, only a fraction of a square yard of homespun linen each, it is true (though cumulatively this mounted up to a good deal), but over ten square yards each of homespun cloth. In Quebec, these figures were far exceeded, there being ten square yards of linen made on every farm and twenty-eight square yards of cloth. The Ontario farm was already a snug place, for it had enough garden and orchard to give every occupant the proportion of an acre per farm and he grew, according to the census, twelve bushels of apples on it, to say nothing of other fruits. No wonder the Canadian farm wife's cellar shelves have traditionally groaned with the weight of their long rows of preserves, all put down against the winter that was just round the corner.

If these dry facts are for the 'average' farmer, then among a large number of persons, some must have been high above the average, while others would be far below it. That is, in this most democratic of occupations and this most democratic of countries, there must already have been a rural class line in the making: this, however, would correspond with the distribution of soils by districts, leaving members of any single rural community on a footing of relative equality. The soil itself sorted out our farmers into groups all the way from big men at the top to a class at the bottom which had all the ear-marks of a peasantry except a peasantry's stability and tradition. It was a class found everywhere in Canada, one grading down to a 'poor white' status, and uncomfortably numerous.

The 'sturdy yeoman' of this chapter is the 'average farmer' whom our statistics depict. He is the fortunate person on reasonably good soil who can win a modest and independent competence. By Confederation it was evident that he was flourishing and after Confederation the marks of his success became more and more evident in good houses, large barns, the improvement of roads, new school buildings—not that formal education was making much of a showing—and the adoption of mechanical improvements as they came along. Yet, in human affairs, as in the sea, the big fish swallow the little ones. If this goes on long enough, the families at the top draw away from the yeoman class, educate their children, become superior to manual work and turn themselves into 'gentlemen farmers'. A further stage is reached when urban wealth begins to buy land and set up plaything farms with employees to run them.

In a new country such as ours, the social processes, as compared with those of the old world, are rapid. In the spoil of North America, land was the most desirable booty from the first and it was secured in every conceivable way, direct and indirect, honest and dishonest; mostly, it might seem, dishonest. But apparently few of the land speculators retained their holdings as family estates: their object was simply resale at a higher price. The home farm of the famous Colonel Talbot, who, with all his faults, was not exactly a land speculator, consisted of about six hundred acres, and it is still intact.[9] Here was 'gentleman farming' continuously from the beginning. There has not been much of it in Canada and of what there has been, not much has been successful. One instance from a later period and province is perhaps illustrative. In the early eighteen-nineties, an English immigrant of the 'gentleman' class bought land in south-western Manitoba and began to farm it: his employees were other young Englishmen of similar type. These young men were required to dress for dinner every night. Hunters were kept. The experiment did not last long. Similar stories are told of the fruit ranchers in the interior of British Columbia.

This mention of British Columbia brings us to a still later period in time, but not in social development. Among the fruit ranchers of the Okanagan there have been many attempts to transfer the 'gentleman farmer' concept to Canada, but few of them have been successful. If this social type is to emerge among us, it will be through evolution from the ranks, and so far, the conditions of our life have made against that occurring. Thus the writer knows two good Ontario farms each of which produced a minister of the crown, but both these men were accustomed to pitch hay and feed the cattle with the rest of the farmers about them.[10] In the same region there formerly were a number of 'gentlemen' (all English) farmers, but gradually they gave way to 'yeomen': nowhere were farms consolidated into 'estates' with rent-paying tenantry.

There have been many instances of urban wealth buying into the land for 'plaything' purposes. One of the earliest of these was that of the Honourable George Brown, who early in the eighteen-sixties acquired 'Bow Park Farm', in a loop of the Grand River near Brantford. Here he raised pure-bred cattle and set up as a country gentleman. A fine residence was built (which is still in use) but eventually Brown's toy ceased to have its original interest and he made it into a limited company. It is still a farm, well managed by a graduate of the Ontario Agricultural College, and producing an immense amount of food every year, but it did not descend to the second generation of Browns. Since 1911, it has been owned and operated by Canadian Canners, Ltd., which company is now as Canadian as the old McLaughlin Motor Car Co., in that it has become a subsidiary of an American firm.[11]

Most cities of any size have had rural retreats on their edges which have been owned by wealthy men and have been used as farms. These 'farms' have been good speculations but they have necessarily been transient. This is especially noticeable around Toronto, where the rapid advance of the city has raised land values astronomically.

On a beautiful autumn day during his first year in the University of Toronto, the writer remembers taking a walk up Spadina Road, over the hill, where 'Pellatt's Castle' now stands, and on to St. Clair Avenue. There at the corner of St. Clair and Spadina Road, were open fields and a farmer with his team working in them. But even by that time, the plaything farms were out beyond this genuine farm, far to the north-east of the city.

In the eighteen-forties there arrived in Upper Canada from northern Ireland a young man named William Tyrrell. He became a successful builder, and an interesting group of houses on King Street in Kingston, still first-class residential property, is his work. In the eighteen-fifties he built a big house in Weston, Ontario. His sons went to the university and both became well known. One of them lived to become the grand old man of Canadian geology, Dr. J. B. Tyrrell, the hero of the epic trip of exploration across the Barren Lands of the Canadian Arctic (1893-1894). Dr. Tyrrell, after making a fortune in northern Ontario gold mining, settled down in his sixties on a farm at the edge of Toronto. He planted an orchard of Northern Spy apples, and lived to harvest many thousands of bushels of apples from it. He had neighbouring farms literally pushed on him by their owners, who seemed to wish nothing so much as escape into a job from the responsibilities of yeoman status. Now his splendid orchards seem about to be engulfed by an advancing city. His heirs will reap the financial gains, but a beautiful and productive bit of countryside will have been turned into dull city streets and a distinguished Canadian name disappear into the relative anonymity of city life.

Ontario has so little good farm land that probably all of it will be suburbanized sooner or later and taken out of production, but it is Ontario which, because of its rapid development, best illustrates the social evolution of the country-side. And, of course, in the post-Confederation period, the Ontario farm was the representative Canadian farm. Rural Ontario was a northern projection of American rural society and most of the points that could be made about the one could be made about the other. In both it was the average man who counted. That average man might be a relative new-comer, as he usually was in Ontario, or he might be of some ten generations on this continent: whichever he was, he followed just about the same way of life, for new-comers rapidly fitted themselves into the prevailing pattern. In this way, the Canadian country-side represents the migration of the country-side of New England and New York, with its customs and attitudes not greatly changed.

The statement would not be valid for French Canada, which has its own way of life, but even there, the environment being similar, relatively the same responses were produced. The major difference would be that the French-Canadian farmer has always had that family attitude towards his farm which has been weak in English Canada. In French Canada, the family farm is an ancestral possession, handed down from father to son (by a peculiar system of inheritance which does not involve the rank in the family of the heir so much as his fitness to carry on). In English Canada, it is much closer to a piece of real estate, and few farmers have ever hesitated to sell out when offered a good enough price. Even so, there are plenty of farms in English Canada on which the family that received the original grant from the Crown still resides. English Canada's system of inheritance is also its own: it seems to consist mainly, though there are no rules, in leaving the farm to a son and requiring him to give mortgages to the other children, share and share alike. During the depression of the nineteen-thirties, the interest payment on these mortgages (which rapidly got out to nephews, nieces and more distant relatives) often became so onerous, that the ocupant of the farm simply surrendered it and moved away. In French Canada, one son seems to expect, and to be expected, to stay on the farm: he may marry and bring his wife home. In English Canada this has never been more than exceptional, and since the father was often quite capable of carrying on for years after his boys grew up, more often than not they struck out for themselves. Then, at the father's death or retirement, the farm would be sold. For reasons such as these there has always been a rapid flux in the English-Canadian ownership of land as compared with French Canada. A comparison of names, farm by farm, as given in the atlases of 1870, with the present occupancy of farms shows huge changes, but in French Canada it is almost normal for the same family to have been on the same farm since the beginning, in some cases three centuries ago.

The consequences of rapid change in ownership have often been disastrous to the land. If a man expects to leave to his son the farm he has himself inherited, then he will probably take care of the soil, the trees and the property. The English-Canadian farmer, necessarily with exceptions, has had little of this respect for the land: he has looked on his farm not altogether as a mine but as something from which he expected to extract the utmost in terms of production. This does not mean that he has invariably been a bad and careless farmer, for where the soil is good enough to withstand his assaults, he is quite likely to have co-operated with it, if only because good farming pays. But poor land makes the owner ruthless. He will overgraze, and cut the trees, squeezing the last ounce of raw material out of his property. The evidences of this are spread all over Canada in the form of eroded hill-sides, filled with great gullies or desolate square miles of bare rocks, and here and there the skeletons of dead trees. A few generations of 'farming' have reduced districts in the Caledon Hills or the Kingston-Belleville neighbourhood to desert. There is not much point of talking about 'sturdy yeomen' in these districts, for the people in them go down with the land.

The clash between rural and urban values

Whether the soil be poor or good, whether the farmer foolish or wise, the temptations of a commercial way of life such as ours must, except in infrequent cases, drive the occupant to forcing his land. It sometimes seems as if the most dangerous man to have on the farm is the farmer. The aristocratic system of the old world at least had the merit, through its tenant farming, of making the farmer behave himself. In Canada tenancy has made things worse, for then neither owner nor tenant has had a full sense of responsibility. Nor does family pride of possession often come to the soil's rescue, for in English Canada the farmer who would count on his son to succeed him would as likely as not get fooled by the son moving off to the nearest town, out West, or over to the States (later to come back, horribly patronizing, as a visitor, to show the old folk 'how well he had done').

Added to all this heavy discount on 'a sturdy yeomanry' was (and is) the endemic 'slap-dashery' of the frontier—the readiness to make do, the shiftlessness, the fixed notion that no job is worth doing really well (after all, the aim is the barn door) and that precision is almost reprehensible: this fumbling carelessness, invariably accompanied by a narrow pride in the values it is supposed to represent as opposed to those of a more advanced external world, has often marked the Canadian farmer. "I don't need no men in books to tell me how to run my farm," said an old farmer to the present writer in his youth.

It is the rapid change in the ownership of land which, among other things, requires us to consider the period after Confederation as not permanent: there can be nothing permanent about the country-side of English America, for it reflects the speed of change that marks our civilization as a whole. The 'sturdy yeoman', therefore, no sooner emerged than he began to change into something else. By modern times he seems to have become either the owner of a machine shop for extracting food values from the soil, a man chained to a herd of cows and the city dairies, a fairly large-scale capitalist, with a capitalist's attitude towards the land—the land as a factory; or at the other end of the scale, a poor white skulking on the margins of the better farming districts. Or it would be fairer to say he is becoming such things, for there are still sturdy farmers left, and there will be until they are submerged by city values.

That is just the point: "submerged by city values!" Country communities to have built up their own way of life must have had long periods of relative isolation. This has produced local customs, dress, dialects. A remote and isolated island would exemplify the extreme case. We have plenty of remote islands in Canada, but few genuinely isolated ones: even the Magdalens have had cable and steamer connection for a century. Nevertheless it is such spots which have built up their own way of life and have been least overwhelmed by city values. The more extensive and richer rural districts have been exposed to these from their first day of settlement, and it is only because cities were themselves weak that a distinctive rural way of life could get established. As we have seen, even so it has been more or less transitory.

The settler no sooner got on the land than he began to leave it, as his descendants still do. For this there are many reasons, the most direct of which is the end of available land, the next, dislike of the drudgery which farm life entailed. Most men who stuck it out through pioneer conditions and raised a family on their holding were anxious to see their sons settled around them, and often by watching their opportunities, they were able to get neighbouring farms, either from the Crown or from other holders. In this way family settlements sometimes expanded over a considerable area. But the process could not go on indefinitely and when virgin land was gone, a man with a number of sons had to have a long purse and buy out his neighbours, if he wished to keep his boys about him. In the process, someone had to go away: talk about keeping youth on the farm has always been nonsense. The only way of keeping youth on the farm would be to subdivide the farm until eventually it would come down to Oriental conditions, with one farmer on an acre. Under Canadian circumstances, the resulting standard of living can be imagined. Youth has always had to leave the farm and always will. Where love of the ancestral acres is strongest—in Quebec—young people leave the farm in greater numbers than they do elsewhere, there being more of them to leave.

A charming account of a youth spent on a farm well past the pioneering stage, yet presenting just the set of conditions whose description has been attempted here, is the semi-autobiographical book *The Master's Wife*, by the late Sir Andrew Macphail, a Prince Edward Islander. Shy, proud, stiff Highlanders fill the pages, transplanted Highlanders whose life revolves around religion, the Scottish psalms, the Scottish Sabbath and work, work, work. They reflect plain living and high thinking, natural delicacy, poise and manners, all the pride of the tribesman. "The truth is, the Highlanders were the last community of gentlemen. . . ." Hence, Macphail says, when great men came among them, there was no sense of inferiority, and no failure of courtesy: there were no rude assertions of equality, just the tribesman's natural assumption of it. But surely here was an attitude which marked many other Canadian country dwellers: there were few among them to pull a subservient forelock, like English labourers in the romantic-novel tradition. And few, too, to play the gentleman. If English people of 'the classes' always received such objectionable demonstrations of equalitarianism in Canada, was it probably not their own fault? The writer once happened to blunder into a log hut where a simple French-speaking Canadian was making maple syrup. While he was there, no less a personage than the Governor General, the late Lord Byng, happened to come in. The syrup-maker received him without the slightest trace of embarrassment, without truckling, without coldness, without fuss! It was Lord Byng who appeared not quite as his ease.

One of Macphail's chapters is entitled "The Escape". What is the escape? It is the escape from the land, from drudgery. And what is the escape route? It is schooling; not education, but schooling, which if it led to the right kind of escape might incidentally, as in the case of the Macphails, become education. One wintry day in Kingston, Sir Andrew's brother, Alexander, was seated before his comfortable fire with a couple of younger men. A workman was visible through the window, shovelling the snow as it fell. 'Sandy' turned to the young men, indicated the contrast presented by the two sides of the window and said one word: "Latin!"

Sir Andrew himself was largely self-educated, with the assistance of his father, a sort of bush-school inspector. He won a scholarship which took him to Prince of Wales College, Charlottetown, for a couple of years and then, aged eighteen, became a school teacher, salary $380.00 a year. But that was riches in 1886! From country school teacher, he went on to McGill and later, a large reputation. How many have followed that escape route from the farm! And how few among them have, incidental to their schooling, found an education! It is no wonder that cultural standards in Canada remain at a low level, when education has had to begin anew at the beginning with each generation and has also so often been regarded merely as a vocational can-opener.

Macphail was entirely frank about it. No Macphail had ever 'worked'—that is, sunk to the status of manual employee (they all 'toiled' hard enough on their farm)—therefore stick to your books! Master the Latin declensions and the mathematical formulae, not for themselves but as keys—keys to the prison that held you. The irony of it is that it probably all came out just as well as the helping-lame-dogs-over-stiles type of thing: "The masters in that Orwell school felt that their whole business was done when they had kept order, so that those who desired to learn were left free in silence . . . no boy was compelled to attend school; he was not inveigled into a scholarly course which he was too feeble-minded to pursue. . . . Best of all, he returned to the land, or to a trade, before he was rendered incapable of dealing with them. . . ."

The Presbyterian Scot has been notorious for following this escape route of education, or rather, schooling. "Father" (in E. A. Corbett's *Father, God Bless Him*[12]) was typical "in never dreaming that any of his children would not go on to the highest type of education attainable." "Father" in this case was a minister, and his sights were raised higher. But every farm, whatever the racial or religious background of the occupants, had to serve as an escape route of some kind, for it was from the farms that virtually the whole population of the country was recruited.[13]

The dispersion of the farm boys

The farm boy came to town and he might end up anywhere from a day labourer to an intellectual, from a pauper to a millionaire. It was largely his energy that lent such a mighty sweep to North American civilization. The Canadian farm not only furnished the recruits for our growing cities, but sent its sons far afield and into every calling: in the eighteen-seventies and eighties, they migrated by the tens of thousands to the American West, where such states as North Dakota became almost more Canadian than anything else. About the same time in our own North West Territories, they were sending that wedge of Anglo-Saxon Protestantism westward along the Canadian Pacific Railway from the Red River to the mountains, and this region to this day remains most faithfully a reflection of eastern Canada.

The farm boys found all the frontiers there were to find. They went into the bush and became lumbermen and river drivers.[14] As river drivers, they developed that pride in their dangerous calling which has spilled over into many a native ballad:—

O ye maidens of Ontario, give ear to what I write,
In driving down these rapid streams where raftsmen take
　　delight,
In driving down these rapid streams as raftsmen they must do,
While these low and loafing farmer boys they stay at home
　　with you.

Oh, these low and loafing farmer boys they tell the girls great
　　tales.
They'll tell them of great dangers in crossing o'er the fields,
While the cutting of the grass and weeds is all that they
　　can do,
While we poor jolly raftsmen are running the Long Soo.

And when the sun is going down, their plows they'll cast aside.
They'll jump upon their horse's back and homeward they will ride.
And when the clock strikes eight or nine, then into bed they'll crawl,
While down on Lake St. Peter we stand many a bitter squall.

In all probability, the writer of that ballad—*Ye Maidens of Ontario*—was himself an Ontario farm boy who had escaped into the larger, more exciting world of the river driver.

Just as farm boys from the Maritimes in preceding generations had taken to that most extensive of all frontiers, the sea, so in central Canada, they took to the lakes. To the lakes they carried their farm nomenclature, so that a shackle is not a shackle to the lake sailor but a clavis. And in one other way, at least, they carried their folk instinct abroad with them. If they made ballads in the bush and on the river, they made them on the lakes:—

> Come all ye young men listen
> While a warning I'll give you,
> Pray never go a-sailing
> To plough those waters blue;
> Oh never go a-sailing,
> No matter what they pay—
> Think of those poor dear fellows
> Drowned on the last of May.
>
> The Steamer "D. D. Calvin"
> The "Bavaria" in tow
> Loaded timber at St. Eguss (*sic*)[15]
> And for Garden Isle did go,
> All started on her homeward trip
> With spirits light and high,
> Never dreaming that so soon
> On the bottom some would lie.
>
> John Marshal was her master,
> A man we all know well,
> For courage as a seaman
> Few could as well excel.
> He leaves a wife and a family
> To mourn his dreadful fate.
> And likewise Felix Compeau,
> Who acted as first mate.

And as for Sandy Berry—
I pen this with regret—
His tall and manly figure
We cannot easily forget.
But the strongest and the bravest
When called upon must go—
We hope to meet in Heaven,
Where high winds never blow.

But there were other victims,
Whose names we only know
But none the less our sympathy
Out to their friends shall go.
For the Lord who reigns above us
And doeth all things well
Has taken them from a troubled earth
And gone with them to dwell![16]

As the farms prospered or became overcrowded, as farmers educated their children or simply were compelled to find room for them somewhere else, the farm boy spread out further and further into the life of the country. He secured his share of places in the professions. He made his contribution to public life. In the United States it used to be thought necessary to believe that presidential candidates had been born in log houses (though few of them had been). In Canada, such a birthplace would have been no demerit for high office, though here again, relatively few could boast it: of the prime ministers of Canada only Arthur Meighen seems to have been a farm boy. But the farms furnished many of the secondary figures, and numbers of the rank and file.

Most fundamental of all, perhaps, the patterns of life worked out in the country-side have gone deep into our outlook. Canada is no longer predominantly a rural country, but a high proportion of its people are still close to their rural origins; their family memories go back to the farm, and a good many of their values. The latter may be simple, but they have nearly always been wholesome. Since there are few really large cities in Canada, these standards have a good chance for survival, through association and renewal. In this way, the era of 'the sturdy yeomen', gone though its finest expression may be, remains a continuing force.

Notes to Chapter 21

1. Witness such books as K. C. Cragg, *Father on the Farm* (Toronto, 1947), John Coburn, *I Kept My Powder Dry* (Toronto, 1950),

Sir Andrew Macphail, *The Master's Wife* (Montreal, 1939), E. A. Corbett, *Father, God Bless Him* (Toronto, 1953), R. S. McLaughlin, *My Eighty Years on Wheels*, as told to Eric Hutton (Maclean's Magazine, Sept. 15th, Oct. 1st, Oct. 15th, 1954), C. L. Burton, *A Sense of Urgency* (Toronto, 1952), Luella Creighton, *High Bright Buggy Wheels* (Toronto, 1951), and many others.

2. The *religion* of the country-side, as contrasted with its denominationalism, is not here discussed. For the most part, under whatever forms it expressed itself, it partook of the semi-pantheism, that regard for the eternal Great Mother, which comes naturally to country people everywhere. Upon this foundation was erected the framework of Christian belief and virtue.

3. See *Weekend Magazine*, Vol. 4, No. 46, 1954. The present writer does not vouch for the details.

4. From an Orillia newspaper of about 1875.

5. Ibid.

6. Toronto *Globe and Mail*, Saturday, May 30th, 1953, in an article by Robert Fulford.

7. These are drawn from the census of 1871.

8. Reapers and mowers, Ontario .21 per farm; Quebec, .04. Horse rakes, Ontario .29; Quebec, .08.

9. And to-day (typically) in the hands of a family living in the United States.

10. But with the introduction of certain new crops the situation is changing. On the good lands of Elgin County there are a number of large farms, whose owners are not only prosperous but wealthy. These men are reported as identifying themselves with the upper *bourgeoisie* of the neighbouring towns and cities.

11. *Globe and Mail*, Nov. 9th, 1956.

12. Toronto, 1953.

13. The statistics show a large immigration between 1871 and 1891, but on looking at the figures for native-born and foreign-born in the two periods, it is impossible to find the immigrants. The returns themselves make it clear that the country in the period grew from itself, that is, mainly from its country-side.

14. See, for example, Ralph Connor, *The Man from Glengarry, Glengarry School Days*, etc., etc.

15. Sandusky? Oak timber used to be brought from such ports for export.

16. Courtesy of Elizabeth Harrison, Kingston, who collected this ballad on Garden Island, Ont.

22: The birth of modern Canada

IN THE PERIOD CENTRING on the turn of the century
—say from about 1890 to 1910—Canada passed through the
earlier stages of adolescence and reached the later. That pre-
war generation was one in which everybody in the country,
from the oldest man to the youngest infant, was growing up.
The essence of provincialism, to refer to Howell's words again,
is having your centre of reference elsewhere. By the outbreak of the First World War, Canadians had made some
progress in transferring their centre of reference to their own
country. They were in about the same position as the youth who,
slowly realizing himself, begins to fear—and hope—that a
dark shade may be coming over his upper lip.

In the attempt to make a picture of this period, the reader's
imagination must see a large map steadily unfolding. Whereas
once upon a time to talk to a Canadian about 'the Red River
of the North' would have been much like talking to him of the
Zambesi, now in this period that straddled the centuries, men
would say "Oh, yes, a neighbour of mine has gone out there
to take up land." To Edward Blake in the eighteen-eighties,
the Pacific coast was as remote as Tibet but by the turn of the
century it had become that part of Canada where winters were
mild and in which somebody in town had just decided to have
a fling at fruit farming. The imaginative leap required is tremendous. The men of the forming generation—the 'Fathers of
Confederation'—had not been able to adjust their eyesight
quickly enough to the new scene that their efforts had brought
into being and the unfortunate results had been the two armed
disturbances of 1870 and 1885. But now, with the turn of the
century, all that was passing away and a vast new Canada was
rising. Provincial minds were being forced to become national,
and in this stretching those who made a move had a natural
advantage over those who stayed at home. From Toronto, only
Toronto was to be seen (with a glimpse of New York), but from
Winnipeg, one could see both Montreal and Vancouver.

The revival of nationalism

It was probably some glint of this new vision which caused a Toronto newspaper to remark early in the eighteen-nineties that "the revival of the national sentiment is again becoming popular."[1] If the eighteen-eighties had seen the idea of the new Dominion sink to a pathetic low, the eighteen-nineties were to see it begin to rise and the nineteen hundreds were to see it grow to fair dimensions. The eighteen-eighties had witnessed the racial-religious struggles centring around Louis Riel and the North West Rebellion (1885), the Honoré Mercier nationalist ministry in Quebec (1886), Mercier's Jesuits' Estates Act (1888) and the consequent movement of Protestant protest which embodied itself in the rebels against Macdonald—that so-called 'Noble Thirteen' who included one of his closest supporters, D'Alton McCarthy. The decade had also witnessed the attempts of the exponents of provincial rights, such as W. S. Fielding of Nova Scotia, seriously to curtail the powers of the central government. All this, plus what seemed like perpetual business depression, had boiled up into the 'Commercial Union' movement of the late eighteen-eighties and its counter-weight, the agitation for 'Imperial Federation'. The two centrifugal forces had battled it out in the election of 1891 in which Macdonald, playing every card of appeal to traditional loyalties ("A British subject. . . .!") was, after hard fighting, returned. Then followed the five years of political doldrums after his death (1891), with four Conservative prime ministers in as many years. The Conservative régime ended with the classic struggle over the Manitoba schools, and the victory of Wilfrid Laurier.

Laurier in his campaign of 1896 had no choice: he had to put his position on the widest possible grounds, for he was appearing as the reconciler, the peacemaker; in his own words, the genial sun that persuades the traveller to take off his coat, not the blustery north wind, which makes him draw it closer to him. Laurier's victory was a victory for compromise and tolerance. Upon these qualities, if upon any, our bicultural state must be built. Their eloquent and clarifying enunciation by Laurier, one of the few men of his time who could see both sides of the racial case, went far to remove the pettiness and division of the preceding decade. He gave all Canadians something they could agree upon—Canada! Of course he was tremendously lucky, for coincident with the beginning of his government, the economic tide turned, and Laurier would have been less than human had he not displayed a certain tendency to identify his own self with the genial sun.

Various as the explanations may be for the turn in the tide, there can be no question of its reality. In the eighteen-eighties such journals of opinion as *The Bystander* and *The Week* had talked Canadian nationalism and had pleaded for national unity. Their readers had been few. In the eighteen-nineties the movement perceptibly broadened. Then in 1893, there was organized, in Hamilton, Ontario, the first Canadian Club. Its objects were discussion of national affairs and promotion of national feeling. Within a short time it had over three hundred members, and similar clubs were being organized in nearby points. This would not have been possible ten years before.

The programme of activities during this first year of the first Canadian Club tells us something of the interests of the times. Papers were presented—"Canadian Patriotism," "The Battle of Stoney Creek," "The National Spirit in Art" and other such subjects. The year rose to two high points, the celebration of Queenston Heights, and a dinner. The spirit in which the Club was launched may be judged by the description given of the banqueting hall:

> At the head of the room . . . were two great Canadian flags,[2] gracefully draped, with the arms of the Dominion. . . . At the opposite end of the room there were also Canadian flags, hanging curtain-wise. On the side walls were fixed shields bearing the arms of the seven provinces of the Dominion. . . . On the wall, half-way down the room, hung a gigantic moose-skin, with the Dominion arms, cunningly carved in wood, resting on it: and opposite to it, against a Union Jack, hung the skin of an immense cinnamon bear. . . . The skins of several Canadian wolves, with the heads intact, hung on the walls. . . ."[3]

The spirit of the Club was purely Canadian, as the titles of the papers indicate. That they drew upon the time-honoured substance of patriotism—the memories of old wars—is nothing to be surprised at in an era when relations between the United States and ourselves were not yet good, and when most adults could remember the overt threats that had come from the south. Moreover in a community such as Canada where the sense of identity has always been weak—if it had not been, it would not have required Canadian Clubs to bolster it—it was legitimate to employ such devices: our neighbours have always done so. The chief reason for weakness in the sense of identity lies in the fact that it has been ground between the upper and the nether millstones of colonialism and localism. A person could give his love to his native town and his devotion to his province and not find that in conflict with his devotion to his Queen, or to that romantic concept 'Britain'. The idea *Canada*, however, was an intrusive: it predicated a new centre of loyalty, and one that it might not always be possible to reconcile with loyalty to the British world beyond our doors.[4] All this Christopher Dunkin had predicted in 1865, in the course of the Confederation debates.

This tension between the two loyalties, the British and the Canadian, has been emphatically reflected in our history: Canadian sentiment has swung back and forth from the one orientation to the other, movements and counter-movements have arisen and high matters of policy have been decided, all on the basis of whether they were strengthening the one allegiance or the other. Thus to the Canadian Club came the riposte of the Empire Club.[5] To the acclaim with which Laurier was received as national leader on his return from the Queen's Diamond Jubilee in 1897[6] the reaction was the intoxication of loyalty to Great Britain with which English Canada responded to the Boer War. After that war came the 'morning after', the bitter disillusions of the Alaska Boundary settlement (1903) when the devil tempted even Torontonians. There is a story to the effect that when one of the late Commissioners, Sir Alan Aylesworth, was to address a meeting on his return to Toronto, it was only with difficulty that he prevailed on the committee to allow the British flag to be exhibited. Then after the Alaska Boundary disappointment came the boom of the West, alternating with the rally to George Foster's sounding of the tocsin in 1908 over the German naval scare, and that in turn with the refusal of naval aid to Great Britain (1910, 1912) and similar refusal to accept economic bounty from the United States (in the defeat of Reciprocity, 1911). This echoing of episode upon episode was capped by the explosion of 1914, which, for Canada, ushered in a new order of things.[7]

Except for one important qualification the two forces, 'imperialism' and nationalism, appear to be in balance during the period. The qualification is important: the very forces that represent tradition are themselves welling up out of the new country. They grow with its growth and they transform themselves in the process from the narrow colonialism of former days to what is called in Canada 'imperialism'. 'Imperialism' in the Canadian sense represents the expansive force of a new, young people expressing itself through the channels of tradition. Of Canadian 'imperialists', the most vociferous were usually Tories in politics, Anglicans in religion and the well-to-do. But they also included the right wing of Liberalism and members of other denominations. The closer one was, by denomination or association, to the traditional ruling class, the more likely he was to be an 'imperialist'. To such people, the word 'imperialism' meant the unity of the English-speaking world under the Crown plus a society with a prominent place for the 'chosen few'—though when the time came, as it did during the Boer War, they had no feeling against taking the attitude towards 'lesser breeds' which is closer to the Marxian conception of 'imperialism'. Canadian 'imperialism' has never been simple: it can at one and the same time be bitterly contemptuous of 'Englishmen' and warmly welcome 'the British connection'. A newspaper in that most 'loyal' of all Canadian cities, Saint John, could write, apropos of a book by an English traveller:— "Canadians might never suspect how coarse, ignorant, conceited and withal, amusing they are if talented Englishmen did not come out occasionally, and write books about them."[8] 'Imperialism' was in its own way a kind of Canadian nationalism.

Canadian nationalists had no desire to part from Great Britain in bad blood, but they did not wish to be committed automatically by 'the parent state' to its decisions and they did not want to see its social system transported artificially to the new world—its titles and other distinctions of rank, its private schools and its state church, all of which have appeared on numerous occasions in these pages. Many an imperialist, especially in this period which saw popular democracy reach its peak in Canada, would have drawn the line at these things too, and it is ironical that when the bestowal of titles in Canada was ended (1917), it was on the initiative of a Conservative member from one of the old Loyalist districts, Mr. W. F. Nickle of Kingston. Beside this determination to end distinctions of rank there might be set the observations of the *Ottawa Free Press* on a similar subject. "Gold lace and swords" had no place in "this democratic country." "It is a subject for congratulation that at the last State dinner, only one deputy minister appeared in uniform. . . . The dress of an ordinary citizen should be quite good enough even for a minister."[9] Monarchy and titles were "flummery." Yet while North American conceptions have strongly marked both camps, their feelings for the traditional and for the new creation respectively have given them material for combat in almost every year of Canadian history, and the end is not yet.[10]

A schooling in imperialism

The wonder is that the tender plant of Canadian nationalism survived at all, for all little Canadian boys and girls have been subjected from the day on which they start to school to an unending steeping in the liquid of 'imperialism' and from the day they can read to an equally unending cultural (or anti-cultural) bombardment from the south. Some excerpts from the life of the Canadian schoolboy in the period, when the two forces in our existence were so constantly in conflict, may illustrate the point.

In the year 1897 youthful minds were dazzled by a grand and spectacular event, the Diamond Jubilee of good Queen Victoria. In one not untypical little town, the approaching apocalypse filled the school days. In church, sermons were preached; even Methodist congregations went to the length of introducing into their services that bit of state church secularism *God Save the Queen*. The streets began to fill with arches, full of loyal mottoes. On the day itself, processions formed, bands played, and the spirits of all children rose. In one little boy's case, a relative arrived from 'the city' and presented to him a 'medal' (probably bought in Eaton's and of American manufacture) with the Queen's head on one side and the British flag on the other. A great float had been built out on the water in front of the town and at night the little row-boats which were so integral a part of that age drifted about it, illuminated with Chinese lanterns. At a given signal, the float burst into flames, which shot to heaven. A band struck up a patriotic air, and a display of fireworks rose from the nearby wharves. To small boys, Queen Victoria, *Rule, Britannia* and Heaven's command seemed all one.

Not long after, the Americans began to fight the Spaniards. American songs drifted up over the border. One of them had a sentimental refrain to the effect that two soldiers, one of whom was thinking of his sweetheart so young and gay and the other of his mother so old and gray, were "dying to-night for the Stars and Stripes—just as the sun went down!" The same small boy heard the song echoing out over the waters of the bay shore on which his family was that summer taking its holiday in the fashion of the day, 'camping'. But the young people who sang it had turned the Yankees' flank: when they sang it, they made the young soldiers "die tonight for the Union Jack—just as the sun went down!" That there were no young Canadians dying for the Union Jack at the moment did not bother them.

Next year, there were, for the Boer War broke out. But Canadians, unimaginative and dumb, have never made their own songs: instead, this time they shouted out a popular English doggerel ballad of the period—"Soldiers of the Queen!"

"It's the soldiers of the Queen, my lads, who's been, my
lads, who've seen, my lads,
In the fight for England's glory, lads, when we have to show
them what we mean,
And when we say we've always won, and when they ask
us how it's done,
We'll proudly point to every one of England's soldiers of
the Queen."

Many an English Canadian at that juncture ached to become
a 'soldier of the Queen' and some had their opportunity. War
in South Africa! Local boys volunteering! Long months of
disappointing half-tragic news! The impossible had happened,
British soldiers had been defeated! And to crown it all, the
very heavens intervened. Going 'down street' one morning
the small boy encountered one of those printed bulletins of
the times which gave the news of the day in headline; on it
in great black type were the staring words: "THE QUEEN IS
DEAD!" Nothing more could happen after this: this was the
end of the world.[11]

Again a snapshot, printed vividly on a small boy's mind.
More arches across the streets. More parades, more military
bands. And high amidst it all, four men in khaki, the town's
contribution to the war, less one (who never came back). In
the midst of civic and clerical dignities, they stood stiffly to
attention as the cheers went up. Speeches were delivered and
presentations made. Traditional military music and the traditional uniform everywhere! It is with something of anti-climax
that the next incident comes: September 14th, 1901. On the
shooting of President McKinley in the neighbouring city of
Buffalo, the local school board in a gesture of sympathy, decides
that school children, anxious to share their neighbours' grief,
can hardly be expected to continue with their studies: a day of
mourning is proclaimed, a glorious September day. One party
of schoolboys (there may have been others!) mourned in high
spirits by resorting to the neighbouring bush and gathering
beech-nuts!

When schoolboys of that day got home and sat down with
a book, as some of them were known to do (and their own
copies, too), they probably opened up *Under Drake's Flag*, or
one of the other innumerable excerpts from English history
written by G. A. Henty. Spanish galleons sailed into view,
'pieces of eight', and tough, indomitable English sea dogs! What
if these heroes did burn Spanish towns and plunder Spanish
ships? How could that be wrong, seeing they were English?
And were they not merely avenging the fires which Spaniards,

working through Bloody Mary, had kindled in Smithfield? Henty, Collingwood, W. H. G. Kingston (*True Blue* and more British naval glories) steeped that generation of reading boys in history, mainly English history, and put the love of the sea (aboard a British man-of-war) into the veins of many a lad who had never seen anything more than an inland lake.

If boys missed such writers at home—and girls the second-hand introduction into the world of 'finishing schools' and the domestic life of the English gentry which was the feminine counterpart of it—they got the same sort of thing at school, through their school 'readers':—

> Ho! breakers on the weather bow
> And hissing white the sea
> About the good ship goes, and leaves
> Old England on the lea!
>
> Oh, for a soft and gentle breeze
> I heard a fair one cry,
> But give to me the soaring wind
> And white waves heaving high.
>
> And white waves heaving high my boy
> The good ship tight and free
> The world of waters is our home
> And merry men are we!

The country school-marms who could translate those words into the language of landlubbers must have been few, but the ideas got across all the same. They came in a dozen different paths:—

> The sea, the sea, the open sea,
> The bright, the blue, the ever-free
> Without a mark, without a bound
> It runs the earth's wide regions round.
>
> I never was on the dull, tame shore
> But I loved the great sea more and more. . . .

Or most direct of all:—

> Ye Mariners of England
> That guard our native seas. . . .
> The meteor flag of England
> Shall yet terrific burn. . . .

At the turn of the century the Canadian public school was not making young Canadians but young Englishmen. It is not surprising that fourteen years later, those boys rushed off across the seas to fight for a country they had never seen—to fight as perhaps men never fought before. It was an unlooked-for turn in the road which eventually brought much of this energy and this emotion into identification not with 'the parent state', but with the home community. But that is a subject for another chapter. Here it is the preliminaries to the turn that are to be glanced at.

A nascent culture

Some years after our little Ontario boy, with throbbing pulse, had watched soldiers coming home from war in South Africa, he was writing a high-school essay which was in itself indicative of the new current in that it was on Canada and its future. Schoolboy fashion, the essay advanced second-hand opinions (mostly 'cribbed' from English quarterlies) on Canada's advances in self-government and on the immense pace at which the West was being settled. The wind was pointing in a different direction now!

A digression is in order here, to enable us to look at the familiar things in the life surrounding that schoolboy of the nineteen hundreds.

In a little town of those days, anywhere in Canada, any school-master encountering any pupil who had found any quarterly would have had cause for rejoicing, for quarterlies and their contents were not the daily fare of small townsmen: they usually predicated a public library and these existed in Ontario alone.[12] The secondary town had nevertheless passed well beyond the stage of being without culture of any sort (as had been the situation in the pioneer phase). Good vocal music of a semi-classical, semi-popular nature was common, its agency being the church choir. On occasion, visiting artists amplified its range. "The Holy City" rolled out by a city tenor like Harold Jarvis could captivate its audience. A clergyman (admittedly of wider horizons than most) could organize a series of winter concerts of high order, acting, as he said, on the principle that "The church provides the best." Never more fully than in this period, the early twentieth century, had the church played its historic role of 'mother of the arts'.

Another aspect of the same situation lies in the development of the theatre outside the cities. "The church provides the best" was a calculated offset to the 'show-play', which continued to be unsparingly denounced from many a Methodist or Baptist pulpit. Other denominations were not so rigid, and coincident with the most zealous church-going era in Canadian history (from about 1880 to 1910), there grew up the local 'opera-house', which provided entertainment upon the stage varying all the way from fairly good to horrible. One of these 'opera-houses' whose entire life story is well known to the writer, may stand as a case history. This theatre, which was aesthetically pleasing in its internal decoration and fully equipped techni-cally, was built about 1897. It was far too ambitious for its community, but the way in which it got built was so vivid a combination of the uneven threads in Canadian life that it will bear repeating. At that time, the last remains of a local family compact still were discernible in the town and county of this incident; as a consequence, a man 'of good family' was county treasurer, apparently a public-spirited citizen and a prominent member of the right, or semi-official, church. Partly as business enterprise, partly as a gesture of regard towards his fellow citizens, he began to build an 'opera-house'. Some of the con-struction material came from the old Salvation Army barracks across the way. Pious people shook their heads and said no good could come of pulling down the Lord's house and putting the materials into a den of iniquity. The local Anglicans, whose church was next to the barracks, were reported as believing that it was a good use for any Salvation Army barracks, espe-cially one that made such evangelical din under their very noses.

The theatre was finished, an extraordinary building for so small at town to have, and opened with a week of Shakespeare —a week of Shakespeare in a town of five thousand! Coinci-dent with the opening it was discovered that the county treas-urer was short in his accounts by the sum which the theatre had cost. But when they came to look for him, he was not to be found, and he never has been found. Meanwhile, the county had the theatre, which it operated through a lessee for many years, until it degenerated into a 'movie', had the inevit-able fire and was reopened as a filling station! The present town, four times as large, has no theatre, no public auditorium and probably could not stand one night of Shakespeare, let alone a week.

The place referred to was not exceptional for the period from about 1890 to 1910 and for the more prosperous parts of the country. Young people before they 'went away' (and of course they nearly all 'went away'), if they desired, could have explored small libraries, listened to a considerable variety of the simpler forms of vocal music, taken part in amateur productions of the Gilbert and Sullivan operas and attended a wide variety of plays (given, naturally, by the second com-panies rather than the first), ranging down from Shakespeare —Robert Mantell, a reputable if 'provincial' actor, used to make an annual tour—through current comedies and melodramas to 'The Marks Brothers," "The Guy Brothers Minstrels," and *Uncle Tom's Cabin* complete with bloodhounds. This is not to say that an original culture was growing up (at one remove from the grass roots) but that a provincial version of the general culture of the English-speaking world was available to those who wished it. Since its expression was mostly through the direct spoken word and human voice, it was superior to the machine-made substitutes that have destroyed it. It may be that history will show the present vain and fearful generation that autos, 'movies' and television have not moved it farther ahead but farther behind.

The formal schooling of the early century was both better and worse than that of mid-century. Country schools were the same then as now or as at any time during the last century. Grade schools in towns have improved in physical equipment, but the quality of the teachers is not much different: all over Canada, we have plenty of twentieth-century schools filled with nineteenth-century teachers. In secondary education, the collegiate institute of the nineteen hundreds, which catered only for fairly bright children, gave to those who wanted it a good education, with enough elements of culture about it to make it more or less complete in itself without the necessity of going on to university.[13] The high-school teacher of the eighteen-seventies and eighties, though seldom an original scholar, had often been an old-fashioned 'learned man': his successor in the nineteen hundreds was apt to be merely a university graduate with a rather poor degree. This was the period in which the change was occurring, so that schools of that era shared two educational experiences; the older, which, at its best, was solid and cultural; the newer, whose exponents were not seldom people with poorer backgrounds and smaller gifts.

The reflections in the schools of the attitudes of the day cast a certain ray of light over the period. One of the author's classical masters used to bring armfuls of books into his classes and encourage his students to take them home. One pupil thanks him "in his place of blissful rest," wherever that may be, for thus introducing him to Herodotus and some of the treasures of Greak art. But when he passed his pictures round the class, with their undraped male figures, the girls began to giggle. This master disappeared after a few months' teaching. So, shortly afterward, did the classics.

But, if the moral tone of the day seems overstrict now, let it be remembered that these were the days—and just about the last days, say around 1905—when ladies still were ladies: it had been only a few years before when an irate father had come home from an evangelistic service, and cast his eyes on a device which, the revivalist had assured his hearers, would lead their daughters straight to the devil, a device with two narrow wheels and a seat whose significance (to the revivalist) Sigmund Freud would have had no trouble explaining; to wit, a bicycle. The father, to save his daughter from her shame, had taken an axe and smashed up the infernal machine.[14]

All this is parenthetical. To return to our schoolboy's essay on 'Canada's Future'. Here, somewhere between 1902 and 1910, the country swung from youthful enthusiasm for the father's cause to concern for and pride in its own growth: it had passed the most trying period of adolescence and was finding the signs of manhood coming over it. There is little doubt as to the factor which accelerated and emphasized the change: it was that one to be described in the next chapter, the opening of the West.

Notes to Chapter 22

1. Toronto *Globe*, March, 1893, quoted in Nina L. Edwards, *The Story of the First Canadian Club*, 1893-1953 (Hamilton, 1953).
2. Presumably the red ensign with Canadian coat of arms.
3. Edwards, op. cit. This interesting little pamphlet contains a number of other items useful for the eighteen-nineties and the revival of national feeling. It constitutes a tribute to two men who have otherwise received little recognition—Sandford Evans and Dr. C. R. McCullough. And for those who like another method of approach to social history, the mass picture of the membership gives statistical confirmation of the exit of the beard for, of some 320 individuals, only some 45 wore beards. Moustaches, of course, were still numerous.
4. All the more noteworthy, then, is the appearance among later presidents of the Hamilton club of certain men who have never made any secret of putting their loyalty to 'Britain' ahead of their loyalty to Canada.
5. See *Empire Club Addresses* (Toronto, 1904-1905): "Imperialism in Canada" by William Wilfrid Campbell; "The Defense of the Empire" by Sam Hughes, M.P.; "Canadians in the Imperial Military Service" by Lieut.-Gen. Benson; and "Canada's Position in the Empire" by W. F. Cockshutt, M.P.
6. The Jubilee, of course, greatly stimulated imperial patriotism. See, for example, J. van Sommer, *Canada and the Empire* (Toronto, n.d. *c.* 1898), a tract of evangelical fervour on the subject.
7. These ideas are developed a little more fully in the present writer's *Canada, Nation and Neighbour* (Toronto, 1953) which was specifically intended as an examination of the growth of Canadian nationalism.
8. *Saint John Telegraph* referring to J. F. Fraser, *Canada as It Is*, and quoted in S. E. Moffett, *The Americanization of Canada* (New York, 1907), p. 18.
9. Ibid., p. 52; *Ottawa Free Press*, Nov. 24th, 1905.
10. In the Suez crisis of 1956 the old distinction between the two camps came out at once.

11. For a most interesting recreation of that bleak January day in 1901 see R. O. Earl, "The End of the World", *Queen's Quarterly*, Summer, 1955.
12. Is this not still the case, with a few exceptions?
13. The present writer would like to pay tribute here to his own Collegiate in Barrie, Ont. and the education it gave him, and especially to a man who greatly influenced him and who set before him the aim of excellence and the grace of our English tongue, its headmaster, T. H. Redditt. He had the support of others of the same type; they have not had many successors.
14. W. J. Healy, "Bicycles were Immoral" in the *Winnipeg Free Press*.

23: The transcontinental country

WITHOUT 'THE WEST' Canada would have continued to be 'a minor show'. Some kind of maturity would have been reached, but it would have been only provincial, such as parts of eastern Ontario and Nova Scotia had already attained. There is an ocean of difference between the relatively mature localism of a secondary urban community and the air that blows through the national capital, Ottawa. This air begins to blow at Montreal, where the meeting of the two cultures makes for unwilling breadth. It strengthens in Ottawa, whose major reason for existence is the duty of seeing in all directions. A current from it runs down to Toronto and the western peninsula of Ontario (only two or three chapters ago, this was 'western Canada'), both of which are rescued from parochialism by the scope of their economic activities. But it is at the head of the lakes that the air begins to blow strong, for with Port Arthur the traveller is in another world, the West. From lakehead to Pacific coast, the same air blows.

The same kind of observation could be made as one goes northward, for here too there is another world. The atmosphere is similar to that of the West. It has the geographical emancipation, the hope, energy, lack of convention, readiness to accept all comers and on equal terms, that mark new societies wherein, the old moulds having been broken, the pieces are set loose and shaken up into new patterns.

The country beyond the lakes

Western society takes its shape, and partly its tone, from its natural circumstances. The habitable country-side runs from Beauséjour, east of Winnipeg, to Banff, a thousand miles. Over this, settlement, once vigorously begun, swept like a prairie fire. In 1873, Archbishop Taché of St. Boniface could write: "If one compares the immensity of [these prairies] with the scantiness of the area which some of the most powerful nations on the globe occupy, . . . one naturally asks if these vast solitudes are always to remain in the state in which providence has kept them down to our day. . . ."[1] At the end of the decade, 1880, the West still had only a handful of people. Twenty years later, the fire had just begun to spread, and thirty years after that again (1930), it had stopped, because it had burned itself out through the occupation of most of the good land. There was an 'old West' around Winnipeg, and another around Victoria, but these little spots of earlier settlement were submerged in the vast tide of the early twentieth century, so that for practical purposes, the West and its mentality are the product of scarcely more than a generation. This in itself gives a certain similarity of outlook, but a larger prop has been the geographic and economic unity of the prairies, with every farmer a wheat farmer and every town a wheat town.[2] Wheat has been to western Canada what fur was to New France.

The stature of the Dominion as a whole, with this new territory and this new staple added to its life, vastly increased. It has continued to grow because of the successive unfolding of other great staple commodities that have vastly increased the complexity of Canadian economic life and the numbers of the Canadian people.

Societies founded upon staple trades all have common characteristics: since these have been discussed in the author's previous book *Colony to Nation*,[3] they may be dismissed briefly. The major socio-psychological effect of a new staple, that is of a commodity whose supply and market alike seem unlimited, is to promote the gambling spirit. Gold is a staple commodity and a gold rush is more or less typical of the spirit that prevails in any staple-trade community. Poor to-day, rich to-morrow! Work like fury extracting the new wealth, then retire to luxurious ease! Or, as often occurred in the Southern cotton society, build a pretentious establishment and, surrounded with servants, horses and dogs, live 'like a gentleman'! A preponderance of males, with all the male traits cast into high relief, and just enough women to make the whole thing piquant or beastly, according to taste. "The lady that's known as Lu" has always had a place in any new society, whether a gold camp, the bush or the prairie. Readers will remember that Frederick Philip Grove makes one of his novels, *Settlers in the Marsh*, turn on the big Swede homesteader who got into the net and ended by marrying one of these. On the edge of every construction job, around every mining camp, in every pioneer town, east or west, conspicuous to the interested eye, though seldom referred to in polite literature, there has appeared the 'fancy lady'.

If the staple is large enough, these days pass, other women come in, families form and the beginnings of a community become discernible. For this line of evolution wheat afforded an adequate basis, with the result that the prairie West got over its youthful measles relatively soon, and a stable society reflecting the East emerged. The mountains and the coast, with their logging and fishing, which segregated the male for long periods, were slower. In the eighteen-nineties Winnipeg, according to old hands, was well supplied with frontier characteristics: its bars were numerous, long and rowdy. The men who frequented them were noisily gay with all the vulgarity familiar to anyone who knows the frontier at first hand. They were nearly all harmless enough—no six-shooters—but they wanted excitement: it was a matter of high jinks in low dives. By the turn of the century Winnipeg was losing the more lurid of these traits. Not that anyone will be innocent enough to believe that merely getting older makes a place more virtuous: rather, a certain cycle seems discernible—first of all, the irresponsibilities which all males exhibit when adrift from the order imposed by kinship and association, then, in conscious contrast, middle-class respectability, and lastly, varying degrees of metropolitan sophistication, with sin slipping into its silken stage at the top and retaining its ugliness at the bottom. Canada's major cities are edging into the third of these phases: one of them, Vancouver, seems an interesting combination of the three of them all at once—and that because it is a modern metropolis on the edge of the bush.

The 'get-rich-quick' mentality of the wheat economy is exemplified in the so-called 'bonanza farm' (also interestingly described by Grove in *An Immigrant's Search for America*). The 'bonanza farm'⁴ was just a gold mine: a huge area, acquired cheaply, worked by large-scale mechanical methods, with all labour 'hired hands' and the proprietor, who was without the slightest feeling for the soil, associating himself with the capitalist class. As the old opportunities for building these huge farms have gone, other holdings have been thrown together and differentiations among western agriculturalists have rapidly emerged (that is, in the course of half a century), with large men at the top, smaller men making up a large middle, and a relative small group of small men, mostly 'New Canadians', on the bottom. Western Canada has thus repeated the experience of Ontario, but at a more rapid pace.

The men who made the West

A new frontier invariably casts up the bizarre and the picturesque in more than average numbers. Some men of this type are merely slightly off-centre, others have a natural flamboyance which prompts them to do what Bill Smith from Nova Scotia did when he got out to the Pacific Coast and blossomed out as the universal democrat, the 'lover of the world', *Amor de Cosmos*. Or release from the inhibitions of 'the folks back home' may bring forth a Bob Edwards, with his *Calgary Eye-Opener*, the very incarnation of the male's frontier. Canadians, not being exhibitionists, have not produced a large crop of such characters: their frontiers have carried relatively subdued colours (though they have been present, even to the 'bad men') and the 'sterling fellow' has been more characteristic of them than the 'cut-up'.[5]

How could it be otherwise when the sedate East was streaming out west in a vast migration that carried all its values along with it?[6] By 1890 Manitoba already had many of the aspects of the Ontario country-side and a narrow wedge of settlement from the East, complete with school-house, church and country store, had forced its way right through to the mountains. Think of the kind of people who made the transfer: sons of substantial farmers looking for land, not fun, small townsmen with respectability in their souls, young doctors, lawyers and clergymen going out west to 'grow up with the country'. Not much material for unruliness in such men as these. A Sunday in Moosomin soon became as sedate as a Sunday in Galt!

Individuals of every type stand out from a crowd—which also they typify! In the early 'eighties a young Presbyterian minister arrived in Winnipeg from Ontario. He was given a horse and a buckboard, and told to drive out to his charge, which was—in Edmonton! The drive took him seven weeks! The young clergyman remained in the West for the rest of his life, helping to build its churches and its colleges. He, Rev. Dr. Baird, was typical of many.

Another 'builder of the West' was a man already mentioned in these pages, Sandford Evans of Hamilton. Evans carried his Canadian nationalism with him to Winnipeg, where until his death in the early nineteen-fifties, he continued quietly to express his point of view, which, the necessary transposition made, was that of his favourite quotation:

". . . How shouldst thou prove aught else but dear and holy
To me, who from thy lakes and mountain-hills,
Thy clouds, thy quiet dales, thy rocks and seas,
Have drunk in all my intellectual life,
All sweet sensations, all ennobling thoughts,
All adoration of the God in nature,
All lovely and all honourable things. . . ."[7]

An immigrant of another type was young George Belton, who came out in 1890 "a strapping and well-strapped lad of fifteen", as he himself says, when he arrived at Moose Jaw and got his first job gathering buffalo bones. That winter, "I sawed wood with a bucksaw, at the back door of a residence in Moose Jaw. I did not see anything humiliating about it, either. . . . I chummed with a lad of my own age whose job was to clean the dining-car at the C.P.R. terminal, and with the son of a well-paid government official; the former is now [about 1940] a big railroad executive . . . and the last I heard of the latter, he was in jail. . . ." Here are all the characteristic attitudes displayed by the English-speaking pioneer of evangelical Protestant background: any honest toil is as honourable as any other; complete equalitarianism; belief in the inevitability of sin in high places; entire confidence in the future. To them add the ease with which the lads of the eastern farms adapted themselves, making the same contrast with immigrants from overseas as had the Loyalists in the eastern forests. As Belton puts it: "Hardship of the pioneers? Bunk! The finest sleep I ever had was slept between a haystack and a henhouse, in the open. . . . Hardships of the pioneers? Tell that to the marines, these were the best days of our lives. We ate like horses, had good food in plenty, wore rough, warm clothing and suffered less from cold in the sod houses than many do now in apartment blocks. . . ."[8]

Another of the pioneers was John Wright Sifton, born on a farm near London, Ontario, an ardent Methodist and Prohibitionist, a stern Protestant crusader in the footsteps of George Brown. He came to Manitoba in 1874. While he could meet the world sufficiently on its own terms to secure, as a good Liberal, a succulent railway contract from the Liberal government of Alexander Mackenzie, the kind of new society that he was likely to envisage would hardly have appreciated that of Bob Edwards.

Sifton's sons succeeded him and were greater than he, one of them being Sir Clifford and the other, almost equally well-known, Arthur. Clifford in his lifetime was often accused of possessing that ambivalent scale of values which has frequently been noted as marking the career of the successful Methodist. At any rate, he became a rich man and ended by breeding horses and 'riding to hounds', at which point he surely ceased to be a Methodist. His sons were brought up in his image and presumably their sons also—and grandsons, for so far does this family now extend. Apart from the West the Siftons are worth studying as a Canadian family: they have not run down as have so many others, and their successive generations are typical. The first Sifton in Canada was a small North Ireland farmer, with all the papist-hunting zeal, one gathers, that marks the type. His sons carved farms out of the Upper Canadian wilderness. It was his grandson, John Wright Sifton, who migrated to Manitoba. His sons, in contrast with their forebears, had formal education at the Methodist university of eastern Canada, Victoria. They became lawyers and rose to the later amplitudes of their political careers.[9] When Sir Clifford left public life (1905), he devoted himself to his private interests, of which one of the chief was the *Manitoba Free Press*. On his death this property passed to one of his sons, and it is still in the family.

The interesting thing about the Sifton family is its attainment in a generation or two of the uppermost rung which ability, wealth and good luck can reach in Canada, and the relatively humble height of that elevation. 'Riding to hounds', which few fellow-Canadians, especially Westerners, could be induced to look at as other than a bit of silly 'play-acting', seems to be as far up the scale as a Canadian family is likely to get.[10] No peerages for the Siftons, after the manner of English press lords! Apart from wealth and local reputation the members of such a family to-day, a century and a half after their evolution began, are in just about the same position and have just the same status as other Canadians of similar capacities. So much at least has the spirit of democracy done for us: it has not prevented men segregating themselves according to their abilities, and enjoying the resulting status, whatever it may be, which is impossible, but it has required that every generation take that test afresh. It has had little interest in a man's family background, much in the man himself. And it has set its face against the creation of a distinct way of life (as, for instance, through the type of school attended) by which those who have 'arrived' can fence themselves off from those who have not.[11]

The name of Clifford Sifton at once recalls that of another Ontario man whose place in building the West was just as large as his—John W. Dafoe, the editor of Sifton's *Free Press*. Dafoe was an eastern Ontario man of Dutch Loyalist ancestry, and like Sifton, of Methodist background. His parentage was humble and at an early age he began to look after himself: in fact, at the incredible age of thirteen, he was 'teaching' in a backwoods school. Dafoe first went west in the eighteen-eighties, then returned at the beginning of the present century as editor of the *Free Press*, a position he retained until his death. As the voice of the grain farmer and grain trade and then later of the West generally, and especially of the old Victorian individualism which saw itself threatened by a rising collectivism, Dafoe made himself a national reputation. As he became more and more widely known, especially from the end of the First World War, this broadened into international proportions, and he grew to be in some measure the voice of Canada, for his westernism easily changed inta nationalism. His position at its widest might be defined as free trade, complete Canadian autonomy, though no cutting of the British tie, and unreserved acceptance of the international order as represented by the League of Nations, in the conviction that only through an international authority could a secondary power like Canada survive, as could the Commonwealth. In these matters men like Dafoe explain the West.

The Sifton-Dafoe group constituted a powerful influence in western Canada, and through it, in all Canada. Its power lay in its quality as representative of the new society, and therefore of the new spirit of Canadian nationalism, which in the West found itself impressively stimulated by the optimism of a new country and the very magnitude of the task in hand. Its success was founded on its attraction of men beyond the ordinary place or power seeker. This in turn rested on the intellectual appeal of its leaders and their quantum of political idealism, both national and international. Hence the innumerable cabinet ministers, judges, civil servants and academics who have been associated with it. Yet few of the men at the centre of the group were fine-fibred: they were well-armoured enough to fight the battle of life as they found it without much squeamishness. They were, as they would have themselves maintained, 'practical men' and their interests lay mainly in what might be called the architectural aspects of society— the broad lines of its material fabric (as, for example, land settlement, railways, freight rates, the tariff). Their objectives, it would seem, did include some kind of social utopia, but it is to be suspected it was one where strong men got what they wanted and where the desirable society consisted wholly of strong men. They attained great power, and some of them wealth, but they never formed a 'family compact'. It was too late in the day for that; there was no Government House to draw them together, no semi-state church to rally around. Responsible Government, moreover, has made the perpetuation of cliques difficult. Again, the West represented the ascendancy of the middle class and of 'non-conformity'.

Of men of another kind, two examples come to mind at once. One was John S. Ewart, fighting for his own conception of a just society, and the other was J. S. Woodsworth, who could never have been contented until he had reached the impossible ideal of establishing the kingdom of God on earth. The present author has written of both these men elsewhere,[12] so little need be said of them here. Ewart's formative days in the West were in the eighteen-nineties, during which period he acted as counsel on behalf of the French Canadians who were fighting for their school rights. As a young Ontario Presbyterian, he had been a follower of George Brown. But Brown's narrow influence did not survive immersion in the West. Although the French lost their legal fight, the spectacle of one man, at a formative stage in the community's growth, attempting to stem the currents of intolerant racialism and standing up, at the cost of popularity, for what he thought was right, is one that furnishes to the portion of posterity which can discern such things, an inspiring example.

Woodsworth's main work lies beyond the bounds of this chapter. Before the First World War, he was known as one of the Methodist Church's young intellectuals, the son of a missionary to the settlers and himself a missionary to the social rags and tags gathered about him in what was appropriately named 'All People's Mission'. It was just at the end of the present period that he found himself beyond the limits of conventional Christianity and preparing to take the leap that later was to make him one of the great figures of Canadian life. The foundations of the man were, however, already visible to those who knew him—his fire of purpose and his complete integrity. Here, as with Ewart in his hard-headed lawyer's way, was a consecrated man. The influence of such men in shaping western Canada went far.

The new western society

Western Canada differs in no respect more fundamentally from eastern in that it was a new *Canadian* society. Eastern Canada's roots lay in the old colonies and in the British Isles; but the formative element in the settlement of the West, being from eastern Canada, had already co-ordinated these heritages into a pattern of its own, and it was this pattern in which the

West grew up. On the debit side, this included the racial differences that had always cursed the country, and on the credit, the absence of the old colonial stuffiness, both secular and denominational, which had applied so many brakes to the wheels of democratic self-government in the East. The traditions of Church and King had been carried to the West, it is true, by the Hudson's Bay Company and the Anglican clergy whom it supported, but for the most part these were not strong. Vestigial 'family compacts' are to be traced in both Winnipeg and Victoria; that in Winnipeg was for a time a little more than vestigial, and its deposits of place and influence were still strong enough in the nineteen-thirties to do scandalous damage to the University of Manitoba. With such exceptions, the West was a blank sheet on which the Canadian people could draw their own portrait. The artists who were to drew it exhibited manifold traits, among which the influences of an old-world society were weak: western Canada was built in the image of the plain man.

This book unfortunately cannot deal in detail with the French Catholic contribution to the building of the West. A good deal was said about it in *Colony to Nation* and there is no space here for repetition. French Catholicism is to be put into the category of pathfinder: its people explored the West, set up the buffalo hunt, built the first college (St. Boniface) and fought the first fight for provincial status and provincial rights. French-speaking Canadians, being few, have not been able to play a pronouncedly positive role in an English-speaking society, but by sticking up for their rights, they have reminded the English that there are other societies than the merely commercial. They have thus constituted a leaven for the West. Canada owes much to a man once execrated, Louis Riel. French-speaking Canadians in the West have displayed all the virtues of a stubborn minority. Long may they continue to do so!

The conceptions held of the West were as varied as the human beings who went there. It was a rich prize to be ravished and the ravishers were many and zealous. It was also an idea, a country to be built, and the builders were numerous and many of them devoted. That is what distinguishes the rise of the prairie West from that of Upper Canada and British Columbia. In both these territories there had been just as many natural prizes to be carried off as in the prairies but in neither is it easy to find so many men of vision and devotion as it was the good luck of the prairies to possess. It is true that Upper Canada eventually obtained its men of devotion such as Ryerson, Mackenzie in his peculiar way, Baldwin, and, for more mundane matters, William Hamilton Merritt, but only after a long painful struggle were they able to guide their province's destinies.

Since the vast empty land beyond the lakes challenged men to begin over again, and since it provided a hard environment, the three prairie provinces from the beginning have been marked by a drive towards efficient collective action. Hence the efforts to get correct surveys and easily obtainable and ascertainable titles to land. Hence the generous town planning of such cities as Saskatoon. The common school was carried westward with the pioneer, but the symmetrical educational pyramid, extending up to the university, was a western conception. The University of Manitoba was begun in 1877, not to teach but to grant degrees, and it was to have a monopoly within the province of the degree-granting powers. This, for better or worse, it still possesses, and the other provinces have followed its example.

The public power, used in one direction for social advance, could be used in another, and its use was always necessary, for the land was wide and the people were few. It was therefore natural that a second stage should comprise some control over the means of production, with such objectives as the prairie attempts to break the tariff privileges of the East and those of the urban grain merchants. The present socialistic governments of Saskatchewan and Alberta are logical evolutions from the original conceptions of social efficiency that a new start called out: the idea of 'co-operative commonwealth' (and indeed the words) long preceded the organization of the party which formally adopted the name, and this idea, growing out of the local circumstances, was far wider than mere party concepts. This is the foundation, this conception of a new, efficient and prosperous society, with all the middle-class virtues, from which, in party as in other matters, the experimentalism of the West springs. In this conception men tracing their antecedents back to the evangelical denominations of the East were to play a leading part.[13] On the prairies Ontario's sturdy yeoman was born anew.

Naturally, the old Adam would out, and the West was to have its share of public scandals. In new communities, with a great deal of natural wealth lying about waiting to be seized, human nature's defences against dishonesty, never robust in the best of societies, break down, and the strong and advantageously placed rush in and get what they can—that is the record of every society known to man, and to it the West was no exception: public honesty in new countries seems to begin when there is nothing much left to steal. The wonder is that there were not more scandals and more rape of the public domain, and the still greater wonder is that this early plundering attitude did not entail a grievous heritage to the future. For the public interest has been served as well and as honestly in the West as we have reason to expect. The citizenry of the West at its most stalwart, which was perhaps the period from about 1910 to 1930, had more cohesive qualities, more sense of the public interest, more anxiety as individuals to take part in serving that interest, than other parts of Canada.

British Columbia was not so fortunate. Its rich natural heritage was tucked out of sight and more difficult to exploit. There two factors opened the way to big enterprises, in contrast to the ordinary man's attack on the land which marked the prairies. The old Crown Colony tradition which lingered on in Victoria for a number of years continued an atmosphere of easy-going privilege. There was also the character of the people. The prairies were made by the hard-working evangelical Protestants of the East, chiefly Ontario, led, as the pages above have indicated, by well-endowed and public-spirited men. While British Columbia drew many people of this class, it also drew a large component of its people direct from England, and while the basic qualities of these new-comers were not very different from those of the prairie people, their experience of the new world was less, and what is more, they established mainly an urban society. To all this add a more or less relaxing climate and the isolation of the mountain valley. The results manifested themselves in a less certain aim, a less homogeneous society, and one not so much impressed with the dreadful fact that it must work, for the night would be coming when man would work no more!

While British Columbia's coastal strip is not another California and its people do not share all of the pagan life which marks southern skies, they have leaned rather farther towards it than have the hard-bitten people who must face the winters of the interior. Nor has there been the same ancestral puritanism among them: there is a world of difference between a gentle Anglican from southern England and some stern Biblical Scot or Irishman, even unto the third and fourth generation. It is not surprising that this magnificent but rather easy-going province should for years have led the country in the high state of its public health, the low number of its births, in the handsomeness of its people's incomes and the frequency with which they divorced each other, but not in leaders of large calibre; and that it should have found for itself no prophets at all.

With the above brief words, the vast sweep of the original Dominion out to the Pacific Coast and the islands of the Pacific Coast must be dismissed. The treatment is inadequate, but for adequacy volumes would be required.[14] Within a generation, the original Dominion, its people undergoing every species of internal division, suffering under chronic economic depression, subject to frequent menacing gestures from its great neighbour and regarded mainly as a nuisance by the mother country, had managed to make its claim good to the entire continent north of forty-nine (except Alaska), and to send out several hundred thousands of its citizens to possess the land. These men carried with them the institutions they knew, and which they had already forged for themselves: their free churches (perhaps the most important of all), their public-school systems, their municipal government, their assemblies, their banks, their insurance companies, their yeoman farms. They carried, too, their attitudes—their instinctive feeling for equality, their man-to-man hospitality and kindliness, their individualism, their yearning for progress and their crude definitions of it. On the other side of the ledger, they took with them their sense of racial superiority, so easily turned into arrogance, their narrow materialistic conceptions, their insularity, their suspicion of 'smart people' who moved in other worlds. They carried with them both their traditional attachment to the Crown and a love of the new land they were building which has made western Canada the principal source of modern Canadian nationalism. They took with them eastern distrust of the big neighbour along with the utmost readiness to fraternize with its citizens. Their reflex action on the East was almost as important as their own achievements in the West.

For the West expanded minds: it made Canadians think of themselves as belonging to a vastly larger world than the original provinces had provided. It made Ottawa a crossroads for everybody from North Sydney to the Queen Charlotte Islands. It added several more 'Queen Cities of the West', gave the easterner scope and hope and brought once more into the country that breath of life which blows over the most magnificent of man's jobs, wherever he has had the good luck to be able to carry it out—the building of a new society.

Notes to Chapter 23

1. Quoted in E. Tassé, *Le Nord-Ouest* (Ottawa, 1880).
2. The modern alternatives, which are perhaps to diversify the West's economy a little, had not arisen in the period of this chapter, roughly, down to 1915.

3. See index to the present writer's *Colony to Nation* (Toronto and London, 1957) s. v. *Staples Trade, Fur Trade, Timber Trade, Wheat,* etc.
4. The term is American and not much used in the Canadian West, although such farms existed. See "The Bell Farm—Once the World's Biggest Farm" in *Echoes of the Qu'Appelle Lakes District* by T. Petly (Indian Head, Sask.). In the farm (1882) there were 50,000 acres and much English capital. As a business venture it was a failure.
5. The American frontier was never as wild as romanticized conceptions of 'the Wild West' imply. See Paul Sharp, *Whoop-Up Country* (Madison, Wis., 1955).
6. Rev. J. H. Riddell, *Methodism in the Middle West* (Toronto, 1946). Riddell himself was another of these 'builders'. He became President of Wesley College, Winnipeg. In contrast to the previous and parallel generation in the East, most such men in the West were natives of Canada. They help to explain the higher degree of national consciousness of the West, as compared with the earlier East.
7. Samuel Coleridge, "Fears in Solitude".
8. *Winnipeg Free Press.*
9. It seems hardly necessary to mention that Sir Clifford, as Minister of the Interior under Laurier, was intimately associated with the later settlement of the West and that Arthur became Premier of Alberta and then a Dominion Cabinet Minister. Both brothers stood for a high degree of Canadian nationalism.
10. See also p. 309.
11. For the Siftons, see J. W. Dafoe, *Clifford Sifton in Relation to His Times* (Toronto, 1931). A relatively formidable hierarchy of classes might have developed had it not been for the barrier interposed in 1917 to the granting of knighthoods and titles; already several peerages had been given to Canadians.
12. In *Colony to Nation,* see index under *Woodsworth,* and in *Canada, Nation and Neighbour,* see index under *Woodsworth, Ewart.*
13. See S. M. Lipset, *Agrarian Socialism: the Co-Operative Commonwealth Federation in Saskatchewan* (Univ. of Calif., 1950) who shows the preponderance in the CCF and other 'progressive' movements of men of substantial middle-class type with a large proportion United Church in religious affiliation (and, let it be whispered, of Anglo-Saxon descent).
14. And many volumes have been written, for there is now a large literature on the settlement of the West. The following may be mentioned: A. M. Bezanson, *Sodbusters Invade the Peace* (Toronto, 1954); Jean Burnett, *Next Year Country* (Toronto, 1951); E. F. Hagell, *When the Grass was Free* (Toronto, 1954); Grant MacEwen, *Between the Red and the Rockies* (Toronto, 1953); W. L. Morton, *The Progressive Party in Canada* (Toronto, 1950); J. H. S. Reid, *Mountains, Men and Rivers* (Toronto, 1954); Paul F. Sharp, *The Agrarian Revolt in Western Canada* (Minnesota, 1948). There are scores of others.

24: New Canadians

A PLEASANT ROAD RUNS north from Winnipeg along the east bank of the Red River. It is edged with a long, straggling settlement, whose first houses were built of squared timber, low-set, whitewashed, with gay-coloured window trimmings. The occasional 'onion'-domed church set amid them could well have made a person imagine that he was in one of the neater country-sides of Russia. To-day, many of the log-cabins have been down-graded to sheds and stables and in front of them new dwellings stand, new houses in the general North American model but with little marks of style about them that associate them with an immigrant racial[1] group. For this is a Ukranian settlement in a Ukranian country-side. Formerly it was lightly peopled by the old Red River colonists, but they are almost gone now, and their survivors appear as strangers in the land of their birth.

The eastern bank of the Red River is typical of the prairies. The three provinces constitute a vast congeries of separate settlements put into the interstices of the original English-Canadian framework, scores of them with their own speech and their own way of life, united only by the *lingua franca* of the English language, by the traditional English institutions of self-government and law, and that powerful agency of community, the school. At the beginning of the century most of these prairie lands were empty, and now they are nearly all occupied. New peoples from the ends of the earth have poured out upon them, all dumped into the common mould of the prairie environment, and all slowly taking on common form from the mould. There, in brief, is the story of the largest migration movement in the history of this country of migrations; that movement which, beginning just before the turn of the century, rose to a peak in the very year in which the First World War broke out and slowly tapered off until we closed our doors in 1930; and which, the moment we opened them after the Second World War, began again and as this book is written (1957) is continuing. At its beginning nearly all Canadians were of British or French stock: at the half-century mark, rather more than one in five traced his origin to some other country, a proportion that was increasing. One in five, or thereabouts, was, in the parlance of the day, a 'New Canadian'.

The 'New Canadians'

The term 'New Canadian' struggled into existence during the first decades of the century, perhaps because it was not so insulting as 'bohunk' or 'dago'. From the first, insular natives were puzzled by the ingress of strangers of whom they had never previously heard—it was like the arrival of Gaelic-speaking Highlanders two or three generations before, only, so to speak, 'more so'. How deep the experience went is illustrated by a simple man of the North's answers to a catechism on this word he used so much, *bohunk*. All the bush camps of those days were full of *bohunks* and no one liked them much. What, then, was a *bohunk*?

"Is a French Canadian a *bohunk*?"
"Certainly not."
"Is a Swede a *bohunk*?"
"No."
"How about Germans?"
"No, about the same as Swedes.
"Are Finns *bohunks*?"
"Well, they might be."
"Are Galicians [later Ukrainians]?"
"Oh, yes, of course they are—Poles, too."

So the *bohunk* evidently was the strange new brand of humanity from the East, the Slav.

Like the earlier waves, the foreign immigration of the twentieth century upset a society just nicely getting on its feet and introduced a range of social problems whose settlement would take many decades. It was as if one were to have his family made over by adopting orphan strangers of unfamiliar habits and various tongues, strange conceptions of family life, peculiar diets and sketchy notions of civic responsibilties. It was all very well to expect the strangers to adapt themselves to you, but how about your having to adapt yourself to them?

In the face of the antagonisms, the hatreds, the surcharged emotions, which arose when new racial groups encountered old—to say nothing of the economic competition which the contact engendered—the mystery is how, within the short space of a generation or so, society succeeded in recapturing any measure of unity. In Europe, where the same situation has occurred time and again, societies so invaded often have dissolved in the chaos of racial war—that is why the Balkans used to be called "the powder keg of Europe". How is it that the new world has escaped the disintegrating processes that have harried the old? These forces exist, but few would contend that they threaten the internal peace of our society. What is the explanation of the mystery?

It has not lain in the dragooning methods of the lands from which so many of the new arrivals came. Our devices were many; some subtle and some easily distinguished. Among the latter the common school stands out, for in it, in district after district, racial differences have worn themselves down against the common background of the English tongue and the Canadian tradition. The need for the English language as the open sesame to the continent's great attraction—improved circumstances, 'getting on' in the old, familiar sense—has powerfully reinforced the work of the common school. Among the more subtle agencies at work was the new land's spirit of freedom. No need to tell the immigrant what that meant! No need to tell anyone what it means who has ever sniffed the air of unfreedom!

In the new land, with English institutions of freedom behind it, there could be little of that close-knit, old-world tribalism, that intense consciousness of the blood-group, which forms a front against all comers and thinks in terms of 'ourselves alone'. The spirit of freedom opens doors. In consequence, Canadian immigration policy, like American, if not 'wide open', has been generous. Neither people has thought of keeping the continent to itself: both have talked in terms of a brave new world, where all the white peoples (note the adjective) could join together in building a North American New Jerusalem. In practice the vision has been more narrowly glimpsed in Canada than in the United States. In the United States, they were building the republic. In Canada, a third of our people were perpetuating the old régime and wished nobody's assistance in that preoccupation. A large proportion of the remainder were building a British colony. The big, overriding national objective with its splendid cement of a common task hardly existed in Canada at the beginning of the immigration flood. The result has been a greater sense of exclusiveness on the part of 'old' Canadians as compared with Americans and a much sharper sense of race: this has delayed the process of society building through intermarriage.

For English Canadians, getting their hearts across the seas has been more difficult than for 'new' Canadians, so possibly one of the services of the new arrivals was to force the old hands to begin to think in terms of this new homeland of theirs rather than of the other homeland, the British Isles, from which most of them were themselves removed by only a generation or two. The new immigration has helped to force a new conception of the Canadian people upon us. No longer can we think of ourselves as overseas British: we have put our feet on the American road and for more than half a century now have been building a new composite. If and when a new 'cake' emerges from all these ingredients we have mixed, we shall have no option about it—it will be of native taste and texture.

There is no important divergence between Canadian immigration experience and American (barring the point noted at the end of the last paragraph but one) except that the Canadian has come a generation or two behind that of its neighbour. Apart from this, everything has been much the same— the adjustments of the immigrant himself, the order in which the immigrant has been drawn from the various countries of the old world, the rural and urban phases of immigration, the progress of the immigrant through the hierarchical structure of the existing society, the changes in that society because of the immigrant, the effectiveness or ineffectiveness of the 'melting pot'—all of these have been almost identical. The tragedy of the immigrant—and his hope—repeated for each and every human immigrant soul but with individual variations, lies exactly in these words 'melting pot', for to use the Biblical phrase, "he must be born again"—he must put off his old way of life, old habits, old associations, old speech, and enter a new and puzzling world which seems to offer him—what? Some kind of spiritual salvation? In infrequent instances (as probably for the Hungarian refugees of 1956-1957), yes. In most cases, merely material betterment. In the process of being born again, many fail, and with them (and, indeed, with the others, too) horrible rifts open up between them and their children. Let no comfortable citizen, living upon the heritage of his emigrating ancestors who had similar adjustments to make of which he has no knowledge, imagine that the way of the immigrant is easy or that it is an easy business to make a new and ordered society out of a myriad disparate individuals. Our Canadian misfortune has been the thoughtlessness, the superficiality, the arrogance, the instinct for exploitation, the greed, which we have manifested towards the immigrant. Where, among all our public men who have had anything to do with forming policy upon it, have we detected a perceptive insight into the social process, where have we heard anything but banal, commonplace views, views stemming mainly from our shallow 'bigger and better' notions?

As a consequence of their different approaches and different historical experiences, the two Canadian races have had different conceptions of immigration. The French attitude has been simple: "Let us keep the kind of society we have, unchanged, and unthreatened by the new-comer. We had to share our house once before with an intruder. We do not wish to do so again". The English Canadian, although by no means devoid of the same attitudes (which manifest themselves in the antagonisms that confront the new-comer) has, as a rule, simply applied his own individualistic outlook to the problem: he will judge the immigrant on his merits (provided he has a white skin) and leave him alone to work out his own salvation. The French Canadian thinks in terms of the old group of *nous autres*, the English Canadian hardly thinks in terms of a group at all: if he has any touchstone, it is personal advantage. To this, Protestant-Catholic rivalry provides a partial exception.

It is still too early to make definitive judgments on the subject of immigration. We have always been building a new society in America. What the new-comer will contribute to Canada cannot therefore be assessed. He has been brought here mainly because of his strong arms. If he has passed on to his daughter a pair of arms also clever enough to make a violin virtuoso out of her, like Donna Gresco, the native is inclined to think of her as a typical Canadian. If he gets into trouble and smashes his wife's head in with an axe, as immigrants have done on occasion, then the native thinks of him as a foreigner. What is certain is that the ingress of hundreds of thousands of strangers has delayed for many a day our attainment of a homogeneous society, growing from within, the parts of which understand and can communicate with each other.[2]

Before World War I it used to be said that some seventy languages could be heard on the streets of Winnipeg. Many of these could be heard, not only in Winnipeg, but in plenty of other places too, though some in diminishing volume.[3] Among them, in those days, English was perhaps not always the most common. There is a story that J. S. Woodsworth, who at that time was pastor of All People's Mission in Winnipeg, on being asked by the census taker what his nationality was, replied 'Canadian'. The official, of foreign birth, was puzzled. Finally, after Woodsworth had spelled out the word for him, he wrote it down, with the remark: "First one of them kind of people I've found around here!" The very idea 'Canadian' was obscure in those days, yet the English-speaking group never lost control: from the first it supplied the high officialdom of the three provinces and nearly all the parliamentarians. It is only in our own day that the 'New Canadians' have got up as far as the office of mayor.[4] The first Ukrainians to move into public life were from Manitoba, in which province several of them began to sit in the Assembly shortly after the First World War, and at least one of them became a provincial cabinet minister. The province's only Communist assemblyman was also a Ukrainian. There have been two or three Ukrainian members of Parliament.[5] The subordinate places, such as teachers in common schools, were among the first to be occupied, and in our own day a rare university chair has gone to someone (mostly Icelandic) not of 'British' descent. This slow climb up the social ladder is an experience common to every group of new-comers, and for each group the rate of climb seems to be roughly proportional to the length of time in the country.

The numerical size of the group also has been a factor (both positive and negative) in its coming into the general society. One of the largest 'New Canadian' groups in Canada is the Ukrainian. Where they are settled in large colonies, as near Vegreville in Alberta, they retain their old ways. But their numbers have secured them representation in parliament and in at least one provincial cabinet, and these representatives are forces for Canadianization.

Scandinavians, who are numerous in Canada, but rather scattered, are usually thought of as solid citizens, quickly becoming integrated into the general community, yet, Icelanders apart, they have contributed no one of prominence to the Canadian political and judicial world, and only one half of Frederick Philip Grove to the literary. The Icelanders rate high on any count—literary figures, public men, judges, professors, have proceeded from this small, concentrated people.

Persons of recent German origin—'New Germans', mostly not from Germany proper—form the largest group among the newer stocks,[6] but they have contributed no one of note to Canadian life.

Every considerable immigrant group, though without separatist ambitions, has had passing dreams of reconstituting its homeland on the new soil. Yet no group represents the complete society from which it was derived and in the new world every group has to find new 'national' leaders. Before it has accomplished this feat, however stubborn the resistance, it has found itself overtaken by North American life, into which its members have slowly merged. In Canada it has only been the pietistic religious groups—the Mennonites, Hutterites and Doukhobors—that have succeeded in maintaining themselves more or less intact, and many members of these groups, too, have passed into ordinary citizenship. Large rural colonies, such as still exist on the prairies, will continue to maintain their language and their folk customs for long periods, but they too will 'melt', and for the simple reason that there is nothing for which most of their members subsequent to the first or second generation are more anxious than to be indistinguishable from other Canadians.[7]

The notion that is sometimes heard about Canada being a 'mosaic', rather than a 'melting pot' like the United States, is not the product of hard thinking. No one in Canada would contemplate with equanimity a dozen little racial enclaves separated from the general community. The only reality there is in such vague nonsense is the fact that, Canadian national symbolism not yet having developed far, the new-comer has not been called upon quite as forcibly to conform publicly. Since we have had no George Washingtons to make "Farewell Addresses", children of foreign parentage do not have to learn "Farewell Addresses" by heart. In ordinary private life there would seem to be just as much pressure for conformity as there is in the United States.

The business of working huge drafts of new elements into a young society that has never had too much fixity of shape itself has constituted a severe strain on the affiliations and traditions of the original groups. Few 'New Canadians', surely, can think of 'the motherland', 'the homeland' (meaning 'Britain'), with the nostalgic affection that surrounds these sentimental terms in the minds of many English Canadians, for they have other motherlands and homelands. Few can think of themselves as sons in one of their father's world-wide estates, which has been an attitude natural to English Canadians. Few can have the same filial affection for the British monarchy. Every circumstance, it would seem, forces them away from colonialism towards nationalism, for they have cut their ties with the past and must find their new homes here. We shall hear more of this in the future than we have in the past: as yet the newer peoples have not had time to do much more than look after their economic well-being, and they have still to explore these subtle questions of the spiritual springs of society. In the meantime, they acquiesce in prevailing patterns. A few become as good royalists as the head of any old Toronto family: a few among the Icelanders, for example. Some go to the opposite extreme and become Communists, as have some Ukrainians and Finns. Some retain their original religion; others, like many among the Scandinavians and Germans, affiliate themselves with some Canadian denomination. Some come to understand our traditional institutions of freedom, though this is the most difficult of all areas to penetrate (as witness the large numbers of those of the old stocks who have not done so), and the one which, it is to be feared, takes the most damage when new citizens are made *en masse*. The one thing that would appear predictable is that in the end the new country will shape them, as it has shaped the rest of us. If in the process that which is valuable in the inherited tradition (and free institutions surely rank highest in it) is preserved, we shall have something to be thankful for.

Consequences—political, social, religious

It is related that when Clifford Sifton's immigrants were arriving by the tens of thousands around the turn of the century, most of the menfolk were found to be able to speak just two words of English: curiously enough, having regard to the dispassionate concern for the new-comers displayed by Sifton's immigration agents, these turned out to be "me Liberal"! Those two words have had something to do with the inability of the Conservative party to make much permanent impression on Saskatchewan and Alberta.

Canada has been a school for the immigrant, wherein he has learned the elements of self-government. She has performed her century-old function of a training ground for American citizens. It has been our job to take in the immigrants, educate them and their children, train them in citizenship and then pass on the better, brighter and more energetic among them to their fuller destiny in the United States. Many remain, of course, but many go. Statisticians tell us that during the last century, the millions of immigrants we have had are just about equal in number to the millions of emigrants. This has been a country of nomads (and it is hard to see how a society of much worth can arise among nomads), who pitch their tents here for a generation or two and then move on to greener fields. To this aspect of migration Canadian statesmanship, past and present, has been almost totally blind.

This perpetual recommencement of our society has had many aspects, bad and good. It has possibly kept us more closely related to the outside world than are our neighbours in the United States, and in this way it may have served a little to relieve the narrowness of a new community. Thus Arthur George Street in his little book *Farmer's Glory*,[8] in talking about his days as a farmhand in Manitoba, claims that the European immigrant, whatever his status, at least had known one other human environment, whereas the native Canadian knew only his own. In competitions in narrowness, the native Canadian would probably win. On the other hand, immigrants' children become just as parochial as those of natives. If parochialism is to be relieved, that must come from circumstances which increase the breadth of society, not from individuals. If Canada becomes more of a centre of things than it has hitherto been, its people will also lose some of their provincialism.[9]

Our subject calls for detailed study rather than passing observation, and, did space permit, it could be pursued indefinitely. It has a dozen different angles—sociological, economic, demographic, and many more. Dry statistical material alone leads into the infinite ramifications of biological pattern as shown in birth and death rates, of religious affiliation, of urban and rural grouping and of mobility within the country. An illustration of this last is the degree of diffusion of the original immigration from the West throughout the rest of the country. Many a young man of, say, Ukrainian parentage, has left Saskatchewan for Vancouver, while his brother has come to Oshawa. The Ukrainians only seem the most conspicuous in this respect because their path is often marked by their 'onion'-domed churches.

An aspect of the new immigration, traceable statistically but needing the interpretation that only observation can give, has been the diversification and perhaps division of Roman Catholicism. The liturgical framework of Catholicism does not differ greatly from country to country, the doctrinal not at all, but few would deny that there are vast differences in the spirit of Catholicism and the attitudes of Catholics. Before our European immigration, the Roman Catholic Church in Canada was divided mainly by the two languages. But in the twentieth century numerous other Catholic groups have pushed in the direction of local autonomy under their own bishops. Some may have succeeded in obtaining this. Polish Catholics in Manitoba, for example, seem to be in a position of semi-independence.

The effect of 'national' churches on the unity of Catholicism must be considerable, for such churches draw their adherents into bodies that do not have much relationship with others and which must therefore find it difficult to unite for large objectives: the numerous Catholic churches of modern Manitoba probably could not present the same united front on school rights as did the French Catholic church of the eighteen-nineties. And when division goes beyond liturgical uniformity, as it does with the Greek Catholics who follow the Greek rite and have their own separate hierarchy,[10] nothing much remains in common except the nominal headship of the pope and the general body of Catholic dogma.

The same kind of observation could be made about Protestantism among the 'New Canadians': immigration has led to its further division. For Protestantism this is, however, not a matter of primary significance, since its genius consists in individual decision. Even so, Protestant division has had its limits. The chief barrier to the infinite fragmentation of 'New Canadian' Protestantism has been presented by one of the traditional Protestant churches, the Lutheran. Before 1900, Lutheranism was weak, resting only on the old German communities of the eastern provinces. It is not strong to-day, but it is much stronger than it was, having come up on the Scandinavian, German and Finnish immigration of the intervening half century. Lutheranism in America has never been fully unified, and since it reflects so many facets of Christianity—all the way from the most intellectual to the most 'fundamental'—it is not likely to become so. Moreover there is no national Lutheran Church in Canada, but the various bodies have their affiliations with their counterparts to the south. This situation will probably change as the lines between the national groups within Lutheranism grow less distinct.

The biological pattern of all immigrant groups is fairly well defined. New-comers usually have to start at the bottom: they are therefore poorer than the average citizen. Not having the advantages of the older classes, they have a higher death rate. But being poorer—and the correlation seems proveable—they have more children. Their children, and more especially their grandchildren, having got accustomed to the way of the country, behave biologically much as everybody else.[11] The same considerations apply to such qualities as industriousness, frugality, thrift and craftsmanship. When you have cut your cables, as have the first-generation immigrants, you have to make good or go under. Therefore, for the most part you work hard—especially since on the average it is the more energetic people who emigrate. Immigrants often 'get on' remarkably well (to the jealousy or admiration, in about equal proportions, of 'old hands') and soon become substantial holders of property. If the English-Canadian immigrant in the United States were identifiable *en masse*, he would display an approximation to the set of qualities marking the Pole or the Italian in Canada.

European immigration into Canada has, however, not consisted of exactly the same type of person as has gone to the United States. Canada early got the reputation of being a quiet country. As a Dutch immigrant said: "I went first to Chicago but I soon decided that that was no place to bring up a family, so I came up here."[12] There has been a constant selection, on this score, which cumulatively is not unimportant. The same selection, of course, has acted upon the native-born: it has tended to be the more able, and especially the spontaneous, the extroverts, 'the up-and-coming' who have gone to the United States. So evident has this tendency been that it is possible for the acute observer to predict fairly accurately which members of a given group of young people will end up in the States. Canada has retained the withdrawn people, the sedate, and those with the least energy and ability. What this century-old export of brains[13] and energy has done to our society cannot be estimated, but it would seem that it has been one of the large factors in keeping it in that state of low water which has always been the object of the Yankee's good-natured scorn. The difficulties of nature have been great in Canada and they have led to its having had to get along with people who would put up with them, who, given the ease with which one can always go somewhere else, have been the passive and the acquiescent. There is no reason to think that the new immigrants are different from the old in these respects.

It would be overstatement to say that Canada consists entirely of second-rate people, but by no means overstatement to say that it has never been over-supplied with first. Donna Gresco, mentioned before, is a useful case in point, for as a young musician of great ability, she has found little place for her talents in Canada. Betty Jean Hagen, an 'old Canadian', is another example—a distinguished violinist from Simcoe County, Ontario, via Edmonton, now married in New York.[14] The idea of new people bringing in their gifts and thus enriching the Canadian scene is of limited force: the best of the new people have taken and will take their gifts out almost as quickly as they bring them in. What the immigrant will contribute permanently will be new names, and the odds and ends of a folk culture, such as those that now remain of Scottish folk culture—most of us can sing one verse of Annie Laurie and we know the tune: so in two or three generations from now, most people of German descent will still know the tune (and a few of the words) of *Ach, du lieber Augustin*.

This negative selection has at least relieved us from certain groups which have not been much of a blessing in the United States. Sicilian and south Italian banditry have not yet got much of a foothold in Canada. Though we are in no position to point a scornful finger at our neighbours, yet the 'boss'-ridden American city has little counterpart in Canada, nor have we yet found a Senator McCarthy (our Catholic Irish have been of a quieter brand than their fellows across the line, especially since one of them made the mistake of assassinating D'Arcy McGee, and the British-hating proclivities of their southern brethren have been only mildly reflected among them).

The new European immigration of the twentieth century has greatly changed many districts in Canada. In some, the immigrant has been the pioneer and has formed colonies. In others, he has shoved out the original English-speaking people, by undercutting them in work and pay. In others he has settled down beside them. He has rarely been freely and frankly accepted. Everyone has been in favour of immigration but against having immigrants. The new tensions that have been introduced into our activity by mass immigration are often painfully obvious but it can at least be said that these lead us unwillingly in the same direction to which every other large factor in Canadian life impel us—to compromise. Everyone hates compromise too, but where you have a country of two primary cultures, two primary religions, and two pulls on fundamental allegiance—one to the past and one to the country—and now, another large, heterogeneous group which must be built into the original structure, only one attitude becomes possible, short of endemic civil war, the attitude of compromise. Whatever the ultimate balance of his account, the 'New Canadian' has at least promoted this most unwelcome of all the Canadians virtues, compromise.

Notes to Chapter 24

1. Since the Germans made so much ado about what they called 'race', the sociologists now hold it to belong with other four-letter unmentionables; they use instead the term 'ethnic' (which means the same thing but sounds more pretentious and therefore, it is to be presumed, pleases them better).
2. In Winnipeg, the great immigration simply built one city alongside the other (north and south of Portage Avenue) and rarely the twain do meet.
3. The census of 1951 enumerates 16 mother tongues.
4. In 1956 Edmonton already had had a 'New Canadian' mayor, as had Fort William, and Winnipeg had just elected one.
5. In 1957, Mr. Diefenbaker included a 'New Canadian'—a Canadian-born Ukrainian—in his Cabinet, the first to be so selected.
6. See next Chapter.

7. The Jews have quickly adapted themselves, but few of them have been absorbed: they resemble no other group.
8. London, 1932.
9. An American observer recently remarked that to him the inhabitants of the best sections of Toronto seemed to be provincial—they were no longer provincial to London, he said, but to New York and Hollywood: that is, these were their centres of reference.
10. They are to be carefully distinguished from the Greek Orthodox Catholics: unfortunately in the censuses they pop into and out of the classification 'Roman Catholic' in such a way as to make it difficult to keep track of them.
11. See the Diagrams at the end of the next Chapter.
12. The same remark was once made to the present writer by one of his Jewish friends.
13. Even to-day (1957) with conditions never so favourable, a high proportion of those graduating from our universities with first-class standing leaves us every year.
14. See *Weekend Magazine*, Dec. 29th, 1956.

25: The immigrant stocks in Canada

F OR THOSE WHO HAVE THE PATIENCE to read them, more can be gathered about our immigrant groups from a few diagrams than from dozens of pages of reading. Those given here,[1] and upon which the text of this chapter is a commentary, are based upon the Canadian Census. The census has given *racial origin* for many decades: this category has recently been deodorized by being cut down to *origin*. The census classifications are stable for the larger stocks, but for the lesser, they wobble about, producing 'races' in one census and extinguishing them in the next. For the censuses from 1931 on, a most useful category has been introduced, mother tongue, and beginning in 1941, tables correlate important data such as religion, mother tongue and racial origin. These tables enable us to find out how many Lutherans were Swedish, how many born in Russia were of German descent, and so on.

If a person has lost his original mother tongue and has learned the language of the new country 'at his mother's knee', it is fairly safe to put him down as a member of the general group—in our case, those who speak English, or rarely, French. Those who speak English in Canada greatly exceed in number those who put down a 'British Isles origin'. The inference is that many from the other groups have been assimilated into the general English-speaking group. The diagrams attempt to show how this applies to several racial stocks: they assume that the difference in numbers between those of a given origin and those who speak the corresponding language roughly represents the number who have passed into the English group. This is the 'area of assimilation' shown on the diagrams. It is of course not mathematically accurate and owing to lack of data, can only be portrayed from 1931 on. This comparison between mother tongue and racial origin can be buttressed by introducing the category 'country of birth'. There are, however, relatively few instances where country of birth, mother tongue and racial origin neatly correspond. A person could reasonably put himself down as born in Czecho-Slovakia, of Polish mother tongue and Ukrainian origin.[2] Further, this person might be of Greek Orthodox religion, Greek Catholic, Roman Catholic, or United Church. But if persons put themselves down as born in Italy, the chances are that they are of Italian racial origin and Roman Catholic in religion, and that their mother tongue is Italian. The correspondence also holds for persons of Scandinavian extraction, but for practically no others. The difficulty lies in the shifting political frontiers of Eastern Europe, from which so many of our immigrants have come. For example, there are persons who call themselves 'Austrians' but speak a Slavic language. Apart from the Canadian Census authorities, no one has yet found an 'Austrian' race: these people are simply ex-subjects of the former Emperor of Austria-Hungary. In like manner, before 1919, there was no Poland and when Poland was reborn, it included some millions of Ukrainians. 'Ukrainians' are a language group, rather than a race: our Canadian Ukrainians stem mainly from the old Austria-Hungary: formerly the census labelled them 'Galicians', 'Bukowinians' or 'Ruthenians'.[3] They are so diverse that the one feature of which we can be sure is their mother tongue, and the number of people who speak it.

The proper adjective 'German' is the most complex of them all. Few Canadian Germans are *Reichsdeutsch* (from Germany), most are *Auslandsdeutsch* (from other lands). They come from Estonia on the north to the Black Sea on the south, from Alsace on the west to the Caspian Sea on the east. In religion, they may be Mennonite, Lutheran, Roman Catholic, or one of our own Protestant denominations. Their native language may or may not be German! They may have been in the country one year or two hundred! As the diagram shows, a large proportion of them speak English. This is not only because Germans assimilate fairly quickly but much more because our population has had large German elements in it from the beginning, such as the Lunenburgers of Nova Scotia, who came in 1753, or the numerous German United Empire Loyalists: it is foolish to think of the descendants of Cassellmans, Shavers or Merkeleys from the old counties of Eastern Ontario as anything other than *Canadian*. Germans who came in the nineteenth century are a little more easily distinguishable because they tended to settle in compact blocks as in Waterloo County, Ontario. But these old German districts are also today in nearly every important sense of the word, Canadian (a Lieutenant Governor of Ontario belonged to one of them).[4]

We should divide our Germans into 'old Germans' and 'new', the 'new Germans' being mainly in the West, and very much subdivided in origin, religion, language and other characteristics. There is the further complication that in the war years, 'German' became unpopular as a term. Hence in 1921, thousands of 'Germans' became 'Dutch'. In 1931, many of them were 'German' once more and in 1941, they had returned to being 'Dutch'. 'German' Mennonites (Russian born) seem never to have recovered from this attack of 'Dutchness'. The only way to deal with this group seems to be to lump Germans and Dutch together statistically, and that is the way the diagrams handle them.

Comments on the diagrams

There follow remarks on the diagrams one by one.

Diagram 6 shows the growth of the Canadian population of the two major stocks, English and French. Since the 'English' stock consists of English, Scots (a few of whom still speak a foreign language), two brands of Irish, Welsh, Americans, and any others who choose to call themselves 'English', the census resolves the complexity by using the phrase 'British Isles origin'. The diagram shows how many more people have English as their mother tongue than give their racial origin as 'British Isles': this difference, it calls 'the area of assimilation'. In similar fashion, it shows the growth of the French stock (almost entirely from natural increase as contrasted with immigration plus natural increase of the English, which accounts for the greater regularity of the curve) and those who give French as mother tongue. The difference between the two indicates a small absorption of the French by

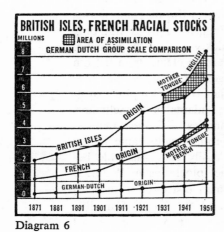

Diagram 6

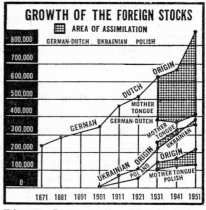

Diagram 7

386 / Canadians in the making

the 'English'. The French group is the simplest of all statistical groups, as it is almost completely homogeneous in the important characteristics. It is, moreover, much more regular in its biological behaviour than is the English, which means that its birth rate does not shrink as much in bad times as does that of the English. This also is reflected in the diagram.

The German-Dutch group is also plotted on Diagram 6 in order to give comparison of the two scales employed.

Diagrams 7 and 11 show the growth and degree of assimilation of the principal immigrant stocks. On Diagrams 8 and 10, birthplaces have been added for Italians and Scandinavians. Both

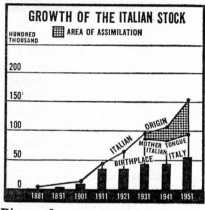

Diagram 8

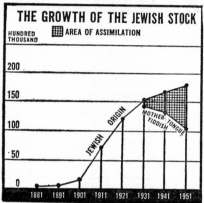

Diagram 9

these groups afford good ground for study of an immigrant group which has taken up its weight. By 1911, the first rush of Italians was over and thereafter, until the recent (1945 on) renewal of the inflow, the number of immigrants born in Italy increased only slightly. But the Italian stock went on growing quite rapidly. Nevertheless, Italian as a mother tongue barely held its own after 1931. The conclusion must be that the Italians (see 'area of assimilation') were passing into ordinary Canadian life. Further analyses for such a group indicate its birth rate in comparison with other groups (No. 15), its religion (No. 17), etc.

The Scandinavians (Swedes, Norwegians, Danes, Icelanders), most would agree, stand closest to the English group and this is reflected in the speed with which they lose their language. A good number of them turn out to be ordinary American immigrants of Scandinavian origin. The bottom line of their diagram (No. 10) indicates that they ceased to come to us after 1931. Those who are here are apparently adopting English at a

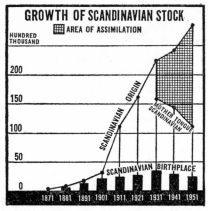

Diagram 10

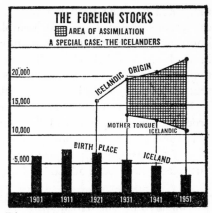

Diagram 11

rapid rate. One sub-group among them is of especial interest, the Icelanders. The Icelanders are our oldest 'New Canadians', having begun to come in the eighteen-seventies. Their compact settlements on Lake Winnipeg and in the city of Winnipeg have prevented their being overwhelmed, that and the fact that they brought with them their own highly literate and literary culture. It is no accident that they have already given a number of authors to Canada. Diagram 11, using an enlarged scale, shows their experience insofar as census records give it. The

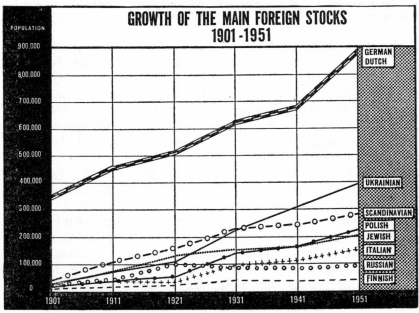

Diagram 12

bottom line shows how rapidly the number of those born in Iceland fell off after 1911 (as the first immigrant generation died off): it shows the same fate overtaking the Icelandic tongue, especially since 1941, with the rise of the third and fourth generations, and the considerable expansion, from a small base, of the total Icelandic stock.

Diagram 12 shows clearly the period of origin of the more important stocks—the beginning of the twentieth century for all of them except the German-Dutch, who also were greatly reinforced after that date. It shows, too, how the cessation of immigration in 1930 slowed down the rate of expansion of the particular group: when immigration was resumed after 1945, the opposite effect is equally clearly visible. Diagram 13 brings this out even more distinctly by putting into percentage form

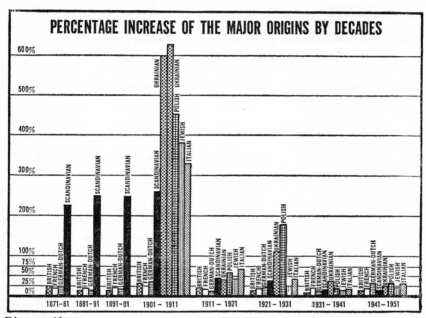

Diagram 13

rates of increase from one decade to another. In the first onset of a new stock, the percentage rate of increase is high (if there is one person here already and two more come, the group will have been increased by 200 per cent!). The high percentages of the newer groups for the decades down to 1901-1911 indicate these initial inrushes. The much lower rates, though the still high ones, for those groups during the period 1911-1931, illustrate the high immigration of those years. For 1931-1941 there was virtually no immigration. This, therefore, is the only

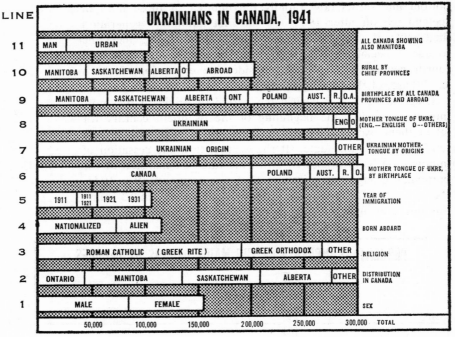

Diagram 14

decade in our history where we can see all the other stocks behaving under the same conditions as the French. From 1871 on, the percentage increases of English and French do not differ excessively (the low English birth rate and high emigration being balanced by much British immigration). During 1931-1941, the English, depending on births alone, almost ceased expanding. The French did not, though they slowed down. The German-Dutch and the Scandinavians followed the same pattern, and were in between the two older stocks, as we should expect from more recent arrivals, many of whom were rural and Catholic. The Ukrainians continued to increase at a rapid rate, entirely by reproduction: this represented their position as the most recent arrivals, the poorest, the least Protestant and the most rural, these being the factors correlating with high birth and death rates.[5] Since 1945, immigration has once again destroyed the symmetry of the picture.

Diagram 14 illustrates the principal points about the Ukrainians for the year 1941, the first year for which so much correlated information became available. The horizontal column at the bottom of the diagram, division into the two sexes, indicates the normal situation in an immigrant group, more men than women. The next column up shows distribution by provinces. The concentration is where it would be expected to be, in the three prairie provinces, with the largest number in Manitoba. The considerable number in Ontario mainly represents the 'spill-over' from the West. The third line gives distribution by religion. In 1941, all former Greek Catholics were converted by the census authorities into Roman Catholics and in 1951, they were reconverted. Greek Catholics are Roman Catholics with a difference. Note the distinction between them and Greek Orthodox. The remainder ('Other' on the diagram) are scattered, with the largest group in the United Church. The fourth line shows that there are still a considerable number of those born elsewhere who are not naturalized. Many of these put themselves down as 'Austrian': presumably they are neglectful old people who came here many years ago. The fifth line shows the period of immigration, with the years before 1911 (and by 1941 immigrants of those years would be passing away quickly) about balancing 1921-1941. Line six shows total persons giving Ukrainian as their mother tongue, with those born in Canada greatly predominating, and Poland and Austria the largest single foreign countries. Line seven shows all those who speak Ukrainian by their racial origin. Note that quite a considerable number who were not Ukrainian in origin gave the language as their mother tongue. This seems to mean that the Ukrainians absorbed members of other groups.

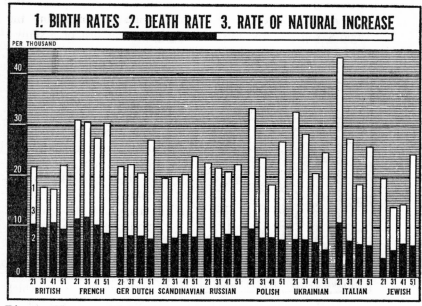

Diagram 15

Line eight shows that there was a small group of English-speaking Ukrainians. Lines nine, ten, and eleven are to be compared with line two. They show that most of our Ukrainians are prairie born, that most of them are still rural and that the major urban concentration is in Manitoba, that is, in Winnipeg.

Diagram 15 portrays the birth and death rates of the various stocks for the four census years for which the available data allow these to be calculated. Our Reports on Births, Marriages and Deaths begin in 1921. If we put these together with the census returns by 'origins', we can strike rates per thousand for each stock: the result the diagram shows. The British stocks have the lowest birth rates and the highest death rates, which means that they have the lowest rate of natural increase. This is in part a reflection of their infertility—which in turn is based on their economic and social status, their urban preponderance and their Protestantism—but in part also of their distribution over a wider segment of time. Compared with them, it might be said that few immigrants have as yet had an opportunity to grow old and therefore they show lower death rates. The French maintain their low death rate by their high birth rate, the death rate being calculated against a steadily widening base at the bottom: the greater youthfulness of any French-Canadian group, as compared with any English-Canadian, is visible to the naked eye. The immigrant stocks approximate to the English pattern in the ratio of their length of residence on this side of the Atlantic. It is remarkable how quickly the birth rates even of Polish Catholics are approximating the Anglo-Saxon pattern: this in itself is another test of assimilation. The marked expansion of the birth rate for all stocks in 1951 should be noted: this in part reflects the new immigration. The lowest of all birth rates has been recorded by the most highly urbanized of all the groups, the Jewish, in the years 1931 and 1941.

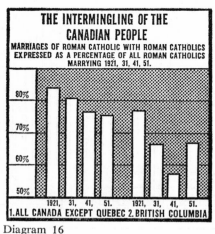

THE INTERMINGLING OF THE CANADIAN PEOPLE
MARRIAGES OF ROMAN CATHOLIC WITH ROMAN CATHOLICS EXPRESSED AS A PERCENTAGE OF ALL ROMAN CATHOLICS MARRYING 1921, 31, 41, 51.

1. ALL CANADA EXCEPT QUEBEC 2. BRITISH COLUMBIA

Diagram 16

Diagram 16 provides another light on assimilation, that coming from intermarriage. The data are drawn from the *Reports on Vital Statistics*, which show the religions of all brides and grooms. The majority of people marry within their denominational group, the smaller the group the more intense being the degree of intermarriage. This is not socially significant except in the case of 'mixed' or Catholic-Protestant marriages. What the results of these are in strengthening or weakening the groups involved by addition of new adherents from the cradle cannot be determined, but it would be reasonable to believe that cases of intermarriage tend to decrease group tensions, for whichever parent the children follow, they must be more familiar with the other group than if both parents were of the same church. In Diagram 16 the degree of intermarriage is shown 1921-1951 for all Canada except Quebec (since Quebec was not available in 1921 and since there is relatively little intermarriage in that province). To show the most extreme departure from denominational marriages, the record of that Canadian province which deviates farthest from the average pattern in these matters, British Columbia, is added.

Diagram 17 analyzes the various stocks by denomination

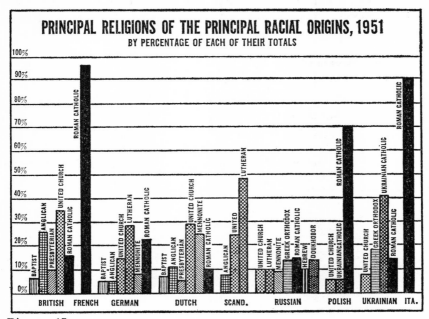

Diagram 17

(1951 Census gives the most convenient data for this). The predominance of 'national' churches is evident. The numbers of adherents among a foreign stock to one of the English Protestant denominations provides another criterion of assimilation: this figure is especially high for the Germans, Dutch and

Scandinavians. Note the distribution of the apparently homogeneous Mennonite group among Germans, Dutch and Russians. Note also the numerous religious divisions of the 'Russians', who evidently are in no sense a homogeneous racial group: the same, to a lesser degree, is true of the Ukrainians. Note the success of the United Church in establishing itself among nearly all foreign stocks: this church, the exact image of middle-class Canadian respectability, may be regarded as the norm of Canadian denominational life.

The diagrams only provide suggestions for further work on a subject which could be carried much further and which could be added to as additional censuses are taken. The writer will guarantee that anyone who gets into this type of analysis and has some flair for it will not readily put it by, for within the heavy volumes of the census, crammed with repellent pages of statistics, is packed a wealth of material on the peoples of Canada. It reaches far beyond their economic activities into the recesses of their philosophical and psychological ways of life. Skill and imagination will make it over into flesh and blood!

Notes to Chapter 25.

1. See the end of this Chapter.
2. The present writer had a student who did so.
3. See the census of 1921, Vol. I, p. 356, where some 70 racial classifications are given.
4. Louis Breithaupt of Kitchener, Lieutenant Governor from 1952 to 1957.
5. The relationship between religion and the birth rate is discussed in the present writer's *Colony to Nation* (Toronto and London, 1957), pp. 64 ff.

26: War's rude alarms

IN THE SUMMER OF 1914, few Canadians, engrossed as most of them were in the rapid growth of their country, thought that war was about to burst on their quiet corner of the world. Four years and some months later, the Dominion came out of the encounter, found itself somewhat dazed but otherwise intact, and prepared to make up for the lost time. No hostile shot had been fired in Canada but the blood-letting overseas had been deep—over sixty thousand men killed from a country that could ill spare them, and countless thousands more wounded and maimed—and the measures taken at home to sustain the conflict had gone far to change the easy-going Canadian shape of things. The First World War was a profound experience for the Canadian people and it had profound effects.[1]

The war affected the different sections in vastly different ways, and many of these effects remain plainly visible. French Canadians had looked on war as defence of the homeland. They had had no tradition of fighting abroad. During the old régime, they were too remote to have had any interest in the European wars of the kings of France, and after the Conquest, down to recent times, they continued to be quite untutored with respect to matters beyond their province: how then could they have interest in the European wars of the kings of England, of which the war against Germany was just another?

"The average French Canadian voter has never come into direct personal contact with the really crucial questions of defence—at all events, not for a hundred years. . . . As for international affairs and the world-wide struggle for existence, well, they may be all right for those who like them, or for those whose special penitence it is to bear them; but, for himself and his own people that's none of their business, and "on est bi'n icitte. . . ."[2]

The *élite* of French Canada were as well informed as those

of the English but intellectual perception is not emotional perception: the feelings of most of the leaders in 1914, like those of the United States, were not engaged.

English Canadians as a group formed a sharp contrast, but if the whole group were broken down into its many sub-groups, much of this would disappear. Most of them then were close to their roots in the British Isles: many of them still had blood connection there.[3] As Chapter 22 has suggested, in their school-days they had been steeped in the romantic aspects of English history and literature, and upon them shone the full glamour of the British military tradition. Whenever war brought the deeper currents of their life into the conscious areas of thought (as the Boer War had already done), most of them probably thought of themselves as mere sundered fragments of a world-wide stock that was always fighting somewhere or other—and, given the evangelical attitudes, fighting was always transmuted into "fighting for the right". This latter determining factor has been almost absent from the psychology of French Canada, as from that of France. Expositors of French-Canadian and English-Canadian attitudes toward war have neglected it, yet upon it could be based a full-dress study of the two civilizations.

The call to arms—and the response

English Canada has been harshly condemnatory of French Canada's short-sightedness with respect to the issues involved in both wars. Perhaps rightly so. It is not, however, the historian's business to condemn but to understand. One important element in understanding is knowledge of the circumstances affecting men and their surroundings. Thus, it was not strange that the first people to rush to arms in English Canada were recently arrived immigrants, for they knew something about the other side of the ocean. A scattering of the native-born did the same: in those who did so, there were marked group affiliations. Some of them had been militiamen before the war. Many officers derived from the old Anglican and Tory 'ruling class'. Many a foot-loose prospector from the North hurried off from his war with the wilderness to another war with the Germans. City people were more immediately affected than country dwellers. The western provinces, where men still had shallow roots, were conspicuous in the manpower they furnished. Certain of the oldest districts of the East, where traditional sentiment might have been expected to have had other results, notoriously lagged behind.

". . . We regret . . . to be compelled to admit that right here in this district where we boast our United Empire Loyalist ancestry and our readiness to prove ourselves worthy of such an ancestry, there have been many neighborhoods . . . that have contributed not one single native-born Canadian son to fight the enemies of our nation. Is Bay of Quinte loyalty, after all, only a cheap, counterfeit sentiment that manifests itself in frantic flag-flapping at election time, perfervid Twelfth of July orations, parading of brilliantly uniformed men to religious services . . . and then, when danger actually threatens, the cyclone cellar for ours?"[4]

The extract corroborates the present author's opinion, elsewhere expressed, that it was not so much high notions of imperial allegiance that had originally brought the Loyalists to Canada as entanglements with the King's shilling. The way in which the editorial writer blends the two imperialist traditions, Loyalism and Orangeism, is also interesting, especially in that both are accused of being laggards in coming forward to fight. But was this not to face native Ontarians with exactly the same accusation as they were about to hurl against the Quebeckers? It was not primarily a matter of 'loyalty' at all: it was a matter of the associations surrounding a man. If he failed to go for a recruit, would it not be because the distant struggle had not touched his imagination and his emotions, because, that is, he had become much more a 'native' than he had actually suspected? The remedy for all this would have been for Canada to be a nation, which in 1915 she was not. Nor was she in 1939, though further on, and as a result of her being further on there was less tension (though quite enough) about the business of volunteering. In 1914 and 1915, after the initial rush to the colours, English Canada's response to recruiting was such as to spread alarm: "This Province (Ontario) is not at war. It doesn't know anything about it. It is at hockey. . . ."[5] Perhaps it was because the burden of so much recruiting exhortation was 'duty to the empire'. Perhaps the day was a little far spent for that. The ephemeral periodical just quoted from reprinted a piece from the front page of the Toronto *Board of Trade News*, February 1915, entitled "Canada's Duty" and called heavy attention to the fact that away down at the end of "duties" such as "Large increase in farm production" or "The purchase and use of goods 'made in Canada' " there came "Furnish her full share of men and materials to the Motherland in defence of civilization"![6]

If native English Canada was slow to awake to its obligations, French Canada, as its history made inescapable, was much slower. The situation was complicated by every conceivable subsidiary issue. Sam Hughes, Minister of Militia, as a fighting Irish Protestant was not the ideal man to enlist the sympathies of French Roman Catholics. Sending English Protestant ministers to drum up recruits under the eyes of their priests may not in retrospect be regarded as the highest wisdom. Keeping high-ranking French officers such as General Lessard cooling their heels on this side of the Atlantic possibly had something to do with keeping French ardour cool also. Exhortations to 'fight for France' as if France were to French Canada what England was to English, showed profound misunderstanding of French Canada's psychology. The expulsion of many monastic orders from France a few years before and their sympathetic reception in French Canada, their subsequent influence, like that of the French clerical refugees after 1789, had helped turn clerical New France away from old and had made it easy, in a community deeply persuaded that the hand of God was visible, to believe that France was being punished for her sins.

None of these things the government of the day seemed to understand. Instead of capitalizing on the initial burst of good will in French Canada, it alienated it: within a year that gap had opened between the races which widened until it came close to civil war and which it has taken the best efforts of a generation to narrow. It is easy to say that 'it would have opened anyway'. But need it have opened as widely if there had been more insight, if the country had been in charge of men who simply put Canada and its unity first? The question will never be answered, but it is significant that in the second war, the gap did not open as widely. In the period since the second war, both parties have modified their positions. French Canada has found out something about the outside world, especially with the threat of atheistic Russian Communism, and English Canada is slowly becoming Canadian. Its right wing, like right wings everywhere, may secretly thirst for war[7] and probably would be as ready to accept American leadership as formerly English, but the mass of the people are not quite as susceptible to the ancestral emotions as once they were. In 1957 English-Canadian and French-Canadian attitudes were visibly closer than a generation before.

Just prior to the First World War, English Canada had found an admirable outlet for its energies in the job of building the West and the North. Two transcontinental railways in a few years were a psychological equivalent for war. They called out many of the same qualities: large- and small-scale organizing abilities, physical hardships to be overcome, physical obstacles as formidable as in many fields of war. The construction north of Lake Nipigon, which was all supported from the C.P.R., a hundred miles to the south, provides an example. In winter the only communications route was over the ice of the lake, by sleigh, with no benefit of gas engines. Many a grim episode in storm and blizzard and bitter cold occurred out there on that great frozen lake whose surface was yet never dependable. Lines of communication in France did not present many terrors to men who had kept open such lines in Canada. Settling the West, with the hardihood that new settlement always involves; the battle with nature; the gamble with one's future; the challenge of building a new country, from sod house to Government House—all this called out attributes similar to those useful in war.

North American life from the beginning has had the aspect of a military campaign. As the continent becomes subjugated and the soft city man everywhere takes over, these old gifts will go (but the car and industry keep us on a semi-military basis) and Canadians will be no more useful or adaptable on the field of battle than others. In the second war that point may already have been reached (though accounts still drifted back of young fellows in the ranks who asked nothing better than to be left on their own without handicap of officers). In contrast, the fighting men of England and Germany, released from the erosions of urbanism, found pioneer qualities once more in war and at the end probably had little to learn from trans-Atlantic friends or foes.

The author remembers a conversation with an English friend in June of 1914. This man was an erratic who had 'knocked about' the north country for years. He was also sensitive and cultured. Both of us were on the point of making a long plunge into the bush.[8] We knew nothing of impending trouble in Europe. Yet on talking over the stage of maturity that Canada had reached, we humourously agreed (and the author can only plead his youth and the thought of the time for what was a silly notion) that a nice little war would be just what the country needed to cap its development and give it a sense of corporate unity. We got the war all right but not the neat little affair we had both predicated. Nevertheless it did for Canada just what we had idly speculated about; it increased its sense of corporate unity. If it did not make a nation, it advanced the making of a people who had not really existed before—the English Canadians.[9] Nowhere did this go further than among the fighting troops: men realized, as they faced death, that around them were their own fellows and that back far behind them was the land from which they had come. If there is one experience more effective than another for discovering one's identity, it is removal from one's familiar surroundings, and the largest removal of all is from one's country. No Canadian has difficulty envisaging Canada once he gets three miles off shore, and usually his sentiment for it rises with the distance. In war, when the uncertainty of seeing familiar surroundings again is heightened, feeling for them is also heightened. Sometimes the expressions of homesickness or the delight at the first glimpse of the native land on return took on a quality which it would hardly become sober history to recount.[10]

English Canadians rushed off to war without knowing much about the issues involved, which they took for granted. There was never any doubt among either the men themselves or their people that they would make good soldiers. There never has been any doubt since. In the army, as elsewhere, their qualities lay about midway between British and American: more discipline than Americans, more adaptiveness than British, less innovating initiative than the Americans, less original genius than the Britsh, more general average capacity perhaps than either of the others. In the Second World War, Canada's fighting forces had an extraordinary percentage in them of men with more than common-school education. The men of the First War had the qualities that might be predicated from this educational average. They were competent in that good, middle-ground way which has been coming out of late years as a major Canadian quality: the quality which belongs to the average plus, but which by that very fact, tends to lack extremes. Canadians are the Swiss of North America. One does not look to the Swiss, with Frenchmen on one side of them and Italians on the other, for original genius. He does, however, look to them for solid dependability. That perhaps explains why Canada has not yet produced a commanding military figure—that and the extreme distaste the average man evinces towards anyone with abilities too far in excess of his own.

War's consequences

The war affected Canadian society in every direction. It made Canada a paradise for the 'profiteer' and while war-profiteering became so obvious and sometimes so corrupt that public indignation grew loud, yet government, faced with a range of problems in social regulation which were quite novel, was ineffective in dealing with it: Canada had as yet no administrative bureaucracy of moment and the old type of civil servant was as useless for the new situation as the old-fashioned banker and lawyer on whom governments had hitherto relied for their *expertise*. Many a Canadian fortune must rest on the profits of the war of 1914-1918. But then, as this book has noticed before, that is no new thing, for there has been no single war, from the American Revolution on, from which individual Canadians have not profited.[11] This also holds good for the country as a whole: other countries may be bled by war, but Canada has invariably found it a stimulus to her production and a well of unsuspected riches. Perhaps this is knowledge that should be withheld from Canadians or they may begin to think aloud, at a point in history when a new situation has arisen, that thought which must be held half-formed and disowned within many a mind, that war is 'a good thing'.

One of the major administrative innovations to come out of the war was the new financial structure. A national debt contracted at home provides an additional anchor for society. Every respectable country should possess a substantial national debt: this Canada found no difficulty in accumulating, and from domestic sources. The second innovation was equally important, the revamping of the tax structure, and especially the inauguration of the income tax. The income tax until recently was optimistically referred to as a 'war tax', but everyone knew that once levied, it would continue. "It's a poor war out of which you can't get a new tax," the late President Taft once jokingly exclaimed. In principle it is a fair tax, and it is a useful device for maintaining a rough equality among disparate economic areas of the country, taking away from metropolitan centres some of the wealth they have extracted from their hinterlands and putting it back. These far-reaching objectives were not envisaged when the tax was initiated. It is only gradually that its potentialities as a socialistic measure have been realized. If it could be administered by gods and angels, it would be ideal for its purposes. As it is, men being men, the phrase 'publicans and sinners' (*publicani*—tax gathers) comes to mind. The income-tax sytsem has forged fetters about the citizen whose effects have hardly yet been suspected, still less evaluated: for one not unimportant department of his life— his money—it provides a combination of Circumlocution Office with secret police that must powerfully affect the whole genius of democracy. For this no alternative has been invented and the end is not yet.

This 'efficient' side of Canada's war experience was probably the most prominent of all the direct effects. It opened the vista of a managed, or planned, society, which is still being pursued: this, in turn, called for personnel, and the call was answered by the pouring into the Canadian public service of a good proportion of the best brains of the country. As a result it is now admitted (by Canadians) that Canada has one of the most efficient civil services in the world: it is no use debating whether she might not have been better off if she still had the easy-going office holders of the nineteenth century, for the times have moved beyond that point and if we are to retain our free society our job is to accept our new masters, the civil servants, and devise restraints to impose on them just as our ancestors imposed restraints on 'divine right' kings.

During the war, three-quarters of a million men—and quite a few women, too—found themselves in uniform, about one in twelve of the country's population. The immediate effects of service life were sharp, the distant ones must have been far-reaching. Not only did men learn to use weapons and to become familiar with the noise of battle and scenes of violence, but they learned to submit themselves to a type of discipline to which most of them had been complete strangers, to give the word of command and to accept gradations of rank.

One typical young Canadian who had been in that typical Canadian occupation, school-teaching, joined up and was picked out for a commission. He was sent to the nearest large city for the usual army course. There he fell under the ministrations of tough old sergeant-majors from whom he learned much about life that he had not suspected to exist. As he himself said, innocence, the innocence of the unsophisticated young fellow in an unsophisticated society, fell from him like a cloak (not that he began to revel in sin) and when he had finished his courses, "he knew how to command men", something he would never have learned as a school-teacher!

Rank, class and Sam Hughes

In our loose-jointed society, distinctions in rank were almost beyond the ken of ordinary men. 'Discipline' was not far from an unknown word. Good order there was, good order based on the home, the school, the church. These institutions supplied the best kind of discipline, discipline from within, but that was not the kind the army imposed on men, which had more analogies to the discipline of the factory. But factories had not been prominent aspects of Canadian life: the average employee had worked on the farm or in the little businesses of the small town. Only in a few large cities had the impersonal discipline of organization become prominent. And, suddenly, the flower of Canada's youth was subjected to it, and to more, for in the fighting services what prevailed was not merely discipline for efficiency, but discipline as an aspect of class. How would Canadians, accustomed to the minimum of restraint, take submission to men who, by official decree, became their social superiors, a class apart, with distinct habits, clothes, privileges? Canadians had always prided themselves on their democratic railways, where one did not, as in England, ride 'first', 'second' or 'third', but all shared the same seats. Myth, if you like, seeing there were parlour cars, but myth believed in. And now, the flower of the country's youth was officially divided into 'first class' and 'third class', with a little group of 'seconds' known variously as corporals, sergeants or sergeant-majors.

Many were the heart-burnings, the fits of anger and mortification, and infinite the devices of adjustment, as this new, horrible fact of class distinction made itself felt. Before the war, no Canadian youth (with the possible exception of the microscopic number who attended private schools) had been accustomed to address others, whether elders or not, as 'sir'. And here they were pitchforked into a situation in which the use of 'sir', the ceremonial salute, and a dozen other minor and major matters were *de rigueur*. The official ritualism of army life (a reflection, as already suggested,[12] of that fully ritualized life which is second nature to the English upper classes, whether expressed in the services of the Established Church, in fox-hunting, or in coronations) for most men was at first 'hard to take'. Harder still was the occasional objectionable display made by men whose officer-status was proving too much for their proper balance, like the captain who in a hotel dining-room, complained because privates were also being served therein. The reverse of that situation was the one depicted in the familiar cartoon in *Punch* where the 'colonial officer' is made to say to his men: "And now, boys, we are to be inspected by an English general. And while he is here, be careful not to call me 'Alf' ". The following, by official attestation, is real; and nothing could illustrate more vividly the difference in hierarchical ideas which obtained on either side of the Atlantic. If this was not frontier democracy speaking through one of its most flamboyant examples, what was it?

Sir Sam marched up to Kitchener's desk. When he arrived at the desk Kitchener spoke up quickly and in a very stern voice said: "Hughes, I see you have brought over a number of men from Canada; they are of course without training and this would apply to their officers; I have decided to divide them up among the British regiments; they will be of very little use to us as they are." Sir Sam replied: "Sir, do I understand you to say that you are going to break up these Canadian regiments that came over? Why, it will kill recruiting in Canada." Kitchener answered: "You have your orders, carry them out." Sir Sam replied: "I'll be damned if I will," turned on his heel and marched out."[13]

The man who was capable of thus treating the great Kitchener was as quick with his pen as with his tongue. Witness what must surely have been one of the most remarkable *General Orders* ever put out to any force. After some rhetoric on the abominations of the enemy, it continued: "Soldiers! The world regards you as a marvel. . . ." and proceeded to detail the remarkable achievements of these marvels in building a camp with, among other things 'three and a half miles of rifle range—twice as long as any other in the world."[14] That would frighten the Germans all right!

Somehow or other, Sam Hughes' army adjusted itself to the English society of ranks and classes and without too much injury to Canadian conceptions of equality. Brother learned to salute brother in the street and, in England at any rate, to patronize the café appropriate to his rank. Those Canadians who became officers quickly understood that they could not play the feudal superior to their men, as English officers were expected to do (not least by their men). Battle experience soon sorted out the genuine article from the counterfeit and the Canadian Army ended the war with no greater strain between officers and 'other ranks' than did others. When the uniforms came off, men dropped back into their previous spheres. Nevertheless something remained, some residual deposit of class distinction that had not been there before. Canada had entered the war a pioneer democracy: she came out of it a more experienced country, with tens of thousands of her people aware of another world, of its class distinctions, of its vices and, mostly in a vague way, of its ancient culture. Most of those who had submitted themselves to the will of others must have enjoyed the experience, for it was not from the old soldiers that the equalitarian reform movements of the next generation were to proceed. The veterans, to judge from their organizations, came to stand for conservatism, a certain imperialistic jingoism and the small favours that they could extract from government. But there were also thousands of ex-servicemen who did not maintain active association with veterans' organizations. University youth, to name no others, came back basically unaffected by the dip into army life and the sophisticated society of the old world, but broadened by the experience and finding it easier to evaluate the petty moralities of Canadain life than it would otherwise have been.

This sudden expansion of view which had come to those who served abroad, affected 'the folks back home' in a dozen ways. 'Returned men', as they were invidiously called by those who did not fight, at once began to prove 'difficult'. The distinction remained until another war came along to renew it— that between those who had seen the world and those who had not. It received its characteristic expression on every social level. Men who had been overseas had outgrown the stuffinesses of the lower-middle-class society that marked most of Canada, that constricted, conventional society which had come in on the heels of pioneer heartiness. "Home-keeping youth have ever homely wits." The soldiers' initiation into ritualism had given them a sense of form that people at home often did not possess—they took their hands out of their pockets when the National Anthem was played. It had equipped some of them with habits that did not help them much in humdrum life: many had to find out that there was no more room in Canadian life for the 'officer and gentleman' type which attempts to live on its 'quality' than there is for the 'bum'. Whatever the individual experience, it never fitted with ideal smoothness into the old grooves of Canadian society. Canadian society itself was changing rapidly: the impact of the ex-fighting men accelerated the change.

But as always, it must be remembered that there were two Canadas and that they had had quite different experiences. French Canada did not see the war as a heroic crusade against wrong. Rather, it saw it as one more attempt of the English to dragoon and coerce. Why should young French Canadians get into the uniform of the British king and serve under English-speaking Protestant officers? If it be suggested that many a young man had done just that in the war of 1812, the historian sees first of all the difference between the known enemy at the gate and the unknown enemy some thousands of miles away, and then the growth of a national and democratic spirit in the century's interval which brooked the outsider less easily than the old seigneurialism had done. Yet in heightening that sense of 'ourselves alone', the war may have brought closer eventual understanding between the two peoples: it at least showed English Canadians of penetration (who in such matters are few) that a people cannot be coerced, but must be understood and persuaded.

For English Canada, where death had come into many a home, where every household hung on reports of battle and where names like Vimy and Ypres became as familiar as those of the next streets, the war, surely one would say, must have constituted a deep spiritual experience. But did it? It is difficult to assess the effect of war in such terms. War matures and hardens national societies. For countless individuals whose loved ones do not return, there is travail of spirit. But in Canada in 1914-1918 individual experience did not mount up into national. Canada was not Hungary in 1956, under the tyrant's feet. A revolutionary war, with its goal of a 'new heaven and a new earth', constitutes a spiritual experience for a people, for in it (as has been previously pointed out) everyone 'must stand up and be counted'. That was not the case for Canada in 1914-1918, where for most people life continued to go along its usual grooves, only more prosperously.

The spiritual experience from war might be expected to crystalize in literature. Yet that seems to come long after the event: it was Tolstoy, decades later, who celebrated Russia's triumph over Napoleon. It was Tennyson, centuries later, who spoke for the Elizabethan sea-dogs, not their contemporary Shakespeare (though they may have been speaking through him). So in Canada's case, the expression of the spiritual experience (which in itself will also *be* the spiritual experience) may show up a century or two hence, when the meaning of our fighting on these distant battlefields becomes clearer. Or it may not. Much of the generous gain that might have come out of World War I, from a sense of duty done, and gratuitously done, was frittered away in the miserable friction between the races. Dozens of specific effects are traceable but no complete assessment is as yet possible except the almost platitudinous statement that the vast communal effort it involved moved us in English Canada closer to becoming a national community.

Notes to Chapter 26

1. The effects of the Second World War must be assumed, for there is no space to deal with them separately. Yet to lump all wars together would be to write not history but a sociological essay. History seeks the concrete: we must study war by studying wars, in this case the First World War.

2. Col. William Wood, "The French Canadian Enclave" in *The Canadian War*, Mar. 13th, 1915, p. 18.

3. Eleven per cent of the people were of direct British birth, and as many more were of British parentage. Some hundreds of thousands were foreign-born or of foreign parentage. English Canadians whose parents were English Canadians numbered in 1921 about 2,800,000 out of a total population of 8,788,000. In 1914 they would have been fewer.

4. Quoted from *The Ontario*, Belleville, in *The Canadian War*, Feb. 6th, 1915.

5. *The Canadian War*, Mar. 13th, 1915, reporting a country conversation.
6. Ibid., Mar. 20th, 1915.
7. There was some evidence of this at the time of the Suez crisis, November 1956.
8. See the present writer's *Unconventional Voyages* (Toronto, 1953).
9. The Second World War carried the process much further—the consolidation of English Canada went on visibly.
10. As when men fell on their knees on landing and kissed the soil.
11. See p. 181 ff.
12. See p. 140.
13. *Official History of the Canadian Forces in the Great War, 1914-1918* (Ottawa, 1938), p. 126; an eye-witness account.
14. Ibid., Vol. II, p. 122.

27: Yesterday and to-day

'WE ARE LIVING IN AN AGE OF CHANGE.' Is there anyone who has not uttered the hackneyed words? And have there been any times in the world's past when they have not been uttered? "Time's ever rolling stream bears all its sons away!"

Constant change, we may agree, is the lot of man. But are there not higher and lower crests in this endless procession of the waves across the sea of history? Historians dearly love to find 'turning points of history'. They refer to 'the fall of Rome', the Renaissance, the French Revolution, as 'ends of an epoch' or 'the beginning of a new age'. Such periods, we may agree, formed major crests. May not our own age mark another? The halcyon days of the nineteenth century ended with the roar of the guns in that August of 1914 and since then two world wars have brought vast changes in every aspect of life, from mere technical devices to the profoundest regions of belief, all in less than a single lifetime Whether the changes that we have witnessed are greater or less in magnitude (and what is the measure of magnitude?) than those of times past is immaterial: they are great.

This book has already referred to previous changes of magnitude: the swing from seventeenth-century puritanism to eighteenth-century rationalism, and the swing away from that 'Age of Reason' to the nineteenth-century romanticism and sentimentalism, with its contrapuntal echo of the seventeenth century. To-day we have swung far from the nineteenth-century orbit of our great-grandfathers and once again, one sometimes thinks, the contrapuntal echo can be heard: an echo, this time, of that eighteenth century long ago, but a distorted echo. We have left behind Victorian prudishness and sentimentality: we stare at life with eyes as hard as those of the 'men of reason', and the buildings that we put up (our best reflections), like theirs, run to lean straight lines, without ornament. But our eyes may be less assured than those of the eighteenth cen-

tury, and there is in them that which was not then present—
dread!

Science and religion

Since we, the living, stand in the midst of change, it is difficult for us to estimate its direction and strength. When the
task is to examine a generation of time and a half-continent
of space, there can be no limit to the detail which should be
examined but cannot be. The attack must be made by looking
at things in the large.

Few would doubt that the major change marking the post-
war period had to do with the fundamentals, with matters of
belief, both as to the nature and destiny of man and the nature
of society. Changes in these depths were necessarily marked
by changes on the surface. In Canada, the revolution in social
action did not become prominent until the hard times of the
nineteen-thirties, but the revolution in belief, and therefore in
manners and morals, had been in the making for some time.

In the world at large the debate between religion and science
had been going on for generations, but it had only come into
the ordinary man's field of vision during the Victorian period.
Its big headings are familiar: the discovery that the earth
revolves around the sun, Newtonian physics, which convinced
thinking men that the universe was not mere accident and
chance, Darwinian survival of the fittest, and so on. In our
own century, along with previous great names, there are those
of Einstein and Freud. Such men have profoundly changed
our conceptions of the nature of things, that is, of religion.
To-day, it would seem as if modern science and traditional
religion were so far apart that they can have nothing in common.

If there still is a heaven 'far above the bright blue sky', it
is now much farther off than previous generations suspected,
at least half a billion light years off, so astronomers tell us,
for with their biggest telescopes they can see out that far. To-
day we have abolished hell—and the devil, too, insofar as he
was an external entity (though possibly we have just transferred him inside ourselves). Yet the churches flourish, and
not merely on the credulity of the simple. After all, with all
our knowledge, we have never moved one inch beyond the
insight of the Psalmist—"If I ascend up into heaven, Thou
art there: if I make my bed in hell, behold, Thou art there . . .
the darkness and the light are both alike to Thee!"

What all this comes down to saying is that, while scientific
findings affect the physical side of life and are echoed in the

attitudes and beliefs of intellectuals, they only slowly affect the accumulation of long tradition. In the formation of this long social and political tradition of ours, Christianity has had a dominant place. The whole complex is too intricate and the process by which it evolved has been too gradual for its pattern to be quickly changed. Hence, though it may be disturbing to reflect that in the scheme of things, if scheme there be, human beings possibly are no more important than maple trees or mosquitoes, people in general are not upset. New views of God, man and the universe must eventually affect society but they filter down in ways uncertain and indirect. Society is not a pool of clear water in which the course of the sinking stone—the idea or the doctrine—may be watched to the bottom. Rather it is a jungle through which the revolutionary conception has to force itself by some inner dynamic of its own—and be changed, often out of recognition, as it goes on its course.

So far away are the innermost recesses of the social jungle from its sunlit spots that it may be debated whether from age to age they undergo much change of any sort. Men have always recognized that there is this residuum in society. Our modern educational services shrink it, but our vast cities make it larger. It is like the bottom of the sea, the deep out of which everything rises. For the social historian satisfactorily to describe it is almost impossible, for it is the portion of society which leaves the smallest record of itself behind.[1] Its religion has probably not altered much from the beginning of time, or its morals either. It rides along on the technical achievements of every age, and when the society that the relatively few have built collapses, it retreats into the anonymity of the merely biological. If such words are used, then, as 'movement', 'change' and 'progress', they must be understood as applying to the different layers of society in different ways and affecting them at different rates.

The post-war revolution

Canada, by its isolated and backwoods nature, has until relatively recently been well insulated against the revolutionary consequences of scientific and critical thought. It was not until the twentieth century that the views of a hundred years before seemed to become part of the common stock of assumptions. When, in 1909, the Rev. George Jackson of Victoria College carried his 'modernistic' opinions on Biblical criticism outside his class-room, he was fiercely attacked by his senior officer, the Rev. Dr. Carman: the controversy reverberated throughout the land, but the weight of sentiment seemed to be on

Jackson's side. At one stage in the proceedings, the editor of the *Globe*, a Presbyterian minister, summed up the sense of his Methodist fellows neatly by quoting John Wesley: "The Methodists do not insist on your holding this or that opinion; but they think and let you think."[2]

With the increasing efficiency of communication, later disintegrating knowledge (such as Freudian psychology, with its tendency to dethrone reason) spread more quickly. The sharpest break with a rather simple past came just after the First World War. *Post hoc, ergo propter hoc*? The intellectual revolution, working underground, must have had much to do with that break.

Until 1914, Canada was steeped in Victorianism.[3] Victorianism is perhaps just a convenient catchword, but on the side of morality and deportment it carries connotations of primness, religiosity, undue piety, the taboos of conduct, stiffness and ceremoniousness; and on the intellectual side, of romanticism, mysticism real or posed, and the mannered thought and conduct which does not spring directly from the actual situation. Those who were brought up in the late autumn of Victorianism will know what it all meant: the utmost of propriety in conduct, the provincial attachment to English giants of the previous age like Tennyson and Dickens, the failure to come to hard intellectual grips with the nature and problems of one's own society.[4]

When the well-brought-up young fellows of middle-class parentage who comprised so large a sector of Canadian society went off to war in 1914, many of them, perhaps the majority, took with them a code of conduct which had trained them against the sins of the flesh, against the use of alcohol and tobacco, against gambling and, for a large minority, against card-playing, against dancing and even against the theatre. Such young men went to church regularly, and took the minister seriously, if not always literally. They genuinely believed they had to help make a better world, and largely by helping their fellows, through traditional forms of charity. Yet they were neither paragons, nor Puritan snobs. As they grew older, they may have found that they had to compromise their attitudes; but with attitudes such as enumerated, it was fairly certain that they, the not-far-from average young Canadians of 1914, would have started life.

To-day nearly all this Protestant asceticism (but not the humanitarianism) then so powerful, has gone. It would be wrong to say that the war blew it away, though the war, by showing thousands of young Canadians wider civilizations, had a good deal to do with that.

In an old book of memoirs, the authoress, writing about 1820, recalls how in her youth, about 1760, Dafoe's *Moll Flanders* could be read aloud in mixed company, old and young, but how by the opening years of the new century, that had become impossible. The twentieth century reversed this trend. *Moll Flanders* would have remained tucked away until the nineteen-twenties, when it might have been taken out and read to a mixed audience without much disturbance of equanimity. At a little later time, the nineteen-thirties, there was at least one hardy soul who was heard at a mixed party reading aloud not *Moll Flanders*, but *Rabelais*, four-letter words and all, and the young ladies present seemed to be taking it quite comfortably in their stride. Yet even in sophisticated London as late as 1910, in the first performance of *Pygmalion*, with what a resounding thwack had the word 'bloody' fallen on the stage floor! In Toronto, where Mrs. Patrick Campbell had shortly come to repeat her London success and where the audience, for so distinguished an occasion, was expectant and 'emancipated', on the repetition of the epithet the thwack was louder still![5]

The intriguing question is whether the change in intellectual outlook, plus the war experience, worked a significant change in conduct also. Did a generation 'go to the devil' because it modified its beliefs and discarded the taboos? It is too easy to say that, if we no longer believe in eternal damnation, we just go in for eating, drinking and living merrily. There is another ethic behind Puritanism, not primarily religious—the ethic of achievement. Achievement, selfish or otherwise, requires qualities: the earnest and ambitious Communist of this last generation exhibited them, just as had Canadians before the first war. Add to the job of building a country, evangelical religion (whether free will Methodist or predestinate Presbyterian, does not matter) and you get that combination of qualities which marked the day and incidentally carried Canada's soldiers to distinction. On the other hand, if we are not "fleeing from the wrath to come," we are apt to take an easier view of life and to be a little more indulgent to human frailty, and this latter would seem to suggest the sounder line of explanation. After the war, tasks were not quite as urgent, we became a little more at home in our world, and a little less eager, not such crusaders as before, and so our almost impossible propriety of speech and conduct was moderated. The qualities associated with the puritanism of achievement—all the 'copy-book virtues' —were not, however, radically affected. We continued to be our industrious, thrifty, energetic and efficient selves.

Nor did there seem much observable change in our humanitarian instincts—except in that humanitarian movements tended to become organized and depersonalized. And always hovering in the wings, as it were, was the scientific attitude. This attitude stood ready to convert fellow-feeling into efficiency, neighbour into social worker: after all, an efficient citizen 'has no right' to be poverty-stricken, incapacitated or diseased. Just a little further off lay that scientific logic which could look at humans as objectively as guinea pigs. Some of Hitler's men of science went over that line. So far we have not crossed it.

The collapse of the Prohibition movement supplies a conspicuous example of the way in which our society 'matured', 'lost its zeal', 'broadened', 'slumped' (take your choice). Before the war, it was not just a few cranks who were rallying their forces against 'the demon rum', but large, intelligent and prosperous sections of nearly every community—every Methodist and Baptist, most Presbyterians, and groups of some size from the Catholics and even the Anglicans. The drive against the liquor traffic was conducted in every form and on every plane, educational, emotional, evangelical, economic. It was compounded of social disinterestedness, religion—from hot and strong to staid and dignified—fanaticism, and detached analysis of the situation. It caught up all ranks and classes, and the debate, which went on with growing intensity through the early years of the century, provided as big an opportunity for education in self-government as this country has ever received. During the war, the Prohibition forces rolled to triumph, and just after it, consolidated their triumph in further victories. Then even more quickly than the achievement came crashing defeat, and the country descended into the ugly and unsatisfactory situation with respect to alcohol in which it has continued. There can be no doubt about the collapse. No middle course for Canadians in the matter of 'the demon rum'. To-day, the Prohibition movement is as dead as the proverbial door-nail. If this is not a dramatic change, what is? And why did it occur?

The change in sexual morals

During the nineteen-twenties, much used to be heard of the loosening of sexual morality. A favourite, and silly, phrase was 'flaming youth'. The American magazines were filled with stories about 'petting' and 'necking', which were apparently new activities for young people (the stories made good 'copy' too). We are under the disadvantage in Canada of having a great deal of our social discussion conducted for us by our American friends and in reference to American conditions, which differ from Canadian: for illustration of this, see the women's pages of almost any daily newspaper. It is therefore difficult to get at our own situation, and dangerous to take the American for the Canadian: thus, our newspapers run columns of advice to the love-lorn on the American plan, which permits as many marriages end to end, so to speak, as the heart of woman can desire, as long as no two of them are conducted side by side. Despite increasing frequency of divorce,[6] which, nevertheless, is still not common, the situation in Canada does not parallel the American abolition of marriage 'for keeps': discussion in American terms has only a secondary relevance for Canadians. Consequently when we hear how youth 'flamed' in the nineteen-twenties, we must first inquire whether it was American or Canadian youth that 'flamed'.

'Flaming' was always understood as referring to hot passions spilling over. The only statistical index to sexual morality (which, presumably, has some connection with our intellectual and religious background) that we Canadians possess (the Americans have their Professor Kinsey) is (appropriately) to be found in the dry-as-dust columns of the *Report on Vital Statistics*, where the curious may see an exact record of illegitimate births, province by province, from 1921 to the present. Illegitimate births may be a reflection of ignorance and their absence not one of good conduct, but nevertheless there is probably some correlation between illegitimacy and lax morals. 'Where there's smoke, there's fire.' For Canada as a whole, for 1921 (the first year of record) they formed 1.97 per cent of all live births. This rate slowly but unvaryingly increased to a peak of 4.47 per cent in 1945. Since then, it has receded slightly, being 3.83 per cent in 1955. In all provinces but two the line would show about the same curve. The two exceptions are Quebec and British Columbia. In Quebec, the illegitimacy rate is low and the variations from year to year small. The maximum 3.4 per cent, was reached in 1939, the minimum, 2.7, in 1946 and to-day it is 3.2. British Columbia began in 1921 with a lower rate of illegitimacy than the average, 1.2, but there is hardly a year since which has not seen this increase, so that in 1954, it stood at 6.20 per cent—that is, one child in every sixteen was illegitimate. British Columbia's only rival in bastardy is the province on the opposite side of the continent, Nova Scotia, which has only recently lost the lead. In 1945, Nova Scotia's illegitimacy rate rose to 7.9, or roughly one in twelve births. Let us hope that the phenomenon does not too closely resemble the iceberg. In all provinces, the rate ascended rapidly during the Second World War, for in any great war, woman reverts (without too much persuasion) to her ancient role of prize of the warrior.

If war-time records are to be relied on, illegitimacy and venereal disease have no coincidence. During 1940 the venereal disease rate among the troops varied from 24 per thousand in British Columbia to 202 in Military District No. 5, Quebec City. Montreal stood next at 116. Toronto, District No. 2, had a rate of 45. These rates decreased in each of the following years, but the order of incidence remained about the same, except that Montreal displaced Quebec in dubious victory. In 1943, the rates were: Montreal—68 per 1,000, Quebec—62, Toronto—31, British Columbia—13.[7] The figures are difficult of interpretation, for bastardy and syphilis ought to occur together. Instead—the more bastardy, the less syphilis! The relation between uniforms, a great city and venereal disease is plain. But why the discrepancy between, say, Montreal and Toronto? Toronto's undoubted virtue? The much lower economic level in the crowded slums of Montreal and Quebec, which forces more girls into prostitution? The superior moral standards of the Protestant areas? The large concentration of soldiers in a city like Quebec? But then Nova Scotia, with Halifax, was much lower than Quebec and it is also half Catholic. Whatever the explanation, in the face of such figures it would appear that male chastity, a strict article of the code before the First World War, was no longer what it had been. But then in this matter of men in masses, perhaps we are looking at those recesses of the jungle mentioned above: perhaps for the entire community, not merely the middle classes, the situation had not been very different before 1914—there is no way of telling.

Temporarily at any rate, the two wars wrested morals out of their older groove, away from the strict and creative puritanism of the nineteenth century, closer to a secularism, and even paganism, that Canadians of an older generation had been accustomed to associate with unregenerate 'foreigners' and such lesser breeds. The old reticences disappeared and manners became freer and conversation, as noticed above, more frank than at the beginning of the century. When in the nineteen-tens a medical man, addressing a group of students, of both sexes, told the young ladies they should get rid of their corsets, their embarrassment on the mention 'out loud' of the intimate word was evident. In the early nineteen-thirties the author well remembers a young lady of eighteen holding forth among her elders on the subject of birth control, without embarrassment to anyone there present. This was all for the good: it was only recapturing for urban children the healthy familiarity with biological processes that country children had always possessed. It probably carried its analogies to the sudden rush in the nineteen-twenties on the part of young ladies to discard not only the heretofore unmentionable corsets but as much as they dared of the rest of their clothing.

This discarding of her clothing probably was related to the new general sense of liberty that woman was experiencing. In the sphere of conduct, she had discovered that the moral code had been more of man's making than her own, a reflection of his idealism and his possessiveness. In the sphere of citizenship, the Canadian woman no more had to fight for political rights (in contrast with England) than had her males before her, and she probably valued them as little. There were no streams bursting their banks, no hordes of women anxious to lose their chains and flaunt their new-found freedom. Woman, on whom pioneer condition had put such a high 'price tag', stepped into the privileges of a youthful society with little protest. Apparently as long ago as the beginning of representative government (1791), if she was a freeholder, her voting was not prevented. This right, or privilege, she later lost and in recapturing it, had her one struggle of consequence,[8] though even that was minor. She had had the right to hold her own property as a married woman given to her (1882) before it had been awarded in Great Britain.

As the freedom of the bush gave way to the Victorian proprieties of the rising cities and towns, nineteenth century Canadian woman found it easy to retreat to the status of 'lady'. She came out of those fastnesses mainly in the period after the First World War, and as easily as she had gone into them. And now at mid-century she is apparently once more in retreat. That at least seems to be the conclusion of one acute analyst of the Canadian scene, Arthur L. Phelps:—

"[Women] are considered sub-standard human beings. . . . It is the ingrained masculinism in our tradition . . . which keeps women frozen out of the first category of humans. I'm all for bringing them in. Seemingly, though, it's a dreadful personal risk. It makes women buzz like hornets to suggest it. It makes them uneasy and vindictive. It seems to threaten their prerogatives and their established methods as females. They would far sooner wheedle and be kept than stand up and be accounted human on their own."[9]

Mr. Phelps's spirited exhortation brought no delegations of infuriated feminists to his door. Forty years before, when a daring young man wrote an article in the University of Toronto *Varsity*, which began with the sentence "Woman is inherently a barbarian",[10] the heavens were rent with protest! To-day, with the five-room bungalow as the object of life and every woman in sight pregnant, the approach of a variant of Victorian domesticity brings neither regret nor deunciation.

Is the world getting better or worse?

That phrase, "a variant of Victorian domesticity", fetches the observer up with a round turn, for it makes him realize that he is already edging forward into a new social climate, to which the observations of the nineteen-twenties, thirties and forties do not too happily apply. During those decades no remark was more common than that 'the age is one of increasing secularism'. People, so it was alleged, had turned away from the traditional religion and morality to a way of life that entertained only material values. To-day, alongside the emphasis on things, the observer must put such phenomena as the increasingly early age of marriage, the greatly increased birth rate, the rather tame domestic ambitions of the rising generation,[11] and the marked increase in church membership. The contradiction is at first sight puzzling—never before so large a place in life for the merely material and at the same time a pronounced return to institutional religion.

In investigating the contradiction, we are hovering on the edge of an old and familiar question: Is the world in general, and Canada in particular, getting better or worse? The question has always been asked and it has invariably been answered according to the predilections of the person asking it. The present writer does not claim to be an exception to the rule. He would also be prepared, did space permit, to add another half-dozen chapters piling up the evidence on both sides.

There is one area of life in which it seems possible to return a cautious affirmative. Surely in alleviation of suffering and in attempts to establish communities that provide some reasonable kind of existence for their members, men are making a better world. The opinion begs the question of the meaning of 'better'. It may be that the original cause of all our woe was eating the apple. It may be that we humans come off second best compared with our four-footed friends, on whom has not been inflicted the burden of self-consciousness. Such judgements would not, however, secure majority votes. Man must follow his destiny, so what alleviates his journey is probably 'better'.

It would be idle to ring the changes on the marvels of modern progress in medicine, surgery, sanitation and the rest: everyone knows them in advance. No age has seen them go forward nearly as fast as our own, and it will soon be possible to take a man wholly apart and put him together again. Let us hope dispassionate experimenters will not be tempted to do so just to observe results. So with the mysteries of nature: thanks to their solution, we are not too far from war over the ownership of the moon.

More interesting material lies closer at hand than the moon, in the way in which we have tried to organize our society in relation to the forces we have let loose, and their concomitants in wealth and power. In Canada, successive groups have held the destinies of the country in their hands, and their actions while in control make up most of the material of our history. After the Conquest, at first there were the predatory wandering traders, then the little groups of semi-aristocrats in 'family compacts' who secured as many good things for themselves as possible and, in order to do so, consolidated their power over government. They were succeeded by the great merchants, such as those who long dominated the economy of the St. Lawrence. The merchants gave place to the industrialists. whose triumph came with the 'National Policy' of Sir John Macdonald.

The rise of the next class of men strong enough to compete for national power was heralded by 'The Patrons of Industry' in Ontario, who made a bid against the government of Sir Oliver Mowat in the eighteen-nineties. The industry these men 'patronized' was agriculture. Eastern agriculture would never have been strong enough alone to control the state, but when the West was settled, that was another story. From the beginning of the twentieth century, the agricultural interest grew powerful, and in 1921, the farmers elected (in 'The Progressive Party') the second largest number of members to parliament. But they lacked cohesion and their party fell to pieces. In any case it was too late for any one interest group to control a country as complex as Canada. Meantime industry as it grew stronger created its own internal divisions: organized labour became the antidote to organized capital. It is hard to see how we could have one without the other, except in a slave society.

Group loyalties and the tensions between groups were strengthened and crystallized by the great depression of the nineteen-thirties. If organized labour, through unemployment, was weakened, the necessity of preventing the labourer starving to death was strengthened. Out of debate, riots, hunger marches, new conceptions of society rapidly emerged. 'New', that is, to a youthful country like Canada, where every newcomer traditionally carved his fortune out of nature. The humanitarianism that had underlain English socialism had been a Canadian inheritance, just as strong in Canada as it had been in England, and traceable to the same evangelical Protestant sources. Like conditions producing like results, collectivism as a political creed and as a social gospel began to make headway in Canada, too, giving us our left-wing parties such as the C.C.F. (Co-operative Commonwealth Federation) and a conspicuous example of the consecrated man in politics, J. S. Woodsworth.

There has always been an element of collectivism in Christianity, though Christians have just as often been successful in avoiding its implications. Nevertheless the long-range, indirect effects of such injunctions as those requiring us to bear each other's burdens or to do good "unto the least of these", have been great: they have accounted for the spirit of our English-speaking world, and as the logic of events worked on, they began to account for much of its structure, too. That is, Anglo-Saxon socialism (or collectivism) boils down to an indirect and unconscious attempt to apply New Testament ethics to specific situations. If 'the labouring man' has been able to better his situation as opposed to 'the capitalist' it is partly because the capitalist has been beaten before he started, overcome by the logic of the ethic on which his society is founded. Evidently there have been other influences, too, such as naked pitting of interest against interest, but these have ridden along on the original swell. Doctrinaire ideas, such as Marxism, have had little influence in Canada except negatively, by way of delaying the logical evolution of industrial society.

The hard times of the nineteen-thirties forced social integration along many channels. Direct methods of 'relief' made many think in terms, not of 'relief' but of justice. Partly as a result, various social devices, now well known, have gradually come into being, such as mothers' and children's allowances, old-age pensions, and a measure of hospitalization. These, after all, are in exactly the same line of descent as say, free schooling. At mid-century, Canada was much closer to a just society than she had been in 1920, though she still had considerable distance to go, notably in adequate standards of housing.

One problem which was not tackled, which was scarcely envisaged, had to do with the numbers and natures of men themselves. How long, it may be asked, can humanity just go on breeding, and expecting that vague entity 'society' to shoulder the consequences. Unlimited breeding, however much approved by religious authority, when transmuted, as it must be, into poverty and poverty's consequences, becomes sin. Religious authority thus puts itself on the side of sin. If western life is to be further ordered in the interests of justice—and all its logic seems to go in that direction—the day will come when men will have to take into their hands the last, most difficult problem of all, that of regulating, by means other than war and famine, their own numbers.

Is social justice a criterion?

Many would refuse to use social justice as a touchstone for the answer to the original question: is the world getting better or worse? They would insist on bringing back the discussion to the primary field, that of religion. They would say that if scientific knowledge has had a vast negative impact on our traditional religion, then the world has got worse. On the other hand, it has yet to be proved that a religious attitude is incompatible with scientific knowledge. If religion, any religion, cannot stretch itself somehow or other to incorporate man's increasing knowledge, then so much the worse for that religion. Christianity, especially on its ethical side, has already shown that it has capacity for adaptability, so that no matter how much its formal doctrines may have to be changed, it will probably continue to hold its place. After the First World War, the Church did lose its appeal for many young people, particularly for those of advanced education and those of little education—top and bottom. Thus many a man who had been proceeding towards the ministry before going overseas did not return to his studies after the war, and the clerical profession in Canada has never recovered from the blow it received at that time, for students in theology suffered a reduction in numbers, in energy and in calibre. But to-day it would appear that organized Christianity in the form of the Church has been more or less able to accommodate itself to the new knowledge, and to stand up to the secularism of the age.

The union of several Protestant bodies into the United Church of Canada was in some respects a rear-guard action and could have been interpreted to mean a conservation of slender resources, a consciousness that the old inspiring fire was no longer there. Yet during the great depression of the nineteen-thirties, the churches acquitted themselves well in coming to the rescue of whole country-sides in Saskatchewan. They did not cease to attract a certain quota of devoted men. War, when it came, should have been their opportunity. And in war, as in depression, the clergy also acquitted themselves well.

At the end of hostilities, there began the economic expansion in Canada which is continuing as these words are written. It was mainly urban and suburban. It dispersed a new level of prosperity in every direction. It moved many a family up into the middle class. And it was accompanied, not by the flight from organized religion which had marked the nineteen-twenties, but by a vigorous movement of expansion in the church. What all this meant it is hard to say. Was the average man any more *religious* than when he had stayed away from church? Was he secretly dreading the rods which scientific knowledge had already made ready for his back—the atomic bombs, the guided missiles, and all the other agents of destruction that one day might fall from the skies? Was he, in his silent Canadian way, registering his awareness that his kind of people throughout the world were in retreat and was his renewed interest in his traditional structure of religion a testimony to his determination, if necessary, to stand and fight? Or was all this church-going and church-building merely a reflection of bourgeois prosperity, the image of the conservative, security-loving generation that had succeeded the high adventurousness of those who had built the transcontinental railways and the new provinces? Is this what the rapid increase of ritualistic formality in the evangelical denominations is to be taken to mean?[12] Since the author's countrymen are rarely able to put thought or emotion into words, the question cannot be answered.

It would be strange, however, if the phenomenon were entirely superficial. It is possible that after the long debate, science and religion may be coming to some kind of reconciliation: a new synthesis may be forming. It is clear that no society of any vitality can endure long without some binding principle to hold it together.

The above paragraphs leave the original question unanswered: "Is society getting better or worse?" Much can be said on both sides. It may be that society, whatever its formal religion and professed convictions, does not change a great deal. We no longer burn witches and we have developed our humanitarian instincts. Yet we kill people on the road with our cars, several thousands of them each year. Society is so complex that it goes in every direction at once. But it registers its main movements in a conspicuous way—by the gods and goddesses that it sets up for worship. If the current gods and goddesses (the real ones, underneath the labels) can be found, then, perhaps, the general direction things are taking can be glimpsed. For that another chapter is necessary.

Notes to Chapter 27

1. Reference has already been made to one example of this: our inability to find out, except by inference, what made simple *habitants* act as they did in 1775. See p. 121.
2. C. B. Sissons, *History of Victoria University* (Toronto, 1952).
3. See Chapter 15.
4. It is not suggested that such standards marked the whole of society, though since they were 'the thing', they penetrated a long way. A perusal of the file of *The Arbour*, published at the University of Toronto about 1911 on, confirms the impression—the utmost propriety and an almost complete failure to penetrate the realities of Canadian life.
5. The author heard the thwack!
6. The Canadian divorce record (each ten years): in 1921, 558; in 1931, 700; in 1941, 2,461; in 1951, 5,263. The peak was reached in 1947 with 8,199. Each post-war period was marked by a sudden uprush of divorces. In previous wars the maladjustments they reflect would have resulted in more or less legal 'separations'. How many 'commonlaw' marriages exist, which divorce statistics do not reflect, it is impossible to say. Experience of social workers points to many.
7. *Winnipeg Free Press*, Feb. 26th, 1944.
8. The municipal franchise may never have been wholly lost: it was accorded again by law, beginning in 1882.
9. In the *Ottawa Citizen*, Jan. 2nd, 1953.
10. W. C. Kester, "Sexism", *The Varsity*, Feb. 11th, 1914.
11. Observable to their instructors, also commented upon from time to time: see Hugh MacLennan in *Maclean's Magazine*, July 21st, 1956, p. 4.
12. Not only in the churches but in most spheres of life is ritualization increasing: in the formalities of speech, song and act, although these have their silly side, some 'service clubs' have reached the High Church plane—they, too, are attesting their own excellence. Formlessness is the mark of a new society, where everything is beginning over again. We are, therefore, some distance along the road, though the ritual marking the various groups within our society has not yet mounted up to embrace the national whole. That is, Canadians, as a people, have not yet begun to testify to their own excellence, as older peoples do.

28: New gods for old

MODERN MAN, SO IT HAS BEEN SAID, is an infant crying for his mother; at least that is what we are told is the basis for the American cult of 'Momism'.[1] Canadians have not been much affected by 'Momism' but not having been able to invent symbols for their own psychology, they have accepted their neighbours'—without knowing the difference. Here, then, close to the centre of being, there may perhaps be found the first of the gods we really worship.[2]

Man has invariably sought a symbol-goddess. In the middle ages he made a stern masculine Deity share His place with a woman, the Mother of God. Mary received short shrift from the Protestant Reformers, whose Calvinist branches, especially prominent in Canada, suspected her sex in nearly all of its aspects. Yet paradoxically it was this Calvinist continent which gave woman her fling, and made its civilization into an altar to the feminine. In woman's hands, thanks to the wills of deceased husbands and fathers, were the majority of shares in its great corporations. Much of its economic life turned about woman, her necessities and her desires—'the shops', 'shopping', the vast domain of feminine adornment. On a more earthy level, the masses, intent on the life-force, welded to the elemental, to the *ewig weibliche* which is both mother and wife, had once again brought back the love-goddesses: crude versions of them, to be sure, and links with Aphrodite rather than with the Virgin and Child. But back the love-goddesses had come, and their images, multiplied a thousand times, might be worshipped in any collection of drug-store pornography. Aphrodite, born anew from the sea foam of photographic puffery, had become one of the great goddesses of our new paganism. The reflection of their dreams, the masses had made her, as they always make religion, as in 1273 they forced transubstantiation on a reluctant papacy.

It may be that the female masses play just the same role in fashioning male gods. Once it was Apollo, the beautiful youth:

in our day it is the latest idol of the screen, groaning out his heart (or stomach) to audiences of 'teen-age girls.

The great god CAR and his associates

That inventive society known in Canada as "the country to the south," could make a new goddess as quickly as it made a new car. But in making new cars, it made a new god. For the god, no better name could be found than simply—CAR!

In one of the annual reports of a great motor-car company during the mid-century years, there might be seen pictured the dignified and elegant ritual which surrounds the birth and renewal of this god—his Easter! The artist who depicts the scene has drawn a great crowd of people, of every conceivable social type, gathered about altars on which current images of the god CAR are displayed. In the upper left of his picture, there is a vast symphonic band of music, possibly a heavenly choir, its every violin bow at the ordained, precise angle. In the centre, richly but decorously dressed ladies grace a stage, beside which fountains play and from whose wings ballet dancers make appropriate obeisance. At the back of the stage, on a higher level than ladies and audience, surrounded by a nimbus of light clouds, at the point reserved in temples for the principal altar of the god, CAR is pictured midway between heaven and earth. "Lo, He comes, in clouds descending," the rapturous beholders seem to cry, as they greet the great god in his form of "The New Model for the Coming Year".

CAR's worship detracted even from that of Aphrodite herself (though the two were not without their intimate relationships). "Cars outshine the stars", says a popular magazine, picturing a daughter of the goddess reclining languidly, though with a second-best look, against one of the elegant new images of the god.[3] All ranks and classes burned incense to CAR— save a few sour intellectuals who thought to avoid the industrial revolution he symbolized by ignoring it. "Yesterday I bought a Cadillac, and realized a lifelong ambition," says one of the gentlemen reported in that anthropological study of a wealthy Toronto suburb, *Crestwood Heights*.[4] CAR's devotees increased with the years. And no wonder. A patient, obedient god who takes you where you want to go, faster than any magic carpet. A comfortable, well-upholstered god. A god whose priests well knew how to gain new worshippers by playing on the qualities of vulgarity and ostentation. And above all, the god of power, who multiplied man's ego manifold. Yet a ruthless god, sometimes, too, who could turn on his idolater and rend him.

CAR brought in his company a whole host of lesser godlets (most of them born of Electra), which their worshippers called 'modern conveniences' or more simply 'progress'—the labour-saving devices that stood in every housewife's kitchen, and the long series of instruments of communication such as the radio, television, and the rest. What this vast upheaval would mean before it reached its logical conclusion — and what is its logical conclusion? — who was to say? We all worshipped CAR and his fellows, that is, the innumerable by-products of science, power and human ingenuity, and some of us thought we saw these gods admitting us to a cheerful, effort-less heaven. Slowly it dawned on the less simple that there was not much satisfaction in that type of 'progress' which eventuates in hydrogen bombs. And so we come again, by another route, to the disillusionments of the day, to that look of dread in human faces that was not there before, and perhaps because of such matters, to that groping back after some other kind of God which the last chapter suggested might be occurring.

Meanwhile, CAR and his associates changed our society out of recognition. They scattered our homesteads far beyond the cities, so that many of us became once more, after a fashion, country dwellers.[5] Others, yielding to the logic of CAR, married themselves to him for better and for worse, moving their habita-tion from place to place under the hauling power that he pro-vided. CAR threatened to turn us all into nomads, and his wheels, like Juggernaut, levelled every physical and psychical obstacle they met. They invaded every urban open space and threatened to destroy every blade of urban grass. They knocked down houses. They called imperiously for straight, wide roads to be carved out of our diminishing fertile fields. They tore up our precious peach orchards and ordained that factories for making new parts of CAR should be erected in their place.

More than that, CAR forced on men, far more effectively than French Revolutionary slogans could ever do, the worship of another great god, Equality (though not of Fraternity), for once surrounded by his metal-and-glass turret, every man became equal to every other man, just as every metal-and-glass turret, despite the efforts of their advertisers to the contrary, was approximately equal in value and in efficiency to every other metal-and-glass turret. But it was not a new brother-hood that our god created for us, for once inside his fortress, a man became a world in himself, proudly independent, to whom the objects shaped like his own were threats which approached and passed, forgotten as quickly as avoided. They might contain millionaires or paupers, good men or rogues: to each other as they whirled by they were just shapes.

Were there no good words to be used of CAR? Of course there were, many. For one thing, CAR gave to many a slave promise of freedom. He offered escape from orders, from routine, from boredom. He made, or seemed to make, the humble masters of their fate. By opening up the vistas of the roads, he brought back to life the pathfinder, the explorer, the romantic in us. He was really a kindly god if worshipped with common sense. But instead his cult often carried his faithful into ecstasy and hysteria.

Men like gods: British style and American

The effects on men of CAR worship, that is of the new mechanical society, are not yet fully discernible. That society is without question one of the most remarkable in history: it is perhaps also, all its aspects considered, the most lunatic. Once again, it has not been our own creation and though Canadians are almost as ardent worshippers at these shrines as are Americans, they have not invented them. They do not resist the modern god, but he is not quite their god in the same sense as he is the Americans'. It has always been Americans who have worked up the folk-lore of this modern religion (as, for example, the stories that used to be told about the old model-T Ford such as giving a squirrel away with each one to follow it and pick up the nuts), just as it has been Americans who have supplied and taken most seriously its high priests, among them the great cardinal who did so much towards establishing it, Henry Ford himself.

Henry Ford was a figure who could hardly have been other than American. Canada did not provide a stage for such as he. Yet this was not on account of lack of opportunities here for accumulating wealth, but rather because that process called for more betting on the sure thing than was necessary across the border. This gave rise to a sub-variety of rich men in Canada, not precisely identical in attitudes with their American opposite numbers. In the United States, when men got tired of piling up millions, they were apt, in gestures of ennui, or in order to ensure monuments to themselves, to hand their money over to 'foundations', charities, universities. This public munificence also proceeded from genuine patriotism, for many such men were aware that they as Americans were building the republic. In Canada public benefaction was a less familiar pattern: the Canadian rich man did not have the same sense of nationalism as the American, and with honourable exceptions, he frequently spent his money in ways which suggest that his patterns of conduct lay outside his own society. There was something of the provincial about the rich man, as about other Canadians. Consequently the sub-god Croesus did not receive the semi-divine honours often accorded him by our neighbours. Nor did the activities associated with him. "The United States' business is business," Calvin Coolidge is alleged to have said. No Canadian prime minister would ever make such a statement.

Shortly before the First World War, there began to rise on the ridge at the north of Toronto, a vast structure which, as it took shape, was revealed to be a feudal castle. Neighbouring barons were peaceful and the townsfolk had not asked protection from them: nevertheless the feudal castle kept on growing. When completed, its towers and turrets boasted no archers, nor its drawbridge men-at-arms. It was merely a house, albeit a very big one, one fitted to the magnificence of the wealthy citizen who had built it. On the occasion of the coronation of George V, this gentleman had taken over to that ceremony, at his own expense, the entire militia regiment of which he was colonel. A knighthood duly followed. He had then built his feudal castle, and for a short time, he lived in it. It later became a kind of museum *cum* dance-hall, ridiculously named in characteristic unoriginal borrowing, *Casa Loma*.[6] The suggestions of baronial grandeur, the military associations, the knighthood, these were aspects of a Canadian pattern of wealth which had no exact counterpart across the line. They led back to deity by a different route.

"Toronto was a beautiful city, fifty years ago" (about 1902), proclaimed a newspaper caption of the nineteen-fifties, placed over a picture of the Governor General of that day and his lady alighting from their coach and four outside the mansion of Sir Joseph Flavelle. The way of life there depicted—coach, postillions, footmen and all—was at any rate elegant and had tradition behind it, if not Canadian tradition. In the same newspaper, about the same time, there was a photograph of a wedding party of mid-century, a very special one: an antique coach, with self-conscious bride and bride-groom and a coachman, still more so, in cocked hat and knee breeches. "Regal transportation of newlyweds", says the heading, in pointing up the 'play-acting', which, we may surmise, had a touch of nostalgia about it. Mr. Skey, M.P. for Toronto Trinity, in deploring the post-war victory of the British Labour party, "likened the present moment (1947) in Great Britain to the time when Huguenots left their native France to enrich other countries with their skills and knowledge. . . . Britain is an occupied country, occupied by an alien form of government (socialism)".[7]

The feudal past, the instincts of a ruling class, wealth, public status (which implies some sense of responsibility), this looking to a state of affairs in Great Britain which in its entirety no longer existed—all these were elements in the make-up of that vast complex which we in Canada called for want of a better name 'Imperialism'; it was one of our Canadian sub-gods.

For a contrast between it and 'tycoonery' pure and simple, let the reader glance at the same paper and read the account of the man who had made his million before he was forty. His style of living expanded in sumptuousness, if not in wisdom, with his wealth: he kept a racing stable; he dashed back and forth across continent and ocean. Requiring a little expansion in the sexual sphere and growing tired of his wife, he arranged with his partner to do an exchange. After that last exploit he died of a hemorrhage at fifty-four. A short time later his son fell foul of the police. The explanation for such men might be found, perhaps, in words used to review an American novel: "When the world of middle-class comfort and Babbitt-like idealism collapses, men go adrift and a way of life becomes hopeless in which there is no success that cannot be measured in material terms, or no goal not expressed in the accumulation of goods and sensations. It is spiritual depression that seems to render all such ends barren and worthless." Our millionaire, if he could have found a cause, might have become a useful citizen and his money might not have destroyed him and his son.

Canada, be it said, did not really produce many pure wasters of this type. Much more typical were the self-made men, who, whatever their road up, gained respectability and became members of university boards of governors or chairmen of the local board of hospital trustees. This is hard to explain, for a "cause" in the Canada of the mid-twentieth century, in the sense of some impelling and noble objective, seemed just what was lacking. Were we the beneficiaries of our retarded development, still living in the substantial nineteenth century, with its religious and domestic values, not yet as far along the road of sophistication as our elder brethren who had had more generations of society-building behind them?

The list of men-as-gods does not stop by any means with those who became prominent because of their wealth. If space permitted, statesmen, soldiers, men of letters, scientists, sportsmen, could all be scrutinized as candidates. What the process involves is finding the hero, that type of man whom a people regard as representative. What came out at once in an examination of Canadian life—English-Canadian—is that there was no hero. Could any one imagine an Eisenhower in Canada—a successful general vaulting into political leadership? Generals were strange beasts who roamed forests shunned by the rest of us, and after they had done their war-time duties, they were to be shot on sight. Even the great air fighters of the First World War, who for a short time seemed to qualify as heroes, were soon forgotten. The officer class in our growing forces was virtually a new phenomenon to us, one not familiar to many. When it became familiar it would not be liked, for it represented a 'throwback' to those old days when there had been superiors and inferiors. Military officers do not make faithful servants of the God Equality. As for men of letters and scholars as 'heroes', perish the thought! The chances of their becoming representative figures in a population such as ours were zero. Entertainers, actors, actresses, we could not believe existed unless they were American. A considerable section of our youth worshipped readily enough at Hollywood shrines, but we had no local national figures of the sort. Merely rich men did not impress us, as they seemed to do our neighbours. Our labour leaders were a class on the way up but as yet they had become neither powerful enough, rich enough, nor wicked enough to have won for themselves anything like the place in national life enjoyed by some of the great tribal chieftains of labour in the United States. Statesmen once had been heroes —one has only to think of Sir John. By mid-century they had become just 'good fellows'—'Mike' or 'John'—one of the boys. Could a new crop of those statues that adorn Parliament Hill in Ottawa be imagined—dignified gentlemen in frock coats, reading portentous speeches? We were left with our professional hockey players: it is possible that Lionel Conacher came close to a national popular figure. But hockey players could at best be the heroes of an hour. Canada might be a land fit for heroes to live in but the genius of the Canadian people seemed emphatically to make against its being a land in which heroes lived! It was a hard country on men-like-gods.

The god Equality

Canadians were always acutely aware of the differences in size, power and wealth between their country and the United States, and it was perhaps the hopelessness of changing this situation that made them indifferent to their own submergence in the American way of life. But the major reason for their indifference was that they worshipped the same gods as did

Americans. To one of these gods the United States as a nation is officially consecrated, the great God Equality, *Equalitas*, to give him the classic name which is his due. "We hold these truths to be self-evident, that all men are created equal. . . ."[8] In Canada, Equality was not given a place in the official pantheon but he had almost as wide a circle of devotees as in the United States itself. To his apotheosis everything conspired: he still lived back in the bush—especially the 'bush' of our minds—and made his sorties thence out into the clearings. He had powerful institutions and priesthoods to serve his cause, and these at mid-century had constrained nearly the whole of society into his service. He rode triumphant on the back of that other god, CAR. It is by no means the least of Canadian paradoxes that the cult of the God Equality seemed to combine well enough with older creeds which ranged men in a pyramid at whose apex was a semi-supreme being receiving quasi-divine honours.

Equalitas is the father-god of a much respected deity whose images by mid-century had girdled the globe, though they were changed out of recognition as they passed from land to land, the god *Democracy*. *Equality* had brought *Democracy* out of the forests which had been his own place of gestation and found human parentage for him in those eighteenth-century frontier intellectuals, such as Thomas Jefferson, who had worked out the philosophical exposition of his cult. Jefferson, fronter versatility magnified, was also the inventor of the six-miles-by-six township, which we Canadians copied in our newer provinces: the six-by-six township, monotonously repeated from the Appalachians to the Rockies, is the reduction of the idea of equality to mathematical expression—the equality, economic, social, political and legal, of masses of identical farmers. Here was the genius of the continent, the god it worshipped in a temple to whose vastness no ancient deity ever could have aspired.

The god Equality is the image of our desires but his off-spring, the god Democracy, reflects our intellects. He proved a much more taxing god than his parent and consequently his temples, while thronged with unperceiving crowds, had fewer genuine worshippers. The evidence, it is to be feared, piled up. Political meetings where Democracy was the unseen presence, once vast, could hardly be held—people preferred to enjoy their equal rights to sit at home watching a 'soap opera' on television! At elections complaints came in over the smallness of the vote. Municipal life—the very matrix of the god's image—quite often could not find men to fill its offices. "A public meeting was adjourned when only twelve electors were in attendance . . . the mayor had been given an acclamation, and all twelve aldermen. . . ."[9] It is not fair to put the blame for such situations solely on the distractions of the great mechanical god CAR. CAR, it is true, was a demanding god, and Democracy could not stand against him in direct combat. But it was not merely warfare among the gods. Democracy had come down to earth and dwelt among us too easily for his own good: we took him for granted and did not value him because we had not wrestled with him.

There are times when every people serve false gods. Equality, a god with aspects of beneficence, could easily become one of them, for if the supporting intellectual and philosophical elements are taken from his worship, the slope goes quickly down to that bog which might be called "simpleton democracy", and from this men have always been fished up via the route of demagoguery and tyranny. At mid-century the bog had not yet been reached but only self-conscious and effective inquiry into the deeper aspects of our religion of Equality would save us from it. Our people would have to learn to tolerate men who were not afraid, for the sake of equality, of being 'unequal', for

> "When everybody's somebody
> Then no one's anybody."[10]

Logic carries the worship of the god Equality into all spheres: age, sex, race, nation, body, mind.[11] As a result many temples were consecrated in North America to Equality in regions where it is hard to see that that worship was justified. One of these regions, a strategic one, was education. It is good Christian teaching that every soul is worth as much as every other soul. But it is a far cry from equality of souls to equality of minds. Yet many managed to convert the one belief into the other, and most of those who did so probably were indirectly influenced by the old Christian doctrine. Once the mind and soul were equally caught up into the theology of Equality, however, the door was open to every absurdity as oblation to the great god. At mid-century a 'half-baked' philosophy had already been emphasizing for a generation the virtues of 'adjustment', that is, conformity. One of the disservices of simpleton 'educators' thus was to forward the trend towards simpleton democracy. Apart from their efforts, the trend had its dynamic, for the worship of the god did not rest quite as directly on the Christian teaching as it had in previous generations. Two wars had caused a hardening process to set in and had given that much more opportunity for another logic to be worked out, that of CAR, a synonym for which was efficiency. If we still organized anti-cancer, anti-polio and anti-other-disease associations (such associations neatly mark the swing in Protestant societies from belief in the worth of souls to belief in the worth of bodies), it was not entirely because of our passionate concern for our fellow men, but also because of our drive towards an efficient society, which CAR demands. Now the logic of the efficient society is the collectivist society: as André Siegfried puts it, "the pursuit of efficiency leads down the same collectivist slope in Pittsburgh as in Magnitogorsk".[12]

Yet it was mainly the old humane attitude which had become responsible for educational and intellectual chaos, for it assumed that "you couldn't have too much of a good thing" and sentimentalized the situation in such cries as "every child should have his chance". This led to keeping as many children in school as long as possible and the enunciation of the doctrine of "exposure". But many did not profit from this "exposure" to education and so the next step was to temper the wind to the shorn lamb. Nothing contributed more effectively to the decay of the inherited culture, though such sentimentality did not succeed in providing a substitute for it. As this book is written there are signs that the worst is over in educational sentimentality and that discipline and order may once more recapture their place. But those engaged in the battle are not tempted to hope too quickly when confronted with such splendid gems as the following comment of a college student in Canadian history on the second prime minister of his country, Alexander Mackenzie:—

> "Mackenzie's grandfather was an official who took part in the William Lyon McKenzie Rebellion. McKenzie himself was not a good leader, although he molded and guided his people.
> As a graduate lawyer from Chicago, he was interested in humanity, and civil liberty. He wrote a book on "Humanity and Industry", which included ideas for social reform. He was called upon by the C.C.F. to implement these ideas but he never did.
> He was wary and cautious in his speech, but against Laurier in the Naval Bill."

Our Canadian school-teachers, but not the pseudo-philosophers of education, made a good fight against the new educational quackeries. Yet while many schools continued to offer the same old reliable brand of goods as before (its age a patent proof of its inferiority in the eyes of the second-raters), others yielded.

One of the major educational tasks of the future would be to escape from too zealous worship of the gods Equality and Democracy, while avoiding the complete desertion of their altars.

Not only in education but in every other field the god Equality required his offerings. All occupations tended to be reduced to the same level: you might choose to be a clergyman, I might prefer to run a dance hall. The idea, carried far enough, would equate the banker and the bank robber. To this pathetic end had Calvinism's belief in 'the calling' (which had had so much to do with building America) been carried.

In the aesthetic world the sacrifice to Equality was, it would seem, disastrous. It allowed a person to say of a work of art, a poem or a play, "well, that may be your preference, but it is not mine"—and no canon of criticism could be set up against such personal judgments, for 'everyone is entitled to his choice'. To this it was no retort to say that the market would determine the outlines of a culture. The great cultures were built by great artists and by men of great taste and discernment, not by Everyman. Everyman has had little taste and he has worshipped the God Equality under his other titles of Sameness or Conformity. Consequently he has invariably taken what the mass producers have given him. At mid-century the major point of the salesmen-priests who forced their products upon him was that these were 'the very latest': the 'very latest', both salesman-priest and those over whom he cast his spells would have agreed, must be 'the very best'. But how could mere change for change's sake have any but accidental relationships to beauty and to worth?[13] Thus the twin gods Equality and CAR (the latter under his cognomen 'Perpetual Industrial Revolution') drove society on towards the deadly average.

The worship of Equality was not all dark rite: it had its services of song and of joy. The god dampened down some of our human irrationalists. He persuaded many an English Canadian to think of French Canadians as fellow citizens rather than as "these French". He lessened anti-Semitic prejudices and induced some tolerance for the foreign immigrant. Though opportunities for the display of them in Canada are limited, he succeeded in having colour prejudices frowned upon.[14] For much of all this, that most ubiquitous and industrious of his altar boys, the public school, was directly responsible.

From out of Equality's Heaven proceeded that upon which we invariably prided ourselves the most: our classless society.

While not even the great god himself was able to prevent some from thinking themselves 'better' than others and from amassing more in the way of power or pelf or education or ancestors than others, while, that is, the class line develops easily and quickly everywhere, yet in general our pride has been founded on fact. As a rule, here in Canada, men have been judged on their own qualifications. Since Confederation, if not before it, not many public men have had any background of education, culture or wealth other than what they have acquired for themselves. We have suffered, as a result, from short-sightedness and the difficulty self-made men have of thinking in general terms, but we have kept our social ladder free for all hands to climb.

After all, it was the god Equality, whether in social visage, political or economic, who focussed every new-comers' piety, for every new-comer prayed for equality—with those who preceded him, if not with those who were to follow him. If the ambition for inequality lies just as deep in man as that for equality, the public doctrines of the god at least served as aids in preventing the rise of those old-world class distinctions from which most of us would feel we had *escaped*. At mid-century, Equality had come close to being the official deity of the Canadian state. In this straining for mystical union with him, whether for better or for worse—and it is not self-evident that a desire to stand the society of men and of nations on its head is for the better—Canada was in the same current that was sweeping along the whole human race. Equality had become a universal deity.

The old culture and the new civilization

In a country like Canada, where the background of most people has been narrow and the opportunities they have had for learning something about the great world few, it is the mass gods who must be worshipped. There was a time in the old pioneer days when men could be individuals but when the bush was cut away and no longer hid them from each other, deviation easily became heresy: it offended the worshippers of the great god Equality. To-day, as yesterday, deviations are reprobated by the average man, precisely because he senses that they stand for an order of things which would displace him from his representative position and threaten his power. 'Democracy', the average man would say, 'has no room for the fellow who wants to be different'. The problem is a vast one: how to maintain a society with the equalitarian values of the pioneer and at the same time gradually build a national culture which in the distinctions it makes is not concerned over-much with the shrine of Equality.

Foremost, perhaps, among modern deviationists is the gifted individual whose intellect carries him into spheres unattainable by the average man, spheres whose existence, indeed, is unsuspected by that man. Such individuals often deny and sometimes ridicule the values of the average man. No more offensive type of heretic could be imagined, as is indicated by the vigour with which such terms as 'high-brows' and 'egg-heads' are hurled about. Men to whom such epithets are applied are sensed by the mass as the new threat, replacing the old ruling class of a century ago. The enduring elements of civilization, the free play of mind, a feeling for which characterizes the intellectual—these are precisely the matters which are anathema to the average, which gives its acclaim to the trivialities of the moment. That which should draw the allegiance of good men and true, it sometimes seems, is something in the nature of the comic strip, while great poetry is to be shunned like the plague.

Does this mean that the old culture which grew up in the countries from which we came is unacceptable to our people, that it will have to be replaced by something else, something created out of native materials? All cultures have to be built out of native materials and the best of them cannot resist time indefinitely, as the fate of the ancient world indicates. But must we jettison everything from the past? In practice we shall not do so, but it sometimes seems as if the dominant pressures were in that direction. The sense of the past is weak in Canada, both our own past and that of our European forebears; and building on the past, rather than tearing down and starting over again, often seems to be regarded not as wisdom but as foolishness. We are in that uncomfortable in-between stage, when we understand neither whence we came nor where we are going.

Such a stage provides the best backgrounds for the philistine, who can join to his natural dislike of everything he cannot understand the weight of all the arguments for the religion of Equality and novelty ('Novelty' is another North American god whose theology would well merit study, did space permit). ". . . The lack of culture mentioned most often in your columns seems to be the dearth of appreciation of the music of the so-called major composers, such as Ravel, Hindemith, Khatcha-turian, Bach, Beethoven, Mozart, Haydn and Schubert, whose 'music' sounds like a group of energetic children hammering a key-board at random. . . ."[15] The quotation surely is the perfect expression of philistinism. Most people in most ages probably have been philistines, cultural barbarians dragged along by the scruffs of their necks, as it were, by their more discriminating brethren, but in what previous age was the barbarian able to shout out and silence individuals who were groping their way upward?

In the nineteenth century, Canadians were fairly generally ready to choose for their government, men who had had more training and experience than themselves.[16] During the present century, in contrast, the class line has received more emphasis —but from below. In the nineteen-thirties and forties several professional hockey players were elected to parliament: good fellows, no doubt, and their constituents probably thought them ideal representatives—themselves magnified! One of our Canadian cities had the bad judgment during the early nineteen-fifties to chose for its mayor a man who was also a professor: this stigma eventually helped to secure his defeat but before that there had been much subterranean grumbling and jealousy. ". . . Since————has had a university professor as mayor, have the ordinary, run-of-the-mill working people been given any consideration? It has been nothing but higher taxes. . . ."[17] One might contrast the opening words of a letter from that benighted country, Germany: "Sehr Geehrter Herr Professor" —"Most honoured Professor"!

The public expressions of the tastes and preferences of the common man, pandered to by those who get his dollars, had become so numerous by mid-century that it would only be boring to cite many of them. There is before the author as he writes, a picture torn out of a leading newspaper, one whose circulation is among the most responsible class of citizen. What is the picture? A sickly 'close-up' of a grinning woman to whose cheek are being applied the protruding lips of an ugly man. The caption: "Reunited after 23 Years." The combination of sentimentality and vulgarity is what we may expect when the 'voice of the people' is heard above all others. Such a picture would not have appeared in the same paper twenty-five years before. That vulgarity which used to be condemned as typically American had by the nineteen-fifties become just as typically Canadian.

This is possibly merely another way of saying that Canada had become more North American. She had moved further from her point of origin in the British Isles, whose life had become more and more remote to her people. Virtually all that remained was the official link of the Crown but when the wearer of the Crown came on special occasions, not to dwell among us, but to pay a short courtesy visit, while the occasion woke up some of the old memories, it seemed for the most part to provide merely an exotic spectacle. By mid-century even English literature was fading out over the Atlantic horizon. Shakespeare, it is true, was, as always and everywhere, indestructible, but the long train of his successors, despite all the labours of the schools, was increasingly unfamiliar. The well-known old poems were like a child's toys, put away in the attic to gather dust, recollected only with an effort or a smile. As Arthur Phelps put it: "The whole social scene of the English novel seems remote to the Canadian student . . . a great deal of English literature is merely by colonial inheritance politically ours. . . ."[18] The Canadian 'mass-man', in short, was cut off from his old roots and he had not sprouted new ones of enduring strength. He might be seen in the abstract, as it were, at a big hockey match. Hockey has been our national game and a fine game it has been: there must be few of the older men in our society who have not had a try at it themselves in their youth. The statement could hardly be made of the rising, or automobile, generation, whose chief function at a hockey match is to watch the gladiators. "The hockey fan likes his games rough. It gives him a thrill to see an opposing player, after a sound body check go flying through the air, his stick in one direction, his teeth in another. . . ."[19] The hockey fan and his kind would probably have liked nothing better than to see the corpses of the vanquished left lying upon the ice. It was the 'hockey fan', the 'average man', who by the nineteen-fifties had reduced Canadian hockey to the lessened figure it was cutting before the world, its teams, once so easily victors, defeated by Americans, defeated even by Russians.

And yet it was around this 'average man', bawling out against the referee, and his average wife, glued to her television screen, and his average daughter, with her lipstick and her chewing gum, that our civilization was revolving, and all too commonly he or more often, she, was held to be its fine and final product. "The big point that strikes the European when he first enters this country is the low cultural level of the people. This is not only their fault—it is also the fault of their educational system, their environment and their way of life. . . ."[20]

The 'average man', armoured in his pride in his shiny car and in his wife's 'dream kitchen', would not have understood what the immigrant who wrote that was talking about but would have contented himself with getting angry and telling the immigrant to 'go back home if he didn't like it here'. But if a people believe that mechanical devices represent the highest good, if they shove aside those of superior intellectual endowments because they are 'different' (unless they happen to be 'scientists', that is, magicians), if they take mediocrity as their social ideal, perhaps there is some point in the immigrant's remarks. The best defence against such charges is not their repudiation but an appeal to historic necessity. On the voyage to the new world, many a cherished object had, it must be admitted, to be cast overboard. The ideas, implements and ways of life that did not fit the new environment had to go. So much was jettisoned that the new society seemed poorer in content than the old. Having rushed down one slope in this way, it then had to climb the hill on the opposite side of the valley and it was finding the climb up a good deal harder than the slide down.

The deities who were presiding over the climb up were proud, young gods. Not only Equality, but Novelty and the shining young goddess Hope. In the new country they all were being worshipped with fervour and despite the disagreeable practices gathering about some of their shrines, it is possible that they might create, not 'a new heaven and a new earth'— their worshippers had abandoned that dream, if they had ever had it—but something worth having, a new civilization in place of an old culture. Canada in particular, with its newly evolved urban industrial and commercial class, must accept the new gods, for these classes worship them in spirit and in truth. And it is permissible to imagine that out of these very classes there would arise that new culture which alone would justify the country's separate existence. The old folk culture was gone, killed by the god CAR. Yet the new cities, with their miles of sprawling streets, were not slums: they contained the vitality of the nation. Their inhabitants, whether 'workmen' or 'office workers', did not mourn their lot. They did not think of themselves as 'toiling masses' but as middle-class people who owned property. They had pride. And pride is a condition of self-expression. If the God Equality would refrain from crushing all individualism out of his worshippers and if he would prevent them from falling into that condition of irresponsibility out of which comes simpleton democracy, then perhaps the city was the hope of the future. Possibly the place of the sturdy yeomanry of a previous generation would be taken by the bright boys of the television studio.

The goddess Canada
The next aspirant to divinity bears a name of good classical stamp: its ending in 'a' assures us of its sex—*Canada*, a youth-

ful goddess ranging herself alongside those older and tougher matrons *Britannia*, *Gallia*, and *America*. At the time of writing, 1957, there is still some doubt as to the lady's existence, though of late there have been pious attendants at her shrine. She is like one of those combination stars of which the astronomers tell us, that are ever and anon blotted out of sight by their larger and brighter companions. "While discussing some news with grades 5 and 6, I discovered that some of the children could tell the name of one country that participated in World War II—it was the U.S.A. The flags they drew were 'stars and stripes'."[21] There must be a country known as Canada, for it appears on the maps and people have been known to admit that they are citizens of it. They are not all "Canadians who are actually just 'half-way Canadians', men who insist upon presenting themselves to American visitors as if they were really British who had the misfortune to live in Canada. . . ."[22]

But then again, possibly there is no such country, or if there is there should not be, for we read that "Lincoln County Orangemen have labelled as subversive and unpatriotic the singing of *O Canada* in St. Catharines schools."[23] We also discover that no flags are flown in this curious country on the day devoted to celebrating its birth because it has no flag to fly,[24] not one that all its people will accept, anyway. If we are to trust one of its leading newspapers, it does not know how to build its own roads (many motorists would agree!): "Canadian engineers should do the detailed planning of the Lake Shore Expressway with U.S. engineers acting as consultants to iron out any snags, in the view of William McBrien, TTC chairman and member of the Lake Shore Expressway co-ordinating committee."[25] Mr. McBrien, it is to be presumed, represents dangerously advanced nationalistic opinions.

Furthermore, according to writers in the same paper, Canada cannot do for itself what would seem to be quite simple things, such as entertaining people at its annual grand jamboree, the Toronto ('Canadian National') Exhibition. The residue of 'national' in 'Canadain National' must be small. "Headline attraction at the 14 day exhibition is to be nine magazine covers by Norman Rockwell. . . . Rockwell is famous for covers in the *Saturday Evening Post.* . . ."[26] Canada—a goddess spurned, apparently, in her very temple.

One wonders at a large and prosperous community leaning helplessly up against the convenient neighbouring lamp-post. One wonders, until he turns up pictures like that which appeared in a Toronto paper, Aug. 28th, 1948, showing a group of persons about to open this same 'Canadian National' Exhibition. Prominent among them was a tall gentleman in white naval uniform, with plenty of medals on his breast. It was he who was about to do the opening. To his right were two short gentlemen, who gazed at him in attitudes of respect. All were smiling pleasantly, but the tall gentleman was not showing the evident signs of restraint visible upon the faces of the two shorter ones: "Full well they laughed with counterfeited glee. . . ." Their faces were lit up by the interior illumination which comes when the faithful stand in the presence of the elect. The tall gentleman was one of the overseas great, a 'prince of the blood'; the shorter ones were two leaders in provincial and municipal life. Here, printed forever upon two human countenances, plain for men of discernment to descry, was the inescapable expression of that lack of self-dependence and self-confidence, coming close to servility, which the small feel in the presence of the great. Here was the explanation, perhaps the major explanation, for the uncertain nature of this otherwise pleasant young goddess *Canada*. "It is true that Canada, of all the English-speaking [*sic*] members of the Commonwealth has the least distinctive flavour. It is virtually without a separate culture of its own. . . ."[27] No wonder.

A similar revealing photograph was used a good deal during the war—Roosevelt, King and Churchill at the Quebec Conference, 1943. Roosevelt and Churchill occupy the centre, and to one side hovers Mr. King. The two great gentlemen are very much aware that they are sharing the spotlight with each other, but they are quite unaware of the presence of Mr. King. Mr. King is smiling desperately at the camera, but it is a separate individual smile, not mingled with that of the other two. The title of the picture should be "Me too". As long as Canada continued to assume "me too" roles, she would not rise to her destiny.

The goddess *Canada* had made a brief appearance here on earth just after Confederation, but as these pages have shown, she had been immediately ushered back whence she came by George Brown and the Toronto *Globe*. After that she flitted about the realm named after her, but never managed to occupy it, still less win its people's hearts. As the Orangemen said, *O Canada* was a subversive sentiment. The might and magnetism of that other lady *Britannia* were sufficient to prevent the young woman from taking possession of her own home, and as *Britannia* changed from a deity to something like an ageing woman who had lost her money, another deity sailed into the sky—the southern sky, of course—and those who formerly had bowed down to one outside altar prepared to genuflect before the other.

Canada from the British Conquest on, had always been under the influence of the southern god. In every year of her history she had been becoming 'Americanized'. Thanks to modern communications and the disappearance of old enmities, the process was probably going on at an intensified rate by mid-century, until all an acute observer could say was: "A Canadian is one who is increasingly aware of being 'American' in the continental sense without being 'American' in the national sense."[28] The actual, if piecemeal, purchase of the country by Americans was a phenomenon which in the end might whittle away even the qualification "in the national sense". "Moffats, Ltd., appliance manufacturers with main plant in Weston, Ont., has been acquired by the Avco Manufacturing Corp. of New York, and will be operated as a subsidiary of the newly formed company, Avco of Canada, Ltd., subsidiary of Avco Manufacturing. . . ."[29] The Moffats had been making stoves at Weston for over a century. Some such brief note could have been found on the financial page of almost every issue during the period after the Second War. "Canners Control sold at Brief, Dull Meeting", announces the headline. "Directors pressured shareholders to accept the offer and presented them with no reasonable alternative. . . . The once Canadian enterprise, Canadian Canners, Ltd., is now a subsidiary of the California Packing Corporation of San Francisco."[30]

To such transactions few Canadians had much to say. Canadian business men accepted American leadership with alacrity, only too ready to snuggle down in the protecting wing of greatness, while the Canadian 'man in the street' had no feeling about ownership of industry one way or another. Labour unions were themselves leaders in the process of Americanization, and their Canadian organizations were but reflections of the greater bodies across the border. Here was a new variant of imperialism, American predominance in Canada and Canadian co-operation in American dominance elsewhere, which in 1957 was just reaching the initial stages of its political phase.

There was a remnant among English Canadians who objected to their goddess being displaced from her own temple by those who served another national deity. They objected, it could be said, to being swallowed even by the most kindly of crocodile-gods. In their resistance they were in harmony with those of French origin, to whom neither alien deity, *Britannia* nor *America*, was acceptable.

French Canada, fortified behind its language and its faith,

had something that English Canada did not possess: a way of life of its own, and a way of life that by mid-century was fast developing its cultural expressions. French Canadians were a people. It still was doubtful if English Canadians were, especially in that the immigration policy of the administration of the day appeared designed to upset whatever social homogeneity they had previously attained. On the other hand, by displacing the Anglo-Saxon, with his mere pushing energy, that administration may have given the land, through the scores of thousands of Europeans whom it brought in, the possibilities of a cultural future of its own and even of a political future, for they would not find *O Canada* subversive. If those who spoke English in Canada and did not find *O Canada* subversive could link up with those who spoke French and join to *O Canada* the words *Terre de nos aïeux*, there might then be some future for the common country.

But what English Canadians had done for French Canadians seems to have been to substitute for the old way of life that had come down from New France the enticing prospect of careers as workmen in English factories and of houses in miserable industrial ant-heaps. Gabrielle Roy's *Bonheur d'Occasion* with its depressing portrait of life in the French slums of Montreal unconsciously depicted English Canada's gift to French Canada: life as underlings, a life to which the individual could make little contribution, a life upon which the English notions of material comfort had been impressed but in which the English capacities and opportunities to achieve material comfort had not been attained. Nor could the bridge be crossed from the French-Canadian way of life to the English, for there was no end to the English section of the bridge—there was no English-Canadian way of life, at least none that could satisfy, none clearly grasped, little that French-speaking Canadians could distinguish from the American.

Yet how sad and sorry Canada must remain as long as it continued to be a pale imitation of the United States. How sad and sorry when the way out appeared so plainly: here was a country of two peoples, of two ways of life, of two cultures. That fact alone gave it any distinction it might happen to possess. The two had lived together for nearly two centuries, never intimately and often not happily, but without flying at each other's throats. That in itself was no mean accomplishment, one to which there were not many parallels elsewhere in the world. They could have powerfully reinforced each other—if the more extreme among the French could have abandoned their touchiness and their lack of interest in everything outside themselves, and if the more extreme among the English their absurd arrogance (what had they to be arrogant about? second-hand American cars?), their silly notions of racial superiority and their narrow intolerance. Canada, bright young goddess as she seemed to her admirers ninety years before, might again become a potency if those who called themselves her votaries could rise to these necessary heights.

The sky was not entirely empty of favourable auspices. As this book drew to its end, Canada, through its government, was asserting itself on the international scene and almost for the first time was discovering for itself a personality.[31] At home, the rear-guard was fighting its unending battle against "our sense of identity",[32] but it was a losing battle, for Canadians were at last beginning to find a little satisfaction in the fact of their own existence: the star of the Goddess *Canada* actually appeared to be in the ascendant. English Canadians would put her future in terms of the number of million barrels of oil she could provide for them. French Canadians might put it in terms of the respect she could command from other nations. The terms may not matter: the point is that they were both beginning to put it in terms of some sort, for in the future these terms might become common terms.

And what a future it could be if Canadians, of both races, had the vision to measure up with the country whose name the goddess bore! Four million square miles of the earth's surface for them to tend and move about in. Much of it might not appear valuable, but it was all God's earth: rightly used, it was not only 'valuable', in the sense that even the dull English Canadian could grasp, but *freedom*. Think for a moment, while the endless lines of cars sent their carbon monoxide fumes into the city streets, of what stretched on and on into the silent North! In Canada there was space, and there always would be space, and the qualities and privileges that come from space.

Here are a few lines, gathered from a short run of daily newspaper issues, which go to indicate the life and qualities that still existed in that northern country which it was the privilege of Canadians to be building: "The speed and vigour with which Canadian mining men can 'face-lift' a wilderness is being shown again . . . on the north arm of Lake Manitou-wadge. Last year, there was a primitive desolation. . . . To-day there's a clearing more than a quarter of a mile long. . . ." The above refers to a copper site that was turned into a modern town. This was the merely mechanical. The merely human excels it in interest: "Up north, where frontier conditions still exist, you can see how rich human character can develop and flourish . . . I can assure you that the frontiers rich in colour and in characters, still exist—not so many miles above the point where Toronto's neat suburban areas end. . . ."[33] And then in the subjoined headline there is the old note of personal heroism (combined with a touch of the bizarre):

ALONE IN HOUSE AT NIGHT, WOMAN
KILLS DRUNKEN BEAR

The bear, it appears, had swallowed a mixture of honey and wood alcohol with which the pioneer woman had attempted to relieve herself of its presence. "The bear only became tipsy. After staggering around the yard, it finally plunged through a window. Mrs. Sidinsky blazed away with her husband's rifle, killing the animal."

Or the ordinary experience of the prairie woman who, returning from town with her husband, had to stay in the car, owing to the fuel line freezing, while he struggled home through a blizzard to get the horses:

"Half of his journey was made walking backward to catch his breath. My concern was for him, lest he collapse: then all would be lost. His concern was for me lest I become panic-stricken and start out too soon. Finally . . . I caught sight of a faint light in the distance. . . . It came nearer and nearer. Soon I heard the rumble of a waggon over the rough roads. In seconds more rattle of trace chains and the snorting of horses, and the sight of a sheep-skin coated man. . . . Though the wind cut like a knife, it was a happy journey home. . . ."

These things were the authentic Canada, the aura of the young goddess, just as truly as the hurly-burly of commercialism, the worship of the golden calf of the bursting cities.

"Wonderful, over the broad lake to hunt here and there in the fast boat. The lake belongs to us alone. I believe the land has so many lakes that almost every Canadian could have one of his own. . . . On the long summer evening, we sit outside in front of the cottage and let our glance sweep over the darkening lake. . . . For days, for weeks, one might stay here, we reflect. . . ."[35]

What a nice, discerning note for a foreign author to sound! He was wrong in only one particular: despite our growing numbers, the land could have given us, in all probability, not one lake each, but two. Think of the European in his crowded countries, constantly tripping over his neighbour, to whom Canada could represent a place "where the world is beginning over again". Here, whatever else there was, there was vitality, resource and hope—hope and the future.

And so, on the edge of things, close to the primitive, where it began, we come to the end of this long book. Three centuries stretch behind us. Every year of each of them has its own individuality, and as they pile up, the aggregate of them becomes more and more complex. They interfuse and intertwine, these flowing years, and the tapestry woven out of them is our history. No matter how long the book, most of the story must be left out, and as it gets down closer and closer to the present more and more of it must be left out. For the people about whom and for whom it has been written, the Canadians, have been getting more numerous and spread out over wider areas as time has worn on. And now they cover half a continent: it is theirs, without serious challenge, theirs to make or mar, theirs to keep in good order physically, theirs to keep sweet and clean and free in matters of the mind and spirit. Many of them, these men who serve their country as civilians now and have served it in battle in times past, possess a document, their commissions, which ends with significant words, words that may serve as the end of this book and as injunction, warning and inspiration to themselves and to their children:—

"HEREOF NOR YOU NOR ANY OF YOU MAY FAIL AS YOU WILL ANSWER THE CONTRARY AT YOUR PERIL"

February 17, 1957.

Notes to Chapter 28.

1. Philip Wylie, *Generation of Vipers* (New York, 1946).
2. No attempt is made here to present a complete discussion of our modern gods. That would require a separate volume. Prominent deities like 'Free Enterprise' and 'Progress' must be omitted. The latter has been alluded to several times.
3. *Weekend Magazine*, Aug. 17th, 1957.
4. John R. Seeley, R. Alexander Sim, and Elizabeth W. Loosley, *Crestwood Heights* (Toronto, 1956).
5. "Rural non-farm" as the census calls it.
6. *Casa Loma*, literally 'House Hill'. As Spanish, so the author's colleague, H. W. Hilborn, Professor of Spanish at Queen's, assures him, it is of the same excellence as the French in the student club name *chez chien*, which is supposed to stand for 'dog house'.
7. Toronto *Globe and Mail*, May 2nd, 1947.
8. The Declaration of Independence, 1776.
9. Dispatch from Barrie, Ont., in the *Globe and Mail*. It was the mayor of this same enlightened town who, in discussing the pollution of the beautiful body of water on which it stands, was reported as having said: "Water pollution must be accepted as one of the

incidents of modern urban life". Barrie was growing, he was proud of it, water pollution from sewage was 'progress' and he was proud of that too!

10. Gilbert and Sullivan in *The Gondoliers* (Savoy Theatre, 1889).
11. The attitude of young people towards old is quite different in countries with a tradition of inequality from those, especially the United States, with a tradition of equality. The same is true of the relationship between the sexes. In one mid-Western University known to the author, staff and students share the same lavatory.
12. André Siegfried, *The Character of Peoples* (London, 1952).
13. Last year's car put completely *hors de combat* by the big new tail fins on those of this year. Next year, out go the tail fins!
14. See article in *Citizen* (Canada, Dept. of Citizenship, 1957): "an attitude of acceptance of the negro came to prevail in Canada to a degree that had not existed before".
15. Letter in the *Globe and Mail*.
16. See C. G. Power, "Career Politicians", *Queen's Quarterly*, winter, 1957.
17. Letter in newspaper of city referred to.
18. *McGill Daily*, McGill University, Mar. 17th, 1949.
19. J. V. McAree, "They Like It Rough", *Globe and Mail*, Mar. 19th, 1953.
20. Immigrant's letter in *Globe and Mail*.
21. Private letter from near Sarnia, Ont., 1954.
22. Private letter from New York, Mar. 25th, 1953.
23. *Kingston Whig-Standard*, Feb. 10th, 1956.
24. J. V. McAree, *Globe and Mail*, July 12th, 25th, 1951.
25. *Globe and Mail*.
26. Canadian Press dispatch, Aug. 16th, 1957.
27. Patrick O'Donovan in *Kingston Whig-Standard*. Young children, the present writer is informed, were insisting on saying 'lootenant' which is what they heard on the American radio. Their elders had long since given up eating with knife in right hand and fork in left, even in 'high society', and had gone back to the American habit of shovelling.
28. A. L. Phelps.
29. *Globe and Mail*.
30. Ibid., Nov. 9th, 1956.
31. Over the Suez question, 1956.
32. See *Our Sense of Identity* (ed. Malcolm Ross, Toronto, 1954).
33. Bruce West in the *Globe and Mail*.
34. *Globe and Mail*, Mar. 9th, 1949.
35. Vitalis Pantenburg, *Hier Fangt die Welt Noch Einmal Ein: auf Kanadas Neuen Strassen* (Here the World is Beginning Over Again: on Canada's New Paths), published in Bremen, Germany, in 1954.

Index

Index

A

Abelard, Pierre, 57
Abercrombie, Lord, 83
Abraham, Plains of, 17
Absolutism, French, 50
Academic Standards, 269
Acadia, 25, 61
Acadians, expulsion of, 84, 87, 92, 185
Acadian Recorder, 279
Accidents, 422
Actors and actresses, 429
Addington, the road, 263
Advertising, 203, 424, 425, 426, 433
Adultery, 77, 104
Adventure, French love of, 23
'Age of Reason', 214
Ages, the Middle, 56
Agnosticism, 420
Agrarian, movement, 418
Agricultural Society of Quebec, 107
Agriculture, 44, 328, 360
Ailleboust, D', 37, 105
Airplane, 425
Alaska Boundary Settlement, 348
Alaska Highway, 141
Alberta, 306, 367
Alcohol, 330, 411, 413
Aliens, 184, 235
Allan, Sir Hugh, 246
Allan, William, 168, 235
Allegiance, oath of, 120
Alline, Henry, 147, 169
All People's Mission, 365, 375
America, the goddess, 438, 441
Americans and American Attitudes, 131, 135, 136, 174, 178, 179, 180, 186; Americans, nature of, 138, 237, 273, 427; Americans, Canadian Attitudes towards, 156, 177, 179, 182, 280, 291, 379; American, census, 386; American flag, 439; American Immigration, 175, 176, 387; American invasion, 174, 422; Americans, military ineptitude of, in War of 1812, 178; American-Can. Relations, *see* Can.-Am. relations, 278 ff; American society, 424, 425; American culture, 426, 429; Americanization, 200, 312, 336, 413, 414, 429, 436, 439, 441, 442, 446
Amherst, Sir Jeffrey, 81, 84
Amherstburg; settlement of, 168
Amiens, Treaty of (1802), 146
'Amusement', definition of, 321
Ancien régime, 64
Andrel, Lieut., 124
Anglicans, Anglicanism, Anglican Church, 22, 64, 72, 97, 98, 130, 137, 139, 140, 141, 142, 147, 159, 160, 161, 162, 165, 170, 171, 172, 183, 184, 197, 199, 215, 216, 218, 219, 237, 243, 271, 276, 285, 330, 348, 366, 368, 403, 413
'Anglo-Canadian', the, 200
Anglo-Catholics, 215
'Anglo-Normans', the, 123
Anglo-Saxons, 143, 419, 442
Animals, 58, 69, 417
Annapolis,
N.S., 170, 226
Basin, 15
Valley, 42, 147, 148, 238, 243, 329

Annexation Manifesto (1849), 123, 236, 276
'*Annus mirabilis*' (1759), 85
Antigonish, N.S., 145
Anti-Americanism, 156, 182, 234, 279, 290, 441
    Catholicism, 216, 284, 332
    clericalism, 125, 275, 398
    democracy, 280
    Republicanism, 174, 181, 281
    Semitism, 433
Aphrodite, worship of, 423
Apollo, worship of, 432
Appliances, modern electrical, 434
Appeals, criminal, 52
Apples, 42, 333, 336
Aquinas, Thomas, 58
Arbour, The, 422
Architecture, 46, 63, 64, 74, 148, 151, 157, 158, 162, 170, 199, 213, 225, 226, 228, 229, 230, 231, 238, 270, 271, 307, 309, 371, 408
Arctic Ocean, 155, 335
Ardagh family, 199
Aristocracy, 97, 98, 113, 139, 141, 142, 235, 236
Armies, Armed Forces, 81, 83, 84, 121, 148, 150, 152, 153, 197, 220, 237, 289, 403, 415, 429
Armouchiquois, the, Indians, 3, 4
Armstrong, C. H. A., 228
Arrêt du Conseil d'Etat du Roi, 75
Aristotle, 58
Arnold family, 271
Arson, 331
Art and Artists, 74, 150, 151, 296, 313, 314, 325, 326, 355, 433, 438
Artisans, 14, 34, 48
'Ascendancy', the, 218
Asceticism, 411
Ashburton, Lord, 279
Assault, crime of, 331
Assembly, Legislative, the, 107, 110, 111, 119, 126, 129, 131, 134, 146, 154, 163, 184
Astronomy, science of, 409,
Atheism, 90, 177, 223, 269, 319
Atlases, 337
Atom bombs, 421
Austria-Hungary, Emperor of, 385

Auteuil, D', 61
Authority, legitimate, 100, 102, 104, 112, 114, 123, 124, 280
Authors, Canadian, 232, 233, 239, 251, 252, 293, 388.
Autonomy, 81, 105
Automobile, the, 355; *see Car*
Avco Company of Canada, Ltd., 441
Avenir, l', 275
Average, Canadian, the, 421
Avocat, the, 48, 109, 110
Axe, the, 78
Aylesworth, (Sir) Allan, 348

B

Baby, M., 236
Backwoodsman, the, 204
Badelart, Dr., 95
Baillef, French Architect, 46
Bailly, Abbé (Tutor to Carleton's children), 99
Baird, Rev. Dr., 361
Baldwin family, 218
Baldwin, Robert, 136, 219, 253, 367
Ballads, 293, 341, 342
Balls, 61, 77, 238, 250
Banff, 358
Banishment, 160, 164, 171, 172
Banks, 369, 401
Banting family, 271
Baptism, 11
Baptists, 147, 160, 161, 162, 206, 217, 243, 267, 268, 276, 319, 353, 413.
Baptist Church, Jarvis St., Toronto, 271
Barclay, Rev. (Presbyterian Minister), 162
Barn raisings, 206, 261
Barré, Col., 96
Baron, feudal, the, 97
Barrie, Ont., 196, 199, 210, 319, 357, 445
Barristers, French, 109
Baseball, 320
'*Bastonnois, Les*', 87, 180
Bastardy, 415
Bath, Ont., 161; Bath Road, 158
Baths, in pioneer era, 203

Baudoin, Abbé, 43, 44
Bay of Chaleur, 243
Bears, 347, 444
Beards, 307, 356
Beauharnois, Gov., 31
Beaumont, church of (1725), 74,
227
Beauport, 20
Beaupré, 20
Beauséjour, 358
Beaver and Beaver Trade, 7, 8, 16,
155, 251
Bédard, Pierre, 128
Bed-warmer, the, 48
Beer, 29, 48, 209
Beggars, 50
Bégon, Intendant, 76; Marie Eli-
zabeth, 77, 78; Michel, 77
Beliefs, 409, 410
Bell farm, 370
Bellarmine, (Spanish Jesuit), 57
Belleville, 305
Bell-Smith, F. M., Artist, 314
Belton, George, 362
Benefactor, the Canadian Public,
426, 428
Berthelot, M., 36
Bérulle, Pierre, 21
Beverages, 48
Bibaud, Michel, 252
Bible, the, 162, 166, 318, 410
Bicycle, the, 356
Biddulph Township, 331
Bidwell, Barnabas, 186
Bidwell, Marshall, 186
Bigeon, Jacques, 31
Bigot, Intendant, 77
Bill of Rights, (1689), 128
Birth Control, 416, 420; Birth
Rate, the, 17, 34, 35, 36, 63, 113,
115, 185, 193, 194, 209, 210,
303, 325, 380, 387, 390, 392,
394, 414, 417, 420; Births, ille-
gitimate, 77, 150
Bishop, the office of, 48, 49, 61, 63,
66, 69, 75, 103, 119, 121, 123,
242
Black family, 271
Blake family, 218
Blake, Edward, 219, 345
Blake, W. H., 225
Blasphemy, 31

Blizzards, 444
Bloodshed, 12
'Bloody Mary', 352
Blossom, H.M.S., 124
Bluenose, The, 241
Board of Trade News, 397
Bobcaygeon, Road, 263
'Bohunk', 372
Bologna, Concordat of, 64
'Bonanza' farm, 370
Bonaventure county, 245
Bons Vieux Temps, les, 45, 225,
238
Books, 80, 286
"Boom", Canada, 1910, 190
Booth, John R., 266, 267
Bossuet, Bishop, 30
Boston, 84
Botany, 75
Boucher family, 20, 45; Boucher,
Pierre, 35, 36, 52
Boudreau, Jean, 110
Bourassa, Henri, 110
Bourgeois, Marguèrite, 24
Bourgeoisie, the, 50, 110
Bourget, Bishop, 220, 224, 276
Bowman, Jacob, U.E.L., 179
Bowman, Peter, U.E.L., 179
'Bow Park Farm', 335
Boxing, 322
Boys, education of, 73
Boys family, 199
Braddock, General, 83
Branch plant, Am., in Can., 312,
441
Branding, 164
Brantford, Town of, 305
Brébeuf, 24
Breithaupt, Louis, 394
Brewing, 266
Briand, Bishop Jean Oliver, 101,
103, 104, 114
Brick, 158, 329
Britannia, the goddess, 438, 440,
441
British-American Relations, 131,
135, 136, 174
British-Americans, 273, 291, 390
British-American Magazine, 292
British attitudes and influences on
Canada, 97, 100, 136, 137, 138,
177, 191, 202, 217, 246, 281,

282, 296, 352, 366, 369, 371, 386, 396, 400, 427, 440
British Columbia, 334, 345, 368, 414, 415
British Columbia, University of, 195
British Empire, 85, 86, 96, 273, 440
British North America, 169, 213, 240, 247, 251, 256, 257, 271, 291
B.N.A. Act, the, 291, 292
Brockville, 1871, 305
Bronson family, 266
Brown, George, 193, 195, 216, 274, 275, 276, 277, 281, 283, 284, 291, 318, 335, 362, 365, 440
Brown-Dorion, Ministry, the, 276
Browning, Robert, 22
Brulé, Etienne, 6
Buckboard, the, 361
Bucksaw, the, 362
Buffalo, buffalo hunting, etc., 169, 329, 362, 366
Buggy, the, 333
Buies, Arthur, 224
Buildings, old manor, 37, 46, 205, 329
'Bukowinians', 385
Bureaucracy, growth of, 402
Burke, Edmund, 96
Burton, C. L., *A Sense of Urgency*, 310
Bush, Canadian, 399, *see Wilderness*; Bushmen, 211; Bushwhackers, *Canadiens*, 249
Businessman, the, 50, 51, 121, 199, 308, 309, 310, 441; Business, Can., Am., 411; *see also Commerce and Industry*
Bustles, 311
Byng, Lord, 340
Bytown, 195, 264, 296
Bystander, The, 296, 316, 317, 347

C

Cabanes (huts), Indian, 46
Cabarets, 75, 76
Cadillac, the car, 424
Caen, 7
Café, 31

California Packing Company, 441
Callières, M. de, 49
Calvinism, 22, 72, 97, 98, 141, 160, 161, 183, 342, 423, 433
Campbell, Sir Alexander, 305
Campbell, Mrs. Patrick, 412
Camp-meetings, 160, 330
Camping, 350, 372
Canada, general aspects of, 5, 8, 28, 30, 53, 72, 79, 85, 86, 88, 99, 102, 109, 111, 117, 125, 136, 139, 140, 174, 178, 180, 181, 182, 185, 188, 189, 192, 195, 198, 200, 212, 213, 218, 219, 220-221, 232, 237, 259, 261, 262, 263, 271, 273, 274, 284, 291, 292, 293, 299, 300, 303, 308, 311, 312, 315, 319, 325, 328-329, 329, 345, 346, 347, 368, 377, 378, 381, 382, 395, 400, 410, 411, 440, 443, 444; Dominion of, the, formation of, 274, 286, 325, 347, 369; 'East', creation of, 257; English, 276, 295, 301, 358, 373, 374, 387, 390, 396, 397, 398, 405, 406, 407, 442; *First,* 296, 298; French, 59, 73, 75, 81, 100, 116, 117, 177, 228, 251, 252, 253, 254, 256, 275, 295, 336. 366, 373, 375, 390, 396, 397, 398, 405, 406, 441, 442; French, *see New France*; goddess, 438, 440, 443, 444; the laws of, 27, 32, 118, 120, 122; relations with United States, 175, 182, 185, 187, 249, 259, 263, 278, 312, 426, 429, 440, 442.
Canada Life Assurance Co., 310
Canada Packers, firm, 267
Canadian Canners Company, Ltd., 335, 441
Canadian Club, the, 347, 348, 356
Canadian National Exhibition, The, 311, 325, 439, 440
Canadian flag, 347
Canadian Journal, 269
Canadian literature, Methodist contribution to, *see also Literature,* 286
Canadian Monthly, 294
Canadian Pacific Railway—*See Railways,*

Canadian Railways, 305, *see Railways*

Canadian Shield, 254, 264

Canadian Society of Etchers, 326

Canadians, general traits of, 14, 17, 36, 56, 138, 160, 179, 200, 201, 207, 259, 273, 274, 276, 278, 279, 282, 285, 290, 297, 302, 303, 313, 314, 316, 319, 321, 324, 338, 339, 340, 345, 348, 351, 352, 353, 365, 373, 374, 375, 376, 377, 379, 392, 398, 399, 400, 406, 411, 412, 417, 418, 421, 427, 428, 434, 437, 438, 439, 440, 441, 445; English, attitudes, traits, etc., of, 72, 85, 88, 96, 123, 126, 135, 136, 173, 177, 188, 189, 214, 229, 230, 262, 316, 336, 337, 375, 390, 392, 396, 433, 442, French, attitudes, traits, etc., of, 36, 50, 51, 53, 58, 71, 76, 77, 78, 80, 82, 85, 86, 87, 88, 90, 98, 99, 102, 103, 104, 111, 112, 113, 116, 117, 122, 123, 125, 126, 128, 136, 143, 173, 176, 177, 180, 188, 213, 222-223, 223, 224, 225, 238, 247, 251, 255, 262, 264, 274, 306, 330, 337, 366, 375, 380, 390, 392, 395, 398, 442

Canadien, le, newspaper, 130, 131, 132, 222, 223, 251, 257

Canals, 188, 194

Candide, by Voltaire, 86

Canoe Routes, 47

Canso, fishing at, 36; Gut of, 145

Cape Breton, 25, 72, 143, 144, 145, 148, 191, 196

Capitaine de Milice, 42, 112

Capitalism, 188, 418, 419

Capitulations, French, 123

CAR, the god, 424, 425

Car, the motor, 45, 320, 422, 425, 426, 430, 431, 432, 433, 437, 438, 443, 446

Card playing, 330, 411

Carignan-Salières, Regt., 33

Carillon, battle of, 90

Carleton, Guy, 96, 98, 99, 100, 112, 113, 114, 119, 121, 125, 126, 130

Carling family, 266

Carling, Sir John, 271

Carnival, Montreal winter, 324

Carman, Rev. Dr., 410

Carmen, Bliss, 244

Carriages, light, of Ont., 333

Cartier, Georges Etienne, 188, 216

Cartier, Jacques, 2, 4, 8, 10, 187

Cartwright family, 165

Cartwright, Richard, 305

Carving, teaching of, 73

Cary, Thomas, 128, 129

Casa Loma, 427, 445

Casgrain, Abbé H. R., 89

Cassellman family, 385

Casson, Dollier de, 35

Casualties, Canadian, World War I, 395

Cathedrals, 229, 230

Catholicism, *see Roman Catholicism*

Cattle, 54, 79, 332

Cavaliers, the, 91, 137, 329

Census, the, 40, 42, 62, 73, 74, 79, 102, 103, 108, 113, 126, 189, 209, 210, 211, 257, 325, 344, 382, 383, 384, 385, 386, 387, 390, 394, 422

Chairs, sedan, 148

Chamber music, 312

Chambly family, 36

Champigny, De, 49

Champlain, Samuel de, 2, 3, 4, 7, 8, 10, 12, 14, 16, 17, 18, 23

Champlain, Lake, foray at, 11

'Change', definition of, 410

Chapais, Thomas, 81, 82, 89, 92

Charbonnel, Bishop, 266

Charity, work, New France, 48, 68; Charities, Upper Canada, 267; Charity, American, 426

Charlevoix, historian, 46

Charlottetown, P.E.I., 145

Charron brothers' school, 73, 74

Charlton, John, 316, 317

Chaste, de, M., 7

Chastity, Canadian, 415

Chateauguay, battle of, 177

Chateau Richer, 62

Chatham, Town of, 305

Chauveau, P.J.O., 225

Cheese, home-made, Ont., 333

Cheniquy, M., 163

Cherrier, family, 110

Chignecto, Isthmus of, 146
Chimney sweeps, 75
Choiseul, Duke of, 86
Choral groups, Toronto, 312
Christianity, 6, 217, 410, 419, 420, 431
Christian Guardian, 285
Christie, Maj. Gabriel, 114
Christie, Robert, 130, 131
Church, churches, in general sense, 56, 61, 64, 77, 87, 88, 96, 97, 124, 125, 297, 370, 393, 420, 421; buildings, 46, 63, 64, 74, 229-230, 312; -going, 68, 320, 409, 411, 417; Union, 331
Churchill, Sir Winston, 83, 440
Circuit-rider, the, 330
Cité d'argent, la, 47
City, the, 1, 46, 259, 273, 292, 304, 305, 312, 328, 335, 341, 360, 367, 368, 402, 410, 415, 438, 444; Cities, *see names of individual*
Citizenship, 184, 281, 416, 430
Civilization, 1, 15, 28, 203, 214, 231, 311, 314, 319, 325, 338
Civil Liberties, 119, 120, 134
Civil Service, Canadian, 163, 284, 297, 400
Civil Wars, English, 96
Clapham Sect, the, 217, 237
Classics, place of in education, 355
Class Line, the, 15, 28, 36, 37, 48, 50, 52, 96, 97, 98, 108, 137, 141, 159, 160, 165, 166, 175, 177, 196, 197, 198, 199, 200, 201, 202, 203, 205, 208, 210, 214, 215, 220, 221, 234, 235, 236, 243, 246, 249-250, 255. 259, 263, 264, 271, 292, 293, 294, 308, 310, 311, 313, 319, 328, 333, 334, 338, 339, 344, 349, 365, 367, 370, 376, 394, 395, 396, 402, 403, 404, 405, 409, 410, 411, 415, 419, 420, 421, 423, 426, 427, 428, 429, 434, 435, 436, 437, 438, 442, 446
Clay, blue, 49
Clear Grits, 276, 282
Clergy, the, 120, 140, 147, 161, 162, 182, 183, 308, 361
Clergy, the Roman Catholic, 28, 43, 44, 48, 62, 63, 102, 103, 122, 162, 249, 275, 276
Clergy, the Four Articles of the, 65
Clergy Reserves, the, 140, 236
Climate, 273
Clipper ships, 241
Cloth, homespun, 333
Clothing, 416
Club, Constitutional, 107
'Coaching Era', 329
Code, legal, New France, 27, 32, 51; civil, English, 119; of Victorianism, 411
Codfish, 169
Coffee, 48
Coffin, W. C. H., 106; Thomas, 106; family, 106, 108
Coke, Lieut., 136
Colbert, 19, 27, 32, 33
Colborne, Ont., 165, 205
Coldwater, Ont., 331
Collectivism, 364, 367, 419, 432
Colleges, 73, 74, 110, 218, 323, 355
Collingwood, R. G., 352
Collins, Enos, 149, 150
Colonialism, 27, 78, 85, 88, 136, 137, 138, 141, 163, 166, 196, 197, 208, 213, 220, 221, 233, 246, 273, 280, 281, 282, 284, 286, 293, 296, 298, 301, 310, 313, 314, 315, 323, 326, 346, 347, 348, 350, 356, 366, 370, 374, 377, 396, 397, 411, 427, 437, 439, 440, 441, 443; Colonial policy, 85, 163; Colonies and colonization, 6, 7, 12, 15, 16, 20, 21, 22, 24, 25, 82, 240; Colonists, 16, 79, 84
Commerce and commercialism, 50, 96, 97, 109, 250, 244, 246, 309, 315, 328
Common Man, 162
Commons, House of, Canadian, 248
Commonwealth, the, 364, 367
Communication, 71, 72, 189, 190, 202, 207, 273, 399, 411
Communists and Communism, 236, 376, 378, 398, 412
Communities, 207, 214, 292, 367, 368
Conacher, Lionel, 429

Concerts, church, 353
Conciliar struggle, the, 64
Concubines, Indian, 44
Conformity, Canadian, 431, 433
Confederation, 81, 123, 195, 236, 243, 253, 266, 273, 277, 279, 280, 281, 283, 289, 290, 291, 292, 293, 294, 295, 296, 297, 298, 299, 300, 304, 313, 324, 328, 330, 332, 334, 345, 348, 434, 440
Conflict of loyalties, 348
Congregation, Sisters of the, 74
Congregationalists, 147
Congress, American, 121
Connaught, Duke of, 309
Conquest, the English, 21, 22, 27, 36, 37, 44, 45, 48, 50, 71, 73, 74, 78, 79, 81, 82, 85, 86, 87, 88, 89, 90, 91, 92, 95, 102, 105, 106, 107, 109, 111, 113, 116, 117, 118, 125, 127, 135, 136, 139, 141, 145, 173, 188, 223, 224, 225, 244, 251, 295, 306, 395, 418, 427, 441
Conquest, the French, of the Quebec English minority, 295
Conscription, 124, 125, 133, 254, 324
Conservative Party, the, 121, 277, 346, 378, 398, 404
Conservatism, Fr. Can., 188
Constitutional Act of 1791, 122, 244, 295, 416; Constitution, the American, 141; Constitutionalism, British, 128
Conversion, 11, 160
Coolidge, Calvin, 427
Co-operative Commonwealth Federation, 419, 432
Copernicus, 409
Copper, 443
Corneille, (Fr. poet), 224
Coronations, 403
Corporations, 423
Corsets, 415
Corvée, la, 108, 112, 121, 124
Cosmetics, 317
Costume, 78, 138, 148, 166, 203, 204, 231, 310, 311, 317, 318, 349, 351
'Côte', definition of, 41, 42
Coudres, Isle aux, 74

Council of New France, the, 49, 52, 119
Counter-reform, 219
Country life, 329, 330
Countryside, 331, 334, 336, 338
County Atlas of Ontario, 329
Coureur-de-bois, the, 48, 54
Coûtume de Paris, la, 29
See also Law
Cox, George A., 309, 310, 325; Harold, 310
Craig, Gov., Sir James, 99, 110, 125, 128, 129, 130, 131, 132, 176, 177
Cramahé family, 109
Crandall, Reuben, 160
Crémazie (poet), 252
Creighton, Prof. D., 188
Creswick family, 199
Crestwood Heights, 424
Crimean War, 220, 259
Cricket, 323
Crime and punishment, 31, 51, 52, 75, 120, 121, 150, 160, 164
Crinolines, 231
Croesus, 427
Cromwell, Oliver, 267
'Crown Colonies', 257
Crown Hill, Ont., 196, 197
Cruikshank, statistician, 176
Culture and Cultures, 6, 28, 29, 61, 71, 72, 73, 74, 75, 77, 80, 107, 127, 144, 154, 205, 224, 252, 293, 296, 298, 306, 312, 313, 325, 340, 351, 353, 355, 357, 424, 426, 429, 433, 434, 435, 437, 438, 440, 441, 442
Curés fixes, 62
Curfew, 51
'Custom of Paris', 27
'Cutter', the, 329

D

Dafoe, John W., 263, 364
Dalhousie University, 181, 218
Dafoe, Daniel, Moll Flanders, 412
'Dago', definition of, 372
Dairies, city, 338
Damours brothers, 43
Dancing, 77, 166, 250, 261, 330, 411, 427
Danes, 387

Darwin, Charles, 407
Dauphinie family, 146
Davies, Robertson 211
Davies, Wm., 267, 269, 271, 272, 276
'Deal' trade, 247
Death rate, 185, 192, 194, 210, 300, 303, 380
De la Roche, Mazo, 210
Declaration of Independence, 141, 445
Defence of Canada Regulations, 134
Demagoguery, 431
'Demoiselle, une', 48
'Democrat' (carriage), 333
Democracy, 28, 42, 136, 137, 139, 140, 143, 163, 183, 184, 198, 199, 208, 235, 236, 256, 279, 280, 281, 318, 320, 339, 349, 366, 368, 402, 403, 404, 405, 429, 430, 431, 434, 436, 438
Denis, Simon, 36
Denison family, 220, 237
Denison, Merrill, 246
Denominations and Denominationalism, 160, 161, 183, 191, 216, 217, 276, 284, 420, 421
Dénonville, Governor, 60
Dénot, Marie, 35
Deportees, 34
Deportment, 138, 411
Depression and depressions, economic, 259, 299, 337, 389, 409, 419, 421
Deschambault, Marie Catherine, Dowager Baroness of Longueuil, 106
Dessaulles, M., 275, 280
Detroit River, settlement along the, 168
Detroit, 233
'Development'—Puritan conceptions of, 188
See also Progress
Deutschland über alles, 221
Diamond Jubilee, 348, 350
Dickens, Charles, 257, 411
Diefenbaker, John, 382, 429
Deities, 423
See also gods

Digby, N.S., 147
Digé, Jean, 110
Discipline, 402
Diseases, 192, 304, 415, 432
Dissent and Dissenters, 98, 142, 147, 160, 161, 169, 170
Distilling, 271
Divine Right of Kings, 402
Divorce, 117, 414, 422
Dobell, Hon. R. R., 248
Doctors, 48, 109, 308-309, 361
Doctrine, religious, 57, 58, 67, 97, 295
See also Ideologies
Dogs, 45, 46
Dollard des Ormeaux, 23
Dominion Day, 439
Dominion Monthly, the, 294
Dominion of Canada, 301-302
Donkeys, 75
'Donnellys, the Black', 331, 334
Dorchester, Lord, 125, 126, *see also Carleton, Guy*
Doukhobors, the, 152, 377
Dorion, A. A., 275, 276, 281
Dosquet, Bishop, 73
Doutre, J., 275
Dowries, 66, 69, 105, 106, 108
Dress, 203
See also Costume
Drinking, drunkenness, 47, 51, 166, 168, 169, 236, 305, 319, 331, 360, 413
Drury family, 196, 210
Duchesneau, Intendant, 30, 53
Dufour, Joseph, 111
Duels and duelling, 164, 172, 235, 322
Duluth, Sieur, 51
Dundas Street, 160
Dunkin, Christopher, 271, 348
Dunn, Hon. John Henry, 220, 236-237
Dunsford family, 200
Dupuy, Intendant, 31
Duquesne, Fort, 84
Durham, Lord, 96, 98, 244, 330
Dutch immigrants, 393
Duval, M., 8, 16
Duvernay, Ludger, 251
Duvert, Dr., 120
Dye-wood, 49

E

Ears, the cutting off of, 100
East, in contrast to West, the, 358, 369
Eastern Townships, 157, 188
  See also Settlement
Eaton, T. Company, the, 144, 310, 312, 350
'Ecclesiastical Chart', 183
Economists and Economics, 117, 223
Economy, the Canadian, 369, 401
Eddy family, 266
Eden, Emily, 139
Edison family, 170
Education, 24, 27, 69, 72, 73, 74, 79, 80, 105, 117, 125, 126, 153, 164, 165, 166, 172, 203, 205, 216, 217, 218, 223, 251, 269, 293, 312, 316, 318, 334, 340, 341, 350, 351, 352, 355, 367, 369, 400, 410, 419, 431, 432, 434, 437, 439
Edwards family, 267, 361, 362
Egerton, Hon. Arthur, 250
'Egg-heads', 435
Eisenhower, Dwight, 429
Einstein, Albert, 409
'Elect', the, 97
Elections, 124, 194, 195, 265, 315, 346, 430
Electra, the goddess, 425
Electrical appliances, 425
Elgin County farms, 344
Elite, the, 75
Elizabethan sea-dogs, 406
Elmsley, Hon. John, 167, 216
Emigres, 77
Emigrants and Emigration, 192, 209, 378, 380, 381, 382
Emily Montague, 111
Empire, *see Imperialism*
Empire Club, the, 348, 356
Engagés, 34
Engineers, 439
'England, my England', 221
England and the English, English Immigration, English Institutions, 25, 53, 65, 71, 79, 82, 83, 85, 95, 96, 108, 138, 142, 144, 196, 197, 198, 200, 207, 210, 215, 220, 223, 371, 373, 404, 406, 428, 436
English as contrasted with French, 245, 276, 295, 337
English language, 371, 384, 386
English thought, 214, 215
Enlightenment, the Age of, 60, 105, 127, 214, 219, 223, 237, 238, 254
Entertainment, 61, 77, 429
Environment, 381, 399
Episcopalianism, American, 142
Equalitas, the god, 430
Equality and equalitarianism, 136, 137, 140, 141, 200, 201, 202, 207, 208, 404, 419, 425, 429, 430, 431, 433, 434, 435, 438, 446
Ernestown, Ont., 161
Erroll, the Earl of, 250
Etchers, Society of, 326
'Ethnic', the term, 382
Etienne, Philippe, 35
Etiquette, 47, 138, 282, 302, 318, 412, 446
Europe, 59, 67, 78, 131, 213, 214, 372, 379, 385
Evangelicanism, 217, 218, 318, 356, 367
Evans, Sandford, 356, 361
'Everyman', 433
Evolution, 58
Ewart, John S., 365, 370
Examinations, University of Toronto, 270
Excellent, H.M.S., 124
Executions, public, 121, 164, 252
Exhibitions, 325
Exodus to United States, 313, 338, 339, 378, 381, 383, 431
Expansion, New France, 72
'Experimentalism', 367
Exploitation of Canadian resources, 441
Explorers and exploration, 25, 26, 72, 155
Exports, 72, 249, 383
'Eye-Opener', the Calgary, 361

F

Factory, the, 402, 442
Fallen Timber, Battle of, 174

Family, the, 333, 437
Family Compact, the, 140, 159, 160, 167, 171, 183, 184, 199
Family Compact-ism, 220, 418
Famine, 36
Farish family, 146, 169
Farmer, the Farms, Farming, 44, 48, 85, 263, 303, 328, 329, 332, 333, 334, 335, 336, 337, 338, 339, 340, 341, 342, 343, 344, 353, 354, 355, 360, 361, 369, 396, 430, 445
Fascism, 298
Fashions, 166
Fathers of Confederation, 292
faux-sauniers, 38, 43
Fenians, Irish, 279
Feudalism in New France, 44, 108, 331
Fiddle, 261
Field, Robert, artist, 150
Fielding, W. S., 346
Filles du roi, les, 33, 34
Finnish immigration, 372, 380
Fireplace, the, 48
Fire prevention, 47, 75
'Firewater', 69
Fireworks, 350
Fishing, 169
Flag, the Canadian, 91, 348, 356, 439
'Flaming youth', 413
Flavelle, Sir Joseph, 427
Fletcher (writer), 206
'Flirting', 316, 317
Folk customs, Folk lore, 45, 204, 261, 377, 381, 426
Folleville, Mme de, 51
Food, 48
Football, 321, 324
Footmen, 427
Ford, the Canadian, 426
Forest, the, 2, 12, 43, 44, 167, 189, 201, 205, 260, 263, 271, 273
Forest fires, 75
'Foreigners', 415
Forges de St. Maurice, 48
Fork, the, 47
Fort Henry, 230
Foster, George E., 348
Foster, W. A., 296, 298

Foster, Stephen, 261
'Foundations', the American, 426
Fox, Charles, 96
Fox, W. S., 272
Fox-hunting, 403
Frame houses, 329
France and the French, 2, 5, 6, 7, 11, 12, 13, 14, 15, 23, 25, 28, 29, 30, 32, 33, 37, 43, 44, 46, 50, 52, 53, 64, 65, 69, 71, 75, 76, 78, 81, 82, 83, 84, 85, 86, 87, 95, 108, 110, 123, 125, 127, 131, 187, 215, 219, 275, 398, 400
Franchise, the, 416, 418, 422
Franciscans, the, 68, 69
Francophobia, 129, 130, 131, 132
Fraser family, 85, 267
Freckles, 317
Fredericton, N. B., 153, 243, 264, 305
Freedom, 30, 32, 50, 52, 100, 117, 124, 128, 134, 160, 173, 277, 373, 378; 'Free Enterprise', 27, 445; Free-thinkers, 318; Free Trade, 364
Freight rates, 364
French language, 53
   See French Canada, Canadians French, Language
Freud, Sigmund, 356, 409, 411
Freeholders, 416
'The Front', along Lake Ontario and the St. Lawrence, 158, 205
Frontenac, Governor, 37, 38, 46, 63
Frontier, the, 28, 43, 44, 45, 46, 47, 157, 158, 200, 201, 206, 207, 217, 256, 263, 318, 321, 331, 332, 338, 341, 359, 360, 361, 370, 443
Fruit, 333
Frying-pan, 48
Fundamentalism, 147
Fundy, Bay of, 243
Funerals, 330
Furniture, Domestic, 43, 47, 171, 231, 329
Fur trade and Fur-trader, 7, 8, 15, 34, 50, 76, 85, 155, 168, 169, 359
Fuyards, les, 24

G

Gaels and the Gaelic Language, 144, 196, 208, 241, 372
'Galician' immigrants, 372
Gallia goddess, the, 438
Gallicanism, 60, 65, 66
Galt, Ont., 361
Galt, Alexander T., 123, 195, 295
Games, 62, 312, 321, 323, 324
Gambling, 62, 322, 359, 411
Garbage disposal, 47
Garibaldi, legion of, 224, 295
Garneau, F. X., 89, 117, 251, 252
Garrison Club, Quebec, 248
Gas, natural, 167
Gas stations, 354
Gaspé, Aubert de, 114, 225
Geddie, Rev. John, 217
Genealogy, 71, 106, 108, 114
Generals, 429
'Gentleman-farmer'
    See Class Line
Gentleman, "Gentry", the, as settlers, etc., 34, 36, 37, 95, 107, 141, 197, 198, 199, 200, 201, 235, 236, 250, 334
George III, 84, 101, 120, 255
George V, 427
George, Lake, 87
Georgian architecture, 231
Gérin-Lajoie, 225
Germans in Canada, 191, 196, 211, 372, 376, 378, 380, 385, 386, 387, 389, 390, 393, 404
Ghent, Treaty of, 187
Gifford, Dr. Robert, 20, 35
Gilbert and Sullivan, 354
Gilding, 73
Gillies family, 267
Gilmore family, 267, 248
Girls, the education of, 24, 73
Girls, wayward., 61
Gladiatorial shows, 322, 324
Gladstone, William Ewart, 139
Glass, window, 47
Globe, the, Toronto, 216, 276, 296, 411, 440
"God Save the Queen", 350
God, 58, 410
Gods and goddesses, 237, 344, 422, 423, 424, 425, 445

Gold, 336, 359
'Golden Age', 225
Gooderham family, 209, 260
Gowan, Sir James, 199, 218, 219
Gourlay, Robert, 171-172
Governor, Governments, 27, 30, 31, 34, 48, 49, 50, 62, 63, 64, 66, 69, 75, 76, 81, 98, 99, 103, 109, 116, 118, 119, 125, 128, 129, 136, 159, 163, 251, 259, 281, 298, 315, 353, 362, 366, 400, 418, 436
Government House, N.S., 226
Government House, Canada, 399
Grand Séminaire, le, 73, 223
'the Grange', 314
Grant family, 106, 107
'Great Awakening', the, 217
Great Lakes, the, 3, 342
Greek Orthodox Catholics, 383, 385, 391
Greek "Uniate" Catholics, 380
Gregory VII, Pope, 56
Gresco, Donna, violinist, 375, 381
Grey County, 193
Groulx, Canon Lionel, 90
Grove, F. P., 359, 360, 376
Guérout family, 106, 109
Gugy family, 109
Guelph, Ont., 305
Guy, the brothers, 355

H

Habeas corpus, writ of, 122, 128, 137
'Habitation', Champlain's, 8
'Habitant', the, 63, 66, 78, 87, 102, 105, 111-112, 113, 114, 119, 120, 121, 122, 124, 125, 131, 422
Hachin, André, 51
Hagen, Betty Jean, violinist, 381
Hair, 318
Haldimand family, 109
Haldimand, Township of, 206
'Half-pay officer', 210
Haliburton, Thomas Chandler, 234, 241, 243
Halifax, N.S., 146, 148, 149, 150, 151, 153, 169, 235, 242, 243, 257, 264, 265, 305, 415
Halifax Club, the, 150

Hamilton, Alexander, 292, 298
Hamilton, Ont., 159, 264, 305, 347
Handicrafts, New France, 74
Handly Mountain, N.S., 147
Hanging and Hangmen, 8, 16, 52, 75, 120, 121, 164
Harris, Mrs. Amelia, U.E.L., 179, 180
Harris, Robert, artist, 314
Harvard College, 73, 153, 162, 323
Hastings road, the, 263
Haude-Coeur, Jean, 52
Head, Sir Edmund, 268
Heating of houses, 48, 329, 331,
Hébert, Louis, 17; Marie, 24
Hector, the, 146
Hemingway, Ernest, 204
Hémon, Louis, 222
Hemp, 126
Henry IV, King of France, 60
Henry VIII, 64, 65
Henry, Alexander, 169
Henty, G. A., 351
Heroes, Heroines, Heroism, 24, 325, 428, 429, 444
Hessian mercenaries, 133
Highlanders, 117, 207, 372
'High-brows', 435
'High' society, 263
Highways, 425, 439
'Hill-billies', 204, 255
Hinman family, 165, 205, 206
Hinterland, the, 123, 246-247
   See also *Frontier, Wilderness, Backwoods*
History and Historians, Canadian, 8, 21, 24, 25, 26, 30, 37, 39, 45, 53, 56, 81, 82, 88, 89, 90, 91, 92, 102, 117, 118, 130, 131, 132, 139, 142, 157, 173, 177, 185, 188, 196, 200, 224, 418, 432, 445
History, English, 396
History, interpretation of, 408, 409
Hitler, Adolph, 173, 413
Hockey, 312, 320, 324, 397, 429, 436, 437
Hobbes, Thomas, 13
Hochelaga, 4
Hocquart, Intendant, 78
Holidays, religious, 112, 114
Holy City, The, 353

Hollywood, 383, 429
Home, discipline of the, 402
Homes for the aged, 48
Hope, Lieut.-Gov., 99, 122
Hope, worship of, 438
Horses, 21, 45, 47, 263, 329, 332, 333; 'Horse and buggy' era, 262, 327, 328, 329, 343-344; Horse-cars, 307; Horse-racing, 322, 344
Hospitals, 48, 68, 419, 428
Hotels, 154, 158, 170, 250
Houses and Housing, 45, 47, 158, 417, 420
Howe, Joseph, 136, 241, 244
Howe, Gen. William, 152
Howells, W. D., 301, 302, 315, 345
Hudson's Bay Company, 18, 25, 123, 155, 168, 321, 366
Hughes, Sam, 397, 403, 404
Huguenots, 7, 10, 21, 22, 53, 60, 65, 77, 427
Humanitarianism, 48, 68, 164, 186, 217, 411, 413, 417, 422, 432
'Hundred Associates', 19
Hungarian immigration, 374
Hunger marches, 419
Hunter, Gen., 159
Hunting, 138
Huronia, 69
Hutchison, Bruce, 230
Hutterites, 152, 377
Hydrogen bombs, 425
Hygiene, cult of, 203

I

Iberville, Lemoyne d', 25, 49
'Ice Palace' of Montreal, 324
Icelanders, Icelandic Language, 376, 378, 387, 388, 389
Ideas and Society, 410
Ideologies, 58, 59, 60, 96, 97, 98, 127, 128, 136, 138, 141, 142, 152, 187, 188, 208, 215, 247, 254, 387, 396, 409, 410, 412, 417, 419, 421, 429, 431, 433, 446
Idols, screen, 424
Illinois, French, 53

Illiteracy, 72, 102, 105, 111, 118, 165, 237
Illegitimacy, 414, 415
Immigrants and immigration, 20, 21, 29, 35, 37, 77, 85, 144, 146, 150, 157, 159, 160, 161, 171, 175, 176, 184, 191, 192, 193, 194, 195, 196, 200, 201, 206, 207, 208, 209, 214, 218, 231, 265, 266, 283, 284, 298, 299, 330, 339, 344, 368, 369, 371, 372, 373, 374, 375, 377, 378, 380, 381, 382, 384, 385, 387, 389, 390, 391, 393, 394, 396, 397, 433, 434, 442
See also under names of racial groups
Imperialism, 66, 79, 85, 86, 88, 96, 214, 220, 221, 233, 237, 315, 348, 349, 350, 351, 352, 400, 404, 427, 428, 441
'Imperial Federation', 315, 318, 346
Imports, 72, 110
Incarnation, Marie de l', 24
Income Tax, 401
Indians, the North American, 3, 6, 7, 8, 11, 12, 13, 14, 15, 23, 25, 36, 43, 46 52, 53, 60, 69, 71, 126, 247, 305, 321
Indentured servants, 34
Individualism, Victorian, 364
Industry, Industries, 27, 49, 72, 97, 141, 328, 399, 418, 424, 441
Infanticide, 150; Infant mortality, 192, 194
Ingersoll, Robert, 319
Inglis, Rev. Charles, 142, 150, 170
Inns, 51, 52
Inquisition, the, 275
Insanity, 48
Institut Canadien, l', 220, 224, 238, 275
Institutions (general sense), 29, 48, 59, 61, 100, 105, 118, 122, 143, 163, 373
Intellectuals, intellectualism, 220, 223, 238, 254, 410, 411, 429, 435, 436
Intendant, the, 27, 30, 31, 45, 49, 50, 61, 62, 66, 75, 76

Intercolonial Railway, 243
Intermarriage, 11, 71, 107, 108, 114, 123, 126, 129, 159, 199, 207, 211, 247, 271, 330, 392, 393
International Relations, internationalism, 295, 395, 440, 443
Intolerance, 21, 130
Introspection, French-Canadian, 225
Invasions, American, 102, 104, 107, 112, 117, 121, 124, 125, 174, 177, 279
Invasion, the Fenian, 279
Inventions, 75
Inventories, 32
Irish in Canada, the, 191, 194, 195, 196, 203, 207, 218, 219, 265, 266, 271, 276, 283, 331, 368, 369, 382, 386
'Ironsides', the, 267
Iron works, 48, 72
Iroquois, Indians, the, 3, 11, 25. 30, 46, 91, 252
Isle Royale, 49
Isle St. Jean *(and see Prince Edward Island)*, 25
Italians and Italian language, 381, 385, 387, 400

J

Jackson, Rev. George, 410
Jails, 52, 164
Jameson, Attorney-General, 197
Jameson, Mrs., 197, 208, 210
Janes, S. H., 309
Jaques and Hay, furniture, 231
Jarvis family, 140, 152, 156, 171, 236, 353
Jay, John, 174
Jeffers, Rev. Wellington, 284
Jefferson, Thomas, 178, 215, 430
Jeffreys, Charles W., 314
Jenkins, Captain, 100
Jennett family, 271
Jesuits, the, 24, 31, 36, 60, 62, 63, 65, 68, 73, 74, 85, 86, 103, 126, 127, 133, 134, 346
Jesuit Martyrs, the, 11, 284
Jesuit *Relations*, the, 85
Jews, the, 108, 383, 392, 433

'Jingo-ism', 404
Jobbery, 167
Johnson, Sir John, 156
Johnson, S. C., 192
Johnson, Dr. Samuel, 270
Johnson, Sir William, 156, 158, 170
Johnston, J. F. W., 241
Johnstown, N.Y., 158
Joliet, the explorer, 25
Journalists and Journalism, 109, 127, 128, 129, 132, 275, 315, 436
Juchereaux family, 20
Judges, the, 109, 119, 122, 126, 163, 376
Jury system, the, 118, 120, 122, 133
Justice, 59, 164, 420

K

Kalm, Peter, 79, 203
Kamouraska, Church of, 227
Kawartha Lakes region, 197
Kempenfeldt Bay, 199
King, William L. Mackenzie, 195, 432, 440
King's College, 312
Kingston, Ont., 159, 171, 182, 213, 229, 235, 255, 264, 265, 282, 305, 349
Kingston, W. H. G., 352
Kinsey Report, 414
Kipling, Rudyard, 237
Kirby, William, 45
Kirke brothers, 18, 19
Kitchen appliances, 437
Knife, use of, 47
Knighthoods, Canadians and, 370, 427
Knox, William, 170

L

Labatt family, 266
La Bouteillerie family, 36
Labour, Labouring class, 246, 273, 360, 418, 419, 429, 438, 441
Labour Party, 427
Lachine, 23, 155
Lacolle, battle of, 177
Lacrosse, 268, 312

Ladies, 118, 416
    See also Women
Lafontaine, L. H., 194, 253
La Galisonnière, Governor, 78
'Laissez-faire', 215
Laissez-passer les raf'mans, 305
Lake sailors, 342
Lally family, 199
Lampman, Archibald, 297
Lanctot, Gustave, 20, 66, 91
Lands, Acts, Crown, grabbing, grants, tenure, titles, etc., 15, 27, 37, 44, 72, 79, 103, 118, 120, 153, 167, 168, 184, 197, 240, 259, 334, 336, 337, 360, 367, 371, 425
Land of Hope and Glory, 220
Langhorne, Rev. John, 161
Langtons, Ann and John, 198, 201, 205, 210
Languages, the English and French in Canada, 114, 117, 119, 120, 126, 127, 131, 138, 256, 384, 446
Language, French, as used in Canada, 53
Languages, foreign, 375, 377, 382, 391
Lanqueteau, François and Jean, 35
La Roche, Marquis de, 7
La Rochelle, 21
La Salle, Robert de, 23, 25
Lateran Council, 219
Latimer, Hugh, 24
Latin, 73, 105, 340
Latrines, 47
Laurier, Sir Wilfrid, 110, 136, 224, 254, 326, 348, 432
Latresse, Simon, 124
Laval, Bishop, 60, 61, 62, 63, 64, 65, 69, 203, 317
Laval University, 57, 73, 79
Lavaltrie, Pierre-Paul, Seigneur de, 105, 108, 109
La Vérendrye, Sieur, 25, 72
Law, English Common, Roman, Lawyers, Legal Systems, 25, 27, 32, 48, 51, 52, 54, 59, 75, 76, 80, 99, 109, 110, 117, 118, 119, 120, 122, 129, 133, 164, 308-309, 331, 361, 371, 401
"Lawn-tennis", 322

Lead roofs, 168
League of Nations, 364
Legend, 'Golden Age', 45
Léger, Jules, 90, 224
Legislature, 105, 111, 130, 163, 280. *See also, Assembly, Council*
'Lend-lease', 237
Lennox family, 271
Leonard family, 154
Lescarbot, Marc, 4, 5, 13, 14, 15, 16
Lespinasse, Jean de, 32
Letters, pastoral, 87
Lettres de cachet, 75
Lemelin, Roger, 115, 133
LeMesurier family, 106
Lemoine family, 35, 36
Lessard, General, 398
Lévis, General, 83, 84, 88
Lévis, Town of, 305
Libel, 129
Liberals and Liberalism, 216, 219, 223, 224, 238, 276, 277, 318, 326, 348, 378
Liberty, conceptions of, 50, 52, 119, 326
Libraries, 74, 107, 223, 353
Lieutenant-Governor, the, 385
Limestone, 158
Lincoln County, 439
Linen, homespun, 333
Lingo, lake sailor, 342
Liquor, 69, 99, 271
Literacy, 72, 162
Literary and Athletic Society, University of Toronto, 269, 272
Literary Garland, 232
Literature in Canada, 73, 74, 144, 145, 152, 154, 198, 202, 210, 224-225, 231, 232, 233, 234, 238, 243-244, 251, 252, 255, 257, 285, 293, 294, 297, 352, 353, 370, 376, 388, 396, 411, 437
"Little Englanders", 86
Liverpool, N.S., 146
Liverpool Packet, the, 149
Lods et ventes, 108
Logging and Logdrivers, 249, 360
London, Ont., 172, 264, 305
Lone Shieling, 232

Longfellow, Henry W., 92
Longley, J. W., 299
'Long Soo', the, 341
Longueuil, Barony of, 45, 106, 107
Loudon, General, 83
Louis XIII, King of France, 21; Louis XIV, 27, 60, 64, 65, 71, 85, 173; Louis XV, 61
Louis, gold, the, 124
Louisiana, 53, 85, 92, 117
Louisbourg, 72, 83, 85, 226
Louvain University, 57
'Love-feasts', 330
Love-making, 413
Love-goddess, worship of the, 423
'Love-lorn', advice to, 414
Lower Canada, 126, 154, 190, 191, 193, 194, 244, 245, 246, 247-248, 249, 250, 251-252, 252-253, 259, 265, 274, 275
Lower classes, 210, 234, 410, 423
Lower, A. R. M., *Colony to Nation,* 359, 366
Loyalty, the question of, 84, 85, 99, 100, 101, 102, 103, 104, 107, 112, 114, 121, 122, 123, 124, 130, 131, 132, 133, 142, 147, 149, 171, 176, 177, 183, 243, 255, 280, 284, 296, 315, 348, 397
Luc, Frère, 74
Lucas, Clarence, 313
Lumber, 189, 241-242, 243, 331, 341
Lunenburg, N.S., 146, 196, 385
Lutherans, the, 160, 380, 384, 385

M

Mabane, Dr. Adam, 122
Macaulay, Zachary, 217
McBrien, William, 439
McCarthy, Dalton, 199, 346
McCarthy, Senator J., 278, 382
McCaul, Rev. John, 232, 269, 312
McCord, John, 99, 114
McCulloch, Dr., 194
McCulloch, Dr., Dalhousie University, 218
McCullough, Dr. C. R., 356
Macdonald, Angus L., 241
Macdonald, Sir John A., 195, 216, 237, 267, 283, 291-292, 298,

302, 305, 309, 315, 346, 418, 429
Macdonell, Miles, 172
Macdonnell family, 156
McDowell, Rev. Robert, 161
McGee, D'Arcy, 121, 265, 290, 298, 382
McGill University, 323, 340
Mackay, Donald, 241
'Mackenzies', the, 195; Mackenzie, Sir Alexander, the explorer, 155, 195; Mackenzie, Alexander, Prime Minister, 195, 198, 291, 362, 432; Mackenzie, N. A. M., President, U.B.C., 195; Mackenzie, Robert, of B.C. and of the London School of Economics, 195; Mackenzie, William Lyon, 136, 195, 212, 255, 367, 432; Mackenzie, Sir William, railway magnate, 195, 309
MacLaren family, 267
McKinley, Pres., 351
McLane, David, 120, 127
McLaughlins, the, of Oshawa, 335
McMaster University, 209, 267
McMaster, William, 267
McNab, Sir Allan N., 268, 276
Macphail, Sir Andrew, author of *The Master's Wife,* 340
Machinery, farm, 333, 344
Madison, Pres., J., 182
Magistrates, 197
Magazines, popular, 413, 423
Maine, 181
Male traits, 359
Man, the average, 435, 437, 441; Mankind, 410, 417, 420, 423, 425; 'Man-hunting', 12; Man-slaughter, 164
Mance, Jeanne, 24
Mandements, bishop's, 87, 88, 104
Manereuille, M., 61
Manitoba, 346, 361, 379, 392; Manitoba College, 230; *Manitoba Free Press, the,* 263, 299; Manitoba University of, 366, 367
Manitoulin Islanders, 145
Manitouwadge, Lake, 443
Mann, Sir Donald, 195
Manners, 47, 138, 409

Manor houses, 227
Mantell, Robert, 354
Manufacturing, pulp and paper, 247
Manure, 44
Maple Leaf and Canadian Annual, The, 233
Maple syrup, 340
Marchington, Philip, 149
Mariage 'au gaumine', 40, 77
Maritimes, the, 144, 145, 146, 147, 148, 150, 151, 152, 153, 154, 211, 240, 241, 242, 243, 244, 245, 342
Marriage and Marriages, 31, 35, 36, 49, 61, 77, 106, 107, 108, 114, 123, 140, 160, 161, 183, 211, 240, 392, 414, 417, 422
Marsh, Township of, 210
Martel family, 146
Martyrdoms, Jesuit, 11, 24, 60, 67
Marxism, 349, 419
Mary, the Virgin, 67, 70, 423.
Masefield, John, 237
Masons, 14
Mass, 40; Mass production, 433; Masses, the, 422, 434, 437
Massey family, 165, 188, 189, 206, 267
Materialism, Canadian, 160-161, 417, 428
Mathematics, 73
Mayflower, the, 152
Medcalf, Francis H., 332
Medievalism, 97
Medicine, practice of, 146, 169, 271, 418
Meighen, Arthur, Prime Minister, 343
'Melting pot', the, 374, 377. *See also Immigration*
Men, self-made, 428
Mennonites, the, 160, 377, 385, 386, 393
Merchants and mercantilism, 19, 22, 50, 76, 100, 107, 121, 122, 129, 141, 155, 159, 166, 195, 242, 243, 247, 248, 257, 367, 418, 433
Mercier, Honoré, 300, 346
Mercury, Quebec, 128, 132
Merkeley family, 385

Merritt, William Hamilton, 367
Mesplet, Fleury, 127
Métis, 168
Methodists and Methodism, 145, 160, 161, 162, 182, 183, 206, 217, 218, 237, 263, 271, 276, 285, 286, 319, 330, 350, 353, 364, 411, 412, 413
Metropolitan Church, Toronto, 307
Metropolitanism, 242, *and see preface*
Michilimachinac, 182
Middle Ages, the, 423
Middleman, the, 155, 182
Middle class, the, 98, 237, 360, 411, 421, 438
Midwives, 75
Migration, 153. *See Emigration, Immigration*
Militia, the, Militia, Captains of, Military, the, 49, 76, 83, 112, 121, 124, 126, 130, 178, 180, 186, 279, 286, 289, 300, 306, 402, 403, 429. *See also Army, Soldiers*
Millionaires, Canadian, 427, 428
Miller, M., artist, 313
Mills, 31, 51
Milnes, Lieut.-Gov., 106, 112, 125
La Minerve, journal, 257
Mines and minerals, 145, 360, 443
Minority rights, 123, 126
Minstrels, 355
Ministry as a profession, the, 420
'Miracles', 68
Miramachi, 243
Mission and Missionaries, 11, 60, 69, 217
Missiles, guided, 421
Modern times, 311, 408
Moffats, Ltd., 441
Molière, J. B. P., 61
Molson, John, 181, 235
Molson family, 209, 246, 266
'Momism', cult of, 423
Monarchy, the, 29, 30, 33, 50, 65, 87, 92, 101, 102, 104, 112, 138, 152, 223, 268, 280, 281, 282, 377, 427, 436, 440
Money, paper, 124

Money, worship of, 309
Monnet family, 109
Monopoly, 237
Monsters, 3
Montcalm, General, 79, 83, 300
Montesquieu, Baron de, 60
Montreal, 23, 27, 46, 47, 48, 49, 51, 60, 62, 63, 64, 74, 76, 81, 107, 111, 124, 126, 129, 154, 155, 181, 182, 189, 193, 194, 195, 227, 236, 245, 246, 247, 249, 256, 257, 264, 271, 296, 304, 306, 309, 316, 358, 415, 442
Montreal, Bank of, 297
Montreal Gazette, 127
Montreal, H.M.S., 182
Montreal, University of, 57, 64, 209
Monts, Sieur De, 7, 8, 15, 16, 22
Moodie, Mrs. S., authoress, 197, 198, 200, 204, 205, 208, 232, 255
Moody, the Evangelist, 318
Moose Jaw, Sask., 362
Morals, 55, 60, 61, 62, 77, 104, 117, 150, 317, 409, 411, 413, 414, 416, 417
Moraudière, Abbé de la, 77
Morel, Abbé, 63
Morgan family, 199
Mormons, the, 205
Mortality rate, the, 10, 422
Mosquitoes, 203
Moustaches, 356
Mothers' allowances, 419
Mother tongue, 284
Mountain, Bishop Jacob, 129, 130, 160
'Movement', definition of, 410
'Movies', the, 312, 320, 354, 355, 424
Mowat, Sir Oliver, 195, 291, 305, 307, 418
Mumford, Lewis, 304
Murder, crime of, 52, 150, 331
Murray, General James, Governor, 83, 84, 98, 99, 100, 102, 103, 107, 118
Music, 206, 261, 308, 312, 313, 351, 353, 354, 435
Musseaux, Sieur., 76

Mutilation as punishment, 164
Mysteries, New World, 3, 4
Mysticism, 411
Myths, 12, 13, 26, 117, 138, 225

N

Nantes, Edict of, 60
Napoleon 1st, Emperor, 117, 123, 131, 137, 150, 173, 406
Narroway, Rev. J. R., 286
Nation, Canadienne, la, 89, 253, 254
Nation, The, periodical, 296, 298, 313, 315
Nation, Nationalism, Nationalists, 26, 53, 64, 65, 66, 71, 72, 77, 78, 79, 82, 88, 89, 90, 91, 92, 117, 124, 125, 126, 127, 128, 129, 131, 132, 138, 144, 173, 179, 180, 181, 182, 185, 188, 208, 210, 221, 222, 223, 234, 237, 238, 239, 251, 258, 276, 283, 284, 285, 286, 289, 291, 292, 293, 294, 296, 297, 298, 300, 305, 315, 325, 346, 348, 349, 356, 361, 364, 369, 370, 373, 374, 397, 400, 401, 405, 406, 407, 412, 422, 426, 428, 429, 437, 438, 439, 440, 442, 443, 445, 446
National Hotel, Toronto, Irish sack of, 266
National Policy, 299, 418
Naturalist, a Provincial, 127
Naturalization, 373, 376
Natural Rights philosophy, 215
Navigation, 73, 181
'Navvies', 194
Navy, Naval Affairs, Naval Policies, 84, 124, 148, 150, 348, 432
Nazism and Catholicism, 298
Negro, the, 43, 207, 278, 433, 446
Nellis family, U.E.L.'s, 179
New Brunswick, 143, 151, 152, 153, 154, 156, 157, 170, 181, 185, 190, 191, 243, 244, 260, 289, 325
New Brunswick, University of, 243
'New Canadians', the, 122, 360, 372, 376, 377, 382, 388

New Dominion Monthly, the, 293
New England, 21, 22, 42, 71, 72, 87, 146, 147, 226, 328
Newfoundland, 143, 144, 145, 299
New France, 6, 8, 18, 19, 20, 21, 22, 23, 24, 25, 28, 29, 30, 32, 33, 34, 35, 36, 37, 38, 40, 41, 42, 43, 44, 45, 46, 47, 48, 49, 50, 52, 53, 56, 57, 60, 61, 63, 66, 71, 72, 75, 78, 81, 82, 83, 84, 85, 86, 87, 88, 89, 91, 92, 98, 109, 442
"New Light" Baptists, N.S., 147, 169
New Orleans, 72
'New Subjects', the, 116, 122
New Testament, 419
New World, the, 1, 2, 12, 23, 45, 207, 215, 373, 376, 377
New York, 383
New York Mercury, 83
Newark, U.C., 159
Newman, Cardinal, 219
Newspapers, 127, 128, 129, 132, 166, 205, 231, 232, 241, 257, 312, 414, 436
Newton, Sir Isaac, 409
'Newtown' (Naples), 141
Niagara-on-the-Lake, U.C., 157, 158, 228
Nickle, W. F., M.P., 349
Night clothes, 311
Nightingale, Florence, 24
Night-watch, New France, 52
Nicolet, Seminary of, 105
Nipigon, Lake, 399
'Nobles' of New France, the, 34, 37
Noblesse du robe, la, 109
'Noble Savage', myth of, 12, 13
'Noble Thirteen', the, 199, 346
Nomadism, as aspect of Canadian society, 378, 425
Non-Conformists and Non-Conformism, 97, 147, 149, 160, 161, 165, 171, 216, 217, 266, 267, 268, 365
Nordheimer, S., 309
Normans, the, Normandy, 13, 29
North America, 25, 29, 34, 78, 140, 141, 157, 399, 425, 433
North, the Canadian, 358, 398, 443, 444

North West Rebellion (1885), 346
North West Territories, 341
'Nor'Westers, the', 128, 155, 168
Northumberland County, Ont., 309
Norwegians in Canada, 387
Notary, the, 32
Notre Dame de Montréal, Church of, 227
Notre Dame, Daughters of the Congregation of, 74
Notre Dame des Victoires, Church of, 74
Nouchet, Joseph, 74
Nova Scotia and Nova Scotians, 143, 146, 147, 148, 150, 153, 170, 181, 190, 226, 235, 241, 242, 243, 245, 255, 260, 283, 289, 298, 325, 358, 375, 414
Novel, the, 437
Novelty, worship of, 435, 438
Nuns of New France, the, 61, 62, 69, 70, 102, 103, 107
Nursing profession, 24

O

'Oaklands' estate, Toronto, 309
Obligations, feudal, 32
Obsolescence, 'built-in', 433
Observateur, l', journal, 282
O Canada, 239, 440, 442
O'Donnell, James, architect, 227
Officers, official, officialdom, 27, 35, 48, 49, 88, 96, 109, 129, 132, 134, 163, 197, 237, 402, 403
Office workers, class of, 438
Oil, 443
Okanagan Valley, B.C., 334
Old age pensions, 419
Ontario, Lake, 87
Ontario, the province of, 207, 216, 238, 298, 300, 303, 313, 326, 329, 330, 331, 332, 333, 335, 336, 344, 345, 346, 353, 358, 361, 391, 397, 425. *See also Upper Canada*
Opera, opera-houses, 312, 353, 354
Orangeism, 194, 195, 266, 268, 282, 284, 318, 331, 397, 439, 440
Orchards, 42, 167, 425
Ordinances, Intendant's, 47
Order of Good Cheer, 13

Orders, religious, 68, 69, 102, 117, 119
Organs, 261, 267, 268
Organizations, veterans', 404
Orillia, Ont., 331
Orleans, Island of, 83
Ottawa City, 264
Ottawa, as capital, 287, 296, 298, 304, 305, 358, 369
Ottawa Free Press, journal, 349
Ottawa and Opeongo Road, the, 263
Ottawa Valley, the, 266
Ouellet, Fernand, historian, 238
Oxen, 157, 329, 333
'Oxford Movement', the, 215, 219
Ozanne, Louis, 35

P

Pacific coast, 155, 257, 360
Paganism, Canadian, 321, 415, 423
Paint, on buildings, 158, 329
Panet family, 109, 115, 124
'Panis', les, 43
Pantheism, 344
Papacy, the, 56, 57, 64, 65, 66, 67, 119, 130, 219, 295, 300, 423
Papal Zouaves, the, 295
Papineau family, 110, 127, 275
Papineau, Louis-Joseph, 110, 115, 136, 212, 222, 223, 224, 238, 244, 274
'Papists', 266, 284
Paper money, 119
Parades, 351
Parent, Etienne, 251
Paris, France, 29, 51; *Paris, Coûtume de,* 27, 28; Paris, Treaty of, 1763, 92, 103, 119
Parish in New France, the, 42, 62
Parkman, Francis, 8
Parliament, the Canadian, 81, 297, 305, 376
Parochialism, 379
Parti anti-Canadien, le, 132; *Parti Canadien, le,* 132; *Parti rouge, le,* 127. *See Rouges, les.*
Passe-dix, game of, 62
Paternalism, 31, 47, 75, 76, 92, 96, 108, 198, 199
Pathfinding, 23

Patrie, la, conception of, 72
Patriotism, 25, 72, 84, 85, 137, 149, 208, 241, 347, 407, 426, 439
Patronage, 129
'Patrons of Industry', Ontario, 418
Paupers, immigrant, 201
Pays, le, newspaper, 275
Pays d'en haut, 47
Pays d'états, 29
Pays, le petit, 72
Peach orchards, Ont., 425
Pearson, L. B., 429
Peasants, peasantry, 45, 328
Peel County, Ont., 193
Peerages, 263, 370
'Pellatt's Castle', Toronto, 335
Penetang Road, Ont., 196
Penn, Wm., 10; Pennsylvania, 87
Periodicals, literary, 231, 232, 233, 234, 257, 285, 292, 293, 294, 298, 325, 403
Perrot family, 36
Persecution, religious, 160
Perth Road, the, 263
Pétain, Marshal, 219
'Peterloo Massacre', the, 137
Petit Séminaire, le, 73
Phelps, Arthur, L., 416, 417, 437
Phenomena, scientific, 75
Philadelphia, 10
Philistinism, Canadian, 435
'Philosophes, les', 60
Philosophy and philosophies, 56, 57, 58, 59, 60, 73, 215, 432
Photography, pornographic, 423
Pictou Academy, 218
Pietists, French, 21
Pigs, 47
Pigeon, wild, 167
Pine, white, 230
Pilgrims, the, 10
Pinhey family, 198, 210
Pioneers and pioneering, 17, 43, 44, 136, 150, 155, 159, 162, 165, 167, 168, 176, 198, 201, 202, 203, 204, 205, 206, 207, 211, 217, 233, 273, 328, 353, 362, 399, 405, 416, 434, 438, 443
Pitt, Fort, 84
Pitt, William, Earl of Chatham, 83, 84, 92, 96

Pittsburg, 84
Pius IX, Pope, 216, 219, 238
Plague, the, 35
Plains of Abraham, Battle of the, 83, 84, 98, 300
Planning, Town, 27. *See also Towns*
Planters, Virginian, 142
Plays, 148, 154, 354
Plessis, Bishop, 131, 238
Poêle, le, la, 48
Poetry, 144, 145, 154, 169, 244, 293, 325
Poles, Polish immigration, 379, 381, 385, 392
Police, the, 150, 331
Politics, Politicians, Political parties, 129, 220, 277, 289, 290, 291, 370, 378, 382, 410, 429, 430, 436. *See also individual parties*
Pollock, Gilmour and Company, 247, 248
Pont-Gravé, 7
'Poor whites', 205, 264, 338
Pope, Alexander, 221
Pope, the, 380. *See also Papacy*
Population, the Canadian, 15, 20, 29, 33, 34, 35, 36, 41, 43, 72, 79, 115, 126, 127, 133, 145, 146, 151, 153, 175, 185-186, 189, 190, 192, 193, 194, 209, 210, 257, 259, 264, 271, 303, 304, 305, 325, 344, 384, 385, 387, 390, 392, 394
Pork, packing of, Upper Canada, 267
Port Arthur, Ont., 358
Port Dover, Ont., 180
Port Hope, Ont., 305
Port Royal, 4, 13, 15, 42, 170
Portrait painting, Robert Field, 150
Postillions, 427
Pottery, 49
Poutrincourt, M. de, 4, 7, 12, 13, 15, 16
Poverty and birth rate, 390, 420
Powell, Chief Justice, 167
Prairies, 358, 359, 444
Pragmatic Sanction of 1436, 64
Preemption, right of, 108

Prejudice, colour, 433
Pre-Loyalists, 150
Pre-Raphaelites, 270
Presbyterians, the, 97, 98, 142, 145, 160, 161, 162, 165, 217, 218, 271, 274, 276, 285, 330, 341, 412, 413
Press-gang, the, 124, 125, 148, 170
Prévert, M., 3, 4
Prevost, Gov. Sir George, 150, 177
Price family, 247, 257
Priests and the priesthood, 15, 23, 43, 44, 61, 62, 63, 66, 103, 119. 120, 121, 123, 124, 125, 130, 133
Prince Edward Island, 143, 145
Prince of Wales, 268, 281, 282, 340
Princess Patricia, 309
Printing press, the, 75, 127
Prisons, 318
Private enterprise, 50
Privateering, 149
Privilege, 129, 130, 136, 137, 159, 197, 199, 214, 234-235, 236
Procès-verbal, the, 32
Proclamation of 1763, 118
Professors, 376, 436
Professions, the, 197, 251, 308, 361, 432, 433
Professionalism in sports, 324
Profiteers, war, 149, 150, 400
'Progress', 168, 188, 189, 237, 249, 408, 410, 418, 425, 433, 437
Progressive Party, the, 418
'Prohibition' movement, 319, 413
'Promoters', 160
Propaganda, Revolutionary, 124, 125
Property, 32, 118, 120, 184, 380, 416, 438
Prosperity, 71, 72, 127, 149, 151. 155, 166, 182, 201, 237, 243, 259, 421
Prostitution, 203, 319, 359, 415
Protestants and Protestantism, 7, 21, 56, 58, 59, 72, 87, 90, 109, 119, 133, 143, 148, 166, 189, 191, 213, 216, 217, 218, 219, 220, 249, 254, 265, 276, 308, 309, 318, 319, 341, 362, 366, 368, 375, 385, 390, 392, 393, 411, 412, 415, 419, 420, 432
Provincialism, 71, 79, 82, 240, 254, 292, 295, 345, 347, 379, 380, 383, 427, 429
Province Building, N.S., 226
Prynne, John, 100
Psychology, as explanatory factor, 58, 245, 411, 423
Punishment and crime, 51, 52, 160. 164
Puritans and Puritanism, 22, 60, 92, 97, 139, 142, 146, 147, 148, 218, 320, 321, 330, 368, 408, 412, 415

Q

Quakers, the, 161
Quartering, punishment of, 164
Quebec Act, 32, 96, 102, 105, 120
Quebec Agricultural Society, 107. 127
Quebec, Bishop of, 103
Quebec City, 8, 10, 16, 17, 18, 19, 20, 22, 27, 46, 47, 48, 49, 50, 63, 64, 68, 74, 76, 79, 83, 84, 85, 87, 107, 111, 115, 121, 123, 124, 126, 133, 155, 160, 164, 170, 181, 187, 189, 191, 193, 194, 227, 228, 235, 244-245, 246, 248, 257, 264, 265, 295, 296, 304, 313, 415
Quebec Conference, 1943, 440
Quebec, district of, 74
Quebec Mercury, newspaper, 129
Quebec, Province of, 1763-1791, 1867-, 59, 81, 122, 123, 154, 226, 246, 254, 257, 275, 300, 303, 326, 333, 344, 346, 393, 398, 414, 442. *See also Lower Canada, New France*
Quebec Seminary of, 74
Quebec, Sovereign Council of, 32, *and see Council*
Queen Anne's War, 23
Queen's University, 162, 196, 209
Queenston Heights, Battle of, 347
'Quilting-bees', 261
Quinte, Bay of, 397
'Quittances', 32

R

Rabelais, 412

Race canadienne, la, 228

Racial Relations, 98, 99, 106, 107, 108, 109, 113, 116, 119, 120, 121, 123, 124, 125, 127, 129, 130, 131, 132, 135, 171, 176, 177, 187, 188, 193, 202, 207, 208, 209, 211, 244, 246, 248, 249, 253, 254, 257, 260, 274, 276, 277, 278, 284, 285, 291, 295, 298, 300, 301, 303, 306, 316, 318, 324, 346, 365, 371. 372, 373, 382, 397, 398, 405, 406, 433, 442

Raçine, the poet, 224

Radcliff family, 211

Radicals and Radicalism, 127, 128, 131, 136, 213, 224, 238, 275, 276

Radio, the, 312, 425

Raftsmen, 341

Raids, border, 71

Railways, 30, 168, 243, 246, 257, 259, 262, 297, 299, 304, 305, 306, 309, 319, 329, 362, 364, 398, 399. *And see names of individual railways*

Ralston, Col., Minister of Defence, 241

Ramezay, de, family, 51, 107

Rank, distinctions in, 402

Rankin family (Kingston pioneers), 159

Rationalism, 214, 219, 274, 408

Raymond, Canon, 152

Reactionaries, political, 137

Reading public, the, 413

Reason, the Age of, 237. *And see Enlightenment*

Rebels, the Nova Scotia, 153

Rebellion of 1837, 122, 123, 140, 184, 188, 224, 236, 244, 252, 255, 256, 275, 432

Rebellion Losses Bill, 236

Rebellions, the Riel, 123, 299, 305, 316, 345, 356

Reciprocity, 259, 348

Recollets, the, 63, 74

Recruiting, 403

Redditt, T. H., Principal, 357

Red River Settlement, 18, 43, 168, 169, 371

Reform, 160

Reformation, the, 57, 58, 59, 60, 274, 423

Reformatories, 318

Reformers, the (political party), 216. *And see Liberals*

Régime militaire, le (1760-1763), 118

'Reign of Terror', Gov. Craig's, 130, 132

Relations, the Jesuit, 26, 85, 86

'Relief', 419

Religion, religious controversy, religious orders, religion as an aspect of society, 24, 46, 48, 51, 56, 58, 60, 66, 68, 104, 117, 119, 121, 138, 139, 140, 142, 147, 148, 160, 162, 177, 183, 202, 203, 217, 220, 268, 270, 274, 319, 320, 326, 344, 362, 371, 378, 394, 398, 408, 409, 412, 413, 417, 420, 421, 423, 428, 441

'Remittance men', 77

Renaissance, the, 408

Répentigny family, 37, 49, 51

'Rep. by Pop.', 193, 260, 277

Representative Government, 107, 116, 120, 122, 123, 126, 129

Republicanism, 140, 152, 202, 224, 268

Resources, natural, their destruction, 167, 168, 169, 172, 441

'Respectability', 139

Responsibility, civic, 163

Responsible Government, 123, 128, 140, 197, 240, 243, 252, 253, 281, 365

Restaurants, 154

Restoration, the Bourbon (1815-1830), 219

'Returned man', the, 405

Revenge, the, Halifax privateer, 149

Revivalism, religious, 217, 218, 222, 330

Revolt, the Hungarian (1956), 406

Revolution and Revolutions, 96, 151, 236, 328, 406, 423; Revolution, the American, 97, 98, 100,

104, 112, 114, 121, 123, 135, 136, 137, 139, 140, 144, 146, 147, 149, 150, 151, 155, 156, 159, 171, 174, 179, 203, 221, 273, 279, 290, 401; Revolution, the French, 65, 90, 118, 123, 124, 125, 126, 131, 137, 177, 213, 219, 221, 222, 223, 236, 238, 265, 280, 398, 408, 411, 425

Révue Canadienne, la, 289

Rhinelanders in N.S., 146

Richard, Maurice ('The Rocket'), 324

Richardson, Rev James, 182

Richardson, Maj. John, author, 233, 239, 251

Richelieu, Cardinal, 18, 19, 21

Riddell, Rev. J. H., 370

Ridout family, of York, U.C., 236

Ridgeway, Battle of (1866), 279

Riel, Louis, 123, 300, 305, 306, 366

Rigs, horse, 331

Riots, 332, 419

Ritualism, 137, 138, 141, 142, 147, 215, 216, 403, 405, 422

Rivard, Adjutor, writer, 225

River drivers, 305, 341

Roads, 160, 263, 273, 328, 329, 439

Robbery, highway, 331

Roberts, Sir Charles, poet, 154, 244

Roberval, 8

Robinson Crusoe, 80

Robinson, Sir John Beverley and the Robinson family, U.E.L., 156, 158, 160, 171, 220, 235, 236, 237, 271

Roebuck, J. A., 215

Roman Catholicism, its nature and doctrine, 2, 7, 11, 22, 24, 28, 40, 48, 50, 51, 56, 57, 58, 59, 60, 62, 64, 65, 67, 68, 70, 91, 101, 102, 109, 111, 112, 119, 124, 125, 131, 145, 177, 188, 215, 216, 219, 220, 222, 224, 234, 254, 266, 295, 326, 379, 385, 391, 413; Roman Catholics, 191, 195, 298, 379, 382, 390; Roman Catholics and

Catholicism, 21, 56, 67, 68, 72. 87, 97, 126, 284; Protestants and, 316, 318, 393; Roman Catholic Church, its status, organization, relationship with the State, etc., 57, 62, 63, 64, 98, 103, 104, 105, 119, 122, 123, 130, 140

Romanticism, 22, 138, 139, 214, 215, 216, 217, 218, 219, 220, 221, 224, 226, 227, 230, 232, 233, 237, 238, 270, 314, 396, 411

Roofs, tin, 47

Roosevelt, F. D., 440

Ross, P. D., journalist, 316

Rouges, les, 224, 254, 274, 276, 280, 282, 326

Rouleau, C. B., writer, 225

Roundhead tradition, the, 97, 137

Rousseau, J. J., 13, 127

Row-boat, the, 350

Rowe, Hon. Earl, 277

Rowsell, Henry, diarist, 272

Roy, Gabrielle, authoress, 442

Royal, Joseph, politician, 289, 290

Royal Newfoundland Regiment, 144

Royal Canadian Institute, 269

Royal Engineers, 150

Royal visits, 436

Royal William, steamer, 189

Rule, Britannia, 350

Ruralism, rural life, 261, 328, 353, 354, 390, 445

Rush-Bagot Agreement, 187

Russian immigrants, 393, 394

Ruthenian immigrants, 385

Ryerse, Port, Lake Erie, 179

Ryerson, Egerton, and the Ryerson family, 156, 161, 162, 175, 179, 185, 216, 285, 366

Ryland, Herman W., 129, 132, 177

S

Sabbatarianism, 318

Sacraments, the, 67

Saddle-horse, 329

Sagard, *The Long Voyage to the Country of the Hurons,* 14

Saguenay, Kingdom of the, 2

'Sahib', the, 96, 131, 246, 247, 257

Sailors, 242
Saints, Catholic, 67, 68, 70
Saint's Day, 112
St. Albertus Magnus, 57
St. Andrew's Presbyterian Church, Toronto, 307
St. Boniface College, Man., 366
St. Catharines, Ont., 305, 439
St. Francis of Assisi, 69
St. Germain, Guillaume, Notary, 32
St. James Cathedral, Toronto, 307
St Jean, Isle, 145
St. Jean Baptiste Day, 251
Saint John, N.B., 153, 243, 264, 305, 349
St. Jean Port Joli, Church of, 227
St. John River Valley, N.B., 151, 152, 153, 191
St. John's, Nfld., 144, 264
St. Laurent, Rt. Hon. Louis, 198, 274
St. Laurent, parish of, 68
St. Lawrence River, 418
St. Lawrence, H.M.S., 182
St. Mary's Roman Catholic Cathedral, Kingston, 332
St. Maurice, Forges of, 72
St. Michael's Cathedral, Toronto, 307
St. Paul, arm-bone of, 68
St. Patrick, 265
St. Pierre, parish of, 68
St. Sacrement, Lac, 87
St. Stephen, N.B., 157
St. Sulpice Seminary, Montreal, 74. *See also Sulpicians*
St. Thomas Aquinas, 68
St. Vallier, Bishop, 61
Salaberry, de, Col., 180
Salesman, the, 433
Salmon, the, 167
Salone, Emile, historian, 20, 74
Salvation Army, 318, 354
Sam Slick, Haliburton's, 241, 257
Sanitation, 10, 11, 47, 154, 203, 211, 418
Sankey, evangelist, 318
Sarrazin, Dr., botanist, 75
Saskatchewan, Province of, 367, 421
Saskatoon, Sask., 367

Saturday Evening Post, 439
Saturday Reader, 293, 294
Sawmilling, 247
Saw, the power, 329
Scaffold, 52
Scandals, public, 367
Scandinavians, 376, 378, 380, 387, 393
Scepticism in *The Enlightenment,* 127
Schools, School-books, Schooling, School-teachers, 51, 68, 73, 74, 126, 165, 277, 300, 312, 340, 351, 353, 355, 373, 376, 402, 403, 429
Science, 58, 75, 409, 413, 418, 420, 421, 425, 437
Scot, the, 107, 142, 144, 145, 146, 148, 159, 161, 191, 195, 196, 202, 203, 210, 211, 241, 248, 276, 330, 368, 381, 386
Sculpture, 74
Scurvy, 8, 10
'Sea-dogs', 351
Seamanship, 242
Secord family, 179
Sects, the, 148, 160
Sectionalism, 299, 300
Secularism, 127, 223, 318, 417
Secular Thoughts, periodicals, 319
Sedition, 128
Seduction, 316-317
Seigneurs and Seigneurialism, 28, 36, 37, 44, 45, 62, 105, 106, 108, 110, 114, 120, 121, 122, 124, 126, 129, 131, 405
Seignobos, C. V., historian, 67
Self-government, 102, 147, 378, 413
Self-made man, 434
Selkirk, Lord Alexander, 18, 168, 169
'Semi-intellectuals', 293
Senate, Canadian, 281
Sentimentalism, 408
Separate Schools, 216, 284, 318, 320, 365
Sergeant-major, the rank of, 402
Servant class, 137, 200
Settlers and settlement, 16, 21, 25, 26, 41, 43, 44, 135, 136, 143, 144, 147, 148, 149, 150, 151,

152, 153, 154, 155, 156, 157, 158, 159, 160, 161, 162, 163, 165, 166, 167, 168, 169, 170, 171, 175, 176, 177, 184, 187, 189, 191, 196, 197, 198, 199, 200, 201, 202, 203, 204, 205, 206, 207, 208, 209, 210, 211, 217, 255, 261, 274, 353, 361, 364, 370, 373, 374, 375, 377, 384, 399, 418, 430

Seven Years' War, the, 88, 149, 174. *See also Wars*

Sewell, Jonathan, Att.-Gen. and Chief Justice, L.C., 129, 130, 132, 177

Sex, 60, 217, 317, 414, 446

Shakespeare, William, 354, 406, 437

Shanty Bay, Ont., 199

Shaw, 167

Shaw, G. B., his *Pygmalion*, 412

Shefford County, L.C., 245

Sherbourne St. Methodist Church, Toronto, 310; Sherbourne Villa, Toronto, 310

Sherbrooke, Gov. Sir John, 150; Sherbrooke County, L.C., 245; Sherbrooke, city of, 264

'Shiners', the Bytown, 195

Ships, Shipping and Ship-building, 72, 149, 152, 153, 209, 241, 242

Shoemaker-preachers, 147

Shops and Shopping, the, 423

Sibbald family, 199, 210

Sidewalks, New France, 47

Sidney, Cape Breton, 144

Siegfried, André, author, 432

Sifton family, 362, 363, 364, 370

Silversmithing, 43

Simcoe, John Graves, 159, 160, 165, 166, 172, 175

Simcoe County, Ont., 218, 270, 381

Sin, the idea of, 356

Sinecures, 129, 159, 163

Singing, choral, 206

Skating, 324

Skey, L., M.P., 427

Skittles, game of, 268

Slavs in Canada, 372, 385. *See also specific races of*

Slavery, 43, 52, 164, 255, 278

Sleigh, the, 202, 399; Sleigh-bells, 329

Slums, 415

Small, Mr., official and duellist, U.C., 164

Smallpox, 316

'Smart Alec', the, 307

Smith family, U. E. L., 156; Smith, Adam, 324; Smith, Goldwin, 264, 314, 329

Smugglers, 38, 43

Snobbery, 166, 198, 403

Snowshoe, the, 45, 324

Snider Rifles, 306

Soap, use of, 10

'Soap-opera', 430

Socialism, 367, 401, 417, 432

Social Services, 48, 68, 419

Society, Social structure, etc. in New France, 27, 28, 29, 31, 33, 34, 36, 37, 40, 43, 44, 45, 47, 48, 49, 50, 51-52, 58, 59, 60, 61, 62, 63, 64, 65, 66, 67, 68, 69, 71, 72, 73, 74, 75, 76, 77, 78, 79, 82, 87, 88 post-Conquest, 1760-1791, Canadian, in general social attitudes, classes, characteristics, structure, by regions and periods, 95, 96, 97, 98, 99, 102-113, 117, 118, 121, 125, 126, 127, 128, 129, 130-131, 135-145, 147-151, 152, 153, 154, 156, 158, 159, 160, 162, 163, 164, 166, 168, 175, 189, 197-203, 206, 211, 234, 235, 243-244, 246, 247, 249-251, 255, 260, 261, 283, 307-309, 314, 315, 317, 318, 320, 321, 328-329, 343, 345, 353, 355, 358, 359, 364, 365, 367, 371, 380, 381, 382, 398, 404, 405, 409, 423, 425, 426, 427, 430-435, 437, 438, 440, 441, 442, 444. *And see under the various social classes separately*

Sociologists' 'lingo', 382

Soil, role of the, in society, 333

Soldiers, 25, 34, 43, 44, 77, 84, 85, 87, 96, 99, 121, 131, 150, 399, 400, 404, 412

Soldiers of the Queen, song, 350

Songs, popular, 178, 261, 293, 350, 351
Sophistication, social, 151, 402, 412
Sorel, P.Q., 305
Souls, 431, 432
Sous-delegué, le, 80
Sovereign Council of New France, 31
Spaniards and the New World, 6
Sports, 138, 312, 320, 321, 322, 323, 324, 334, 437
Spruce tea, 8
Spruce gum, 13
Square Timber Trade, 247. See also Timber, Trade
Squirearchy, the, 45, 96, 160. See also Gentry
Stadacona, 10
Stanstead, P.Q., 157, 245
Staples and the Staple Trades, 359, 360
Stark's Corps, 140
Starvation, 10
State, the, 66, 101, 102, 104
Statesmen, attitudes towards, 429
Stations, fishing, 144
Status, economic, and birth rate, 392
Steamer, the, 202
Stewart family, 199
Still, a primitive, 13
Stocks, punishment in the, 164
Stoves, 48, 168, 329, 441
Stone cutters, 14
Stoney Creek, Battle of (War of 1812), 342
Strachan, Bishop John, 161, 165, 183, 216, 271, 326
Strange, Maj.-Gen. (1885), 306
Strathy family, 199
Street, A. G., author, 379
Streets, 47, 154, 157, 168
Strickland family, 197, 198
Stuart, Rev. Geo. Okill, 162
Students, 73, 432
Subjects, the New, 99
Suburbanization, 186, 328, 421, 425
'Suisse, un', 109, 115
Sulpicians, the, 31, 36, 63, 74, 125, 126

Sulte, Benjamin, historian, 20, 90, 102
Summa Theologica, 59
Sunday Observance, 268, 317
'Superintendant of the Romish Church', the, 103
Superior Council of New France, 75
Supremacy, the Act of (1534), 65
Surgical progress, 418
Surveyors, Land-, 110
Survival, the Miracle of (la Survivance), 81, 82, 89, 91, 116-132
Swearing, 31
Swedes in Canada, 372, 387
Swift, Dean, 97
Swiftsure, the steamer, 186
Swiss, the, 109, 400
Syllabus of Errors, the, 219, 221
Syphilis, 415

T

'Taboos', 330
Taché, Archbishop, 358
Talbot, Colonel, 197, 210, 229, 334, 344
Talent, Canadian, export of, 381. See also Exodus
Talon, Intendant Jean, 27, 31, 33, 38
Tariff, the, 364, 367
Tartuffe, Le, Molière's, 61
Taschereau family, 109, 115
Taste, standards, 433, 436
Taverns, 75, 99
Taxation, 50, 66, 76, 112
'Tax war', 401
Tea drinking, 48
Teetotallers, 268
Teaching, 402
Technology, 190, 425
'Teen-ager', 437
Telephone, 310
Television, 320, 355, 425, 430, 438
Telescopes, 409
Temperance movement, 203, 206, 255, 268, 271, 318, 319, 320
Tennyson, Alfred, Lord, 238, 270, 406, 411
Terrebonne, 1841, Election at, 194
Terre-Neuve, 25. See Newfoundland

Test Act, the, 118, 119
Théâtre du Marché à Foin, at Quebec, 154
Theatre, the, 61, 148, 154, 257, 272, 330, 353, 411, 429
Thériault, M. W., 57
Thermometer, 75
Theocracy of New France, the, 22, 28
Theology, 56, 57, 58, 67, 68, 73, 160, 162, 420
Timber Trade, the, 155, 247, 257, 259, 266, 304
Tin roofs, 47
Titles, 349, 370
Tithe, the, 66, 117, 120, 124
Tobacco, 52, 329, 330, 411
Toboganning, 250, 317
Toleration, 103, 126, 422
Tonnancour, de, family, 106
Toronto, 167, 168, 193, 228, 230, 255, 264, 265, 266, 267, 269, 271, 272, 297, 304, 305, 306, 307, 308, 309, 310, 312, 322, 325, 332, 335, 348, 358, 383, 412, 415, 427, 444; Toronto Lawn Tennis Club, 323, 326; Toronto Industrial Exhibition, 271; Toronto, Normal School, 271, 312; *Toronto Old and New,* 307; Toronto Stock Exchange, 271; Toronto Transportation Commission, 439; Toronto, University of, 57, 216, 269, 270, 272, 307, 335, 417, 422
Torture in Canada, 11, 12, 14, 51, 52, 75, 120
Tories and Toryism, 96, 120, 129, 142, 268, 276, 348, 398. *See also Conservatives, Upper Classes*
Townsman, the, 48
Town planning, 33, 38, 46, 157, 167, 168, 367
Townships, Jeffersonian, 430
Toynbee, Arnold, 23, 67
Tracy, Marquis de, 23
Traill, Mrs., 198
Transportation, sentence of, 164
Transportation, 311. *See the various modes of*
Transubstantiation, 423
Trade, Traders, Trading-posts, 1,

14, 15, 19, 50, 51, 52, 72, 73, 97, 98, 99, 100, 145, 155, 182, 418. *See also Business, Commerce, and specific trades*
Tradition, 96, 97, 128, 135, 136, 140, 141, 145, 146, 152, 156, 157, 160, 163, 176, 181, 197, 222, 348, 396, 416, 427, 438
Travel and travellers, 137, 202, 349
Treason, crime of, 120, 155, 156, 164
Trees, cutting and clearing, 155, 156, 337. *See also Forest*
Trials, 55, 120, 121, 128, 164
Tribalism, 324, 373
Trinity Church, Barrie, Ont., 216, 219
Trois Rivières, P.Q., 20, 27, 63, 264, 305
Trudel, Marcel, historian, 127
Truro, N.S., 146
Twelfth of July, 397
'Tycoons', 428
Tyrrell family, 335

U

Ukrainians, 371, 376, 378, 379, 385, 390, 391, 394
Ultramontanism, 65, 66, 125, 295, 318
'Uncle Tom's Cabin', 355
'Underground Railway', 278
Unemployment, 419
Uniform, 349, 402
Union of Upper and Lower Canada, 1840, 252, 253, 257, 277, 283
Union Jack, 347, the
United Church, the, 161, 385, 391, 394, 420. *See also Church*
United Empire Loyalists, 122, 137, 139, 140, 145, 146, 151, 152, 153, 154, 155, 156, 157, 160, 174, 175, 179, 180, 243, 362, 385, 396, 397
United States in relation to Canada, the, 30, 43, 143, 174, 182, 187, 209, 221, 279, 290, 292, 298, 299, 301, 303, 312, 335, 347, 348, 350, 369, 378, 380,

381, 383, 396, 413, 423, 426, 429

Unity, Canadian, 399

Universe, concept of, 410

'*Université mixte*', 105

Universities, the, 57, 165, 209, 404, 426, 428

Upham family, 154

Upper Canada, 143, 145, 153, 155, 156, 157, 158, 159, 160, 161, 162, 163, 164, 165, 166, 167, 168, 175, 176, 181, 182, 183, 190, 193, 195, 197, 198, 199, 200, 201, 202, 205, 206, 207, 208, 209, 210, 211, 215, 216, 228, 229, 230, 234, 235, 236, 237, 252, 254, 255, 256, 258, 259, 260, 261, 265, 266, 270, 271, 274, 276, 277, 284, 291, 325, 366, 432

Upper Classes, the, 129, 130, 132, 137, 138, 140, 151, 152, 197, 205, 208, 266, 396, 403

Urbanism, 1, 260, 262, 312, 321, 327, 335, 338, 339, 341, 343, 344, 367, 368, 374, 392, 396, 399, 416, 421, 438

Urban industrial classes, 438

Ursulines of Quebec, the, 24, 36, 72, 73, 74, 88, 98

Utensils, table and cooking, 47, 48

'Utilitarianism', 214

Utrecht, Treaty of, 1713, 71

V

Vaccination, 316

Vanbrugh, the architect, 227

Vancouver, city of, 360; Vancouver Island, 145, 205, 323

Varennes family, 36

Varsity, the, journal, 417

Vaudreuil, Governor de, father, 49, 69, 71; Vaudreuil, Governor de, son, 71, 76

Vegreville, Alta., 376

Verchères, Madeleine de, 25

Versailles, 49

Veterans' organizations, 404

Victoria College and University, 263; Victoria Cross, the, 220; Victoria Day, 212; Victoria, B.C., 248, 359, 366, 368; Vic-

toria, reign of Queen, 212, 213, 237, 309, 350, 351, 356, 357; Victorianism, Canadian, 212, 213, 214, 218, 408, 409, 411, 416, 417, 422; Victorian architecture, 231

Vimy Ridge, Battle of, 406

Virgin Mary, cult of, 423. *And see Mary*

Virginia, 139, 142

Vision, quality of, 5

Vital Statistics, 392, 414, 415

Voltaire, 60, 75, 86, 127, 213, 223, 238

Volunteering, 396, 397

Vote, the, voters, 416, 430. *See Franchise*

W

Wacoustah, by John Richardson, 233

Wagon, the, 444

Walker's Ear, 100, 114

Wallace, *Wooden Ships and Iron Men,* 242

War and Wars, 149, 173, 396, 398, 399, 401, 406

War, American Civil, 261, 278, 279, 298; American invasions of 1838-1839, 278, 279

War, Spanish-American, 350

War, American Revolutionary. *See Revolution, American*

War, Boer, 348, 350, 351, 396

War of 1812, 131, 144, 149, 156, 157, 174, 176, 177, 178-182, 184-186, 193, 194, 204, 239, 256, 278, 405, 406

War, English Civil, 97, 98, 141

Wars, French-Indian, 23

Wars, French-English, 19, 71, 84, 100, 174

War, the Seven Years, 81, 83, 84, 85, 87, 88, 149

Wars, the Napoleonic, 123, 150, 213, 247

Wars, World War I, 88, 309, 321, 345, 348, 364, 365, 371, 375, 395, 396, 397, 398, 399, 400, 401, 402, 404, 405, 406, 408, 409, 411, 415, 421, 429, 431

Wars, World War II, 88, 219,

381, 397, 398, 399, 400, 406, 408, 415, 431, 439, 441
Warden of the North, 150
Warner, Charles Dudley, 303
Washington, George, 79, 138, 152, 377
Water company, first public, 154
Waterloo, Battle of, 213
Watson, Homer, artist, 314
Watts, Isaac, 145
Ways of life, 98, 139, 141, 142, 143, 147, 187, 188, 249, 254, 366, 402, 405, 410, 412, 442
Wealth, 311, 426, 427, 428, 429
Week, the, periodical, 299, 300, 314, 315, 317, 326, 347
Wellington, the Duke of, 131, 186
Wesley, John, 160, 217, 237, 285, 411
Wesleyanism, 146. See *Methodism*
Wesley College, Winnipeg, 370
Wesleyan Repository and Literary Herald, 285, 303
West, the (mainly in reference to the prairie west), 72, 135, 168, 187, 259, 302, 328, 348, 358, 359, 360, 361, 362, 364, 365, 366, 367, 369, 376, 380, 398
West Coast, *see Pacific*
West, Benjamin, artist, 142
West Indies, 72; West Indies Company, 31
Westmacott, Capt., 150
Weston, Ont., 441
Wheat, 259, 332, 359, 360, 367
Wheel, breaking on the, 52
Whigs, the English, 96
Whiskey, 206
White, Att.-Gen., U.C., duellist, 164
'White House', the, Bath Road, 158
Wilberforce, Wm., 217
Wigs, wearing of, 148, 166
Wilderness, the Canadian, its nature and effects, 1, 10, 11, 15, 16, 23, 40, 43, 44, 47, 136, 137, 140, 145, 148, 153, 154, 155, 156, 169, 201, 205, 263, 273, 319, 320, 367, 396, 399, 416, 434, 443. *See also Forest, frontier*

William III, 166
Williams, Gen., of N.S., 220
Williamsburg, Va., 230
Wilmot, Township of, population, 257
Wilson, Sir Daniel, 270
Wine, 29, 48, 52, 148
Winnipeg, Man., 230, 319, 358, 360, 366, 375, 382, 388
Winslow Papers, N.B., 152, 154
Winslow family, 153, 154, 159
Winters, Canadian, 155, 399
Witch-burning, 51, 422
Wives, supply of. *See Woman*
Wolfe, Gen. James, 74, 84, 88, 106
Woman, women, supply of, status of, nature of, 16, 17, 25, 27, 33, 34, 38, 48, 51, 59, 60, 61, 75, 77, 78, 79, 104, 203, 204, 302, 316, 317, 352, 355, 359, 411, 415, 416, 417, 422, 423, 424, 437
Wood, Col. Wm., historian, 106
Wood, as staple product, 189; Wood ashes, 75; Wood carving, art of, 74; Wood-piles, 75; Wood-sawyers, 14
Woodsworth, J. S., 365, 370
Wordsworth, William, 238
Workers, office, 108
World Affairs, Canada and, 407, 443
World, the state of the, 417, 420, 440
Worts family, distillers, 207
Wycliffe College, 219
Wounding, 265, 266

Y

'Yankees', 200. *See Americans*
Yarmouth, N.S., 146
Yeomen farmers, 197, 327, 328, 334, 335, 337, 343, 367, 438
Yonge Street, Toronto, 160
York, U.C., 159, 166, 167, 168, 182, 186, 233, 235, 236
York Almanac, the, 235
York, Archbishop of, 57
Yorkshire Methodists in N.S., 146
Youth, 411, 420, 424, 429
Ypres, Battle of, 406

This book has been set in Times Roman,
a contemporary type face originally commissioned
by *The Times* of London from Stanley Morison.
It is one of the most pleasant and unobtrusive
of type faces since it is large on the body
and quite free from any mannerisms.

The paper is Provincial's Olde Vale Antique
Laid.

The book was designed by Arnold Rockman
and printed and bound by
T. H. Best Printing Company Limited.

The plates were printed gravure by Sun Printers
Limited.